Frankfort

uisville

Lexington

own ★ Harrodsburg ★ Richmond

Perryville

ENTUCKY

VIRGINIA

Mill Springs

Cumberland
Gap

Bristol

Bull's Gap

Greeneville

Knoxville

NORTH
CAROLINA

hester

Chattanooga
Chickamauga

Dalton

GEORGIA

WITHDRAWN

Marietta

Atlanta

TENNESSEE'S WAR
1861-1865

TENNESSEE'S WAR
1861-1865
Described by Participants

Compiled and Edited

by

Stanley F. Horn

Nashville • 1965

TENNESSEE CIVIL WAR CENTENNIAL COMMISSION

Copyright © 1965 by Stanley F. Horn
Second printing, 1973
Third printing 1980
Fourth printing, 1985
Fifth printing, 1990
Library of Congress Catalog Card Number: 65:64988
ISBN 0-87402-019-0 (cloth: alk. paper)
Distributed for the Tennessee Historical Commision by
The University of Tennessee Press, Knoxville

To those who lost and those who won

CONTENTS

FOREWORD

A T THE *outset, it should be understood that this book does not attempt to supply a detailed history of the Civil War in Tennessee. It is, rather, an arrangement of selected material from the writings of those who took part in or were contemporaneous observers of those four years of war in this state, in an effort to show the first-hand impression made then by the war on these individuals —civilian, military and political; men and women; Northerners and Southerners.*

There are many books available giving the historians' and the fiction writers' accounts of these events, based on the writers' study and research. Here, however, will be found what was written, mostly at the time, by those who were telling about what they themselves had seen and experienced. Linked together by some supplied connective material, these excerpts show how the war in Tennessee impressed those who took part in it, as expressed in their own words.

These selections embrace the written recollections and opinions of observers and participants on both sides, including an occasional neutral bystander. Naturally, it being wartime, a large part of the material pertains to soldiers' life and battles, but there are also reflections of the impact of the war on the social and economic life of the non-combatants.

Accounts of battles written by those engaged in the fighting are necessarily written from a limited point of view and are seldom objective or impartial. The official reports of officers are frequently colored by self-interest; indeed, in reading the reports of an engagement written by opposing commanders it is sometimes hard to realize that both are referring to the same action. Likewise, the private soldier, with only a worm's-eye view of the proceedings, was generally only vaguely informed (if at all) as to the tactics involved or the overall objectives sought; but it was the man in the ranks who experienced the actual shock of battle and suffered the privations, the hunger and the blood-letting of army life. And it was

[9]

the people back home who patiently bore their share of the shock of the war's tragedy and destructiveness.

From all these sources, the raw material of history, carefully balancing the conflicting statements in the light of the more detached viewpoint made possible by the passage of a century, we may be able to gain a better understanding of what actually took place in Tennessee during those desolating four years than can be derived from the carefully polished prose of the historical writers of later years.

No one person could ever read all the thousands of books, magazine articles, diaries and letters pertaining to the Civil War. Here, however, within the covers of one book—a sort of anthology or compendium or scrapbook—will be found a sampling of the written words of those who were here when the war was fought, which it is hoped will give the reader a look at the war from the point of view of the time it happened.

In 1887 Senator John Sherman, brother of General William Tecumseh Sherman of the Union Army, was invited to Nashville to make a speech at a patriotic celebration. In the course of his remarks, referring to the losses and sacrifices of the Civil War, he said: "The courage, bravery and fortitude of both sides are now the pride and heritage of us all. Think not that I come here to reproach any man for the part he took in that fight, or to revive in the heart of anyone the triumph of victory or the pangs of defeat. . . . No man in the North questions the honesty of purpose or the heroism with which the Confederates maintained their cause, and you will give credit for like courage and honorable motives to Union soldiers, both North and South."

It is in the same spirit of recognition of the valor and devotion of the men and women, North and South, who experienced the trials and tragedies of those wartime years that this book is presented.

S. F. H.

Nashville, Tenn.
June 30, 1965

PROLOGUE

☆ *Tennessee Goes to War*

WHATEVER else may be said of Tennessee's participation in the War Between the States, or Civil War, it can not be charged that she rushed into the conflict with any undue lack of deliberation. On the contrary, an examination of the historical records reveals clearly her reluctance to leave the Union and the earnest efforts made by her political leaders in the Sixties to avoid secession.

It was once remarked by a commentator on Tennessee history who valued colorful expression above historical accuracy that "Tennessee never seceded from the Union, but Isham G. Harris seceded and took Tennessee along with him." But this flippant aphorism misrepresents the facts.

It is a matter of record that Tennessee did separate itself from the other states of the Union by entirely formal and deliberate action—an ordinance of the General Assembly which was ratified by the vote of the people. The fact that this action was taken only a few weeks after these same citizens of the state had voted not to secede has been considered by some so anomalous as to be attributable only to the sinister influence of a fire-eating Governor who was determined to sever the state's connection with the Union, regardless of the will of the people.

It is true that a majority of the people of the state did, indeed, have great respect for Harris and his views. Actually, however, the passage of the secession ordinance by the state's legislative body, in May 1861, and its prompt and decisive ratification by the vote of the people, was but a logical reflection of the sharp and swift change in the prevailing public sentiment in Tennessee in reaction to the sudden alteration in the political situation that had developed since the balloting less than four months before.

The feeling of a majority of the citizens of the state in this trying time of crisis seems to have been closely parallel to the feeling of Governor Harris. He believed sincerely that the sovereign states of the Union had an entirely legal and constitutional right to withdraw at their pleasure from the compact into which they had voluntarily entered. He believed that (regardless of the moral aspects of the question) the ownership of slaves was on the same legal basis as the ownership of any

[11]

other variety of property and that these property rights, like other property rights, should be respected by all the citizens of all the states of the Union. Harris was not, however, a pro-slavery demagogue, nor was he at first one of those who clamored for Tennessee's withdrawal from the Union. On the contrary, although he firmly believed in the right of a state to secede, the record shows that he was by no means eager to see Tennessee exercise that right. He counseled moderation and restraint until the fatal hour of decision in April, 1861, when Tennessee was forced to decide whether to furnish the troops demanded of her to make war on the other Southern states or to withdraw from the Union.

When that hour came, Governor Harris and the people of Tennessee realized that the time for temporizing had passed. A natural reluctance to sever the ties of union with her sister states was one thing; furnishing troops to coerce the states that had seceded was quite another. War was no longer an abstraction; it had now become a tragic reality. Tennessee now must fight; the only question left open was whether she should fight for or against her friends. Harris was but reflecting the aroused sentiments of a preponderant majority of the people of Tennessee when he replied to President Lincoln's call for troops in terse terms of blazing defiance: "Tennessee will not furnish a single man for purposes of coercion, but 50,000 if necessary for the defense of our rights and those of our Southern brothers." Impressive evidence of the validity of his defiance, as a spokesman for the people, was provided a few weeks later when more than two-thirds of the voters of the state cast their ballots in favor of the secession against which they had voted only a short time before when there seemed still to be hope of a peaceful settlement of the differences between the North and the South. Changing events brought about a change in public opinion; and it was Harris who sparked this change into dynamic action.

Isham Green Harris was born in 1818 in Franklin County, Tennessee, one of the southern tier of counties adjoining the state of Alabama. Like many another statesman, he studied law and was admitted to the bar at an early age. In 1847, at the age of 29, he was elected to the State Senate—the first of what was to be an unbroken record of victories at the polls in some fifty years of political activity. He later served Tennessee in various public offices, including service in Washington as a member of the House of Representatives; and in 1857 was elected governor of the state on the Democratic ticket.

If by any chance there were any who entertained any doubts as to just where Harris stood on the question of states' rights, they were enlightened by the plain and emphatic declaration in his inaugural address when he took over the Governor's chair from Andrew Johnson on November 3, 1857:

"The formation of our domestic institutions and the administration of our domestic affairs are amongst the highest and most important powers' reserved to the states and to the people', the exclusive exercise of which by the states is the surest bulwark against anti-republican tendencies and certainly affords to the citizens a greater amount of security for life, liberty and property, and in the pursuit of happiness, than can be secured under any other government that has ever existed. And any attempt on the part of the Federal Government or a sister state to interfere with the domestic institutions or policy of a State Government, or the formation of the domestic institutions of a new state, would be a palpable usurpation of power and an officious intermeddling, fraught with the most serious dangers and resulting probably in the most disastrous consequences."

During the two years of Harris's first term as Governor there were continuing rumbles of premonitory thunder presaging the impending storm as the clash of ideas between the North and South continued to carry them along the pathway to war, but his administration was occupied principally with the state's internal problems. The people and the newspapers discussed slavery and abolitionism from time to time and there were occasional publicly expressed suggestions of the possibility of secession as a last resort; but there was nothing recorded in the official utterances or papers of Governor Harris to indicate that these were burning issues or that he was particularly concerned with them.

In March of 1859 the Democratic State Convention was held in Nashville, and a platform was adopted which among other things endorsed the recent Dred Scott decision of the Supreme Court and expressed "undiminished confidence" in President Buchanan and Governor Harris, but did not make any reference to secession. Harris, without a suggestion of opposition, was nominated as the party's candidate for another term as Governor.

In the course of the ensuing campaign Harris again reiterated his strongly pro-Southern stand on the sectional questions then troubling the country. He emphatically endorsed the Democratic platform's approval of the Dred Scott decision, and warned of the danger to the South emanating from "the anti-slavery fanaticism of the North." That the people of Tennessee were preponderantly in agreement with his views is indicated by the fact that in the election he received the largest vote ever polled for any candidate in the state up to that time.

Governor Harris in his first message to the General Assembly devoted his remarks very largely to the state's financial affairs and banking problems, with no comment whatever on slavery or the widening rift between North and South. But even as he was reading his message to the legislators, the fanatic John Brown was gathering his fellow-conspirators about him preparatory to the attack on Harper's Ferry that would bring the slavery agitation to a quick and bloody crisis. Within ten days after that affair, the General Assembly of Tennessee adopted strongly worded resolutions denouncing the "recent insurrection at Harper's Ferry". It was, they said, "the natural fruits of the treasonable 'irrepressible conflict' doctrine of the Black Republican party", and they expressed appreciation of the promptness with which the National Administration had taken stern action to check the abolition conspiracy.

Events were now moving swiftly to their tragic climax, and early in 1860 the questions of slavery, states' rights and secession were brought prominently into the spotlight of public attention in the South in a manner requiring a definite and official stand by the state of Tennessee.

South Carolina in December 1859 had adopted some vigorously worded "Resolutions in Relation to Federal Affairs". These resolutions asserted her right to secede from the Union, pointed out the Northern abolitionists' assault upon "the institution of slavery and the rights and equality of the Southern States", and called for a meeting of representatives of the slave-holding states "to concert measures for united action". A copy of this resolution was sent by Governor Gist of South Carolina to Governor Harris, with the request that the documents be laid before the legislature of Tennessee, expressing the hope that "Tennessee will not hesitate to confer with her Southern sisters."

Harris dutifully submitted the resolution to the members of Tennessee's General Assembly in a special message February 26, 1860, again avowing his "jealous regard for the rights of the states", but expressing the opinion that resistance to "any unjust and unconstitutional warfare upon them or their institutions should be by the use of all the Constitutional means in our power, to the end that the Union may be preserved as it was formed." His message concluded with these placatory words:

"Whilst there is much in the present attitude of parties, states and public men in the northern portion of the country to cause apprehension as to the security of our rights and the continuance of fraternal feeling, yet there is a probability, and I hope a strong one, that wise, temperate and firm counsel may avert the impending evils. Therefore, before widening the breach in the manner designated in the resolution herewith submitted, our policy should be to exhaust every means consistent with honor and the Constitution, in an earnest effort to check the tide of aggression and restore the era of good feeling and fraternity throughout the whole country."

Governor Harris's soothing counsel of moderation evidently impressed the legislators. After considerable debate, a resolution was adopted which expressed due appreciation of the gravity of the problems facing the Southern States, but advanced the suggestion "that the most efficient policy for preserving our liberties and the Union will be found in such direct legislative action upon the part of the Southern States as may be necessary, and by offering united opposition at all times to the sectional party known as the Black Republican party, and that such a line of policy is more likely to attain the great end in view than the agency of an assemblage which can exercise no powers except to debate and advise." In conclusion it was declared that "In the opinion of the General Assembly it is inexpedient to appoint deputies to the congress proposed by South Carolina."

This, temporarily at least, officially established Tennessee and its Governor in a position outside the orbit of those warm-blooded leaders in other Southern states who felt that the limit of patience and endurance had just about been reached. And so matters rocked along during the ensuing months of 1860 on a basis of uneasy peace, with mounting apprehension as the Presidential campaign developed and campaign oratory aroused the feelings of the people.

The supreme crisis came in November of 1860 when the balloting resulted in the selection of Abraham Lincoln, the candidate of the Republican party. This new political party was definitely anti-Southern in its basic principles, and the bitterness of defeat for those who opposed Lincoln and his party was intensified by the fact that he did not receive a majority of the popular vote.

The so-called "Cotton States" registered a quick reaction to the news of Lincoln's election. South Carolina seceded from the Union in December 1860, and Alabama in January 1861. They were followed in quick succession by Georgia, Florida, Mississippi, Louisiana and Texas. Recognizing the full import of these events, Governor Harris called a special session of the General Assembly of Tennessee to meet in Nashville January 7, 1861. He submitted to the legislators a message in which he declared that:

"The systematic, wanton and long continued agitation of the slavery question, with the actual and threatened aggressions of the Northern states and a portion of their people upon the well-defined constitutional rights of the Southern citizens, the rapid growth and increase in all the elements of power of a purely sectional party, whose bond of union is uncompromising hostility to the rights and institutions of the fifteen Southern states, have produced a crisis in the affairs of the country unparalleled in the history of the past, resulting in the withdrawal from the confederacy of one of the sovereignties which compose it, while others are rapidly preparing to move in the same direction."

As a means of peaceably settling the slavery question Harris suggested five amendments to the Constitution of the United States which would spell out and guarantee the Southern slave-holders' rights. He expressed the view that if the adoption of these principles was accepted by the Northern people "peace will again establish her court in the midst of this once happy country, and the union of these states be restored to that spirit of fraternity, equality and justice which gave it birth." Secession he spoke of as a "fearful alternative"; and the possible arraying of the states of the Union into two seperate confederacies he termed "a calamity".

Realizing, however, that there was a growing feeling that the people of the state should have a means of expressing their views on the subject of secession, Harris recommended that the General Assembly submit to a vote of the people the question of whether there should be held in Nashville a convention "to take into consideration our Federal relations, and determine what action shall be taken by the State of Tennessee for the security of the rights and the peace of her citizens."

The election was held on February 9, and the result indicated that the people of Tennessee were still inclined to shrink from the dreadful spectre of secession as they voted: For the Convention, 57,798; No Convention, 69,675. A majority of the people of the state, obviously, were not ready even to talk about the drastic step of secession; so, temporarily at least, Tennessee continued as one of the United States of America.

It should be mentioned, however, that—technically speaking—it was not the entire state of Tennessee that remained in the Union. In Franklin County, snuggled up against the northern boundary of Alabama, which was one of the charter members of the infant Confederate States of America, the vote in the election was pro-Southern by a ratio of six to one—1240 to 206. When the anti-secession result of the state's referendum was officially announced on February 24th, a mass meeting of the Franklin County citizens was held in Winchester, the county seat, deploring and protesting the action of Tennessee's voters as "a source of unfeigned mortification and regret." Peter Turney, one of the county's leading secessionists, offered a resolution declaring that the people of the county were compelled by the vote to stay in the Federal Union "against our wills and earnest desire, when our hearts, sympathies and feeling are with the Confederate States of America." The resolution concluded by declaring Franklin County "out of the Union", with a petition to the state legislatures of Alabama and Tennessee, asking that the boundary line between the two states be officially altered so that Franklin County would be physically and geographically separated from Tennessee and joined to the state of Alabama, thereby giving to the citizens of that country "a government having our consent".

That these resolutions were not merely "sound and fury, signifying nothing" was demonstrated by the raising of the Confederate flag in Winchester "on a pole 100 feet high". Even more substantial evidence of the pro-Confederate zeal of the citizens of this new annex to Alabama was afforded by the fact that Peter Turney within a few days raised a regiment of volunteers to serve the Southern Confederacy, which regiment left for Virginia on May 1, and fought in that area until surrendered at Appomattox in April 1865.

Most of the other Tennesseans, however, not so bellicose as the Franklin Countians, appeared willing to accept the verdict rendered by the voters at the polls, at least for the time being, and the secession agitation in the newspapers and among the people subsided to some extent—but not for long.

On April 12 the whole country was rocked by the news of the bombardment of Fort Sumter. War was now an actuality, and the pro-Confederate sentiment in Tennessee quickly became more vigorously manifest. Then on April 17 came the electrifying news of Governor Harris's bold repudiation of President Lincoln's call on Tennessee to furnish two regiments of the 75,000 troops to be used to subdue the seceded states, and hardly a murmur of disapproval of his defiance was heard from the people. Precipitated by Lincoln's call for troops, there developed almost overnight a swift and impressive change in popular sentiment. A majority of the people seemed to recognize the unwelcome fact that now the time had come when they must take sides in the conflict that had already begun, and that spiritually and philosophically there was only one side they could take.

Events now moved rapidly. Governor Harris, recognizing the change in public sentiment, issued a proclamation calling for an extra session of the General Assembly to meet in Nashville on April 25, basing his call on an avowal that "An alarming and dangerous usurpation of power by the President of the United States has precipitated a state of war between the sovereign states of America." Immediately upon the assembling of this extra session, Harris presented them with a formal message briefly outlining the recent events and vigorously denouncing "the bloody and tyrannical policy of the Presidential usurper" and "his hordes of armed soldiery marching to the work of Southern subjugation." The essence of his message was contained in one sentence: "I respectfully suggest that our connection with the Federal Union be formally annulled in such manner as shall involve the highest exercise of sovereign authority by the people of the state."

The carefully guarded words used by Governor Harris reflected his consciousness of the fact that there were still a good many people in Tennessee who had an innate inclination to shy away from the word "secession", which to the lovers of the old Union had taken on an almost unholy connotation. In making his specific recommendation for action, therefore, he said: "I respectfully recommend the perfecting of an ordinance by the General Assembly, formally declaring the independence of the State of Tennessee of the Federal Union . . . and that such ordinance, when it shall have been thus perfected by the Legislature, shall at the earliest practicable time be submitted to a vote of the people, to be by them adopted or rejected." He further suggested an ordinance, also to be submitted to the voters, providing for the state's admission as one of the Confederate States of America.

The members of the General Assembly, it developed, were overwhelmingly in favor of enacting such an ordinance as the Governor suggested. Also they carefully followed his cue in distinguishing between the right of secession and the right to revolt, and on May 6th passed "An Act to submit to a vote of the people a Declaration of Independence". This formal Declaration of Independence opened with this pronouncement: "We, the people of the State of Tennessee, waiving any expression of opinion as to the abstract doctrine of secession, but asserting the right as a free and independent people to alter, reform or abolish our form of government in such manner as we think proper, do ordain and declare that all the laws and ordinances by which the State of Tennessee became a member of the Federal Union of the United States of America are hereby abrogated and annulled . . and do hereby henceforth become a free, sovereign and independent state."

The philosophical foundation for the terms of the proposed legislation was carefully explained by the General Assembly in its "Legislative Address to the People of Tennessee" which was issued along with the call for the election, and which declared: "While differences of opinion exist as to the abstract right of secession, no one denies the right of a people to revolutionize. The right to 'change, alter or abolish' their form of government is a principle engrafted in the fundamental laws of the state. Your representatives have therefore steered clear of the mooted question of secession, and submitted a revolutionary document which, if ratified by the popular vote, will sever the ties that bind Tennessee to her enemies and oppressors—and that, after all, is the object to be attained, by whatever name it may be called."

As might naturally be supposed, the Confederate authorities at Montgomery were acutely interested in the turn of events in Tennessee. The original seven Confederate states were keenly aware of the desirability of having the border states join them, and the secession of Tennessee seemed especially desirable, as Tennessee in the Confederacy would provide a geographical buffer along the northern frontiers of Alabama, Georgia and Mississippi. It is not surprising, therefore, to find that when the state legislature assembled in April, there appeared in Nashville a distinguished citizen of Alabama, the Hon. Henry W. Hilliard, who bore the imposing entitlement of "Commissioner from the Confederate States to the State of Tennessee." Mr. Hilliard let it be known that he would accept an invitation to address the General Assembly; and, such an invitation having been extended, he appeared before them on April 20 and delivered what the newspapers of the day described as an oration of great eloquence and impressiveness.

"Mr. Hilliard," wrote an admiring Nashville editor, "manifests none of the vindictiveness which seems to be considered a staple article by many public men of late, but rather chooses to treat of events and actors from a more elevated and statesmanlike standpoint than that of a coarse and unreasoning denunciator. It is true he spoke in strong terms of the treachery and perfidy of Lincoln, but he took care to show clearly and reasonably the grounds upon which he based his charge." Mr. Hilliard told the legislators that he came to Tennessee for the purpose of establishing a temporary alliance between the state and the Confederate states, to continue until Tennessee should decide for or against adopting the Constitution of that government and becoming one of the Confederate States of America.

Mr. Hilliard was able to return to Montgomery with a report of "mission accomplished", for the General Assembly did pass a law providing for a Military League with the Confederacy, to become effective May 7, even though the "declaration of independence" had not yet been ratified and Tennessee was still legally one of the United States.

An act was also passed providing for the raising of a provisional army of 55,000 volunteers "for the defense of the state", directing the governor to take charge of this military force, and authorizing the issuance of $5,000,000 of state bonds to raise funds to support the military forces.

Fortified with this legislation, Governor Harris promptly proceeded with an energetic program of preparation for war. As authorized by the legislation, he announced on May 9th the appointment of a Military and Financial Board consisting of three prominent Tennesseans: Neill S. Brown, William G. Harding and James E. Bailey. Gideon J. Pillow and Samuel R. Anderson, who had served as officers in the Mexican War, were named major generals in the "Provisional Army of Tennessee", along with a full complement of other military officials. Companies of volunteers were raised in all parts of the state and mustered into service. Training camps for troops were established, the banks of the Mississippi River above Memphis were fortified, and efforts to form a defensive alliance with the governor of Kentucky were instituted.

When at length the referendum election was held on June 8, the result was such a foregone conclusion as to be a sort of anti-climax, the voters ratifying the withdrawal from the Federal Union and alliance with the Confederate States of America by a vote of more than two to one.

Most of the negative votes were cast in the counties constituting East Tennessee, and the outcome of the election was violently protested by the Union sympathizers in that section. Following the legislative enactment of the "Declaration of Independence" in May there had been held at Greeneville a protest meeting at which the action of the General Assembly was denounced as "hasty, inconsiderate and unconstitutional", calling upon the people of the state to vote against it in the June 8th election. When the result of that election was made known, another convention was held at Greeneville and a memorial was adopted and submitted to the General Assembly at Nashville, denouncing the legislation and the referendum as "unconstitutional and illegal, and therefore not binding upon us as loyal citizens," and asking the consent of the Assembly that the dissident East Tennessee counties "may form and erect a separate state".

The separatists' memorial, however, was ignored by the General Assembly, and on June 24th Governor Harris officially announced that "an overwhelming majority" of the voters had signified their approval of "separation", and he declared Tennessee "a free, independent government". Technically the state continued as a "free and independent government" for almost a month, but on July 22nd Tennessee was formally admitted to membership in the Confederate States of America.

Actually, the election was to a great extent a mere formality, ratifying what had already been done. By the legislative acts of early May the Governor and the General Assembly had made Tennessee an ally though not a member of the Southern Confederacy, and by the time the election was held the state had twenty-four regiments of troops in the field, three of them already mustered into the service of the Confederate States.

So, for better or for worse, Tennessee cast its lot with the Southern Confederacy; so began the most tragic four years of the state's history.

CHAPTER 1

☆ *Preparing for War*

THE INITIAL steps taken in Tennessee to prepare for the war are summarized by James D. Porter in the *Confederate Military History*. Porter served as adjutant general on the staff of General Pillow, and played an important part in the organization of the provisional army of Tennessee, so he speaks with knowledge and authority:

On the 9th of May, 1861, the governor appointed, by and with the advice and consent of the General Assembly, to be major-generals, Gideon J. Pillow and Samuel R. Anderson; brigadier-generals, Felix K. Zollicoffer, B. F. Cheatham, Robert C. Foster 3rd, John L. T. Sneed and William R. Caswell; adjutant-general, Daniel S. Donelson; inspector-general, William H. Carroll; surgeon-general, B. W. Avent; chief of artillery, John P. McCown; assistant adjutant-generals, W. C. Whitthorne, James D. Porter, Hiram S. Bradford and D. M. Key, with assistants for all departments; and on the 28th of June following he appointed Bushrod R. Johnson, colonel and chief of engineers, and made Moses H. Wright captain and chief of ordnance. For military and financial board, Neill S. Brown, James E. Bailey and William G. Harding were selected. V. K. Stevenson was made colonel and chief quartermaster, with a full complement of assistants. Maj. George W. Cunningham was placed in charge of the depot at Nashville for the accumulation of supplies, and there, and subsequently at Atlanta, Ga., he exhibited extraordinary skill and energy in the discharge of his duty. The Military and Financial Board rendered great assistance to the chiefs of the several departments of the army. The services of the members of the board were recognized as of the first importance; their functions ceased with the transfer of the troops to the Confederate States.

John Heriges, keeper of public arms, reported in January, 1861, that the state arsenal contained 8,761 muskets and rifles, 350 carbines, four pieces of artillery, and a small lot of pistols and sabers, with 1,815 muskets and rifles, 228 pistols and 200 sabers in the hands of volunteer companies. Of the muskets in the arsenal, 280 were percussion, the balance were flint-lock, and over 4,300 of them were badly damaged; the carbines were flint-lock and unserviceable, and two of the four pieces of artillery were in the same condition. The governor reported in his message, dated April 2, 1861, that since the date of the report of the keeper of public arms, he had "ordered

[19]

and received at the arsenal 1,400 rifle muskets." This constituted the armament of the State of Tennessee.

The chief of ordnance, Capt. M. H. Wright, thoroughly educated to the duties of his place, soon organized a force for the repair of arms, the manufacture and preparation of ammunition and the equipments of the soldiers, and for the conversion of the flint-lock muskets to percussion; and, aided by patriotic citizens like Samuel D. Morgan, established a plant for the manufacture of percussion caps. Thus he was able to supply the troops of Tennessee as they took the field. Shipments of caps were made to the authorities at Richmond, who used them very largely at the first battle of Manassas. About 3,000 pounds of powder were being manufactured daily. Foundries for the manufacture of field guns were constructed at Nashville and Memphis, and by November guns of good pattern were turned out at both points at the rate of six a week. Capt. W. R. Hunt, of the ordnance department, was the efficient head at Memphis.

Nashville soon became a great depot of supplies for the Confederate States. The manufacture of powder was stimulated, fixed ammunition was made in large quantities, large supplies of leather and material for the manufacture of shoes and hats on a large scale were established. Great stores of bacon and flour and everything required by an army were provided. From these stores supplies were sent to Virginia and all points in the Southwest, and Nashville attained a degree of importance it never before enjoyed and perhaps will not soon again enjoy.

Major-General Pillow established his headquarters at Memphis and very soon organized the Provisional Army of Tennessee. Before the close of the month of May, twenty-one regiments of infantry were armed and equipped and in the field, and ten artillery companies and one regiment of cavalry were organized and mustered into the service of the state, besides three regiments of infantry then in Virginia already mustered into the service of the Confederate States. More than double that number of troops had tendered their services to the state, as the governor stated in his message of June 18th, "without even a call being made;" but their services were declined until the necessities of the state required a larger force and until arms could be provided. Before the close of the year 1861, the official records of the office of the Secretary of State show, seventy-one regiments of infantry and twenty-two batteries of artillery were mustered into the service of the state, and twenty-one regiments of cavalry, nine battalions, and enough independent companies and partisan rangers to have constituted eight full regiments were organized.

In the summer of 1861 all the troops were transferred to the service of the Confederate States, and the following-named general officers of Tennessee were commissioned Confederate brigadier-generals by President Davis: Gideon J. Pillow, Samuel R. Anderson, Felix K. Zollicoffer and B. F. Cheatham. These were soon followed by the appointment of John P. McCown, Bushrod R. Johnson, Alexander P. Stewart and William H. Carroll to the same rank.

Tennessee's entry into the war, of course, brought about an immediate and complete upheaval in the pattern of the people's lives, both private and public. The effect of this, as experienced and recorded by a woman who lived in Nashville through those stirring days, is to be seen in a little book published soon after the war by Mrs. Irby Morgan. Mrs. Morgan was the wife of a prominent Nashville business man who became active in Tennessee's preparations for the war effort, and in her *How It Was; Four Years Among the Rebels* she has left an impressive and moving record of one woman's experiences as she followed the Confederacy through its four tragic years. In the first chapter of her book she tells how, as soon as Tennessee withdrew from the Union, "every one commenced planning and trying to do something to aid the South":

Drums were beating, fifes playing, the boys coming in troops to enlist for the war, and anxious fathers and mothers could be met at every point. All were earnest and anxious, as few had anticipated the result of the wrangling the country had had for years; and now war was upon us, and we totally unprepared for it.

We of the South were in a dilemma what to do; but we went on the presumption that "where there's a will there's a way," to get us out of difficulty, and the result proved it. All the old guns and muskets to be found were brought into requisition, and many consulted as to how to use them, how they could be remodeled, etc.

Mr. V. K. Stevenson and others formed a company to gather war materials, and my husband, Mr. Irby Morgan, was selected by him to go to New Orleans, Louisville, and other points to get sulphur and other material for making percussion caps.

Col. Samuel D. Morgan took great interest in the cap factory, and it was a success, for in a short time they were making thousands. Mr. Irby Morgan brought home two of the first perfect caps, and requested me to keep them as souvenirs of the war. The caps that were used at Manassas and Bull Run were made in our cap factory of the material bought by my husband.

After this factory had proved a success, Mr. Morgan and others were sent to hunt wool to make clothes for our soldiers, and he went to Texas and other points and bought four hundred and fifty thousand pounds and had it shipped to Nashville, and from there he took it to factories in Mississippi, Alabama, Georgia, and East Tennessee to be made into Confederate gray. He went to the factories and got the cloth, and the last he procured Gen. Roddy had to send an escort to guard the wagons, and he delivered to the department in Atlanta five hundred thousand yards of Confederate gray which he had made at a cost of seventy-five cents a yard, when it was selling in the market at five dollars a yard.

During the summer of 1861, while Tennessee was in the throes of effecting its formal separation from the United States, Bishop Leonidas Polk of the Episcopal Church visited Sewanee, Tennessee, in connection with the Church's plan for the establishment of a university at that location. On this occasion he encountered Governor Isham G. Harris, who (knowing that Polk was a graduate of the Military Academy and that he and Jefferson Davis had been class-mates at West Point) asked the Bishop if he would go to Richmond and use his influence with Davis to obtain armanent and equipment for the Tennessee troops and also to impress on the President the importance of prompt measures for the defense of the Mississippi River and its Valley.

Polk went to Richmond, where he was cordially received by his old friend, now burdened with the multiplying responsibilities of the Presidency of the infant Confederate States of America. It happened that at the same time there was in Richmond a delegation of men from the Mississippi Valley, who had come to urge Davis to appoint some competent officer to defend that area. The upshot of this combination of circumstances was that Davis asked Polk to accept a commission as Major General in the Confederate army, an appointment which Polk, after prayerful consideration, reluctantly accepted. In writing to his wife, telling her of his decision to accept, he said: "I find my mind unable to say No to this call, for it seems to be a call of Providence. . . . I will do what I can for my country, our hearthstones and our altars. And may the Lord have mercy upon me, and help me to be wise, to be sagacious, to be firm, to be merciful, and to be filled with all the knowledge and all the graces necessary to qualify me to fill the office." Accordingly, on June 25th, Polk was issued his commission as a Major General in the provisional Confederate army, and on July 4th was assigned to the command of Department No. 2, with headquarters at Memphis.

Upon assuming command of the Department on July 13, he issued his "General Orders No. 1", which constituted a stirring declaration of principles:

Having been assigned to the charge of the defense of that part of the valley of the Mississippi which is embraced within the boundaries of Department No. 2, I hereby assume command. All officers on duty within the limits of said department will report accordingly. In assuming this very grave responsibility, the general in command is constrained to declare his deep and long-settled conviction that the war in which we are engaged is one not warranted by reason or any necessity, political or social, of our existing condition, but that it is indefensible and of unparalleled atrocity.

We have protested, and do protest, that all we desire is to be let alone, to repose in quietness under our own vine and under our own fig tree. We have sought and only seek the undisturbed enjoyment of the inherent and indefeasible right of self-government, a right which freemen can never relinquish, and which none but tyrants could ever seek to wrest from us. Those with whom we have been lately associated in the bonds of a pretended fraternal regard have wished and endeavored to deprive us of this, our great birthright as American freemen. Nor is this all. They have sought to deprive us of this inestimable right by a merciless war, which can attain no other possible end than the ruin of fortunes and the destruction of lives; for the subjugation of Christian freemen is out of the question.

A war which has thus no motive except lust or hate, and no object except ruin and devastation, under the shallow pretense of the restoration of the Union, is surely a war against heaven, as well as a war against earth. Of all the absurdities ever enacted, of all the hypocrisies ever practiced, an attempt to restore a union of minds, hearts, and wills like that which once existed in North America, by the ravages of fire and sword, are assuredly among the most prodigious. As sure as there is a righteous Ruler of the universe, such a war must end in disaster to those by whom it was inaugurated, and by whom it is now prosecuted with the circumstances of barbarity which, it was fondly believed, would never more disgrace the annals of a civilized people.

Numbers may be against us, but the battle is not always to the strong. Justice will triumph; and an earnest of this triumph is already beheld in the mighty uprising of the whole Southern heart. Almost as one man this great section comes to the rescue, resolved to perish rather than yield to the oppressor who, in the name of freedom, yet under the prime inspiration of an infidel horde, seeks to reduce eight millions of freemen to abject bondage and subjugation. All ages and conditions are united in one grand and holy purpose of rolling back the desolating tide of invasion, and of restoring to the people of the South that peace, independence, and right of self-government to which they are by nature and nature's God as justly entitled as those who seek thus ruthlessly to enslave them.

The general in command, having the strongest confidence in the intelligence and firmness of purpose of those belonging to this department, enjoins upon them the maintenance of a calm, patient, persistent, and undaunted determination to resist the invasion at all hazards and to the last extremity. It comes bringing with it a contempt for constitutional liberty and the withering influence of the infidelity of New England and Germany combined. Its success would deprive us of a future. The best men among our invaders opposed the course they are pursuing at the first, but they have been overborne or swept into the wake of the prevailing current, and now, under the promptings of their fears or the delusion of some idolatrous reverence supposed to be due to a favorite symbol, are as active as any in instigating this unnatural, unchristian, and cruel war.

Our protest, which we here solemnly repeat in the face of the civilized world, has been hitherto unheeded, and we are left alone, under God, to the resources of our own minds and our own hearts, to the resources of manhood. Upon them, knowing, as he does, those whom he addresses, as well as those with whom you are co-operating throughout the South, the general in command feels he may rely with unwavering confidence. Let every man, then, throughout the land arm himself in the most effective manner, and hold himself in readiness to support the combined resistance. A cause which has for its object nothing less than the security of civil liberty and the preservation of the purity of religious truth, is the cause of Heaven, and may well challenge the homage and service of the patriot and Christian. In God is our trust.

One of General Polk's biographers, his son Dr. William M. Polk, says that "General Polk was well aware that he had been assigned to the most important military position in the Confederacy", but he goes on to say:

The difficulties with which he had to contend were very great. The militia of the State of Tennessee had not yet been transferred to the Confederate Army, and the only troops which were legally under his authority were a few regiments at Corinth and some unarmed companies in Memphis and Vicksburg; but until a regular and legal transfer could be made, the Tennessee authorities consented that the state troops should serve under General Polk's orders. Within the limits of the department there were about ten thousand men of this description; but, notwithstanding the most energetic efforts of their commander, General Pillow, many of them were without arms, and ordnance supplies of all sorts were still entirely inadequate. To these deficiencies General Polk first turned his attention and, with the assistance of Captain Richard Hunt as ordnance officer, he soon had that branch of the service in working order.

That Captain William Richardson Hunt was a competent and energetic ordnance officer is clearly indicated by a letter he addressed, from his office in Memphis, to General Polk on August 12. In this letter he summed up the existing conditions and the outlook, with suggestions as to the steps needed to be taken, with a presience and far-seeing appreciation of the magnitude of the task facing them which was not shared by all those in authority in the Confederacy:

Sir: If this war should unfortunately be prolonged, the valley of the Mississippi must ultimately become its great theater, for the enemy now working to subjugate the South knows the value of our great artery of commerce and of the prominent cities upon it too well for us to doubt that he will bend all his energies to control them. To prepare for such a defense as may be commensurate with the interests involved, we may have to invoke all the resources of this valley, and I feel satisfied that they are amply adequate to the emergency.

You now have in the section under your command, already finished and to be finished in the next 30 days, 75 field guns of various caliber, and I beg you will allow me to suggest and recommend that 50 batteries, of six guns each, be put into the field as early as possible.

To effect this, it will be best to send agents to Vicksburg, Jackson, New Orleans, Mobile, Montgomery, Huntsville, and Nashville, to make contracts for, say, 165 field pieces; two 12-pounder rifled Parrott guns; one 12-pounder howitzer; one 24-pounder howitzer; making a total of 74 6-pounder field pieces; 74 12-pounder Parrott guns, rifled; 37 12-pounder howitzers; 37 24-pounder howitzers.

For the moving of this artillery we shall require 2,500 sets of artillery harness; 225 gun carriages, and 225 caissons; 38 battery wagons, and 38 battery forges.

The cost will be [giving detailed figures] $515,825. This estimate is based upon the number of pieces allowed per thousand men by the United States Government. Three hundred pieces would be the supply allowed for 100,000 men, two pieces per thousand men for battery purposes, and the third piece to be held in reserve, in case the pieces in battery should be disabled by any casualty. Should you fail to get the number of pieces contracted for, yet you could not fail to get a large supply of them, and the entire manufacturing enterprise of the country would be enlisted in the manu-

facture of cannon or of any and all kinds of ordnance, as they would have abundant
machinery in readiness for turning its powers into any required channel.

The history of all wars of independence teaches us that the fires of patriotism burn
more brightly at the outbreak than towards their close. Men in the outset of such a
contest are more oblivious of personal discomfort, less selfish, than they become as
the struggle progress, and more willing to contribute in all way the means of winning
independence. Our Revolution of '76 is an instance to illustrate this truth. The paper
of the Government passed current at first, though rejected as worthless towards the
close, yet that Government was surely better able to make good its contracts at the
end of that struggle than at the beginning. May not such be the result in this contest,
and does not wisdom point out the necessity of securing such war material as we can
while our Government is in good credit?

For the 300 field pieces will be required ammunition costing say, $100,000; making
a total cost for the 225 field pieces and ammunition for one campaign, say, $640,000.

I would also respectfully recommend that contracts be made for 25,000 sword
bayonets for Mississippi rifles and 10,000 for double-barreled shotguns. These bayonets
complete will cost about $9 each, making a total cost of $315,000 for the 35,000.
Bayonet and gun barrels for rifles ready forged out for rifling can be procured in any
quantity at $3.00 each from Hillman Brothers, on Tennessee River. The dies for locks
and nipples are being made here and can be turned out in large quantities. A foundry
and shop in this city can turn out gun stocks at the rate of 100 to 200 per day, and
we can thus have a weapon equal in all respects to the Mississippi rifle, while it will
not be so heavy.

Two machines for rifling cannon will be in operation here this week, and, if successful, they can turn out six pieces daily. Contracts may be made at other points
for casting and boring guns, while the rifling could be done here whenever required.

The spirit animating the United States Congress and people, and the great preparations made for a war upon a grand theater, induce me to urge upon you the importance of a timely and efficient preparation on our part, and the plan for equipping
ourselves.

On his way back to Nashville from Richmond, Polk in coming through East
Tennessee became strongly aware of the strong pro-Union sentiment prevailing
among the people in that part of the state and their disinclination to accept
the decision of the majority of their fellow-Tennesseans in voting for secession.
He stopped in Nashville to see Governor Harris and impress on him the gravity
of the disaffection in the eastern part of the state, and after conferring with the
governor he sent a telegram to President Davis urging the vital importance of
sending to East Tennessee a strong body of Confederate troops under an able
commander. For some reason, not entirely clear, Polk recommended the appointment of Felix K. Zollicoffer (a Nashville editor and member of Congress) for
commander of these troops, although Zollicoffer had had only a smattering of
military experience in the Mexican War. Zollicoffer, however, was commissioned
brigadier general and sent off to Knoxville with a motley force of raw recruits,
numbering some 3,000 or 4,000.

When Polk was in Richmond urging Davis to appoint a single commander
for the over-all direction of military activities in the Confederate West, he suggested only two names: Albert Sidney Johnston and Robert E. Lee. Of the two,
Johnston was his first choice. Johnston was a graduate of the Military Academy at
West Point, but he had had little actual experience in command of combat troops.
Nevertheless, he was at the time generally considered a military man of exceptional
ability. Davis in after years said: "I hoped and expected that I had others who

would prove to be generals; but I knew that I had one, and that was Sidney Johnston." Johnston was on army duty in California when the war began in 1861, but he promptly resigned his command, and made his way overland across the hot, sandy wastes of Arizona, New Mexico and Texas to New Orleans and thence to Richmond, where he arrived on September 5th and offered his services to the Confederacy. Davis was delighted when Johnston put in his appearance at the Confederate White House, and promptly commissioned him a full general in the Confederate Army and sent him to Tennessee with the resounding title of "General Commanding the Western Department of the Army of the Confederate States of America."

Jefferson Davis, in his *Rise and Fall of the Confederate Government,* tells of Johnston's taking over his new command:

General Johnston, on his arrival at Nashville, found that he lacked not only men, but the munitions of war and the means of obtaining them. Men were ready to be enlisted, but the arms and equipment had nearly all been required to fit out the first levies. Immediately on his survey of the situation, he determined to occupy Bowling Green in Kentucky, and ordered Brigadier General S. B. Buckner, with five thousand men, to take possession of the position. This invasion of Kentucky was an act of self-defense, rendered necessary by the action of the government of Kentucky and by the evidence of intended movements of the forces of the United States. It was not possible to withdraw the troops from Columbus in the west, nor from Cumberland Ford in the east, to which General Felix K. Zollicoffer had advanced with four thousand men . . . East of Columbus, Fort Henry, Fort Donelson and Hopkinsville were garrisoned with small bodies of troops; and the territory between Columbus and Bowling Green was occupied by moving detachments which caused the supposition that a large military force was present and contemplated an advance. A fortified camp was established at Cumberland Gap as the right of General Johnston's line, and an important point for the protection of East Tennessee against invasion. Thus General Johnston located his line of defense, from Columbus on the west to the Cumberland Mountains on the east, with his center at Bowling Green, which was occupied and intrenched.

Granting that his difficulties were monumental, some military critics have questioned whether General Johnston made the best possible use of his limited facilities. His line across the state of Kentucky, it is true, left much to be desired from many standpoints, military and otherwise. But its location was limited and governed by practical conditions which are well set out by his son and biographer, William Preston Johnston:

In determining his line of operations, General Johnston had to consider the geography of the theatre of war, the political complexion of the population, and the strength and disposition of the forces opposed to him. Each of these conditions was of such a character as to put him at a disadvantage. . . . As Columbus and the Cumberland Mountains had become the extremeties of the Confederate line by force of natural conditions, so Bowling Green, likewise, became the salient. . . . Any point in advance of Bowling Green (was) unsafe; while Bowling Green itself, situated on the turnpike, railroad and river, was a good position for defense. . . . The line was not all that could be wished; it ran through an unfriendly or lukewarm population, and it was pierced by two great rivers (the Tennessee and the Cumberland) whose mouths were in possession of the enemy; but every other line had equal or greater advantages. In war, as elsewhere, we must take things as we find them, not as we would have them.

Following the formal entry of Tennessee into the Confederate States of

America, the Military and Financial Board (Messrs. Neill S. Brown, W. G. Harding and James E. Bailey) on October 1, 1861, made their official report to the state's General Assembly, summarizing their activities since the Board was created in May of that year:

The undersigned, members of the Military and Financial Board, beg leave respectfully to report that they were organized under the act of May last, soon after its passage, and have been engaged ever since in the execution of the arduous and difficult trusts imposed upon them. Prior to their organization and in anticipation of the passage of the act of May, a preliminary and informal board was instituted at the instance of the Governor of the State, by whose agency large supplies of clothing, provisions, and material of war were purchased and shipped to Nashville. The sequel has shown the wisdom and forecast of this early movement, as it enabled the state to secure a large amount of articles of indispensable necessity that in a short time afterward could not be purchased at any price; and much of what was still attainable and important to the service soon rose to enormous rates.

Contemporaneously with this original board, there were established by private citizens at Nashville, Knoxville, Memphis, and other places boards of supply that rendered efficient and valuable services as auxiliaries in the great work of preparation. And to the liberality and patriotism of the citizens of those and other localities the state is largely indebted for whatever has been achieved in organizing and fitting out the Provisional Army.

The undersigned, of course, found many difficulties to encounter. A large army, such as Tennessee had never furnished before, had to be raised, organized, equipped, clothed, fed, and paid. The task was a new one, and the facilities in many respects not abundant. Arms and ammunition, the most important items in such an emergency, were the most difficult of attainment. The blockade then and still existing all around the Southern States rendered the importation of these articles almost impossible. At the time of the organization of this board there was not a cap factory in the whole South, nor a powder mill in operation, nor a manufactory of small arms to any extent, and but one cannon foundry. In this state of things there was no appeal except to our own resources. Under the auspices of Samuel D. Morgan, esq., a manufactory of caps was established in this city, which from small beginnings has been made to produce within the last four months over 12,000,000 caps, and is now producing daily enough to sustain the waste of a great battle. Much credit is due Mr. Morgan for his aid in this and other matters connected with the public service. The capacity of this establishment is believed to be adequate to meet the demands of the whole Confederate States.

Cannon enough have been cast, both bronze and iron, to supply the whole Provisional Army of Tennessee for the present. This has been done principally in Nashville and Memphis, and to some extent in Chattanooga, and can now be carried on to any limit. The manufacture of small-arms, such as guns and sabers, has also been pressed with the utmost diligence. A large amount of capital and skill has been brought into requisition for this purpose in Nashville, Memphis, Knoxville, and other places, and while the production up to this time has not been great, the foundation has been laid by which, in a few months, there will have been more guns manufactured in the state than were to be found in the arsenal at the commencement of the present struggle. The skill employed in this important branch is rapidly improving, and the most confident hopes are indulged that the success will be complete.

On the subject of powder, the undersigned have encountered the greatest difficulty. By timely action a large amount of sulphur was obtained by purchase at different points, but the supply of saltpeter was limited, and not to be had in the markets of the South. To supply this indispensable article, resort was had to the caves of Tennessee, Georgia, Alabama, and Arkansas, and, at considerable expense and delay, contracts were made in all these localities which, with varied success, promise in the aggregate to afford a sufficient amount for the current demand. In many instances liberal advances had to be made to induce the investment of capital and labor in that uncertain and precarious business, and it has been impossible to procure the manufacture of the article at all, except at high prices.

The undersigned also, by advances, procured one powder mill that had been out of use for some time to be refitted with increased capacity, and it has been in operation for several weeks past. They procured also in like manner to be erected a new mill, which is now about completed, with large capacity. These two mills, if they meet with no accident, it is believed will be able to furnish powder enough to meet the current demands of the whole Government during the war.

The expenses of all these operations have been considerable and greatly enhanced by the increase in the price of materials, and in certain branches of mechanical labor. Arms of every description soon rose to enormous rates, but the undersigned, while seeking to practice economy as far as possible, did not hesitate to pay high prices where it was necessary to arm and sustain the soldier and prepare for the impending struggle. Much of the expense incurred resulted from the failure of Confederate authorities promptly to muster our troops and to prepare for their support. The consequence was that the state has been compelled, until a recent date, to pay, clothe, and sustain her army, notwithstanding it was virtually turned over by the vote of the 8th of June and the proclamation of the Governor. This, however, can only prove a temporary inconvenience, as the Government has admitted its readiness to pay our troops from and after the 31st of July, the date of the Governor's proclamation, and such as have not been paid by the state since that period will be paid by the Confederate paymaster, and of course the advances by the state on this account refunded.

General Johnston was fully aware of the magnitude of the problems confronting him, and he was exerting every energy personally to improve the quantity and quality of his armament. One of his aides, Samuel Tate, reported to him from Memphis on November 4th as to the results of his efforts there:

Dear Sir: I arrived at home last night. I find the foundries of Nashville are prepared to work on a large scale, but have engagements for some time ahead; but in case of emergency I have no doubt you can get the guns they are making for the Government. I can get six guns a week cut and bored at Huntsville, from 6-pounder to 24-pounder howitzers. I can have completed here about twelve guns a week after the order is received and patterns made. The Parrott gun seems a failure; cast and wrought iron will not do combined. We are making a Dahlgren cast-iron 6-pounder gun that can be rifled, that will do, weighing about 900 pounds. Colonel Hunt tells me he has fifteen field guns here, 6-pounders on carriages, not appropriated. He also has copper and tin to cast about fifty more, and is having them turned out about one per day. Would you prefer them rifled or not? How many brass 12-pounder howitzers would you like in proportion to 6-pounder smooth and rifled guns?

Colonel Carroll tells me he is ordered to East Tennessee; is waiting for his guns to be repaired; says he can have it done at the rate of 100 per day. He says he will move 900 men this week. I think you had better write him to go, without waiting to have anything done to his guns except ordinary repairs. Colonel Reynolds has a regiment at Iuka, 100 miles east of here; no guns. General Walker has a brigade at Huntsville and no guns. M. Walker is sick; his regiment has but few guns, about 100; expects more this week. A Texas regiment is here, I learn, without guns. I have not seen them. Colonel Looney's regiment here expect guns this week.

I have great fears for Zollicoffer's safety if he does not get help soon.

Could you not get the War Department to give us some submarine batteries on the river above here? I have my doubts about stopping these iron gunboats, but I am sure we could blow them out of water with proper batteries. They would cost but little; the scarcity of powder is the only trouble. Fort Pillow and Columbus I fear, from what Captain Lynch said to me a few days ago, is deficient in quality as well as quantity of powder. Morgan, of Nashville, assured me when I was there that their mills were now making 2,800 pounds per day. We have made requisitions on them for 35,000 pounds for our forts above, but get no response. I have been running around all day to find out what I could, and write now in great haste to go by train in a few minutes. Let me know how many and what kind of guns you want, and I will try and get them made as rapidly as possible. Say whether you want carriages or not.

P. S.—Colonel Forrest's regiment of cavalry, as fine a body of men as ever went to the field, has gone to Dover or Fort Donelson. Give Forrest a chance and he will distinguish himself.

Neill S. Brown's service on the Military Board had so impressed him with the gravity of the situation on the Tennessee and Cumberland Rivers that on December 14th he wrote from Nashville a personal letter to Secretary of War Benjamin appealing for help; and, to emphasize the importance of the matter, Mayor R. B. Cheatham of Nashville carried the letter to Richmond and presented it to Benjamin in person. In his letter Brown said:

Sir: This will be presented to you by R. B. Cheatham, esq., mayor of Nashville. After an interview with General A. S. Johnston, he visits Richmond for the purpose or urging the expediency of constructing gun-boats for the use of the Cumberland and Tennessee Rivers, or rather of converting steam-boats into gun-boats. I commend him to your kind and respectful notice as a gentleman of intelligence and energy and who is familiar with our wants, our territory, and necessities. I will add on this subject my own conviction of the utility of one or more gun-boats on each river. I am of opinion that our city, with all its public stores, is in imminent peril. You are aware that the force of the enemy in front of Bowling Green is not less than 75,000, and perhaps 100,000. We have not half that number to oppose them. Our new forces now assembling will be indifferently armed and our stock of lead is lamentably short. Can we not get a supply of lead from Virginia? We wish the real lead for rifles. I respectfully urge upon you also the necessity of appointing a brigadier-general of the interior for this place, to attend to the thousand and one items that are oppressing the service and will not admit of delay. Among his other duties should be added the entire care of the railroad bridges of the State and to have them well guarded. Such an officer should be a brigadier general to give him weight and influence, and if he is a painstaking man, popular and energetic, he could do more good than if he were in the field winning victories. The necessity of such an appointment here is obvious. As it is, there is confusion and delay and the commanding general is constantly harassed with these details, and less able to attend to them than one specially assigned.

One of the things most apparent to all observers on both sides from the very first days of the war was that the Tennessee and Cumberland Rivers offered an inviting double pathway to the heart of the Confederacy. The Tennessee has its headwaters in the mountains of East Tennessee, whence it flows south in a big bend through northern Alabama, touches the northeastern corner of Mississippi, and then runs north through western Tennessee and Kentucky to the Ohio. The Cumberland rises in eastern Kentucky, curves in a wide sweep through Middle Tennessee to where Nashville stands on its southern bank, thence flows northwest to its confluence with the Ohio. Smithland at the mouth of the Cumberland is only twelve miles from Paducah at the mouth of the Tennessee. There is an odd geological formation in Western Kentucky and Tennessee, as a result of which the two rivers in this area flow almost due north, while the Mississippi, about a hundred miles away, pursues a roughly parallel channel due south. The Tennessee could carry an invading Northern army into north Alabama as far as Florence just below Muscle Shoals and into control of the important Memphis & Charleston Railroad. The Cumberland could lead them straight to Nashville, the capital of Tennessee, a city the Confederacy could ill afford to lose.

Nashville was one of the largest and most important cities south of the Ohio River, and occupied an important strategic position. Besides being on the Cumberland River, it had railroads leading north to Louisville, south to Decatur, southeast to Chattanooga and Atlanta, and westward toward the Tennessee. Since the outbreak of the war it had been converted into a giant arsenal and depot of supplies.

The importance of the Cumberland and Tennessee Rivers had not escaped the notice of Governor Harris. One of the first things he did after Tennessee seceded was to order the construction of forts on the rivers to control them and repel invaders. Selection of the best possible location for the forts was delegated to General Daniel S. Donelson, a West Point graduate—and, incidentally, a nephew of General Andrew Jackson's wife. The only limitation on Donelson's choice was that the forts should be as far north (down the rivers) as possible, but must be within the borders of Tennessee, since Kentucky was at that time maintaining the figment of neutrality. Donelson reported that the strongest point on the Cumberland was a high bluff on the west bank a mile below the village of Dover. Dover was forty miles from the river's mouth, and, aside from its communication by river, was connected with Nashville, seventy-five miles away, by a road passing through Charlotte. In General Donelson's judgment there was no particularly good location for a fort on the Tennessee within the borders of the state, but he selected a point on the east bank, almost due west of the chosen site on the Cumberland and about twelve miles from it, as being the best available.

Accordingly, with some misgivings, the places selected were ordered fortified. The one on the Cumberland at Dover was named in honor of General Donelson; that on the Tennessee was called Fort Henry for Gustavus A. Henry, Confederate Senator from Tennessee. The surveys were entrusted to a competent civil engineer, Adna Anderson, assisted by W. F. Foster (later General A. P. Stewart's chief engineer) and they started work on May 10.

Jefferson Davis in Richmond was not unaware of the acute nature of the military problems presented by these rivers. In writing about it after the war he says:

When the State of Tennessee seceded, measures were immediately adopted to occupy and fortify all the strong points on the Mississippi, as Memphis, Randolph, Fort Pillow, and Island No. 10. As it was our purpose not to enter the State of Kentucky and construct defenses for the Cumberland and Tennessee Rivers on her territory, they were located within the borders of Tennessee, and as near to the Kentucky line as suitable sites could be found. On these sites were commenced the construction of Fort Donelson on the west side of the Cumberland, and Fort Henry on the east side of the Tennessee, and about twelve miles apart. The latter stood on the low lands adjacent to the river about high-water mark, and being just below a bend in the river and at the head of a straight stretch of two miles, it commanded the river for that distance. It was also commanded by high ground on the opposite bank of the river, which it was intended should be occupied by our troops in case of a land attack. The power of ironclad gunboats against land defenses had not yet been shown, and the low position of the fort brought the battery to the water-level, and secured the advantage of richochet firing, the most effective against wooden ships.

Fort Donelson was placed on high ground; and the plunging fire from its batteries, was thereby more effective against the ironclads brought to attack it on the water side. But on the land side it was not equally strong, and required extensive outworks and a considerable force to resist an attack in that quarter.

In September, 1861, Lieutenant Dixon, of the Confederate Engineer Corps, was instructed to make an examination of the works at the two forts. He reported that Fort Henry was nearly completed. It was built, not at the most favorable position, but it was a strong work, and, instead of abandoning it and building at another place, he advised that it should be completed, and other works constructed on the high lands just above the fort on the opposite side of the river. Measures for the accomplishment of this plan were adopted as rapidly as the means at disposal would allow.

In relation to Fort Donelson, it was his opinion that, although a better position might have been chosen for this fortification on the Cumberland, under the circumstances surrounding the command, it would be better to retain and strengthen the position chosen.

The opinion of an experienced naval gunner as to the location and strength of the forts is expressed by Captain Jesse Taylor, who at the outbreak of the war had been placed in command of a "camp of artillery instruction" near Nashville:

About the 1st of September, I received a visit from Lieutenant-Colonel Milton A. Haynes of the 1st Regiment Tennessee Artillery, who informd me of the escape of a number of our steamers from the Ohio River into the Tennessee, and of their having sought refuge under the guns of Fort Henry; that a "cutting-out" expedition from Paducah was anticipated, and that as there was no experienced artillerist at the fort the Governor (Isham G. Harris) was anxious that the deficiency should immediately be supplied; that he had no one at his disposal unless I would give up my light battery (subsequently Porter's and later still Morton's) and take command at Fort Henry. Anxious to be of service, and convinced that the first effort of the Federals would be to penetrate our lines by the way of the Tennessee River, I at once, in face of the loudly expressed disapproval and wonder of my friends, consented to make the exchange.

Arriving at the fort, I was convinced by a glance at its surroundings that extraordinarily bad judgment, or worse, had selected the site for its erection. I found it placed on the east bank of the river in a bottom commanded by high hills rising on either side of the river, and within good rifle range. This circumstance was at once reported to the proper military authorities of the state of Nashville, who replied that the selection had been made by competent engineers and with reference to mutual support with Fort Donelson on the Cumberland, twelve miles away. Knowing that the crude ideas of a sailor in the Navy concerning fortifications would receive but little consideration when conflicting with those entertained by a "West Pointer," I resolved quietly to acquiesce, but the accidental observation of a water-mark left on a tree caused me to look carefully for this sign above, below and in the rear of the fort. My investigation convinced me that we had a more dangerous force to contend with than the Federals, namely, the river itself.

Inquiry among old residents confirmed my fears that the ground on which the fort was not only subject to overflow, but that the highest point within the fort would be—in an ordinary February rise—at least two feet under water. This alarming fact was also communicated to the state authorities, only to evoke the curt notification that the state forces had been transferred to the Confederacy, and that I should apply to General Polk, then in command at Columbus, Ky. This suggestion was at once acted on—not once only, but with a frequency and urgency commensurate with its seeming importance—the result being that I was again referred, this time to General A. S. Johnston, who at once dispatched an engineer (Major Jeremy F. Gilmer) to investigate and remedy. It was now too late to do so effectually, though an effort was made looking to that end, by beginning to fortify the heights on the west bank (Fort Heiman).

The armament of Fort Henry at the time I assumed command consisted of six smooth-bore 32-pounders and one six-pounder iron-gun. February 1st, 1862, by the persistent efforts of General Lloyd Tilghman and Colonel A. Heiman, this had been increased to eight 32-, two 42- and one 128-pounders (Columbiad); five 18-pounder siege guns. All of these were smooth-bore metal and it was deemed best to subject them to a test; and as two of them burst with an ordinary charge, the others were set aside as useless incumbrances. The powder supplied was mostly of a very inferior quality, so much so that it was deemed necessary to adopt the dangerous expedient of adding to each charge a proportion of quick-burning powder.

Fort Henry got all the attention at first and the site of Fort Donelson was quite neglected, but in October Colonel R. W. McGavock with three companies of Tennessee troops was sent to Dover, and he signed communications as "Commanding at Fort Donelson." Work on the fortifications still languished, however, and Senator Henry (who was keeping an eager eye out) wrote General Polk apprehensively that only these 300 men, with four guns, stood between the Ohio River and Nashville. "There is no part of the whole West," he said, "so exposed as the Valley of the Cumberland." He stressed the importance of defending the iron furnaces in this valley which were manufacturing iron for the Confederacy.

As soon as General Johnston was assigned to the West and arrived on the scene, he saw that both river forts must be put under a competent commander who would aggressively push them to completion. In early October he asked that Major A. P. Stewart be appointed a brigadier for this purpose, but Secretary Judah P. Benjamin named instead a Kentuckian, Lloyd Tilghman, who assumed duty on November 17. It did not take Tilghman long to realize what he was up against. On December 16 he wrote to General Johnston:

I deem it only just to myself to say I am not secure at either Henry or Donelson. Have 1,500 unarmed men. Have asked for two companies for heavy artillery; have no answer. Think movements at Cairo look to Cumberland and Tennessee certain. Waiting on Captain Shaw to organize MacGavock's regiment.

Receiving no assistance from his immediate commander, Tilghman in his desperation resorted to the expedient of a personal letter to President Davis, telling of the precarious situation of the forts:

Sir: This will be handed to you by Colonel Bailey, of one of the Tennessee regiments stationed at this post. The exposed position of this command and the impossibility of obtaining arms here has induced us both to make an effort to secure them at Richmond. Knowing the difficulties we all labor under on this score, permit me simply to state that I feel deeply solicitous about our condition on the Tennessee and Cumberland, and believe that no one point in the Southern Confederacy needs more the aid of the Government than these points. Colonel Bailey will be presented to you under such auspices as will, I am sure, command for him your especial consideration.

The scarcity of materiel was intensified on December 23rd when the ordnance depot at Nashville and its store of munitions and supplies was destroyed by fire. Moses H. Wright, who had been appointed Chief of Ordnance by Governor Harris when Tennessee seceded, reported the sad news to Colonel Josiah Gorgas, Confederate Chief of Ordnance at Richmond:

Sir: I have the honor to report by letter the destruction and entire loss of the ordnance depot and supplies, reported by telegram this a.m. The fire originated between 3 and 4 a.m., how or where I am unable to ascertain. I had a sentinel at both doors (house fronts on two streets) and private watch inside. The watchman inside reports that the first he knew of it flames burst from the room above him where I kept such articles as flints, shoe thread, lanyards, &c., on one side and percussion caps and friction-primers on the other. In a few moments after discovering the fire, an explosion occurred of the percussion caps and a case of rockets (which were also in the room) and the primers. A man (corporal of the guard) reports that the fire commenced in an adjoining building, but the truth of the case has not yet been fully developed. Notwithstanding the guards, &c., I am constrained to believe that it was the work of an incendiary, inasmuch as if it had been from spontaneous combustion of the caps or primers (which I think could not have occurred, as everything was so carefully dry) an explosion would have been heard in the first instance. No oil nor anything of the kind was in that portion of the house at all, and special pains have always been taken to keep every portion thoroughly cleaned, and in no case has it ever been allowed for rubbish to accumulate in any portion of the house. The loss is of course heavy, principally artillery harness and equipments generally. Say from 400 to 600 sets artillery harness, 300 cavalry saddles, from 8,000 to 15,000 sets of equipments and accouterments for infantry, 2,000,000 percussion caps, 5,000 friction primers, two dozen rockets, &c., 300 reams cartridge-paper. A full report will be made as soon as possible. I have asked for a board of survey from General Johnston.

A few days later, Mayor John Park of Memphis issued a proclamation "To the Citizens of Memphis", which was printed in the *Appeal* of December 28th:

TO THE CITIZENS OF MEMPHIS:

You have been indolent in every respect—I mean the real estate owners of the city of Memphis. You have taken no interest in the proceedings of the PLEBIANS, who are the rulers, and why? Because you preferred the downy couch, believing outsiders who were not identically interested in the welfare of the City, could be inveigled into the service of standing guard, which you should have done, and which you have refused to do.

From my personal observation of twenty years' standing, it is this:—When men become possessed of wealth, no matter how they may have been before, they imagine they are superior to the commonality, but in this they are most egregiously disappointed.

I have to say one thing to the community at large, who are identified with the interests of the City and their own property; come out and show the community where you stand, whether neutral, Lincoln or Davis.

JOHN PARK, Mayor.

Today's reader of this proclamation may find it somewhat incoherent and not entirely clear as to just what impelled the Mayor thus to address his fellow-citizens. General Polk's friend, Samuel Tate, however, found it alarming, and sent a copy of it to General Polk as evidence of the unhappy state of affairs in Memphis:

I inclose you [wrote Mr. Tate] a proclamation issued this morning by John Park, our mayor. You will see from it where we stand. Our city is in a terrible condition with such a man at its head. You can plainly see his aims. Nothing in my judgment will do but strict military law as long as he is at the head of affairs. Our prisoners are not safe. I learn there is frequently no guard around them. Your ordnance, commissary, and quartermaster's stores are unsafe, only two to four men at each place at night to guard them, and the town full of rascals and incendiaries, and the mayor issuing proclamations saying he will protect them, and offering inducements virtually to bring in more. For heaven's sake don't let any supplies be burnt up for want of proper guards. Nashville has suffered enough. Don't let us repeat it. We have no one here with any authority over the city who is disposed to protect the right.

Meanwhile the seeds of discontent and rebellion in East Tennessee were ripening into open rebellion against the Confederate authorities. R. R. Hancock of the Second Tennessee Cavalry, McNairy's Battalion, which had been sent to that section with General Zollicoffer, summarized the situation thus:

East Tennessee was now ablaze with excitement on account of the uprising and open rebellion of the Union men. They were flying to arms in squads of from fifty to five hundred. Several bridges along the East Tennessee and Georgia, and Virginia and Tennessee Railroads were burned. It appears that William Blunt Carter, of East Tennessee, (brother of Col. S. P. Carter) was the prime mover and chief instigator of the revolt and bridge burning, and the following communication dated September 30, 1861, from Brigadier General George H. Thomas, commanding the forces at Camp Dick Robinson, to Major General George B. McClellan will show the beginning of his plans:

"I have just had a conversation with Mr. W. B. Carter, of Tennessee, on the subject of the destruction of the Grand Trunk Railroad through that state. He assures me that he can have it done if the Government will intrust him with a small sum of money to give confidence to the persons to be employed to do it. It would be one of the most important services that could be done for the country, and I most earnestly hope you will use your influence with the authorities in furtherance of his plans, which he will submit to you, together with the reasons for doing the work."

Suffice it to say that he received satisfactory encouragement from the Federal Government, and, setting out on his mission about the middle of October, Carter arrived in the neighborhood of Montgomery, Morgan County, Tennessee, on the 22d, and under that date he wrote to General Thomas:

"I reached here at 2 P. M. to-day. I am in six miles of company of rebel cavalry. . . . You will please furnish the bearers with as much lead, rifle powder, and as many caps as they can bring for Scott and Morgan Counties. You need not fear to trust these people. They will open the war for you by routing these small bodies of marauding cavalry. . . . . Hasten on to our aid. To-morrow night I hope to be near our railroad. . . . . You shall hear from me again soon"

On the 27th, near Kingston, Roane County, he wrote again to Thomas as follows:

"I am now within a few miles of the railroad, but I have not yet had time to obtain all the information I must have before I decide on the course best for me to adopt. If I can get half a dozen brave men to 'take the bull by the horns' we can whip them completely and save the railroad. If I cannot get such leaders we will make a desperate attempt to destroy all the bridges, and I firmly believe I will be successful . . . The Union men of East Tennssee are longing and praying for the hour when they can break their fetters . . . . Men and women weep for joy when I merely hint to them that the day of our deliverance is at hand. . . . I beg you to hasten on to our help, as we are about to create a great diversion in General McClellan's favor. You must bring some small arms with you. I am satisfied that you will have to take the road by Monticello and Jamestown, unless you come by Cumberland Gap."

Having succeeded in maturing his plans, the execution of which resulted in the bridge burning, as previously mentioned. Mr. W. B. Carter set out on his return November 11th, and arrived at his brother's headquarters at "Camp Calvert," near London, Kentucky, on the 16th, and on the same day his brother, Colonel S. P. Carter (afterward General), sent the following report to General Thomas, whose headquarters had been moved forward from Camp Dick Robinson to Crab Orchard:

"My brother William has just arrived from East Tennessee. . . . He reports that on Friday night, 8th instant, of last week, he succeeded in having burned at least six, and perhaps eight bridges on the railroad, viz.: Union bridge, in Sullivan County, near the Virginia line; Lick Creek bridge, in Green County; Strawberry Plains, in Jefferson County, fifteen miles east of Knoxville, partially destroyed; Hiwassee bridge seventy miles south-west of Knoxville, and on the East Tennessee and Georgia Railroad; two bridges over the Chickamauga; one between Cleveland and Chattanooga; and the other between Chattanooga and Dalton, Georgia. These bridges are certainly destroyed. The Long Island bridge, at Bridgeport, on Tennessee River, and a bridge below Dalton, on the Western and Atlantic road, are probably destroyed."

Only five bridges were actually burned, as is shown by the following dispatch dated November 11, 1861, to Adjutant General Cooper from Colonel W. B. Wood, Sixteenth Alabama, who had been for some time guarding the railroad as best he could with the small force at his command:

"Three bridges burned between Bristol and Chattanooga, two on Georgia road. Five hundred Union men were threatening Strawberry Plains. Fifteen hundred assembling in Hamilton County, and a general uprising in all the counties. I have about one thousand men under my command."

In order to put down this revolt of the Unionists, Stovall's Battalion and a light field battery were sent from Richmond, Virginia, to Bristol, Tennessee (11th); the Seventh Alabama, Col. S. A. M. Wood, from Pensacola to Chattanooga (14th); General W. H. Carroll, with two regiments, though mostly unarmed, from Memphis to Chattanooga (15th); and General Zollicoffer sent the Twenty-ninth Tennessee, Colonel S. Powell, from Jacksborough to Knoxville (10th).

On the 11th Col. Danville [sic] Leadbetter, of the Engineer Corps, was ordered by President Davis to proceed at once from Richmond to East Tennessee, assume command of all the troops to be stationed for the protection of the railroad between Bristol and Chattanooga, reconstruct bridges, and repair and keep open the line of communication between those points.

On the 20th Colonel W. B. Wood wrote to the Secretary of War thus:

"The rebellion in East Tennessee has been put down in some of the counties, and will be effectually suppressed in less than two weeks in all the counties. Their camps in Sevier and Hamilton Counties have been broken up, and a large number of them made prisoners. Some are confined in jail at this place and others sent to Nashville. The prisoners we have tell us that they had every assurance that the (Federal) army was already in the state, and would join them in a very few days; that the property of Southern men was to be confiscated and divided among those who would take up arms for Lincoln."

In answer to an inquiry in reference to what he should do with his prisoners, Colonel Wood received the following from Secretary of War Benjamin:

"All such as can be identified as having been engaged in bridge burning are to be tried summarily by drum-head court-martial, and, if found guilty, executed on the spot by hanging. It would be well to leave their bodies hanging in the vicinity of the burned bridges. All such as have not been so engaged are to be treated as prisoners of war, and sent with an armed guard to Tuscaloosa, Alabama, . . . and held in jail till the end of the war. Such as come in voluntarily, take the oath of allegiance and surrender their arms are alone to be treated with leniency."

Some, I know not how many, were found guilty by a "drum-head court martial" and hung.

As a general thing these bands of traitors would disband and flee to the mountains on the approach of an armed force of Confederates, therefore it was a difficult matter to do any thing with them.

Some interesting details as to the difficulties encountered by the Confederate authorities in East Tennessee are set out in a report sent November 17th to

General Bragg at Pensacola by Colonel S. A. M. Wood of the Seventh Alabama Volunteers who had been sent with his regiment to Chattanooga:

Dear Sir and General: I have the honor to report to you for your information the following with regard to the Seventh Regiment:

We arrived at this place on Thursday, at 5 o'clock. I came through and arrived on Thursday morning, but the burning of the bridge forced the regiment around by Cleveland, where I met it at 11 o'clock, and came down with it. At Cleveland I arranged with Col. W. B. Wood by telegraph to make a joint movement on the forces of the insurgents, and ordered him to proceed by way of Cottonport and Decatur to their camp ground on Sale Creek. I also ordered 300 mounted Home Guards, under Colonels Gillespie and Tibbs, accompanied by a lieutenant of my command, to move in two parties across the river, one to cross at daylight Friday morning 8 miles above where my regiment would cross and the other 8 miles below me. Between sundown and 11 o'clock Thursday night the Seventh Regiment prepared rations for three days, and I chartered a steamboat for three days for $100, and put the whole regiment on it. At daylight we landed 27 miles from this place and 9 miles from the camp of the traitors. Column was formed, skirmishers thrown out, and we marched through, detaining men, women, and negroes, as we went on, to prevent any information to the enemy. We arrived at the camp ground (formerly a Cumberland Presbyterian Camp meeting place) at 11 o'clock. A body of 300 mounted Home Guards reached the camp ground from Rhea County five minutes before us, and had advanced 200 yards towards us in a lane. In some houses near there a large number of women, seeing our approach, were screaming, and one or two Lincolnites were trying to escape—one on foot we had just captured. Our skirmishers surrounded the house, which increased the noise, and commanded the horsemen, now forming line of battle, to halt, but they turned and fled. Five shots were fired at them, wounding slightly one man in the foot, and one of their horses; also wounding a Lincolnite, who was flying about 200 yards beyond them, in the shoulder. The whole squadron was then soon out of sight at a fierce gallop. Their captain caught sight of our banner and returned, and we found them friends. The Lincolnites number 300; had met the night before our arrival, and voted on three propositions:

1st. Should they fight? Ayes 4, noes 296.

2d. Should they go to Kentucky? Ayes 65, noes all the others.

3d. Should they disperse? Ayes about 230, noes about 70.

They then all fled the camp, the four fighting men going with the colonel, named Clift; the 65 towards Kentucky, with their major, named Sullivan; the others, with the lieutenant-colonel, scattering to their homes and the mountains.

Col. William B. Wood was now within seven miles of me. My mounted men had not come up. I ordered Colonel Wood back to Knoxville, and I ordered all the mounted men to pursue and capture the 65 going to Kentucky. Staid all night at the camp ground. Many good citizens, who had been robbed of their guns and property, came to see us. The next morning took a different road to return, ordering the steamboat up the river. Arrested about 12 traitors, five with guns and knives, bound for Sullivan's camp. They are the most miserable, ignorant, poor, ragged devils I ever saw. Reached the boat at 11 o'clock, came down 16 miles, landed, and sent out two companies under Major Russell (I accompanying them) to visit the house of Colonel Clift. He was not there. His house looks as if it belonged to some crazy man—a large two-story frame building with half the windows out; no furniture, and all in decay. Found a letter from him to Shelton (lieutenant-colonel), dated November 6, giving the place of the rallying. Returned, and reached this place at 9 o'clock at night.

This morning have moved the regiment out to the burned bridges, 15 miles, so as to get out of the way of whisky, and to encamp among the Lincolnites. When I arrived Colonel Leadbetter was not here. A Tennessee regiment without arms was just arriving.

All in confusion; a general panic; everybody running up and down, and adding to the general alarm. I issued an order taking command; put the town under martial law; shut up the groceries [grog-shops], forbade an exit, by railroad or otherwise, without a permit from provost-marshal; had every avenue guarded; arrested about 12 persons who were talking Lincolnism before I came. Arrested a man myself on the cars as I went to Cleveland, and brought him back. Found him one of their traveling agents, going off with the news of my arrival. I have relieved all our friends in this country. All were alarmed; all are now resting easy. I have run all the Lincolnites.

Upon my return here I find that Brigadier-General Carroll, of the Provisional Army, formerly postmaster at Memphis, Tenn., is here with two more Tennessee regiments and one company of flying artillery. General Carroll has just been appointed. He has been drunk not less than five years. He is stupid, but easily controlled. He knows nothing, and I believe I can do with him pretty much as I please. He is going to send two pieces of artillery and 500 men to march up and down Sequatchie Valley—a useless expenditure of money. The presence of so many troops here is wholly unnecessary. He has, however, only 800 stand of arms. What the others will do I do not know. He speaks of going to Knoxville in a few days.

Colonel Leadbetter telegraphed me from Bristol to disperse the traitors, station guards at bridges, and move on to Knoxville, but if I station guards my regiment is all gone. I am now dispersing the insurgents, and shall keep at it from this point until I hear from the War Department or you, or again from Colonel Leadbetter. General Carroll will not detain me. I refer you to a letter inclosed for some of my private views. I desire, unless I can get some command here, to come back to you. If I cannot order and have the same discipline, then let me come where I will find it.

Colonel Daniel Leadbetter, who had been sent to East Tennessee by the Richmond authorities, to command the Confederate forces trying to restore order in that region, on November 30th, issued a conciliatory proclamation from his headquarters at Greeneville:

PROCLAMATION

HEADQUARTERS,

Greeneville, East Tenn., November 30, 1861.

TO THE CITIZENS OF EAST TENNESSEE:

So long as the question of Union or disunion was debatable, so long you did well to debate it and vote on it. You had a clear right to vote for the Union; but when secession was established by the voice of the people you did ill to distract the country by angry words and insurrectionary tumult. In doing this you commit the highest crime known to the laws.

Out of the Southern Confederacy no people possess such elements of prosperity and happiness as those of East Tennessee. The Southern market which you have hitherto enjoyed only in competition with a host of eager Northern rivals will not be shared with a few states of the Confederacy equally fortunate politically and geographically. Every product of your agriculture and workshops will now find a prompt sale at high prices, and so long as cotton grows on Confederate soil so long will the money which it brings flow from the South through all your channels of trade.

At this moment you might be at war with the United States or any foreign nation and yet not suffer a tenth part of the evils which pursue you in this domestic strife. No man's life or property is safe, no woman or child can sleep in quiet. You are deluded by selfish demagogues who take care for their own personal safety. You are citizens of Tennessee and your state (is) one of the Confederate States.

So long as you are up in arms against these states can you look for anything but the invasion of your homes and the wasting of your substance? This condition of things must be ended. The Government commands the peace and sends troops to enforce the order. I proclaim that every man who comes in promptly and delivers up his arms will be pardoned on taking the oath of allegiance. All men taken in arms against the Government will be transported to the military prison at Tuscaloosa and be confined there during the war.

Bridge-burners and destroyers of railroad tracks are excepted from among those pardonable. They will be tried by drum-head court-martial and be hung on the spot.

D. LEADBETTER,
Colonel, Commanding.

On December 8th Colonel Leadbetter sent to General Samuel Cooper at Richmond a cheery report, which displayed excessive and premature optimism on his part:

It is believed that we are making progress toward pacification. The Union men are taking the oath in pretty large numbers and arms are beginning to be brought in. Captain McClellan, of the Tennessee cavalry, stationed by me at Elizabethton reports that Carter County is becoming very quiet and that with the aid of a company of infantry he will enter Johnson County and disarm the people there. I shall send the company without delay.

The execution of the bridge-burners is producing the happiest effect. This coupled with great kindness toward the inhabitants generally inclines them to quietude. Insurgents will continue for yet a while in the mountains but I trust that we have secured the outward obedience of the people.

Colonel Leadbetter's optimism, however, proved to be a good example of wishful thinking. Contrary to his expressed expectations, things went from bad to worse in East Tennessee. A crushing blow to the prestige and authority of the Confederate States of America was provided by the defeat suffered when the troops under the command of General Crittenden and General Zollicoffer assumed the offensive and advanced into Kentucky. At the battle of Fishing Creek (also called Mill Springs, also called Logan's Cross-roads) on January 19th Zollicoffer was killed, and the shattered Confederate forces were sent reeling back into a disorderly retreat to the south side of the Cumberland River, a retreat that did not end until the demoralized remnants of Crittenden's army reached Chestnut Mound, a short distance above Carthage. A depressing summary of the bleak outlook at the beginning of the New Year, 1862, is to be found in a letter to Jefferson Davis from Dr. J. G. M. Ramsey of Knoxville. Dr. Ramsey was a man of parts: historian, physician and banker, president of the Knoxville branch of the Bank of Tennessee. He was also officially recognized by the Confederate government as a *quasi* member of the Confederate Congress from Tennessee, and on January 24th in this capacity he wrote frankly and forcibly to the President:

Dear Sir: When I wrote you a few days since, amongst other things I told you of simultaneous stampedes of the Union men in the direction of Kentucky. I thought at the time that they had news from that state of which we were entirely uninformed, and forewarned our bridge officers of the necessity of increased vigilance and more guards at the exposed points on the railroads and the provision store-houses, and even suggested the removal of the stores to places of greater security. Large numbers of Tories unarmed and on foot have stealthily withdrawn from nearly all East Tennessee, and are no doubt in the enemy's service, and if the invasion of the border counties is prosecuted further these refugees will come against us; and acting as pilots through that mountain region will endanger several important points.

The disaster to Zollicoffer on last Sunday you have already been informed of. Those of our forces engaged in that fight are returning home one by one in rapid succession, and from many of them I hear that Crittenden's whole army is perfectly demoralized and refused to serve under him, imputing to his constant inebriation the unfortunate advance of General Zollicoffer, and against his own earnest protest. Imputations of a graver character against the loyalty of the commanding officer are freely spoken of in the camp and believed.

I hope this latter is without foundation, but the soldiers believe it and assert it, and whether true or false, its effect is the same. His army is disaffected, mutinous, and will never be reorganized under him. And yet these men are brave, patriotic, and loyal, excepting always those of them late Union men and recruited from that party. These can never be trusted till they are subdued. But I fully believe if an officer could be sent here at once in whose experience, loyalty, and freedom from Union associations and sympathies they can repose implicit confidence, the Army can be organized and the invasion repelled. I fully believe that this will have to be done or East Tennessee will be invaded and held, the bridges burned again, and our territorial disintegration temporarily effected.

Let a competent man be sent here from beyond the influence of Tennessee politics, known to us as of unquestionable loyalty—one who is perfectly sober, who has had experience in arms, who has enterprise as well as courage—and these Tennessee troops now mortified and chagrined at the late disaster and anxious to wipe out the accidental disgrace will rally to his standard and not stop this side of the Ohio. Had Zollicoffer not been ordered to make that unwise advance all would have been now right. We should first have a new commander, a stranger to our people by an antecedents and political sympathies with reconstruction, &c., who will reassure our soldiers, stimulate the efforts of our own people, and impart to them a new vitality, and the late defeat will be converted into victory. If you have not yet accepted the resignation of Pillow he will be able to restore order out of this chaos; but I do not presume to suggest for you or the Secretary of War, but I think it no presumption in me to give my opinion that the necessities of the occasion demand the transfer of Crittenden to another field. I would have also suggested General Elzey, with the hope of getting Colonel Vaughn (who is under him) on our frontier. But I hear, too, that he is not sober, and besides you may not be able to weaken your Potomac line. Many of our friends will telegraph you to-day on this subject.

P.S. I understand that General Caswell, of this city, is an applicant for the position of brigadier-general. He does not equal in his claims either Colonel Vaughn or Colonel Cummings, both of whom have experience and capacity, and are original States' rights men, and entirely temperate. Floyd or Pillow I think should come here at once.

As bodies of troops from other Southern states were sent forward in response to Albert Sidney Johnston's frantic call for reinforcements, the civilian population of Tennessee began to see more of the seamy side of war, as the massing of troops destroyed any remnants of the pre-war tranquillity. A notable example of this was provided by the arrival in the city of a regiment of Texas cavalry that was to become famous in the annals of the war: Terry's Texas Rangers. This body of more than a thousand red-blooded, energetic young Texans, recruited by Colonel B. F. Terry, was temporarily camped in Nashville awaiting mounts before moving forward to Bowling Green. Full of animal spirits and with time hanging heavy on their hands, they created a notable stir in the city as they galloped their horses through the streets and at their camp at the West Side Fair Grounds gave daily exhibitions of the horsemanship that had made the Texas cowboys famous. One of their number, J. K. P. Blackburn, tells entertainingly of an incident that served to exhaust the city's hospitality for their spirited visitors from Texas, and hastened their movement forward to the front:

Colonel Terry, as a precaution against possible trouble, had arranged for guards to be placed around the camp every night to prevent the men from going up town. The men, undisciplined as they were, looked upon this as an unnecessary restriction upon their general liberty, and so some of the most determined ones would manage to get out and go up every night, and sometimes they would get unruly or noisy from drink and fall into the hands of the police and be locked up; but generally they were released after short detention and a promise of good behavior in the future. In this way there was some bad blood between the "cops" and the Texans, which soon brought on a crisis and bloodshed and death to some of the police force.

One night three or four soldiers slipped by the guards, went up town, imbibed too freely of booze, went to the theater and took their seats in the gallery. Captain John Smith's expected execution and Pocahontas' rescue as related in early history of the Colonies was the drama staged for the night. When that part of the play was reached where Captain John Smith, condemned to die by his Indian captors, was bound hand and foot and his head placed upon a rock, the executioner drew back his bludgeon to strike the fatal blow, Pocahontas thrust her own body between Smith's head and the descending bludgeon, one of the boozy soldiers in the gallery whipped out a six-shooter and fired upon the supposed executioner with the remark that "his mother had taught him to always protect a lady when in danger." This shot missed its mark, but created consternation and stopped the play. The police rushed in to arrest the offender, the other soldiers helped him to resist arrest, and shooting began, resulting in the death of two policemen and the wounding of another one and the freedom of the soldiers to return unmolested to camp.

This tragedy was reported to the Governor of Tennessee and immediately telegraphed by the Governor to General Johnston, who ordered Colonel Terry to come immediately on the first train to Bowling Green and report to him. By daylight next morning the regiment was in the train on their way to their destination, nearer to the scenes that should soon be enacted between contending lines of battle.

CHAPTER 2

☆ *The Fall of The Forts*

THE CONFEDERATE authorities' heavy-footed and apathetic attention to the vital matter of maintaining control of the Cumberland and Tennessee Rivers was in marked contrast to the Federals' recognition of the opportunity offered them by this thinly protected approach to the vitals of the Confederacy. As early as the middle of October, 1861, the gunboat *Conestoga* made its way from the Ohio up the Tennessee on a reconnaissance and threw a few shells at Fort Henry to develop the location and range of the Confederate guns. As a follow-up, during the ensuing winter, the *Conestoga,* accompanied by the *Lexington,* made frequent appearances below Fort Henry, firing a few shells and then retiring.

In January, as a diversion in favor of the Federal forces in eastern Kentucky, there was a reconnaissance in force by both infantry and gunboats. Major General McClernand marched overland from Cairo with 6,000 men to menace the Confederate stronghold on the Mississippi at Columbus, Kentucky; Major General C. F. Smith with two brigades moved from Paducah down into western Kentucky, threatening Fort Henry and all the Kentucky country between the fort and Columbus; and Admiral Foote and his gunboats steamed up the river in concert with Foote.

At this time the water in the Tennessee was barely deep enough to float the gunboats, but the season of the rises was approaching, and enough had been learned of the Confederate weakness for Grant confidently to telegraph Halleck at St. Louis on January 28: "With permission, I will take Fort Henry on the Tennessee and establish and hold a large camp there." The requested permission was given, and on February 2 the campaign was launched, with Grant and 17,000 troops and Foote with seven gunboats moving up the river, which was now at a high stage and rising rapidly. On the morning of the 4th, the gunboats were in formation about three miles below the fort and began to shell the position, while the transports were discharging their blue-clad cargo. The main body of troops, under Grant, landed on the east bank of the river at Bailey's Ferry, but 6,000 under General C. F. Smith were detached to the west side to take Fort Heiman, which they found unfinished and unoccupied. Not until late afternoon of the 5th were all the troops disembarked, and then the gunboats moved in closer to renew their fire, which was answered by the Confederate gunners. After a few rounds the gunboats dropped back downstream and the action ceased.

At the time of the first attack on the 4th, General Tilghman was not in the fort, having gone with Colonel Gilmer to inspect Fort Donelson, leaving Colonel Heiman in command. Hearing the firing, however, Tilghman returned to Henry the night of the 4th and assumed active charge of the defense there on the morning of the 5th. He telegraphed General Johnston, advising him of the attack and asking for reinforcements, concluding his message: "The high water threatens us seriously". As a matter of fact, the river was now rising so rapidly that it was an open question whether the first enemy to enter the fort would be the Yankees or Old Man River.

The official report of any unsuccessful military commander, in the nature of things, consists to some extent, of explanations and excuses for his failure. General Lloyd Tilghman's report of the fall of Fort Henry is no exception to the rule; but his report makes it clear that to a great extent he was a victim of circumstances. Given an untenable position to hold with inadequate forces, assailed by an overwhelmingly superior force, he had but little choice—to save as many of his men as possible, to fight as long as he could, and in the end to surrender on the best terms available. Extracts from his report to General Samuel Cooper at Richmond give an impressive picture of the military and personal crisis confronting him and the gallantry with which he met it:

Early on the morning of the 6th, Captain Padgett reported the arrival of five additional transports, and the landing of a large force on the west bank of the river. From that time up to 9 o'clock it appeared as though the force on the east bank was again re-enforced, which was subsequently proven to be true. By 10 a. m. it was plain that the boats intended to engage the fort with their entire force, aided by an attack on the right and left flanks from the two land forces in overwhelming numbers.

To understand properly the difficulties of my position it is right that I should explain fully the unfortunate location of Fort Henry in reference to resistance by a small force against an attack by land co-operating with the gunboats, as well as its disadvantage in even an engagement with boats alone. The entire fort, together with the entrenched camp spoken of, is enfiladed from three or four points on the opposite shore, while three points on the eastern bank completely command the both, all at easy cannon range. At the same time the entrenched camp, arranged as it was in the best possible manner to meet the case, was two-thirds of it completely under the control of the fire of the gunboats.

The history of military engineering records no parallel in this case. Points within a few miles of it, possessing great advantage and few disadvantages, were totally neglected, and a location fixed upon without one redeeming feature or filling one of the many requirements of a site for a work such as Fort Henry. The work itself was well built, it was completed long before I took command, but strengthened greatly by myself in building embrasures and epaulements of sand bags. An enemy had been to use their common sense in obtaining the advantage of high water, as was the case, to have complete and entire control of the position.

I am guilty of no act of injustice in this frank avowal of the opinions entertained by myself, as well as by all other officers who have become familiar with the location of Fort Henry; nor do I desire the defects of location to have an undue influence in directing public opinion in relation to the battle of the 6th instant. The fort was built when I took charge, and I had no time to build anew. With this seeming digression, rendered necessary, as I believe, to a correct understanding of the whole affair, I will proceed with the details of the subsequent movements of the troops under my command.

By 10 A. M. on the 6th the movements of the gunboats and land force indicated an immediate engagement, and in such force as gave me no room to change my previously conceived opinions as to what, under such circumstances, should be my course. The case stood thus: I had at my command a grand total of 2,610 men, only one-third of whom had been at all disciplined or well armed. The high water in the river filling the sloughs gave me but one route by which to retire, if necessary, and that route for some distance in a direction at right angles to the line of approach of the enemy, and over roads well-nigh impassable for artillery, cavalry, or infantry. The enemy had seven gunboats, with an armament of fifty-four guns, to engage the eleven guns at Fort Henry. General Grant was moving up the east bank of the river from the landing, three miles below, with a force of 12,000 men, verified afterwards by his own statement, while General Smith, with 6,000 men, was moving up the west bank, to take a position within 400 or 500 yards, which would enable him to enfilade my entire works. The hopes (founded on a knowledge of the fact that the enemy on the two previous days had thoroughly reconnoitered the several roads leading to Fort Donelson) that a portion only of the land force would co-operate with the gunboats in an attack on the fort were dispelled, and but little time left me to meet this change in the circumstances which surrounded me.

I argued thus: Fort Donelson might possibly be held, if properly re-enforced; even though Fort Henry should fall, but the reverse of this proposition was not true. The force at Fort Henry was necessary to aid Fort Donelson either in making a successful defense or a holding it long enough to answer the purposes of a new disposition of the enemy from Bowling Green to Columbus, which would necessarily follow the breaking of our center, resting on Forts Donelson and Henry. The latter alternative was all that I deemed possible. I knew that re-enforcements were difficult to be had, and that unless sent in such force as to make the defense certain, which I did not believe practicable, the fate of our right wing at Bowling Green depended upon a concentration of my entire division on Fort Donelson and the holding of that place as long as possible, trusting that the delay by an action at Fort Henry would give time for such re-enforcements as might reasonably be expected to reach a point sufficiently near Fort Donelson to co-operate with my division, by getting to the rear and right flank of the enemy, and in such a position as to control the roads over which a safe retreat might be effected.

I hesitated not a moment. My infantry, artillery, and cavalry, removed of necessity to avoid the fire of the gunboats to the outworks, could not meet the enemy there; my only chance was to delay the enemy every moment possible and retire the command, now outside the main work, towards Fort Donelson, resolving to suffer as little loss as possible. I retained only the heavy artillery company to fight the guns, and gave the order to commence the movement at once.

At 10:15 o'clock Lieutenant-Colonel MacGavock sent a messenger to me, stating that our pickets reported General Grant approaching rapidly and within half a mile of the advance work, and movements on the west bank indicated that General Smith was fast approaching also. The enemy, ignorant of any movement of my main body, but knowing that they could not engage them behind our entrenched camp until after the fort was reduced or the gunboats retired, without being themselves exposed to the fire of the latter, took a position north of the forks of the river road, in a dense wood (my order being to retreat by way of the Stewart road) to await the result.

At 11 a. m. the flotilla assumed their line of battle. I had no hope of being able successfully to defend the fort against such overwhelming odds, both in point of numbers and in caliber of guns. My object was to save the main body by delaying matters as long as possible, and to this end I bent every effort.

At precisely 11:45 a. m. the enemy opened from their gunboats on the fort. I waited a few moments until the effects from the first shots of the enemy were fully appreciated. I then gave the order to return the fire, which was gallantly responded to by the brave little band under my command. The enemy, with great deliberation, steadily closed upon the fort, firing very wild until within 1,200 yards. The cool deliberation of our men told from the first shot fired with tremendous effect.

At 12:35 p. m. the bursting of our 24-pounder rifled gun disabled every man at the piece. This great loss was to us in a degree made up by our disabling entirely the *Essex* gunboat, which immediately floated down-stream. Immediately after the loss of this valuable gun we sustained another loss, still greater, in the closing up of the vent of the ten-inch columbiad, rendering the gun perfectly useless and defying all efforts to reopen it. The fire on both sides was now perfectly terrific. Ten enemy's entire force was engaged, doing us but little harm, while our shot fell with unerring certainty upon them and with stunning effect.

At this time a question presented itself to me with no inconsiderable degree of embarrassment. The moment had arrived when I should join the main body of troops retiring toward Fort Donelson, the safety of which depended upon a protracted defense of the fort. It was equally plain that the gallant men working the batteries, for the first time under fire, with all their heroism, needed my presence. Colonel Heiman, the next in command, had returned to the fort for instructions. The men working the heavy guns were becoming exhausted with the rapid firing. Another gun became useless by an accident, and yet another by the explosion of a shell striking the muzzle, involving the loss of two men and disabling several others. The effect of my absence at such a critical moment would have been disastrous. At the earnest solicitation of many of my officers and men I determined to remain, and ordered Colonel Heiman to join his command and keep up the retreat in good order, while I should fight the guns as long as one man was left, and sacrifice myself to save the main body of my troops.

No sooner was this decision made known than new energy was infused. The enemy closed upon the fort to within 600 yards, improving very much in their fire, which now began to tell with great effect upon the parapets, while the fire from our guns (now reduced to seven) was returned with such deliberation and judgment that we scarcely missed a shot. A second one of the gunboats retired, but I believe was brought into action again.

At 1:10 p. m., so completely broken down were the men that, but for the fact that four only of our guns were then really serviceable, I could not well have worked a greater number. The fire was still continued with great energy and tremendous effect upon the enemy's boats.

At 1:30 p. m. I took charge of one of the 32-pounders to relieve the chief of that piece, who had worked with great effect from the beginning of the action. I gave the flag-ship *Cincinnati* two shots, which had the effect to check a movement intended to enfilade the only guns now left me. It was now plain to be seen that the enemy were breaching the fort directly in front of our guns, and that I could not much longer sustain their fire without an unjustifiable exposure of the valuable lives of the men who had so nobly seconded me in this unequal struggle.

Several of my officers, Major Gilmer among the number, now suggested to me the propriety of taking the subject of surrender into consideration. Every moment I knew was of vast importance to those retreating on Fort Donelson, and I declined, hoping to find men enough at hand to continue a while longer the fire now so destructive to the enemy. In this I was disappointed. My next effort was to try the experiment of a flag of truce, which I waved from the parapets myself. This was precisely at 1:50 p. m. The flag was not noticed, I presume, from the dense smoke that enveloped it, and leaping again into the fort continued the fire for five minutes, when, with the advice of my brother officers, I ordered the flag to be lowered, and after an engagement of two hours and ten minutes with such an unequal force the surrender was made to Flag-Officer Foote, represented by Captain Stembel, commanding gunboat *Cincinnati*, and was qualified by the single condition that all officers and men should be treated with the highest consideration due prisoners of war, which was promptly and gracefully acceded to by Commodore Foote.

Captain Jesse Taylor, the experienced naval gunner who was in personal charge of Fort Henry's rather limited artillery and who personally made the formal surrender of the fort to the victorious Federals, has left a detailed and spirited account of these momentous proceedings:

The forenoon of February 6th was spent by both sides in making needful preparations for the approaching struggle. The gun-boats formed line of battle abreast under the cover of the island. The *Essex*, the *Cincinnati*, the *Carondelet*, and the *St. Louis*, the first with four and and the others each with 13 guns, formed the van; the *Tyler*, *Conestoga*, and *Lexington*, with 15 guns in all, formed the second or rear line. Seeing the formation of battle I assigned to each gun a particular vessel to which it was to pay its especial compliments, and directed that the guns be kept constantly trained on the approaching boats.

Accepting the volunteered services of Captain Hayden (of the engineers) to assist at the Columbiad, I took personal supervision of the rifle. When they were out of cover of the island (one mile below the fort) the gun-boats opened fire, and as they advanced they increased the rapidity of their fire, until as they swung into the main channel above the island they showed one broad and leaping sheet of flame. At this point, the van being a mile distant, the command was given to commence firing from the fort; and here let me say that as pretty and as simultaneous a "broadside" was delivered as I ever saw flash from the sides of a frigate.

The action now became general, and for the next twenty or thirty minutes was, on both sides, as determined, rapid, and accurate as heart could wish, and apparently inclined in favor of the fort. The iron-clad *Essex*, disabled by a shot through her boiler, dropped out of line and the fleet seemed to hesitate; but then a succession of untoward and unavoidable accidents happened in the fort and thereupon the flotilla continued to advance. First, the rifle gun, from which I had just been called, burst, not only with destructive effect to those working it, but with disabling effect on those in its immediate vicinity. Going to the Columbiad as the only really effective gun left, I met General Tilghman and for the first knew that he had returned to the fort; I supposed that he was with his retreating army. While consulting with him a sudden exclamation drew me to the Columbiad, which I found spiked with its own priming wire, completely disabled for the day at least.

The Federal commander, observing the silence of these two heavy guns, renewed his advance with increased precision of fire. Two of the 32-pounders were struck almost at the same instant, and the flying fragments of the shattered guns and bursted shells disabled every man at the two guns. His rifle shot and shell penetrated the earthworks as readily as a ball from a navy Colt would pierce a pine board, and soon so disabled other guns as to leave us but four capable of being served.

General Tilghman now consulted with Major Gilmer and myself as to the situation, and the decision was that further resistance would only entail a useless loss of life. He therefore ordered me to strike the colors, now a dangerous as well as a painful duty. The flag-mast, which had been the center of fire, had been struck many times; the top-mast hung so far out of the perpendicular that it seemed likely to fall at any moment; the flag halyards had been cut by shot, but had fortunately become "foul" at the crosstrees.

I beckoned—for it was useless to call amid the din—to Orderly Sergeant Jones, an old "man-o'-war's man," to come to my assistance, and we ran across to the flag-staff and up the lower rigging to the cross-trees, and by our united efforts succeeded in clearing the halyards and lowering the flag.

The view from that elevated position at the time was grand, exciting, and striking. At our feet the fort with her few remaining guns was sullenly hurling her harmless shot against the sides of the gun-boats, which, now apparently within two hundred yards of the fort, were, in perfect security, and with the coolness and precision of target practice, sweeping the entire fort. To the north and west, on both sides of the river, were the hosts of "blue coats," anxious and interested spectators, while to the east the feeble forces of the Confederacy could be seen making their weary way toward Donelson.

On the morning of the attack, we were sure that the February rise of the Tennessee had come. When the action began, the lower part of the fort was already flooded. When the colors were hauled down, the water was waist-deep there; and when the cutter came with the officers to receive the formal surrender, she pulled into the "sally-port". Between the fort and the position which had been occupied by the infantry support was a sheet of water a quarter of a mile or more wide, and running like a mill-race. If the attack had been delayed forty-eight hours, there would hardly have been a hostile shot fired; the Tennessee would have accomplished the work by drowning the magazine.

The fight was over; the little garrison were prisoners; but our army had been saved. We had been required to hold out an hour; we had held out for over two.

We went into the fight with nine guns bearing on the river approach. We had two more 42-pounders, but neither shot nor shell for them. Of these all were disabled but four. Of the 54 men who went into action, five were killed, 11 wounded or disabled, and five missing. When the *Essex* dropped out of the fight I could see her men wildly throwing themselves into the swollen river. Admiral Foote reported that his flagship was struck thirty-eight times, and the commanding officers of the gun-boats (with several of whom I had enjoyed a warm personal acquaintance) complimented me highly on what they termed the extraordinary accuracy of the fire. I believe that with effective guns the same precision of fire would have sunk or driven back the flotilla.

The formal surrender was made to the naval forces; Lieutenant-Commander Phelps acting for Flag-Officer Foote, and I representing General Tilghman. The number captured, including Tilghman and staff, hospital attendants and some stragglers from the infantry, amounted to about seventy.

Henry Walke, commander of the *Carondelet,* tells about the attack on Fort Henry from the viewpoint of the victorious attacker:

The 6th dawned mild and cheering, with a light breeze, sufficient to clear away the smoke. At 10:20 the flag-officer (A. H. Foote) made the signal to prepare for battle, and at 10:50 came the order to get under way and steam up to Panther Island, about two miles below Fort Henry. At 11:35, having passed the foot of the island, we formed in line and approached the fort four abreast—the *Essex* on the right, then the *Cincinnati, Carondelet* and *St. Louis* . . . About noon the fort and the Confederate flag came suddenly into view, the barracks, the new earthworks, and the great guns well manned. The captains of our guns were men-of-war's men, good shots, and had their men well drilled. The flagsteamer, the *Cincinnati,* fired the first shot as the signal for the others to begin. At once the fort was ablaze with the flame of her eleven heavy guns. The wild whistle of their rifle-shells was heard on every side of us.

The firing from the armored vessels was rapid and well-sustained from the beginning of the attack, and seemingly accurate, as we could occasionally see the earth thrown in great heaps over the enemy's guns. Nor was the fire of the Confederates to be despised; their heavy shot broke and scattered our iron plating as if it had been putty, and often passed completely through the casemates. But our old man-of-war's men, captains of the guns, proud to show their worth in battle, infused life and courage into their young comrades. When these experienced gunners saw a shot coming toward a port, they had the coolness and discretion to order their men to bow down, to save their heads.

From the number of times the gun-boats were struck it would appear that the Confederate artillery practice, at first at least, was as good, if not better, than ours . . . The Confederate soldiers fought as valiantly and as skillfully as the Union sailors. Only after a most determined resistance, and after all his heavy guns had been silenced, did General Tilghman lower his flag. . . .

When I took possession of the fort the Confederate surgeon was laboring with his coat off to relieve and save the wounded; and although the officers and crews of the gun-boats gave three hearty cheers when the Confederate flag was hauled down, the first inside view of the fort sufficed to suppress every feeling of exultation and to excite our deepest pity. On every side the blood of the dead and wounded was intermingled with the earth and their implements of war. Their largest gun, a 128-pounder, was dismounted and filled with earth by the bursting of one of our shells near its muzzle; the carriage of another was broken to pieces and two dead men lay near it, almost covered with heaps of earth; a rifled gun had burst, throwing its mangled gunners into the water. But few of the garrison escaped unhurt.

The actual fighting that resulted in the fall of Fort Henry was all on the part of the naval forces, as General Grant's infantrymen floundered in the muddy river bottoms. Grant's men, however, occupied the fort late in the afternoon of the 6th, and it was Grant who sent the glad news to Halleck. Halleck notified President Lincoln, and the Northern states went wild with joy as the newspaper extras' headlines screamed: "Fort Henry Has Fallen!"

Albert Sidney Johnston at Bowling Green was naturally shocked, although probably not entirely surprised, to learn of the Confederate disaster, and he hurriedly made such arrangements as were possible to prepare Fort Donelson for the assault there which might logically be expected to follow. The troops at Donelson were now left without a commanding officer, with Tilghman started on his way to a Northern prison. Temporarily the command was assigned to Brigadier General Bushrod R. Johnson; but on February 7th General Pillow, with all the troops under him at Clarksville, was ordered to move to Donelson and assume command.

Johnston, who had no great faith in the impregnability of Fort Donelson, ordered Pillow to hold it as long as possible, then evacuate the position and march to Nashville by way of Charlotte. Pillow assumed command on the 9th, and went to work energetically to make as strong a defense as possible. One of his first problems was to restore the morale of the troops, sadly shaken by the Fort Henry surrender and by the legend of terrible invincibility which the quick success of the gunboats had created. Colonel Gilmer was put to work strengthening the fortifications on the river and also on the land side—and an appeal was made to Johnston for reinforcements.

Johnston was now confronted with the baffling problem of how best to utilize his limited force to the greatest possible advantage. Nashville had not been fortified, and it was his conviction that the fight to hold Nashville must be made at Fort Donelson. Bowling Green was no longer tenable; and the troops there, he felt, must fall back on Nashville. Beauregard, called into council, favored concentrating all the troops at Fort Donelson, there to force a decisive battle with Grant, but Johnston was unwilling to risk the destruction of his whole army by permitting it to get penned in between Grant and Buell. At length on February 7th it was agreed between Johnston, Beauregard and Hardee that Hardee with his division should retreat from Bowling Green to Nashville, that Beauregard should return to Columbus and make "a desperate defense" of the Mississippi at that point, and that the other available troops would be concentrated at Fort Donelson for a last-ditch defense of that vital position.

Immediately there ensued that confusion of counsel and conflict of opinions that was to prove fatal to the Confederates. Floyd with his brigade, in obedience to orders, had moved from Clarksville to Cumberland City, sixteen miles above (that is, south of) Fort Donelson, where the railroad crossed the river. Floyd thought the principal stand should be made there, and he ordered Buckner (who was under his command) to leave the fort, and join him at Cumberland City. Pillow, who thought the fight for control of the Cumberland River should be made at the Fort, refused to permit Buckner to leave to join Floyd. Pillow appealed to Johnston for support, and accordingly Johnston ordered Floyd to move his force into Fort Donelson. Floyd arrived there during the early hours of the 13th and, by reason of his senior rank, assumed command—the fifth commander the fort had had within one week.

Meanwhile the Federals, although exhilarated by their easy success at Fort Henry, seemed uncertain as to just what to do next. In reporting the capture of Fort Henry to Halleck, Grant (with excessive optimism) had flatly stated: "I shall take and destroy Fort Donelson on the 8th and return to Fort Henry." But the designated time-table did not work out quite so simply. The steadily rising river flooded the low ground and the roads were under water for a space of two miles, making it impossible for the infantry to move. Then there were morale problems. Grant's men were largely inexperienced and undisciplined, and that their enforced idleness had a bad effect on their conduct is indicated by a "General Field Order" issued by Grant on the 9th:

The pilfering and marauding disposition shown by some of the men of this command has determined the general commanding to make an example of some one, to fully show his disapprobation of such conduct. Brigade commanders, therefore, will be held accountable for the conduct of their brigades, regimental commanders for their regiments, and company commanders for their companies. If any one is found guilty of plundering or other violation of orders, if the guilty parties are not punished promptly the company officers will be at once arrested, or if they are not known the punishment will have to come upon the regimental or brigade commanders. Every offense will be traced back to a responsible party.

In an enemy's country, where so much more could be done by a manly and humane policy to advance the cause which we all have so deeply at heart, it is astonishing that men can be found so wanton as to destroy, pillage, and burn indiscriminately, without inquiry.

This has been done but to a very limited extent in this command so far, but too much for our credit has already occurred to be allowed to pass without admonition.

But Grant had other problems than the misconduct of his troops. On February 8th, with his staff and part of a cavalry regiment, he made a personal reconnaisance within a mile of the works at Fort Donelson. In his *Memoirs,* written in 1894, Grant in a characteristic but ill-advised expression of contempt for his opponents says:

"I had known General Pillow in Mexico, and judged that with any force, no matter how small, I could march up to within gunshot of any intrenchments he was given to hold. I said this to the officers of my staff at the time. I knew that Floyd was in command, but he was no soldier and I judged that he would yield to Pillow's pretensions."

In truth, however, Grant's keen analysis in 1885 of his opponents' weaknesses was necessarily based on knowledge after the event. As a matter of fact, neither Pillow nor Floyd was in the fort on the 8th. On the other hand, Grant's expressed confidence in his ability to make a quick capture of the fort was evidently diminished by what he saw on his reconnaissance. At any rate, on the 10th he telegraphed Foote, commanding the gunboat flotilla, asking for his help and cooperation:

I have been waiting very patiently for the return of the gunboats under Commander Phelps, to go around on the Cumberland, whilst I marched my land forces across to make a simultaneous attack upon Fort Donelson. I feel that there should be no delay in this matter, and yet I do not feel justified in going without some of your gunboats to co-operate. Can you not send two boats from Cairo immediately up the Cumberland? To expedite matters, any steamers at Cairo may be taken to tow them. Should you be deficient in men, an artillery company can be detached to serve on the gunboats temporarily.

Please let me know your determination in this matter, and start as soon as you like. I will be ready to co-operate at any moment.

Apparently, however, cooperation between the army and the navy was not entirely automatic. General Halleck found it necessary to back up Grant's appeal to Foote with a telegram sent on the 10th to Brigadier General Cullum at Cairo asking, him, if possible to try to "persuade Flag-Officer Foote to send gunboats up the Cumberland." Still Foote seemed to be in no hurry to move.

Knowing, as we now do, of the inadequacy of the Confederate forces and their confusion of purpose, it is interesting to observe that Halleck entertained an almost ludicrously inaccurate idea as to what his enemy might do, as evidenced by his telegram of the same day to General George B. McClellan, then commander of all the Federal forces in the field:

It is said that Beauregard is preparing to move from Columbus, either on Paducah or Fort Henry. Have you fully considered the advantage which the Cumberland affords to the enemy at Nashville? An immense number of boats have been collected, and the whole Bowling Green force can come down in a day, attack Grant in the rear, and return to Nashville before Buell can get half-way there. The bridges are all destroyed and the roads rendered impassable. If Buell must move by land, why not direct him on Clarksville? I can do no more for Grant at present. I must stop the transports at Cairo to observe Beauregard. We are certainly in peril.

Then, for good measure, emphasising his unwarranted fear of counter-attack by the Confederates, Halleck telegraphed Grant:

If possible destroy the bridge at Clarksville. Run any risk to accomplish this. Strengthen land side of Fort Henry, and transfer guns to resist a land attack. Picks and shovels are sent. Large re-enforcements will soon join you.

At length Grant regained some measure of his confidence and began a somewhat cautious approach to the siege of Fort Donelson. McClernand's division started the forward movement on February 11th, with Grant following with the main body of troops on the 12th, leaving General Lew Wallace with 2500 men temporarily at Fort Henry. Foote and the gunboats started on the 11th, accompanied by transports carrying six regiments of reinforcements who had arrived at Fort Henry just as Grant was preparing to set out. At Paducah the convoy picked up eight more transports loaded with troops—10,000 additional soldiers for Grant.

The Twelfth Regiment of Iowa Infantry was one of the units in General C. F. Smith's division that made the overland march from the Tennessee River to take part in the investment of Donelson. Major David W. Reed of that regiment has set down an account of their experience that may be accepted as typical of that of the investing Federal forces:

On the 12th the regiment was ordered out in "light marching order, with three days' rations in haversacks." The weather was warm and pleasant, and, remembering the burden of overcoats on the recent march, the men accepted the order as it read ("light marching order"), and fell into ranks without overcoats, taking only one blanket each. Marching twelve miles, the regiment bivouacked at night in line of battle before Fort Donelson.

Early on the morning of the 13th the line was advanced, the Twelfth moving in line of battle toward the fort. The men soon experienced the first shock of hearing the discharge of artillery, knowing that the pieces were aimed "this way," and the greater shock which comes to every man the first time he sees wounded men borne to the rear of a battle line.

The regiment moved forward to the brow of the hill, within easy range of the fort and separated from it by a ravine filled with fallen timber, making an abatis entirely impassable by a regiment in line, and nearly impenetrable by a skirmish line. Here the regiment halted and Company A was detailed as skirmishers and sent forward into the abatis to drive out the rebel sharp-shooters. No attempt was made during the day by any of Smith's division to advance farther than to get into position and wait for the gunboats.

During the afternoon of the 13th rain began to fall, and soon after the weather turned colder, so that the men were obliged to wrap their blankets around them as they stood in line. None of them had at that time been provided with rubber blankets and, of course, all were soon thoroughly drenched. About dark the rain turned to snow and continue to fall very fast until it lay five or six inches on the ground, the cold increasing until it was below freezing. Fires could not be lighted on account of nearness to rebel lines, and as the only resource left to prevent freezing to death, the men, laying aside their now stiffly frozen blankets, commenced running around in a circle, and through the live-long night kept up that "By company, in a circle, double quick, march!"—entirely new to Casey's tactics. Major Brodtbeck was found during the night seated at the foot of a tree so completely chilled that he could not move. He was roused with some difficulty, and as he afterwards said, "Someone gave me something out of a canteen that warmed me, but I ask no question what it is." One company at a time was kept on picket at the front, but these were frequently changed during the night. About daylight of the 14th the whole regiment was relieved and marched to the rear where the men built fires and made coffee, dried their clothes and took some needed rest.

The severity of the weather, especially painful as it followed so closely the preceding balmy days, is commented on by all those participants in this campaign who left a record of their experiences. All join in setting it down as a night of horrid suffering. The freezing north wind drove stinging snow spitefully against blue and gray alike, shivering in an unusually low temperature of 10 degrees. The lines were so close together that fear of the unsleeping sharpshooter's deadly aim made fires impossible. The thinly clad Confederates huddled miserably in their shallow trenches: as across the intervening hollows the Northern troops suffered equally, regretting their improvident casting aside of their overcoats on the gay march from Fort Henry, deceived by the treacherous mildness.

General Grant, in his post-war writing about the Fort Donelson campaign, commented on the failure of the Confederates to impede his approach, apparently unaware of the fact that while he was marching across from Fort Henry to Donelson, there had not yet been attained any unity of command at the latter. In fact, as Grant was deploying his men on the morning of the 13th, General Floyd was just arriving at the Dover landing and hurrying his men into position behind the breastworks, as he assumed command of the nondescript forces he found there. Floyd's accession brought the total garrison to a force of somewhat less than 15,000; Grant, with his reinforcements, had about 27,000 men.

The Confederate batteries on the river-front had just been completed and manned on the morning of the 13th, and the inexperienced artillerists were in the process of being taught the rudiments of how to handle the big guns when the first of Foote's flotilla, the *Carondelet,* appeared and gave them their baptism of fire. Captain B. G. Bidwell of the Thirtieth Tennessee Infantry, the only officer connected with the heavy batteries who was fortunate enough to escape, a few weeks later wrote to J. P. Benjamin, Secretary of War, giving him a first-hand account of the engagement with the gunboats:

Fort Donelson was on the crest of a hill, on the south bank of the Cumberland, about one mile below the little town of Dover. The vicinage around was very broken below the fort. Running back from the river was a deep ravine or gorge, filled with backwater for a mile back. Breaking off from this was another deep hollow, which ran up behind the fort, making almost all of the fort on the crest of the hill. Just above the main part of the fort a hollow makes out from the river, which runs diagonally across the fort, making the inner fort nothing but a hollow and the side of the hill. The most of the work was tolerably good earthwork, the remainder nothing but rifle pits, thrown up after the fall of Fort Henry.

There was in the fort one large howitzer (a good one) and two small 9 or 12-pounders, made in Clarksville, of very little account. Below the fort, and just at the foot of the hill, was our battery of eight 32-pounders and one 10-inch columbiad. On the extreme left, just above the river bank and on the point of the hill above, was another battery, including one rifled gun and two old carronades or ship's guns, which were worthless there or anywhere else. Their trunnions, being too small, were bent. This battery was separated from the other by another hollow and point of land projecting to the river bank between them. The 32-pounders were in good condition. Four of them were under the charge of Captain Beaumont and the other four commanded by myself. The rifled gun was under the charge of Captain Ross.

One boat made its appearance around the point above two miles and a half below us on Thursday, February 13, and fired a few rounds at us, to which our battery replied pretty warmly until she retired. The next to the last shot from the boat came through the embrasure of the second gun in my battery, striking the left cheek of the carriage, shivering it, and disabling the gun, killing Captain Dixon, of the Engineer Corps, who had, by order of General Pillow, been placed in command of the entire heavy artillery as chief. Upon his death Captain Culbertson, of the old Army, took command.

All was quiet until the evening of the 14th (Friday), when four boats came around the point, arranged themselves in line of battle, and advanced slowly, but steadily, up the river to within 200 yards of our battery, and halted, when a most incessant fire was kept up for some time. We were ordered to hold our fire until they got within range of our 32-pounder. We remained perfectly silent while they came over about 1½ miles, pouring a heavy fire of shot and shell upon us all the time. Two more boats came around the point and threw shell at us.

Our gunners were inexperienced and knew very little of the firing of heavy guns. They, however, did some excellent shooting. The rifled gun was disabled by the ramming of a cartridge while the wire was in the vent (it being left in there by a careless gunner), and being bent, it could not be got out. But the two center boats were both disabled, the left center (I think) by a ricochet shot entering one of the port-holes, which are tolerably large. The right center boat was very soon injured by a ball striking her on top, and also a direct shot in the port-hole, when she fell back, the two flank boats closing in behind them and protecting them from our fire in retreat. I think these two were not seriously injured.

They must have fired near 2,000 shot and shell at us. Our Columbiad fired about twenty-seven times, the rifled gun very few times, and the 32-pounders about 45 or 50 rounds each. A great many of our balls took effect, being well aimed.

I am confident the efficiency of the gunboat is in the gun it carries rather than in the boat itself. We can whip them always if our men will only stand to their guns. Not a man of all ours was hurt, notwithstanding they threw grape at us. Their fire was more detructive to our works at two miles than at 200 yards. They over-fired us from that distance.

Our men all did well. I probably ought not to make any distinction, but will refer to the gallant conduct of John G. Frequa, a private and gunner. At the highest gun in my battery he stood perfectly straight, calm, cool, and collected. I heard him say, "Now, boys, see me take a chimney." The chimney and flag both fell. He threw his cap in the air, shouting to them defiance. "Come on, you cowardly scoundrels; you are not at Fort Henry," were his words to them. Very soon he sent a ball through a port-hole and the boat fell back. This boy is one of the prisoners so unnecessarily and wrongfully surrendered at Donelson—surrendered, with his comrades, while at his post Sunday morning, without any knowledge of what was being done and no chance for escape.

I was sent for by a colonel of a Tennessee regiment and was at Dover when the white flags were sent out early Sunday morning, and had no chance to communicate with my men or save them.

Impressive evidence of the crashing effectiveness of the Confederate gunners' fire is to be found in the account of the repulse of the gunboats' attack written by Henry Walke, commander of the *Carondelet:*

At 3 o'clock in the afternoon [of the 13th] our fleet advanced to attack the fort, the *Louisville* being on the west side of the river, the *St. Louis* (flag-steamer) next, then the *Pittsburgh* and *Carondelet* on the east side of the river. The wooden gunboats were about a thousand yards in the rear. . . . When within a mile of the fort the *St. Louis* opened fire, and the other ironclads followed—slowly and deliberately at first, but more rapidly as the fleet advanced. As we drew nearer, the enemy's fire greatly increased in force and effect . . .

We heard the deafening crack of the bursting shells, the crash of the solid shot, and the whizzing of fragments of shell and wood as they sped through the vessel. Soon a 128-pounder struck our anchor, smashed it into flying bolts, and bounded over the vessel, taking away a part of our smoke-stack; then another cut away the iron boat-davits as if they were pipe stems, whereupon the boat dropped into the water. Another ripped up the iron plating and glanced over; another went through the plating and lodged in the heavy casemate; another struck the pilot house, knocked the plating to pieces, and sent fragments of iron and splinters into the pilots, one of whom fell mortally wounded and was taken below; another shot took away the remaining boat-davits and the boat with them; and still they came, harder and faster, taking flag-staffs and smoke-stacks, and tearing off the side armor as lightning tears away the bark from a tree. Our men fought desperately, but under the excitement of the occasion loaded too hastily, and the port rifled gun exploded. . . .

When within about four hundred yards of the fort, our pilot house was struck again and another pilot wounded, our wheel was broken, and shells from the rear boats were bursting over us. All four of our boats were shot away and dragging in the water. On looking out to bring our broadside guns to bear, we saw that the other gun-boats were rapidly falling back out of line. The *Pittsburgh,* in her haste to turn, struck the stern of the *Carondelet* and broke our starboard rudder, so that we were obliged to go ahead to clear the *Pittsburgh* and the point of rocks below. The pilot of the *St. Louis* was killed, and the pilot of the *Louisville* was wounded. The *St. Louis* and the *Louisville,* becoming unmanageable, were compelled to drop out of the battle, and the *Pittsburgh* followed; all had suffered severely from the enemy's fire. Flag-Officer Foote was wounded while standing by the pilot of the *St. Louis* when he was killed.

Colonel Nathan Bedford Forrest had viewed the naval engagement, purely as a spectator, from a point of vantage on the river-bank where he had ridden with his second in command, Major D. C. Kelley. In his official report Forrest paid a deserved tribute to the gallantry displayed by both sides:

No one could do justice in description to the attack or the defense. More determination could not have been exhibited by the attacking party, while more coolness and bravery never were manifested than were seen in our artillerists.

As he watched, Forrest grew excitedly apprehensive over the outcome, seeing the apparently irresistible avalanche of shot and shell from the gunboats. Turning to Major Kelley, a former minister, he cried: "Parson, for God's sake pray! Nothing but God Almighty can save that fort!"

Similar fears were felt by Floyd who, in the midst of the bombardment, telegraphed Johnston to inform him of the gunboats' onslaught, closing his message with the ominous (and erroneous) prediction: "The Fort can not hold out twenty minutes."

Floyd, however, was more to be pitied than censured. He was not a trained soldier, and his only military experience had been gained in the brief and unsuccessful campaign in West Virginia which had convinced Robert E. Lee of Floyd's incompetence. He had not the least familiarity with the task of holding a fortified position like Fort Donelson, and he undertook its defense reluctantly. His natural vacillation was intensified by the conflicting advice he received from his two associates, Pillow and Buckner—and harmonious relations were not improved by the fact that Pillow and Buckner were bitter personal enemies, still nursing an old feud from the Mexican War.

Before the gunboats began their action on the 13th Floyd had called a council of war, at which it was unanimously agreed that the fort should be evacuated. The strategy decided upon was an immediate attack on the right wing of the investing Federal land forces, in an effort to seize the road leading to Charlotte and thus open up the way for the withdrawal of the fort's garrison to Nashville. This attack was to be made by Pillow's massed division, and about noon on the 13th his men were ordered out of the trenches and into formation to the rear and left of their occupied line. To Buckner's division was assigned the task of covering the withdrawal, should Pillow's sortie prove successful. Buckner was preparing for this movement when he got word early in the afternoon that it had been deferred, as Pillow had decided that it was too late in the day to launch the planned attack. And so the day ended, with no action taken by the Confederate land forces.

One of the divisions in the Federal army of investment was commanded by General Lew Wallace, who after the war was the famous author of the best seller *Ben Hur*. General Wallace, with his literary skill, and with the advantage of his personal participation in the events of which he writes, is able to give a graphic account from the Federal point of view, of the deploying of the Confederate and Union forces as Fort Donelson was invested:

The morning of the 13th—calm, spring-like, the very opposite of that of the 6th—found in Fort Donelson a garrison of 28 regiments of infantry: 13 from Tennessee, two from Kentucky, six from Mississippi, one from Texas, two from Alabama, four from Virginia. There were also present two independent battalions, one regiment of cavalry, and artillerymen for six light batteries, and 17 heavy guns.

General Buckner's division—six regiments and two batteries—constituted the right wing, and was posted to cover the land approaches to the water-batteries. A left wing under General Pillow was organized into six brigades, commanded respectively by Colonels Heiman, Davidson, Drake, Wharton, McCausland, and Baldwin, and posted from right to left in the order named. Four batteries were distributed amongst the left wing. General Bushrod R. Johnson, an able officer, served the general commanding as chief-of-staff. Dover was converted into a depot of supplies and ordnance stores. These dispositions made, Fort Donelson was ready for battle. . . .

On the morning of the 13th of February General Grant, with about twenty thousand men, was before Fort Donelson. We have had a view of the Confederate army in the works ready for battle; a like view of the Union forces outside and about to go into position of attack and assault is not so easily to be given. At dawn the latter host rose up from the bare ground, and, snatching bread and coffee as best they could, fell into lines that stretched away over hills, down hollows, and through thickets, making it impossible for even colonels to see their regiments from flank to flank. . . .

In a clearing about two miles from Dover there was a log-house, at the time occupied by a Mrs. Crisp. As the road to Dover ran close by, it was made the headquarters of the commanding general. All through the night of the 12th, the coming and going had been incessant. Smith was ordered to find a position in front of the enemy's right wing, which would place him face to face with Buckner, McClernand's order was to establish himself on the enemy's left, where he would be opposed to Pillow.

A little before dawn Birge's sharp-shooters were astir. Each was a preferred marksman, and carried a long-range Henry rifle, with sights delicately arranged as for target practice. In action each was perfectly independent. They never maneuvered as a corps. When the time came they were asked, "Canteens full?" "Biscuits for all day?" Then their only order, "All right; hunt your holes, boys." Thereupon they dispersed, and, like Indians, sought cover to please themselves behind rocks and stumps, or in hollows. Sometimes they dug holes; sometimes they climbed into trees. This morning they dispersed early to find places within easy range of the breastworks.

The movement of Smith and McClernand was begun about the same time. A thick wood fairly screened the former. The latter had to cross an open valley under fire of two batteries, one on Buckner's left, the other on a high point jutting from the line of outworks held by Colonel Heiman of Pillow's command. . . . As always in situations where the advancing party is ignorant of the ground and of the designs of the enemy, resort was had to skirmishers, who are to the main body what antennae are to insects. Theirs it is to unmask the foe. Behind the skirmishers, the batteries started out to find positions, and through the brush and woods, down the hollows, up the hills the guns and caissons were hauled. In the gray of the dawn the sharp-shooters were deep in their deadly game; as the sun came up, one battery after another opened fire, and was instantly and gallantly answered; and all the time behind the hidden sharp-shooters, and behind the skirmishers, who occasionally stopped to take a hand in the fray, the regiments marched, route-step, colors flying, after their colonels . . .

It is now—morning of the 14th—easy to see and understand with something more than approximate exactness the oppositions of the two forces. Smith is on the left of the Union army opposite Buckner. My division, in the center, confronts Colonels Heiman, Drake, and Davidson, each with a brigade. McClernand, now well over on the right, keeps the road to Charlotte and Nashville against the major part of Pillow's left wing. The infantry on both sides are in cover behind the crests of the hills or a thick woods, listening to the ragged fusillade which the sharp-shooters and skirmishers maintain against each other almost without intermission. There is little pause in the exchange of shells and round shot. The careful chiefs have required their men to lie down. In brief, it looks as if each party were inviting the other to begin. . . .

The sharp-shooting and cannonading, ugly as they may seem to one who thinks of them under comfortable surrounding, did in fact serve a good purpose the day in question in helping the men to forget their sufferings of the night before. All night the tempest blew mercilessly upon the unsheltered, fireless soldier, making sleep impossible. Inside the works, nobody had overcoats; while thousands of those outside had marched from Fort Henry as to a summer fete, leaving coats, blankets, and knapsacks behind them in the camp. More than one stout fellow has since admitted, with a laugh, that nothing was so helpful to him that horrible night as the thought that the wind, which seemed about to turn his blood into icicles, was serving the enemy the same way; they, too, had to stand out and take the blast.

Grant's original plan of battle was for the troops to hold the Confederates in their lines while the gunboats attacked the land batteries and silenced those guns if possible. It was hoped that some of the gunboats might be able to run by the batteries and get above Dover and that, in cooperation with the land forces, they might thus force the surrender of the Confederate garrison. The repulse of the gunboat attack, however, nullified this hope, and, later, Grant wrote:

The sun went down on the night of the 14th of February, leaving the army confronting Fort Donelson anything but comforted over the prospects. The weather had turned intensely cold; the men were without tents and could not keep up fires where most of them had to stay. . . . Two of the strongest of our gunboats had been disabled. . . . I retired this night not knowing but that I would have to intrench my position, and bring up tents for the men or build huts under the cover of the hills.

General Grant, however, might not have felt so perturbed had he been aware of the simultaneously increasing apprehension of the Confederate commanders. That evening Floyd called another council of war. Despite the river batteries' driving off the gunboats, he still thought it impossible to hold the fort, and again there was unanimous agreement that they would try to force their way out to Nashville by the Charlotte Road.

Planning to march at dawn, the Confederates worked tirelessly at realignment through the bitter cold night. Over the icy roads, through the snow and frozen mud, the men and guns were pulled out of the advanced trenches and assembled in new positions on the left. At 5 A.M., promptly on schedule, Pillow moved to the attack against the Federal right under McClernand.

Grant apparently had no thought that the beleagured Confederates might come out of their works and launch an assault against him. At any rate, early that morning he had left his headquarters and gone to visit Foote on his flagship, leaving behind him definite instructions to each of his division commanders not to move from their positions without his explicit order. These strange instructions, it developed, had almost fatal consequences.

Pillow's attack on McClernand was signally successful. As he was being steadily forced backward, McClernand appealed to General Lew Wallace for assistance. Wallace sent to Grant's headquarters for permission to march to McClernand's support—but Grant was not there. However, Pillow's relentless advance pushed McClernand into complete and precipitate retreat, driving him for two miles right into Wallace's division, forcing Wallace in self-defense to join in the fighting. But Pillow's resistless advance continued, with Buckner joining in on the flank, and by early afternoon the end sought by the sortie had been achieved: The Charlotte road was completely in the Confederates' control, and McClernand's and Wallace's men were retreating in confusion, crying "All's lost! Save yourselves!"

General Wallace gives a participant's vivid account of the effective culmination of the Confederate sortie:

> Buckner flung a portion of his division on McClernand's left, and supported the attack with his artillery. McClernand, watchful and full of resources, sent batteries to meet Buckner's batteries. The roar never slackened. Men fell by the score, reddening the snow with their blood. The smoke in pallid white clouds clung to the underbrush and tree-tops as if to screen the combatants from each other. Close to the ground the flame of musketry and cannon tinted everything a lurid red. Limbs dropped from the trees on the heads below, and the thickets were shorn as by an army of reapers. . . .
>
> It was now 10 o'clock, and over on the right Oglesby was beginning to fare badly. The pressure on his front grew stronger. The "rebel yell", afterward a familiar battle-cry on many fields, told of ground being gained against him. His right companies began to give way, and as they retreated, holding up their empty cartridge-boxes, the enemy were emboldened and swept more fiercely around his flank, until finally they appeared in his rear. He then gave the order to retire the division. . . .
>
> By 11 o'clock Pillow held the road to Charlotte and the whole of the position occupied at dawn by the First [McClernand's] Division, and with it the dead and all the wounded who could not get away. Pillow's part of the programme arranged in the council of the night before was accomplished. The country was once more open to Floyd. Why did he not avail himself of the dearly bought opportunity and march his army out?

General Wallace's rhetorical question is one that has since been asked countless times, but as yet there has been no satisfactory answer. The only logical conclusion seems to be that Pillow lost his head, and also lost his nerve, at this critical point. After pausing to send an absurdly vainglorious telegram to Johnston at Nashville: "On the honor of a soldier, the day is ours!", he ordered the whole army (including Buckner's division) back to their positions in the works. Buckner, very properly, questioned Pillow's authority to change the plan of battle or to give orders to him. At this juncture Floyd arrived on the scene and Buckner appealed to him. Floyd agreed that the original plan should be adhered to, and instructed Buckner to stay where he was. Upon consulting Pillow, however, Floyd reversed himself and ordered all the men, Buckner's included, back into the fort.

Meanwhile Grant had at last returned to the battlefield. Informed of the Confederates' successful break-through, he correctly concluded that the concentration on their left must have weakened their right. He accordingly ordered Smith to attack the Confederate right and, at the same time, ordered his right wing to retake the positions lost to Pillow. As Pillow was by now on his way back to the position he had occupied before the attack, McClernand's advancing columns merely followed the withdrawing Confederates. By the time Buckner's troops had made their way back to their original position, they found that Smith's men were already occupying Buckner's former works, and the best Buckner could do was to take possession of a hill overlooking the position, placing his artillery there, thereby stopping the Federal advance for the day.

That night, in the Confederate command post at the old Dover Hotel, there was a gloomy gathering of the general and field officers in a climactic council of war. It was agreed that still the best course for the Confederates was to evacuate the fort and withdraw to Nashville, but scouts had reported (erroneously, Forrest later said) that the Federals had occupied the only possible road of egress, and surrender was the only alternative.

Just exactly what was said at this conference, and who said what, became a matter of controversy afterwards. It seems plain, however that it was General Buckner who was the leading spirit in advocating the surrender of the fort and its troops, deeming its defense hopeless, so it is enlightening to read what he had to say about it in his official report:

When the information of our reinvestment was reported, General Floyd, General Pillow and myself were the only members of the council present. Both of these officers have stated the views of the council, but my recollection of some of the incidents narrated differs so materially from that of General Pillow, that without intending any reflection upon either of those officers, I feel called upon to notice some of the differences of opinion between us.

Both officers have correctly stated that I regarded the position of the army as desperate, and that an attempt to extricate it by another battle, in the suffering and exhausted condition of the troops, was almost hopeless. The troops had been worn down with watching, with labor, with fighting. Many of them were frosted by the intensity of the cold; all of them were suffering and exhausted by their incessant labors. There had been no regular issue of rations for a number of days and scarcely any means of cooking. Their ammunition was nearly expended. We were completely invested by a force of nearly four times the strength of our own. In their exhausted condition they could not have made a march. An attempt to make a sortie would have been resisted by a superior force of fresh troops, and that attempt would have been the signal for the fall of the water batteries and the presence of the enemy's gunboats sweeping with the fire at close range the positions of our troops, who would have thus been assailed on their front, rear, and right flank at the same instant. The results would have been a virtual massacre of the troops, more disheartening in its effects than a surrender.

In this opinion General Floyd coincided, and I am certain that both he and I were convinced that General Pillow agreed with us in this opinion. General Pillow then asked our opinion as to the practicability of holding our position another day. I replied that my right was already turned, a portion of my intrenchments in the enemy's possession—they were in position successfully to assail my position and the water batteries—and that, with my weakened and exhausted force, I could not successfully resist the assault which would be made at daylight by a vastly superior force. . . . I expressed the opinion that it would be wrong to subject the army to a virtual massacre when no good could result from the sacrifice, and that the general officers owed it to their men, when further resistance was unavailing, to obtain the best terms of capitulation possible for them. General Floyd expressed himself in similar terms, and in this opinion I understood General Pillow to acquiesce.

For reasons which he has stated, General Floyd then announced his purpose to leave, with such portions of his division as could be transported in two small steamers, which were expected about daylight. General Pillow, addressing General Floyd, then remarked that he thought that there were no two persons in the Confederacy whom the Yankees would prefer to capture than himself and General Floyd, and asked the latter's opinion as to the propriety of his accompanying General Floyd. To this inquiry the latter replied that it was a question for every man to decide for himself. General Pillow then addressed the inquiry to me, to which I remarked that I could only reply as General Floyd had done, that it was a question for every officer to decide for himself, and that in my own case I regarded it as my duty to remain with my men and share their fate, whatever it might be. General Pillow, however, announced his purpose to leave; then General Floyd directed me to consider myself in command. I remarked that a capitulation would be as bitter to me as it could be to any one, but I regarded it as a necessity of our position, and I could not reconcile it with my sense of duty to separate my fortune from those of my command.

General Grant in his *Memoirs* relates the details of the exchange of notes that sealed the terms of the capitulation of the Fort:

Before daylight General Smith brought to me the following letter from General Buckner: "Sir:—In consideration of all the circumstances governing the present situation of affairs at this station, I propose to the Commanding Officer of the Federal forces the appointment of Commissioners to agree upon terms of capitulation of the forces and fort under my command, and in that view suggest an armistice until 2 o'clock today."

To this I replied: "Sir:—Yours of this date, proposing armistice and appointment of Commissioners to settle terms of capitulation, is just received. No terms except unconditional surrender can be accepted. I propose to move immediately upon your works."

To this I received the following reply: "Sir:—The distribution of the forces under my command, incident to an unexpected change of commanders, and the overwhelming force under your command, compel me, notwithstanding the brilliant success of the Confederate arms yesterday, to accept the ungenerous and unchivalric terms which you propose."

General Buckner, as soon as he had dispatched the first of the above letters, sent word to his different commanders on the line of rifle-pits, notifying them that he had made a proposition looking to the surrender of the garrison, and directing them to notify National troops in their front so that all fighting might be prevented. White flags were stuck at intervals along the line of rifle-pits, but none over the fort. I had been at West Point three years with Buckner and afterwards served with him in the army, so that we were quite well acquainted . . . He asked permission to send parties outside of the lines to bury his dead, who had fallen on the 15th when they tried to get out. I gave directions that his permit to pass our limits should be recognized. I have no reason to believe that this privilege was abused, but it familiarized our guards so much with the sight of Confederates passing to and fro that I have no doubt many got beyond our pickets unobserved and went on.

One of those who got beyond the Federal pickets "and went on" was no less a personage than General Bushrod R. Johnson. His somewhat naive account of his escape is found in his report for duty, when he joined Johnston's army a few days later:

Many of the men and officers commenced to leave Fort Donelson as soon as they were aware of the proposed surrender, and hundreds of them no doubt have made their way to their homes and to the Army. I have not learned that a single one who attempted to escape met with any obstacle.

Almost immediately upon discovering that steps had been taken towards surrendering our forces, the question occurred to me whether the example of our commanding general was an appropriate one, under the circumstances in which I was placed, to be followed, especially as I had no part in the surrender, and had only on an emergency taken command of the troops with which I had not been previously identified. I, however, concluded to stay with the men, promote their comfort as far as possible, and share their fate.

By Tuesday, February 18, the troops of my command had been separated from me, having been sent down the river on board of steamers, and I concluded that it was unlikely that I could be of any more service to them. I, however, formed no purpose or plan of escape.

In the afternoon, towards sunset, of February 18 I walked out with a Confederate officer and took my course towards the rifle pits on the hill formerly occupied by Colonel Heiman, and finding no sentinel to obstruct me, I passed on and was soon beyond the Federal encampments. I had taken no part in the surrender; had received no orders or instructions from the Federal authorities; had not been recognized or even seen by any of the general officers; had been given no parole, and had made no promises. If my escape involves any question of military law, duty or honor, I desire it may be thoroughly investigated, and I shall submit with pleasure to any decision of the proper authorities.

General Nathan Bedford Forrest, it will be recalled, was a participant in the last charge against the Federal right wing on the 15th which drove McClernand's men into retreat. In his official report he tells of the subsequent events, in his usual vigorous style:

The fight here ended about 2:30 p. m., without any change in our relative positions. We were employed the remainder of the evening in gathering up the arms, and assisting in getting off the wounded. I was three times over the battle-field, and late in the evening was two miles up the river on the road to the Cumberland forge. There were none of the enemy in sight when dark came on. Saturday night (the 15th) our troops slept, flushed with victory, and confident they could drive the enemy back to the Tennessee river the next morning.

About 12 o'clock at night I was called in council with the generals who had under discussion the surrender of the fort. They reported that the enemy had received 11,000 re-enforcements since the fight. They supposed the enemy had returned to the positions they had occupied the day before.

I returned to my quarters and sent out two men, who, going by a road up the bank of the river, returned without seeing any of the enemy, only fires, which I believed to be the old camp fires, and so stated to the generals; the wind, being very high, had fanned them into a blaze.

When I returned General Buckner declared that he could not hold his position. Generals Floyd and Pillow gave up the responsibility of the command to him, and I told them that I neither could nor would surrender my command. General Pillow then said I could cut my way out if I chose to do so, and he and General Floyd agreed to come out with me. I got my command ready and reported at headquarters. General Floyd then informed me that General Pillow had left, and that he (Floyd) would go by boat.

I moved out by the road we had gone out the morning before. When about a mile out we crossed a deep slough from the river, saddle-skirt deep, and filed into the road to Cumberland Iron Works. I ordered Major Kelley and Adjutant Schuyler to remain with one company at the point where we entered this road, where the enemy's cavalry would attack if they attempted to follow us. They remained until day was dawning. Over 500 cavalry had passed, a company of artillery horses had followed, and a number of men from different regiments, passing over hard-frozen ground. More than two hours had been occupied in passing. Not a gun had been fired at us. Not an enemy had been seen or heard.

The enemy could not have reinvested their former position without traveling a considerable distance and camping upon the dead and dying, as there had been great slaughter upon that portion of the field, and I am clearly of the opinion that two-thirds of our army could have marched out without loss, and that, had we continued the fight the next day, we should have gained a glorious victory, as our troops were in fine spirits, believing we had whipped them, and the roads through which we came were open as late as 8 o'clock Sunday morning, as many of my men, who came out afterwards, report.

I made a slow march with my exhausted horses to Nashville, where we arrived on Tuesday morning, and reported myself to General Floyd, who placed me in command of the city on Thursday, at the time of his leaving. I remained in the city until Sunday evening, during which time I was busily engaged with my regiment restoring order to the city and removing public property.

CHAPTER 3

☆ *Terror in Nashville*

G ENERAL JOHNSTON had reached Nashville from Bowling Green, in advance of
Hardee's retreating division, on the morning of the 15th. He had set up his
headquarters in Edgefield, then a separate town across the river from
Nashville, and there he had received the exultant telegrams from Floyd and Pillow announcing "a victory complete and glorious" at Fort Donelson on the 15th.
Johnston lay down to sleep that night feeling comparative ease after several days of
intense anxiety; but before daybreak he was aroused by a messenger with another
telegram from Fort Donelson, this one bearing the heartbreaking news of the
decision to surrender.

Johnston had been fully aware of the difficulty of defending Fort Donelson,
but his apprehensions had been temporarily allayed by the sanguine reports he
had received. Now he was stunned by the portent of the shocking news from
the surrendered fort. In his mind's eye he could clearly see the bleak picture
confronting him: The collapse of his whole defensive line, loss of the slender
foothold in Kentucky, the over-running of a large part of Tennessee by the Federals
and, worst of all, the loss of Nashville. But, with Fort Donelson lost, Nashville was
militarily indefensible, especially as he now had only Hardee's scant 10,000 men
to oppose the converging armies of Grant and Buell.

When Johnston crossed over the river to Nashville that Sunday morning,
February 16th, he found the city joyously celebrating the supposed glorious victory
of the preceding day. But after Johnston informed Governor Harris of the fort's
fall the news quickly leaked out, and, spreading like quicksilver, transformed the
citizens' elation to gloom. And, as exaggerated rumors multiplied, the gloom grew
into hysteria and panic.

A graphic and detailed account of the terror that prevailed among the civilian
population of Nashville at this time was written shortly afterwards by a qualified
eye-witness, John Miller McKee. Mr. McKee was a Nashville newspaper man,
a trained observer, who knew how to write about what he had observed. Under
the heading of "The Evacuation of Nashville" he wrote a serialized article for a

short-lived publication known as "The Annals of the Army of Tennessee", published in Nashville in the Seventies by Dr. Edwin L. Drake, a former lieutenant colonel in the Confederate army. This article was later reprinted in a pamphlet (now scarce) entitled "The Panic". Mr. McKee's personal pro-Union sentiments served to give his article a slightly sardonic tone, but he provides a vivid picture of the terror-stricken city when it received the stunning news of Fort Donelson's surrender:

A large concourse of people from the surrounding country, eager to hear the news from Fort Donelson, had assembled in the city on Saturday, and the successive "extras" that were issued, announcing the result of the fight as it progressed, were bought up and their contents devoured with the greatest avidity. On every corner the exploits of the Confederates formed the staple of conversation, and the highest tributes were paid to Southern valor.

The excitement ran higher Saturday night, if possible, than during the day, and the dispatches, as they came in, were listened to with an eagerness which plainly told the interest that was felt in the contest which then hung, as it were, upon the evenly poised balance of fate. Still, there were those who feared for the result of Sunday's work, since the Federals were being so largely reinforced by fresh troops. They felt that the fate of Fort Donelson hung upon the next day's fight, and that the Federals would go into the contest with the advantages all in their favor, having fresh troops, while the Confederates were worn out with four days' terrible fighting. Notwithstanding this was the feeling of quite a number, the great body of the people of Nashville retired to their couches strongly impressed with the belief that the Confederates, who had already fought four days with victory seemingly theirs, would conquer on the fifth. So passed Saturday night in Nashville.

Before 10 o'clock Sunday morning a rumor (vague and indefinite, it is true) that Fort Donelson had surrendered, and that the entire Confederate force had been taken prisoners, had found its way into the streets of the city, and was spreading with a rapidity which only such rumors can spread. It was the rebound which was least expected by the great mass, and it assumed the most terrible proportions as it traveled. This rumor was accompanied with the statement that General Buell, with thirty-five thousand men, was then at Springfield, only twenty-five miles distant, and that a fleet of Federal gun-boats had passed Clarksville, and would reach Nashville by 3 o'clock in the afternoon, by which time Buell's army would arrive in Edgefield, when the city would be shelled, without notice, and laid in ashes. These rumors created a consternation which it would be impossible to portray. A reign of terror and confusion ensued, the like of which was never witnessed in Nashville.

The town was in a perfect tumult—a furor that lashed into a phrenzy those who were regarded perfect models of the calm and passionless—and the wave was spreading with fearful rapidity. Not a man was there in all the goodly city who stepped forth to tell the people that there was no cause for the alarm to which they had given way. It was understood that the intelligence of the fall of Fort Donelson had been communicated to Governor Harris by General Johnston, and that it was from the former the rumor proceeded. His office at the Capitol was besieged by anxious inquirers, and he was appealed to, through one of his aids, to issue a proclamation setting forth the facts as far as they were in his possession, which, of itself, would quiet the people. . . . The Governor, however, declined to issue a proclamation. Some thought that General Johnston should issue a proclamation, others that the Mayor should, and still others that the editors of the respective papers, who were quite proficient in "making the worse appear the better part," should issue extras assuring the people that matters were not half so bad as they appeared. Nothing, however, was done to quiet the people, who were almost deranged with excitement, and hundreds were seen hurrying to and fro, preparing to flee, as for dear life, before the approach of an enemy they feared but little less than if they had been semi-barbarians.

About 11 o'clock a report was put in circulation, as coming from Governor Harris, that the women and children must be removed from the city within three hours, as at the expiration of that time the enemy would shell the place and destroy it. This outrageous story created the most terrible alarm wherever it went, and it spread like wildfire.

It is due to Governor Harris to say that he never intimated any such thing. There is no doubt, however, that this rumor hurried hundreds from the city, as the contradiction traveled much slower than the original story. Men and women were to be seen running to and fro in every portion of the city, and large numbers were hastening with their valuables to the several railroad depots, or escaping in private conveyances to some place of fancied security in the country. The hire of private conveyances was put up to fabulous prices, and it was only the wealthy that could enjoy the luxury of a ride on that day. Large numbers, in their eagerness to escape from the city, left on foot, carrying with them such articles as they wished to preserve, either as mementoes or for their comfort, and, of course, these must necessarily have been few.

Upon the receipt of the intelligence of the capitulation of Fort Donelson, General Johnson advised Governor Harris to remove the archives of the state to some place of safety, as it might become necessary to evacuate Nashville. In accordance with this suggestion, the archives were packed up and shipped in a special train during the afternoon of Sunday to Memphis, whither they were accompanied by the Governor and heads of departments. The Legislature met at an early hour of the morning, and went through the formality of adjourning to meet upon the call of the Governor, and the following notice was served on the members:

"EXECUTIVE OFFICE, Nashville, February 16, 1862.

"The members of the General Assembly of the State of Tennessee will assemble at Memphis, Tenn., on Thursday next, the 20th inst., for the despatch and transaction of such business as may be submitted to them.

ISHAM G. HARRIS"

This temporary removal of the seat of government was done in accordance with a resolution adopted by the two houses of the General Assembly in secret session a few days previous.

These movements of the Governor and Legislature had a tendency to increase the excitement, while the passage through the city at an early hour in the day of a large portion of General Johnston's army from Bowling Green, was another incentive to the growth of the panic, which continued to spread until it seemed to have seized upon almost every one. Go where a person would, the question met him at almost every other step, "What are you going to do?" or, "I don't know," with here and there an exception, "I shall stay and take care of my family." Very few appeared inclined to give advice in the midst of such a panic, even to their most intimate friends, so that the second question was rarely answered, and each man was left to decide for himself whether he should leave the city, and go, he knew not where, nor for why, or remain and take his chances with those who had prudence enough to stay quietly at home, and those—more fortunate—who could not get away.

Every available vehicle was chartered, and even drays were called into requisition, to remove people and their plunder, either to the country or to the depots, and the trains went off crowded to their utmost capacity, even the tops of the cars being literally covered with human beings. It was a lamentable sight to see hundreds of families thus fleeing from their homes, leaving nearly everything behind, to seek among strangers protection and the comforts and luxuries they had abandoned.

Monday morning, the 17th, came, but it brought no gunboats or Federal troops. It had rained considerably the previous night, and the streets were full of mud, yet the Confederate troops continued to pour in in a continuous stream, and the city was soon filled with soldiers—wet, hungry and worn out by long and continuous marches. As the day wore away they gradually fell back southward, so that comparatively few remained in the city over night.

The excitement of the previous day had abated but little. Business of all kinds was suspended, and the stores and shops remained closed. Almost everybody seemed to be upon the streets, hurrying to and fro, many seeking friends to advise with, while, perhaps, the same friends were out upon a similar mission; others were to be seen congregated in little groups upon the corners discussing the probabilities of the future, or listening to the miraculous stories of some soldier who had escaped from Fort Donelson, and had made his way to this city.

During the morning of Monday, the 17th, a small portion of the public stores was distributed, but an order from General Floyd was soon promulgated countermanding the distribution and many a poor, lone woman, and not a few men, who had reached the scene just in time to be too late, turned away grievously disappointed. It was announced as the determination of General Floyd, who was in command of the post, to ship off the stores for the use of the army, and impressments of wagons and men were extensively made with the view of getting the provisions and other stores, not needed for the hospitals, to the railroad depots and placed in the cars, and large amounts were sent off during the day.

The timid were not yet assured that a battle would not be fought on the opposite side of the river, and their fears were heightened by rumors that Generals Johnston, Pillow and Floyd had determined to make a stand a few miles out of the city, and the counter-marching troops, in the rain which continued to pour down most of the forenoon, gave color to these rumors. So general had become the conviction that a battle was to be fought almost upon the confines of the city, that it became necessary for General Barrow and Mayor Cheatham to again confer with General Johnston, to ascertain whether he had changed his purposes with regard to Nashville. Upon their return they each briefly addressed the eager crowd assembled upon the Public Square, stating that they had the assurance of General Johnston that, at a council of war held that morning, Generals Pillow and Floyd fully agreed with him that . . . the Confederate army would retire before the arrival of the Federal troops, and leave the city to be quietly turned over to General Buell.

During his remarks Mayor Cheatham stated that the remainder of the public stores would be distributed to the people under the supervision of competent and reliable gentlemen, to be designated by himself, who would see that a fair and equitable distribution was made, so that everybody in the city who needed should get a fair proportion. This announcement was satisfactory to the crowd, and they quietly dispersed.

Late in the afternoon a handbill was issued announcing that General Pillow would address the people on the Public Square at seven o'clock that evening. At the time appointed General Pillow addressed the people briefly, not occupying exceeding five minutes' time, informing them that no stand would be made here for the purpose of defending the city, that it would be left for the civil authorities to surrender it into the hands of the Federals, and counseling them to remain quiet and orderly at home. "The Federals," he said, "will be with you only for a time, and I pledge you my honor that this war will not end until they are driven across the Ohio river. The officers who will come among you are gentlemen, and, of course, will behave as such toward you." After some remarks about the terrible fight at Fort Donelson, General Pillow retired, and left immediately upon the cars for his home near Columbia. . . .

During the night of Monday, the 17th, the two boats that were being converted into gunboats were burned at the wharf by order of the military authorities, and as the fire-bell pealed out its terrifying notes of warning, thousands were aroused from their slumbers expecting, from the bright glare that met their gaze as they hastily peered through their windows, to see the city one vast conflagration. It had been freely circulated during that and the previous day, that some of General Johnston's troops had sworn in their wrath that they would reduce the city to a heap of ashes sooner than see it turned over to the Federals. These threats were mainly attributed to the Texas Rangers, and it is due to General Johnston to say that he had sent them South among the first troops that passed through the city on Sunday, and that only a few straggling Rangers were in the city afterward. Whether these rumors had any foundation in reality was of little consequence; they served the purpose of frightening thousands of people almost out of their wits, and they were only assured when the cause of the alarms was ascertained.

The morning of Tuesday, the 18th, dawned cloudy, damp and chilly, but with it came no intelligence of the gunboats, except a repetition of the idle rumors of the previous day.

The distribution of the Government stores was again commenced, and large amounts of various kinds were given out during the day. This distribution created much excitement, and serious fears of a riot were entertained. Indeed, it was all the Mayor and city police, in connection with the military, could do to keep even an approach to order in one or two localities. A good deal of the stores, especially in the Quartermaster's department, was turned over to thousands of poor women who had labored faithfully for the Confederate Government for months previous, in satisfaction of the balances due them. The rush made to the Quartermaster's store by hundreds of women and men, who hoped to get a portion of the goods distributed, was closely akin to a mob, and the wonder is that many were not seriously injured.

It was known to a good many citizens on Monday that the destruction of the railroad and suspension bridges had been determined on as "a military necessity," and this work was expected to have been accomplished Monday night, but it was not done. The fact became generally known on Tuesday, and urgent appeals were made to General Floyd (General Johnston and Pillow having left the city) to spare the suspension bridge, as it was of the highest importance to the people of Nashville to have uninterrupted communication with the other side of the river, from whence, for a time, at least, they would have to draw all their market supplies. His uniform answer was, that the destruction of both bridges was regarded as "a military necessity," and that it was his imperative duty to put into execution the plans agreed upon.

Tuesday night (the 18th) the torch was applied to the railroad bridge, and in a short time all that remained of that splendid structure were the naked pillars and abutments and a few smoking fragments of timber. The precaution had been taken in this instance to prevent the fire-bells giving the alarm, so that the burning of the bridge was witnessed by comparatively few persons, and the event did not arouse the fears of those who had expected a general conflagration. This bridge was one of the finest draw-bridges in the country, and was built for the joint use of the Louisville & Nashville and Edgefield & Kentucky Railroads, at a cost of $250,000.

The wires of the suspension bridge were cut about the same time that the railroad bridge was fired, and the morning revealed a complete wreck of this magnificent structure. This fine bridge was about seven hundred feet long, and its height one hundred and ten feet above low water mark. It was built during the year 1850. The architect was Colonel A. Heiman, of Nashville, who was in command of the Tenth (Irish) Tennessee Regiment at Fort Donelson, and was taken prisoner at the surrender of that post. The contractor was M. D. Field, brother of Cyrus W. Field, who superintended the laying down of the Atlantic Telegraph Cable. This bridge was owned by a joint stock company, chartered by the State Legislature under the name of the Broad Street Bridge Company, and it paid handsome dividends to the stockholders. It had been stated by letter-writers from this place, and perhaps others, that the late General Zollicoffer owned a large amount of stock in this company; that nearly all he was worth consisted of this stock; and that, by the destruction of the bridge, his children (all girls) had been left in destitute circumstances. Such was not the case. General Zollicoffer owned only $8,000 of the stock of the company, and he was esteemed one of the "solid men" of Nashville. The rents from his improved property in the city alone yielded a handsome income in ordinary times.

The distribution of provisions and other government stores was resumed Wednesday morning, the 19th, but was shortly afterward suspended by order of General Floyd, who, it appears, came to the conclusion that the Federals were not as near Nashville as had been supposed, and that supplies could yet be shipped off for the use of the Confederate army. Squads of cavalrymen were stationed in front of each store to keep off the crowds of people who had been drawn hither in expectation of getting a portion of what was to be distributed.

A vigorous effort was made to get the provisions and other stores transferred to the railroad depot, and a large number of wagons from both the city and the surrounding country was impressed into the service, as were numbers of the citizens of Nashville. There was no system, however, in what was done, and every thing went on pell-mell, and the consequence was, much remained undone that might have been accomplished.

The impression got out, and prevailed pretty generally Friday morning, that the goods and clothing in the Quartermaster's department, on the corner of Front Street and the Public Square, would be distributed that day to the poor and needy. It is said, however, the intention was to distribute what remained of these stores to those who had been working for the Confederate Government, especially the women, and had not been paid, as compensation for their services. The rumor attracted an immense crowd, and it was a motley one. The excited crowd swayed to and fro, and grew more clamorous for the promised distribution. The efforts of the police and military to preserve order were of no avail, and a serious riot was imminent. The Mayor appeared and appealed to the crowd to disperse, but his appeal was unheeded. . . . It was a critical moment, and luckily the Mayor bethought himself of an expedient which proved more effective than the bayonets of the soldiers. He ordered out the steam-fire engine, and soon the muddy waters of the Cumberland were pouring down like an avalanche upon the excited populace. The effect was magical. Two or three men were knocked down by the powerful stream, many were thoroughly drenched, while others were well sprinkled, whereat those who escaped laughed most heartily. The passions of the people, wrought almost to demoniac phrenzy, were cooled down, everybody was soon in a good humor, the crowd was dispersed, and a disgraceful riot prevented. So much for cold water!

A sharp little vignette of one Nashville family's reaction to the approach of the war to their own doorstep is given by Mrs. Irby Morgan:

The rumor was all over town that the army would make a stand, and every one who could shoulder a musket must help to defend Nashville to the last ditch. My husband thought it best for us to go, and he would stay and fight if necessary. So we started to Fayetteville. . . . I packed my trunk, took my nurse Ella and children, and my little son ten years old to drive the barouche, and we started, leaving Mr. Morgan there to await coming developments.

Events soon showed that instead of making a stand the army was retreating, and the roads were filled with every kind of vehicle of which the imagination could conceive. Artillery, wagons, ambulances, furniture wagons, carts and every kind of conveyance to which a horse could be hitched. They were driving, lashing, yelling and galloping—and my little children and myself in the midst of them.

We got to Murfreesboro after dark, but found that the army had beaten us there and all the hotels were filled. There we were in the crowded street, not knowing where to go or what to do, when I heard the voice of Frank Eakin, my old hackman, who had waited on me in that capacity for many years whenever a hack was needed. Never did a voice sound so sweet, he ran up and said "Is that you, Miss Julia?" And I said: "Yes, what is left of me." He said: "I will take you out to Miss Julia Eakin's; Miss

Myra Eakin is there—just come all the way from New York, got there this evening." So I gladly followed Uncle Frank, until we got to Mrs. David Spence's house, and there received a hearty welcome. Early next morning old Frank had everything in readiness, trunks securely strapped, harness adjusted, etc., and many directions to my son how to drive to prevent an accident. Then, after Mrs. Spence had prepared us a sumptuous lunch, we bade them good-bye.

The chaotic state of affairs in Nashville at this time is graphically presented, from the military standpoint, by General Basil W. Duke in his *Morgan's Cavalry:*

During the first night after the army reached Nashville, when the excitement and fury were at the highest pitch, and officers and privates were alike influenced by it, it seemed as if the bonds of discipline would be cast off altogether. Crowds of soldiers were mingled with the citizens who thronged the streets all night, and yells, curses, shots rang on all sides. In some houses the women were pale and sobbing, and in others there was even merriment, as if in defiance of the worst. Very soon all those who had escaped from Donelson began to arrive.

Forrest had cut his way through the beleaguering lines and brought off his entire regiment. He reached Nashville on the day after it was entered by the army. It was impossible for the infantry men who escaped to make their way from the scene of disaster except in small detachments. They were necessarily scattered all over the country, and those who reached Nashville in time to accompany the army upon its farther march, came in as stragglers and without any organization. Neither men nor officers had an idea of how or when they were to do duty again. The arrival of these disbanded soldiers, among whom it was difficult to establish and enforce order, because no immediate disposition could be made of them, increased the confusion already prevailing. Rumors, too, of the near approach of the enemy were circulated, and were believed even by officers of high rank.

Buell's army, which then was really not far south of Bowling Green, was reported to be within a few miles of the city, and the Federal gunboats, which had not yet reached Clarksville, were confidently declared to be within sight of Fort Zollicoffer, only seven miles below Nashville.

Upon the second day matters had arrived at such a state, and the excitement and disorder were so extreme, that it became necessary to take other precautions to repress the license that was prevailing besides the establishment of guards and sentinels about the camps where the troops lay, and General Johnston ordered the establishment of a strong military police in Nashville.

The First Missouri Infantry, one of the finest and best disciplined regiments in the service, was detailed for this duty, and Morgan's Squadron was set to assist it. Our duty was to patrol the city and suburbs, and we were constantly engaged at it until the city was evacuated.

General John B. Floyd, of Virginia, was appointed commandant of Nashville, and entrusted with the enforcement of discipline and with all the details of the evacuation. His task was one of no ordinary difficulty. It was hard, at such a time, to know how to begin the work. In such a chaos, with such passions ruling, it seemed folly to hope for the restoration of order. Those who remember the event will recall the feeling of despair which had seized upon the soldiery; the entire army seemed, for the time, hopeless of any retrieval of our fortunes, and every man was thoroughly reckless. Few excesses were committed; but, with such a temper prevailing, the worst consequences were to be apprehended, if the influence of the officers should be entirely lost and the minds of the men should be directed to mischief. . . .

General Floyd's first care (after satisfying himself by active scouting that there was no truth in the reports of the proximity of the enemy, and burning the bridge at Edgefield Junction), was to make arrangements for saving as many of the supplies as was possible, giving the preference to ordnance stores. For this purpose he ordered an impressment of transportation in Nashville and the vicinity, making a clean sweep of every thing that ran on wheels. He issued orders that the citizens should be permitted to help themselves to the remaining stores, and a promiscuous scramble for clothing, blankets, meat, meal, and all sorts of quartermaster and commissary stores, commenced and lasted three days. Occasionally, a half-drunken, straggling soldier would walk into the midst of the snatches, with gun on shoulder and pistol at his belt, and the citizens would stand back, jackal like, until he had helped himself.

Crowds would stand upon the pavements underneath the tall buildings upon the Court House square, while out of their fourth and fifth story windows large bales of goods were pitched, which would have crushed any one upon whom they had fallen. Yet numbers would rush and fasten upon them while other bales were already in the air descending. Excitement and avarice seemed to stimulate the people to preter-natural strength. I saw an old woman, whose appearance indicated the extremest decrepitude, staggering under a load of meat which I would have hardly thought a quartermaster's mule could carry.

Twice during the first day of these scenes orders were received by a portion of Forrest's regiment, drawn up on the Square, to stop the appropriation of stores by the citizens, and they accordingly charged the crowd (deaf to any less forcible reason) with drawn sabres; several men were wounded and trampled upon, but fortunately none were killed.

Nothing could have been more admirable than the fortitude, patience, and good sense which General Floyd displayed in his arduous and unenviable task. . . . He soon found that he could (with no exertion) maintain perfect order or rescue more than a fragment from the wreck, and he bent all his energies to the task of repressing serious disorders, preventing the worst outrages, and preserving all that was most absolutely required for the use of the army and that it was practical to remove.

At last the evacuation was completed, the army was gotten clear of Nashville, the last straggler driven out, all the stores which could not be carried off nor distributed to the citizens, burned, and the capital of Tennessee (although we did not know it then) was abandoned finally to the enemy. Morgan's Squadron was the last to leave, as it was required to remain in the extreme rear of the army and pick up all the stragglers that evaded the rear guards of the infantry. Our scouts left behind, when we in turn departed, witnessed the arrival of the Federals and their occupation of the city.

The authorities at Richmond, misled by the optimistic reports they had been receiving from Fort Donelson, were totally unprepared for the shocking news of the fall of the Fort and the precipitate evacuation of Nashville. In an effort to discover whether everything possible had been done to prevent the disastrous loss of stores and materiel incident to the evacuation, an investigation was instituted by the Confederate House of Representatives. "Interrogatories" were sent to those concerned in the evacuation, and the frank views of an able military man are expressed in the answers to the interrogatories by Colonel Nathan Bedford Forrest:

Interrogatory 1st. I was not at the city of Nashville at the time of its surrender, but was there at the time the enemy made their entrance into that part of the city known as Edgefield, having left Fort Donelson, with my command, on the morning of its surrender, and reached Nashville on Tuesday, February 18, about 10 a.m. I remained in the city up to the Sunday evening following.

Interrogatory 2d. It would be impossible to state, from the data before me, the value of the stores either in the Quartermaster's or Commissary Departments, having no papers then nor any previous knowledge of the stores. The stores in the Quarter-master's Department consisted of all stores necessary to the department—clothing especially, in large amounts, shoes, harness, &c. with considerable unmanufactured material. The commissary stores were meat, flour, sugar, molasses, and coffee. There was a very large amount of meat in store and on the landing at my arrival, though large amounts had already been carried away by citizens.

Interrogatory 3d. A portion of these stores had been removed before the surrender. A considerable amount of meat on the landing, I was informed, was thrown into the river on Sunday before my arrival and carried away by citizens. The doors of the commissary depot were thrown open, and the citizens in dense crowds were packing and hauling off the balance at the time of my arrival on Tuesday. The quartermaster's stores were also open, and the citizens were invited to come and help themselves, which they did in larger crowds, if possible, than at the other department.

Interrogatories 4th and 5th. On Tuesday morning I was ordered by General Floyd to take command of the city, and attempted to drive the mob from the doors of the departments, which mob was composed of straggling soldiers and citizens of all grades. The mob had taken possession of the city to that extent that every species of property was unsafe. Houses were closed, carriages and wagons were concealed to prevent the mob from taking possession of them. Houses were being seized everywhere. I had to call out my cavalry, and, after every other means failed, charge the mob before I could get it so dispersed as to get wagons to the doors of the departments to load up the stores for transportation. After the mob was partially dispersed and quiet restored, a number of citizens furnished wagons and assisted in loading them. I was busily engaged in this work on Friday, Saturday, and Sunday. I transported 700 large boxes of clothing to the Nashville and Chattanooga Railroad depot, several hundred bales of osnaburga and other military goods from the Quartermaster's Department, most, if not all of the shoes having been seized by the mob. I removed about 700 or 800 wagon loads of meat. The high water having destroyed the bridges so as to stop the transportation over the Nashville and Chattanooga Railroad, I had large amounts of this meat taken over the Tennessee and Alabama Railroad. By examination on Sunday morning I found a large amount of fixed ammunition in the shape of cartridges and ammunition for light artillery in the magazine, which, with the assistance of General Harding, I conveyed over seven miles on the Tennessee and Alabama Railroad in wagons, to the amount of 30-odd wagon loads, after the enemy had reached the river. A portion was sent to Murfreesborough in wagons. The quartermaster's stores which had not already fallen into the hands of the mob were all removed, save a lot of rope, loose shoes, and a large number of tents. The mob had already possessed themselves of a large amount of these stores. A large quantity of meat was left in store and on the river bank and some at the Nashville and Chattanooga Railroad depot, on account of the break in the railroad. All stores left fell into the hands of the enemy, except forty pieces of light artillery, which were burned and spiked by order of General Floyd, as were the guns at Fort Zollicoffer. My proposition to remove these stores, made by telegraph to Murfreesborough, had the sanction of General A. S. Johnston.

Interrogatory 6th. No effort was made, save by the mob who were endeavoring to possess themselves of these stores, to prevent their removal, and a very large amount was taken off before I was placed in command of the city.

Interrogatory 7th. It was eight days from the time the quartermaster left the city before the arrival of the enemy, commissaries and other persons connected with these departments leaving at the same time. With proper dilligence on their part I have no doubt all the public stores might have been transported to places of safety.

Interrogatory 8th. Up to Saturday the railroads were open and might have been used to transport these stores. Saturday the bridges of the Nashville and Chattanooga Railroad gave way. Besides these modes of conveyance, a large number of wagons might have been obtained, had the quiet and order of the city been maintained, and large additional amounts of stores might by these means have been transported to places of safety.

Interrogatories 9th and 10th. I saw no officer connected with the Quartermaster's or Commissary Departments except Mr. Patton, who left on Friday. I did not at any time meet or hear of Maj. V. K. Stevenson in the city during my stay there.

Interrogatories 11th, 12th, and 13th. From my personal knowledge I can say nothing of the manner in which Major Stevenson left the city. Common rumor and many reliable citizens informed me that Major Stevenson left by a special train Sunday evening, February 16, taking personal baggage, furniture, carriage, and carriage-horses, the train ordered by himself, as president of the railroad.

Interrogatory 14th. All the means of transportation were actually necessary for the transportation of Government stores and sick and wounded soldiers, many of whom fell into the hands of the enemy for want of it, and might have been saved by the proper use of the means at hand. The necessity for these means of transportation for stores will be seen by the above answers which I have given.

I have been compelled to be as brief as possible in making the above answers, my whole time being engaged, as we seem to be upon the eve of another great battle. The city was in a much worse condition than I can convey an idea of on paper, and the loss of public stores must be estimated by millions of dollars. The panic was entirely useless and not at all justified by the circumstances. General Harding and the mayor of the city, with Mr. Williams, deserve special mention for assistance rendered in removing the public property. In my judgment, if the quartermaster and commissary had remained at their post and worked diligently with the means at their command, the Government stores might all have been saved between the time of the fall of Fort Donelson and the arrival of the enemy at Nashville.

General Johnston, following his evacuation of Nashville, promptly reported to Secretary of War Benjamin his reasons for taking that step. His report, dated at Murfreesboro on February 25th, 1862, is a candid presentation of the situation as he saw it:

The fall of Fort Donelson compelled me to withdraw the remaining forces under my command from the north bank of the Cumberland and to abandon the defense of Nashville, which but for that disaster it was my intention to protect to the utmost . . . The situation left me no alternative but to evacuate Nashville or sacrifice the army. By remaining the place would have been unnecessarily subjected to destruction, as it is very indefensible, and not adequate force would have been left to keep the enemy in check in Tennessee.

Under these circumstances I moved the main body of my command to this place on the 17th and 18th instant, and left a brigade under General Floyd to bring on such stores and property as were at Nashville, with instructions to remain until the approach of the enemy, and then to rejoin me. This has been in a great measure effected; and nearly all the stores would have been saved by the heavy and unusual rains, which have washed away the bridges, swept away portions of the railroad, and rendered transportation almost impossible. General Floyd has arrived here.

The rear guard left Nashville on the night of the 23d. Edgefield, on the north bank of the Cumberland, opposite the city, was occupied yesterday by the advanced pickets of the enemy.

I have remained here for the purpose of augmenting my forces and securing the transportation of the public stores. By the junction of the command of General Crittenden and the fugitives from Fort Donelson, which have been reorganized as far as practicable, the force now under my command will amount to about 17,000 men. General Floyd, with a force of some 2,500 men, has been ordered to Chattanooga, to defend the approaches towards Northern Alabama and Georgia and the communication between the Mississippi and Atlantic and with the view to increase his forces by such troops as may be sent forward from the neighboring states.

The quartermaster's, commissary and ordnance stores which are not required for immediate use have been ordered to Chattanooga, and those which will be necessary on the march have been forwarded to Huntsville and Decatur. I have ordered a depot to be established at Atlanta for the manufacture of supplies for the Quartermaster's Department and also a laboratory for the manufacture of percussion caps and ordnance stores, and at Chattanooga depots for distribution of these supplies. The machinery will be immediately sent forward.

President Davis, shocked by the fall of Fort Donelson and the loss of Nashville, was disturbed by the failure of General Johnston to make any public defense of his conduct in the face of public censure. Johnston was Davis's personal friend, but on March 12th he wrote to him a letter which, though couched in friendly language, broadly intimated to Johnston that the President expected to have some explanation of that disaster:

We have suffered great anxiety because of recent events in Kentucky and Tennessee, and I have been not a little disturbed by the repetition of reflections upon yourself. I expected you to have made a full report of events precedent and consequent to the fall of Fort Donelson. . . . You have been held responsible for the fall of Donelson and the capture of Nashville. 'Tis charged that no effort was made to save the stores at Nashville and that the panic of the people was caused by the army. Such representations have been painful to me and injurious to us both; but, worse than this, they have undermined public confidence and damaged our cause. A full development of the truth is necessary for future success. I respect the generosity which has kept you silent, but would impress upon you that the subject is not personal but public in its nature; that you and I might be content to suffer, but neither of us can willingly permit detriment to the country.

Johnston promptly replied, pointing out that the exigencies of the retreat from Nashville had made it impossible for him to gather the facts for a detailed official report. He did outline in his letter all the circumstances and movements in connection with the Fort Donelson campaign and evacuation of Nashville, concluding with these words:

The blow was most disastrous and almost without remedy. I therefore in my first report remained silent. This silence you were kind enough to attribute to my generosity. I will not lay claim to that motive to excuse my course. I observed silence, as it seemed to me the best way to serve the cause of the country. The facts were not fully known, discontent prevailed, and criticism or condemnation were more likely to augment than to cure the evil. I refrained, well knowing that heavy censures would fall upon me, but convinced that it was better to endure them for the present. . . . The test of merit in my profession with the people is success. It is hard rule, but I think it right. If I join this corps to the forces of Beauregard (I confess a hazardous experiment,) those who are now declaiming against me will be without an argument.

The Federal army of occupation had been in Nashville less than a week when they got their first taste of the dashing exploits of a Confederate cavalry leader whose name was to become famous for reckless daring before the war was over. John Hunt Morgan, then only a captain in command of a cavalry squadron, was hovering on the outskirts of Nashville on the Murfreesboro Pike, when he was informed by his superior officer that the Federals were using a steamboat, the *Minnetonka,* to bring troops into Nashville and that "General Hardee deems it important that the steamboat should be burnt, and wishes you to have it done if it can be done." With the audacity that characterized his activities throughout the war, Captain Morgan proceeded without delay to demonstrate that it was possible to satisfy General Hardee's desire, even though it involved Morgan's penetrating the Federal picket-line and making his way into the city through the back-waters with a small group of his troopers to fire the steamboat in question. It was a relatively small affair, but it gave a foretaste of the reckless daring and personal courage of the great Confederate cavalryman. In his report to General Breckinridge, dated February 27, 1862, he said:

Sir: I have the honor to report that on yesterday, the 26th instant, I left camp with twelve men for Nashville. About 300 yards this side of the last tollgate towards town, I left this pike and crossed through Mr. Trabue's farm to the Lebanon pike, leaving one man near the pike, to bring us intelligence of the enemy, if any should come along the pike. We then followed the Lebanon pike until we reached the city.

When inside the city limits, I found the pike covered with water, it having been backed up by the great rise in the river. Just at that point we met a farmer, who said he was a Union man. Pressed him in, and made him guide us over the back-water. He took us for Federals, as he afterwards told me. We proceeded into the city on Front street, as far as the water-works, and there saw a steamboat—the *Minne Tonka*. She laid about 300 yards out in the vast field which covered the whole valley. She was chained, fore and aft, to trees. She lay not over 500 yards above the gunboats and their large fleet of transports. Could see the soldiers distinctly sitting upon the boats, and they were full of them.

Young Buckner, Warfield, and Garrett took possession of a skiff, and made oars of a piece of plank fence; boarded the steamboat; found several men on board, who seemed preparing to get up steam, to drop down the stream to the gunboats; made the crew leave in a boat, and set fire in several places to the steamer, and reached the shore in safety. The troops in the transports could see what we were doing. My orders were to fire the boat, and then cut her loose, and let her drop down stream and set the other boats on fire; but this I found impossible to do, on account of the steamer being so securely moored with chain cables.

At least 2,000 citizens gathered around us while we were waiting for the boys to get back from the steamer. They begged us to leave; told us the Federal cavalry were scouring the city; that a large party of cavalry had just passed through the streets we were on. Sent all my men but five out the pike, with direction to halt at the cemetery. Remained with the five men about thirty minutes, until I saw a large body of cavalry going out to the Murfreesboro pike at a rapid rate, then started after my command. When we were half-way through the water that was upon the pike, a large body of Federals rode after us until they reached the water, when they halted, much to my satisfaction. We then retraced our steps back to the pike; reached our man who was standing picket just before sundown. About three minutes before we reached him he said seven officers—and one of them a general—had passed through, and stopped at the gate where he was standing, not twenty yards distant. He was in a clump of cedars. When we reached him the officers were not over 700 yards distant.

Kept our position about an hour. A Mr. James came out and informed us that there were men encamped at the toll gate, that had refused him a permit to leave the city, but he walked along with them as they came out, and as they were going into camp he passed along. He had just left when another man rode up. I halted him. He asked me if I was one of our pickets. I replied, if he meant Federals, we were. He said that was what he meant. I then asked him for his pass. He pulled out one from General Mitchell, allowing him to pass and repass the lines. He did not want me to keep it, but I told him it might be forgery, and then I wished to take it in, and see if it was all right. He had been professing to be a Southern-right (man); he is a Lincolnite.

Lieutenant West and myself then rode up to the toll gate. I asked the man who lived there, who were the officers who had just passed through. Said he did not know, but that they were looking out for a place to camp. While talking, heard a body of cavalry approaching. We fell back to the place where our men were. I waited a few minutes. The night being very dark, could not see more than fifty yards ahead of us. While sitting listening, I heard the clink of sabers about sixty yards from us. They had left the pike, and were riding on the dirt along the side of the pike, to keep their horses from making a noise.

We were close to the fence behind cedar trees. They rode up within fifty feet of us, and stopped about five minutes. I dismounted and took a shot-gun and started for the fence, where I could easily have killed two or three of them. Just as I was raising to put my gun through the fence, they called to each other to fire, which they did, and then ran for the city. We returned the fire. One of my men (Peter Atherton) was severely wounded, being shot through the thigh. Reached camp at 12 O'clock last night.

CHAPTER 4

☆ *From Fort Donelson to Shiloh*

F OLLOWING THE surrender of Fort Donelson and the evacuation of Nashville, both armies experienced a period of some confusion—the Federals the confusion incident to victory and the Confederates the confusion of defeat. Johnston in defeat, of course, received plenty of adverse criticism; but President Jefferson Davis expressed undiminished confidence in Johnston's ability and entertained no idea of supplanting him. Grant, on the other hand, although the victor, was so unfortunate as to incur the distrust of his immediate superiors, and his successful military career came very close to being nipped in the bud at that time. General George B. McClellan, who was in Washington in supreme command of all the Federal armies at this time, tells about it thus:

By the 26th of February Nashville was in our hands, and by the 3rd of March Columbus, Kentucky. In the course of these operations Halleck delivered himself of several prophetic statements in regard to "good strategy", each of which proved to be ridiculous.

On the morning of Sunday, March 2, 1862, desiring to give orders for the further movements of Buell's and Halleck's commands, I went to the military telegraph office, and caused communication to be cut off from all wires except those leading to Halleck's headquarters at St. Louis and Buell's at Nashville. I then called Buell and Halleck to their respective offices, and asked for a full report of the condition of affairs, numbers, position and condition of their troops, that of the enemy, etc. Halleck replied the same day:

"I have had no communication with Gen. Grant for more than a week. He left his command without my authority and went to Nashville. His army seems to be as much demoralized by the victory of Fort Donelson as that of the Potomac by the defeat of Bull Run. It is hard to censure a successful general immediately after a victory, but I think he richly deserves it. I can get no returns, no reports, no information of any kind from him. Satisfied with his victory, he sits down and enjoys it without any regard to the future. I am worn out and tired with this neglect and inefficiency. C. F. Smith is almost the only officer equal to the emergency."

To this I replied: "The success of our cause demands that proceedings such as Grant's should be at once checked. Generals must observe discipline as well as private

[73]

soldiers. Do not hesitate to arrest him at once, if the good of the service requires it, and place C. F. Smith in command. You are at liberty to regard this as a positive order, if it will smooth your way."

On the 4th Halleck telegraphed me: "A rumor has just reached me that since the taking of Fort Donelson Grant has resumed his former bad habits. If so, it will account for his repeated neglect of my often repeated orders. I do not deem it advisable to arrest him at present, but have placed General Smith in command of the expedition up the Tennessee. I think Smith will restore order and discipline."

Grant gives this version of this interesting episode:

From the time of leaving Cairo I was singularly unfortunate in not receiving dispatches from General Halleck. . . . Cairo was the southern end of the telegraph wire. My dispatches were all sent to Cairo by boat, but many of those addressed to me were sent to the operator at the end of the advancing wire and he failed to forward them. This operator afterwards proved to be a rebel; he deserted his post after a short time and went south taking his dispatches with him. . . .

On the 2nd of March I received orders dated March 1st to move my command back to Fort Henry, leaving only a small garrison at Donelson. From Fort Henry expeditions were to be sent against Eastport, Mississippi, and Paris, Tennessee. We started from Donelson on the 4th and the same day I was back on the Tennessee River. On March 4th I also received the following dispatch from General Halleck: "You will place Maj.-Gen. C. F. Smith in command of expedition, and remain yourself at Fort Henry. Why do you not obey my orders to report strength and positions of your command?"

I was surprised. This was the first intimation I had received that General Halleck had called for information as to the strength of my command. On the 6th he wrote to me again: "Your going to Nashville without authority, and when your presence with your troops was of the utmost importance, was a matter of very serious complaint at Washington, so much so that I was advised to arrest you on your return." This was the first I knew of his objecting to my going to Nashville. That place was not beyond the limits of my command which, it had been expressly declared in orders, were 'not defined'. . . . I turned over the command as directed and then replied to General Halleck courteously, but asked to be relieved from further duty under him. . . .

Thus in less than two weeks after the victory at Donelson, the two leading generals in the army were in correspondence as to what disposition should be made of me, and in less than three weeks I was virtually in arrest and without a command.

On the 13th of March I was restored to command, and on the 17th Halleck sent me a copy of an order from the War Department which stated that accounts of my misbehaviour had reached Washington and directed him to investigate and report the facts. He forwarded also a copy of a detailed dispatch from himself to Washington entirely exonerating me. When I reassumed command on the 17th of March I found the army divided, about half being on the east bank of the Tennessee at Savannah, while one division was at Crump's Landing on the west bank about four miles higher up, and the remainder at Pittsburg Landing, five miles above Crump's.

On receipt of the order restoring me to command, I proceeded to Savannah on the Tennessee, to which point my troops had advanced. General Smith was delighted to see me and was unhesitating in his denunciation of the treatment I had received. He was on a sick bed at the time, from which he never came away alive.

Following the capture of Fort Donelson, General Halleck did not seem to have any very definite idea as to what to do next. In ordering the movement of Grant's forces up the Tennessee River, in the direction of Alabama and Mississippi, Halleck said:

The main object of this expedition will be to destroy the railroad bridge over

Bear Creek near Eastport, Mississippi, and also the connections at Corinth, Jackson and Humboldt. . . . Avoid any general engagement with strong forces. It will be better to retreat than to risk a general battle. . . . Having accomplished these objects, or such of them as may be practicable, you will return to Danville and move on Paris.

It appears that Halleck's ultimate objective at this time was Memphis on the Mississippi, and that Grant's movement was subsidiary to a planned advance in force down the Mississippi River. But when Halleck later learned of the concentration of Confederate forces at Corinth he changed his plans. Accordingly, on March 15th, Buell was ordered to move from Nashville and unite his force with Grant, thus forming a strong force to oppose the Confederates either offensively or defensively.

An authoritative summary of the Confederate strategy at this time is provided by President Jefferson Davis:

It had been the object of General Johnston, since falling back from Nashville, to concentrate his army at Corinth and fight the enemy in detail—Grant first and Buell afterward. The troops under General Polk had been drawn back from Columbus. The War Department ordered General Bragg from Pensacola, with his well-disciplined army, to the aid of Johnston. A brigade was sent by General Lovell from Louisiana, and Chalmers and Walker were already on the line of the Memphis and Charleston railroad with considerable commands. . . . General Bragg, in a sketch of the battle of Shiloh, thus speaks of General Johnston's army:

"In a period of four weeks, fragments of commands from Bowling Green, Kentucky, under Hardee; Columbus, Kentucky, under Polk; and Pensacola, Mobile and New Orleans, under Bragg, with such new levies as could be hastily raised, all badly armed and equipped, were united at and near Corinth, and for the first time organized as an army. It was a heterogeneous mass, in which there was more enthusiasm than discipline, more capacity than knowledge, and more valor than instruction. Rifles, rifled and smooth-bore muskets—some of them originally percussion, others hastily altered from flint-locks by Yankee contractors, many with the old flint and steel- and shot-guns of all sizes and patterns, held place in the same regiments. The task of organizing such a command in four weeks and supplying it, especially with ammunition, suitable for action, was simply appalling. It was undertaken, however, with a cool, quiet self-control, calling to his (Johnston's) aid the best knowledge and talent at his command, which not only inspired confidence but soon yielded the natural fruits of system, order and discipline.

"This force, about forty thousand of all arms, was divided into four corps, commanded respectively by Major Generals Polk, Bragg and Hardee, and Brigadier-General Breckinridge."

The withdrawal of General Polk's command from the Confederate stronghold on the Mississippi River at Columbus, Kentucky, following the fall of Fort Donelson, left the Confederacy's defenses on the Mississippi in perilously precarious position. The northernmost of these defenses now consisted of the forces under General John P. McCown at New Madrid, on the Missouri side of the river, and at Island Number 10 in the river adjacent to New Madrid, just at the northwestern corner of Tennessee.

General McCown had a total of some 8,500 men in these positions. Before being placed in command there he had been called to Jackson and told in person by Beauregard that they could not send him any reinforcements, and that he must make the best possible defense with what he had. Unfortunately for the Confederacy, however, it developed that McCown was of a nature not very well suited to last-ditch duty.

McCown's hour of trial was not long in coming. Simultaneous with and parallel to the movement of General Grant and General Buell to Pittsburg Landing, General Halleck had ordered General John Pope down the west side of the Mississippi in Missouri, with 25,000 men equipped with an ample supply of artillery, with a thrust aimed at McCown's position. Pope appeared before New Madrid on March 3rd, but skirmished around in that neighborhood for more than a week before delivering his attack on the 12th.

McCown quickly decided that he could not hold out against Pope's superior force, and withdrew from New Madrid on the night of the 13th. Part of his garrison he transferred to Island No. 10 and the rest moved across the river to the Tennessee side. Beauregard described it witheringly as "the poorest defense made by any fortified post during the whole course of the war," and on March 31 Gen. McCown was supplanted by General W. W. Mackall, who had been commissioned for that purpose.

No matter how competent or incompetent the Confederate commander might be, however, Island No. 10 was not an easily defended position. Admiral Henry Walke, in charge of the Federal flotilla which reduced the island fort to capitulation gives a spirited and graphic account of the successful assault by the Federal gunboats:

On March 15th the flotilla and transports arrived in the vicinity of Island Number Ten about nine in the morning. The strong and muddy current of the river had overflowed its banks and carried away every movable thing. Houses, trees, fences, and wrecks of all kinds were being swept rapidly down-stream. The twists and turns of the river near Island Number Ten are certainly remarkable. Within a radius of eight miles from the island it crosses the boundary line of Kentucky and Tennessee three times, running on almost every point of the compass. We were greatly surprised when we arrived above Island Number Ten and saw on the bluffs a chain of forts extending for four miles along the crescent-formed shore, with the white tents of the enemy in the rear. And there lay the island in the lower corner of the crescent, with the side fronting the Missouri shore lined with heavy ordnance, so trained that with the artillery on the opposite shore almost every point on the river between the island and the Missouri bank could be reached at once by all the enemy's batteries.

On the 17th an attack was made on the upper battery by all the iron-clads and mortar-boats. The *Benton* (flag-steamer), lashed between the *Cincinnati* and *St. Louis,* was on the east side of the river; the *Mound City, Carondelet,* and *Pittsburgh* were on the west side; the last, however, changed her position to the east side of the river before the firing began. We opened fire on the upper fort at 1:20, and by order of the flag-officer fired one gun a minute. The enemy replied promptly, and some of his shot struck the *Benton,* but, owing to the distance from which they were fired, did but little damage. We silenced all the guns in the upper fort except one. During the action one of the rifled guns of the *St. Louis* exploded, killing and wounding several of the gunners,—another proof of the truth of the saying that the guns furnished the Western flotilla were less destructive to the enemy than to ourselves.

From March 17th to April 4th but little progress was made in the reduction of the Confederate works—the gun-boats firing a few shot now and then at long range, but doing little damage. The mortar-boats, however, were daily throwing 13-inch bombs, and so effectively at times that the Confederates were driven from their batteries and compelled to seek refuge in caves and other places of safety. But it was very evident that the great object of the expedition—the reduction of the Confederate forces—could not be effected by the gun-boats alone, owing to their mode of structure and to the disadvantage under which they were fought in the strong and rapid current of the Mississippi. This was the opinion not only of naval officers, but also of General Pope and other army officers. . . .

After the evacuation of New Madrid, which General Pope had forced by blockading the river twelve miles below, at Point Pleasant, the Confederate forces occupied their fortified position on Island Number Ten and the eastern shore of the Mississippi, where they were cut off by impassable swamps on the land side. They were in a cul-de-sac, and the only way open for them to obtain supplies or to effect a retreat was by the river south of Island Number Ten. General Pope, with an army of twenty thousand men, was on the western side of the river below the island. Perceiving the defect in the enemy's position, he proceeded with great promptness and ability to take advantage of it. It was his intention to cross the river and attack the enemy from below, but he could not do this without the aid of a gun-boat to silence the enemy's batteries opposite Point Pleasant and protect his army in crossing. He wrote repeatedly to Flag-officer Foote, urging him to send down a gun-boat past the enemy's batteries on Island Number Ten, and in one of his letters expressed the belief that a boat could pass down at night under cover of the darkness. But the flag-officer invariably declined, saying in one of his letters to General Pope that the attempt "would result in the sacrifice of the boat, her officers and men, which sacrifice I would not be justified in making."

During this correspondence the bombardment still went on, but was attended with such poor results that it became a subject of ridicule among the officers of Pope's army, one of whom (Colonel Gilmore, of Chillicothe, Ohio) is reported to have said that often when they met, an inquiry was made respecting the operations of the flotilla, the answer would generally be: "Oh! it is still bombarding the State of Tennessee at long range." And a Confederate officer said that no casualties resulted and no damage was sustained at Island Number Ten from the fire of the gun-boats.

On March 20th Flag-Officer Foote consulted his commanding officers, through Commander Stembel, as to the practicability of taking a gun-boat past the enemy's forts to New Madrid, and all except myself were opposed to the enterprise, believing with Foote that the attempt to pass the batteries would result in the almost certain destruction of the boat. I did not think so, but believed with General Pope that, the cover of darkness and other favorable circumstances, a gun-boat might be run past the enemy's batteries, formidable as they were. . . .

The flag-officer called a formal council of war of all his commanding officers, on board the flag-steamer, on the 28th or 29th of March, and all except myself concurred in the opinion formerly expressed that the attempt to pass the batteries was too hazardous and ought not to be made. When I was asked to give my views, I favored the undertaking, and advised compliance with the requests of General Pope. When asked if I was willing to make the attempt with the *Carondelet,* I replied in the affirmative. Foote accepted my advice, and expressed himself as greatly relieved from a heavy responsibility, as he had determined to send none but volunteers on an expedition which he regarded as perilous and of very doubtful success.

Having received written orders from the flag-officer, under date of March 30th, I at once began to prepare the *Carondelet* for the ordeal. All the loose material at hand was collected, and on the 4th of April the decks were covered with it, to protect them against plunging shot. Hawsers and chain cables were placed around the pilot-house and other vulnerable parts of the vessel, and every precaution was adopted to prevent disaster. A coal-barge laden with hay and coal was lashed to the part of the port side on which there was no iron plating, to protect the magazine. It was truly said that the *Carondelet* at that time resembled a farmer's wagon prepared for market. The engineers led the escape-steam, through the pipes aft, into the wheel-house, to avoid the puffing sound it made when blown through the smoke-stacks.

All the necessary preparations having been made, I informed the flag-officer of my intention to run the gauntlet that night, and received his approval. Colonel N. B.

Buford, who commanded the land forces temporarily with the flotilla, assisted me in preparing for the trip, and on the night of the 4th brought on board Captain Hottenstein, of the 42nd Illinois, and twenty-three sharp-shooters of his command, who volunteered their services, which were gratefully accepted. Colonel Buford remained on board until the last moment, to encourage us. I informed the officers and crew of the character of the undertaking, and all expressed a readiness to make the venture. In order to resist boarding parties, in case of being disabled, the sailors were well armed, and pistols, cutlasses, muskets, boarding-pikes, and hand-grenades were within reach. Hose was attached to the boilers for throwing scalding water over any who might attempt to board. If it should be found impossible to save the vessel, it was designed to sink rather than burn her. During the afternoon there was a promise of a clear, moonlight night, and it was determined to wait until the moon was down, and then to make the attempt, whatever the chances. Having gone so far, we could not abandon the project without an effect on the men almost as bad as failure.

At 10 o'clock the moon had gone down, and the sky, the earth, and the river were alike hidden in the black shadow of a thunder-storm, which had now spread itself over all the heavens. As the time seemed favorable, I ordered the first master to cast off. Dark clouds now rose rapidly over us and enveloped us in almost total darkness, except when the sky was lighted up by the welcome flashes of vivid lightning, to show us the perilous way we were to take. Now and then the dim outline of the landscape could be seen, and the forest bending under the roaring storm that came rushing up the river. With our bow pointing to the island, we passed the lowest point of land without being observed, it appears, by the enemy. All speed was given to the vessel to drive her through the tempest. The flashes of lightning continued with frightful brilliancy, and "almost every second," wrote a correspondent, "every brace, post, and outline could be seen with startling distinctness, enshrouded by a bluish white glare of light, and then her form for the next minute would become merged in the intense darkness." When opposite Battery No. 2, on the mainland, the smokestacks blazed up, but the fire was soon subdued. It was caused by the soot becoming dry, as the escape-steam, which usually kept the stacks wet, had been sent into the wheelhouse, as already mentioned, to prevent noise. With such vivid lightning as prevailed during the whole passage, there was no prospect of escaping the vigilance of the enemy, but there was good reason to hope that he would be unable to point his guns accurately. Again the smoke-stacks took fire, and were soon put out; and then the roar of the enemy's guns began, and from Batteries Nos. 2, 3, and 4 on the mainland came the continued crack and scream of their rifle-shells, which seemed to unite with the electric batteries of the clouds to annihilate us. . . .

Having passed the principal batteries, we were greatly relieved from suspense, patiently endured, however, by the officers and crew. But there was another formidable obstacle in the way—a floating battery, which was the great "war elephant" of the Confederates, built to blockade the Mississippi permanently. As we passed her she fired six to eight shots at us, but without effect. One ball struck the coal-barge, and one was found in a bale of hay; we found also one or two musket-bullets. We arrived at New Madrid about midnight with no one hurt, and were most joyfully received by our army. At the suggestion of Paymaster Nixon, all hands "spliced the main brace."

On Sunday, the 6th, after prayers and thanksgiving, the *Carondelet*, with General Gordon Granger, Colonel J. L. Kirby Smith of the 43d Ohio, and Captain Louis H. Marshall of General Pope's staff on board, made a reconnoissance twenty miles down, nearly to Tiptonville, the enemy's forts firing on her all the way down. We returned their fire, and dropped a few shells into their camps beyond. On the way back, we captured and spiked the guns of a battery of one 32-pounder and one 24-pounder, in about twenty-five minutes, opposite Point Pleasant. Before we landed to spike the guns, a tall Confederate soldier, with cool and deliberate courage, posted himself behind a large cottonwood tree, and repeatedly fired upon us, until our Illinois sharpshooters got to work on him from behind the hammock nettings. He had two rifles, which he soon dropped, fleeing into the woods with his head down. The next day he was captured and brought into camp at Tiptonville, with the tip of his nose shot off. After the capture of this battery, the enemy prepared to evacuate his positions on Island Number Ten and the adjacent shores, and thus, as one of the historians of the Civil War says, the *Carondelet* struck the blow that secured that victory.

CHAPTER 5

☆ *Shiloh*

T HUS THE STAGE was set for the bloody battle of Shiloh. This was the first big-scale battle in the western theatre of the war, a battle which by its savage ferocity and high casualties gave to both North and South shocking and stunning evidence of the gravity of the war in which they were engaged.

The battle was fought on April 6th and 7th around Shiloh Church near Pittsburg Landing on the Tennessee River. The Confederates launched their attack on Grant's army there in the early morning of the 6th and were signally successful. Before night ended the fighting they had driven the Federals almost into the river, with heavy losses. General Johnston was killed in the afternoon of this first day and was succeeded in command by General Beauregard. During the night Grant was reenforced by the arrival of Buell and his 25,000 fresh troops, and the fighting was resumed on the morning of the 7th. The Confederates were driven steadily backward, losing all the ground they had gained the first day, and they retired from the field in the late afternoon.

The armies engaged in the battle were the largest ever assembled on this continent up to that time—about 40,000 on each side the first day, with the augmented Federal force about 25,000 greater the second day. The losses were correspondingly great, the total of killed, wounded and missing amounting to nearly 11,000 Confederate and more than 13,000 Federal.

In many ways the Battle of Shiloh was unique. Its outcome was disappointing to both sides, though both claimed the victory. It gave rise to more intense and sustained controversy between supporters of rival leaders on both sides than any other battle.

Grant and Sherman were violently assailed in the North for being surprised by the Confederates the first morning of the battle and for not pursuing them when they withdrew the next afternoon. Some of Grant's critics even went so far as to contend seriously that he deliberately tried to lose the battle as part of a deep-laid conspiracy to prolong the war for political purposes. This preposterous suggestion was based on the theory that his handling of the battle was so grossly at fault it could not have been the result of mere ineptitude but must have been

[80]

due to something more sinister! Grant himself freely indulged in sharp and open criticism of associates and subordinates. For his reflections on General Lew Wallace he was forced twenty years later to make belated apology. Buell alleged that Sherman deliberately prevaricated in his account of Shiloh, and even charged that Sherman had conspired with Grant to change the official map of the field to cover up their errors.

In the South there was an almost universal belief that nothing but the death of Albert Sidney Johnston had prevented the capture or annihilation of the Federal army on the first day of the battle. Many people, even now, believe that when he fell Johnston had a great victory within his grasp, and that Beauregard, suddenly thrust into command, threw it away. Beauregard through the rest of his life tried to defend himself, but the South would not listen. It had made up its mind about Shiloh and did not want to change. Johnston was the martyred hero, Beauregard the scapegoat.

The story of Shiloh, as written by both sides, is peppered with ifs and punctuated with question marks. Why wasn't Grant present when his army was attacked? Why wasn't Sherman more alert and watchful? Did Grant slow down Buell's march from Nashville and delay his arrival at Savannah? Would the Federal army under Grant have been destroyed if Buell had not arrived when he did? Why did it take the Confederate army so long to get from its Corinth camps to the battlefield? Did Beauregard stop the fighting too soon on the evening of the first day? What would Johnston have done if he had lived? Could General Van Dorn have moved his army from Arkansas to Corinth in time for the battle? Would his 20,000 men have given the needed power to clinch the victory? These are questions that are still debated and still unanswered.

General Beauregard's official report of the battle gives a good account of the opening activities from the Confederate point of view:

By April 1st our united forces were concentrated along the Mobile & Ohio railroad from Bethel to Corinth, and on the Memphis & Charleston railroad from Corinth to Iuka.

It was then determined to assume the offensive, and strike a sudden blow at the enemy, in position under General Grant on the west bank of the Tennessee at Pittsburg, and in the direction of Savannah, before he was re-enforced by the army under General Buell, then known to be advancing for that purpose by rapid marches from Nashville via Columbia. About the same time General Johnston was advised that such an operation conformed to the expectations of the President.

By a rapid and vigorous attack on General Grant, it was expected he would be beaten back into his transports and the river, or captured, in time to enable us to profit by the victory, and remove to the rear all the stores and munitions that would fall into our hands in such an event before the arrival of General Buell's army on the scene. It was never contemplated, however, to retain the position thus gained and abandon Corinth, the strategic point of the campaign.

Want of general officers needful for the proper organization of divisions and brigades of an army brought thus suddenly together, and other difficulties in the way of an effective organization, delayed the movement until the night of the 2nd instant, when it was heard from a reliable quarter that the junction of the enemy's armies was near at hand. It was then at a late hour determined that the attack should be attempted at once, incomplete and imperfect as were our preparations for such a grave and momentous adventure. Accordingly, that night at 1 a.m. the preliminary orders to the commanders of corps were issued for the movement.

On the following morning the detailed orders for the movement were issued, and the movement, after some delay, commenced; the troops being in admirable spirits. It was expected we should be able to reach the enemy's line in time to attack him early on the 5th instant. The men however, for the most part, were unused to marching; and the roads, narrow and traversing a densely wooded country, became almost impassable after a severe rainstorm on the night of the 4th, which drenched the troops in bivouac. Hence our forces did not reach the intersection of the roads from Pittsburg and Hamburg, in the immediate vicinity of the enemy, until late Saturday afternoon.

The unexpected delays in the movement of the troops having thus thrown the operation, at the very outset, twenty-four hours behind the planned schedule, there was some apprehension among the Confederate commanders that the element of surprise might have been removed and that perhaps the attack might better be abandoned. Accordingly, that night Johnston called a council of war for a reappraisal of the situation; but, after thorough discussion, it was decided to launch the attack the next morning as originally planned.

William G. Stevenson, an observant and literate private in the ranks of the Confederate cavalry, with a typical private soldier's curiosity as to what was going on, cautiously made his way to a point of vantage from which he was an unobserved observer of that fateful discussion. With some flair for dramatic narrative, he later wrote an eye-witness account of the momentous council:

In an open space, with a dim fire in the midst, and a drum on which to write, you could see grouped around their "little Napoleon," as Beauregard was sometimes fondly called, ten or twelve generals, the flickering light playing over their eager faces, while they listened to his plans and made suggestions as to the conduct of the fight. He soon warmed with his subject, and throwing off his cloak to give free play to his arms, he walked about in the group, gesticulating rapidly, and jerking out his sentences with a strong French accent. All listened attentively, and the dim light just revealing their countenances showed their different emotions of confidence or distrust in his plans.

General Sidney Johnston stood apart from the rest, with his tall straight form standing out like a specter against the dim sky, and the illusion was fully sustained by the light-gray military cloak which he folded around him. His face was pale, but wore a determined expression, and at times he drew nearer the center of the ring and said a few words, which were listened to with great attention. It may be he had some foreboding of the fate he was to meet on the morrow, for he did not seem to take much part in the discussion. General Breckenridge lay stretched out on a blanket near the fire, and occasionally sat upright and added a few words of counsel. General Bragg spoke frequently and with earnestness. General Polk sat on a camp-stool at the outside of the circle, and held his head between his hands, seeming buried in thought. Others reclined or sat in various positions.

What a grand study for a Rembrandt was this, to see these men, who held the lives of many thousands in their power, planning how best to invoke the angel Azreal to hurl his darts with the breaking of morning light.

For two hours the council lasted, and as it broke up and the generals were ready to return to their respective commands, I heard General Beauregard say, raising his hand and pointing in the direction of the Federal camps, whose drums we could plainly hear: "Gentlemen, we sleep in the enemy's camp tomorrow night".

Beauregard's report tells of the conference, and succinctly sums up the action on the first day of the battle:

It was decided that the attack should be made on the next morning at the earliest hour practicable, in accordance with the orders of movement; that is, in three lines of battle, the first and second extending from Owl creek on the left, to Lick creek on the right, a distance of about three miles, supported by the third and the reserve. . . .

At 5 a.m. on the 6th instant, a reconnoitering party of the enemy having become engaged with our advance pickets, the commander of the forces gave orders to begin the movement and attack as determined upon. . . .

At 5:30 a.m. our lines and columns were in motion, all animated, evidently, by a promising spirit. The front line was engaged at once, but advanced steadily, followed in due order with equal resolution and steadiness by the other lines which were brought successfully into action with rare skill, judgment, and gallantry by the several corps commanders as the enemy made a stand with his masses rallied for the struggle for the encampments.

Like an Alpine avalanche our troops moved forward, despite the determined resistance of the enemy, until after 6 p.m., when we were in possession of all his encampments between Owl and Lick creeks but one; nearly all of his field artillery; about thirty flags, colors and standards; over 3,000 prisoners, including a division commander (General Prentiss) and several brigade commanders, thousands of small arms, an immense supply of subsistence, forage and munitions of war and a large amount of means of transportation—all the substantial fruits of a complete victory, such indeed as rarely have followed the most successful battles; for never was an army so well provided as that of our enemy.

The remnant of his army had been driven in utter disorder to the immediate vicinity of Pittsburg, under the shelter of the heavy guns of his iron-clad gunboats, and we remained undisputed masters of his well selected, admirably provided cantonments, after over twelve hours of obstinate conflict with his forces, who had been beaten from them and the contiguous covert, but only by a sustained onset of all the men we could bring into action. . . .

It was after 6 p.m., as before said, when the enemy's last position was carried, and his forces finally broke and sought refuge behind a commanding eminence covering the Pittsburg landing, not more than a half mile distant, and under the guns of the gunboats, which opened on our eager columns a fierce and annoying fire with shot and shell of the heaviest description.

Darkness was close at hand; officers and men were exhausted by a combat of over twelve hours without food, and jaded by the march of the preceding day through mud and water. It was, therefore, impossible to collect the rich and opportune spoils of war scattered broadcast on the field left in our possession, and impracticable to make any effective dispositions for their removal to the rear.

I accordingly established my headquarters at the Church of Shiloh, in the enemy's encampments, with Major-General Bragg, and directed our troops to sleep on their arms in such positions in advance and rear as corps commanders should determine, hoping, from news received by a special dispatch, that delays had been encountered by General Buell in his march from Columbia, and that his main force, therefore, could not reach the field of battle in time to save General Grant's shattered fugitive forces from capture or destruction on the following day.

Afterwards, both Sherman and Grant (through his aide and mouthpiece, Adam Badeau) were vociferous in protesting that they were not surprised by Johnston's attack at Shiloh. Most students of the battle, however, have remained unconvinced by these protests. Among the Federal officers participating in the battle who certainly thought they were surprised was Captain Ephriam H. Otis, who later wrote:

No one can read the dispatches of General Grant and General Sherman the day preceding the battle without realizing that it [the attack] was a complete surprise of the Federal forces. It will be remembered that when General Ammen [of Buell's army] offered to march his command up to Pittsburg Landing on Saturday, he was assured by General Grant that there would be no battle at that place and was directed to wait until boats could be sent down to transport his men up the river to Pittsburg Landing.

On the 5th of April Grant reports to Halleck that "The main force of the enemy is at Corinth, with troops at different points east; also at Bethel, Jackson, and Humboldt are small garrisons. The numbers at these places seem to constantly change." Another dispatch to Halleck the same day reports skirmishing between his advance and the enemy, with the loss of a few prisoners on each side. Halleck was assured by Sherman, in a dispatch from Pittsburg Landing, on the 5th of April, that: "I have no doubt that nothing will occur to-day, more than some picket-firing. The enemy is saucy, but got the worst of it yesterday and will not press our pickets far. I will not be drawn out far unless with certainty of advantage, and I do not apprehend anything like an attack on our position."

Everything that General Sherman said and did shows conclusively that he did not believe a battle was imminent, and probably he never realized that the Confederate army was before him until the camp of the 53d and 77th Ohio in front of Shiloh Church was attacked on Sunday morning, and his own orderly was killed at his side by a volley from the Confederate skirmishers. It is impossible to believe that these dispatches of General Grant and General Sherman would have been written if they had for a moment supposed that there was a Confederate army in line of battle within less than two miles of the camp, only waiting orders to advance.

It is reported that on the night before the battle, General Albert Sidney Johnston gave the most strict orders to preserve silence in his camps, in order that no knowledge of his presence might be communicated to the Federal army. During Saturday evening a Confederate staff officer was sent out with orders to put a stop to the bugle-calls which were distinctly heard at Confederate headquarters. He was astonished to learn that these bugle-calls came from the camp of the Union forces.

The fact that the battle was a surprise, in the military sense of that term, is perhaps the only excuse that can be offered by the friends of Generals Grant and Sherman for the utter want of preparation on the part of the Federal forces. No directions had been previously given to the division commanders in case of an attack by the enemy, nor had any line of defense been selected. The different commands were widely separated, giving no support to each other, and Sunday morning inspection was going on in the most advanced camps when the battle began.

The reason assigned by General Grant afterwards for not constructing earthworks to protect his front was that he intended his army to act on the offensive, and did not wish them to learn to rely on fortifications. This, however, can hardly be accepted as a sufficient reason for not taking the most common and ordinary precautions observed by a hostile army, operating in an enemy's country, with an impassable river directly in the rear. It would seem clear that the conduct of neither Grant nor Sherman can be explained upon any other ground than that they had no idea that a battle was likely to occur at Pittsburg Landing.

In view of what is now well established, it is curious to note the dispatches of General Halleck to Secretary Stanton on May 2, in which he officially reports as follows: "The newspaper accounts that our divisions were surprised are utterly false. Every division had notice of the enemy's approach hours before the battle commenced."

Later, in transmitting a topographical map of the field, he again asserted that "the impression which at one time seemed to have been received by the Department that our forces were surprised on the morning of the 6th is entirely erroneous. I am satisfied from a patient and careful inquiry and investigation that all our troops were notified of the enemy's approach some time before the battle commenced."

It is safe to say that General Halleck, in sending these dispatches to the War Department, never looked forward to the publication of all official reports of the battle, where the evidence of a complete surprise of General Grant's army on Sunday morning is absolutely overwhelming.

Just how complete was General Sherman's surprise when the storm of battle broke on his front is told in impressive and gripping detail by one who was there, among those surprised, Ephraim C. Dawes:

Colonel Appler of the 53d Ohio Regiment was up at break of day. He woke up his adjutant and took him to the open field at the left of the camp. The picket sent out the evening before came in. Their report was that they had seen what seemed to be a reconnoitering party of the enemy pass along the road through the woods at the end of the field a number of times and heard a good deal of firing apparently about half a mile in front. The firing of Major Powell's party began and Colonel Appler sent a man to the nearest picket post, about three hundred yards distant, to learn its meaning. Before the messenger returned a soldier of the 25th Missouri, wounded in the side, came through the woods and called out, "The rebels are coming! Get into line!"

Reveille had sounded, the companies had had roll-call, and the men were engaged in cooking breakfast. Colonel Appler ordered the long roll and sent a mounted officer to Colonel Hildebrand and another to General Sherman with the information obtained from the wounded man. The regiment formed on its color line. The messenger sent to General Sherman galloped back and reported that General Sherman gave no directions, but said, "You must be badly scared over there." The messenger sent to Colonel Hildebrand brought an order to send two companies at once to report to Major Fearing and support the picket-line, now sharply engaged throughout. The 57th Regiment formed on its color line.

A messenger from Captain McCormick came to Major Fearing of the 77th asking reenforcements for the pickets. Major Fearing was in bed. He ordered the regiment into line and directed Captain Mason to take his company at double-quick to Captain McCormick's support, requested that two companies of the 53d Regiment be also sent, and, hastily dressing, rode to General Sherman's tent with the message sent by Captain McCormick. General Sherman told him to obey the order given to Colonel Hildebrand the night before and take the 77th Regiment to the See house.

Major Fearing returned, and putting the regiment in motion, rode forward to the pickets, who were now falling back, but with a firing-line. A glance showed him the situation and he rode back to the regiment and placed it in position across the western Corinth Road and east of the bridge over Oak Creek. The 57th moved its right forward a few yards to connect with the left of the 78th. Buckland's brigade was now in line and the 48th Ohio Regiment was directed to go out to support the pickets.

The two companies of the 53d had barely left the color line to go to the pickets when an officer of the regiment who had just got out of bed came hurriedly to Colonel Appler and told him that a large force of the enemy was marching across the end of the Rea field south of the camp. This information was sent to Colonel Hildebrand, who directed Colonel Appler to form his regiment on the left of its camp perpendicular to its color line and facing south. Colonel Appler gave the commands and directed the adjutant to conduct the left of the regiment to the proper point, which he designated as opposite the line of officers' tents. As the regiment filed left, one of the companies which had been sent to the pickets came back through the brush, its captain exclaiming as he took his place in the line, "The rebels up there are thicker than fleas on a dog's back."

The adjutant halted the regiment at the proper point, and looking to the right saw the Confederate line of battle apparently within musket-shot and moving directly towards the right flank of the regiment. The sun had arisen in a cloudless sky and the bright gun-barrels of the advancing line shone through the green leaves. The adjutant gave the command, "Front, left dress," and hastening to Colonel Appler, who was in rear of the centre of the regiment said in a low tone, "Colonel, look to the right." Colonel Appler looked up and with an exclamation of astonishment said, "This is no place for us," and commanded "Battalion about face, right wheel." (At this time, about 6:45 A.M., the sick were still in the camps, the sentinels were pacing their beats, the officers' servants and company cooks were preparing breakfast, the details for brigade guard and fatigue duty were marching to their post, and in our regiment, at least, the sutler shop was open.) This order brought the regiment back through its camp. Colonel Appler, marching in front cried out a number of times in the loudest tones of his shrill, clear voice, "Sick men to the rear!" It is needless to add that they obeyed. . . . The regiment halted at the brow of the elevation in rear of the officers' tents, marched ten paces forward, faced about and the men lay down in the brush where the ground began to slope the other way.

While the men were marching back through the camp the Confederate skirmishers fired upon them. No one was hit and there was no confusion. Two pieces of artillery of Waterhouse's battery took position on the right of the regiment as it halted and General Sherman and staff rode along its front, stopping a few paces in front of the sixth company. General Sherman with his glass was looking on the prolongation of the regiment at the troops marching across the end of the Rea field and did not notice the line on his right. Lieutenant Eustace H. Ball of Company E, 53d Ohio, had risen from a sick-bed when he heard Colonel Appler's command and was walking along in front of the line of his company. He saw the Confederate skirmishers emerge from the brush which fringed the little stream in front of the regiment's camp, halt, and raise their guns. He cried out, "General, look to your right." General Sherman dropped his glass, and looking to the right saw the advancing line of Hardee's corps, threw up his hand, and exclaimed, "My God, we are attacked!"

General Beauregard's business-like summary of the first day of the battle in his report gives a terse account of the day's events from the viewpoint of one of the commanding officers. But the action he so crisply describes was provided by some 40,000 youthful private soldiers. What did they think about it? One of the Confederate regiments taking part in the attack that Sunday morning was the Sixth Arkansas Volunteers. An inconspicuous young private in Company E of that regiment was Henry M. Stanley, later to gain worldwide fame as a writer and explorer. A native of England, Stanley was living in Arkansas in 1861, and he was shamed into enlisting when one of the local girls sent him a package containing a petticoat, intended as a more or less gentle hint that his place was in the army.

His career as a Confederate soldier was brief. Shiloh was his first battle, and he was taken prisoner by the Federals early in its second day. He has, however, in his *Autobiography,* left us a vivid picture of his youthful emotions as his company, recruited as the "Dixie Greys", moved into action:

After two days of marching, and two nights of bivouacking and living on cold rations, our spirits were not so buoyant at dawn of Sunday, the 6th April, as they ought to have been for the serious task before us. Many wished, like myself, that we had not been required to undergo this discomfort before being precipitated into the midst of a great battle. . . .

Generals Johnston and Beauregard proposed to hurl into the Tennessee River an army of nearly 50,000 rested and well-fed troops, by means of 40,000 soldiers, who for two days had subsisted on sodden biscuit and raw bacon, who had been exposed for two nights to rain and dew, and had marched twenty-three miles! Considering that at least a fourth of our force were lads under twenty, and that such a strenuous task was before them, it suggests itself to me that the omission to take the physical powers of those youths into their calculation had as much to do with the failure of the project as the obstinate courage of General Grant's troops. . . .

At four o'clock in the morning, we rose from our damp bivouac, and, after a hasty refreshment, were formed into line. We stood in rank for half an hour or so, while the military dispositions were being completed along the three-mile front. Our brigade formed the centre; Cleburne's and Gladden's brigades were on our respective flanks.

Day broke with every promise of a fine day. Next to me, on my right, was a boy of seventeen, Henry Parker. I remember it because, while we stood-at-ease, he drew my attention to some violets at his feet, and said, "It would be a good idea to put a few into my cap. Perhaps the Yanks won't shoot me if they see me wearing such flowers, for they are a sign of peace." "Capital," said I, "I will do the same." We plucked a bunch, and arranged the violets in our caps. The men in the ranks laughed at our proceedings. . . .

We loaded our muskets, and arranged our cartridge-pouches ready for use. Our weapons were the obsolete flintlocks, and the ammunition was rolled in cartridge-paper, and contained powder, a round ball, and three buckshot. When we loaded we had to tear the paper with our teeth, empty a little powder into the pan, lock it, empty the rest of the powder into the barrel, press paper and ball into the muzzle, and ram home.

Then the Orderly-sergeant called the roll, and we knew that the Dixie Greys were present to a man. Soon after, there was a commotion, and we dressed up smartly. A young Aide galloped along our front, gave some instructions to the Brigadier Hindman, who confided the same to his Colonels, and presently we swayed forward in line, with shouldered arms. Newton Story, big, broad, and straight, bore our company-banner of gay silk, at which the ladies of our neighbourhood had laboured.

As we tramped solemnly and silently through the thin forest, and over its grass, still in its withered and wintry hue, I noticed that the sun was not far from appearing, that our regiment was keeping its formation admirably, that the woods would have been a grand place for a picnic; and I thought it strange that a Sunday should have been chosen to disturb the holy calm of those woods.

Before we had gone five hundred paces, our serenity was disturbed by some desultory firing in front. It was then a quarter-past five. 'They are at it already,' we whispered to each other. 'Stand by, gentlemen,'—for we were all gentlemen volunteers at this time—said our Captain, L. G. Smith. Our steps became unconsciously brisker, and alertness was noticeable in everybody. The firing continued at intervals, deliberate and scattered, as at target-practice. We drew nearer to the firing, and soon a sharper rattling of musketry was heard. 'That is the enemy waking up,' we said. Within a few minutes, there was another explosive burst of musketry, the air was pierced by many missiles, which hummed and pinged sharply by our ears, pattered through the tree-tops, and brought twigs and leaves down on us. 'Those are bullets,' Henry whispered with awe.

At two hundred yards further, a dreadful roar of musketry broke out from a regiment adjoining ours. It was followed by another further off, and the sound had scarcely died away when regiment after regiment blazed away and made a continuous roll of sound. 'We are in for it now,' said Henry; but as yet we had seen nothing, though our ears were tingling under the animated volleys.

'Forward, gentlemen, make ready!' urged Captain Smith. In response, we surged forward, for the first time marring the alignment. We trampled recklessly over the grass and young sprouts. Beams of sunlight stole athwart our course. The sun was up above the horizon. Just then we overtook our skirmishers, who had been engaged in exploring our front. We passed beyond them. Nothing now stood between us and the enemy.

'There they are!' was no sooner uttered, than we cracked into them with levelled muskets. 'Aim low, men!' commanded Captain Smith. I tried hard to see some living thing to shoot at, for it appeared absurd to be blazing away at shadows. But, still advancing, firing as we moved, I, at last, saw a row of little globes of pearly smoke streaked with crimson, breaking out, with spurtive quickness, from a long line of bluey figures in front; and, simultaneously, there broke upon our ears an appalling crash of sound, the series of fusillades followed one another with startling suddenness, which suggested to my somewhat moidered sense a mountain upheaved, with huge rocks tumbling and thundering down a slope, and the echoes rumbling and receding through space. Again and again, these loud and quick explosions were repeated, seemingly with increased violence, until they rose to the highest pitch of fury, and in unbroken continuity. All the world seemed involved in one tremendous ruin!

Stanley's account of his youthful reaction points up a notable feature of the battle of Shiloh, that a large proportion of the men engaged on both sides, officers as well as men, were totally inexperienced in the bloody business in which they now found themselves engaged. Basil Duke, then a young lieutenant in Captain John H. Morgan's Cavalry, tells of how it became impressed on him that April morning that he was not engaged in a romantic outing but in a serious activity which might well have grave consequences for the participants:

While the fighting was going on in front, Morgan's Squadron moved along with Breckinridge's division (in the reserve), and we listened to the hideous noise and thought how much larger the affair was than the skirmishes on Green river and around Nashville. We soon learned to distinguish when the fight was sharp and hotly contested and when our lines were triumphantly advancing, and we wondered if those before us would finish the business before we got in.

We had not marched far before we saw bloody indications of the fierce work that had been done upon the ground over which we were passing. The dead and the wounded were thick in the first camp and, thence, onward. Some of the corpses of men killed by artillery showed ghastly mutilation. In getting up our glowing anticipation of the day's program we had left these items out of the account, and we mournfully recognized the fact that many who seek military distinction will obtain it posthumously, if they get it at all. The actual sight of a corpse immensely chills an abstract love of glory. The impression soon wears off, however, and the dead are very little noticed.

Toward 10 or 11 o'clock we wandered away from the infantry to which we had been attached, and getting no orders or instructions, devoted ourselves to an examination of the many interesting scenes of the field, which we viewed with keen relish. The camps whence the enemy had been driven attracted special and admiring attention. There was a profusion of all the necessaries, and many of the luxuries of military life. How we wondered that an army could have ever permitted itself to be driven away from them!

While we were curiously inspecting the second or third encampment and had gotten closer than at any time previously to the scene of the fighting, a single incident interrupted, for a moment, the pleasure of the investigation. Some of the enemy's shells were bursting over our heads, and as we were practically ignorant of the artillery, we were at first puzzled to know what they were. In the general thunder of the fight no special reports could be heard to lead to a solution of the particular phenomena. Suddenly a short yell of mingled indignation and amazement announced that one of the party had some practical information on the subject. He had been struck by a fragment on the shoulder, inflicting a severe gash and bruise. Not knowing how the missile had reached him, he seemed to think himself a very ill-treated man.

Just as Breckinridge's division was going into action, about 12 N., we came up on the left of it, where the Kentucky troops were formed. The bullets were beginning to fly thick about us. Simultaneously the squadron and the regiment nearest to us struck up the favorite song of the Kentuckians, "Cheer, Boys, Cheer". The effect was animating beyond all description.

About this time, while the right and left of the Confederate line was still pressing on, the left center met with a serious check before a strong position which the enemy held tenaciously. The Federal troops at this point were posted upon an eminence, covered with underbrush, and in front of which was a ravine. Eighteen or twenty pieces of artillery, strongly supported, were planted on this hill, and were playing furiously. For perhaps an hour Hardee's efforts to advance were foiled. The position was taken, I believe only after it had been enfiladed. Our squadron approached this point while the advance was thus checked and General Hardee sent an aide to learn "what cavalry that was?" When told that it was Morgan's he expressed pleasure and said that he would send it "to take that battery." This was a truly gratifying compliment, but we received it with sobriety; and as we formed for the charge, which we were told would soon be ordered, indulged in no extravagant expressions of joy. I am even inclined to believe that we were not so sanguine of the result as General Hardee seemed to be. The General sat on his horse near Shoup's gallant battery, which was replying, but ineffectually, to the vicious rain of canister and shell which poured from the hill. He seemed indifferent to the hot fire, but very anxious to take those guns.

We had never seen anything like that before. We had occasionally been fired upon by a single piece of artillery, when we had closely approached the enemy's encampments on Green river; and we used to think that hardly fair. Now the blaze and "volleyed thunder" of the guns on that hill seemed to our excited imaginations like the output of a volcano in active operation.

An hour or two previously, a young fellow, belonging to some Confederate battery which had been disabled, had asked permission to serve with us for the rest of the day. He was riding an artillery horse and had picked up a rifle and a cartridge box on the field, so I put him in the ranks. While we were expecting the order to charge, my eye happened to fall on this youngster, and it occurred to me that I might get from him valuable information germane to the business on hand. I therefore took him aside, and remarked: "You say you have served in the artillery for a year, and you ought to know a good deal about it. Now, General Hardee is going to order us to charge that Yankee battery yonder, and I want you to post me about the way to charge a battery."

"Why, good Lord, Lieutenant!" he exclaimed with much emhpasis. "I wouldn't do it, if I was you. Why your blamed little cavalry won't be deuce high agin' them guns."

I became angry, because I was not feeling hopeful or comfortable, and his prediction "mingled strangely with my fears."

"Haven't I told you," I said, "that General Hardee will order us to take those guns? Now, don't express any opinion, but answer my question, 'What's the best way to charge a battery?' "

He looked me squarely in the eye for a few seconds, and then said very earnestly: "Lieutenant, to tell you the God's truth, thar' ain't no good way to charge a battery."

The order to charge was not given: I will confess, greatly to our relief. At the first slackening of the fire some of our infantry regiments dashed forward successfully; but the enemy quitted the position because they were about to be surrounded. Several of the guns were taken.

At about 2:30 P. M. on that Sunday afternoon there occurred what many have always regarded as the turning point of the battle when a stray Minie ball struck General Johnston, inflicting a wound from which he bled to death in a few minutes. Isham G. Harris, governor of Tennessee, who served as a volunteer aide de camp on the staff of the General, tells of the circumstances attending Johnston's death. At the General's suggestion, Harris had personally led a

Tennessee regiment in the charge that was successful and drove the Federals back on their reserve line on a ridge. Then, Harris goes on:

Just as the line on our extreme right (with which I had moved forward) was established, casting my eye upon the line to the left I saw General Johnston sitting upon his horse a few feet in rear and about the center of the line. He was alone. I immediately galloped to him to ascertain if, in his new position, he wished to send orders.

I had never in my life seen him looking more bright, joyous and happy . . . The charge he had led was heroic. It had been successful, and his face expressed a soldier's joy and a patriot's hope.

As I approached him, he said "Governor, they came very near putting me hors du combat in that charge", holding out and pointing to his foot. Looking at it, I discovered that a musket-ball had struck the edge of the sole of his boot, cutting the sole clear across and ripping it off to the toe. I asked eagerly "Are you wounded? Did the ball touch your foot?" He said "No", and was proceeding to make other remarks when a Federal battery opened fire from a position which enfiladed our line just established. He paused in the middle of a sentence to say, "Order Colonel Statham to wheel his regiment to the left, charge and take that battery." I galloped to Colonel Statham, only about two hundred yards distant, gave the order, galloped back to the general where a moment before I had left him, rode up to his right side and said, "General, your order is delivered and Colonel Statham is in motion"; but as I was uttering this sentence, the general reeled from me in a manner that indicated he was falling from his horse. I put my left arm around his neck, grasping the collar of his coat, and righted him up in the saddle, bending forward as I did so and, looking him in the face, said, "General, are you wounded?" In a very deliberate and emphatic tone he answered, "Yes, and I fear seriously."

At that moment I requested Captain Wickham to go with all possible speed for a surgeon, to send the first one he could find, but to proceed until he could find Dr. Yandell, medical director, and bring him. The general's hold upon his rein relaxed, and it dropped from his hand. Supporting him with my left hand, I gathered his rein with my right, in which I held my own, and guided both horses to a valley about 150 yards in rear of our line where I halted, dropped myself between the two horses, pulling the general over upon me, and eased him to the ground as gently as I could. When laid upon the ground, with eager anxiety I asked many questions about his wounds, to which he gave no answer, not even a look of intelligence.

Supporting his head with one hand, I untied his cravat, unbuttoned his collar and vest, and tore his shirts open with the other, for the purpose of finding the wound, feeling confident from his condition that he had a more serious wound than the one which I knew was bleeding profusely in the right leg; but I found no other and, as I afterward ascertained, he had no other. Raising his head, I poured a little brandy into his mouth, which he swallowed, and in a few moments I repeated the brandy, but he made no effort to swallow; it gurgled in his throat in his effort to breathe, and I turned his head so as to relieve him.

In a few moments he ceased to breathe. I did not consult my watch, but my impression is that he did not live more than thirty or forty minutes from the time he received the wound.

Colonel William Preston Johnston, in his biography of his father, the General, contributes a touching and regretful foot-note:

The mortal wound was from a Minie ball, which tore the popliteal artery of the right leg, where it divides into the tibial arteries, as Dr. Yandell informs me. He did not live more than ten or fifteen mintues after receiving it. It was not necessarily fatal. General Johnston's own knowledge of military surgery was adequate for its control by an extemporized tourniquet, had he been aware of or regardful of its nature.

Dr. D. W. Yandell, his surgeon, had attended his person most of the morning; but, finding a large number of wounded men, including many Federals, at one point, General Johnston ordered Yandell to stop there, establish a hospital, and give them his services. He said to Yandell: "These men were our enemies a moment ago, they are prisoners now; take care of them." Yandell protested against leaving him, but he was peremptory, and the doctor began his work. He saw General Johnston no more. Had Yandell remained with him, he would have had little trouble with the wound. It was this act of unselfish charity which cost him his life.

Colonel Johnston, concluding his account of the battle, gives a picture of the situation the evening of April 6th that has been accepted as an accurate one by all those who believe that it was only the death of General Johnston that prevented the annihilation of Grant's army:

The last attack of the day was about to be made, and in sufficient force to insure its success. Most of the Confederate brigades were swarming to the front, converging their lines upon the sole point of defense. Their ability to take it seems scarcely to admit a doubt. That little screen thrown down, the Federal army lay at the absolute mercy of its antagonist. The Confederates, in possession of the heights, could have poured concentrated destruction and slaughter into the confused mass below and compelled instant surrender. All the fruits of victory seemed within the grasp of the Confederate army, when the prize so dearly bought was suddenly snatched away. . . . All was shattered by one word. "On!" would have made it history; but the commanding general said "Retire". It was all over. That bloody field was to mean nothing in all time but a slain hero and 25,000 dauntless soldiers stretched upon a bloody field.

Beauregard spent most of the rest of his life in attempting to refute the allegation that it was his lack of energy and enterprise that had cost the Confederates a great victory. Colonel Alfred Roman in his *Military Operations of General Beauregard,* generally regarded as having been substantially the product of Beauregard's own pen, has this to say on the subject:

The blame for having withdrawn the Confederate troops too soon from the fight, on the evening of the 6th, "just as"—it is alleged—"a last concentrated effort was about to be made by some of the subordinate commanders" has been entirely disproved by the reports of brigade and regimental commanders. The cessation of hostilities was not ordered until "a last concentrated effort" had been made shortly after 4 P.M., under General Beauregard's own eyes, and not until he was satisfied, from the condition of his troops, that no further attack on our part would meet with success. . . . It was not until about 6 P.M., shortly before sunset, that the order was given to cease the contest, and collect and reorganize the various commands before it should be too dark to carry out the order effectually. But before these instructions could be generally distributed, the fighting had in reality ceased on the greater part of the field.

Jefferson Davis, in his *Rise and Fall of the Southern Confederacy,* spared no words in heaping blame on General Beauregard for losing, through his own ineptitude, the battle which Johnston by his great military skill had all but won:

When General Johnston fell the Confederate army was so fully victorious that, had the attack been vigorously pressed, General Grant and his army would before the setting of the sun have been fugitives or prisoners. . . . Not for the first time did the fate of an army depend upon a single man, and the fortunes of a country hang, as in a balance, on the achievements of a single army. To take an example far from us, in time and place, when Turenne had, after months of successful maneuvering finally forced his enemy into a position which gave assurance of victory, and had marshalled his forces for a decisive battle, he was, when making a preliminary reconnaissance, killed by a chance shot; then his successor, instead of striking, retreated, and all which the one had gained for France, the other lost. . . . I believe that again in the history of war the fate of an army depended on one man; and more, that the fortunes of a country hung by the single thread of the life that was yielded on the field of Shiloh.

President Davis's reference to the experience of Marshal Turenne at Sassbach in 1675 as analogous to General Johnston at Shiloh in 1862 was especially distasteful to General Beauregard, who retorted (through the pen of Colonel Roman):

The falsity of the comparison is too flagarant to need more than a passing notice. First, it was at the suggestion of General Beauregard that General Johnston had marched his small army to Corinth in order to form a junction there and fight the battle of Shiloh, not "after months of successful maneuvering", as was the case with Marshal Turenne, but on the contrary after months of irreparable disasters which had brought the country to the brink of despair and led General Johnston to believe that he had lost the confidence of both the people and the army. Second, it was General Beauregard—not General Johnston—who "had marshalled our forces for a decisive battle" at Pittsburg Landing, as has already been fully and clearly established. Third, when the commanding general fell, the battle had been in progress fully eight hours. His "successor" continued the attack, with all the vigor and energy possible, as long as daylight and the physical condition of his men allowed him to do so. . . . Fourth, the victory was by no means assured at the hour of General Johnston's death. All that can be said is that our right was then in the act of driving back the enemy's left; but there still remained his right and centre which, though hard pressed, had not yet been routed and only began to give way in confusion after General Beauregard had assumed command.

This unseemly post-war wrangling among the Confederate leaders had its counter-point on the Federal side. Grant was strangely unwilling to admit that the timely arrival of Buell and his army had been a decisive factor in winning the battle, and Buell was justifiably incensed at Grant's attitude. Buell had been understandably horrified when, late in the afternoon of Sunday, he arrived on the west bank of the river with the first units of his command and was confronted with the inescapable evidence that Grant's army had suffered a disastrous defeat, with demoralizing consequences. As he tells it:

The face of the bluff was crowded with stragglers from the battle. The number there at different hours has been estimated at from five thousand in the morning to fifteen thousand in the evening. The number at nightfall would not have fallen short of fifteen thousand, including those who had passed down the river, and the less callous but still broken and demoralized fragments about the camps on the plateau near the landing.

At the top of the bluff all was confusion. Men mounted and on foot, and wagons with their teams and excited drivers, all struggling to force their way closer to the river, were mixed up in apparently inextricable confusion with a battery of artillery which was standing in park without men or horses to man or move it. The increasing throng already presented a barrier which it was evidently necessary to remove, in order to make way for the passage of my troops when they should arrive.

In looking about for assistance I fell upon one officer, the quartermaster of an Ohion regiment, who preserved his senses, and was anxious to do something to abate the disorder. I instructed him to take control of the teams, and move them down the hill by a side road which led to the narrow bottom below the landing, and there park them. He went to work with alacrity and the efficiency of a strong will, and succeeded in clearing the ground of the weapons. It proved before night to have been a more important service than I had expected, for it not only opened the way for Nelson's division, but extricated the artillery and made it possible to get it into action when the attack occurred at the landing about sunset.

In one of the Indiana regiments in Buell's reinforcing army was a buck private named Ambrose Bierce. In post-war writing of his wartime experiences he has left a sharply etched eye-witness's picture of that confusion referred to by General Buell:

Along the sheltered strip of beach between the river bank and the water was a confused mass of humanity—several thousands of men. They were mostly unarmed; many were wounded; some dead. All the camp-following tribes were there; all the cowards; a few officers. Not one of them knew where his regiment was, nor if he had a regiment. Many had not. These men were defeated, beaten, cowed. They were deaf to duty and dead to shame. A more demented crew never drifted to the rear of broken battalions. They would have stood in their tracks and been shot down to a man by a provost-marshal's guard, but they could not have been urged up that bank. . . .

Whenever a steamboat would land, this abominable mob had to be kept off her with bayonets; when she pulled away, they sprang on her and were pushed by scores into the water, where they were suffered to drown one another in their own way. The men disembarking insulted them, shoved them, struck them. In return they expressed their unholy delight in the certainty of our destruction by the enemy.

Historians generally agreed that the timely arrival of Buell's army saved the day for the Federals. Grant, however, in his account of the closing action on the first day of the battle belittles the value of Buell's reinforcement:

There was a deep ravine in front of our left. The Tennessee River was very high, and there was water to a considerable depth in the ravine. Here the enemy made a last desperate effort to turn our flank, but was repelled. The gunboats *Tyler* and *Lexington,* with the artillery under Webster, aided the army and effectually checked their further progress.

Before any of Buell's troops had reached the west bank of the Tennessee, firing had almost entirely ceased. . . . As his troops arrived in the dusk, General Buell marched several of his regiments part way down the face of the hill, where they fired briskly for some minutes, but I do not think a single man engaged in this firing received an injury: the attack had spent its force.

General Lew Wallace, with 5,000 effective men, arrived after firing had ceased for the day, and was placed on the right. Thus night came, Wallace came, and the advance of Nelson's division came, but none—unless night—in time to be of material service to the gallant men who saved Shiloh on that first day against large odds. . . . The presence of two or three regiments of Buell's army on the west bank before firing ceased had not the slightest effect in preventing the capture of Pittsburg Landing.

General Hurlbut, of Grant's army, however, in his account of the ending of the day's fighting clearly give the impression that it was the arrival of Buell's advance brigade [Ammen's] that was decisive:

About 6 P. M. this movement (for a final Confederate attack at the landing) was reported to General Hurlbut. He at once took measures to change the front of two regiments, or parts of regiments, and to turn six pieces of artillery to bear upon the point of danger. At that instant, he being near the head of the Landing road, General

Grant came up from the river, closely followed by Ammen's Brigade of Nelson's division. Information of the expected attack was promptly given, and two of Ammen's regiments deployed into line, moved rapidly forward and after a few sharp exchanges of volleys from them, the enemy fell back, and the bloody series of engagements of Sunday at Pittsburg Landing closed with that last repulse.

General Buell in a post-war article bitterly refuted Grant's account of what took place. He says:

The reports of all the officers who took part in the action at the landing—Nelson, Ammen and the regimental commanders—fully sustain the main point in these accounts, and are totally at variance with General Grant's statement in his *Century* article. . . . The attack was not repelled until Ammen arrived, and it can not be affirmed under the circumstances that the action of his brigade in delaying and repelling the enemy was not of the most vital importance. Had the attack been made before Nelson could arrive, with the means which the enemy had abundantly at hand, it would have succeeded beyond all question.

Buell also claims, and apparently on substantial grounds, that it was his troops who took the initiative in the Federal attack the next morning:

The engagement was brought on, Monday morning, not by General Grant's order but by the advance of Nelson's division along the River Road in line of battle, at the first dawn of day, followed by Crittenden's division in column. The enemy was encountered at 5:20 o'clock, and a little in advance of Hurlbut's camp Nelson was halted while Crittenden came into line on his right. By this time the head of McCook's division came up and was formed on the right of Crittenden. Before McCook's rear brigade was up, the line moved forward.

General Beauregard in his report of the battle states that at the close of the first day's fighting he "directed our troops to sleep on their arms". But not all the Confederates spent the night in slumber. Colonel Nathan Bedford Forrest and his regiment had taken an active part in the fighting that day, and at nightfall went into bivouac on the Confederate right near the river. But the coming of night did not put a stop to the ever-alert Forrest's activities. In one of the captured Federal tents he had found a supply of blue army overcoats. Dressing a dozen of his troopers in them, he sent them to reconnoitre within the Federal lines. Thomas Jordan, who in 1867 was co-author of a biography of Forrest, tells how these scouts discovered Buell's 25,000 reinforcements crossing the river, and hurried back to report their discovery:

Completely successful, the scouting party returned in an hour and reported that, reaching the Landing, they had seen heavy reinforcements coming rapidly by water. Also, in their opinion, such was the disorder prevailing that, if an attack were made in full force at once, they might be readily pushed into the river.

Forrest, ever a man of prompt action, mounted his horse instantly to convey this startling intelligence to the nearest corps commander; and, soon coming upon Generals Hardee and Breckinridge, made known what his scouts announced. He also bluntly added his opinion that either the Confederates should immediately resume the battle or quit the field to avoid a damaging conflict with overwhelming odds. Hardee directed him to communicate his information to General Beauregard, and with that object he rode forth again; but after a diligent search through the woods and darkness, unable to find that General, he became so deeply solicitous that he hurried back to his pickets. Finding all quiet, he again dispatched his scouts within the Federal lines. It was two o'clock A. M. before they returned and reported the continued arrival of fresh troops. Again Forrest repaired and reported to General Hardee the state of affairs, but was instructed to return to his regiment, keep up a vigilant, strong picket-line, and report all hostile movements.

Completely frustrated, Forrest sadly abandoned his efforts to arouse his superiors and lay down to snatch a few hours' rest before the resumption of fighting the next morning. Beauregard, in his official report, takes up the story of the battle, from the Confederate point of view, as it developed with the dawning of the battle's second day, April 7th:

During the night the rain fell in torrents, adding to the discomforts and harassed condition of the man . . . About 6 o'clock . . . a hot fire of musketry and artillery, opened from the enemy's quarters on our advanced line, assured me of the junction of his forces, and soon the battle raged with a fury which satisfied me I was attacked by a largely superior force. But from the outset our troops, notwithstanding their fatigue and losses from the battle of the day before, exhibited the most cheering, veteran-like steadiness.

On the right and center the enemy was repulsed in every attempt he made with his heavy columns in that quarter of the field. On the left, however, and nearest to the point of arrival of his re-enforcements, he drove forward line after line of his fresh troops, which were met with a resolution and courage of which our country may be proudly hopeful. Again and again our troops were brought to the charge, invariably to win the position in issue; invariably to drive back their foe. But hour by hour thus opposed to an enemy constantly re-enforced, our ranks were perceptibly thinned under the unceasing, withering fire of the enemy, and by 12 m. eighteen hours of hard fighting had sensibly exhausted a large number.

My last reserve had necessarily been disposed of, and the enemy was evidently receiving fresh re-enforcements after each repulse. Accordingly at 1 p. m. I determined to withdraw from so unequal a conflict, securing such of the results of the victory of the day before as was then practicable.

Officers of my staff were immediately dispatched with the necessary orders to make the best disposition for a deliberate, orderly withdrawal from the field, and to collect and post a reserve to meet the enemy should he attempt to push after us.

About 2 p. m. the lines in advance, which had repulsed the enemy in their last fierce assault on our left and center, received the orders to retire. This was done with uncommon steadiness and the enemy made no attempt to follow.

The line of troops established to cover this movement had been disposed on a favorable ridge commanding the ground of Shiloh Church. From this position our artillery played upon the woods beyond for a while, but upon no visible enemy and without reply. Soon satisfied that no serious pursuit would be attempted, this last line was withdrawn, and never did troops leave the battlefield in better order; even the stragglers fell into the ranks and marched off with those who had stood steadily by their colors.

A second strong position was taken up about a mile in the rear, where the approach of the enemy was awaited for nearly an hour, but no effort to follow was made, and only a small detachment of horsemen could be seen at a distance from this last position warily observing our movements.

Arranging through my staff officers for the completion of the movements thus begun, Brigadier-General Breckinridge was left with his command as a rear guard to hold the ground we had occupied the night preceding the first battle, just in front of the intersection of the Pittsburg and Hamburg roads, about four miles from the former place, while the rest of the army passed to the rear in excellent order.

On the following day General Breckinridge fell back about three miles, to Mickey's, which position we continued to hold, with our cavalry thrown considerably forward in immediate proximity to the battlefield.

Unfortunately, toward night of the 7th instant, it began to rain heavily. This continued throughout the night; the roads became almost impassable in many places, and much hardship and suffering now ensued before all the regiments reached their encampments; but despite their heavy casualties of the two eventful days of April 6th and 7th, this army is more confident of ultimate success than before its encounter with the enemy.

Thomas Jordan, Beauregard's adjutant general, gives a graphic first-hand account of the circumstances in connection with the commanding general's decision to break off the battle on the second day and withdraw to Corinth:

Up to half-past two o'clock on the 7th of April, or second day's conflict, General Beauregard had his headquarters at the Shiloh Chapel, or immediately at Sherman's former headquarters. The Confederate troops, now hardly 20,000 men, were all either directly in advance of that position, or to the right and left of it, somewhat in advance, hotly engaged, having only receded from the places occupied during the night sufficiently to be better massed and organized for fighting. But our losses were swelling perilously, and the straggling was growing more difficult to restrain. A little after two o'clock Governor Harris of Tennessee, who, after the death of General Johnston, had joined the staff of Beauregard in action, taking me aside asked if I did not regard the day as going against us irremediably, and whether there was not danger in tarrying so long in the field as to be unable to withdraw in good order. I answered that I thought it would soon be our proper course to retreat. Having an opportunity a moment later to speak a word to General Beauregard in private, I brought the subject before him in almost these words:

"General, do you not think our troops are very much in the condition of a lump of sugar thoroughly soaked with water, but yet preserving its original shape, though ready to dissolve? Would it not be judicious to get away with what we have?"

"I intend to withdraw within a few moments," was his reply.

Calling upon his aides-de-camp present, he dispatched them with orders to the several corps commanders to begin the rearward movement.

One of the veterans of a Tennessee regiment has left an account of what was perhaps the last exchange of fire between the contending armies on the last day of the battle:

Reaching the old church on the retreat that last evening, General Cheatham ordered the Thirty-eighth to hold the position until a lot of caissons, ammunition wagons, and wounded men in ambulances had crossed a little bridge over a ravine hard by. The men formed across a little graveyard by the church, and sat down, saving the one round of ammunition they had for the most effective use. Generals Beauregard, Breckinridge, Cheatham and others dismounted and waited to encourage them in the fight. Soon the enemy came up, flushed with success, in great force, and delivered a destructive fire. But the Tennesseans waited until Governor Harris, of Beauregard's staff, gave the word, when they fired their last round, and made "the last charge at Shiloh," with fixed bayonets, driving the line in their front back for a quarter mile, after which they returned in good order in time to see the last wagon cross the ravine.

William Stevenson, the observant private in the Confederate cavalry, was one of the dispirited thousands involved in that bitter retreat from the Shiloh battlefield. The horrified reaction of a young raw recruit is reflected in his recountal of his first shocked recognition of the tragic destination of "paths of glory":

In this ride of twelve miles alongside of the routed army, I saw more of human agony and woe than I trust I will ever again be called on to witness. The retreating host wound along a narrow and almost impassable road, extending some seven or eight miles in length. Here was a long line of wagons loaded with wounded, piled in like bags of grain, groaning and cursing, while the mules plunged on in mud and water belly-deep, the water sometimes coming into the wagons. Next came a straggling regiment of infantry pressing on past the train of wagons, then a stretcher borne upon the shoulders of four men, carrying a wounded officer, then soldiers staggering along, with an arm broken and hanging down, or other fearful wounds which were enough to destroy life. And to add to the horrors of the scene, the elements of heaven marshaled their forces—a fitting accompaniment of the tempest of human desolation and passion which was raging. A cold, drizzling rain commenced about nightfall, and soon came harder and faster, then turned to pitiless blinding hail, which fell in stones as large as partridge eggs, until it lay on the ground two inches deep.

Captain Ephriam A. Otis was among those in the Federal army who thought that General Grant was inexplicably lacking in energy in pursuing the retreating Confederates, and he did not mince any words in saying so when wrote his account of the battle:

There was no pursuit of the Confederate army, though Wood's fresh division came on the field shortly after the battle was over. John Fiske states that he once asked General Sherman why the retreating rebels were not pursued, and the reply was: "I assure you, my dear fellow, that we had quite enough of their society for two whole days, and were only too glad to be rid of them on any terms." I am not aware that any other or satisfactory explanation has ever been given of the failure to pursue the enemy on Monday evening. General Grant, in his "Memoirs," says that he did not have the heart to demand more work from his jaded men, and as Buell commanded a separate army, and had only been subject to his orders for a few hours, he felt delicate about giving orders for the pursuit by his army. But he was the senior officer present on the field, and the responsibility for the failure to pursue the Confederate forces would seem to rest upon General Grant. Seldom in the history of war has there been an occasion where a vigorous and energetic pursuit of a defeated army was so imperatively demanded. The Confederate forces were completely broken and demoralized by two whole days of fierce and destructive battle ending in final defeat. The official reports are full of evidence of the disorganized condition of the troops. Bragg reported the following morning that his men were "utterly disorganized and demoralized."

Breckinridge, who was stationed at Monterey a few miles distant from the field, to cover the Confederate retreat, in a dispatch to General Beauregard, says: "My troops are worn out and I don't think can be relied on after the first volley."

A vigorous pursuit with the fresh troops then arriving on the field would certainly have resulted in the complete destruction of the Confederate army and the capture of its artillery and trains.

General Buell says, in "Battles and Leaders":

I make no attempt to excuse myself or blame others when I say that General Grant's troops, the lowest individual among them not more than the commander himself, appeared to have thought that the object of the battle was sufficiently accomplished when they were reinstated in their camps; and that in some way that idea obstructed the reorganization of my men until a further advance that day became inmpracticable.

When the history of the Civil War is finally written neither the explanation of General Grant nor that of General Buell will be accepted as a sufficient excuse for not following up the victory which had been achieved on Monday evening. The result was that Shiloh was one of the many fiercely contested but indecisive battles of the War, where victory meant simply possession of the field.

Beauregard withdrew his broken columns to Corinth without pursuit or opposition, and the army he commanded continued to confront the Army of the Cumberland during all its campaigns for two and a half years more.

Beauregard took his badly battered army back to its camps in Corinth, where the losses suffered on the battlefield were intensified by the rapid increase in sickness in his army. Shiloh had been the first great battle in this section of the country, and its impact was terrific on a people happily unfamiliar with war and its bloody consequences. The people of Corinth were horrified at the ghastly spectacle as the trains of army wagons lumbered in from the battlefield, dripping blood from their heaped-up piles of groaning, suffering wounded. No less than 5,000 wounded men, Federal and Confederate, were dumped into the little town, which was totally unprepared for such an abnormal demand on its hospitalization facilities. Maimed and suffering men lay everywhere—on porches, on sidewalks, on platforms of railroad stations. The supply of doctors and nurses was pitifully inadequate, and this emergency was accentuated as disease—dysentery, typhoid and measles—put 18,000 of Beauregard's soldiers on the sick list.

Fortunately for Beauregard, however, General Halleck, who had now assumed active command of the Federal army at Shiloh, exercised extreme caution in pursuing the defeated Confederates. Not starting his movement until April 29th, Halleck crept slowly forward, the troops entrenching themselves every night after the day's march. By this tedious process Halleck spent the whole month of May in advancing the twenty-two miles from Shiloh to the neighborhood of Corinth. Then, before Halleck could launch an attack in force, Beauregard on the night of May 29th executed a skilful retreat to Tupelo, with Halleck making but a feeble effort at pursuit.

Beauregard himself was in feeble health, and when in June he left the army on sick leave, President Davis (who keenly disliked Beauregard) relieved him of his command, and replaced him with General Braxton Bragg.

CHAPTER 6

☆ *Memphis Falls*

FOLLOWING his success at Island No. 10, General Pope planned to move southward along the river and besiege the Confederate fortifications at Fort Pillow. One of Halleck's first acts, however, upon assuming personal direction of the forces under his command was to order Pope and his 20,000 men to reinforce the troops under Grant and Buell. But Fort Pillow, even though it was not attacked, was incapable of defense after the fall of Island No. 10. So on June 1 it was evacuated by the Confederates, as was Fort Randolph. This left Memphis as the next point of Confederate defense on the Mississippi—and Memphis was but feebly defended, with a handful of infantry troops and a nondescript "fleet" composed of a few river craft hastily transformed into makeshift warships.

Captain J. E. Montgomery of the Confederate Navy in his official report tells of the gallant, but unsuccessful, effort made by the flimsily armored Confederate gunboats to stop the strong and ably commanded Federal squadron as it steamed down the river:

After having deterred the enemy from attempting to pass Fort Pillow since the 11th of April, we were compelled to retire to Memphis, being nearly out of coal. The fleet reached Memphis at 12 m. on June 5. I immediately began to supply the boats with all the coal that could be found in the city. At dark of the same day the Federal fleet made their appearance above Memphis. In view of their overwhelming strength I would have retreated, but only one boat had sufficient coal to reach Vicksburg; consequently there were but two alternatives left me—to destroy our boats or fight. I determined to do the latter. . . .

At 6 o'clock on the morning of the 6th of June I ordered Captain J. H. Burke, of the gun-boat *General M. Jeff Thompson,* and Capt. J. C. Delancy, of gun-boat *Colonel Lovell,* to take positions immediately above the city. The enemy's boats were in line of battle, moving down the river. Captain Burke opened on them with his eight-inch gun, and in a few moments the fight became general. As Captain Delancy was directing his boat at one of the Federal rams, one of his engines got out of order and his boat became unmanageable. The Federal ram *Queen of the*

[99]

West then struck his boat amidships, with disastrous effect. The next moment his boat was again struck by the Federal ram *Monarch* and was sunk. Captain Delancy and most of his crew swam ashore. The *Sumter*, Captain W. W. Lamb, struck the Federal ram *Queen of the West* and sunk her. The *General Price*, Capt. J. E. Henthorne, struck the Federal ram *Lancaster* and sunk her. He then gave chase to the Federal ram *Eastport.*

The *General Beauregard*, Capt. J. H. Hurt, was at the same time coming down the river after the same boat. The *Eastport* backed out from between our two boats before they could reach her, she being much more easily wielded, which caused the *General Beauregard* to run into the *General Price's* wheel, thereby disabling her. Whilst they were thus entangled they were run into and sunk by a re-enforcement of Federal rams.

At this time the flag-ship *Little Rebel*, in the act of striking a Federal gun-boat, was struck by a cannon-ball below the water line, which passed through her boilers, leaving her in a sinking condition. Myself and most of the crew escaped by swimming ashore.

The *Sumter* and *General Bragg* unfortunately got aground on a sand bar and were captured by the enemy. Most of their crews made their escape. Capt. J. H. Burke, finding himself surrounded and overpowered, ran his boat ashore and set her on fire to keep her from falling into the enemy's hands. The *General Van Dorn*, Capt. Isaac D. Fulkerson, succeeded in making her escape. W. H. Cabel, pilot of the *Colonel Lovell*, was killed as his boat was in the act of sinking. Capt. J. H. Burke was wounded in the arm. Capt. W. W. Lamb had a finger shot off.

I am not able to state the number lost in this engagement, but fear it large, as the enemy shot our men in the water. The Federals claim to have taken 161 prisoners. Signal Quartermaster J. Sullivan shot Commodore Ellet, of the Federal ram fleet. He was taken to Cairo and died a few days after. The *General Earl Van Dorn* and the store-boat *Paul Jones* made good their escape up the Yazoo River to the raft. The *Paul Jones* had on board a large amount of powder, shell and cannon balls taken from Fort Pillow, also commissary stores, which were shipped to Yazoo City and turned over to Lieutenant Brown, of the C. S. Navy.

A Federal account of this helter-skelter, dog-fight type of naval battle, replete with colorful details, is given by Alfred W. Ellet, who took an active part in the operation as commander of the *Monarch*. He tells first how his eminent brother, Charles Ellet, Jr., "the inventor of the steam-ram as a vehicle of war destruction", had foretold the possibility of such a catastrophe as did actually occur in March, 1862, when the Confederate ironclad ram *Virginia* (or *Merrimac*) single-handedly almost annihilated the Federal naval force in Hampton Roads. "Upon the startling verification of his neglected admonitions afforded by the *Merrimac*," he writes, "Mr. Ellet was called to the War Department and, after a short conference with Secretary Stanton, was given authority to purchase, refit, man and command, with the rank of colonel, any number of vessels deemed in his judgment necessary to meet and defeat the fleet of iron-clad rams known to be in process of construction on the lower Mississippi River." He then goes on:

Never was work more promptly or more effectually performed. Colonel Ellet purchased a number of steamboats at different points on the Ohio River, the best he could find in the short time at his disposal. He took some old and nearly worn-out boats, strengthened their hulls and bows with heavy timbers, raised bulkheads of timber around the boilers, and started them down the river to Cairo as fast as they could be got off the ways. They were the *Dick Fulton, Lancaster, Lioness, Mingo, Monarch, Queen of the West, Samson, Switzerland,* and *T. D. Horner.*

While the work was progressing, and before any one of the rams was nearly completed, information was received that the Confederate fleet had come out from under the batteries of Fort Pillow, had attacked our fleet of gun-boats lying near Craighead's Point, and had disabled two of them. Colonel Ellet received most urgent telegrams from the Secretary of War to hurry the rams forward at the earliest possible moment. In consequence of these demands, five of them were immediately dispatched down the river under my command, work upon them being continued as they proceeded and for several days after their arrival at Fort Pillow. The other rams followed, and about the 25th of May Colonel Ellet joined the fleet on board the *Switzerland,* and the ram-fleet was now ready for action.

Colonel Ellet at once conferred with Flag-Officer Charles H. Davis on the propriety of passing Fort Pillow, and engaging the enemy's fleet wherever found. Flag-Officer Davis did not approve the plan suggested, but offered no objection to Colonel Ellet's trying the experiment. Accordingly, immediate preparations were begun for running the batteries with the entire ram-fleet. During this period of preparation, constant watch was kept upon the fort and the enemy's fleet.

On the night of the 4th of June I crossed the timber point in front of the fort, and reported to the colonel commanding my conviction that the fort was being evacuated. About 2 o'clock in the morning I obtained permission, with many words of caution from Colonel Ellet, to run down opposite the fort in a yawl and, after lying off in order to become assured that the place was abandoned, to land, with the assurance that the rams would follow in case my yawl did not return before daylight. I landed with my little band, only to find the fort entirely deserted; and after planting the National colors upon the ruins of one of the magazines, we sat down to wait for the coming of daylight and the rams. They came, followed by the entire fleet, and after a short stop all proceeded down the river, the rams taking the lead, to Fort Randolph, where they delayed long enough to plant the National flag and to examine the abandoned fortifications, the gunboats at this point taking the advance.

After leaving Fort Randolph the ram-fleet proceeded without incident to within about twenty-five miles of Memphis, where they all rounded to and tied up for the night, with orders of sailing issued to each commander; instructions to be ready to round out at the signal from the flag-ship, and that "each boat should go into the anticipated fight in the same order they maintained in sailing." At the first dawn of day (June 6th) the fleet moved down the river, and at sunrise the flag-ship rounded the bend at "Paddy's Hen and Chickens," and immediately after came in sight of the Federal gun-boats anchored in line across the river, about a mile above Memphis. Colonel Ellet promptly signaled his vessels to tie up on the Arkansas shore, in order of their sailing, as he desired to confer with Flag-Officer Davis before passing further.

The *Queen of the West* came to, first, followed by the *Monarch* and other rams in regular succession. The *Queen of the West* had made the land, and passed out line to make fast; the *Monarch* was closing in just above, but had not yet touched the shore. At this moment, and as the full orb of the sun rose above the horizon, the report of a gun was heard from around the point and down the river. It was the first gun from the Confederate River Defense Fleet moving to attack us. Colonel Ellet was standing on the hurricane-deck of the *Queen of the West.* He immediately sprang forward, and, waving his hat to attract my attention, called out: "It is a gun from the enemy! Round out and follow me! Now is our chance!" Without a moment's delay, the gun-boats had opened their batteries, and the reports of guns on both sides were heavy and rapid.

The morning was beautifully clear and perfectly still: a heavy wall of smoke was formed across the river, so that the position of our gun-boats could only be seen by the flashes of their guns. The *Queen* plunged forward under a full head of steam, right into this wall of smoke and was lost sight of, her position being known only by her tall pipes which reached above the smoke. The *Monarch* following, was greeted while passing the gun-boats with wild huzzas from our gallant tars. When freed from the smoke, those of us who were on the *Monarch* could see Colonel Ellet's tall and commanding form still standing on the hurricane-deck, waving his hat to show me which one of the enemy's vessels he desired the *Monarch* to attack, —namely, the *General Price*, which was on the right wing of their advancing line. For himself he selected the *General Lovell* and directed the *Queen* straight for her, she being about the middle of the enemy's advancing line. The two vessels came toward each other in most gallant style, head to head, prow to prow; and had they met in that way, it is most likely that both vessels would have gone down. But at the critical moment the *General Lovell* began to turn; and that moment sealed her fate. The *Queen* came on and plunged straight into the *Lovell's* exposed broadside; the vessel was cut almost in two and disappeared under the dark waters in less time than it takes to tell the story. The *Monarch* next struck the *General Price* a glancing blow which cut her starboard wheel clean off, and completely disabled her from further participation in the fight.

As soon as the *Queen* was freed from the wreck of the sinking *Lovell,* and before she could recover headway, she was attacked on both sides by the enemy's vessels, the *Beauregard* on one side and the *Sumter* on the other. In the melee one of the wheels of the *Queen* was disabled so that she could not use it, and Colonel Ellet, while still standing on the hurricane-deck to view the effects of the encounter with the *General Lovell,* received a pistol-ball in his knee, and, lying prone on the deck, gave order for the *Queen* to be run on her one remaining wheel to the Arkansas shore, whither she was soon followed by the *General Price* in a sinking condition. Colonel Ellet sent an officer and squad of men to meet the *General Price* upon her making the shore, and received her entire crew as prisoners of war. By this time consternation had seized upon the enemy's fleet, and all had turned to escape. The fight had drifted down the river, below the city.

The *Monarch,* as soon as she would recover headway after her conflict with the *General Price,* drove down upon the *Beauregard,* which vessel, after her encounter with the *Queen of the West,* was endeavoring to escape. She was thwarted by the *Monarch* coming down upon her with a well-directed blow which crushed in her side and completely disabled her from further hope of escape. Men on the deck waved a white flag in token of surrender, and the *Monarch* passed on down to intercept the *Little Rebel,* the enemy's flag-ship. She had received some injury from our gun-boats' fire, and was making for the Arkansas shore, which she reached at the moment when the *Monarch,* with very slight headway, pushed her hard and fast aground; her crew sprang upon shore and ran into the thick woods, making their escape. Leaving the *Little Rebel* fast aground, the *Monarch* turned her attention to the sinking *Beauregard,* taking the vessel in tow, and making prisoners of her crew. The *Beauregard* was towed by the *Monarch* to the bar, where she sank to her boiler-deck and finally became a total loss.

The others of the enemy's fleet were run ashore and fired by the crews before they escaped into the adjoining Arkansas swamps. The *Jeff Thompson* burned and blew up with a tremendous report; the *General Bragg* was secured by our gun-boats before the fire gained headway, and was saved. The *Van Dorn* alone made her escape, and was afterward burned by the enemy at Liverpool Landing, upon the approach of two of our rams in Yazoo River, in order to prevent her from falling into our hands. . . .

After the *Monarch* had towed the *Beauregard* into shoal water, from which, it was hoped, she might be raised, I received the first intelligence, from a dispatch-boat bearing orders, that Colonel Ellet was wounded. The orders I received from him were: "Continue the pursuit as long as there is any hope of overtaking the flying enemy."

Toward the close of the engagement, Colonel Ellet was informed that a white flag had been raised in Memphis, and he immediately sent his young son, Medical Cadet Charles Rivers Ellet, ashore with a party of three men and a flag of truce, to demand the surrender of the city. They landed in a row-boat and delivered Colonel Ellet's dispatch to the mayor, and received his reply; then, surrounded by an excited and threatening crowd, they proceeded to the post-office, ascended to the top of the building, and, while stoned and fired upon by the mob below, young Ellet lowered the Confederate colors and raised the National flag over the city of Memphis. This incident occurred a considerable length of time before the formal surrender of the city into the possession of the United States troops under command of Colonel G. N. Fitch. . . .

The scene at this battle was rendered most sublime by the desperate nature of the engagement and the momentous consequences that followed very speedily after the first attack. Thousands of people crowded the high bluffs overlooking the river. The roar of the cannon and shell shook the houses on shore on either side for many miles. First wild yells, shrieks, and clamors, then loud, despairing murmurs, filled the affrighted city. The screaming, plunging shell crashed into the boats, blowing some of them and their crews into fragments, and the rams rushed upon each other like wild beasts in deadly conflict. Blinding smoke hovered about the scene of all this confusion and horror; and, as the battle progressed and the Confederate fleet was destroyed, all of the cheering voices on shore were silenced. When the last hope of the Confederates gave way, the lamentations which went up from the spectators were like cries of anguish. . . .

General Jeff Thompson, noted in partisan or border warfare, having signally failed with those rams at Fort Pillow, now resigned them to their fate. It was said that he stood by his horse watching the struggle, and seeing at last his rams all gone, captured, sunk or burned, he exclaimed, philosophically, "They are gone, and I am going," mounted his horse, and disappeared.

An enormous amount of property was captured by our squadron; and, in addition to the Confederate fleet, we captured at Memphis six large Mississippi steamers, each marked "C. S. A." We also seized a large quantity of cotton in steamers and on shore, and the property at the Confederate Navy Yard, and caused the destruction of the *Tennessee*, a large steam-ram, on the stocks, which was to have been a sister ship to the renowned *Arkansas*. About one hundred Confederates were killed and wounded and one hundred and fifty captured. Chief of all results of the work of the flotilla was the opening of the Mississippi River once for all from Cairo to Memphis, and the complete possession of Western Tennessee by the Union forces.

Memphis, under the domination of an army of occupation, reacted in about the same manner as any other occupied city. Some of the citizens, basically Union sympathizers, welcomed the Federal army; the great bulk of the citizenry were still loyal to the Confederacy and more or less openly antagonistic to the occupying army; some, although still sympathetic to the Confederacy, found it expedient to collaborate with the conquerors. In the latter classification, apparently, was John Hallum, a prominent Memphis attorney, who in later years wrote with surprising candor of his experiences during the Federal occupation:

As soon as the army of occupation took possession of the city an order was issued commanding all citizens within a prescribed time to take the oath of allegiance to the National Government. Non-compliance meant banishment beyond the lines. This was gall and wormwood to all who had given their adhesion to the Confederate States. Rather than submit to its terms, I resolved to go South with my family, and teach school when my physical condition permitted. I was then suffering with an aggravated enlargement of the pleura of long standing, my system was much swollen and skin almost as white as cotton. In this condition I applied for a pass through the lines for my family and myself and household goods, clothing, etc., but was promptly informed I could not take any kind of property, not even a change of clothing. I had no national currency at the time, but fortunately John C. Lanier, the old Clerk and Master, a short time after called me into the Gayoso Bank and paid me $1,500 in greenbacks, money due me. This was a Godsend at the time.

A few days after I had applied for a pass through the lines, a strange gentleman came to me who said he was a "Moses" who could lead me out of the wilderness of my troubles, and I told him I was very much in need of just such a person.

"How can you help me?"

"You are an ex-Confederate soldier, and of course it's rough on you to be compelled to take the oath. That can be avoided and every object accomplished. I can bring the papers to you already made out, and all you will have to do is to sign your own name to them; no oath whatever required. You need not go to the office; I will bring them to you—but it costs money to secure these valuable privileges."

"How much?" said I.

"Five hundred dollars."

"Well, my friend, call around in a day or two. I will think this matter over, and look into it, and if I find or become satisfied that your representations are true, I will invest and take stock in 'Moses'."

No man could pursue any avocation, do any business, or purchase supplies without a permit based on the oath of allegiance, and specifying what he was permitted to purchase. I soon found that "Moses" knew what he was doing, and that a very lively cash trade had sprung up in the patriotic office where the oath was supposed to be *bona fide* administered, in fact was often administered there to those applying for and willing to take it. There were two departments, Division Nos. 1 and 2. No. 2 was the cash division, where *sub rosa* men presided, where "division and silence" was observed.

When "Moses" called again we struck a trade. He took my height, color of hair and eyes, and the description *personne*, retired, and in an hour I was a loyal man; "paid the cash and took my choice," and swore to nothing.

"Moses" did an immense business; he was a shrewd trader. I afterward found that his scale of prices was graduated on adjustable scales, always fixed at standards suited to the customer's financial status. This scale ranged up and down from $10 down to $500 up. Unfortunately for me, I struck the wrong end of the pole, but did not know it at the time "Moses" tapped me.

Splendid trader, "Moses" was. His exchequer balances rapidly increased. There was much "silence" but little "division", and abundance of *sub rosa*. He was eminently practical, reduced everything to commercial standards, had a Bureau in every branch of the service, and an army at his beck and call . . . How he secured immunity was nobody's business.

Recalcitrants gave him no trouble. They understood that "an ounce of fear was worth more than a ton of love" when it came to kicking against the army of occupation and its followers. The army had great confidence in "Moses." He often outgeneraled the Secretary of War. He was a good fellow. Simon Cameron, the first Secretary of War under President Lincoln, admired him and "monkeyed" with him until he lost his place in the Cabinet; but "Moses" did not get a set-back, but took in more *sub rosa* . . . Cameron started the first "Moses" in national contracts, it was charged; Simon got out, "Moses" stayed.

I was as green and innocent as a gosling on a grassy lawn when I first met "Moses" and his family, and did not know the interpretation of that bright lexicon of Yankee youth, where it speaks of being "on the make," and reduces soul and body to commercial standards. . . . An unwilling, a compulsory novitiate in the history of war, to stand aloof as a silent spectator was impossible—an actor I must be, no choice. Society was in an upheaval like Aetna in eruption, a cyclone like the French Revolution was in progress, and I was a citizen of conquered territory, in hourly contact with my conquerors, and forced to deal with them on their terms, not mine.

Hallum's naive explanation and justification of his course of conduct at this critical time may be taken as typical of the reasoning of others who took the same course at this time:

"To be or not to be" was the question of the hour: Go South with a penniless and helpless family without food or clothing and a fearfully deranged physical system, or to practically ride the storm with the wings and army of "Moses" after renewing my health? Although every fiber, woof, and web of the heart and soul was in deepest sympathy with my native South . . . I chose to stay with and protect my family if I could, to ride the storm if I could. Penny-whistlers have criticised my conduct, knowing as little of the circumstances which surrounded me, of the impulses which moved and impelled me, as the Indian does of the diplomacy which obtains with civilized people . . .

After purchasing five hundred dollars' worth of patriotism from my friend Moses, I opened a suite of offices on the ground floor on the south side of Court Square . . . The Bastile of the revolution, the Irving Block, was being filled from cellar to dome with prisoners—citizens and Confederate soldiers . . . Letters poured on me in immense numbers; every man wanted assistance, from the blockade runner by water and land to the impoverished citizen and destitute soldier. Sometimes one hundred of these letters came to me in one day. All these letters were read by officers in charge of the prison before they reached me. Hundreds of these distressed men in their great anxiety for relief promised large fees, when in fact they had nothing at command. These letters inspired Moses with visions of wealth.

It will be readily seen from the volume of business daily, almost hourly, pouring in on me, that it would require an enormous amount of time to go through the slow and formal process of a military court in trying these cases, and that if a more expeditious method was not found but little could be done. In addition to that my notarial business was voluminous sometimes, and often bringing me a revenue of $500 per day. Added to all this much time was devoted to consultations with merchants, traders and blockade runners. A corps of clerks were employed, everything systematized, and a large volume of business was dispatched every day with the greatest facility. . . .

The Bastile was in charge of a young man of thirty, my own age at that time, whom I cannot better describe than by saying he was double-geared lightning, and continually propounded to himself: "What am I here for?" It devolved on him, this shrewdest of all the Moses family I ever came in contact with, to read the voluminous correspondence coming to me hourly from the Bastile. He saw every department, military and civil, in all of their ramifications, embracing every available opportunity to make money, and he caught the contagious fever, and determined to subordinate his opportunities to that end. Not knowing me, he at first tried to divert my business to an attorney from the North, who had followed along in the wake of the army, but he signally failed in that. Then he sought a private interview with me, not at either his or my office, but a secluded suite of rooms on the west side of Main street.

He was excessively cautious, wise beyond his years, and I can pay no higher tribute to his genius than by saying the combination which he sought and formed with me never made a failure. He simply offered for a stipend, graduated to a basis which my clients could pay to secure, their release and to furnish, when desired, passes through the Federal military lines. Of my large volume of other business he knew nothing and had nothing whatever to do, and never knew the large amount of revenue I devoted from other sources of income to release a large number of penniless clients in the Bastile.

I told him frankly that at least four-fifths of that class of my clients were penniless, although every one without exception, in their letters to me, promised liberal fees, and that in these cases he must expect no compensation whatever; that I must be the sole judge of their ability to pay; that I had never charged but one Confederate soldier, and that I did not intend ever to charge another; and that he must be as vigilant and prompt with these poor men as with the wealthiest blockade runner. And it was further stipulated that I was to be entirely relieved from going to the Bastile to confer with my clients—that they must be sent when I demanded, to my office, under one or more of his guards on my order for them in writing sent by one of my clerks. This was all agreed to and promptly carried out. We never had the slightest misunderstanding or disagreement. In six months I gave him $65,000. and he released for me many hundreds of Southern citizens and hundreds of Southern soldiers, and gave all who wanted them passes through the lines. . . .

A hint of the profits to be derived from "trading with the enemy, is to be found in his recital of the methods pursued in this popular and profitable pastime:

Blockade running was one of the industries of the war period. The patriotism of the Northman succumbed to his cupidity and avarice, and they swarmed on the heels of the army like the locusts of Egypt. The contagion embraced every guild of traders, from the capitalists to the man limited to a few hundred dollars . . . As soon as a city or town fell within the protection of the Federal army it was filled with competing merchants and large stocks of goods. A fleet of trading boats were anchored behind the ironclad flotilla weeks before the fall of Memphis, and they tied up at the landing before the emblem of National authority, the flag, reached the shore. Eager purchasers swarmed the decks of these boats. Vacant stores in the city were filled as soon as the merchandise could be conveyed and opened up. If a storehouse was found vacant (and four-fifths were in that condition), the eager merchant did not wait to find the owner or his representative, but was put in possession under the "Abandoned Property Act" and the rents paid to that department. Residence property was subjected to the same confiscation. The rural population soon ventured in, and either bought or subscribed to the oath of allegiance, a condition precedent to the purchase of the limited supplies permitted under military regulation. Family medicines were in great demand, $10 to $15 being paid anywhere outside of Federal lines for an ounce of quinine. Whisky commanded from $10 to $15 per gallon beyond the lines. Cloth for uniforms commanded fabulous prices.

After the occupation of the city, many dead animals had to be conveyed beyond the picket lines. Their stomachs were cut open and filled with goods, then sewed up and thus transported beyond the lines; dealers in quinine made large profits in this way before detection. The details of such operations, with Memphis as a base, would fill a large volume. Blockade runners from the North in quest of Eldorado, soon began to elbow each other. Both civilians and a few army officers were equally devoted to patriotism and commerce. This clash of pursuits and interests soon filled prisons with patriotic civilians who were anxious to pay handsomely for relief. So many came and brought with them the means to gratify their love of gain by trading with the rebels, that a military order was necessary to check this hegira South, an order to seize and confiscate all moneys being brought into territories occupied by the Federal armies.

Military developments were slow following Beauregard's retreat and the Federal occupation of Corinth. General Halleck seemed paralyzed by indecision or caution. Having concentrated an army of 120,000 men, he promptly took steps to break it up. On June 10th Pope was transferred to Virginia to try his hand against Lee, who had just crushed McClellan in the Seven Days battles around Richmond. Buell was on the 11th ordered to take off with his army in the direction of East Tennessee, along the Memphis & Charleston railroad, assigned the task of repairing the railroad as he went along, which naturally slowed his progress. Halleck remained with Grant, virtually in command of what was supposedly Grant's army, Grant describing his position as unbearable, "with a nominal command and yet no command". When Memphis was captured, he asked permission of Halleck to remove his headquarters to that city. This permission was granted, and on June 21st, accompanied by his staff and a cavalry escort, he started for Memphis, by way of LaGrange. In his *Memoirs* he tells how, after leaving LaGrange, he came with a hair's breadth of being captured:

With my staff and small escort I started at an early hour on the 23rd of June, and before noon we arrived within twenty miles of Memphis. At this point I saw a very comfortable-looking white-haired gentleman seated at the front of his house, a little distance from the road. I let my staff and escort ride on ahead while I halted and, for an excuse, asked for a glass of water. I was invited at once to dismount and come in. I found my host very genial and communicative, and stayed longer than I had intended, until the lady of the house announced dinner and asked me to join them. The host, however, was not pressing, so that I declined the invitation and, mounting my horse, rode on.

About a mile west from where I had been stopping a road comes up from the southeast, joining that from LaGrange to Memphis. A mile west of this junction I found my staff and escort halted and enjoying the shade of forest trees on the lawn of a house located several hundred feet back from the road. I too stopped, and we remained there until the cool of the afternoon, and then rode into Memphis.

The gentleman with whom I stopped twenty miles from Memphis was a Mr. DeLoche, a man loyal to the Union. He had not pressed me to tarry longer with him because in the early part of my visit a neighbor, a Dr. Smith, had called and, on being presented to me, backed off the porch as if something had hit him. Mr. DeLoche knew that the rebel General W. H. Jackson was in the neighborhood with a detachment of cavalry. His neighbor was as earnest in the Southern cause as was Mr. DeLoche in that of the Union. The exact location of Jackson was unknown to Mr. DeLoche, but he was sure that his neighbor would know it and would give information of my presence, and this made my stay unpleasant to him after the call of Dr. Smith.

A day or two after I entered Memphis I learned that Jackson was very much disappointed that he had not captured me; that he was six or seven miles south of the Memphis and Charleston railroad when he learned that I was stopping at the house of Mr. DeLoche and had ridden with his command to the junction of the road he was on with that from LaGrange and Memphis, where he learned that I had passed three-quarters of an hour before. He thought it would be useless to pursue with jaded horses a well-mounted party with so much of a start. Had he gone three-quarters of a mile farther on he would have found me with my party quietly resting under the shade of trees and without even arms in our hands with which to defend ourselves.

A day or two later Mr. DeLoche called on me in Memphis to apologize for his apparent incivility in not insisting on my staying for dinner. He said that his wife accused him of marked discourtesy, but that after the call of his neighbor he had felt restless until I got away. I never met General Jackson before the war, but have met him since at his very comfortable summer home at Manitou Springs, Colorado. I reminded him of the above incident, and this drew from him the response that he was thankful now he had not captured me. I certainly was very thankful too.

Grant's stay in Memphis was short.   On July 11 General Halleck was called
to Washington to assume supreme Federal command.   As one unfriendly Northern
critic acidly commented: "Halleck's demonstrated unfitness for his position induced the administration to find a higher position for him. . . . Unable to command successfully one army, he was ordered to Washington to command all the
armies." Grant was ordered to Corinth to replace Halleck in command of the
district of West Tennessee, and Sherman (with his three brigades and Hurlbut's
division) was sent to Memphis to replace Grant there. Sherman posted his troops
on the river-bank, in and near Fort Pickering, and undertook the task of ad-
ministering the military rule of the conquered city. He tells of some of the difficulties he encountered:

When we first entered Memphis, July 21, 1862, I found the place dead; no business doing, the stores closed, churches, schools, and every thing shut up. The people
were all more or less in sympathy with our enemies, and there was a strong prospect
that the whole civil population would become a dead weight on our hands. Inasmuch
as the Mississippi River was then in our possession northward, and steamboats were
freely plying with passengers and freight, I caused all the stores to be opened, churches,
schools, theatres, and places of amusement to be reestablished, and very soon Memphis
resumed its appearance of an active, busy, prosperous place. I also restored the mayor
(whose name was Parks) and the city government to the performance of their public
functions, and required them to maintain a good civil police.

Up to that date neither Congress nor the President had made any clear, well-
defined rules touching the negro slaves, and the different generals had issued orders
according to their own political sentiments. Both General Halleck and Grant regarded the slave as still a slave, only that the labor of the slave belonged to his
owner, if faithful to the Union, or to the United States, if the master had taken up
arms against the Government, or adhered to the fortunes of the rebellion. Therefore,
in Memphis, we received all fugitives, put them to work on the fortifications, supplied
them with food and clothing, and reserved the question of payment of wages for
future decision. No force was allowed to be used to restore a fugitive slave to his
master in any event; but if the master proved his loyalty, he was usually permitted
to see his slave, and, if he could persuade him to return home, it was permitted.

Cotton, also, was a fruitful subject of controversy. The Secretary of the Treasury,
Mr. Chase, was extremely anxious at that particular time to promote the purchase
of cotton, because each bale was worth, in gold, about three hundred dollars, and
answered the purpose of coin in our foreign exchanges. He therefore encouraged the
trade, so that hundreds of greedy speculators flocked down the Mississippi, and resorted to all sorts of measures to obtain cotton from the interior, often purchasing it
from negroes who did not own it, but who knew where it was concealed. This whole
business was taken from the jurisdiction of the military, and committed to Treasury
agents appointed by Mr. Chase.

It did not take Sherman long to recognize the magnitude of the task undertaken by the Federal government in attempting to bring the seceded states back
into the Union by military force.   Within a few weeks he wrote a frank personal
letter to Secretary Chase, expressing views that at that time were by no means
unanimously held by the Federal press and officialdom:

I will write plainly and slowly, because I know you have no time to listen to
trifles. This is no trifle. When one nation is at war with another, all the people of
the one are enemies of the other: then the rules are plain and easy of understanding.
Most unfortunately, the war in which we are now engaged has been complicated with
the belief on the one hand that all on the other are not enemies. It would have been

better if, at the outset, this mistake had not been made, and it is wrong longer to be misled by it.

The Government of the United States may now safely proceed on the proper rule that all in the South are enemies of all in the North; and not only are they unfriendly, but all who can procure arms now bear them as organized regiments, or as guerrillas. There is not a garrison in Tennessee where a man can go beyond the sight of the flagstaff without being shot or captured.

It so happened that these people had cotton, and, whenever they apprehended our large armies would move, they destroyed the cotton in the belief that, of course, we would seize it, and convert it to our use. They did not and could not dream that we would pay money for it. It had been condemned to destruction by their own acknowledged government, and was therefore lost to their people; and could have been without injustice, taken by us, and sent away, either as absolute prize of war, or for future compensation.

But the commercial enterprise of the Jews soon discovered that ten cents would buy a pound of cotton behind our army; that four cents would take it to Boston, where they would receive thirty cents in gold. The bait was too tempting, and it spread like fire, when here they discovered that salt, bacon, powder, fire-arms, percussion-caps, etc., were worth as much as gold; and, strange to say, this traffic was not only permitted, but encouraged. Before we in the interior could know it, hundreds, yes thousands of barrels of salt and millions of dollars had been disbursed; and I have no doubt that Bragg's army at Tupelo, and Van Dorn's at Vicksburg, received enough salt to make bacon, without which they could not have moved their armies in mass; and that from ten to twenty thousand fresh arms, and a due supply of cartridges, have also been got, I am equally satisfied.

As soon as I got to Memphis, having seen the effect in the interior, I ordered (only as to my command) that gold, silver, and Treasury notes were contraband of war, and should not go into the interior, where all were hostile. It is idle to talk about Union men here: many want peace, and fear war and its results; but all prefer a Southern, independent government, and are fighting or working for it. Every gold dollar that was spent for cotton was sent to the seaboard, to be exchanged for bank-notes and Confederate scrip, which will buy goods here and are taken in ordinary transactions. I therefore required cotton to be paid for in such notes, by an obligation to pay at the end of the war, or by a deposit of the price in the hands of a trustee, viz., the United States Quartermaster. Under these rules cotton is being obtained about as fast as by any other process, and yet the enemy receives no "aid or comfort." Under the "gold" rule, the country people who had concealed their cotton from the burners, and who openly scorned our greenbacks, were willing enough to take Tennessee money, which will buy their groceries; but now that the trade is to be encouraged, and gold paid out, I admit that cotton will be sent in by our open enemies, who can make better use of gold than they can of their hidden bales of cotton.

CHAPTER *7*

☆ *Post-Shiloh Interim*

BEAUREGARD WAS exceedingly bitter over the manner in which he was relieved
from the command of the army he had commanded from Shiloh to Tupelo.
He knew that Jefferson Davis was unfriendly, and he felt that Davis had
eagerly grasped this opportunity to vent his personal hostility. Beauregard, however,
had no feeling of personal resentment against his successor, Braxton Bragg, and he
corresponded with Bragg as to what method of campaign should be adopted for the
army's future activities.

When Bragg assumed command, his first official act was to issue a turgid
address to the troops, "the brave men of Shiloh and Elkhorn" (the latter reference
to include Van Dorn's men, who had finally joined up). In this address he
emphasized the advantages of discipline, and called attention to the need for
aggressive action against "an insolent but wary foe". He promised: "A few more
days of needful preparation and organization and I shall give your banners to the
breeze." He would lead them, he said to "additional honors to those you have
already won on other fields"; then he added grimly: "But be prepared to undergo
privation and labor with cheerfulness and alacrity."

Despite his brave words, Bragg was beset by numerous difficulties and un-
certainties, and was by no means sure just what course he should pursue. But,
whatever his other shortcomings, Bragg had a talent for organizing and training
troops, and while he was deliberating as to what could be done, he was hammering
his army into a disciplined, efficient fighting machine.

Meanwhile, General Halleck, with incredible ineptitude, was effectively breaking up the army of some 120,000 men of which he had assumed command after
Shiloh. As a part of this dispersal, Buell was ordered to "occupy East Tennessee",
moving along the Memphis & Charleston Railroad, repairing it as he went. By
the latter part of July Buell had arrived at Stevenson, Alabama, in a position to
menace Chattanooga, which seemed to be his immediate and logical objective.
Whatever his plans might have been, his presence in the neighborhood was
recognized by the Confederates as a serious threat. General Edmund Kirby Smith

was in command of the Confederate forces in East Tennessee, and he telegraphed Bragg at Tupelo that Buell had gone so far from his base that it seemed a propitious time to move against him.

Bragg, however, needed no prodding. He had been keeping a weather eye on Buell, and when he received Kirby Smith's suggestion he was already putting into action a plan of offensive strategy he had worked out in his own mind. He wrote a personal letter to Beauregard, explaining his plan of campaign, asking his "candid criticism" and expressing the hope that "in view of the cordial and sincere relations we have ever maintained" Beauregard would approve his plan. Describing his movement, Bragg wrote:

I am moving the army, 34,000 effectives, to East Tennessee, to join with Smith's 20,000 and take the offensive. My reasons are, Smith is so weak as to give me great uneasiness for the safety of his line—to lose which would be a great disaster. They refuse to aid him from the east or south, and put the whole responsibility on me. To aid him at all from here necessarily renders me too weak for the offensive against Halleck, with at least 60,000 strongly intrenched in my front. With the country between us reduced almost to a desert by two armies and a drought of two months, neither of us could well advance in the absence of railroad transportation. It seemed to me then, I was reduced to the defensive altogether or to the move I am making. By throwing my cavalry forward towards Grand Junction and Tuscumbia, the impression is created that I am advancing on both places, and they are drawing in to meet me. The Memphis and Charleston has been kept cut, so they have no use of it, and have at length given it up. Before they can know of my movement, I shall be in front of Buell at Chattanooga and, by cutting off his transportation, may have him in a tight place. Van Dorn will be able to hold his own with about 20,000 on the Mississippi. Price stays here with 16,000. I leave tomorrow for Mobile, thence to Chattanooga. Our cavalry is paving the way for me in Middle Tennessee and Kentucky.

Beauregard replied to Bragg's letter, agreeing that an offensive was the indicated strategy for the Confederate forces. He concluded his letter by saying: "I am happy to see that my two lieutenants, Morgan and Forrest, are doing such good service in Kentucky and Tennessee. When I appointed them I thought they would leave their mark wherever they passed."

Bragg's statement that "Our cavalry is paving the way for me in Middle Tennessee and Kentucky" was no mere perfunctory compliment. The energy of Morgan and Forrest, foreshadowing their later greatness, had hampered and bewildered the Federals to such a point as almost to paralyze them, and Beauregard's expression of pride in their demonstration of their prowess was thoroughly justified. After his retreat from Corinth to Tupelo, and before he was succeeded in command of the army by Bragg, he had taken the action which at the time seemed of relatively minor importance but which thrust into positions of great effectiveness these two men who were to write their names high on the pages of the history of the Civil War.

John Hunt Morgan, as a Kentucky cavalry captain, had attracted favorable attention on the retreat of the Confederate forces from Bowling Green through Nashville to Murfreesboro and subsequently in the battle of Shiloh. After falling back to Tupelo, Beauregard increased Morgan's command to four companies, with authorization to recruit a brigade if possible. He also directed the Army Quartermaster to provide Morgan with $15,000, with the explanation that Morgan was starting on "an important military expedition beyond the Tennessee."

Nathan Bedford Forrest, as one of Beauregard's last official acts, had been recommended for promotion to the rank of brigadier general and assigned to the command of cavalry regiments under independent commanders then operating in eastern Tennessee.

On July 6th Forrest left Chattanooga with about 1000 men, headed for Middle Tennessee. Buell had his eyes on McMinnville as a strategic point between Nashville and Chattanooga, and had collected at Murfreesboro a brigade of 1,750 men which was intended to occupy McMinnville. On July 13th (his 41st birthday) Forrest swooped down on Murfreesboro in an audacious dash and captured the entire force, including all its officers and its commander, General T. T. Crittenden, together with stores valued at almost a million dollars.

The various outfits making up the Federal force at Murfreesboro had not yet been consolidated into a unified command and were camped in widely separated locations on the outskirts of the town. Forrest divided his attacking force into separate detachments to assail the Federal camps, while he with a small body of his troops charged into the public square and surrounded the court-house, the jail and the hotel where General Crittenden made his headquarters. Crittenden and his staff were quickly bagged, and the attacking troopers turned their attention to the jail, which was crowded with military and political prisoners, six of whom were under sentence of death. Among the latter was a Confederate officer, Captain William Richardson, falsely accused as a spy, who was to be executed at sunrise. In later years he wrote of his hair-breadth deliverance:

Just about daylight on the morning of the 13th I was aroused from sleep by my companion, who had caught me by the arm and was shaking me, saying, "Listen! listen!" I started up, hearing a strange noise like the roar of an approaching storm. We both leaped to our feet and stood upon an empty box, which had been given us in lieu of a chair, and looked out through the small grating of our prison window. The roar grew louder and came nearer, and in a very few seconds we were sure we could discern the clatter of horses' feet upon the hard turnpike. In a moment more there could be no doubt as to the riders of these horses, for on the morning air there came to our ears with heartfelt welcome the famous rebel yell, the battle-cry of the Confederate soldiers. Almost before we could speak, the advance-guard of the charging troopers came into sight and rushed by us on the street, some halting in front of the jail.

Within the prison yard one company of Federal troops had been stationed, and seeing they were about to be surrounded by the Confederates and that our rescue was sure, several of these soldiers in wicked mood rushed into the passageway in front of our cell and attempted to shoot us before they ran from the building. We only saved ourselves by running forward and crouching in the corner of the cell by the door, a position upon which they could not bring their guns to bear. Before leaving the jail one of the Federal guards struck a match and, lighting a bundle of papers, shoved this beneath the flooring of the hall-way where the planks were loose and, to our horror, we realized that he was determined to burn us to death before the rescuing party could break open the door When the Southern riders reached us the fire was already under good headway, and the jailer had fled with the keys. It seemed as if we were still doomed. The metal doors were heavy, and it was not until some of our men came in with a heavy iron bar that the grating was bent back sufficiently at the lower corner to permit us to be dragged through as we laid flat upon the floor.

At this moment Forrest dashed up and inquired of the officer in charge if he had rescued the prisoners. He said they were safe, but added that the jail had been set on fire to burn them up, and the guard had taken refuge in the court house. Forrest said, "Never mind, we'll get them". I shall never forget the appearance of General Forrest on that occasion: his eyes were flashing as if on fire, his face was flushed, and he seemed in a condition of great excitement. To me he was the ideal of a warrior. . . . After the fighting had ceased and the Federal prisoners were all brought together, General Forrest came to me and said: "They tell me these men treated you inhumanly while in jail. Point them out to me." I told him there was but one man I wished to call his attention to, and that was the one who had set fire to the jail in order to burn us up. Forrest asked me to go along the line with him and point that man out. I did so. A few hours later, when the list of the private soldiers was being called, the name of this man was heard and no one answered. Forrest said, "Pass on, it's all right."

General Buell at Huntsville was immediately notified of Forrest's swoop on Murfreesboro, and he was much upset by the news. It was feared that Forrest would next move on Nashville, and Buell hastened reinforcements to that point under General Nelson, with orders to re-take Murfreesboro and McMinnville. Buell also telegraphed the bad news to General Halleck, saying that "The worst feature of Forrest's attack was the interruption of the Chattanooga railroad, just completed . . . A large portion of the 50,000 rations of forage forwarded to Murfreesboro have been captured or burned." The raid, he said, "has caused serious delay in the means of supplying the army so that it can move on the Decatur route. The force (at Murfreesboro) was more than sufficient to repeal the attack. Take it in all its features, few more disgraceful examples can be found in the history of our war."

Forrest was informed of Nelson's advance, but, giving thus early evidence of that enterprising audacity which characterized his military career, instead of re-treating to safety, he swept around in Nelson's rear and destroyed four of the bridges between him and Nashville. Forrest got so close to Nashville that Military Governor Andrew Johnson grew panicky. He magnified the raid into an attempt to capture the city, and ordered that it be promptly and strongly fortified. For his personal protection he had the State Capitol ringed about with a stout palisade of timbers and breastworks of cotton-bales protecting artillery emplacements, with an infantry guard camped on the Capitol grounds and within the building.

Forrest, of course, with his meagre force had no serious intention of attempting to capture Nashville, but he continued to hover around the outskirts of the city, with occasional hostile demonstrations sufficient to keep the Federals in a state of acute anxiety. Being informed that there was a force of 500 Federal cavalry stationed at Lebanon, he conceived the idea of surprising and capturing them, and by a forced march reached the suburbs of the town early in the morning of the 20th. Colonel Jordan tells the story of this typically Forrestesque action:

Making all necessary dispositions at once for the occasion, he dashed with his now confident command into the place, but had the keen disappointment to see that his enemy had been forewarned and was leaving at full speed by the Nashville road with such a start as to make pursuit fruitless. Posting pickets on all the approaches, so to guard against the possibility of a surprise, Forrest remained with his command in observation at Lebanon until the next morning, the recipients meanwhile of unbounded hospitality from the open-handed people of the place and neighborhood. His men were not only fed, during their stay, upon poultry, choice hams and roasted pigs, but more than three days' rations of these danities were supplied spontaneously for the march.

After leaving Lebanon, the line of march brought the command, about 1 P.M., to the Hermitage—in his lifetime the favorite home and in death the burial place of the illustrious Jackson. The Confederate leader, halting here, gave his men an hour to visit the precincts redolent with martial memories of peculiar interest and value to the young men of his brigade, and well calculated to influence them "To matchless valor and adventures high". And here, too, a pleasant incident served to brighten the wearisome and perilous routine of the expedition. A party of ten or twelve young ladies, escorted by a few gentlemen, appeared upon the scene to celebrate in its groves the first anniversary of the battle of Manassas and at the same time do honor to the tomb and fame of the great Tennessean. With these charming daughters of the neighborhood the moments sped pleasantly and with happy effect upon their young countrymen.

Soon after leaving the Hermitage, going in the direction of Nashville, Forrest's scouts informed him that General Nelson with a force of 3,500 men had left Nashville for Murfreesboro in pursuit of him. This was just the kind of situation Forrest relished. After charging and capturing part of the pickets on the Lebanon road outside Nashville, he crossed on a by-lane to the Murfreesboro pike where he drove in the pickets on that road, attacking with such vigor and uproar that the Federals in Nashville thought a serious attack was impending. "The long roll and other signals of alarm were to be heard on all sides", Jordan relates. After burning a few bridges and capturing some scattered outposts, Forrest was informed that Nelson, hearing the firing, was retracing his steps on the Murfreesboro pike and was drawing near. Forrest withdrew his command to a position on a by-road then known as the Chicken Pike, and went into camp in a woodsy location from which it was possible to hear Nelson's men marching back to Nashville on the turnpike.

The next morning Forrest and his force started on their way back in the direction of Murfreesboro. Nelson, as soon as he learned of this, again staged a counter-march in pursuit. Forrest turned off in the direction of McMinnville and, in the words of Colonel Jordan: "Nelson, finding his adversary out of his reach and his own infantry thoroughly footsore and fatigued, gave up the operation as useless, expressing his disgust in energetic terms, and denouncing the folly of attempting to catch cavalry with infantry."

Meanwhile Morgan's "important military expedition" got off to a bad start, with an unsuccessful brush with the enemy at Lebanon. He proceeded to Knoxville, however, where he got together a force of about 800 men and staged a sensational raid into Kenutcky, which created great alarm among the Federals in that area. He was back in Tennessee early in August, having marched over a thousand miles in 24 days, captured and paroled 1,200 prisoners, and lost less than a hundred of his own men, killed and wounded.

Later in August Morgan went on the rampage again in Tennessee, north of Nashville, and on the 22nd captured Gallatin and its garrison. Most important, he destroyed several of the railroad bridges and the tunnel between Gallatin and Nashville, thus shutting off the shipment of supplies from Louisville for several weeks. Buell sent a force of cavalry under General R. W. Johnson to drive Morgan out of Tennessee, but Morgan met it on the outskirts of Gallatin on the morning of August 21st and administered a stinging defeat. Summarizing the results of this action in his official report, Morgan proudly said:

My command, not exceeding 700 men, succeeded in defeating a brigade of 1,200 chosen cavalry, sent by General Buell expressly to take me or drive me out of Tennessee, killing and wounding some 180 and taking 200 prisoners, including the brigadier general (Johnson) commanding, and a greater part of the regimental officers. My loss amounted to five killed, eighteen wounded and two missing.

Following this affray, Morgan established his temporary headquarters at Hartsville, a few miles north east of Gallatin, where he rested and recruited his command, until he was ordered to join General Kirby Smith in Kentucky, in September.

An interesting and novel by-product of the stay of Morgan's men in Hartsville before the battle at Gallatin was the launching of the *Vidette,* a publication which became a sort of "house organ" of Morgan's command, issued at irregular intervals and at various locations between raids. Colonel Duke (with a suggestion of tongue-in-cheek) tells of the brief but brilliant life of this unique publication:

While we were at Hartsville a case of types and a printing press had been found in the deserted room once occupied as a printing office, and were immediately put to use. Poor Niles, who had once been an editor, went to work and organized a corps of assistants from among the practical printers, of whom there were several in the Second Kentucky, and issued a small sheet which he called the *Vidette.* It was conducted after his death by Captain Alston.

It was printed on any sort of paper that could be procured and consequently, although perfectly consistent in its politics, it appeared at different times in different colors. Sometimes it would be a drab, sometimes a pale rose color, and my recollection is that Boone's surrender (at Gallatin) was recorded upon a page of delicate pea-green. Colonel Morgan, finding the pleasure it gave the men, took great pains to promote the enterprise.

The *Vidette* was expected with as much interest by the soldiers and country people as the *Tribune* by the reading public of New York. General orders were published in it, promotions announced, and complimentary notices made by Colonel Morgan of the deserving. Full accounts of all our operations were published, and the reports of the various scouting parties filled up the column devoted to "local news". The editors indulged in the most profound and brilliant speculations on the political future, and got off the ablest critiques upon the conduct of the war. As every thing "good" was published, some tremendous and overwhelmingly descisive Confederate victories, of which the official records make no mention even by name, were described in the *Vidette,* and the horrors of Federal invasion were depicted in terms which made the citizen reader's blood freeze in his veins.

While Forrest and Morgan were so effectively "paving the way" for Bragg's advance into Tennessee and Kentucky, he was actively proceeding with preparations for that movement. Bragg's course bristled with complications, involving as it did the longest march of the largest troop movement during the entire war. Aside from the basically important and vexing problems of transportation and subsistence, a further difficulty was imposed by the fact that he was contemplating operations in a section officially under the jurisdiction of General Edmund Kirby Smith. General Smith was a seasoned soldier, a graduate of West Point, and he had served with the Confederate army in Virginia before being given command of the "Department of East Tennessee, North Georgia and Northwest Carolina" in February 1862, with headquarters at Knoxville.

The advance of Bragg's army reached Chattanooga on July 24th, and Bragg himself got there on the 29th. Smith went to Chattanooga from Knoxville to confer with Bragg, and Bragg reported to General Samuel Cooper in Richmond that they had "arranged measures for mutual support and effective cooperation." It appears that each made an honest attempt to carry out these measures, Smith gracefully waiving any claims to precedence he might have in East Tennessee; but the promised "effective cooperation" did not work out very satisfactorily.

The plan of operation agreed upon, as reported to General Cooper on August 1st, was for Kirby Smith to move at once from Knoxville against General George

W. Morgan's Federal force at Cumberland Gap, while Bragg waited at Chattanooga for the rest of his trains to come up. If Kirby Smith was successful at Cumberland Gap, Bragg said, they would join forces and go into Middle Tennessee "with the fairest prospect of cutting off General Buell".

It now seems plain that at this time Bragg had no intention of launching an expedition into Kentucky, his whole concern being the driving out of Buell and the redemption of Middle Tennessee. Ten days later, Bragg wrote to Kirby Smith that it would be a week before he could start his movement from Chattanooga, going on to say: "Information I hope to receive will determine which route I shall take—to Nashville or Lexington [Kentucky]. My inclination now is to the latter." The next day he wrote to General Price, back in Mississippi: "As soon as my transportation comes up, we shall move into Middle Tennessee and, taking the enemy's rear, strike Nashville or, perhaps, leaving that to the left, strike for Lexington and Cincinnati, both of which are entirely unprotected."

It was a brilliantly conceived campaign, and it started off successfully enough in its execution. Kirby Smith started from Knoxville on August 14th. He turned the Federal position at Cumberland Gap, leaving about half of his force there to invest that stronghold, and then struck across the mountains into Kentucky. At Richmond on August 30th he was confronted with a force of about 6,000 Federals under General Nelson; but this force, thanks largely to the brilliant work of General Patrick R. Cleburne, was given a destructively severe drubbing, entirely eliminating it as an effective fighting unit. Nelson's official report of his casualties was 206 killed, 844 wounded and 4,303 captured; with the loss of all his wagon trains and supplies, nine pieces of artillery and 10,000 stand of small arms. The Confederate loss was 78 killed, 372 wounded and 1 missing.

With practically all organized opposition eliminated, Kirby Smith swept on to Lexington where he remained in virtual control of central Kentucky through the entire month of September, making occasional cavalry raids northward to the environs of Louisville and Cincinnati.

Bragg began his forward march from Chattanooga on August 28th, with his army of 27,816 officers and men divided into two wings, the right under General Leonidas Polk and the left under General Hardee. Buell had a much larger force than Bragg (variously estimated in different official reports at from 45,000 to 59,000), but he had a wholesome respect for his opponent's ability, and he went cautiously about interposing his force between Bragg and Nashville.

When Bragg started out from Chattanooga, Buell's right was at Stevenson, his center at Decherd on the Nashville-Chattanooga railroad, and his left at McMinnville. He had a strong force in observation at Altamont, but Wheeler drove them out when Bragg started forward. Buell then ordered a concentration at Murfreesboro, but when he arrived there he received the disquieting news of Nelson's crushing defeat at Richmond, and so he marched his whole army into Nashville and prepared to defend it against the attack he thought was coming. Meanwhile Bragg was advancing northward across Tennessee—up through the Sequatchie Valley, through Pikeville to Sparta, then on to Carthage and Gainesboro on the Cumberland River. On the march he too had learned of Nelson's destruction by Kirby Smith, who wrote urging Bragg "to move into Kentucky and, effecting a junction with my command and holding Buell's communications, to give battle to him with superior forces and with certainty of success." Bragg, apparently influenced by this advice, advanced in the direction of Glasgow, Kentucky, where, he later said, he hoped to join Kirby Smith and gain such a decisive victory over the Federal forces as would attract the enlistment of pro-Southern Kentuckians and give him strength for further conquest.

It did not take Buell long to sense the crystallization of Bragg's plans for the Kentucky invasion, and he promptly set out for Louisville with most of his army, leaving only 6,000 men under General James S. Negley to hold Nashville. While Buell was advancing, Bragg moved on to Munfordville, where he captured the Federal fort and garrison of 5,000, with all its stores, artillery and small arms.

These initial successes by Kirby Smith and Bragg, coming almost simultaneously with Lee's victory over Pope in Virginia at Second Manassas, naturally threw the whole Confederacy into a state of the most intense elation. It marked the high water mark of Confederate offensive military operations. But Lee's invasion of Maryland following his victory at Manassas proved unsuccessful; and Bragg's Kentucky campaign after its auspicious start, inexplicably fizzled.

Everybody expected Bragg to have Kirby Smith's army joined with his and give battle, probably successfully, to Buell—but there was no battle. "Here," General Basil Duke says, "was the first exhibition of that vacillation, that fatal irresolution, which was to wither the bright hopes his promises and his previous action and aroused"; and Duke goes on to lament "the strange contrast exhibited by the nerve and purpose of his plan and the timidity and vacillation of his conduct." Anyhow, Bragg, for reasons which have never appeared sound or convincing, decided to march on to Bardstown without further contesting Buell's advance to Louisville. During Buell's march his right flank was, of course, dangerously exposed, but Bragg surprisingly made no effort to seize the inviting opportunity to strike a damaging blow to his adversary.

From then on, Bragg's Kentucky campaign was one succession of anti-climaxes, marked by confusion, overlooked opportunities and indecision. Buell, after strengthening and refreshing his army at Louisville, moved out of that city on October 1 to offer Bragg battle at Bardstown. Bragg, however, was not at Bardstown; he was in Frankfort (the state capital) preparing to stage elaborate ceremonies inaugurating Richard Hawes as Provisional Governor of Kentucky under the Confederate government. The ceremonies got under way on October 2, but Hawes was interrupted in the midst of his inaugural address by the sound of Federal shells bursting in the city, and Bragg was forced to turn from political to military activities.

The next few days were, for both Federals and Confederates, a nightmare of marching and counter-marching, orders and rescinded orders, misunderstandings and recriminations, with elements of both armies badly scattered and considerably confused. On October 8th a part of Bragg's army was at length brought face to face with a part of Buell's army at Perryville. Here was fought a ferociously contested battle, with some of the most desperate hand-to-hand fighting of the whole war, with heavy losses on both sides. The outcome was considered a definite victory for the Confederates, and Bragg's men expected to renew the battle the next morning, confident of continuing to drive Buell's forces before them. But Bragg, to the amazement of the Federals, and to the distress of his own generals, decided not to follow up his victory but to abandon further prosecution of the campaign that had started out so promisingly and to carry his army back to Tennessee with its avowed mission unaccomplished.

The retreat from Kentucky was a dismal but picturesque affair. A brigade of cavalry led the way, followed by great herds of beef cattle, sheep and hogs, driven along the road by shouting cowboys and herders, recruited from the ranks of the Texas cavalry regiments.   There was a long caravan of refugees and their families, with carriages, stage-coaches, omnibuses and farm wagons piled with household furniture strung out down the road for miles.   Trains of army wagons, heavily loaded down with captured provisions, firearms, ammunition and merchandise, creaked along. Conspicuous among them were the 4,000 shiny new wagons, with the U.S. brands on their canvas, which Kirby Smith had captured from Nelson.   The route was by way of Crab Orchard, Lebanon and Barboursville to Cumberland Gap, then on to Morristown and Knoxville in East Tennessee.   Buell kept up the semblance of a pursuit for a short while, but soon abandoned the chase and took steps to transfer his army back to Nashville in anticipation of Bragg's ultimate move against that city.

After the pursuit had been abandoned, Bragg's retreating army settled down to its march with no greater obstacles than rocky roads (mighty hard on barefoot soldiers whose shoes had been marched into shreds), deep fords and steep mountain passes.   But, footsore and defeated though they were, the elan of the army was indestructible, as is evidenced by Sam Watkins' light-hearted recollections of that memorable march:

Along the route it was nothing but tramp, tramp, tramp, and no sound or noise but the same inevitable, monotonous tramp, tramp, tramp, up hill and down hill, through long and dusty lanes, weary, worn out and hungry. No cheerful warble of a merry songster would ever greet our ears. It was always tramp, tramp, tramp. You might, every now and then, hear the occasional command, "Close up!" but outside of that, it was but the same tramp, tramp, tramp. I have seen soldiers fast asleep, and no doubt dreaming of home and loved ones there, as they staggered along in their places in the ranks. I know that on many a weary night's march I have slept, and slept soundly, while marching along in my proper place in the ranks of the company, stepping to the same step as the soldier in front of me did.

Sometimes, when weary, broken down and worn out, some member of the regiment would start a tune, and every man would join in. John Branch was usually the leader of the choir. . . . He would commence on a lively, spirit-stirring air to the tune of "Old Uncle Ned."   Now, reader, it has been twenty years ago since I heard it, but I can remember a part of it now. Here it is:

"There was an ancient individual whose cognomen was Uncle Edward.
He departed this life long since, long since.
He had no capillary substance on the top of his cranium,
The place where the capillary substance ought to vegetate.

His digits were as long as the bamboo piscatorial implement of the
    Southern Mississippi.
He had no oculars to observe the beauties of nature.
He had no ossified formation to masticate his daily rations,
So he had to let his daily rations pass by with impunity."

Walker Coleman raises the tune of "I'se a gwine to jine the rebel band, a fightin' for my home." That is all I can now remember of that very beautiful and soul-stirring air. But the boys would wake up and step quicker and livelier for some time, and Arthur Fulghum would holloa out, "All right; go ahead!" and then would: "Toot! toot!" as if the cars were starting, "Puff! puff!" and then he would say, "Tickets, gentlemen, tickets, gentlemen," like he was a conductor on a train of cars.

This little episode would be over, and then would commence the same tramp,

tramp, tramp, all night long. Step by step, step by step, we continued to plod and nod and stagger and march—tramp, tramp, tramp. After a while we would see the morning star rise in the east, and then after a while the dim gray twilight, and finally we could discover the outlines of our file leader, and after a while could make out the outlines of trees and other objects. And as it would get lighter and lighter, and day would be about to break; "Cuckoo, cuckoo, cuckoo," would come from Tom Tuck's rooster. (Tom carried a game rooster, that he called "Fed" for Confederacy, all through the war in a haversack.) And then the sun would begin to shoot his slender rays athwart the eastern sky, and the boys would wake up and begin laughing and talking as if they had just risen from a good feather bed, and were perfectly refreshed and happy.

We would usually stop at some branch or other about breakfast time, and all wash our hands and faces and eat breakfast, if we had any, and then commence our weary march again. If we were halted for one minute, every soldier would drop down and, resting on his knapsack, would go to sleep. Sometimes the sleeping soldiers were made to get up to let some General and his staff pass by. But whenever that was the case, the General always got a worse cursing than when Noah cursed his son Ham black and blue.

The outcome of Bragg's Kentucky campaign was, like the battle of Shiloh, unsatisfactory to both sides. Bragg's failure to capitalize on the strong strategic position he achieved and then let slip through his fingers caused outspoken complaint against his generalship among the people of the Confederacy and also among his subordinate generals. Recognizing this, as soon as he had his army safely back in Tennessee Bragg went to Richmond to make a personal report to President Davis. In his talks with Davis he fastened the blame for his failure on General Polk. Polk, Bragg said, had not obeyed orders. Anything that Bragg said was generally accepted at face value by Davis, but Polk also was a favorite of his, and he was not willing to condemn Polk without hearing his side. Polk accordingly was summoned to Richmond, and he obeyed with alacrity.

Davis subjected Polk to something like a cross-examination, and Polk gave blunt answers to his old school-mate's blunt questions. Generously according Bragg all proper credit for his skill as an organizer and disciplinarian, Polk expressed the candid opinion that Bragg was "wanting in the higher elements of generalship." Polk said flatly that the campaign had been a failure, that both Kirby Smith and Hardee thought so, and that Bragg had lost the confidence of his generals.

That Bragg's criticism of Polk had not undermined him in the President's esteem was demonstrated by Polk's promotion to the rank of lieutenant general, and similar promotions were given to Hardee and Kirby Smith. Kirby Smith, upon his return to Tennessee, had asked Davis to relieve him of any further service in which he would be subject to Bragg's orders, the outcome of which was that within a few months he was designated to command the Trans-Mississippi department, after some of his troops had been transferred to Bragg's command.

On the Federal side there was bitter criticism of General Buell's conduct of the Kentucky campaign. Both Abraham Lincoln and Andrew Johnson were strongly antagonistic to Buell; so it was little surprise to him when, as he was moving his army back in the direction of Nashville, he received on October 30th an order from Washington to turn his command over to General William S. Rosecrans, who had attracted the attention of the Federal high command by his successes in Mississippi.

For a while a similar fate seemed about to overtake Bragg, but President Davis was stubbornly reluctant to believe him as incompetent as his many critics claimed. Davis therefore adopted the halfway remedial measure of appointing General Joseph E. Johnston department commander, with supervision over the commands of both Bragg and Kirby Smith and also over General Pemberton at Vicksburg. Johnston recognized this as a practically impossible assignment, but he reluctantly accepted and left Virginia for Chattanooga.

Bragg's force, upon its return to Tennessee, went first to Knoxville, then to Chattanooga and from there to Shelbyville. Forrest, who had accompanied the army into Kentucky, had been sent back to Tennessee before the battle of Perryville with orders to establish headquarters at Murfreesboro and organize the scattered cavalry commands in that area. Later General John C. Breckinridge was sent to Murfreesboro with his infantry division; and, still later, Bragg moved up from Shelbyville to Murfreesboro and established the army headquarters there.

Before General Bragg got to Murfreesboro, General Breckinridge had conceived the idea of staging a noisy demonstration against the Federals in Nashville, primarily as a show of force, and not with any actual expectation of capturing the city. The attacking force consisted of the cavalry commands of Forrest and Morgan, acting independently, supported by an infantry brigade under General Hanson. This affray was not a military operation of great proportions; but it is interesting to read the accounts of it written by participants on both sides. These accounts are so greatly at variance, it is hard to realize that they all refer to the same action.

Basil Duke writes from the viewpoint of Morgan's attacking force, in which Duke was a leading spirit:

Breckinridge was desirous of impressing the enemy at Nashville with an exaggerated idea of his strength, so that the army of Rosecrans might not be in any too great haste to drive him away when it reached Nashville. General Bragg was limping on so slowly that it was by no means certain that a swinging march (by the Federals) would not put the enemy in possession of the whole of Middle Tennessee (with scarcely a skirmish) and shut Bragg up in East Tennessee. With the instinct, too, which he felt in common with all men who are born soldiers, Breckinridge wished to press upon the enemy and strike him if he discovered a vulnerable point.

He learned that a large lot of rolling-stock (of the Louisville and Nashville Railroad), had been collected in Edgefield (across the river from Nashville). There were, perhaps, three hundred cars in all. If these were burned, the damage done the enemy and the delay occasioned him would be very great. The cars were collected at a locality commanded by the batteries on the Capitol hill, and so near the river that all the forces in the city could be readily used to protect them. Breckinridge depended upon Morgan to burn them, but planned a diversion on the south side of the river which he hoped would attract the enemy's attention strongly and long enough to enable Morgan to do his work.

The day after we arrived at Gallatin a dispatch was received from General Breckinridge, communicating his plan. Forrest was to move on the southeastern side of Nashville, supported by the Kentucky infantry brigade [Hanson's], and Morgan was instructed to dash into Edgefield and burn the cars while Forrest was making his feigned attack.

Our brigade moved all night (of the 5th) and striking through the woods came upon the northern side of Edgefield. Just as we struck the pickets, we heard Forrest's guns on the other side of the river. The Second Kentucky was in advance, and as the head of the column was struggling over a very rough place in the railroad it was opened upon by a company of infantry pickets, who came out from behind a small house about sixty yards off. I never saw men fight better than these fellows did. They were forty or fifty strong and had to retreat about half a mile to reach their lines. The timber of the ground over which they had to retreat had been cut down to leave the way clear for the play of artillery and we could not charge them. Few men beside those in the advance guard got a chance at them. They turned and fought at every step. At least eight or ten were killed, and only three captured. I lost three of my advance guard. . . .

We pressed on to within a hundred yards of the railroad embankment in the bottom near the river, and quiet through Edgefield. Some little time was required to get all the regiment up, and Hutchinson and I had just formed it and the line was advancing when Colonel Morgan ordered us back. He had reconnoitered, and had seen a strong force of infantry behind the embankment; and the fire slackening on the other side induced him to suppose that more infantry, which we could see double-quicking across the pontoon bridge was the entire garrison of that side coming to oppose him. It turned out that the force coming over the bridge was small, but the Sixteenth Illinois and part of another regiment were stationed behind the embankment and among the cars we wished to burn. We succeeded in burning a few. A good deal of firing was kept up by the enemy upon the detail engaged in the work of destruction, but without effect.

So little attention was paid to what Forrest was doing that when we drew off altogether, the enemy followed us a mile or two. As the column filed off from the by-road (by which it had approached Edgefield) on to the Gallatin pike, the enemy drove back the pickets which had been sent down the pike.

Colonel Jordan, of Forrest's staff, gives this spirited account of what General Duke called Forrest's feigned attack—and, incidentally, does not mention that Morgan's men were involved in the affair:

The movement of General Bragg had completely isolated the Federal force at Nashville from all available support or relief, and, knowing that force to be weak, General Forrest now proposed to his superior to attack it in concert with Hanson's infantry. General Breckinridge giving his assent, the plan of attack was duly arranged for the 6th of November.

As the greater portion of his men were raw and Tennesseans, Forrest thought it expedient to explain to them beforehand what he proposed to attempt, and to invoke a sturdy, resolute effort to recover their state capitol from the hands of invaders. The effect was evidently good, for an admirable spirit was clearly dominant. At the time appointed, all needful preliminaries having been arranged, the troops, distributed in columns, moving by the Franklin, Charlotte, Nolensville and Murfreesboro turnpikes, were pushed forward in close proximity to the city, driving the Federal pickets and cavalry back behind their works. Forrest at the head of about one thousand cavalry, moving on the Murfreesboro road, supported closely by Hanson, was at the Lunatic Asylum—six miles from the heart of Nashville—by daylight. The rifle-pits in advance in this quarter were speedily carried, and, Hanson having become eager to engage his men, the main attack was ordered. It was now about sunrise; the utmost confidence animated both infantry and cavalry, and in a few moments the assault would have been essayed, when an order was received from General Breckinridge countermanding the operation, under express instructions from General Bragg. Hanson was therefore counter-marched to LaVergne.

However, leaving a squadron to picket that approach, Forrest moved the remainder of his immediate force across to the Nolensville turnpike where Dibrell was in position skirmishing with the Federals, who were in their works in his front. Here ascertaining that a strong Federal force was outside of the lines on the Franklin road in front of Starnes, taking Dibrell's regiment and Gunter's battalion, with Freeman's artillery,

General Forrest moved across and was soon engaged in an animated skirmish with the main Federal force, artillery being freely used on both sides at very short range. The Eighth Tennessee was here brought to its first charge, and executed it so handsomely, in the teeth of two infantry regiments firing from behind a fence, that the Federals retired rapidly in rear of their works. In this affair Freeman's artillery, actively employed, gave earnest of its future brilliant services. Shot and shell plowed the ground and covered his gunners, while fragments of shell were scattered among the guns and carriages, killing and crippling a number of horses. For a time, in fact, it seemed that the battery would be destroyed; but all stood staunchly at their posts, and plied their pieces with coolness, and so skillfully as to make this battery thenceforward a favorite both with the General and his men.

In obedience to the orders of his superiors—leaving Dibrell to hold and observe the Nolensville pike, Starnes the Franklin and Morgan the Murfreesboro highway— Forrest now retired to LaVergne, deeply chagrined that he had been forced, by orders given at such a distance from the threatre of operations, to abandon an enterprise the success of which he was satisfied was almost an absolute certainty.

The recovery of Nashville at that juncture was so clearly fraught with moral, political and military advantages that those charged with the general conduct of military affairs at Richmond surely ought to have initiated measures to insure the operation. . . . It was one of those numerous occasions to seize patent opportunities which, in the study of this war hereafter, will amaze and puzzle the military student and, indeed, all thoughtful readers.

After these somewhat divergent accounts of this action by two of the Confederate participants, it is interesting to read an account of it from the Federal standpoint, written by John Fitch, provost judge of the Federal Army of the Cumberland:

The rebel forces concentrated at Murfreesborough to operate against Nashville were under the command of Major General John C. Breckinridge. He had succeeded in accumulating about five thousand infantry, an unknown force of cavalry, and a large amount of artillery, principally of a heavy character, and on November 5 made an attack on the city with his cavalry. At two o'clock on the morning of the 5th, Forrest, with three thousand men and four pieces of artillery, opened fire on our pickets on the Lebanon and Murfreesborough roads, driving them in—they, in accordance with orders, making but feeble resistance, General Negley indulging in the hope of drawing the enemy under the fire of the forts.

About the same hour a similar cavalry force under Morgan, two thousand five hundred strong, with one gun, attacked the works on the north side of the river, defending the approaches to the railroad and pontoon bridges, to destroy which was probably their purpose. The forces holding these defences quickly and gallantly repulsed the enemy; while about the same time, the guns of Fort Negley opening on Forrest, his forces were dispersed and driven back. The enemy, however, soon rallid on the south, and took position with their cavalry and infantry a little beyond the original picket-line. Colonel Roberts, with two regiments of infantry and one section of artillery, advanced on the Murfreesborough road, while General Negley, with the 69th Ohio, 78th Pennsylvania, 14th Michigan, and a cavalry force, marched out on the Franklin road, quickly driving the enemy from their position there, who then fell back, closely pursued, seven miles from the city. At this point Colonel Stoke's Tennessee Cavalry was ordered to charge the rear of the retreating rebels; but their main body had succeeded in making a detour to the left and, in the excitement of the charge, the cavalry and infantry pursued a small force in the direction of Franklin.

The enemy, with the view to cut off Negley from the city, soon appeared in his rear with the force making the detour, and planted a battery near the road. On learning of this movement, General Negley changed front and advanced on the enemy in their new position. The artillery was soon got into action, and the battery of the rebels was disabled—shortly after which they retired in confusion, with heavy loss. It was soon after ascertained that the enemy, greatly outnumbering our forces, were about to make a charge with cavalry on Negley's flanks; and he slowly retired towards the city and to more favorable ground. Stokes's cavalry were so disposed as to divert the expected charge upon the rear; and the 14th Michigan was stationed in such manner that when the charge came the enemy were received with so destructive a fire that they were driven back in great disorder.

They then attempted to plant their artillery on the turnpike, but were driven from that position before the guns could be discharged. General Negley still continued to retire towards the city, the enemy making one more effort to get in his rear. In this attempt they were completely foiled by the reserve force, which had been ordered forward.

Colonel Roberts on the Murfreesborough road met with equal success, and drove the enemy back in confusion.

On the following day the advance of the Army of the Cumberland appeared at Nashville, and the famous siege was raised.

The first elements of Rosecran's army reached Nashville the morning of November 7th. Rosecrans himself, accompanied by his staff, left Bowling Green on the morning of the 10th on a special train that carried them as far as Mitchellsville. Here the railroad services ended, due to the depredations of Morgan's cavalry, and the general and his party, accompanied by a squadron of cavalry, left the cars and mounted horses for the forty-mile ride to Nashville. The war correspondent of the Cincinnati *Commercial,* accompanying the cavalcade, tells of its progress:

The first acre of Tennessee soil betrayed the ruthless track of war. Fallow fields were spread out before the vision, and the voice of the planter was not needed to prove that the peaceful plowshare had been transformed into the biting sword. Fences had been absorbed in campfires; the click of the old mill wheel had ceased; broken windows and shattered frames stared from deserted homesteads and charred chimneys begrimed with smokestains stood in stark solitude in the bosom of deflowered gardens and blistered groves—painful monuments of rebellion and grim pictures of its bitter fruits. Ravage and desolation everywhere. There were no little children gamboling on cabin thresholds. Hardly a dog barked at the rattling cavalcade. Now and then a woe-stricken woman peered sadly through a broken window-pane. Yonder, a rugged and ragged and wretched man in butternut jeans, clinging with the resolution of desperation to the last rafter of the dear old homestead, scowled ferociously at the passing strangers in his country's uniform.

But, as if deliberate purpose had not afflicted the land with fell visitation, carelessness and chance were now aggravating havoc. Idle soldiers or heedless teamsters kindling bivouac fires among the dry leaves of autumn, had communicated flames to the forests, and consuming conflagrations were streaming like whirlwinds through their brittle branches. . . . A gloomy pall of smoke, fit emblem of the mournful pestilence which desolated that sad land, hovered over the scorched and blistered face of nature in dismal clouds, through which the Southern sun, like an angry globe of fire, but dimly scattered its enfeebled blaze—the abomination of desolation, but fitting retribution for parricidal war. . . .

Night had ensabled the prospect long before the cavalcade discovered the feeble glimmer of the distant city. The groves and hillsides were blazing with cheerful biovouac fires. The merry to-bed tattoo rataplanned cheerily in the deep valleys of the Cumberland, and the good-night taps of great drums rolled up their solemn diapason ere the horse-hoof clatter of the coming chief echoed in the dismal streets of desolate Nashville. . . .

Headquarters were established in the Cunningham mansion, a spacious and elegant edifice well adapted to the patriotic use to which it was appropriated. The staff enjoyed it, but the elite of rebellious Nashville did not seem to appreciate their comfort. Cunningham was a Quartermaster in the rebel service and a Federal Quartermaster was now occupying the dwelling of his neighbor, Colonel Stevenson, also a rebel Quartermaster. A little later the Provost Marshal General was elbowed out of the Cunningham house, and occupied the former residence of General Zollicoffer. Many other private and public buildings were also appropriated to Federal uses, and they were found quite convenient. Nashville was now a military city.

Now that Nashville was indeed a military city, the Federal army of occupation was confronted with the considerable task of endorcing some semblance of loyalty on a hostile and rebellious population. Provost Judge Fitch tells of the problem, as he saw it:

Nashville was a rebel city, occupied as conquered territory, and swarming with traitors, smugglers and spies. Of its male inhabitants a large number were in the rebel army; and its women, arrogant and defiant, were alike outspoken in their treason and indefatigable in their efforts to aid that cause for which their brothers, sons and husbands were fighting. The city, in fact, was one vast "Southern Aid Society," whose sole aim was to plot secret treason and furnish information to the rebel leaders. To purify this tainted atmosphere, to establish order by the application of military law, and to impress this people with a sense of the strength and power of the Government was the task to which General Rosecrans assiduously devoted himself while waiting for the accumulation of sufficient food, clothing, ammunition and camp equipage to make a further advance.

The police and secret-service department was organized and put into successful operation. The secret haunts of treason were penetrated, and its agents dragged forth to exposure and punishment. Smugglers and spies were pursued with a vigor so relentless that detection became the rule and escape the exception. Goods were seized and their owners sent to prison or expelled from the department, thus virtually putting an end to the contraband trade which had been of incalcuable benefit to the rebels. . . .

With all this care for the civil affairs of the department, the army was not neglected. No effort was spared to perfect its drill, discipline and equipment. An efficient signal corps was established. A new system of inspections was devised and adopted. A more careful attention to the proper performance of guard duty was strictly enjoined. Sutlers were checked in their illegal and injurious practices. The authority obtained from the War Department to dismiss from the service incompetent and drunken officers was freely exercised. A cowardly trick of voluntarily surrendering to the enemy to be paroled and thus escape the service was summarily ended by the publication and subsequent enforcement of an order directing that all thus practically guilty of desertion should have their heads encased in white cotton night-caps and, thus publicly branded as cowards, be marched through the streets and camps and sent North. The effect of this discipline was soon apparent; and in the six weeks spent in Nashville a long stride towards perfection was made by the army, thanks to the energy of its commander and the fidelity of its officers.

Bragg, in establishing his headquarters at Murfreesboro, announced his determination to "occupy Middle Tennessee in force and, if possible, to hold for the coming winter the country between the Cumberland and Tennessee rivers." Joe Johnston had set up his headquarters at Chattanooga, but late in November he spent several days in Murfreesboro inspecting the army of about 40,000 which

Bragg had assembled and which Johnston now officially called the Army of Tennessee—the name it was to make lustrous.

Soon after his return to Chattanooga Johnston became involved with President Davis in a clash of opinions as to the proper distribution of the troops in his department. Davis wanted to strengthen Pemberton in Mississippi by sending him reinforcements detached from Bragg. Johnston protested that Bragg could not send any part of his force to Mississippi "without exposing himself to inevitable defeat," and he suggested that Pemberton be aided by sending to him the considerable force in Arkansas under General Holmes, then idle. Davis was displeased by Johnston's attitude, and on December 10th, accompanied by his aide, General G. W. C. Lee (Robert E. Lee's son) he went to Murfreesboro to size up Bragg's army for himself.

After spending three days there, Davis went to Chattanooga and there instructed Johnston to order Bragg to send General C. L. Stevenson with his division of 10,000 men to Mississippi to help Pemberton. Johnston, the good soldier, obeyed the President's order, but he did not attempt to conceal the fact that he considered it a fatally ill-advised act. Bragg also strenuously opposed this weakening of his army, but to no avail. If attacked, Davis told him, "Fight if you can, and fall back beyond the Tennessee. Davis, shaking off all objections, returned to Richmond, leaving both Johnston and Bragg in an unhappy frame of mind, and leaving the Army of Tennessee in a dangerously weakened condition.

Bragg, recognizing that it was not feasible to attack the army under Rosecrans in Nashville, assumed a defensive position anchored on Murfreesboro, where his center under General Polk was stationed. His left was at Triune and Eagleville, twenty miles west of Murfreesboro, under General Hardee; with his right at Readyville, 12 miles to the east, under General McCown.

In the reorganization of his forces, Bragg had rewarded Joe Wheeler's good work in the Kentucky campaign by promoting him to the rank of major general and putting him in command of all the cavalry. This placed both Forrest and Morgan under Wheeler, a boyish-looking, slender young man of 26, who had only recently graduated from West Point. If Forrest or Morgan felt any dissatisfaction at their subordination they did not show it, and kept at their work with undiminished energy. The cavalry serving directly under Wheeler was now attached to Hardee's corps, with Wharton's mounted forces assigned to Polk. The Confederate pickets extended to within two miles of Nashville, and the cavalry patrolled all the intervening country.

While he was encamped on the Murfreesboro line, Bragg made good use of his cavalry, sending them on spectacular raids on the Federal communications and interfering seriously with the enemy's plans. Typical of these raids was Morgan's brilliant swoop (December 7) on Hartsville, fifty miles north of Nashville. At Hartsville there was encamped a Federal brigade, commanded by an Illinois colonel, later described by a Northern newspaper correspondent as "without experience and without moral determination."

Cloaking his attack by an advance of two of Cheatham's infantry brigades against LaVergne on the Nashville road, and a similar feint by Hanson's brigade toward Lebanon, Morgan surprised the Hartsville camp and after a sharp engagement overwhelmed it. Colonel Basil Duke, Morgan's right-hand man (and incidentally his brother-in-law) gives us this animated account of the affair, replete with all the colorful details that only a participant could give:

Just at daylight the cavalry, who were marching in front, came upon a strong picket force about half a mile from the encampment, who fired and retreated. We were thus prevented from surprising the enemy before they formed . . .

Stoner's battalion was not taken across the river, but was ordered to move with the two small howitzers (the "Bull Pups") to a point on the southern bank just opposite the left of the enemy's encampment, and, if possible, produce the impression that the attack would be delivered thence. While Stoner could inflict little damage with either musketry or the fire from his little pieces, he nevertheless attracted the attention of the enemy so successfully that the Federal artillery, directed upon him, did not annoy us until after we had formed for attack.

Colonel Morgan had estimated the strength of the garrison, from the reports of his scouts, to be about fifteen hundred, chiefly infantry. It was considerably stronger than that. It consisted of the One hundred and Fourth Illinois Infantry, One hundred and Sixth Ohio Infantry, One hundred and Eighth Ohio Infantry, Third Indiana Cavalry, one company of the Eleventh Kentucky Cavalry and one section of the Thirteenth Indiana Battery—aggregate effective strength, two thousand and ninety-six. . . . The two guns of the Indiana Battery were three-inch rifled Parrotts.

A large part of my column, at least five hundred, had not crossed the river when I moved to rejoin Colonel Morgan, and they did not arrive until after the conclusion of the fight. Of the cavalry which was up, Bennett's regiment was sent into the town of Hartsville and to watch the roads leading to Gallatin and Castalian Springs. At the latter place, a garrison was stationed, estimated to be from six to eight thousand strong; and as it was only six miles distant, attack from that quarter was to be apprehended, so soon as the troops there should be alarmed by the firing at Hartsville and could march to the assistance of their comrades.

Of the force under my command, therefore, Cluke's and Chenault's regiments together numbered, after deducting horse-holders, only four hundred and fifty men, so that our number actually engaged was less than twelve hundred. The enemy was encamped on wooded ground, slightly elevated above the surrounding meadows. . . . When we came in sight of the enemy and saw his line deploying it was immediately apparent that he was much stronger than he had been reported.

I said to Colonel Morgan: "You have more work cut out for you than you bargained for." "Yes", he answered, "and you gentlemen must whip and catch these fellows and cross the river in two hours and a half, or we'll have six thousand more on our backs."

He then ordered me to form my command opposite to and partially outflanking the right of the enemy's line. I was expected to defeat that flank and drive it back upon the rear of the enemy's centre, and then our infantry was to complete the work. I formed Cluke and Chenault at a gallop—Cluke just in front of the regiment which composed the enemy's right flank; Chenault obtusely to Cluke and on the latter's left, and in a position to completely enfilade the Federal line when at close range. My line dismounted at about four hundred yards from the enemy and at once advanced rapidly . . .

Our open formation enabled us to cover the entire front of the force to which we were opposed with a smaller number of men; and also, while affording less exposure to the fire, the men could aim to better advantage. The Federal line fired by rank, the volleys doing less harm because our men had reached the hollow. Little time was given them to reload. When within about eighty yards our fellows opened in earnest, Clukes still pressing on the front, and Chenault having swept so far around and then closed in that the Federal line was taken almost completely in reverse. It gave way, at first slowly, but in a short time in complete disorder.

We kept close after them, the two regiments swinging around until they were at right angles to the direction of their original formation, and the troops which had confronted them had been driven back upon the rear of the Federal centre and left.

This part of the fight was of some twenty minutes' duration. In the meantime Cobb's battery had been hotly engaged with the enemy's Parrotts, which had been brought back from the Federal left so soon as it became apparent where our real attack would be made. One of Cobb's caissons was blown up, doing smart damage, but occasioned no slacking of his fire, which was extremely effective.

Just as our success on the left was completed, Colonel Hunt had formed the infantry and sent them in *en echelon,* the Second Kentucky leading, against the enemy's centre and right. The infantry had marched quite thirty miles, over slippery roads and through the chilling cold, and I saw some of them stumble as they charged with fatigue and numbness; but the brave boys rushed in as if they were going to a frolic.

The Second Kentucky dashed across the ravine, and as it emerged in some slight disorder, the command was unfortunately giving it to halt and "dress". There was no necessity for the order; the regiment was within fifty yards of the enemy, who were dropping and recoiling under its fire. Several officers sprang to the front and called on the men to advance, and Color Sergeant John Oldham pressed forward with the colors. The regiment rushed forward again, but in that brief halt sustained the greater part of its loss. Just then the Ninth Kentucky came up, the men yelling and bounding along like panthers. The enemy gave back in confusion, and were again pressed in the rear by Cluke and Chenault, who were at this juncture reinforced by seventy-five men of the Third Kentucky under Lieutenant-Colonel John Huffman, who during Gano's absence was commanding that regiment.

A few minutes then sufficed to finish the affair. The enemy were crowded together like sheep in a pen, and were falling fast. The white flag was hoisted in a little more than an hour after the first shot was fired. Our loss in killed and wounded was one hundred and twenty-five. . . . The loss of the enemy in killed and wounded was two hundred and sixty-two and in prisoners eighteen hundred and thirty-four.

Men could not possibly behave better in battle than our troops did in this one. Every officer and man exhibited dauntless resolution, and moved confidently and irresistibly against everything that confronted him. The sudden discovery at the beginning of the fight that the enemy was so much stronger than we had supposed him to be seemed only to stimulate their courage. They had literally made up their minds not to be beaten. . . .

No pursuit was attempted and we marched leisurely back through Lebanon, regaining our camps late in the night. Two splendid pieces of artillery were among the trophies, which did good serviec in our hands until they were recaptured upon the "Ohio raid." This expedition was justly esteemed the most brilliant thing that Morgan had ever done and was referred to with pride by every man who was in it. . . .

The victory of Hartsville brought Colonel Morgan his long-expected and long-delayed commission of brigadier-general. . . . General Hardee urged that Morgan's commission should be made out as major-general, but Mr. Davis said, "I do not wish to give my boys all of their sugar plums at once."

A few days after Morgan's sensational success at Hartsville, Forrest was ordered to proceed to West Tennessee with a pick-up brigade of four depleted regiments and Freeman's four-gun battery of artillery, for the purpose of creating sufficient alarm to check Grant's advance into Mississippi. Forrest's men, largely untrained recruits, were armed principally with shotguns and flintlock rifles —and he did not have even a sufficient supply of flints for the rifles or caps for the shotguns. He had been promised modern rifles, but they were never furnished him and, despite his repeated appeals for adequate arms, he had been ordered to ride into the enemy's country west of the Tennessee, armed just as he was.

Forrest with his makeshift command left Columbia on December 10th, and on the 15th reached Clifton, on the Tennessee River 75 miles west of Columbia. In two small flatboats and a few skiffs, the force of about 1800 men completed the crossing of the river on the 17th. Meanwhile the Federals, informed of Forrest's approach, had gathered a force of infantry, cavalry and artillery, consisting principally of the 11th Illinois, commanded by Colonel Robert G. Ingersoll and the Second West Tennessee (Federal) Cavalry under Colonel Hawkins. Forrest advanced on Lexington and launched an immediate assault, whereupon the Tennessee Federal and Ohio cavalry retreated in such disorder that, as Colonel Ingersoll reported, "it was impossible to stop them". The remainder of the Federal force, including Colonel Ingersoll, was forced to surrender, the booty including two three-inch steel rifled Rodman cannon, 300 small arms and ammunition, and about 200 horses and some wagons.

Two of the guns in Freeman's battery were commanded by Lieutenant John W. Morton, later chief of Forrest's artillery. Writing in later years (and in the third person) about the affair at Lexington, Morton said:

The capture of Colonel Ingersoll, Major Kerr and the four other officers was considered a brilliant feat, well calculated to inspire the needy Confederates with confidence and hope; but in the eyes of Lieutenant Morton, serving with a portion of a borrowed battery, the proudest achievement of the whole affair was the capture of the two guns, rifled Rodmans, which were given into his possession, enabling him to return to Captain Freeman the two which had been loaned. No subsequent capture ever brought the same pleasure as did that of these two well-equipped guns, and they accompanied him and gave good service during the remainder of the war. When later service and advancement had taken him from the immediate command of these two pieces, he was always careful to select them for his immediate supervision. The claim may be made that the valorous General Forrest himself had a more than ordinary affection for these two particular pieces, for he was heard to say on more than one occasion that he had no fear of the outcome of an attack if Morton and his Rodmans were with him.

Forrest and his men galloped on from Lexington to Jackson, where he made a feint at an attack, but after giving the garrison there a false impression of great strength, turned north and captured Trenton, Humboldt, and Union City, tearing up many miles of railroad track and cutting Grant's communications with the North. Circling through West Tennessee, he soon found himself hotly pursued by such a large force of Federals that it seemed inevitable that he must be surrounded and captured, but at Parker's Cross Roads, near Huntingdon, he made a stand and fought off his pursuers. Retreating through Lexington, on January 1st he was back at the Tennessee River and within eight hours had crossed the river with his five pieces of artillery, six caissons, sixty wagons and four ambulances, equipments of all kinds, and the whole command of men and horses.

A summary of his accomplishments during that crowded two weeks in West Tennessee is given by Bennett H. Young:

Fourteen days had elapsed since the passage of the river, but what marvellous experiences had Forrest and his raw levies passed through. They had traveled over 300 miles, had been in three sternly contested engagements, with daily skirmishing, had destroyed 50 large and small bridges on the Mobile & Ohio Railroad, and had burned trestles, so as to make it useless to the enemy; had captured 20 stockades, captured and killed 2500 of the enemy, taken and disabled 10 pieces of artillery, carried off 50 wagons and ambulances with their teams, had captured 10,000 stands of excellent small arms and hundreds of thousands of rounds of ammunition, had returned fully armed, equipped and mounted; had traversed roads with army trains at that season were considered impassable even by horsemen. Only one night's rest in 14 days had been enjoyed, unsheltered, without tents, and in a most inclement winter, constantly raining, snowing and sleeting; but these wonderful men had endured all these hardships, neither murmuring, complaining nor doubting, but always cheerful, brave and resigned to do any and every duty that sternest war could bring.

This one campaign had made Forrest's new troopers veterans. There was now no service for which they were not prepared. They were ready to follow their leader at any time and everywhere, and thereafter no troops would perform more prodigies of valor or face a foe with more confidence or cheerfulness.

During the Confederate army's brief stay in the environs of Murfreesboro the social life of the town burgeoned. Two events of that gay interlude were of special interest and significance: a visit to the army by President Jefferson Davis, and the marriage of General Morgan to Miss Mattie Ready of Murfreesboro. The wedding ceremony was performed by General-Bishop Polk, who mentioned both events in a letter to his wife on December 17th:

We have had a royal visit from a royal visitor. The President himself has been with us. He arrived on Friday, reviewed my corps of three divisions on Saturday, dined with a party of general officers at Bragg's, and left on Sunday. The review was a great affair; everything went off admirably, and he was highly gratified with the result—said they were the best-appearing troops he had seen, well appointed and well clad. The sight was very imposing and, as it was my corps, very gratifying to me, as you may suppose. . . . We had a great wedding the other day, as you will also see by the accompanying notice. It was no other than the redoubtable John Morgan. He was married, as you see, by a lietutenant-general, a select company present—Generals Bragg, Hardee, Breckinridge, Cheatham, etc. It is an historical event.

General Polk's son relates that, due to the General's settled determination to avoid all public exercise of his priestly functions, he was at first inclined to decline the request that he officiate at the marriage, but at length concluded to gratify Morgan, "who at Hartsville had just accomplished a brilliant feat . . . and who then was upon the eve of departure upon an expedition into Kentucky for the purpose of harassing the communications of the enemy."

General Morgan's marriage was a gala social affair, and the handsome general and his pretty wife were showered with congratulations. Basil Duke writes frankly of the misgivings of some of Morgan's military associates:

On the 14th of December an event occurred which was thought by many to have materially affected General Morgan's efficiency and subsequent fortunes. He was married to Miss Ready, of Murfreesboro, a lady to whom he was devotedly attached and who deserved to exercise over him the great influence she was thought to have possessed. The marriage ceremony was performed by General Polk, by virtue of his commission as bishop, but in full lieutenant-general's uniform. . . . The bridegroom's friends and brothers-in-arms and the commander-in-chief and Generals Hardee, Cheatham and Breckinridge felt called upon to stand by him on this occasion. Grenfel was in a high state of delight; although he had regretted General Morgan's marriage, thinking that it would render him less enterprising.

The arm-chair military strategists in Washington had a weakness for censuring the commanders of troops in the field because of their alleged lack of aggressiveness. There were numerous and repeated instances of this "let's you and him fight" attitude on the part of President Lincoln and his advisors: McClellan on the Peninsula in 1862; McClellan after the battle of Sharpsburg; Meade after the battle of Gettysburg; Thomas before the battle of Nashville. All these were considered laggards by the Washington experts, and Rosecrans had not been in Nashville long before he got a taste of it in a telegram on December 4th from General Halleck:

The President is very impatient at your long stay in Nashville. The favorable season for your campaign will soon be over. You give Bragg time to supply himself by plundering the very country your army should have occupied . . . Twice have I been asked to designate some one else to command your army. If you remain one more week at Nashville, I can not prevent your removal. As I wrote you when you took the command, the Government demands action, and if you can not respond to that demand some one else will be tried.

With his natural indignation and irritation bristling in every word, Rosecrans replied to Halleck by telegraph the same day:

I have lost no time. Everything I have done was necessary, absolutely so; and has been done as rapidly as possible. . . . If the Government which ordered me here confides in my judgment, it may rely on my continuing to do what I have been trying to do; that is, my whole duty. If my superiors have lost confidence in me, they had better at once put some one in my place and let the future test the propriety of the change. . . . I need no other stimulus to make me do my duty than the knowledge of what it is. To threats of removal or the like I must be permitted to say that I am insensible.

Halleck's reply the next day was explanatory rather than placatory, still insisting that Rosecrans should "move more rapidly", and citing the diplomatic overtones of the military situation:

My telegram was not a threat but merely a statement of facts. The President is greatly dissatisfied with your delay, and has sent for me several times to account for it. He has repeated to me time and again that there were imperative reasons why the enemy should be driven across the Tennessee River at the earliest possible moment. He had never told me what those reasons were, but I imagine them to be diplomatic and of the most serious character. You can hardly conceive his great anxiety about it. . . . It has been feared that on the meeting of the British Parliament, in January next, the political pressure of the starving operatives [in Manchester?] may force the Government to join France in an intervention. If the enemy be left in possession of Middle Tennessee, which we held last July, it will be said that they have gained on us. . . . Tennessee is the only state which can be used as an argument in favor of intervention by England. You will thus perceive that your movements have an importance beyond mere military success. The whole Cabinet are anxious, inquiring almost daily, "Why don't he move?" Can't you make him move?" You will thus perceive that there is a pressure for you to advance much greater than you can possibly have imagined. It may be, and perhaps is, the very turning point in our foreign relations.

The record does not show to what extent, if any, Rosecrans was impressed by Halleck's admonition. At any rate, it was three weeks later before Rosecrans made his forward movement, and during the interim his preparations for battle were not impeded by any further nagging telegrams from the General-in-Chief, which was Halleck's official title.

As Christmas approached, the social life among both officers and men at Murfreesboro approached a climax. Christmas day was featured by horse racing, card playing and other gay doings traditional to Christmas celebrations in the South. It is easy to understand the lament of one of Wheeler's young cavalry captains: "The morning after Christmas day. . . . I felt feeble; but, being anxious to be with my men, reported for duty." Invitations had been sent out for a big ball to be held the day after Christmas—but all festivities were forgotten in the Confederate camp the day after Christmas when news reached Murfreesboro that Rosecrans was that day launching the advance of his army from Nashville. The news of the departure of Stevenson's division for Mississippi had soon leaked through the Federal lines to Nashville, and is supposed to have been one of the deciding factors in Rosecrans' determination to advance against his weakened foe. This resolve was encouraged also by the knowledge that both Forrest and Morgan had been sent away on raids, and that Bragg's ability to withstand an attack would be lessened by his absence of about two-thirds of his cavalry.

Any military leader has an abundance of problems in connection with the movement of his forces into position for the fighting of a major battle. But General Rosecrans, as he started the movement of his forces in the direction of Murfreesboro had an unexpected and unusual problem, one seldom if ever before experienced by any commander of American troops on the eve of a big battle—a mutiny, no less!

The mutineers were a cavalry regiment from Philadelphia described in one of the official documents as "Buell's Body Guard, otherwise the Anderson Troop, otherwise the Anderson Cavalry, otherwise the 15th Pennsylvania Cavalry, otherwise the 116th Pennsylvania Volunteers", but more usually referred to as the Anderson Cavalry. This organization was a sort of blue-stocking group, "none being accepted unless coming well recommended by some well-known, influential person or persons", and it was recruited for the avowed purpose of serving as a body-guard to General Don Carlos Buell. Membership in such a group was attractive, of course, to all those young men who wished to escape the odium of draft-dodging, but also desired to escape the discipline, drudgery and danger incident to serving in the ranks.

After they had been mustered into service and while they were on the way to Nashville they learned that General Buell had been relieved of his command, but they declared their willingness to serve as a bodyguard for General Rosecrans, and continued on their way. Arriving in Nashville on Christmas Eve, 1862, they were promptly informed that General Rosecrans did not desire their services as a body-guard, but they were welcomed as reinforcements for the army's cavalry force. This was not the kind of service they were expecting to perform, and they recoiled from the prospect of actual combat. In the words of an official brief they later prepared:

"So on the morning of December 26th, when requested by our officers to prepare to march to the front, the regiment, in a quiet and gentlemanly manner, stacked their arms in front of their tents, as previously agreed upon. Subsequently, however, upon the representation of General Stanley that, if the regiment would move, it would be held as a reserve, and upon the assertion of Major Rosengarten that our forces had been repulsed and that every man was needed at the front, about 200 were induced to go with the officers, the others firmly adhering to their original design."

Rosecrans at this time was deeply involved in the difficult logistics of the advance of his army on Murfreesboro, and he was infuriated when informed of the recalcitrance of his rejected "body guard". He telegraphed: "I will not submit to their whims. If they do not come to the front at once I will disgrace them and make them regret their folly."

After an incredible amount of discussion and parleying with the obstinate mutineers, they were eventually placed under arrest and locked up in the Nashville

work-house and jail. While all this talk was going on, about 350 of the Pennsyl-
vanians were listed as "missing"—apparently a euphemism for desertion. When
the fighting 200 returned from Murfreesboro, they again resumed their rebellious
attitude, refusing to obey orders, and they too were arrested and jailed.

The mutineers apparently had influential friends and relatives at home, for
Secretary Stanton sent an Assistant Inspector General to Nashville to investigate
"everything connected with the arrest and confinement of these men". Stanton also
personally telegraphed General Mitchell, garrison commander at Nashville, directing him to "treat them in a humane manner, cause them to be imprisoned in
a proper place, and properly supplied and cared for," also asking "when they are
to be tried, and whether you have made any threats or expressed any ill-will
against them."

General Mitchell replied tartly that "They have been treated as all other
soldiers are treated placed in confinement for high crimes". As to the "threats"
and "ill-will", Mitchell reported: "I have said to them that mutiny in the face
of any enemy was punishable by death, and unless they reconsidered their action
some of them would be made examples of. I have further said to them and their
friends that their course was cowardly in the extreme, a disgrace to themselves
and their state. . . . A court-martial assembled today for the trial of these men, by
order of Major General Rosecrans."

The Inspector General reported to Stanton that

As a class they are very intelligent young men, but [for various causes, including]
the interference and influence of friends at home, they have become demoralized and
wanting in discipline; they have become tired of the service, are determined to get out
of it and, therefore, unreasonably magnify their grievances and seek pretexts for
neglecting their duty and disobeying orders. They have set the authority of the
Government at defiance, and have been assured that money and influence will not be
spared in 'their behalf in their course of conduct. . . . In a military sense, all reasonable
means have been exhausted to induce them to return to duty, and awaken in them a
feeling of pride and a proper sense of their sacred obligations to their Government
and country without avail . . . There is no good excuse for their mutinous and dis-
obedient conduct, and hundreds if not thousands of other troops in the Department of
the Cumberland are closely watching the action of the Government in this case. . . .
That the good of the service requires an example to be made of a portion of this
regiment I have no doubt.

Apparently the mutineers were not in error in supposing that "money and
influence" would not be spared in supporting their defiance of the Government.
Several of them were discharged on direct orders from the War Department, "for
no apparent reason whatever", their former Colonel said, "except that their friends
at home, aided by Congressional influence, have applied for it." That this strong
influence extended to General Rosecrans is indicated by the fact that, although he
had been insisting that some of the ringleaders at least be executed, he wilted
under the pressure and eventually agreed that all the mutineers be released from
confinement and meekly consented to the reorganization of the mutineers into a
regiment under their original commanding colonel. Nobody was shot, nobody was
punished—and apparently nobody felt disgraced.

CHAPTER 8

☆ *Battle of Murfreesboro*

R OSECRANS having determined to launch an offensive against Bragg's army
at Murfreesboro, the Federal forces moved out of Nashville on the morning of December 26th in three columns: McCook, with three divisions,
advanced by the Nolensville pike in the direction of Triune, in the vicinity of
which Hardee's troops were stationed. Thomas, with two divisions, advanced on
McCook's right, along the Franklin and Wilson pikes, in a movement designed to
threaten Hardee's right and then to fall in by the crossroads of Nolensville. Crittenden, with three divisions, advanced directly along the Nashville-Murfreesboro pike,
through LaVergne. Rosecrans planned, with Thomas at Nolensville, for McCook
to attack Hardee at Triune. If the Confederates reinforced Hardee, Thomas was
to reinforce McCook. If Hardee was driven back, or retreated voluntarily, and
the Confederates were encountered at Stewart's Creek, Crittenden was to attack
there. Thomas would then come up on Crittenden's right flank, while McCook
pursued or threatened Hardee.

By the time McCook arrived at Triune, however, Hardee had been withdrawn
towards Murfreesboro, necessitating a change in Rosecrans' plans. The three
corps advanced slowly during the next three days, harassed by the Confederate
cavalry and impeded by the fire-and-fall-back tactics of the infantry skirmishers.

While Rosecrans was engaged in bringing his army into position before
Murfreesboro, Bragg had not been idle. Colonel David Urquhart of Bragg's staff
tells of how Bragg got the news of Rosencrans' advance from Nashville and of
his prompt reaction:

On the 26th General Wheeler, commanding the cavalry outposts, sent dispatches
in quick succession to headquarters reporting a general advance of Rosecrans' army.
Soon all was bustle and activity. General Hardee's corps at Triune was ordered to
Murfreesboro. Camps were at once broken up and everything was made ready for
active service. On the 27th of December our army was moving. On Sunday,
December 28th, Polk and Hardee met at General Bragg's headquarters to learn the
situation and his plans.

[133]

Rosecrans was advancing from Nashville with his whole army. Wheeler with his cavalry was so disposed at the moment as to protect the flanks, and, when pressed, to fall back toward the main army. Hardee's corps now constituted the right wing, with its right resting on the Lebanon Pike and its left on the Nashville road. Polk's corps . . . was to take post with its right touching Hardee on the Nashville road and its left resting on the Salem Pike; McCown's division was to form the reserve and to occupy our center. Such was the position of the Confederate army on the 29th of December.

On Tuesday, December 30th, Rosecrans was in our front, a mile and a half away. . . . At 3 o'clock the Federal infantry advanced and attacked our lines, but were repulsed. . . . But night soon interposed, quiet prevailed, and the two armies bivouacked opposite to each other.

General Bragg was on the field the entire day, but returned to his headquarters that evening at Murfreesboro. He called his corps commanders together and informed them that his advices convinced him that Rosecrans, under cover of the day's attack, had been massing his troops for a move on our left flank. It was then agreed that Hardee should at once move to the extreme left Cleburne's division of his corps and the reserve (McCown), and that next morning Hardee should take command in that quarter and begin the fight.

While the opposing commanders were moving their infantry units into position, like pieces on a giant chess-board, General Joe Wheeler and his cavalry on the night of December 29th made a spectacular raid around Rosecrans' entire army. In his official report of the battle, General Bragg devoted only a few brief sentences to Wheeler's raid:

On Monday night Brigadier General Wheeler proceeded with his cavalry brigade and one regiment from Pegram's, as ordered, to gain the enemy's rear. By Tuesday morning, moving on the Jefferson pike around the enemy's left flank, he had gained the rear of their whole army, and soon attacked the trains, their guards and the numerous stragglers. He succeeded in capturing several hundred prisoners and destroying hundreds of wagons loaded with supplies and baggage. After clearing the road he made his way entirely around and joined the cavalry on our left.

Bragg's brief and colorless mention of Wheeler's raid tends to minimize the importance of what was actually an outstanding achievement. The indelible impression made on the enemy by the raid is revealed in the on-the-spot observation of Lieutenant Colonel G. C. Kniffin of General Crittenden's staff:

During the night of the 29th General Wheeler, who had moved from the left to the right of Murfreesboro, advancing by the Lebanon and Jefferson pikes, gained the rear of Rosecrans' army and attacked Starkweather's brigade of Rousseau's division at Jefferson at daylight on the 30th. The head of his brigade train, consisting of sixty-four wagons, had just arrived in camp and was driving into park when Wheeler dashed down upon it with three thousand cavalry. But he had encountered an antagonist as vigilant as himself. Wheeler's men, dismounted, advanced gallantly to the charge, when they were as gallantly met. After two hours' contest, twenty wagons in the rear of the train were taken and destroyed, but the assault upon the brigade was handsomely repulsed. The Confederates fell back, followed by Starkweather for more than a mile, when he returned to camp. The Union loss in killed, wounded and missing was 122.

From Jefferson Wheeler proceeded toward LaVergne, picking up stragglers and a small forage train, arriving at LaVergne about noon of the same day, where he captured the immense supply trains of McCook's corps, moving slowly forward under insufficient guard.

Several hundred prisoners and nearly a million dollars' worth of property was the penalty paid by the Government for not heeding the requests of the commanding general for more cavalry. The work of paroling prisoners, burning wagons, exchanging arms and horses and driving off mules commenced at once and occupied the remainder of the day and night. Early on the morning of the 31st Colonel M. B. Walker's Union brigade . . . on its night march from Nolensville to Stewartsboro, arrived within two and a half miles of LaVergne and advanced at once to the scene of devastation. The turnpike, as far as the eye could reach, was filled with burning wagons. The country was overspread with disarmed men, broken-down horses and mules. The streets were covered with empty valises and trunks, knapsacks, broken guns and all the indescribable debris of a captured and rifled army train. . . . A train at Rock Spring and another at Nolensville shared the fate of that at LaVergne, and three hundred paroled prisoners were left to carry the tidings back to Nashville.

At 2 o'clock on the morning of the 31st Wheeler came up bright and smiling upon the left flank of the Confederate army in front of Murfreesboro, having made the entire circuit of Rosecrans' army in forty-eight hours, leaving miles of road strewn with burning wagons and army supplies, remounting a portion of his cavalry, and bringing back to camp a sufficient number of minie-rifles and accounterments to arm a brigade.

When Wharton captured some of the Federal wagons in the raid to the rear of the advancing army, the spoils included some of the official correspondence of General Rosecrans, which made interesting reading for the Confederates. Productive of considerable merriment and satisfaction was a wailing letter to General Rosecrans from George D. Prentice, the violently pro-Union editor of the Louisville *Courier Journal;* dated at Louisville, November 10, 1862.

Some months ago Mr. John W. White received from me $5,000 in gold, which he invested for me in cotton, investing at the same time a large amount for himself and others. The cotton bales were received at Nashville and used for the fortifications, Government receipts being given for them. They are there yet, I learn. Now it seems to me that when cotton is so very valuable—a bale being worth, say, $240—that cheaper material ought long since to have been substituted in the fortifications. The cotton, I am told, is scandalously wasted by the soldiers. I have written a brief article for my paper on the subject, and I will have a copy sent to you. I beg that you will give a little thought to my suggestions. It is a sad thing for a poor editor to have to sustain a pecuniary loss in such times as these.

With a sense of appreciation of the dramatic detail of combat, and an unusual ability to recapture the fury of battle, Private Sam Watkins of Company H, First Tennessee Infantry gives a private's-eye view of a clash with the enemy as the opposing forces jockeyed for position along Stone's River on December 30th.

The next day, the Yankees were found out to be advancing. Soon they came in sight of our picket. We kept falling back and firing all day, and were relieved by another regiment about dark. We rejoined our regiment. Line of battle was formed on the north bank of Stone's River—on the Yankee side. Bad generalship, I thought.

It was Christmas. John Barleycorn was General in Chief. Our Generals, and Colonels, and Captains had kissed John a little too often. They couldn't see straight. It was said to be buckeye whiskey. They couldn't tell our own men from Yankees. But here they were—the Yankees—a battle had to be fought. We were ordered forward. I was on the skirmish line. We marched plumb into the Yankee lines, with their flags flying.

I called Lieutenant-Colonel Frierson's attention to the Yankees, and he remarked, "Well, I don't know whether they are Yankees or not, but if they are, they will come out of there mighty quick." The Yankees marched over the hill out of sight.

We were ordered forward to the attack. We were right upon the Yankee line on the Wilkerson turnpike. The Yankees were shooting our men down by scores. A universal cry was raised, "You are firing on your own men"; "Cease firing, cease firing." I hallooed, in fact the whole skirmish line hallooed, and kept on telling them that they were Yankees, and to shoot; but the order was to cease firing, you are firing on your own men.

Captain James, of Cheatham's staff, was sent forward and killed in his own yard. We were not twenty yards off from the Yankees, and they were pouring the hot shot and shells right onto our ranks; and every man was yelling at the top of his voice, "Cease firing, you are firing on your own men."

Oakley, color-bearer of the Fourth Tennessee Regiment, ran right up in the midst of the Yankee line with his colors, begging his men to follow. I hallooed till I was hoarse, "They are Yankees, they are Yankees; shoot, they are Yankees."

The crest occupied by the Yankees was belching loud with fire and smoke, and the Rebels were falling like leaves of autumn in a hurricane. The leaden hail storm swept them off the field. They fell back and re-formed. General Cheatham came up and advanced. I did not fall back, but continued to load and shoot, until a fragment of a shell struck me on the arm, and then a minie ball passed through the same, paralyzed my arm, and wounded and disabled me. General Cheatham, all the time, was calling on the men to go forward, saying, "Come on, boys, and follow me."

The impression that General Frank Cheatham made upon my mind, leading the charge on the Wilkerson turnpike, I will never forget. I saw "Victory or death" written on his face. When I saw him leading our brigade, although I was wounded at the time, I felt sorry for him, he seemed so earnest and concerned, and as he was passing me I said, "Well, General, if you are determined to die, I'll die with you." We were at that time at least a hundred yards in advance of the brigade, Cheatham all the time calling upon the men to come on. He was leading the charge in person. Then it was that I saw the power of one man, born to command, over a multitude of men then almost routed and demoralized. I saw and felt that he was not fighting for glory, but that he was fighting for his country, because he loved that country, and he was willing to give his life for his country and the success of our cause. He deserves a wreath of immortality, and a warm place in every Southern's heart, for his brave and glorious example on that bloody battle-field of Murfreesboro. Yes, his history will ever shine in beauty and grandeur as a name among the brightest in all the galaxy of leaders in the history of our cause.

Now, another fact I will state, and that is, when the private soldier was ordered to charge and capture the twelve pieces of artillery, heavily supported by infantry, Maney's brigade raised a whoop and yell, and swooped down on those Yankees like a whirl-a-gust of woodpeckers in a hail storm, paying the blue-coated rascals back with compound interest; for when they did come, every man's gun was loaded, and they marched upon the blazing crest in solid file, and when they did fire, there was a sudden lull in the storm of battle, because the Yankees were nearly all killed. I cannot remember now of ever seeing more dead men and horses and captured cannon, all jumbled together, than that scene of blood and carnage and battle on the Wilkerson turnpike. The ground was literally covered with blue-coats dead; and, if I remember correctly, there were eighty dead horses.

By this time our command had re-formed, and charged the blazing crest.

The spectacle was grand. With cheers and shouts they charged up the hill, shooting down and bayoneting the flying cannoneers, General Cheatham, Colonel Field and Joe Lee cutting and slashing with their swords. The victory was complete. The whole left [right?] wing of the Federal army was driven back five miles from their original position. Their dead and wounded were in our lines, and we had captured many pieces of artillery, small arms, and prisoners.

When I was wounded, the shell and shot that struck me, knocked me winding. I said, "O, O, I'm wounded," and at the same time I grabbed my arm. I thought it had been torn from my shoulder. The brigade had fallen back about two hundred yards, when General Cheatham's presence reassured them, and they soon were in line and ready to follow so brave and gallant a leader, and had that order of "Cease firing, you are firing on your own men," not been given, Maney's brigade would have had the honor of capturing eighteen pieces of artillery, and ten thousand prisoners. This I do know to be a fact.

As I went back to the field hospital, I overtook another man walking along. I do not know to what regiment he belonged, but I remember of first noticing that his left arm was entirely gone. His face was as white as a sheet. The breast and sleeve of his coat had been torn away, and I could see the frazzled end of his shirt sleeve, which appeared to be sucked into the wound. I looked at it pretty close, and I said "Great God!" for I could see his heart throb, and was horrified at the sight. He was walking along, when all at once he dropped down and died without a struggle or a groan.

That even grim war could, and did, have its benign interludes, however, is indicated by an anecdote told by one of Rosecrans' men of an incident that occurred as the two armies were squaring off for the sanguinary battle of Murfreesboro:

One of the most remarkable features of this war is the absence of vindictiveness among the soldiery of the two sections. When parties have met with flags of truce, the privates will freely converse, drink from each other's canteens, and even have a friendly game of cards in a fence corner. Especially upon picket-duty has this friendliness broken in upon discipline—so much so that in many instances orders have been issued strictly forbidding such intercourse. The following incident is related by a member of the 8th Kentucky:

On the 27th of December, our army arrived at Stewart's Creek, ten miles distant from Murfreesboro. The following day, being a Sabbath, and our general being devout, nothing was done except to cross a few companies on the left as skirmishers, our right being watched by the enemy's, as well as ours, both extending along the creek on opposite sides. Despite of orders, our boys would occasionally shut an eye at the Confederates, who were ever ready to take the hint. This was kept up until evening, when the boys, finding they were effecting nothing at such long range, quit shooting, and concluded they would "talk it out", whereupon the following occurred:

Federal (at the top of his voice)—"Halloo, boys! what regument?"

Confederate—"8th Confederate".

F.—"Bully for you!"

C.—What's your regiment?

F.—8th and 21st Kentucky

C.—All right.

F.—Boys, have you got any whiskey?

C.—Plenty of her.

F.—How'll you trade for coffee?

C.—Would like to accommodate you, but never drink it while the worm goes.

F.—Let's meet at the creek and have a social chat.

C.—Will you shoot?

F.—Upon the honor of a gentleman, not a man shall. Will you shoot?

C.—I give you as good assurance.

F.—Enough said. Come on.

C.—Leave your arms.

F.—I have left them. Do you leave yours?

C.—I do.

Whereupon, both parties started for the creek to a point agreed upon. Meeting almost simultaneously, we (the Federals) were, in a modulated tone, addressed in the usual unceremonious style of a soldier, by—

C.—Halloo, boys! how do you make it?

F.—Oh, bully! bully!

C.—This is rather an unexpected armistice.

F.—That's so.

F.—Boys, are you going to make a stand at Murfreesboro?

C.—That is a leading question; nothwithstanding, I venture to say it will be the bloodiest ten miles you ever traveled.

Thus the conversation went on for some time, until a Confederate captain (Miller, of General Wheeler's cavalry) came down, requesting an exchange of newspapers. On being informed we had none, he said he would give us his anyhow and, wrapping a stone in the paper, threw it across. Some compliments were passed, when the captain suggested that, as it was getting late, we had better quit the conference; whereupon both parties, about twenty each, began to leave, with "Good bye, boys; if ever I meet you in battle, I'll spare you." So we met and parted, not realizing that we were enemies.

W. J. Worsham, of the Nineteenth Tennessee Infantry, was one of those who took part in the brisk and bloody skirmishing of December 30th and was glad when the quick winter twilight put an end to the fighting and the soldiers on both sides settled down to bivouac. An incident of that cheerless evening, impressive in its sentimental implications, was related by Dr. Worsham in later years:

Our line ran principally through the cedars and rocks, and this cold winter evening, when all nature presented a dreary outlook, these thick cedars and boulders seemed to cast a double mantle of dreariness over everything. Yet on this Tuesday evening of December the 30th, when the two lines of battle lay in waiting for each other, there occurred an incident in which both armies took a part, and which is not often recorded in the history of battles. With us both armies spoke the same language, learned the same tunes and played the same airs. . . . The night before the battle, after the bands had finished their usual evening serenade, after the sounds of the last piece were dying away in the distance, a Federal band struck up slow and softly: "Home, Sweet Home."

Out in the darkness of this cold December night, amidst the dense cedars and rough boulders along the banks of Stone's river,

"Whose sad, slow stream, its noiseless flood
    Poured o'er the glancing pebbles
All silent now, the Federals stood,
    All silent stood the Rebels.
No heart or soul had heard unmoved
    That plaintive note's appealing,
So sweetly, 'Home, Sweet Home' but stirred
    The hidden fount of feeling."

I tell you this was a soul-stirring occasion. During the stillness of the night, each soldier of both armies was holding communion with his own soul, his mind occupied with the thought of what to-morrow would bring, whether wounds or death, and would he ever see home again, when the notes of this inspiring tune came floating on the stillness of the night. Immediately a Confederate band caught up the strain, then one after another until all the bands of both armies were playing "Home, Sweet Home." And after our bands had ceased playing, we could hear the sweet refrain as it died away on the cool, frosty air on the Federal side. What a thrill of memories was brought to the minds of all that night!

But by the night of the 30th, everybody on both sides realized that the fraternizing and the skirmishing was over, and that the next day would see a full-scale battle. Rosecrans in his official report tells how he called his corps commanders to his headquarters that evening and explained to them his plan of action. The Federal troops were now arrayed in the positions from which he intended to launch his attack on Bragg the next morning, with Crittenden on the left, Thomas in the center and McCook on the right. With these three corps leaders before him, Rosecrans tells how he outlined to each of them the part they were expected to play in the battle to start the next morning:

McCook was to occupy the most advantageous position, refusing his right as much as practicable and necessary to secure it, to receive the attack of the enemy or, if that did not come, to attack himself sufficient to hold all the force on his front; Thomas and Palmer to open with skirmishing, and engage the enemy's centre and left as far as the river; Crittenden to cross Van Cleve's division at the lower ford . . . and to advance on Breckinridge; Wood's division to follow by brigades, crossing at the upper ford and moving on Van Cleve's right, to carry everything before them into Murfreesboro.

This would have given us two divisions against one and, as soon as Breckinridge had been dislodged from his position, and the batteries of Wood's division, taking position on the heights east of Stone's river in advance, would see the enemy's works in reverse, would dislodge them, and enable Palmer's division to press them back and drive them westward across the river or through the woods, while Thomas, sustaining the movement on the centre, would advance on the right of Palmer, crushing their right; and Crittenden's corps, advancing, would take Murfreesboro and then, moving westward on the Franklin road, get in their flank and rear and drive them into the country towards Salem, with the prospect of cutting off their retreat and probably destroying their army.

It was explained to them that this combination, insuring us a vast superiority on our left, required for its success that General McCook should be able to hold his position for three hours . . . Having thus explained the plan, the general commanding addressed General McCook as follows: "You know the ground; you have fought over it; you know its difficulties. Can you hold your present position for three hours?" To which General McCook responded, "Yes, I think I can." . . . The officers then returned to their commands. At daylight on the morning of the 31st the troops breakfasted and stood to their arms, and by 7 o'clock were preparing for the battle.

In the order of battle issued by Rosecrans on the night of the 30th, Van Cleve's division of Crittenden's left wing was assigned the first movement the following morning. Captain Ephraim A. Otis, assistant adjutant general on Van Cleve's staff, tells of this opening action, which so quickly aborted:

Van Cleve was in line and began the movement at daylight, but as he had been placed in reserve in the rear of our left, and had a river to cross before the troops could be formed for attack, a considerable time elasped before the battle could be opened on our part. It was for this reason that the battle opened on our right before our attack could be made, thus giving the Confederates an immense advantage, and placing Rosecrans on the defensive from the very beginning.

I recall as distinctly as if it were only yesterday how the fierce roar of battle broke out in our extreme right as we moved rapidly forward on the left, forded the river, formed in line of battle on the other side, and were moving forward to attack whatever forces lay before us. Before this could be accomplished the significant sounds of battle on our extreme right grew more distinct and nearer, and the conviction grew into a certainty that McCook had been attacked and was being forced back. Shortly afterwards hurried orders were received from General Rosecrans to re-cross the river immediately, leave a brigade to guard the ford, and march to the right of the army, which was in most urgent need of assistance.

The extreme right of our army was commanded by General R. W. Johnson, who had one brigade in line, a second brigade slightly refused on his right flank, and another in reserve. They were not well posted, and although they were in line of battle before daylight they had been led to believe that they would not be attacked in force, and that the real battle was to be decided by Rosecrans' movement on the extreme left. They were veteran soldiers commanded by able and experienced officers, but they were not expecting such an attack as Hardee was about to make, and were largely outnumbered. At the angle of Johnson's line, where he had only three brigades, the enemy had eight brigades in line, with their left reaching far beyond Johnson's right.

There was a light fog early in the morning, but it soon cleared away, and shortly after daylight the long gray line swept swiftly forward and Johnson's whole division was furiously attacked in front and flank, and after a short but gallant defence was driven clear off the field in great disorder with heavy loss. It was said at the time that Johnson's headquarters were too far from the line of battle; that his troops were surprised, and that the artillery horses were sent back to be watered, so that many of the guns were captured because they could not be hauled to the rear. Johnson, however, asserts that he breakfasted at three o'clock that morning, and was on his horse a short distance from the line when the attack was made; that his men had stood in line of battle with guns in their hands long before it began, and that the number of dead artillery horses killed in the attack, and left on the field, showed that a few only had been sent to the river.

Johnson had observed the movement of the enemy during the night, and reported it to McCook, but received no new instructions as to the position he was to occupy. General Willich, commanding Johnson's right brigade, allowed his men to stack arms and make coffee, and just before the attack rode back a short distance to Johnson's headquarters, leaving at the point where the assault was made no one above the rank of regimental commander to give orders or direct the movements of the troops. Willich in attempting to rejoin his brigade rode straight into the Confederate lines and was taken prisoner within half an hour after the first shot was fired. I think it will be conceded that while there may have been no surprise in a military sense, yet Johnson was not prepared for the furious assault in front and on his right at the same moment.

Whatever the cause, the disaster to Johnson's command was complete, and his whole division was driven back in great disorder, leaving nearly all the artillery and many prisoners in the hands of the enemy.

General Bragg, in his official report, tells tersely of the auspicious opening of the battle when McCown's men, followed by Cleburne, surged out of the cedars and hit the Federal right like a thunderbolt:

The enemy was taken completely by surprise. General and staff officers were not mounted, artillery horses not hitched and infantry not formed. A hot and inviting breakfast of coffee and other luxuries, to which our gallant and hardy men had long been strangers, was found upon the fire unserved, and was left while we pushed on to a more inviting feast—that of captured artillery, fleeing battalions and hosts of craven prisoners.

The Federal brigade commanded by Brigadier General E. N. Kirk was on the front line of the extreme right of the Federal army and caught the full force of the Confederate attack on the morning of the 31st. Col. J. B. Dodge of the 30th

Indiana, who succeeded to the command of the brigade when Gen. Kirk was wounded in the first few minutes of the attack, tells of how the attacked Federals reacted when the thunderbolt struck them:

A strong picket line was thrown out from 150 to 200 yards in front, with a cornfield in front of their (the picket) line. Every precaution that was possible was taken to prevent surprise and to give reasonable warning of the approach of the enemy. The brigade was up and under arms for nearly or quite an hour before daylight.

Just after daylight a part of the horses of the battery were unhitched from the caissons and taken to water, which was close by. Just at this moment the enemy made his appearance on our front and right in immense force and formed in close columns, with a front equal to the length of a battalion in line, and ten or twelve ranks in depth. General Kirk immediately ordered the 34th Illinois to advance to near where the picket was stationed, in order to check (at least) the advance of the enemy and save the battery if possible, which movement was promptly executed under an awful fire, which almost annihilated the picket line, or line of skirmishers which it really was, and killed or wounded a large number in the line some 150 or 200 yards in the rear.

The battery under command of Captain Edgarton immediately opened with canister upon the enemy, and only had time to fire eight rounds before the battery was taken. . . . General Kirk was seriously wounded at almost the first fire, and I succeeded to the command of the brigade. . . . The fire the enemy received from us, although well directed and as effective as a fire from two ranks generally is, produced no visible effect upon him as he moved his heavy column forward upon a double quick. . . . The enemy then moved to the left, oblique or nearly by his left flank, until his centre was opposite our extreme right, when he moved forward again, changing direction to his right as he did so, so as to bring his whole force upon our most exposed point. We held our ground until our ranks were not more than twenty yards from the enemy, when I was forced to retire, having no support and seeing that it was a needless waste of life to contend in that position.

General Kirk's brigade was supported by the brigade commanded by Brigadier General A. Willich, who was wounded and captured early in the action. Command of the brigade then devolved on Colonel W. H. Gibson, who has this to say about the Confederates' early morning attack:

At dawn of day orders were received to build fires and make coffee. In a few moments after, I met General Willich, who remarked that he would be absent a few moments at the headquarters of General Johnson, and in case anything occurred in front of our pickets, he directed me to rally the 39th and 32nd [Indiana] to their support. At twenty-five minutes past six, and soon after meeting the general, firing was heard on General Kirk's right. The brigade was instantly ordered to take arms, and Lieutenant Miles of the staff was despatched for General Willich. He was found and started for his command, but his horse was shot under him and he was made a prisoner before giving an order.

The enemy advanced upon our position with four heavy lines of battle, with a strong reserve held in mass. All these were in full view before the lines of General Kirk gave way. His (the enemy's) left extended a great distance beyond our extreme right, and was thrown forward so that his lines were to some extent oblique to ours. To the right of our position and near the Franklin road he took position with an immense force of cavalry. . . . His lines were advanced with great rapidity, and his force could not have been less than thirty-five thousand, besides cavalry.

The lines of General Kirk soon yielded to an assault which no troops in the world could have withstood. . . . With cavalry on the right, infantry assailing them on the left, and heavy masses rushing to the assault in front, these regiments were directed to retire, as the only escape from annihilation or capture. . . . Unchecked the foe rushed on. . . . At this juncture, learning nothing of General Willich, I felt it my duty to exert myself as far as possible to save the command. . . . From my position, looking to our centre, I could see our whole line falling back rapidly in some disorder. . . . [Later] We moved rapidly and in considerable disorder to the Nashville road, closely pursued by the enemy's cavalry. Here the colors of the 39th Indiana were captured. At this moment I learned that a considerable portion of this brigade had reached the centre; that General Willich had been killed or captured, and that Colonel Wallace was in command of the brigade. A complete panic prevailed; teams, ambulances, horsemen, footmen and attaches of the army, black and white, mounted on horses and mules, were rushing to the rear in the wildest confusion.

As the Confederates' initial assault was taken up by the troops on the right of McCown and Cleburne, General A. P. Stewart's brigade moved forward to attack General Negley's line in his front. Alexander F. Stevenson, who was one of those on the receiving end of that attack tells of the Federals' brave but unsuccessful resistance to the Confederate onslaught:

When General Stewart came closer to the Forty-second Illinois the firing again became terrific. Hescock's famous First Missouri battery and Bush's Fourth Indiana also exerted themselves as never before, while a part of Negley's division had a splendid cross-fire on Stewart's right regiments, and the rebel brigade lost many men. But the number of the Confederates was too great. Many of Roberts' men had expended the last cartridge, and, the enemy also coming in the rear, orders were given to fall back. Captain Hescock and Captain Bush, who had fought their guns with the greatest valor, were likewise forced to the rear. Each of the batteries had fired nearly eleven hundred rounds up to that hour, and the firing was at such close range that two of Bush's guns fell into the enemy's hands, as almost every horse belonging to them had been killed.

What a scene! Death and blood everywhere. Colonel Harrington, bravely leading his Twenty-seventh Illinois, was struck by a piece of shell, which tore the jaws from his face; Lieutenant-Colonel Swanwick, of the Twenty-second Illinois, wounded and unable to be moved; nearly forty per cent of the Forty-second and Twenty-second killed or wounded; gallant Captain Houghtalling carried away barely alive, the blood, as it flowed from his wound, leaving a track on the stones; and Lieutenant Tallioferro, who had never flinched, even in the hottest fire, but who seemed to grow in stature as the fire became more intense, shot dead between his cannons. Houghtalling's men, heroes every one of them, refused to leave their guns, and defended them with their revolvers, sabers, and ramrods, till they were finally overpowered and many taken prisoners. . . .

So conspicuous had been the bravery of Colonel Roberts that even the rebels admired him, and so splendidly had the men fought there that the Confederate General Stewart said, in his report: "The force which was engaged in this famous cedar brake was composed, at least in part, of regulars; the brigade was commanded by Colonel Roberts, who fell while gallantly attempting to rally his men opposite the centre of my line. He was buried Saturday evening, and the spot marked by a stone having his name scratched upon it with the point of a bayonet." And so it was, for by that stone we found the grave that held his sacred remains.

J. W. Burke, Lieutenant Colonel of the 10th Ohio Volunteer Infantry, commanding the Headquarters Guard, was posted with eight companies of his regiment at the bridge over Stewart's Creek on the Nashville-Murfreesboro pike, entrusted with the duty of providing protection for the trains. He was not engaged in the action on December 31st, but intercepted a large number of stragglers ("over 1,000" he reported), who had lurid stories to tell of the unhappy outcome of the day's fighting. It was not until the next day, however, that the full force of the fleeing stragglers was impressed on him. As he relates it in his official report:

About one o'clock a squadron of affrighted negroes came charging at full gallop from Murfreesboro towards Stewart's creek, and with such impetuosity and reckless-ness that over one hundred passed the bridge before I could check the progress of the main cavalcade. They were dismounted and some of them ducked by my men. This was the advance of what seemed to me to be the whole army—cavalrymen with jaded horses, artillery and infantry soldiers, breathless and holding on to wagons, relating the most incredible stories of defeat and annihilation of the army, as their respective regiments came streaming down the road and pouring through the woods on their way towards the bridge.

In vain did my small guard stationed on the road try to check the panic. Officers drew their revolvers, but the fugitives heeded them not. My regiment was in line on the hill-side, and I promptly fixed bayonet, marched at double quick to the bridge and drew up a line before it, sending out at the same time two companies deployed as skirmishers on the right and left to prevent the passing of the creek by fording. The fugitives crowded in thousands, and at one time pressed closely up to the bayonets of my men. . . . At this time I was rendered most valuable assistance by Lieutenant Runderhook, 4th United States Cavalry, and his men. . . . Riding through the panic-stricken crowds, the cavalrymen drove them into a field, where a good line was formed and every straggler taken and made "dress up".

The Confederate attack and follow-through was so fierce and irresistible that by 10 A. M. they had put Johnson's and Davis's divisions of McCook's corps to complete flight in a wide sweep of four or five miles to the Nashville pike. Sheridan's division put up sterner resistance, but was at length driven from the field, conducting a fighting withdrawal, despite stunning losses. Out of an effective force of about 6,500 men, Sheridan lost 1796 men and 72 officers killed and wounded, including his three brigade commanders killed.

By noon Bragg's first objective had been attained: the Federal line was doubled back like a jack-knife blade, until its right wing was at right angles to the original line of battle. But the Confederates were not able to deliver the knockout punch. The divisions of Van Cleve and Wood, numbering 12,000 fresh men, had been moved over from the left by Rosecrans to bulwark the badly beaten right wing. Backed up against the Nashville pike, supported by a bristling array of artillery, they were in position to make a desperate stand to hold communication with the rear. Cleburne's and McCown's elated but exhausted divisions, now facing to the east, confronted this fresh line as they emerged from the cedar glade into the open fields east of the pike.

One more push, it seemed, and the rout of the right wing would be complete— but that one more push was not forthcoming. Faced by the double line of reserves along the Nashville pike and the railroad, backed by artillery fire, the impetus of the Confederate drive on the Federal right spent its force, and the Confederates were driven back into the cedars from which they had come. The importance of this repulse, from the Federal point of view, is told by A. F. Stevenson:

The importance of this success cannot be over-estimated. If the Confederates had succeeded in taking and holding the Nashville pike there can be little doubt that the battle would have been lost, and a large part of the army captured. Near the Nash-ville pike were our ammunition trains, which would have fallen into their hands. The pike was the only road that connected us with Nashville, our base of supplies, and, in case a retreat was necessary, the only road on which the army could fall back.

But, more important still, it would have enabled the Confederates to enfilade General Thomas's corps, and to fire on Palmer's and Wood's divisions from the rear as well as from the front.

Under the demoralizing influence of the defeat of Davis's and Johnson's divisions, but few troops could have stood a double fire like this, and they would most likely have been compelled to fall back. But in what direction? There was only one, towards the north, between river and pike; but this space was only a few yards more than one-fourth of a mile in width, and partly covered with timber. A more serious state of affairs cannot be contemplated, and only the best-disciplined troops would have succeeded in fighting their way through.

About 10 A. M., as the Confederate drive against the strengthened Federal right began to slow down, Bragg called on Breckinridge to send two brigades to Polk's support. Breckinridge, however, had been the victim of some extraordinarily inept scouting, and was totally misinformed as to the situation on his front. When Van Cleve began to cross the river early in the morning, in accordance with Rosecrans' original plan of battle, Breckinridge was informed of the movement. But, for some unexplained reason, his scouts did not observe the quick withdrawal of Van Cleve's men—or, at least, did not tell Breckinridge about it—leaving that commander under the delusion that he was being threatened with immediate attack. He so informed Bragg earlier in explaining his inability to send reinforcements. By the time he became aware of the fact that the threatened attack on his front was imaginary, Hardee's men had run up against the fresh Federal line along the Nashville pike and had been driven back to the protection of the cedars.

The new position of the Federal line, as established late in the forenoon, created a sharp salient at the center, where Thomas's left joined Crittenden's right. Within this angle, on a slight elevation just to the east of the Nashville pike and on both sides of the railroad track, was a thick clump of trees covering an area of about four acres, which was referred to in the officers' reports as the "Round Forest". Here Rosecrans assembled every available brigade not already in action and buttressed them with field artillery massed on the high ground back of the forest. This stronghold was maintained against the successive waves of attacking Confederates through the rest of the day. Late in the afternoon Breckinridge's brigades began to come onto the field from across the river, in accordance with Bragg's instructions, and Bragg threw them into action as they arrived. One by one the brigades of Adams and Jackson and Preston and Palmer were hurled against the Round Forest position, with a courage and abandon that won the admiration of the defenders—but it was all in vain. One of the defending Federals tells vividly of the Confederates' last charge that day:

On they came in splendid style, full six thousand strong. Estep's case-shot tore through their ranks, but the gaps closed up. Parsons sent volley after volley of grape-shot against them, and the 6th and 26th Ohio, taking up the refrain, added the sharp rattle of minie-rifles to the unearthly din. Still the line pressed forward, firing as they came, until met by a simultaneous and destructive volley of musketry. They staggered, but quickly re-formed and, reinforced by Preston and the Confederate Palmer, advanced again to the charge. The battle had hushed on the extreme right, and the gallantry of this advance is indescribable. . . . The Confederates had no sooner moved into the open field from the cover of the river bank than they were received by a blast from the artillery. Men plucked the cotton from the bolls at their feet and stuffed it in their ears. Huge gaps were torn in the Confederate line at every discharge. The Confederate line staggered forward half the distance across the fields, when the Union infantry lines added minie-balls to the fury of the storm. Then the Confederates wavered and fell back, and the first day's fight was over.

At length the short winter twilight deepened to darkness, putting an end to the fighting—to the great relief of both exhausted and decimated armies. Colonel Thomas B. Van Horne summarizes the situation existing at the close of the day's fighting:

Neither army commander had fully executed his plan of battle, although General Bragg had approached very nearly the completion of his. He had turned a flank of the national army, bent back the right to the rear of the center, but had failed to turn its left or reach its rear, and hence had not gained the extreme advantages which he had anticipated in assuming the offensive and had seemingly attained at the grand crisis of the battle. He had assaulted boldly and persistently from first to last, but had completely exhausted his army without gaining a decisive victory. General Rosecrans had fought a battle radically different from the one he had proposed for himself. Instead of turning the right of the Confederate army and taking its center in reverse, according to his plan, he had been forced into the most emphatic straits in maintaining the defensive from flank to flank. Both commanders had lost heavily; General Bragg by continuous assaults with massed forces, and General Rosecrans by resistance at each point to superior numbers, and by frequent recessions under the guns of the enemy. . . .

It is seldom that an engagement of such dimensions has left two commanding generals so much in doubt as to the course that either would adopt, and hence each determined to await developments, and each was ignorant of the purpose of the other. Of the two, General Bragg was the more hopeful; not because he had strength for further offense, but from his belief that such was the condition of the opposing army that its retreat was a necessity. And the question of retreat was doubtless at first an open one with General Rosecrans and his subordinate commanders. General Rosecrans' report indicates that he was at first in doubt as to the propriety of attempting to remain on the field. . . . Being aware of his own heavy losses in men and materials, and having his right flank bent back upon his line of communications after a battle which he had provoked by positive offense, he could hardly avoid hesitation in maintaining the defensive in that position.

Thus closed the first day of a battle that was really two separate battles, two distinct engagements separated by a day of relative inactivity. In this first day's fighting, the Federals were driven from their positions on their right for a distance of four or five miles, and the Confederates held the field at the close of the day. Both armies had suffered shocking losses, but the Confederates were justified in feeling that the days was theirs. With an impetuosity he probably regretted later, Bragg exultantly telegraphed President Davis that he had won a great victory and "the enemy is falling back".

The enemy was not falling back, however, although it later developed that Rosecrans did come close to retreating. That evening, in his headquarters in a cabin by the side of the Nashville pike, he conferred with his corps commanders as to what course to pursue. McCook, who had taken such a savage pummeling that day, advised a retreat to Nashville; so did General Stanley, commanding the cavalry. Thomas and Crittenden were non-commital, but assured Rosecrans they would support him in whatever decision he made. Rosecrans, in his report, sums up the result of these deliberations:

After careful examination and free consultation with corps commanders, followed by a personal examination of the ground in rear as far as Overall's Creek, it was determined to await the enemy's attack in that position; to send for the provision train, and order up fresh supplies of ammunition; on the arrival of which, should the enemy not attack, offensive operations should be resumed.

"God has granted us a happy New Year," Bragg exulted in his premature victory telegram to President Davis. When the first day of the new year dawned, however, he probably began to suspect that it might not prove to be so happy as he had predicted. By pressing forward his skirmishers he soon determined that the Federals, instead of retreating, were in a strong defensive position in the adjusted line they had established during the night and early morning. To straighten his line, Rosecrans had withdrawn from his salient in the Round Forest, and Polk promptly moved up into this position—the bastion before which so many of his and Breckinridge's men had fruitlessly sacrificed their lives the previous day.

January 1st was a day of relative inactivity. Rosecrans, in his new and stronger position, seemed satisfied with the respite from attack. Bragg, disappointed at Rosecrans' failure to retreat as expected, seemed undecided what to do. In his official report, Bragg summed it up:

> Our forces, greatly wearied and much reduced by heavy losses, were held ready to avail themselves of any change in the enemy's position, but it was deemed inadvisable to assail him as then established. The whole day . . . was passed without an important movement on either side, and was consumed by us in gleaming the battlefield, burying the dead and replenishing ammunition.

As a matter of fact, each side did make an "important movement" during that day of lull in active combat. Breckinridge, with the brigades he had brought across the river as reinforcements the preceding afternoon, was returned to his original position east of the river. This move was countered by Rosecrans' ordering Crittenden to move Van Cleve's division (now commanded by Colonel Samuel Beatty), supported by Grose's brigade, across the river, where they formed a line of battle about a mile from Breckinridge's front. On the high ground on the west side of the river, supporting Beatty, were the other elements of Crittenden's corps: Negley's division and Hazen's and Cruft's brigades of Palmer's division, with their batteries.

The presence of Beatty's division on the east side of the river was observed by Bragg on the morning of the 2nd, and this precipitated his attack on the Federal left that afternoon which proved to be the determining factor in turning victory into defeat. He tells about this in his official report:

> Observation excited my suspicion in regard to a movement having been made by the enemy across Stone's River immediately in Breckinridge's front. Reconnaissances by several staff officers soon developed the fact that a division had crossed unopposed and established themselves on and under cover of an eminence, from which Lieutenant General Polk's line was both commanded and enfiladed. The dislodgement of this force or the withdrawal of Polk's line was an evident necessity. The latter involved consequences not to be entertained. Orders were accordingly given for the concentration of the whole of Major General Breckinridge's division in front of the position to be taken. . . . Major General Breckinridge was sent for and advised of the movement and its objects, the securing and holding of the position which protected Polk's flank and gave us command of the enemy's by which to enfilade him. He was informed of the forces placed at his disposal, and instructed with them to drive the enemy back, crown the hill, intrench his artillery, and hold the position. . . . General Breckinridge at 3:30

p.m. reported he would advance at 4 o'clock . . . The contest was short and severe; the enemy was driven back and the position was again yielded.

Our forces were moved, unfortunately, so far to the left as to throw a portion of them into and over Stone's River, where they encountered heavy masses of the enemy, while those against whom they were intended to operate on our side of the river had a destructive enfilade on our whole line. Our second line was so close to the front as to receive the enemy's fire, and, returning it, took their friends in rear . . .

Learning from my own staff officers, sent to the scene, of the disorderly retreat being made by General Breckinridge's division, Brigadier General Patton Anderson's fine brigade of Mississippians (the nearest body of troops) was promptly ordered to his relief. On reaching the field and moving forward, Anderson found himself in front of Breckinridge's infantry, and soon encountered the enemy's light troops close upon our artillery, which had been left without support. This noble brigade, under its cool and gallant chief, drove the enemy back and saved all the guns not captured before its arrival. . . . Anderson's men held a position next the enemy, corresponding nearly with our original line, while Breckinridge's brigade commanders collected their scattered men as far as practicable in the darkness, and took irregular positions on Anderson's left and rear. At daylight in the morning they were moved to the front and the whole line re-established without opposition.

It is generally agreed that the turning-point of the second day's battle was when the drive of the charging Confederates was checked and turned into a repulse by the torrent of artillery fire from the Federal guns on the north side of Stone's River. It was Captain John Mendenhall of the Fourth Artillery, Rosecrans' Chief of Artillery, who massed those guns there, and he tells of how he did it:

About 4 p.m., whilst riding along the pike with General Crittenden, we heard heavy firing of artillery and musketry on the left. We at once rode briskly over, and arriving upon the hill near the ford saw our infantry retiring before the enemy. The general asked me if I could not do something to relieve Colonel Beatty with my guns; Captain Swallow had already opened with his battery.

I ordered Lieutenant Parsons to move a little forward and open with his guns; then rode back to bring up Lieutenant Estep with his 8th Indiana battery. Meeting Captain Morton with his brigade of pioneers, he asked for advice, and I told him to move briskly forward with his brigade, and send his battery to the crest of the hill, near the batteries already engaged. The 8th Indiana battery took position to the right of Lieutenant Parsons. Seeing that Lieutenant Osborn was in position (between Lieutenants Parsons and Estep), I rode to Lieutenant Stevens (26th Pennsylvania battery), and directed him to change front, to file to the left and open fire; and then to Captain Standart, and directed him to move to the left with his pieces; he took position covering the ford. I found that Captain Bradley had anticipated my wishes, and had changed front to fire to the left and opened upon the enemy; this battery was near the railroad. Lieutenant Livingston's 3rd Wisconsin battery, (which was across the river), opened upon the advancing enemy and continued to fire till he thought he could no longer maintain his position, when he crossed over, one section at a time, and opened fire again. The firing ceased about dark.

During this terrible encounter of little more than an hour in duration, forty-three pieces of artillery, belonging to the left wing, the Board of Trade battery of six guns, and the batteries of fifty-eight pieces, opened fire upon the enemy. The enemy soon retired, our troops following; three batteries of the left wing, besides those of General Davis, crossed the river in pursuit.

Mendenhall, being an artillery officer, barely mentions the work of the infantry in putting the finishing touches on Breckinridge's repulse. Van Horne, however, is of the opinion that the charge of the infantry, led by Miller's brigade of Negley's division, was the deciding factor. But for this infantry charge, he thinks Breckinridge's forces might have reformed upon their objective and held it.

General Bragg in his official report accepts full responsibility for the decision to retire from the field, virtually admitting defeat. As a matter of fact, however, the idea that the army should retreat after the debacle on January 2 originated with his own subordinate commanders.

Following Breckinridge's repulse, Bragg not only sent Anderson's brigade across the river to help cover his retreat, but later in the evening also sent Hardee with Cleburne's division and also McCown's. This left only the divisions of Cheatham and Withers west of the river. Cheatham had suffered the staggering loss of 36% during the battle, and Withers 28%, and the combined strength of the two divisions was only about 7000 effectives. This disparity became more marked during the night as the river rose rapidly following a heavy rain, and Rosecrans drew to the west of the river all the troops from the east side, thus concentrating his whole army in front of the depleted divisions of Cheatham and Withers. These generals did not then know of the concentration of the enemy's whole force in their front, but they did know that they were unsupported on their side of the river—and, above all, they were convinced that their commanding general was unequal to handling the army as things then stood. General Polk's son tells of the result of their apprehension:

What they heard concerning the state of Breckinridge's division that night, and what they knew of the condition of McCown's and Cleburne's, who had just been alongside of them, did not tend to reassurance upon the general situation. In the absence, then, of the all-essential confidence in the commanding general, and speaking only for themselves, Cheatham and Withers wrote General Bragg at 12:15 A. M., January 3, saying that they thought the army should be put promptly in retreat, adding:

You have but three divisions that are at all reliable, and even some of these are more or less demoralized from having some brigade commanders who do not possess the confidence of their commands. Such is our opinion, and we deem it a solemn duty to express it to you. We do fear great disaster from the condition of things now existing, and think it should be averted if possible.

This note was sent through the corps commander, General Polk, who endorsed upon it:

I send you the enclosed paper as directed, and I am compelled to add that after seeing the effect of the operations of to-day, added to that produced upon the troops by the battle of the 31st, I very greatly fear the consequences of another engagement at this place on the ensuing day. We could now, perhaps, get off with some safety and with some credit if the affair was well managed. Should we fail in the meditated attack, the consequences might be very disastrous. . . .

Lieutenant Richmond, General Polk's aide, took the note to General Bragg, who, upon reading it, replied, "Say to the general we shall maintain our position at every hazard."

General Polk sent the correspondence to General Hardee with General Bragg's reply, for his information, and said: "I think the decision of the general unwise, and am compelled to add, in a high degree. I shall of course obey his orders and endeavor to do my duty. I think it due you to let you know the views of myself and my two division commanders, especially as we all believe the conflict will be severe in the morning." . . .

At ten o'clock on the following day General Polk met General Hardee at army headquarters. General Bragg then stated that he had reason to believe that Rosecrans' strength was greater than he had at first supposed, and as he was then receiving additional reinforcements he felt that, in view of the condition of his own army, a retreat should be made.

In this General Hardee and General Polk concurred, and that night the army withdrew. Hardee marched to Tullahoma by way of the Manchester road, and Polk retired to Shelbyville on Duck River.

General Bragg himself rode to Winchester, fifty miles from Murfreesboro, where he established his headquarters, it being his intention to place his army upon the line of the Elk River. As the enemy showed no disposition to press forward, however, Polk had halted at Shelbyville, twenty miles from Murfreesboro, and reported the fact to General Bragg. He was then directed to remain at the position. Hardee was next moved up to Wartrace, and army headquarters were placed at Tullahoma.

Bragg, in speaking of the reinforcements received by Rosecrans during the night of the 2nd, seems to have been misled into magnifying the number of men that had been added to the Federal force. The only reinforcements actually received that night were Spears's brigade of Tennesseans and the 85th regiment of Illinois Volunteers. The reports of Bragg's scouts may have exaggerated the strength of these fresh units; but to some extent Bragg's impression that the enemy was receiving heavy reinforcements may have been due to an elaborate scheme of deception devised by Rosecrans. Rosecrans mentions this briefly in his report; one of his officers tells about it in more detail:

General Davis's division having been sent across Stone's river, the extreme right became rather weak, and General Rosecrans deemed it, therefore, wise to give the enemy the impression that he was receiving large reinforcements. In order to deceive General Bragg, he organized a large number of men endowed with stentorian voices, who were to represent the commanding officers of companies, regiments, and brigades, composing a division. As soon as these men were properly stationed a loud voice could be heard calling out: "Fourteenth Division, halt!" Immediately afterwards other voices could be heard commanding brigades and regiments to halt, followed by a number of company commands. A few minutes intervened and again these loud voices could be heard, in the stillness of the night, giving the necessary orders by which the imaginary regiments were to take their respective camping-grounds, and companies to stack arms and break ranks. A short time after this had taken place General Rosecrans ordered men to build camp-fires in front of these supposititious new reinforcements.

Whether this ruse had the effect of preventing an attack is perhaps doubtful, though General Bragg states, in his report, that the Federal army had been largely reinforced.

The losses, on both sides, in proportion to the numbers engaged were very heavy. The effective strength of Bragg's army was about 37,712, and he suffered casualties of 10,266, killed, wounded and missing. Rosecrans had 43,400 effectives, with 13,249 casualties.

General Hardee, in his official report of the battle, made an interesting (if not entirely objective) comment on the comparative merits of the two armies:

It is worthy of remark that at Murfreesboro, whenever the fight was confined principally to musketry, and the enemy had no advantage in artillery, we were successful. It was only when they had masked heavy batteries under cover of the railroad embankments that we were repulsed. In every form of contest in which mechanical instruments, requiring skill and heavy machinery to make them, can be used, the Federals are our superiors. In every form of contest in which manly courage, patient endurance and brave impulse are the qualities and conditions necessary to success, we have invariably been successful. Long-range cannon and improved projectiles can be made only by great mechanical skill, heavy machinery and abundant resources. The enemy is therefore superior in artillery. Infantry constitutes the great arm of the service, and its appointments and equipments are simple. The Federal infantry, unsupported by artillery, has not in a single instance fought successfully with ours, when the odds were less than three to two.

Some idea of the extraordinary violence of this battle, and of the surprising quantity of ammunition used, may be gathered from the fact that the report of the Federal ordnance officer shows that during the action their artillery fired 20,000 rounds and their infantry fired 2,000,000 rounds of musketry.

General Rosecrans, a pious man, closed his report of the battle by quoting the first verse of the 115th Psalm: *"Non nobis, Domine, non nobis, sed nomine tuo da gloriam"* (Not unto us, O Lord, not unto us, but unto thy name give the glory).

☆ Six Months Between Battles

THE FIRST SIX months of 1863 passed without any major military activity on the part of the two armies confronting each other in Middle Tennessee. Both Bragg and Rosecrans had plenty of other problems to occupy their attention without either seeking to stir the opposing army into full-scale combat.

Bragg had hardly got his army encamped in its new position before he found himself confronted with such an uproar of censure of his withdrawal from Murfreesboro that he felt it necessary to establish a formal defense against his critics. Relying on that letter from Cheatham and Withers, with its endorsement by Polk, he committed the sad error of making an issue of it, writing the following letter to each of his corps and division commanders on January 11th:

General: Finding myself assailed in private and public, by the press, in private circles, by officers and citizens, for the movement from Murfreesboro, which was resisted by me for some time after advised by my corps and division commanders and only adopted after hearing of the enemy's reinforcements by large numbers from Kentucky, it becomes necessary for me to save my fair name, if I cannot stop the deluge or abuse which will destroy my usefulness and demoralize this army.

It has come to my knowledge that many of these accusations and insinuations are from staff-officers of my generals, who persistently assent that the movement was made against the opinion and advice of their chiefs and while the enemy was in full retreat. False or true, the soldiers have no means of judging me rightly, or getting the facts, and the effect on them will be the same—a loss of confidence and a consequent demoralization of the whole army.

It is only through my generals that I can establish the facts as they exist. Unanimous as you were in council in verbally advising a retrograde movement, I cannot doubt that you will cheerfully attest the same in writing. I desire that you will consult your subordinate commanders and be candid with me, as I have always endeavored to prove myself with you.

If I have misunderstood your advice and acted against your opinions, let me know it in justice to yourselves. If, on the contrary, I am the victim of unjust accusations, say so, and unite with me in staying the malignant slanders being propagated by men who have felt the sting of discipline.

If Bragg had ended his letter right there, he would have been on safe ground. His subordinate commanders would be compelled to admit that they had advised or willingly concurred in the retreat from Murfreesboro. But in the fervor of his indignation and wounded feelings, he added a paragraph that opened up a Pandora's box of criticism which it can well be assumed he did not intend to unleash:

General Smith has been called to Richmond—it is supposed with a view to supersede me. I shall retire without a regret, if I find I have lost the good opinion of my generals, upon whom I have ever relied as upon a foundation of rock. Your early attention is most desirable, and is urgently solicited.

Bragg's request for candid comment met with the wholehearted cooperation of his generals to whom it was addressed. All exonerated him from responsibility for originating the idea of the retreat. But his statement that he would retire without regret if he found he had lost the good opinion of his generals gave them just the opportunity they had been looking for, and they embraced it with enthusiasm.

When Bragg's letter reached Polk's headquarters, Polk was absent on a short leave and the corps was temporarily in command of General Cheatham. Cheatham and Withers talked it over and decided that they should postpone making a detailed reply until they had an opportunity to discuss the matter with Polk. Cheatham, however, did not shirk admitting his responsibility for the note written Bragg from the battlefield and, speaking for himself, he promptly sent a reply saying:

Since the army commenced falling back from Murfreesboro, I have upon all occasions, public and private, stated that I myself was one of the first to suggest the movement, and fully endorse it.

Hardee in his reply emphasized "the delicate character of the inquiries you institute". He took pains to point out that neither he nor his division commanders had made any proposal to retreat, although he admitted that he had concurred in Bragg's decision to retire when it was announced to him on the morning of the 3rd. Then, specifically referring to Bragg's statement in his letter that he would retire without regret if he had lost the good opinion of his generals, Hardee wrote this stinging paragraph:

I have conferred with Major-General Breckinridge and Major-General Cleburne in regard to this matter, and I feel that frankness compels me to say that the general officers, whose judgment you have invoked, are unanimous in their opinion that a change in the command of this army is necessary. In this opinion I concur. I feel assured that this opinion is considerately formed, and with the highest respect for the purity of your motives, your energy, and your personal character; but they are convinced, as you must feel, that the peril of the country is superior to all personal considerations.

Cleburne was equally obliging with his candid views:

I have consulted with all my brigade commanders . . . and they unite with me in personal regard for yourself, in a high appreciation of your patriotism and gallantry, and in a conviction of your great capacity for organization; but at the same time they see, with regret, and it has also been my observation, that you do not possess the confidence of the army in other respects in that degree necessary to secure success.

Breckinridge, who was nursing a keen feeling of resentment at Bragg's comments on the action of his troops on the 2nd, was not reluctant to be just as frank as Cleburne:

Acting with the candor you invoke, they [his brigade commanders] request me to say that in their opinion the conduct of the military operations in front of Murfreesboro made it necessary and proper for our army to retire. They also request me to say that while they entertain the highest respect for your patriotism, it is their opinion that you do not possess the confidence of the army to an extent that will enable you to be useful as is commander. In this opinion I am bound to state that I concur.

Kind-hearted Polk, when he got back on January 30, tried to escape the necessity of voicing his opinion on Bragg's fitness for command. Bragg's letter of inquiry, Polk wrote in reply, seemed to present two points: First, whether the corps and division commanders were willing to give a written statement on the responsibility for the retreat; and, second, whether Bragg had lost the confidence of his officers as military commander. "To avoid being placed in a false position", he asked Bragg to advise him whether he was correct in this interpretation. Not being particularly eager for any more "candid" statements, Bragg grasped at the straw. He replied promptly that his letter contained only one point of inquiry—that about the retreat. "The paragraph relating to my supersedure," he said, "was only an expression of the feeling with which I should receive your replies, should they prove I had been misled in my construction of your opinion and advice."

This gave the bishop-general his desired loophole for not wounding Bragg's feelings. He answered simply that the original letter written by Cheatham and Withers, with Polk's endorsement, showed plainly enough their support of the retreat.

Polk was not to get off so easily, however. He learned two days later that Hardee and his officers felt that Polk had dodged the real issue—the question of confidence in Bragg as commander of the army. They thought Polk's evasive action had left them in the attitude of insubordinate malcontents. Polk, though unwilling to do his brother officers an injustice, did not see how, in the light of Bragg's explanatory letter, he could have expressed to the man himself a judgment of his capacity. Polk therefore chose the course of writing a letter to President Davis, attaching all the correspondence. Commenting on it at some length, he said:

This correspondence has been very unfortunate, and its inauguration ill-judged; but it is now a part of the history of the times, and I feel it to be my duty to transmit to you copies of the letters which have passed between the general and myself. That correspondence speaks for itself.

Then, after pointing out that, by the device of his letter to Bragg and Bragg's reply not insisting on an expression of his opinion as to Bragg's fitness, he had avoided going on record as to that delicate question, Polk went on:

I feel it a duty to say to you that, had I and my division commanders been asked to answer, our replies would have coincided with those of the officers of the other corps. You have known my opinions on this subject since my visit to Richmond. I have only to add, if he were Napoleon or the great Frederick, he would serve our cause at some other point better than here. My opinion is he had better be transferred . . . His capacity for organization and discipline, which has not been equaled among us, could be used by you at headquarters with infinite advantage to the whole army. I think, too, that the best thing to be done in supplying his place would be to give his command to General Johnston. He will cure all discontent and inspire the army with new life and confidence. He is here on the spot, and I am sure will be content to take it.

Johnston was indeed "on the spot", both literally and in the now current vernacular. About two weeks previously President Davis, having been informed

of Bragg's controversy with his generals, had ordered Johnston to go to Murfreesboro and investigate the matter. Davis told Johnston of Bragg's unhappy correspondence with his subordinates, commenting: "Why General Bragg should have
selected that tribunal and have invited its judgments upon him is to me unexplained.
It manifests, however, a condition of things which seems to me to require your
presence. . . . Although my confidence in General Bragg is unshaken, it can not
be doubted that, if he is distrusted by his officers and troops, a disaster may
result."

In his *Narrative* General Johnston tells of how he reacted to the President's
order and how he resisted any inclination he may have had to supersede Bragg in
the command of the Army of Tennessee:

While inspecting the defenses of Mobile on the 22nd of January, I received a
telegram from the President, directing me to proceed "with the least delay, "to the
headquarters of General Bragg's army", and informing me that "an explanatory letter
would be found at Chattanooga." The object of his visit, as explained in the letter found
in Chattanooga, was to ascertain the feeling toward the general entertained by the army
—"whether he had so far lost its confidence as to impair his usefulness in his present
position"; to obtain such information as would enable me "to decide what the best
interests of the service required"; and "to give the President the advice which he
needed at that juncture." Mr. Davis remarked, in this letter, that his own confidence in
General Bragg was unshaken.

I bestowed three weeks upon this investigation, and then advised against General
Bragg's removal, because the field-officers of the army represented that their men were
in high spirits, and as ready as ever for fight; such a condition seeming to me incompatible with the alleged want of confidence in their general's ability. . . .

[Later] As there were no indications of intention on the part of the Federal commander in Tennessee to take the offensive soon, and as my presence seemed to me more
proper in Mississippi than in Tennessee, I left Chattanooga for Jackson on March 9th,
and at Mobile (when continuing on the 12th the inspection interrupted by the President's
telegram on the 22nd of January), I received the following despatch from the Secretary of War, dated March 9th: "Order General Bragg to report to the War Department here for conference; assume yourself direct charge of the army in Middle Tennessee." In obedience to these instructions I returned immediately to Tennessee, and
reached Tullahoma on the 18th, and there, without the publication of a formal order
on the subject, assumed the duties of commander of the army. In consequence of information that the general was devoting himself to Mrs. Bragg, who was supposed to
be at the point of death, I postponed the communication of the order of the Secretary
of War to him, and reported the postponement and the cause to the Secretary. . . .

I soon found myself too feeble to command an army, and in a few days became
seriously sick; so that, when the state of General Bragg's domestic affairs permitted him
to return to military duty, I was unfit for it. He therefore resumed the position of
commander of the Army of Tennessee.

Although lack of confidence in Bragg's ability was evidently prevalent among
his subordinate generals, the records show that this feeling was not absolutely
unanimous. He had at least one staunch friend and defender in General William
B. Bate, commander of the Second Brigade of General McCown's Division. In
a strong letter written on March 24th to Landon C. Haynes, one of Tennessee's
Senators in the Confederate Congress, Bate spoke out clearly and boldly in
Bragg's defence:

Senator: It is thoroughly understood in the Army of Tennessee in the last few
days that General Bragg has been relieved from the command of the Army of Ten-

nessee. Can it be possible that is or will be so? The moment it is done our army here will gradually begin to degenerate into an armed mob, and six months will not pass until it is virtually disintegrated.

Except for an official interview, I do not personally know General Bragg, and cannot be influenced by any other than patriotic motives. While on my crutches I have, as you are aware, been in rear of his army in command of the District of North Alabama and at Chattanooga, which afforded me a fine opportunity to witness the effect of his force of character and discipline. Recently I have been in the field under him, and my convictions as to the necessity of his presence in this army has strengthened daily.

General Bragg exacts military duty from officers as well as men, and hence many of the former, as well as the latter, have become his *critiques par excellence*. I understand from high sources that his standing with his officers and men has been made a cause of complaint to the Government. My opinion is that the very men who make the complaints will rue it in three months from to-day should he be removed. The truth is, Senator, the captious wishes of officers who are ambitious should not be yielded to merely for their gratification. It is a dangerous precedent in an army to gratify the malcontents.

I am for proper discipline and drill, and there is no man in our entire army who is the equal of General Bragg in organizing, disciplining, and keeping together a large command. General Joseph E. Johnston is his superior in many respects I do not doubt, but together we have a happy combination. Keep it so. Those of us who wish the success of our cause above all personal considerations have a right to speak to those who are upon the watch-tower of our liberties and give them the benefit of our personal and official observation, and hence I write you, as one of our guardians who I hope has to the proper extent the ear of the President, and will not hesitate to make known to him the honest and patriotic opinion of one of his officers who feels that the necessity for retaining General Bragg in his present command is urgent. Suppose this army has to fall back south of the Tennessee, and General Bragg is disconnected with it—the terror and awe of his name to deserters lost—what will become of it? It will become a skeleton from desertion—the shadow of its now substantial parts. . . .

Would it not be consistent with your sense of duty to have an interview with the President and urge the retention of General Bragg in his present command?

Whether Senator Haynes did communicate General Bate's views to President Davis is not known; at any rate, the President took no further action at the time. General Johnston's illness continued for about a month. Meanwhile, Bragg seems to have forgot his declared willingness to "retire without regret" if he had lost his generals' good opinion. They, with unparalleled frankness, had made it plain that he had indeed lost their confidence; but Bragg held on to his command, and the unhappy Army of Tennessee continued to function as best it could under the impossible condition of command by a man whose ability was openly and unreservedly distrusted by most of his subordinates.

The relations between Bragg and his generals naturally remained strained, but they all accepted conditions as they existed, without sulking or recrimination, and the army showed no falling off in its efficiency and morale during its six months' encampment on the Shelbyville-Tullahoma line. Bragg was at his best in such circumstances, where there was no need for maneuvering of troops in combat against the enemy. Here, during these months of military inactivity, he had an opportunity to exercise those talents for organization which everybody admitted he possessed, and there was not in the whole Confederacy at that time a more excellently drilled and disciplined body of soldiers than the Army of Tennessee.

While General Bragg was devoting so much of his time to the protection of his reputation from the onslaughts of his critics, General Rosecrans was having a taste of the same bitter dose. As the days and weeks went by and he did not show signs of mounting an immediate offensive, he was subjected to the all too familiar barrage of criticism and admonition from the Washington authorities, who always seemed to find it difficult to conceal their impatience with what they considered the slowness of movement of the armies in the field, regardless of their own ignorance of the problems confronting the commanders.

On May 28th President Lincoln telegraphed Rosecrans: "I would not push you to any rashness, but I am very anxious that you do your utmost, short of rashness, to keep Bragg from getting off to help Johnston against Grant." Rosecrans replied, noncommittally: "I will attend to it." Halleck a few days later, probably inspired by Lincoln, prodded Rosecrans again: "If you can not hurt the enemy now he will soon hurt you." Then, on June 11, Halleck took another jab: "I deem it my duty to report to you the great dissatisfaction that is felt here at your inactivity."

The harassed Rosecrans replied the same day, telling of the preparations he was perfecting for a forward movement by his infantry and cavalry. The great majority of his corps and division commanders, he stated, were of the opinion that an advance was not advisable at that time, going on to say: "Admitting these officers to have a reasonable share of military sagacity, courage and patriotism, you perceive that there are graver and stronger reasons than probably appear at Washington for the attitude of this army. I therefore counsel caution and patience at headquarters."

In acknowledging this, Halleck repeated that "The prolonged inactivity of so large an army in the field is causing much complaint and dissatisfaction, not only in Washington, but throughout the country." As to counseling "caution and patience" on the part of "the authorities here", he said sharply: "I have done so very often; but after five or six months of inactivity, with your force all the time diminishing and no hope of any immediate increase, you must not be surprised that their patience is pretty well exhausted."

That Washington's patience had indeed been exhausted was made plain to Rosecrans four days later, on June 16, when Halleck sent this terse telegram: "Is it your intention to make an immediate movement forward? A definite answer, yes or no, is required." Evidently nettled, Rosecrans replied: "If immediate means to-night or to-morrow, no. If it means as soon as all things are ready, say five days, yes."

At length, on June 21, Rosecrans wrote Halleck a somewhat lengthy letter, detailing the military aspects of the situation as he saw it; then on June 24th he telegraphed Halleck: "The army begins to move at 3 o'clock this morning."

While all this controversey was going on, there had not been a total cessation of military operation. On the contrary, the cavalry on both sides had been almost constantly engaged in some form of activity. Conspicuous for its failure was an apparently ill-advised attempt to recapture Fort Donelson made by Wheeler and Forrest late in January. Henry M. Cist tells about this abortive effort from the standpoint of the victorious Federals:

On January 26th Bragg ordered Wheeler on an expedition to capture Fort Donelson. Wheeler directed Forrest to move his brigade with four guns on the river road via the Cumberland Iron Works to Dover, which was the real position occupied and fortified by the Federal forces and not the old site of Fort Donelson, while Wheeler with Wharton's command of some twenty-five hundred men moved on a road to the left.

Rosecrans, hearing from his scouts that this movement was contemplated, ordered Davis in command of his division and two brigades of cavalry under Minty, to march by the Versailles road and take Wheeler in the rear. Steedman was directed to watch Wheeler's movements by way of Triune. Davis despatched Minty to move with his cavalry around by way of Unionville and Rover, while he moved with the infantry directly to Eagleville. At Rover, Minty captured a regiment of some three hundred and fifty men. Davis and Steedman's forces united at Franklin, the latter marching by way of Eagleville.

Wheeler, advancing rapidly, passed between the troops in pursuit, and on February 3rd his entire force attacked the post at Dover occupied by Colonel Harding with the Eighty-Third Illinois, some six hundred men in the command. The rebels opened fire at once, and made a vigorous assault in force upon Harding's position. His little command repulsed the enemy with heavy loss. Again they advanced, making a more determined assault than before, and again they were driven back, with still greater loss. In this last repulse Harding ordered his men to charge beyond the works, which they did with great gallantry, capturing 42 of the rebels. Wheeler then withdrew with a total loss of 150 killed, 400 wounded, and 150 captured. Colonel Harding lost 16 killed, 60 wounded and 50 captured.

General Wheeler, in his report of this tragic fiasco, explains that:

After maturely considering the matter, we concluded that nothing could be lost by an attack on the garrison at Dover and, from the information that we had, there was good reason to believe that this post could easily be captured."

If Wheeler meant that "we" to include General Forrest, it was definitely misleading. When the attack was first proposed, Forrest minced no words in protesting against it, mentioning a shortage of ammunition and pointing out that "the expedition did not promise results in any wise commensurate with inevitable losses and possible hazard of serious disaster". Dr. Wyeth in his biography of Forrest says:

The premonition of disaster weighed upon Forrest so heavily that on the morning of the engagement he spoke of the matter in strict confidence to his chief-of-staff, Major Charles W. Anderson, and to Dr. Ben Wood, then a surgeon connected with his command. He said: "I have a special request to make of you in regard to the proposed attack on Fort Donelson. I have protested against the move, but my protest has been disregarded, and I intend to do my whole duty and I want my men to do the same. I have spoken to none but you on this subject, and I do not wish that anyone should know of the objections I have made. I have this request to make: If I am killed in this fight, you will see that justice is done me by officially stating that I protested against the attack, and that I am not willing to be held responsible for any disaster that may result."

Forrest, true to his promise, spared no energy in pushing the assault, and he had been painfully injured as two horses were shot from under him as he led his men in two desperate but fruitless attacks on the Federal works. Wyeth tells how the defeated Confederates went into bivouac that night about four miles from Dover, and of the spirited exchange between Wheeler and Forrest that evening:

Here, in a road-side house, by the light of a log fire, Generals Wheeler, Wharton and Forrest talked over the dismal failure of the day. . . . Forrest was in uncontrollable mood, nor was his irritability rendered more easy by the injury he had received and the great fatigue of the day. . . . Wheeler was dictating his report to one of his staff. Forrest was lying down on his water-proof coat in front of the fire, his head on a turned-up chair, and his feet well on the hearth. Then (as Wharton was dictating his report) Forrest interrupted him, saying in an angry and excited tone, "I have no fault to find with my men. In both charges they did their duty as they have always done". At this moment General Wheeler remarked, "General Forrest, my report does ample justice to yourself and to your men." Forrest replied, "General Wheeler, I advised against this attack, and said all a subordinate officer should have said against it, and nothing you can say now or do will bring back my brave men lying dead or wounded and freezing around that fort tonight. I mean no disrespect to you; you know my feelings of personal friendship for you; you can have my sword if you demand it; but there is one thing I do want you to put in that report to General Bragg—tell him that I will be in my coffin before I will fight again under your command." . . .

Wheeler both knew and appreciated Forrest, admired his wonderful genius, and loved him devotedly. Moreover he knew that when the tempest was raging in this wild and rugged nature he could appeal to it more by gentle word and manner than by the strict rules of military discipline. "Forrest," he said, quietly and with great feeling, "I can not take your sabre, and I regret exceedingly your determination. As the commanding officer I take all the blame and responsibility for this failure."

After this Wheeler respected in perfect faith Forrest's whim and determination. . . . The methods of these two soldiers were entirely different and, pursuing them, both won undying fame. Their friendship remained steadfast to the end, and Forrest had no greater admirer than his former chief of cavalry."

But, it should be added, Forrest never again fought under Wheeler's command, no matter how steadfast their personal friendship may have been.

An interesting and attractive picture of the Army of Tennessee and its leaders during this summer is provided by the journal of a distinguished visitor to Shelbyville while Bragg had his army there in 1863. Lieutenant Colonel Arthur Fremantle, a personable young professional soldier, and officer in the famous Coldstream Guards of the British Army, had made his way into the Confederacy through Mexico and into Texas. He then started on a trip through the Confederate states which finally included a short stay with the Army of Northern Virginia and his presence at the battle of Gettysburg, but his first objective was the Army of Tennessee. When he got back to England he set down his observations in an interesting and well-written book entitled *Three Months in the Confederate States,* from which we get some charmingly intimate sidelights on Confederate leaders, as well as fresh and objective views of contemporary army and civilian life. Concerning his visit to Bragg's army Colonel Fremantle says:

28th May (Thursday)—I arrived at Chattanooga (Tennessee) at 4:30 A. M., and after breakfasting started again at 7:30 by train for Shelbyville, General Bragg's headquarters. This train was crammed to repletion with soldiers rejoining their regiments, so I was constrained to sit in the aisle on the floor of one of the cars. I thought myself lucky even then, for so great was the number of military, that all "citizens" were ordered out to make way for the soldiers; but my gray shooting-jacket and youthful appearance saved me from the imputation of being a "citizen." Two hours later, the passport officer, seeing who I was, procured me a similar situation in the ladies' car, where I was a little better off.

After leaving Chattanooga, the railroad winds alongside the Tennessee River, the banks of which are high and beautifully covered with trees. The river itself is wide, and very pretty; but from my position in the tobacco juice I was unable to do justice to the scenery. I saw stockades at intervals all along the railroad, which were constructed by the Federals, who occupied all this country last year.

On arriving at Wartrace at 4 P. M., I determined to remain there, and ask for hospitality from General Hardee, as I saw no prospect of reaching Shelbyville in decent time. Leaving my baggage with the provost marshal at Wartrace, I walked on to General Hardee's headquarters, which were distant about two miles from the railroad. They were situated in a beautiful country—green, undulating, full of magnificent trees, principally beeches—and the scenery was by far the finest I had seen in America as yet.

When I arrived, I found that General Hardee was in company with General Polk and Bishop Elliott of Georgia, and also with Mr. Vallandigham. The latter (called "the Apostle of Liberty") is a good-looking man, apparently not much over forty, and had been turned out of the North three days before. Rosecrans had wished to hand him over to Bragg by flag of truce; but as the latter declined to receive him in that manner, he was, as General Hardee expressed it, "dumped down" in the neutral ground between the lines, and left there.

He then received hospitality from the Confederates in the capacity of a destitute stranger. They do not in any way receive him officially, and it does not suit the policy of either party to be identified with one another. He is now living at a private home in Shelbyville, and had come over for the day, with General Polk, on a visit to Hardee. He told the Generals that if Grant was severely beaten in Mississippi by Johnston, he did not think the war could be continued on its present great scale.

Clement L. Vallandigham was a prominent Democratic politician of Ohio, a former member of the U. S. House of Representatives who had been a vigorous and outspoken critic of the Lincoln administration and its conduct of the war. Arrested and convicted on the charge of "expressing sympathies for those in arms against the United States" he had been sentenced to confinement for the duration of the war, which sentence Lincoln had changed to banishment from the United States. Bragg refused to receive him officially, but gave him temporary asylum as "a distressed wayfarer" until he could be helped to make his way to Canada.

Fremantle continues:

When I presented my letters of introduction, General Hardee received me with the unvarying kindness and hospitality which I had experienced from all other Confederate officers. He is a fine, soldier-like man, broad-shouldered and tall. He looks rather like a French officer, and is a Georgian by birth. He bears the reputation of being a thoroughly good soldier, and he is the author of the drillbook still in use by both armies. Until quite lately, he was commanding officer of the military college at West Point. He distinguished himself at the battles of Corinth and Murfreesboro, and now commands the *2d corps d'armée* of Bragg's army.

He is a widower, and has the character of being a great admirer of the fair sex. During the Kentucky campaign last year, he was in the habit of availing himself of the privilege of his rank and years, and insisted upon kissing the wives and daughters of all the Kentuckian farmers. And although he is supposed to have converted many of the ladies to the Southern cause, yet in many instances their male relatives remained either neutral or undecided. On one occasion General Hardee had conferred the "accolade" upon a very pretty Kentuckian to their mutual satisfaction, when, to his intense disgust, the proprietor produced two very ugly old females, saying, "Now then, General, if you kiss any you must kiss them all round," which the discomfited general was forced to do, to the great amusement of his officers, who often allude to this contretemps.

Another rebuff which he received, and about which he is often chaffed by General

Polk, was when an old lady told him he ought really to "leave off fighting *at his age.*" "Indeed, madam," replied Hardee, "and how old do you take me for?" "Why, about the same age as myself—seventy-five." The chagrin of the stalwart and gallant general, at having twenty years added to his age, may be imagined.

Lieutenant General Leonidas Polk, Bishop of Louisiana, who commands the other *corps d'armée,* is a good-looking, gentleman-like man with all the manners and affability of a "grand seigneur." He is fifty-seven years of age—tall, upright, and looks much more the soldier than the clergyman. He is very rich; and I am told owns seven hundred negroes. He is much beloved by the soldiers on account of his great personal courage and agreeable manners. I had already heard no end of anecdotes of him told me by my traveling companions, who always alluded to him with affection and admiration. In his clerical capacity I had always heard him spoken of with the greatest respect. . . .

Bishop Elliott, of Georgia, is a nice old man of venerable appearance and very courteous manners. He is here at the request of General Polk for the purpose of confirming some officers and soldiers. He speaks English exactly like an English gentleman. So, in fact, does General Polk, and all the well-bred Southerners, much more so than the ladies, whose American accent can always be detected. General Polk and Mr. Vallandigham returned to Shelbyville in an ambulance at 6:30 P. M. . . . After Bishop Elliott had read prayers, I slept in the same room with General Hardee.

29th May (Friday)—I took a walk before breakfast with Dr. Quintard, a zealous Episcopal chaplain, who began life as a surgeon, which enables him to attend to the bodily as well as the spiritual wants of the Tennessean regiment to which he is chaplain. The enemy is about fifteen miles distant, and all the tops of the intervening hills are occupied as signal stations, which communicate his movements by flags in the daytime, and by beacons at night. A signal corps has been organized for this service. The system is most ingenious, and answers admirably.

We all breakfasted at Mrs. _____'s. The ladies were more excited even than yesterday in their diatribes against the Yankees . . . It has often been remarked to me that, when this war is over, the independence of the country will be due, in a great measure, to the women. Men declare that had the women been desponding they could never have gone through with it; but, on the contrary, the women have invariably set an example to the men of patience, devotion, and determination. Naturally proud, and with an innate contempt for the Yankees, the Southern women have been rendered furious and desperate by the proceedings of Butler, Milroy, Turchin, &c. They are all prepared to undergo any hardships and misfortunes rather than submit to the rule of such people; and they use every argument which women can employ to infuse the same spirit into their male relations.

At noon I took leave for the present of General Hardee, and drove over in his ambulance to Shelbyville, eight miles, in company with Bishop Elliott and Dr. Quintard. The road was abominable, and it was pouring with rain. On arriving at General Polk's, he invited me to take up my quarters with him during my stay with Bragg's army, which offer I accepted with gratitude.

After dinner General Polk told me that he hoped his brethren in England did not very much condemn his present line of conduct. He explained to me the reasons which had induced him temporarily to forsake the cassock and return to his old profession. He stated the extreme reluctance he had felt in taking this step. He said that as soon as the war was over, he should return to his episcopal avocations, in the same way as a man, finding his house on fire, would use every means in his power to extinguish the flames, and would then resume his ordinary pursuits.

At 6:30 P. M., I called on General Bragg, the Commander in chief. This officer is in appearance the least prepossessing of the Confederate generals. He is very thin. He stoops, and has a sickly, cadaverous, haggard appearance, rather plain features, bushy black eyebrows which unite in a tuft on the top of his nose, and a stubby iron-gray beard; but his eyes are bright and piercing. He has the reputation of being a rigid disciplinarian, and of shooting freely for insubordination. I understand he is rather unpopular on this account, and also by reason of his occasional acerbity of manner.

He was extremely civil to me, and gave me permission to visit the outposts, or any part of his army. He also promised to help me towards joining Morgan in Kentucky, and he expressed his regret that a boil on his hand would prevent him from accompanying me to the outposts. He told me that Rosecrans's position extended about forty miles, Murfreesboro (twenty-five miles distant) being his headquarters. The Confederate cavalry inclosed him in a semi-circle extending over a hundred miles of country. He told me that West Tennessee, occupied by the Federals, was devoted to the Confederate cause, whilst East Tennessee, now in possession of the Confederates, contained numbers of people of Unionist proclivities. This very place, Shelbyville, had been described to me by others as a "Union hole."

After my interview with General Bragg, I took a ride along the Murfreesboro road with Colonel Richmond, A. D. C. to General Polk. . . . During our ride I met Major General Cheatham, a stout, rather rough-looking man, but with the reputation of "a great fighter." It is said that he does all the necessary swearing in the 1st *corps d'armee*, which General Polk's clerical character incapacitates him from performing.

Colonel Richmond gave me the particulars of General Van Dorn's death, which occurred about forty miles from this. His loss does not seem to be much regretted, as it appears he was always ready to neglect his military duties for an assignation. In the South it is not considered necessary to put yourself on an equality with a man in such a case as Van Dorn's by calling him out. His life belongs to the aggrieved husband, and "shooting down" is universally esteemed the correct thing, even if it takes place after a lapse of time, as in the affair between General Van Dorn and Dr. Peters. . . .

Colonel Fremantle here refers to the then recent killing of General Earl Van Dorn by a Dr. George B. Peters of Spring Hill, Tennessee, in Van Dorn's headquarters at that place. Dr. Peters justified his act as an avenging of Van Dorn's alleged intimate relations with the Doctor's wife. Van Dorn's friends said there was no basis for such a charge, describing the killing as a cold-blooded murder. Colonel Fremantle goes on:

I slept in General Polk's tent, he occupying a room in the house adjoining. Before going to bed, General Polk told me an affecting story of a poor widow in humble circumstances, whose three sons had fallen in battle one after the other, until she had only one left, a boy of sixteen. So distressing was her case that General Polk went himself to comfort her. She looked steadily at him, and replied to his condolences by the sentence, "As soon as I can get a few things together, General, you shall have Harry too." The tears came into General Polk's eyes as he related this episode, which he ended by saying, *"How can you subdue such a nation as this!"*

30th May (Saturday)—It rained hard all last night, but General Polk's tent proved itself a good one. We have prayers both morning and evening by Dr. Quintard, together with singing, in which General Polk joins with much zeal. Colonel Gale, who is son-in-law and volunteer aid-de-camp to General Polk, has placed his negro Aaron and a mare at my disposal during my stay.

General Polk explained to me, from a plan, the battle of Murfreesboro. He claimed that the Confederates had only 30,000 troops, including Breckenridge's division, which was not engaged on the first day. He put the Confederate loss at 10,000 men, and that of the Yankees at 19,000.

With regard to the battle of Shiloh, he said that Beauregard's order to retire was most unfortunate, as the gunboats were doing no real harm, and if they (the Confederates) had held on, nothing could have saved the Federals from capture or destruction. The misfortune of Albert Johnston's death, together with the fact of Beauregard's illness and his not being present at that particular spot, were the causes of this battle not being a more complete victory.

Ever since I landed in America, I have heard of the exploits of an Englishman called Colonel St. Leger Grenfell, who is now Inspector General of cavalry to Bragg's army. This afternoon I made his acquaintance, and I consider him one of the most extraordinary characters I ever met.

Although he is a member of a well-known English family, he seems to have devoted his whole life to the exciting career of a soldier of fortune. He told me that in early life he had served three years in a French lancer regiment, and had risen from a private to be a *sous* lieutenant. He afterwards became a sort of consular agent at Tangier, under old Mr. Drummond Hay. Having acquired a perfect knowledge of Arabic, he entered the service of Abd-el-kader, and under that renowned chief he fought the French for four years and a half. At another time of his life he fitted out a yacht, and carried on a private war with the Riff pirates. He was brigade major in the Turkish contingent during the Crimean War, and had some employment in the Indian mutiny. He has also been engaged in war in Buenos Aires and the South American republics.

At an early period of the present troubles he ran the blockade and joined the Confederates. He was adjutant general and right-hand man to the celebrated John Morgan for eight months. Even in this army, which abounds with foolhardy and desperate characters, he has acquired the admiration of all ranks by his reckless daring and gallantry in the field. Both Generals Polk and Bragg spoke to me of him as a most excellent and useful officer, besides being a man who never lost an opportunity of trying to throw his life away.

He is just the sort of a man to succeed in this army, and among the soldiers his fame for bravery has outweighed his unpopularity as a rigid disciplinarian. He is the terror of all absentees, stragglers and deserters, and of all commanding officers who are unable to produce for his inspection the number of horses they have been drawing forage for. . . .

He talked to me much about John Morgan, whose marriage he had tried to avert, and of which he spoke with much sorrow. He declared that Morgan was enervated by matrimony, and would never be the same man as he was.

31st May (Sunday)—The Bishop of Georgia preached today to a very large congregation in the Presbyterian church. He is a most eloquent preacher; and he afterwards confirmed about twenty people—amongst others, Colonel Gale (over forty years old) and young Polk. After church, I called again on General Bragg, who talked to me a long time about the battle of Murfreesboro (in which he commanded). He said that he retained possession of the ground he had won for three days and a half, and only retired on account of the exhaustion of his troops, after carrying off over 6000 prisoners, much cannon, and other trophies. He allowed that Rosecrans had displayed much firmness, and was "the only man in the Yankee army who was not badly beaten."

Colonel Grenfell called again, and I arranged to visit the outposts with him on Tuesday. He spoke to me in high terms of Bragg, Polk, Hardee, and Cleburne; but he described some of the others as "political" generals, and others as good fighters, but illiterate and somewhat addicted to liquor. He deplored the effects of politics upon military affairs as very injurious in the Confederate Army, though not so bad as it is in the Northern.

At 2 P. M. I traveled in the cars to Wartrace, in company with General Bragg and the Bishop of Georgia. We were put into a baggage car, and the General and the Bishop were the only persons provided with seats. Although the distance from

Shelbyville to Wartrace is only eight miles, we were one hour and ten minutes in effecting the *trajet,* in such a miserable and dangerous state were the rails.

At Wartrace Colonel Fremantle was met and entertained by Major General Cleburne, a native of Ireland. General Cleburne gave the visiting Britisher a brief sketch of his history, which Fremantle duly recorded:

He is the son of a doctor at or near Ballincolig. At the age of seventeen he ran away from home and enlisted in Her Majesty's 41st regiment of foot, in which he served three years as private and corporal. He then bought his discharge, and emigrated to Arkansas, where he studied law, and eschewing politics, he got a good practice as a lawyer. At the outbreak of the war he was elected captain of his company, then colonel of his regiment, and has since, by his distinguished services in all the Western campaigns, been appointed to the command of a division (10,000 men)—the highest military rank which has been attained by a foreigner in the Confederate service. . . . He is now thirty-five years of age; but his hair having turned gray, he looks older. Generals Bragg and Hardee both spoke to me of him in terms of the highest praise, and said he had risen entirely by his own personal merit.

At 5 P. M. I was present at a great open-air preaching at General [S.A.M.] Wood's camp. Bishop Elliott preached most admirably to a congregation composed of 3000 soldiers, who listened to him with the most profound attention. Generals Bragg, Polk, Hardee, Withers, Cleburne, and endless brigadiers, were also present. It is impossible to exaggerate the respect paid by all ranks of this army to Bishop Elliott; and although most of the officers are Episcopalians, the majority of the soldiers are Methodists, Baptists, &c. Bishop Elliott afterwards explained to me that the reason most of the people had become dissenters was because there had been no bishops in America during the "British dominion." And all the clergy, having been appointed from England, had almost without exception stuck by the King in the Revolution, and had had their livings forfeited.

I find that it is a great mistake to suppose that the press is gagged in the South, as I constantly see the most violent attacks upon the President, upon the different generals and their measures. Today I heard the officers complaining bitterly of the *Chattanooga Rebel,* for publishing an account of Breckinridge's departure from this army to reinforce Johnston in Mississippi, and thus giving early intelligence to the enemy.

1st June (Monday)—We all went to a review of General Liddell's brigade at Bellbuckle, a distance of six miles. There were three carriages full of ladies, and I rode an excellent horse, the gift of General John Morgan to General Hardee. The weather and the scenery were delightful. General Hardee asked me particularly whether Mr. Mason had been kindly received in England. I replied that I thought he had, by private individuals. I have often found the Southerners rather touchy on this point.

General Liddell's brigade was composed of Arkansas troops—five very weak regiments which had suffered severely in the different battles, and they cannot be easily recruited on account of the blockade of the Mississippi. The men were good-sized, healthy, and well clothed, though without any attempt at uniformity in color or cut; but nearly all were dressed either in gray or brown coats and felt hats.

I was told that even if a regiment was clothed in proper uniform by the government, it would become parti-colored again in a week, as the soldiers preferred wearing the coarse homespun jackets and trousers made by their mothers and sisters at home. The generals very wisely allow them to please themselves in this respect, and insist only upon their arms and accoutrements being kept in proper order. Most of the officers were dressed in uniform which is neat and serviceable—a bluish-gray frock coat of a color similar to Austrian yagers. The infantry wear blue facings, the artillery red, the doctors black, the staff white, and the cavalry yellow; so it is impossible to mistake the branch of the service to which an officer belongs—nor is it possible to mistake his rank. A second lieutenant, first lieutenant, and captain, wear respectively one, two and three bars on the collar. A major, lieutenant colonel, and colonel, wear one, two and three stars on the collar.

Before the marching past of the brigade, many of the soldiers had taken off their coats and marched past the general in their shirt sleeves, on account of the warmth. Most of them were armed with Enfield rifles captured from the enemy. Many, however, had lost or thrown away their bayonets, which they don't appear to value properly, as they assert that they have never met any Yankees who would wait for that weapon. I expressed a desire to see them form square, but it appeared they were "not drilled to such a maneuver" (except square two deep). They said the country did not admit of cavalry charges, even if the Yankee cavalry had stomach to attempt it.

Each regiment carried a "battle flag," blue, with a white border, on which were inscribed the names "Belmont," "Shiloh," "Perryville," "Richmond Kentucky," and "Murfreesboro." They drilled tolerably well, and an advance in line was remarkably good; but General Liddell had invented several dodges of his own, for which he was reproved by General Hardee.

The review being over, the troops were harangued by Bishop Elliott in an excellent address, partly religious, partly patriotic. He was followed by a Congressman of vulgar appearance, named Hanley, from Arkansas, who delivered himself of a long and uninteresting political oration, and ended by announcing himself as a candidate for re-election. This speech seemed to me (and to others) particularly ill-timed, out of place, and ridiculous, addressed as it was to soldiers in front of the enemy. But this was one of the results of universal suffrage. The soldiers afterwards wanted General Hardee to say something, but he declined. I imagine that the discipline in this army is the strictest in the Confederacy, and that the men are much better marchers than those I saw in Mississippi.

A soldier was shot in Wartrace this afternoon. We heard the volley just as we left in the cars for Shelbyville. His crime was desertion to the enemy; and as the prisoner's brigade was at Tullahoma (twenty miles off), he was executed without ceremony by the provost guard. Spies are hung every now and then; but General Bragg told me it was almost impossible for either side to stop the practice.

In the evening I made the acquaintance of General Wheeler, Van Dorn's successor in command of the cavalry of this army, which is over 24,000 strong. He is a very little man, only twenty-six years of age, and was dressed in a coat much too big for him. He made his reputation by protecting the retreat of the army through Kentucky last year. He was a graduate of West Point, and seems a remarkably zealous officer, besides being very modest and unassuming in his manners.

General Polk told me that, notwithstanding the departure of Breckinridge, this army is now much stronger than it was at the time of the battle of Murfreesboro. I think that probably 45,000 infantry and artillery could be brought together immediately for a battle.

2nd June (Tuesday)—Colonel Grenfell and I rode to the outposts, starting on the road to Murfreesboro at 6 A. M. It rained hard nearly all day. He explained to me the method of fighting adopted by the Western cavalry, which he said was admirably adapted for this country; but he denied that they could under any circumstances stand a fair charge of regular cavalry in the open. Their system is to dismount and leave their horses in some secure place. One man is placed in charge of his own and three other horses, whilst the remainder act as infantry skirmishers in the dense woods and broken country, making a tremendous row, and deceiving the enemy as to their numbers, and as to their character as infantry or cavalry.

In this manner Morgan, assisted by two small guns, called "bulldogs," attacked the Yankees with success in towns, forts, stockades, and steamboats. By the same system, Wheeler and Wharton kept a large pursuing army in check for twenty-seven days, retreating and fighting every day, and deluding the enemy with the idea that they were being resisted by a strong force composed of all three branches of the service.

Colonel Grenfell told me that the only way in which an officer could acquire influence over the Confederate soldiers was by his personal conduct under fire. They hold a man in great esteem who in action sets them an example of contempt for danger; but they think nothing of an officer who is not in the habit of leading them. In fact such a man could not possibly retain his position. Colonel Grenfell's expression was, "every atom of authority has to be purchased by a drop of your blood." . . .

For the first nine miles our road was quite straight and hilly, with a thick wood on either side. We then reached a pass in the hills called Guy's Gap, which, from the position of the hills, is very strong, and could be held by a small force. The range of hills extends as far as Wartrace, but I understand the position could be turned on the left. About two miles beyond Guy's Gap were the headquarters of General Martin, the officer who commands the brigade of cavalry stationed in the neighborhood. . . .

General Martin told me that skirmishing and bushwhacking went on nearly every day, and that ten days ago the enemy's cavalry, by a bold dash, had captured a field-piece close to his own quarters. It was, however, retaken, and its captors were killed.

One of General Martin's staff officers conducted us to the bivouac of Colonel Webb (three miles further along the road), who commanded the regiment on outpost duty there—51st Alabama Cavalry. This Colonel Webb was a lawyer by profession, and seemed a capital fellow. He insisted on riding with us to the vedettes in spite of the rain, and he also desired his regiment to turn out for us by the time we returned.

The extreme outposts were about two miles beyond Colonel Webb's post, and about sixteen miles from Shelbyville. The neutral ground extended for about three miles. We rode along it as far as it was safe to do so, and just came within sight of the Yankee vedettes. The Confederate vedettes were at an interval of from 300 to 400 yards of each other. Colonel Webb's regiment was in charge of two miles of the front; and, in a similar manner, the chain of vedettes was extended by other corps right and left for more than eighty miles. Scouts are continually sent forward by both sides to collect information.

Rival scouts and pickets invariably fire on one another whenever they meet; and Colonel Webb good-naturedly offered, if I was particularly anxious to see their customs and habits, to send forward a few men and have a little fight. I thanked him much for his kind offer, but begged he wouldn't trouble himself so far on my account. . . .

The woods on both sides of the road showed many signs of the conflicts which are of daily occurrence. Most of the houses by the roadside had been destroyed; but one plucky old lady had steadfastly refused to turn out, although her house was constantly an object of contention, and showed many marks of bullets and shell.

Ninety-seven men were employed every day in Colonel Webb's regiment to patrol the front. The remainder of the 51st Alabama were mounted and drawn up to receive Colonel Grenfell on our return from the outposts. They were uniformly armed with long rifles and revolvers, but without sabers, and they were a fine body of young men. Their horses were in much better condition than might have been expected, considering the scanty food and hard duty they had had to put up with for the last five months, without shelter of any kind, except the trees. Colonel Grenfell told me they were a very fair specimen of the immense number of cavalry with Bragg's army.

I got back to Shelbyville at 4:30 P. M., just in time to be present at an interesting ceremony peculiar to America. This was a baptism at the Episcopal Church. The ceremony was performed in an impressive manner by Bishop Elliott, and the person baptized was no less than the commander in chief of the army. The bishop took the general's hand in his own (the latter kneeling in front of the font), and said, "Braxton, if thou hast not already been baptized, I baptize thee," &c. Immediately afterwards he confirmed General Bragg, who then shook hands with General Polk, the officers of their respective staffs, and myself, who were the only spectators.

Dr. Quintard, who was chaplain of Maney's 1st Tennessee regiment, tells in his *Journal* of the part he personally played in bringing about this memorable ceremony:

As soon as I found that the Bishop [Elliott] was able to give us a visit, I made very earnest appeals to the officers and soldiers of our army to confess Christ before men. But there was one man in the army whom I felt I could never get at. He was the Commander-in-chief, General Braxton Bragg. He had the reputation of being so stern and so sharp in his sarcasm that many men were afraid to go near him. Yet I had often thought of him in connection with my work. He never came to the Holy Communion, and I never heard of his being a member of any religious denomination.

Immediately after I received notice of Bishop Elliott's proposed visit, I determined to have a talk with General Bragg. It was late one afternoon when I started for his headquarters. I found two tents and a sentry at the outer one, and when I asked for General Bragg the sentry said: "You cannot see him. He is very busy, and has given positive orders not to be disturbed, except for a matter of life and death."

That cooled my enthusiasm and I returned to my own quarters; but all the night long I blamed myself for my timidity.

The next day I started out again, found the same sentry and received the same reply. This time, however, I was resolved to see the General, no matter what happened, so I said:

"It *is* a matter of life and death."

The sentry withdrew and in a few minutes returned and said: "You can see the General, but I advise you to be brief. He is not in a good humour."

This chilled me, but I went in. I found the General dictating to two secretaries. He met me with: "Well, Dr. Quintard, what can I do for you? I am quite busy, as you see."

I stammered out that I wanted to see him alone. He replied that it was impossible, but I persisted. Finally he dismissed the secretaries, saying to me rather sternly: "Your business must be of grave importance, sir."

I was very much frightened, but I asked the General to be seated, and then, fixing my eyes upon a knot-hole in the pine board floor of the tent, talked about our Blessed Lord, and about the responsibilities of a man in the General's position. When I looked up after a while I saw tears in the General's eyes and took courage to ask him to be confirmed. At last he came to me, took both my hands in his and said: "I have been waiting for twenty years to have some one say this to me, and I thank you from my heart. Certainly I shall be confirmed if you will give me the necessary instruction."

Colonel Fremantle continues with his reminiscences of his visit to Shelbyville:

I had intended to leave Shelbyville tomorrow with Bishop Elliott; but as I was informed that a reconnaissance in force was arranged for tomorrow, I accepted General Polk's kind offer of further hospitality for a couple of days more. Four of Polk's brigades with artillery move to the front tomorrow and General Hardee is also to push forward from Wartrace. The object of this movement is to ascertain the enemy's strength at Murfreesboro, as rumor asserts that Rosecrans is strengthening Grant in Mississippi, which General Bragg is not disposed to allow with impunity. The weather is now almost chilly.

In the evening, after dark, General Polk drew my attention to the manner in which the signal beacons were worked. One light was stationary on the ground, whilst another was moved backwards and forwards over it. They gave us intelligence that General Hardee had pushed the enemy to within five miles of Murfreesboro, after heavy skirmishing all day.

It is evident to me that a certain degree of jealous feeling exists between the Tennessean and Virginian armies. This one claims to have had harder fighting than the Virginian army, and to have been opposed to the best troops and best generals of the North.

I have been agreeably disappointed in the climate of Tennessee, which appears quite temperate to what I had expected.

4th June (Thursday)—Colonel Richmond rode with me to the outposts, in order to be present at the reconnaissance which was being conducted under the command of General Cheatham. We reached the field of operations at 2 P. M., and found that Martin's cavalry (dismounted) had advanced upon the enemy about three miles, and, after some brisk skirmishing, had driven in his outposts. The enemy showed about 2000 infantry, strongly posted, his guns commanding the turnpike road. The Confederate infantry was concealed in the woods, about a mile in rear of the dismounted cavalry.

This being the position of affairs, Colonel Richmond and I rode along the road so far as it was safe to do so. We then dismounted and sneaked on in the wood alongside the road until we got to within 800 yards of the Yankees, whom we then reconnoitered leisurely with our glasses. We could only count about seventy infantry soldiers, with one field-piece in the wood at an angle of the road, and we saw several staff officers galloping about with orders.

Whilst we were thus engaged, some heavy firing and loud cheering suddenly commenced in the woods on our left. Fearing to be outflanked, we remounted and rode back to an open space, about 600 yards to the rear, where we found General Martin giving orders for the withdrawal of the cavalry horses in the front, and the retreat of the skirmishers.

It was very curious to see three hundred horses suddenly emerge from the wood just in front of us, where they had been hidden—one man to every four horses, riding one and leading the other three, which were tied together by the heads. In this order I saw them cross a cotton field at a smart trot, and take up a more secure position. Two or three men cantered about in the rear, flanking up the lead horses. They were shortly afterwards followed by the men of the regiment, retreating in skirmishing order under Colonel Webb, and they lined a fence parallel to us. The same thing went on on our right.

As the firing on our left still continued, my friends were in great hopes that Yankees might be inveigled on to follow the retreating skirmishers until they fell in with the two infantry brigades, which were lying in ambush for them. It was arranged, in that case, that some mounted Confederates should then get in their rear, and so capture a good number; but this simple and ingenious device was frustrated by the sulkiness of the enemy, who now stubbornly refused to advance any further.

The way in which the horses were managed was very pretty and seemed to answer admirably for this sort of skirmishing. They were never far from the men, who could mount and be off to another part of the field with rapidity, or retire to take up another position, or act as cavalry as the case might require. Both the superior officers and the men behaved with the most complete coolness; and, whilst we were waiting in hopes of a Yankee advance, I heard the soldiers remarking that they "didn't like being done out of their good boots"—one of the principal objects in killing a Yankee being apparently to get hold of his valuable boots.

A tremendous row went on in the woods during this bushwhacking, and the trees got knocked about in all directions by shell; but I imagine that the actual slaughter in these skirmishes is very small, unless they get fairly at one another in the open cultivated spaces between the woods. I did not see or hear of anybody being killed today, although there were a few wounded and some horses killed. Colonel Richmond and Colonel Webb were much disappointed that the inactivity of the enemy prevented my seeing the skirmish assume large proportions, and General Cheatham said to me, "We should be very happy to see you, Colonel, when we are in our regular way of doing business."

After waiting in vain until 5 P. M., and seeing no signs of anything more taking place, Colonel Richmond and I cantered back to Shelbyville. . . .

After dark, General Polk got a message from Cheatham, to say that the enemy had after all advanced in heavy force about 6:15 P. M., and obliged him to retire to Guy's Gap. We also heard that General Cleburne, who had advanced from Wartrace, had had his horse shot under him. The object of the reconnaissance seemed, therefore, to have been attained, for apparently the enemy was still in strong force at Murfreesboro, and manifested no intention of yielding it without a struggle.

I took leave of General Polk before I turned in. His kindness and hospitality have exceeded anything I could have expected. I shall always feel grateful to him on this account, and I shall never think of him without admiration for his character as a sincere patriot, a gallant soldier, and a perfect gentleman.

His aides-de-camp, Colonels Richmond and Yeatman, are also excellent types of the higher class of Southerner. Highly educated, wealthy, and prosperous before the war, they have abandoned all for their country. They, and all other Southern gentlemen of the same rank, are proud of their descent from Englishmen. They glory in speaking English as we do, and that their manners and feelings resemble those of the upper classes in the old country. No staff officers could perform their duties with more zeal and efficiency than these gentlemen, although they were not educated as soldiers.

While it was marking time at Murfreesboro, the Federal Army of the Cumberland, unfortunately for posterity, had no such observant and literate visitor as Colonel Fremantle to leave behind him such a revealing and entertaining account of that army's doings. We have, however, from the pen of John Fitch, Rosecrans's provost judge, a somewhat flowery word-picture of life in the Federal camp which, while by no means objective, does tell us something of the happenings during "A Day at Headquarters", which is the title of Mr. Fitch's piece:

The Army of the Cumberland, we will estimate, in round numbers, at fifty thousand men—an extensive family, whose subsistence, discipline, and health are the daily care of its commander.

We are encamped at Murfreesborough,—have been located there for five full— but not solitary—months. Why so long a stay there? involves a combination of answers which the author does not feel called upon to give as "in duty bound." But the reasons are sound, as the result has shown. General Rosecrans moves when he is ready; and he knows the full meaning of that word. In all his military movements, without a single exception, he has made his "good ready", and by that sign has he conquered. In Western Virginia, at Iuka and Corinth, Mississippi, at Murfreesborough, and now upon his march into the vitals of central rebeldom, he has prepared for victory, and so carefully and practically, that he has not yet failed in his advance, nor has he lost a foot of the ground, thus gained, by a forced retreat. When he moves on, it is to CONQUER and to POSSESS.

Say you, good reader, that here is a digression, and that we are no further on in our chapter than Murfreesborough? Not so. We do not propose to journey: We have aimed to "spend the day" at General Rosecrans's head-quarters with his bustling family. So sit you down, and, if it be your wont, fill up and light your pipe, ply your crochet, or unroll your knitting, and let us witness a day of in-door army life and appreciate this stated preparation for victory.

Let us first make ourselves masters of the position. Our army is drawn around Murfreesborough, in an elliptical circle, one and a half miles in diameter. Upon first entering the town, after the battle, this circle was much more extended,—say four miles in diameter, some of the division head-quarters being three miles from the court-house. This was needless; and the general commanding wisely reduced his lines, to avoid unnecessary travel, teaming, and picket-duty. So here we are, our divisions posted at every point of the compass from the court-house; and walk where we may, in any given direction, by day or by night, at the outer line of pickets (for we have town-pickets, street-patrol, &c. in addition) we are sure to bring up against a soldier, gun in hand, pacing his walk of fifty to two hundred feet, with a commanding "Halt!" And thus it is that if those "boys" on picket but do their duty, nor man, nor dog, nor rabbit, hardly, can steal into or out from this devoted town. We may add that far beyond the general picket-line, on every road, lane, and field susceptible of approach, we have posted cavalry pickets, singly, by groups, or in squads, as may be deemed prudent so that surprise is impossible.

Thus surrounded by his great family, General Rosecrans has his headquarters in the heart of the town. He has taken possession of the Keeble residence (if the author remembers the name correctly). It is a fine, two-story, country-town house, with a large, pretty garden attached. Its owner was a lawyer, county clerk, and secessionist, and now holds a position in the rebel army. He fled with Bragg after the Stone River defeat, during the memorable Saturday night, taking his wife and smallest children. The flight we know was sudden; it could not have been in the least anticipated by him, for on the next Monday, upon our entering, his house was found filled with family goods, as though he and his had simply turned the key and gone upon a stay-over-night visit. Of course this was all quite convenient, even to the kitchen-quarters, which shone with burnished stove-ware. Also gleamed there the ivories of a group of great and small Africans, mainly of the feminine gender. These were not quite so convenient, and were "sent to the rear." General Rosecrans and staff, who had been almost constantly in the rain and mud for ten days, now luxuriated upon white sheets and spring-mattresses, and "Philip," his steward, concocted dinners from army rations which were "fit to set before a king" in war-times. Truly, the "Yankee invaders" had arrived, and not only at this house, but at Colonel Ready's—where General John H. Morgan had been married to his daughter, in the presence of Jefferson Davis, Bragg, Bishop Polk, and other rebel potentates, three week before— and at the other best houses in the town.

True, these "Yankees" had only come to the possession and enjoyment of their "rights", after all. This house is but a concatenation of Yankeeism pure and (now) undefiled. Look about with us for a moment. It was planned by a "Yankee," or patterned after some pretty Northern double-story-porch-and-wing. It was built by educated "Yankee" labor, we are sure. It is painted with Northern oil and lead. Every carpet comes from the land of "white slavery," as also the tasty window-curtains, the bedspreads, and the snowy pillow-cases. See you those genuine "Yankee" mirrors and elegant picture-frames and mantel-ornaments? And, alas! we "see ourselves as others see us," by reflection from those highly-polished black marble fire-fronts, wrought by miserable Vermont "mudsills" from quarries away up under the shadows of the old Green Mountains. Why, the elegant chair you sit in, friend, and the sofas and tables and stands and what-nots before you, were manufactured by low plebians in the greasy town of Cincinnati; the clear white table-ware you notice spread out for dinner was sent here by some firm of sand-treading, clam-baking Jerseymen; while the knife and fork you may soon be invited to ply so industriously "grew", like Topsy, alongside of a counterfeit nutmeg, in some lowly vale of Connecticut.

And open the carved doors of those showy library cases. Ah! what a concentration and intensity of Yankeeism! The brain of a Kent and of a Story finely preserved in Massachusetts calf for Keeble; the glories of Irving and Bancroft and Willis, gorgeously clothed in "purple and fine linen" and tipped with gold by enterprising Northern publishers. Here, there, upon every shelf, are stored emanations of Northern art and genius, almost heaven-born, so beautiful and rare are they, by which are brought to view the lights and shadows of far-away foreign lands, the images of grand old mountains and the flashings of darksome ocean-caves, the fire-flash and the roaming buffalo of the prairie, the thunders of Niagara, Titus breaching the walls of fated Jerusalem, the landing of Christianity and democracy from the Mayflower upon the lonely rock, and Angelo's grand conception of the Resurrection.

The possession of all this, the creation of Yankeeism, adorning hundreds of mansions in the "sunny South," and relieving the tedium of many a lazy hour, is the boast, while the creators are the sneer, of a race of uncreative aristocrats. Yes, here, there, everywhere, is the sign of the "Yankee"—in every pane of glass and in every nail of this house "we live in;" and where, then, the impropriety of the Yankee coming to his own?

Surely here has been another digression. But what then?—we are getting slowly on, and to step aside and pluck a fragrant flower now and then relieves the tedium of a journey.

The preliminaries settled, we are ready to spend our "day at headquarters." We are there at nine o'clock in the morning—no sooner; for the general arises at eight, and has just breakfasted. Ah! rather slow, say you? Well, no—considered in the abstract. Great men have great ways, or, at any rate, various ways. Franklin arose at four to make ready to harness the lightning and drive sky-high. Humboldt arrived at four hours of constitutional sleep along about midnight. *Per contra,* the grandest brains of an age have incubated in bed after late breakfast-hours, and the finest poem of a century was written upon a stale pillow at hours as late as eleven o'clock in the forenoon. And there was Newton, who arrived at immortality just after an afternoon nap under an apple-tree. However, before we conclude, we believe the "earliest bird" of a reader will not be severe upon our general's breakfast-hour.

The day of our devotional general commences, we are sure, with the morning prayer. This we have not seen, but, knowing him, we know it to be true. After breakfast the first business in order is the morning reports of any thing stirring "on the front" during the past dark hours. Then reports from his chiefs of staff of what large matter on hand for to-day. Then comes the supervision and signing of important orders to corps commanders, or to the commanders of posts at Franklin, Nashville and elsewhere. And now begin to flock in the daily round of visitors— generals, colonels and captains, upon this or that errand, or for verbal instructions. A heavy army contractor (perhaps heavy in a double sense) must confer with him— is not satisfied with the views or decision of an underling. An old, rich planter is in trouble, and obsequiously squirms into the general's presence—unless, more likely, he has sent his wife, a sallow, plain, dejected appearing woman. She was once, no doubt, a pretty Southern belle; but Southern flowers fade as early as they bloom. By this time there has assembled a crowd of people—officers upon errands, sutlers in trouble, and women with children, and the distinct entity yclept "young ladies", all after passes, or the restoration of property or other "rights"; and all desire a full conference with the general upon their tiny affairs, but are mainly attended to by his polite and excellent aides.

Thus the busy work goes on, let us say, until two o'clock P. M., when the general and his staff officers, with perhaps some distinguished visitors from "abroad", will mount and take a view of the camps, inspect the progress of the fortifications, or call at the quarters of one of his sub-commanders. This is the gala-hour at head-quarters. They have excellent horses; and why not? They are dressed very neatly, as they should be—for then the general is "to be seen of men;" and we all know the value of good example. As he rides along the lines, where the troops are drilling by regiment or battalion, vociferous cheering always greets him; and along the fortifications the same. For stretched all around him is a great army of men who love their commander as but few are loved, and he has shown a full return of affection for them, and that he is ever ready to do battle with them, and, if it is to be, to die by them.

The dinner-hour at head-quarters is four o'clock P. M. That might seem rather after the "St. Nicholas" and "Continental" style. But then it is the supper-hour also—two meals per day; and thus the style is peculiar to our general. After dinner come a leisure hour and a siesta, a cigar and the daily papers. And so Sol marches flaming down the western slope, with his banner of light softly streaming in golden bars through the cedars and among the rocks of the yet torn and crumpled battlefield, and melts away beyond the forests which skirt the lonely river, the lamps are lighted; and now commences the second, and really the most important, half of the day.

From this time until long past midnight a continued stream of business pours into head-quarters. A hundred letters and notes are to be dictated, or to be perused, studied, and answered. Reports of many kinds; of courts-martial, as to "family jars;" of provost-marshal's matters of trade, passes, and concerning refugees and deserters; of sub-commanders respecting the enemy's movements along their fronts; to hear a written report of some spy just come in, and, if important, to see and question the man; to read and consider and answer telegrams from Nashville, Louisville, and Washington, often of vast importance; to confer, privately, with one or a group of his generals, and occasionally to hold a grand council of them; to have a kind, fatherly talk in private with some brave but erring officer; to call an old favorite—perhaps General Thomas, the "Nestor" of the camps—into "his corner," wheel around his chair against intrusion, and, in an under-tone, submit some important fact or uncertain point, and ask for an opinion which he knows well how to value—all this goes on, and much more! Ah! here are decisions being made and plans laid affecting the lives of hundreds, and perhaps of thousands, of human beings—which involve possibly, the fortunes of an army, the fate of a government, or even those liberties which are the natural birthright of a great people.

While thus spending our day at head-quarters, good reader, you will be pleased to observe, we doubt not, the gentleness, almost quietness, which pervades the premises. The officers of staff, the visiting officers, and the secretaries, clerks, and orderlies in attendance, are neatly dressed, and are gentlemanly in their deportment. No shouting, nor loud talking, nor rude, boisterous laughter. An oath is rarely heard—a loud one, never. The inordinate use of liquors is rarely noticeable—is frowned upon. Due respect is paid to the Sabbath-day, the general attending his church-meeting invariably in the forenoon. We have not heard an angry word pass between members of this household during many months. Among the higher officers of our army, respect, confidence, and affection is the very general rule: the exception is rare. Especially has this been the case since the battle of Stone River. That great furnace of affliction seemed to purify and bring together in closer bonds the Army of the Cumberland. Men's hates and ambitions, passions and vices, assumed at least a much milder form, as though all were living in perpetual remembrance of those awful hours and of the dead. And the private soldier was thus equally affected with the officer. Truly, after that trial we had a better army of better men. As with our army, so it will be with the nation:—the gold is purified by the refiner's fire. Meriting this great trial as a people, we are being tried. And if we prove ourselves worthy of preservation, so will we be preserved, and will march on, higher and higher up the scale of national existence.

"Like master like man" is the trite saying of olden times; and it holds equally well in the new. The pleasing results just stated are easily traceable to their source. A cursing and carousing commander-in-chief gathers around him kindred spirits. The Christian and the gentleman, when invested with might and power, surrounds himself with the good and the true, "whose ways are pleasantness and their paths peace."

Such has been our path, you will concede, kind reader, during our day's visit at head-quarters. Let us now retire, presuming it to be three o'clock in the morning—an average hour of retiring for our general during the past eight months. And, while re-tiring, will you not join with him in what you may be assured is his earnest prayer to God, that peace and unity may soon be restored to our beloved and distracted country?

Judge Fitch also provides an equally flowery (and non-objective) chapter in his book entitled "The Army Police and its Chief". The chief of the army police, the notorious and malodorous "Colonel" William Truesdail, was not only heartily detested by the native Tennesseans who felt the weight of his heavy hand; he was openly accused of corruption and depravity by many of his fellow-Federals, in-cluding Military Governor Andrew Johnson.   James D. Porter, later governor of Tennessee, writing after the war, said:

No Tennessean complained of the burthens put upon his people by a state of war; but official robbery and oppression, insults to the old men and to their mothers, their wives and daughters, taxed the endurance of brave men to the utmost.   The rule of the Federal authorities in Tennessee was worse than an iron one.

And Charles A. Dana, in a dispatch to Secretary Stanton, said that:

Governor Johnson complains of the tardiness of Rosecrans, and these long months of precious time wasted. He (Rosecrans) has fallen under bad influence, and especially under that of his chief of detectives, a man named Truesdail. This man is deep in all kinds of plunder, and has kept the army inactive to enable his accomplices and himself to become rich by jobs and contracts. Truesdail's methods so revolted Governor John-son that, in a telegram to President Lincoln, he denounced him as "wholly incompetent, if not corrupt in the grossest sense of the term", and said that the activities of Trues-dail and his secret police were "causing much ill feeling and doing us great harm".

But no reader of Fitch's book would ever have any reason to doubt that Truesdail and his force of secret police, detectives, spies and counter-spies were selfless patriots, clothed in spotless white, as he reads the glowing tribute to their efficiency and patriotism:

At Bowling Green the army mail system was organized, and policemen were put at work, not only there, but in the larger towns along the line of the Louisville & Nashville Railroad, and a surprising amount of knavery, smuggling, and guerrillaism was discovered. Upon reaching Nashville the police business at once assumed vast proportions.   The city was full of violent and confessed rebels, most of whom were both smugglers and spies, as opportunity offered. The army had drawn thither its usual corrupt and festering element of camp-followers. The entire community was rotten, morally and socially. Murder, robbery, drunkenness, and all the nameless vices of rebeldom and war, were openly and shamelessly rampant. The Government was vic-timized at every turn.   Horses and mules, stolen from neighboring farms and stables, were hawked about the streets for purchasers, at prices ranging from ten to fifty dol-lars per head. Arms were pilfered and sold for a trifle. Boots, shoes, uniforms, camp-equipage, ammunition, and supplies of every kind, serviceable to the rebel army, were daily sent beyond our lines in every possible way that the ingenuity of bad men and women could devise.

In our necessarily contracted space we cannot hope to give even an outline of the work accomplished by the Army police.   Suffice it to say that in a short time its influence was felt in every part of the city and army. His patrols were upon every road leading from the city, arresting and searching rebel emissaries, and at times confiscating considerable amounts of contraband goods. His detectives were in every hotel, and upon cars and steamers. Assuming the role of rebel sympathizers, they were introduced into the proudest and wealthiest secession families. Passing them-selves off, in many cases, as spies of Wheeler, Bragg, and Morgan, they acquainted themselves with the secrets, the hopes, and the intentions of that entire people. Men were also busy among our own camps, detecting army vice and fraud. Their searching eyes were on the several army departments, hospitals, theatres, houses of ill-fame, and every centre of public interest. A minute report of all these investigations and their results would thrill the land; but better that it be not told to blanch the cheek and chill the heart of many a true wife and fond parent.

Many offenders thus detected were vigorously dealt with; and yet the police records of the department reveal instances of young men made wiser and better by the kind-ness shown and the advice given them. Humane, benevolent, and far-seeing, yet prompt to visit with merited punishment the hardened offender, none more ready than our Chief of Police [Truesdail] to temper justice with mercy. The many instances of charity to the destitute, of forgiveness to youthful follies of the young men whom he has aided and counselled, of widows and orphans he assisted to fuel and bread during the hard winter at Nashville, of the young women found in male attire whom he and his assistants have decently clothed and sent to their homes, and of deserted children for whom he has found asylums, would of themselves fill many pages of this work.

In brief, the influence of the army police was felt in every ramification of army and city life throughout the Department of the Cumberland. True, errors and wrongs may have been committed by its officials; many an arrest may have been made without good reason therefor, and many goods seized that ought to have been untouched; true, many bad men may have wormed themselevs into its service; but, where such has been the case, none more ready to make restitution, none more severe in punishment of official treachery and knavery, than its justice-loving chief. All in all, he has done well, and has exercised the utmost care in the selection of his subordinates. For be it always remembered that there are but few men fitted for the business of a detective, and a still less number are found to follow it. In large cities, and with armies, the detective is a necessity; and yet it is a profession whose follower is and must be one continued counterfeit. Bad men can make it detestable; but pure-minded, upright officers, operating secretly and in disguise though they may, *CAN* perform their duties with marvellous certainty in the detection of crime, with incalculable benefit to the public, and without injury to the innocent.

That the most worthy motives actuate the subject of this sketch in all his official dealings, the author has abundant reason to know. Colonel Truesdail (he is called "colonel" by general consent, though a civilian and quite regardless of titles) is possessed of a handsome private fortune, which thus far has been diminished, rather than increased, by his army labors. Though a Southern man as regards the location of a great portion of his property and by reason of many years' residence in the slave states, he has been an original and uncompromising friend of the Union.

The results of the army police operations have been immense, both in gain to the Government and prevention of crime. Hundreds of horses and mules have been seized and turned over to the quartermaster's department. Scores of smugglers and spies have been detected and punished, thus largely curtailing this underground trade, alike beneficial to the rebels and detrimental to us. Large amounts of goods and medicines have been confiscated and sold, where the parties implicated were found *flagrante delicto;* and thus this branch of the army has considerably more than repaid its entire cost to the Government. Connected with it, also, is the spy department, from which a line of communication has been constantly maintained throughout the rebel States, to the extreme limits of the Southern Confederacy. This interesting feature in its opera-tions, systematic as it is under the watchful eye of the Chief of Police and under the personal direction of the general commanding, must, for obvious reasons, be imagined rather than described.

Judge Fitch in his book tells of numerous cloak-and-dagger incidents in which Colonel Truesdail's men frustrated the Rebel evil-doers; but (moved perhaps by his Victorian sense of propriety) he makes no mention of one hilarious episode which is solemnly recorded in the *Official Records*.

Rudyard Kipling in one of his "Barrack Room Ballads" mentions the fact that "Single men in barracks ain't no bloomin' saints," and this has been true of single men in barracks in many wars in many lands for many years. The authorities in command of the Federal army of occupation in Nashville early in 1863 were soon confronted with the acute problems created by the flocking to Nashville of so many of the type of women euphoniously designated as "camp followers". In the summer of that year General J. D. Morgan came to the conclusion that there were too many of the "ladies of easy virtue" in the city, and he took prompt and drastic steps to put an end to the operations of the too-numerous practitioners of the oldest profession. Rounding up all of them, he ordered them banished from the city, and took immediate steps to put his order into effect.

It happened that a steamboat captain by the name of John M. Newcomb had just built him a new steamboat and had chartered it to the U. S. Government for use of the army. General Morgan decided that Captain Newcomb's new vessel, the *Idaho,* would be the very craft to convey the ladies elsewhere, so he loaded them aboard the *Idaho* and ordered Newcomb to transport them to some other place, any other place, down the river.

Newcomb protested plaintively that such a passenger list would forever ruin the reputation of his steamboat; and, in a letter to Secretary E. M. Stanton a few months later, he stated that it had done that very thing and that the *Idaho* had since borne "an unprintable nickname". In his letter to Stanton, seeking payment for damages suffered on that history-making cruise, he told the sad story of his unhappy experience:

I protested against their putting these women on my boat, she being a new boat, only three months built, her furniture new and a fine passenger boat. I asked General Morgan how I was to feed the women, and he told me to subsist them myself. I entreated of him to let the government subsist them, that it could do so for much less than I could. His reply was, "You subsist them." When I found Gen. Morgan determined that I should subsist them, I had to buy meat and vegetables at enormous high prices from store-boats along the river, and in addition at many places to buy ice and medicines. I applied to the commissaries along the route for commissary stores to feed these women, but at each place I was refused by the officers in charge, and the civil as well as the military authorities would not allow my boat to land, and put guards along the shore to prevent me from doing so.

Newcomb went on to relate that, although he had asked Morgan for a guard to accompany his passengers, a guard was denied. Without any guard to regulate their conduct, he said, whenever the boat was anchored along the river boatloads of "uncouth men" were attracted to the *Idaho,* and when Newcomb tried to keep these unwelcome visitors off his boat "they and these bad women damaged my boat and her furniture to a great extent."

Captain Newcomb attempted to land his unmanageable cargo at Louisville, but General Boyle, in command of the army post there, ordered him to sail on to Cincinnati—but Boyle did provide an army guard to control the women. Continuing in his narrative of his misadventures, Newcomb wrote to Stanton:

Because I was not allowed to land, I remained in the stream opposite Cincinnati for 13 days, when I was ordered to Nashville again with my cargo. I am here now one week, going from one office to another to see to get my papers and to effect a settlement, which I have not yet done, unless your honor will please to direct payment.

Not until October was Captain Newcomb paid his claim, amounting to $5,316.04. Of this total $1,000 was for damages to his boat and the balance for money paid out for food and medicine for the ladies.

In its passing through the bureaus' red tape, the claim had endorsed on it by one anonymous official who signed with his initials "JCK": "The whole charge should really fall upon General Morgan, who should have surmised that no community would tolerate such an importation, and should not therefore have put the government to this expense."

What was done with the ladies when they returned to Nashville is not revealed in the official record of Captain Newcomb's case. According to local legend, however, they were eventually shipped from the city again, this time by a special railroad train—but whether they stayed away or were perhaps replaced by others of the same profession, the record is silent.

Nashville, however, was not the only place in Tennessee that was plagued by the "corrupt and festering element of camp followers" of whom Judge Fitch complained so feelingly. Charles A. Dana, the roving assistant Secretary of War, was astounded at the corruption springing up as the victorious Federal armies occupied the conquered Southern territory. In a letter written to Secretary Stanton from Memphis in January, 1863, he urged corrective steps to stop the graft and profiteering involved in the illegal "trading with the enemy", saying:

You will remember our conversations on the subject of excluding cotton speculators from the regions occupied by our armies in the South. I now write to urge the matter upon your attention as a measure of military necessity.

The mania for sudden fortunes made in cotton, raging in a vast population of Jews and Yankees scattered throughout this whole country, and in this town almost exceeding the numbers of the regular residents, has to an alarming extent corrupted and demoralized the army. Every colonel, captain, or quartermaster dreams of adding a bale of cotton to his monthly pay. I had no conception of the extent of this evil until I came and saw for myself. Besides, the resources of the rebels are inordinately increased from this source. Plenty of cotton is brought in from beyond our lines, especially by the agency of Jewish traders, who pay for it ostensibly in Treasury notes, but really in gold.

What I propose is that no private purchaser of cotton shall be allowed in any part of the occupied region. Let quartermasters buy the article at a fixed price, say 20 or 25 cents per pound, and forward it by army transportation to proper centers, say to Helena, Memphis, or Cincinnati, to be sold at public auction on Government account. Let the sales take place on regular, fixed days, so that all parties desirous of buying can be sure when to be present. But little capital will be required for such an operation. The sales being frequent and for cash, will constantly replace the amount employed for the purpose. I should say that $200,000 would be sufficient to conduct the movement. I have no doubt that this $200,000 so employed would be more than equal to 30,000 men added to the national armies.

My pecuniary interest is in the continuance of the present state of things, for while it lasts there are occasional opportunities of profit to be made by a daring operator; but I should be false to my duty did I, on that account, fail to implore you to put an end to an evil so enormous, so insidious, and so full of peril to the country. My first impulse was to hurry to Washington to represent these things to you in person; but my engagements here with other persons will not allow me to return East so speedily. I beg you, however, to act without delay if possible.

P. S.—Since writing the above I have seen General Grant, who fully agrees with all my statements and suggestions, except that imputing corruption to every officer, which, of course, I did not intend to be taken literally. I have also just attended a public sale by the quartermaster here of 500 [sic] bales of cotton confiscated by General Grant at Oxford and Holly Springs. It belonged to Jacob Thompson and other notorious rebels. This cotton brought to-day over $1,500,000 cash. This sum alone would be five times enough to set on foot the system I recommend, without drawing upon the Treasury at all. In fact, there can be no question that by adopting this system the quartermaster's department in this valley would become self-supporting, while the army would become honest again and the slave-holders would no longer find that the rebellion had quadrupled the price of their great staple, but only doubled it.

Bragg, during that spring and summer of 1863, seemed to concentrate most of his thoughts and activities on defense, building elaborate fortifications along his front and waiting for Rosecrans to make the next move. There was some talk about the possibility of another invasion of Kentucky, but the only gesture in that direction was Morgan's ill-fated raid through Kentucky into Indiana and Ohio which resulted in the capture of the daring raider and practically all his men. Morgan was imprisoned in the Ohio State Penitentiary at Columbus, and although he escaped late in November and made his way back to the Confederacy, his days of usefulness to the Army of Tennessee were over.

The cavalry remaining attached to the Army of Tennessee, however, was constantly and vigorously astir, as the Federal and Confederate troopers probed each other's defenses. Some of these skirmishes developed into small-sized battles, to two of which General Bragg on March 31st gave official recognition in an official General Order to the army, announcing "with pride and gratification two brilliant and successful affairs achieved by the cavalry of Major General Van Dorn":

On the 5th inst. Major General Van Dorn made a gallant charge upon a large force of the enemy at Thompson's Station. He routed them, killed and wounded a large number, and captured 1221 prisoners, including 73 commissioned officers and many arms. On the 25th, Brigadier General Forrest, with the troops of his command, daringly assailed the enemy at Brentwood, who could not withstand the vigor and energy of the attack and surrendered. The result of this successful expedition was the capture of 750 prisoners and 35 commissioned officers, with all their arms, accoutrements, ammunition and sixteen wagons and teams. The skilful manner in which these generals achieved such success exhibits clearly the judgment, discipline and good conduct of the brave troops of their command. Such signal examples of duty deserve the applause and gratitude of their comrades in arms and their country.

The affair at Thompson's Station, though involving relatively small bodies of troops, was a classic example of a well planned and well conducted engagement, reflecting great credit on the skill of the Confederate leaders, especially General Forrest, who commanded a brigade under Van Dorn, and who took a prominent and decisive part in this brilliantly executed engagement.

General Earl Van Dorn, who had recently been transferred from Mississippi to take command of the Confederate cavalry operating in Middle Tennessee, had arrived at Columbia in February with three brigades of cavalry, about 4,500 men, and established his command post there. On the night of March 4th Van Dorn's scouts reported that a large body of Federal cavalry were moving toward Spring

Hill on the Franklin-Columbia turnpike. Van Dorn promptly made arrangements to meet the advancing enemy at Thompson's Station, between Franklin and Columbia, and his men were in position there early on the morning of March 5th awaiting the coming of the Federals. His troops were skilfully arranged, with Forrest and some 2000 men on the extreme right, Armstrong on Forrest's left, and Whitfield's Texas brigade further to the left commanding the Columbia turnpike. General Jordan describes the ensuing action:

The enemy appeared about half-past nine AM, moving on the Columbia turnpike, with five regiments of infantry, some 600 cavalry and a field battery. Posting the latter upon the right-hand ridge, the Federal infantry was deployed across the pike and rightward, astraddle the railroad. King's Battery (with Whitfield) opened vigorously with shell, but the Federals pushed on handsomely, resolutely upon the Confederate position, and up to within 150 yards. Then Armstrong's and Whitfield's brigades sprang forward and met them, and a sharp exchange of musketry fire took place for full half an hour before the Federal line faltered and fell back.

Forrest, with his apt soldier's eye, now observing that no enemy was likely to appear in his front, determined to detach Colonel Starnes with two regiments to move around by the right upon the Federal artillery and its supports, while he with the remainder of his force, present on the field, led it further to the right and rearward in order to cut off the route of retreat upon Franklin. Meanwhile, Starnes executing his orders with habitual energy, opening with a deadly fire of his rifles, had driven the Federal artillery from their strong vantage ground rapidly to the rear, down the turnpike, and forced the infantry across westward of the railroad to another position upon the ridge in that quarter, where they made a most stubborn stand.

In the meanwhile, apparently observing Forrest's movement, a considerable Federal detachment fell back and took shelter behind a strong stone fence. From this position General Forrest made two sustained attempts to dislodge these men, who maintained it with genuine courage. At the second charge, however, they were overcome and, surrendering, were sent from the field, the General having his horse shot in the affair.

Moving still rearward and to the west of the railroad, he succeeded quickly in getting in a position to cut off the route of retreat of the enemy, who still fought with signal resolution and spirit. Forming his command, including his escort, in line, Forrest now dashed forward with it up the steep slope of the ridge so stoutly held by the Federal infantry, who poured a galling fire upon his men as they followed their leader. The loss was heavy. . . . But this did not check the Confederate advance, and in a few moments Forrest stood within 30 paces of the Federal commander, Colonel Coburn, whose surrender he demanded under the stress of a leveled revolver. Further resistance was in vain, and his brave adversary, thoroughly beaten at all points, was forced to succumb. . . . General Forrest conducted and introduced Colonel Coburn to General Van Dorn, and then returned to look after his wounded, collect and fitly care for the dead, and reorganize the command. . . .

A portion of his men, mounted, had meanwhile followed and endeavored to cut off the runaway cavalry, artillery and some of the infantry, that had fled from the field before the last part of the conflict, but they were obliged to return without more than 75 captured stragglers; the remainder effected their retreat to Franklin, though followed hotly to within two miles of that place. The command surrendered consisted of . . . an aggregate of 2,200—a fine body of men, as shown by their stout fighting. The success was acquired at the cost to the Confederates of about 30 killed and 25 wounded.

In a man of General Forrest's fierce combative spirit the sentimental side was seldom revealed, but during the clamor of the battle of Thompson's Station there occurred an incident which did stir the General's deepest sentiments—the death of his favorite horse, Roderick. Writing about it a few years after the war, one of Forrest's troopers said: "General Forrest rarely alluded to it, and then with evidences of deep emotion which often found vent in tears, belonging as it did to that class of memories which often, with men of his strong and passionate nature, became more sacred with the lapse of years." Writing as an eye-witness of the touching event, the narrator goes on:

During his brilliant and memorable movement against the flank and rear of Colonel Coburn, at the battle of Thompson's Station, General Forrest was mounted that day on his favorite horse, Roderick, and desiring to press the enemy from a strong position across an open field, he appeared upon the flank of one of his regiments as it lay taking the fire and, in his characteristic words, ordered it to "move up". At the command the men leaped to their feet and, with loud cheers, dashed forward under a hot fire.

The General, attended by his son, Lieutenant William Forrest, accompanied the charge, as was his wont when the point to be gained was of importance. In the brief conflict, which resulted in the overthrow of the enemy, Roderick was wounded in three places. This event gave the General so much concern that he immediately dismounted, and charged his son to lead Roderick to the rear and have his wants well attended to by the hostlers in charge of his extra horses. He then mounted his son's horse, which had also been wounded, and pressed forward in pursuit of the enemy.

On reaching the hostlers, Lieutenant Forrest had the wounded animal stripped of saddle and bridle for his comfort, supposing that he was too badly hurt to attempt to get out of the way. As soon as he was at liberty, Roderick, still restless under the excitement of battle, began to nose among the group, evidently in search of his master, a habit he had frequently indulged in at camp, where he was rarely put under the restraint of the halter. In the progress of affairs at the front at this stage, General Forrest's voice, clear and unmistakable, was heard in the distance, directing his line in another attack. Roderick instantly pricked up his ears to get the direction and, neighing eagerly in answer, dashed away before he could be intercepted, guided by the sound of battle, which at that moment broke out afresh.

Lieutenant Forrest, fearing his father's displeasure, immediately mounted and, with several attendants, gave chase with a view of capturing the wounded horse before he could get far away; but the latter went at such speed that he outstripped his pursuers, and when found was following quietly at the heels of the General, having leaped three fences in his progress, besides getting another wound from which he was bleeding freely. As expected, the General was in great wrath over the supposed negligence; but when the nature of the case was explained, he burst into tears and, caressing Roderick for the last time, he turned away from the scene and a short time later received the surrender of Colonel Coburn and two thousand of his men.

Truly the cypress was entwined with the laurel for him on that day, in the death of Roderick, which occurred in the moment of victory. By his order, the faithful animal was interred on the field of battle where his brave spirit passed away, a fitting sacrifice to the God of War, and with a name that will blend for all time with the deeds of his matchless rider.

A Federal account (Colonel Van Horne's) gives these details of the engagement at Thompson's Station as seen from the loser's point of view:

On March 4th General Gilbert (at Franklin) sent an expedition under Colonel John Coburn of the 33rd Indiana south from Franklin. The objects were to form a junction with a column moving toward Columbia from Murfreesboro, and the collection of forage to fill a train of 80 wagons. Colonel Coburn's command embraced his own regiment (with three other infantry regiments), six hundred cavalry under Colonel Thomas J. Jordan, and Aleshire's 18th Ohio battery.

Colonel Jordan moved in advance of the infantry, and met the enemy about three miles from Franklin, moving north. Both forces quickly formed lines of battle, but Colonel Jordan was first in readiness for action, and Aleshire opened with his guns. After a sharp conflict for some hours, the enemy withdrew and retreated toward Spring Hill. The next morning the column advanced, but before reaching Thompson's Station the enemy was again found, and this time in position. There were rumors of other forces on the left flank, and some troops were in sight on high ground in proximity, in that direction.

Colonel Jordan charged the enemy on a line of hills in front of the station, with his men dismounted, when a new position was taken on another range of hills beyond the station. Colonel Coburn pursued to the vicinity of the station, where the column was arrested by shells from a battery on a hill to the left, and soon by the fire of another on the right which, from the direction of the advance, enfiladed the line.

Colonel Coburn had, the day before and that morning, advised General Gilbert of these indications and of direct information that he was meeting the enemy in strong force; yet, as his orders had not been modified, he determined to advance and charge the annoying battery on the right. He placed his own battery by sections on opposite sides of the turnpike and railroad, which are separated by a narrow space; placed the cavalry in immediate support, and disposed three regiments for the attack, his fourth being in the rear to guard the train. The line advanced under the fire of both batteries, when suddenly they ceased firing and the enemy's infantry was seen in motion to attack.

The situation was now fully developed. There was infantry with the two batteries, while cavalry was reported on the left and rear. Colonel Coburn now resolved to retreat; but it was necessary first to repel the enemy. After some sharp fighting in front, the retrograde movement was commenced from the midst of large forces of infantry, cavalry and artillery. Colonel Jordan was ordered to collect his command and cover the retreat, who, soon seeing the infantry of the enemy moving to his rear to cut him off, ordered the battery to move to the rear, and dismounted the detachments of Majors Scranton and Jones to hold the enemy in check to enable Captain Aleshire to save his battery, and then effect a junction with the infantry regiments to the east. But the cavalry and infantry were here separated. The infantry regiments, by changing front to resist attacks from various directions, moved backward and to the east. The cavalry, artillery and the 124th Ohio which, upon being threatened by the enemy, retreated with the train, followed the turnpike road. Colonel Jordan deemed it vain to attempt to resist the heavy masses of the enemy, and, finding himself in a short time surrounded, surrendered the three regiments with him. The other forces escaped. . . .

The reports of Colonels Coburn and Jordan are conflicting as to the exact situation when the latter commenced to retreat. Colonel Jordan asserted that his retreat was necessary to save himself from being cut off by a force moving to his rear, west of the road, which was the direct line for the retrograde movement, and that the situation was then hopeless, as it was vain to resist an army. Colonel Coburn had hope of saving his whole force if its unity had not been broken.

The affair at Brentwood, mentioned by General Bragg in his congratulatory order, is described in some detail by General Jordan:

Having learned, through reliable sources, that the troops who had escaped from the affair at Thompson's Station, on the 5th of the month, were in position at Brentwood Station on the Franklin and Nashville Railroad, guarding the railroad bridge over the Little Harpeth, nine miles rearward of Franklin, General Forrest received permission from General Van Dorn to attempt a *coup de main,* with his division, upon them. This he proceeded to execute on or about the night of the 24th of March.

Starnes with his own, under McLemore, and Edmonson's regiment, moved forward on a by-way, crossing the Harpeth some six miles rightward of Franklin, and thence through fields and woods, deftly threading and eluding the enemy's pickets without discovery, to the point of destination. General Forrest himself, with his escort—Biffle's Regiment, the Tenth Tennessee under Major DeMoss, and Armstrong with the First Tennessee, Third Arkansas, Second Mississippi and Sounder's battalion of his brigade, and a section of Freeman's battery under Lieutenant Huggins—made a detour leftward by the way of Hillsboro, crossing the Harpeth at the Granny White-Nashville turnpike, some six miles north of Franklin, whence he moved rapidly and directly upon Brentwood.

Reaching the place just at dawn, the General made his disposition at once for the attack, although Armstrong—impeded by the artillery—had not yet come up, and Starnes was not in sight. With his force in hand, brushing some pickets aside, he moved rapidly around the position by the right or east, with his escort and Captain Forrest's company, so as to foil the effort to escape which was already being attempted. Securing this position, he then demanded the surrender of the place, which was made without further parley. Armstrong, in the meantime, having come up in their immediate front, deployed his line and planted his artillery so as to command the position.

The troops capitulated, as General Forrest anticipated, proved to be those that had escaped from the field at Thompson's Station under Lieutenant Colonel Bloodgood, who had quite the ground at the height of the conflict, and embracing, according to Federal accounts, some 529 officers, men and teamsters, with 16 or 17 wagons, and three ambulances and teams; also the arms of the men and all the baggage of Coburn's late command, all which was secured with the loss of one man killed and two wounded. The Federals, besides prisoners, lost about 10 killed in the skirmish preceding the capitulation.

After the surrender had been arranged, Starnes came upon the ground with his command, and the prisoners and spoils of war, which were abundant, were placed in his charge. General Forrest then moved at a gallop, with the Tenth Tennessee and Freeman with one of his guns, on the road toward Franklin to the bridge, which he found defended by a stockade strongly garrisoned, the surrender of which, straightway demanded through his aide de camp, Captain C. W. Anderson, was curtly declined. A single shot, however, from Freeman's gun, hurtling and crashing through the stockade, wrought an immediate change of purpose and brought the display of white flags. The men at this point, some 230, the remnant of the Twelfth Michigan Volunteer Infantry, another of Coburn's regiments, made the sum total of prisoners 759. The bridge and stockade being burned to the ground, the objects of the expedition were fully accomplished, making it one of the most skilfully executed of the war.

The set-back at Thompson's Station, however, did not discourage the Federal troopers. Throughout the spring months they were kept busy, making almost daily expeditions in the general direction of the Confederate front, seeking information and the capture of enemy troops, wagon trains or supplies. A contemporaneous account by a participant tells of a typical foray of this kind by the Brigade of Mounted Rifles commanded by Col. John T. Wilder. On April 1st they started out from Murfreesboro in the direction of Lebanon, going on without opposition to Rome and Carthage. Then, says the narrator:

After resting and scouting in this vicinity for some time, the command turned towards the south in the direction of Alexandria, up Caney Fork and Smith's Fork, marching over hills and mountains where the people had never before seen a Federal soldier. Even artillery went rattling over by-roads where scarcely even a wagon had gone before. Hearing that a body of Wharton's cavalry had returned to Liberty and Snow Hill, whence General Stanley had driven a similar force but a few days before, Colonel Wilder laid his plans to capture them. His plan was perfect, and its execution would have succeeded even beyond his expectations, but for a mistake in a single road. Those ordered to take the rear wheeled to the right into the first cross-road, when they should have taken the second. This brought them into the main road of rebel retreat near the rear of their column, while the other would have placed them directly in Wharton's front. . . .

Many Union families were found entirely destitute, and many rebels with abundance. The goods of the latter were distributed among the former, and many hearts made glad. To one a dollar's worth of captured cotton yarn would be thrown; to another a tired-out horse or mule would be given; and so the expedition marched through the country, stripping the rebels and supplying several families that had lost their all for the sake of the Union. . . .

The result of the expedition was as follows: Five hundred head of good horses and mules; $8000 worth of tobacco and cigars, paid for by the Confederacy only two days before; $4000 worth of spun yarn; about 86 tons of hay and forage; 4000 bushels of corn; a large quantity of flour and meal; 104 prisoners, including eight officers who were enforcing the Confederate conscription; a rebel mail and mail-carrier, and 194 able-bodied negroes. The expedition is recognized by all as one of the most brilliant and successful of the campaign, reflecting great credit upon the gallant officer in command.

The excursions of General Wilder and his men were not always so benevolent. One of his troopers tells of how their practices hardened as the war progressed:

In February, Colonel Wilder, on learning that General Roscrans was anxious to increase his mounted force, but could get no horses, sought and obtained authority from that commander to mount his command by raiding the country to the flanks and rear of the army and impressing animals wherever found. Our operations in this enterprise extended east to the base of the Cumberland range of mountains, from McMinnville north to the Cumberland River, and back to Lebanon and the Hermitage. Besides over-running this country, we made two or three excursions to the southwest. All this extensive and rich section we stripped of horses and mules, and by the middle of April the entire brigade was mounted on fairly good animals.

Up to this period of the war our forces had, as a rule, respected the property rights of citizens. Now a new policy had come into operation, and we were its pioneers —the first of all the Army of the Cumberland to commence a system of forcing the disloyal inhabitants of the South to contribute to the support of the army. Not only animals, but vast quantities of forage and other supplies were regularly gathered in by us, and distributed to the troops. Henceforth this policy was largely followed by the western armies.

The practice of stripping the country marched over of all available supplies of war soon became a matter of course and expected by the inhabitants. But not so in the commencement. Our wholesale confiscation of property was looked upon by the sufferers simply as wholesale robbery, and hence a very bitter feeling was entertained toward us. So much so, that at one time rebel commanders of cavalry—numerous small commands of which were constantly encountered by us—felt justified in executing any of our men who happened to fall into their hands. Two of my regiment were shot after being captured near Lebanon. We had a report which we then believed to be true, but which I now doubt, that the Rebel authorities had officially declared our brigade outlaws. Be that as it may, we were in a position to put a stop to any such practice, and we did. Soon after learning of the shooting of the two men above referred to, some of our men hanged four Rebel cavalrymen to a tree fifteen miles north of Murfreesboro. Other acts of retaliation might be mentioned.

During the period of our horse-stealing adventures we constantly encountered Rebel cavalry, principally belonging to John Morgan's command, from which we captured a great many prisoners, while we scarcely lost a dozen men. We aimed to take nothng from Union men, and so long as we kept west of the foothills of the Cumberland range we were in little danger of so doing. But when we reached the mountains great discrimination was necessary, for in these regions a preponderance of the population was intensely loyal.

Captain Marshall P. Thatcher, one of the company commanders in General Stanley's cavalry command, in later years wrote his recollections of those months of semi-truce, preceding the forward movement of Rosecrans' army in June:

As we look back over the intervening twenty years it appears to us as in a dream— those pleasant valleys of Middle Tennessee where the corn had ceased to wave, but the green hills were just as rich in verdure, the early bird-song just as enchanting, the marvelous beauty of flower and shrub and tree undimmed; but our duty was not all poetry and romance. The hard realities of life met us every hour, whether by night or day; at the bugle's shrill call every man "to horse" and away, meeting the enemy on their own grounds, and, if necessary, attacking them in their strongholds. Every foot of ground between Franklin and Columbia became as familiar to us as our neighborhood roads at home. We picketed every road and scouted over every plantation, and he who crept near our lonely videttes at midnight or early morning, when eyes were heaviest, found him as alert as at midday.

At the same time it became necessary to study the people. There were the loyal, the professedly loyal, the conservative Southerner and the bitter secessionist, and as our mission was against armed foes only, it often became a very difficult task to discriminate between the loyal and the professedly loyal; but all were watched alike and our dealings with them made as agreeable as possible under the circumstances.

As a rule, whatever was taken for food was paid for; yet as our army was the natural refuge of some of the worst elements of our Northern society, as well as the same element from Canada, the better portions of our army—though largely in the majority—were often powerless to prevent outrages. Two worthless vagabonds to a single company would give to that company a very bad record—except for fighting. While they often were found in the thickest of the fight, they appeared bullet-proof; in fact, the devil seemed anxious to preserve them for some special job, when they were sure to be on hand. Yet the regiment made many warm friends at Franklin and that friendship was appreciated.

During the month of May the usual routine of camp life was followed—including scouts, skirmishes, foragings and alarms—and we still had time left for the enjoyment of much that was pleasant in that beautiful valley around Franklin—its Roper's Knob, surmounted by fortifications, the headquarters of the signal corps, the clear-running Harpeth, broad plantations dotted with pleasant Southern homes, surrounded by groves of fruit and forest trees. But this apparent inactivity was only a breathing spell to give the country roads a chance to thoroughly dry while the wet season was passing, and on the 2d of June, 1863, we marched out of Franklin, leaving only a small garrison there, while our lines were being contracted to our left, our right resting for a time on Triune, and our active campaign for the summer was begun. . . .

John Will Dyer, Confederate cavalryman, in his post-war *Reminiscences,* tells of his part in one of the numerous skirmishes with the Federals during this time, and of its interesting aftermath:

Our army was camped about Tullahoma and kept up communication with Richmond via Chattanooga and Knoxville. Colonels Bird and Sanders had recruited two (Federal) regiments from the mountains of East Tennessee, Kentucky and Virginia, and were moving down the Clinch river valley with the purpose of cutting Bragg's communications by destroying the railroad bridge at Loudon. We moved across the mountain to intercept them. Our route led through Jamestown, a county-seat stuck into the side of the mountain, and Wartburg, a Swiss colony on the summit, where everything looked as described in histories of the Fatherland, and we could almost imagine that we were soldiering in the mountains of Switzerland.

We got across the mountain and crossed Clinch river at Kingston in time to get in front of Colonel Bird, but as he had a force of 1,800 men and two three-inch rifled cannon, and our force was but 600 men and two mountain howitzers, we did not like to tackle him in the open. Besides, the enemy were "hardy mountaineers" and supposed to be very bloodthirsty, so we gradually fell back to the breastworks at Loudon, hoping for reinforcements or a right good chance to run away. But we got down in the ditches, got our little "bulldogs" in position and waited the attack with a full determination to put up the best fight we could.

The enemy finally begun to show himself, run out his two cannon, and after some delay turned them loose at us. By some means they were unable to throw their shells near us and we soon felt quite secure from any harm from them. They were the poorest gunners I ever knew, and if all the artillerists of the armies had been like them there never would have been a man killed by a cannon unless it might have been the gunner himself. Finally, they moved up their line and prepared to charge on us. When the order was given to charge they came in a rush for about fifty yards, when our skirmishers turned loose on them and sent them back in a hurry. This same performance was gone through with the third time, when Colonel Scott decided to give them a lesson and prepared to charge them. Our howitzers began to throw shells among them and worked so fast and furious that their line was soon demoralized, when over we went after them with that "rebel yell". They didn't stop to see us but, mounting their horses, struck out, every fellow for himself, like the old Harry was after them, throwing away everything that encumbered. We mounted and chased them into the mountains, scattering them so that I never heard of them any more during the war. We captured their two rifled cannon, which were the finest field pieces I ever saw, all their camp equipages, numbers of small arms and hats enough to equip our regiment.

About eight years ago, in the rotunda of the Willard Hotel at Louisville, I met an old comrade who was a member of Scott's regiment. It was the first time we had met since the war and, like old soldiers do, we were talking over old times and fighting over the old battles, in which the Bird and Sanders raid, as we called it, was pretty freely discussed. I noticed that a tall, slim, red-faced old man, dressed in a black suit and wearing a "plug" hat who was sitting near, seemed to be very much interested in our talk. My friend had to leave on the train and I went out on the sidewalk to see him off.

After he had gone this old man approached me and said, "I heard you telling about the Loudon fight."

"Yes," said I, "do you know anything about it?"

"I do," said he. "I'm Colonel Bird."

"Well, Colonel," said I, "did we tell it about right?"

"Not quite," said the Colonel, "it was a heap worse than you said it. I never saw as scared a lot of men in my life. I lived at Clinton and thought I would get to stop and kiss my wife and daughters good-bye, but I didn't even have time to look towards the house. I thought I had two of the best regiments in the army and we could carry everything before us, but they were a set of damned cowards. They could do a heap of blowing, shoot from behind a tree or a rock, but couldn't stand cold lead on open ground.

"Well, the war is over now, let's go and take a drink."

I drank with the old Colonel and we settled our part of the fight then and there.

The armies of Bragg and Rosecrans during this period were separated by a range of high foothills, through which roads connecting Murfreesboro and Tullahoma crossed at three defiles: Hoover's, Guy's and Liberty Gaps.

Bragg occupied a strong position north of Duck river, his infantry front extending from Shelbyville to Wartrace, with his cavalry divided between McMinnville on his right and Spring Hill and Columbia on his left. At Shelbyville Polk's corps was strongly entrenched, with a detachment thrown forward to Guy's Gap. Hardee held the other gaps with strong detachments from his corps.

Rosecrans recognized the defensive strength of Bragg's position, and was reluctant to try a frontal attack on the Shelbyville entrenchments. His eventual plan of attack contemplated turning Bragg's right, which necessitated driving the advanced Confederate detachments from the gaps to the right and left of the main position. Endeavoring to create the impression that a direct attack would be made on Shelbyville, he made his first advance in that direction on June 23rd, with a heavy demonstration in Polk's front. Strong pressure drove the defending units from Hoover's and Liberty Gaps, striking at Hardee's right and rear, and by the 27th the corps of McCook and Crittenden were concentrated at Manchester, threatening to flank Hardee. Guy's Gap was forced by General Stanley's cavalry, routing General Joe Wheeler's over-matched mounted men, opening the way into Shelbyville.

Early on the morning of the 28th, Wilder's mounted brigade pushed through to Decherd, destroying a long stretch of the railroad track in Bragg's rear, and the Confederate commander found himself in a most perilous predicament. Polk and Hardee fell back to Tullahoma, and on the morning of the 29th Bragg's entire army was in the Tullahoma works.

Rosecrans' forces advancing along the Shelbyville pike were hampered by the torrential rains that fell for several days, and also harassed by Wheeler's Cavalry. Martin's division of Wheeler's force had been sent to join Forrest at Spring Hill about the time the Federal advance began, but as soon as Rosecrans' objective became apparent Wheeler ordered both Forrest and Martin to join him at Shelbyville. When Wheeler reported to Bragg in person, he found that Polk had already been ordered out of Shelbyville and was then in full retreat, with his wagon trains following, and Wheeler was ordered to interpose his cavalry between Polk's wagons and any pursuit that might develop. Wheeler reached Polk's abandoned breastworsk shortly before noon of June 27th, when Polk's last wagon had just crossed the bridge over Duck River, which was then in flood.

A Confederate account of Wheeler's handling of this precarious situation as he received the full force of the advancing Federal cavalry is given by one of his troopers, John W. DuBose:

Martin had spent the night in bivouac where he could feed his horses. It rained all night. Word was sent to him to hasten on. Just before noon he came up in a drenching rain, every man soaked to the skin and nine out of ten rifles too wet to shoot. Forrest was on the road behind, advancing.

Colonel James D. Webb of the 51st Alabama, one of Martin's favorite regiments, sent Major Dyke with seven men forward upon an eminence commanding a view of the pike. This scout reported that, as far as the eye could reach, the broad white pike was filled with the mounted men and artillery of the foe, advancing steadily and confidently.

The fight began; Martin had slept on the ground, in the rain, the night before; he took position in drenching rain; not one gun in ten would fire. Russell's 4th Alabama fought bravely. The 51st Alabama was driven in toward Shelbyville, some three miles, Major Dyke and many others being captured. The whole cavalry line fell back in confusion. They were a mere handful.

Wheeler fell back to the town, or was driven back. . . . Wheeler formed his men, perhaps 600 of them, on the court-house square. Up the street the enemy formed for the charge, thousands of them. Men, women and children crowded the doors and windows, waving the stars and strips and shouting welcome to the foe. As was his custom, Wheeler rode to the head of his column. As the serried ranks of the innumerable foe advanced, he cried, "Charge!" The impact was terrific. Two guns he had planted on the street sent shells fiercely into the advancing enemy, but the missing places in their ranks were at once filled. The fighting was hand to hand, with clubbed pistols and clubbed carbines. Wheeler rode here and there on the front. "Kill him! Shoot him! That's Wheeler!" rang out from the lips of mad invaders. Wounded horses neighed, unhorsed riders were ridden down on every side, the red sun sank upon the scene of carnage.

Thirteen thousand to six hundred! "Every man for himself!" shouted Wheeler. Then there came a wild rush for the bridge, the one narrow bridge. Alas a broken wagon blocked it. The routed horsemen spurred their chargers to leap into the raging stream. The enemy opened a rattling fire upon them from the land. . . . Martin was slightly wounded. Wheeler and Martin both reached the river bank. The former struck it where it was perhaps fifteen feet above the water. He spurred his horse to the leap, lost his seat in the descent; but, clinging to the neck of the animal, guided him, swimming to the opposite bank in safety. Martin trotted down an easier incline to the water. His horse struck the steep place on the opposite side and with great difficulty ascended lower down.

Captain Thatcher of Stanley's cavalry was among those taking part in the Federals' slashing attack on Bragg's too-lightly held left flank, and he gives a participant's impression of the attack and its successful outcome:

When the regiment moved through Eagleville, June 23d, artillery confronted them, and a portion of the regiment dismounted and routed them; then mounting they drove the enemy three miles. In this movement the enemy's artillery continued to fire until the Second were within eighty rods, when they limbered up and galloped away. This was a very hot day and men were falling out continually, and soon a flank firing was heard, followed by a charge from the enemy. This was handsomely met by a counter-charge from the First Tennessee (Federal) and the flankers retired in confusion.

At this moment a single horseman was seen to leave the enemy's ranks and charge down alone upon our brigade in front of the First Tennessee. Nearly every man in that regiment and not a few from the Second fired at the charging figure, and at last stopped in blank amazement that the man was able to sit bolt upright in face of that shower of bullets. But he still came thundering on, while hostilities ceased on both sides to look and wonder if the man was made of iron, or had he a charmed life. He soon rode in among the Federal troops and the mystery was explained. A bullet had cut both reins, and the horse refused to cease charging; all that the rider could do was grasp the horse's mane and pommel of the saddle and hang on. His clothes were riddled and the horse had many a scratch, but the man's skin was whole, though it may be doubted if he breathed during his ride.

Camping at Rover for the night, the march was resumed at 8 o'clock next morning, through Versailles and Middleton, where the enemy's cavalry made another stand, but our revolving rifles soon dislodged them, with severe punishment for the time engaged. Rains again set in and all roads except the macadamized turnpikes became next to impassable, while the discomfort of the troops was great. Wagon trains could not keep up and our bivouacs were in the rain, no covering but our wet blankets and ponchos—and such rains as only Tennessee can boast of; while the red clay and black muck formed a barrier more serious than armed foe or frowning battlements.

With such discouragements it was no wonder men should murmur, "Surely the Lord is not on our side—if He has anything to do with this weather."

General Rosecrans had evidently intended to throw his strong right arm around Bragg and crush him before he should cross the Tennessee. We were a part of that strong arm. But our trains and artillery were hopelessly stranded in the mud. Granger, Stanley and Mitchell were all here, but *push* we could not. However, as the cavalry corps came to Fosterville, and drove in the enemy's skirmishers, Stanley determined to abandon the mud-bound trains and artillery to their fate and strike with the cavalry alone.

Guy's Gap was before us, three-quarters of a mile away, and along its crest stretching out to the right and left were earthworks breast high; between us an open plain, ascending to the hill. The sun burst through the heavy clouds and shone full in the faces of 10,000 cavalry, in two lines, division fronts; banners flying, bands playing and the command marching in as perfect lines as if on a parade. Such a sight was rare in the history of the war—a corps of cavalry about to charge earthworks across an open field, and up a hill.

"Steady! steady!" was heard in low distinct tones along the line, though at every step the dreaded grape or canister was expected. A half mile, and yet no sign from the enemy; another quarter and still no curling smoke nor screeching shell. Casting our eyes for a moment to the earthworks not a man nor gun was in sight. At this instant General Stanley ordered Colonel Minty, of the Fourth Michigan Cavalry, to lead the charge with his brigade, and right gallantly was the order executed, Colonel Campbell following next with his brigade, and the entire corps close in the rear in columns of fours and platoons.

The enemy had become frightened and fled precipitately, three pieces of artillery halting long enough on the hill at the entrance to Shelbyville to give us a few shots, then, wheeling again, dashed through the town, hotly followed by Minty and his brigade, while Campbell with his brigade, taking a street to the left, reached Duck river at the further edge of town in time to see hundreds of the enemy plunge in and endeavor to swim across, not half of whom ever gained the other shore, while Minty gained the bridge in time to cut off numerous prisoners from Wheeler's cavalry and capture one piece of artillery on the bridge. The roads were too heavy to follow the fleeing enemy far, and we returned to Guy's Gap for the night, having captured three pieces of artillery and 500 prisoners.

It was at Shelbyville that we were greeted by the pleasant sight of many flags bearing the "Stars and Stripes" suddenly flung out from chamber windows, and shouts of welcome from women and aged men who had lived like prisoners in their own homes; and colored women crying, "Bress de Lord, we knowed you'd come." And it was here, too, that we recaptured one of our female spies, the famous Major Belle Boyd, who had only saved herself from rebel prison pen or the gallows by feigning sickness, which she counterfeited admirably.

Captain Thatcher's reference to "one of our female spies, the famous Major Belle Boyd" reflects some confusion in his recollection. Belle Boyd, of course, was a Confederate spy who operated in Virginia, and who never boasted a military title. He evidently refers to Miss Pauline Cushman, a famous actress of that time, who was serving as a Federal spy and had been given the honorary title of "Major" by the bogus "Colonel" Truesdail under whom she served in Nashville. Employed by Allen's New Theatre in Nashville, she had openly made statements indicating sympathy for the South, and for these spurious evidences of disloyalty to the Union she was publicly and ostentatiously ordered out of the Federal lines, in conformity with the prevailing policy of banishing "Rebel sympathizers" to the South. Then, posing as a refugee from Yankee oppression, she made her way into the lines of General Bragg's army and, according to her own subsequent story, for some time provided valuable information to General Rosecrans. Within a few weeks, however, she was arrested by Confederate scouts and taken to Shelbyville, where she was tried as a spy and sentenced to death. Upon learning of her sentence she was reported "prostrated", and by her illness (probably feigned) postponed her decreed execution. In the gushing words of a eulogistic post-war biography, written by a Philadelphia lawyer, "carefully prepared from her notes and memoranda":

As yet she was too much prostrated by sickness to allow the dread mandate of her enemies to be carried out. The rebels were inhuman enough to do almost anything, but even among them there was none found quite fiendish enough to suggest that she should be carried to the gallows in the state in which she then was. She was then free to this extent, that she need not fear anything immediate; and as the military surroundings were liable to undergo a violent change at any moment there was still room for hope. It might happen that the brave Union boys would yet triumph, as they had often done before, over the base minions of secession and save her. That Shelbyville was the point which they were aiming at was well ascertained, and of itself gave a glimpse for the rainbow tints of hope; but our heroine thought of none of this; she had made her peace with the world and was prepared to die—ignominiously, if need be, as far as outward appearance went, but honorably and high purposed in truth, as her own heart well knew. She was resigned, therefore, hailing each effort made to please her or sympathize with her in her fearful misfortunes with an angelic gratitude that won the love of all observers.

At this dramatic moment, news reached Bragg of the approach of Rosecrans's army, and upon the Confederate evacuation of Shelbyville it was decided that Miss Cushman was too ill to be moved with the retreating army but would be removed to the home of "a certain Doctor Blackburn . . . an excellent physician whom it is well known is a Union man at heart." Then, her admiring biographer goes on in a welter of purple prose:

From that time forth she was treated very kindly, for Doctor Blackman was really a good Unionist, and both he and his amiable wife vied with each other to assist and relieve our heroine. Indeed the dark cloud which had so long enshrouded her fate began slowly to pass away, and the golden gleam of hope's bright sun to cast its warming beams upon her. . . . At length one day it was rumored that a large body of Federal soldiers was just outside the town, and great was the stir and bustle in consequence. Staunch rebels got to work to make Union flags, so as to protect their property, while the true Union people came forth to drink in eagerly the news of the coming succor. At last the battle opened by the dread roar of the artillery. Nearer and nearer the conflict came, deepening and rolling toward her like the waves upon some ocean shore. . . . Crack! would go the deadly rifle, while loud above the clatter of cavalry and whistle of minie-ball would sound the dread artillery. At length the heavy tramp of the retreating rebel columns could be heard and, heaven be praised, the loud shout of victory of our brave, brave boys charged into the heart of the town, their banners flying and their bands playing.

Attenuated as she was, nay almost dying, she felt new life surging through every vein and, springing from her bed, she staggered to the open window. Aroused into a fictitious strength by the stirring events of the day, she was for the moment restored to comparative health and vigor and, wrapping a blanket about her, she stood upon the balcony of her room window until every noble fellow of the Union army had passed. . . . "Thank God!" cried Pauline, in a perfect delirium of joy. "I am safe at last! I'm safe!"

After the Federals had destroyed the N&C railroad at Decherd and interrupted Bragg's communications with the rear, he called a council of war (June 29th). After reciting the critical state of affairs, Polk expressed the opinion that the army should fall back in the direction of its base, so as to keep the connecting line covered all the time. Lieutenant, Richmond tells of the colloquy that followed:

General Bragg said: "That is all very well, but what do you distinctly propose to have done?" General Polk replied that he should fall back or retreat immediately, as he did not think there was a moment to spare. "Then," said General Bragg, "you propose that we shall retreat?" General Polk said: "I do, and that is my counsel." General Hardee was then asked what he thought. He replied that General Polk's views carried great weight, but he was not prepared to advise a retreat. He thought it would be well to have some infantry sent along the line to support the cavalry, and to wait for further developments. It was agreed that this should be done, and that the infantry should be ordered back upon the line. This closed the conference.

The next night Bragg, finding that Rosecrans was pressing to gain his rear, withdrew to a position on the south side of Elk River where it was then planned to dispute the further progress of the Federals. On the evening of July 1, as Rosecrans' pressure increased, Bragg at Decherd sent a note to Polk:

"The enemy has reached your front; close up. The question to be decided instantly: shall we fight on the Elk or take post at foot of mountains at Cowan's?"

General Polk replied: "Take post at foot of mountain at Cowan's." He then wrote a note to General Hardee in which he expressed anxiety as to the situation, but said: "My mind is in part relieved by the decision, which I have no doubt will be made to fight at the mountain. If asked under the circumstances named in my letter whether we ought to fight or retreat, my mind inclines now to the latter course."

The next day, July 2, Bragg moved his army to Cowan, where he drew up in line of battle. Rosecrans declined the implied challenge, and Bragg then moved his army across the mountain and on into Chattanooga, where the Confederate force arrived on July 6th, in good order and unpursued.

As the retreating army paused for rest on top of the mountain that night, General Polk found himself stirred with sadly mingled emotions. In 1856, as Bishop of the Episcopal Church, he had recommended that the Church establish an educational institution, and the next year the University of the South was formally organized and chartered by the state of Tennessee. A tract of some ten thousand acres of land on top of Sewanee Mountain was acquired. Pledges for an endowment fund were obtained, and in 1860 the corner-stone of the main building was laid and the location formally christened "University Place", as Bishop Polk devoutly offered up thanks for the approaching fulfillment of his dream.

Then came the outbreak of war, and the progress of the University movement was stopped. Now, for the first time since the laying of the corner-stone, Polk was back at Sewanee. But now his episcopal vestments were displaced by the gray coat of a Confederate general, and as he looked sadly at that neglected corner-stone, he was surrounded by the tired and ragged rank and file of his retreating army instead of by the college students with whom his mind's eye had fondly peopled the wooded domain.

It was Polk's last look at Sewanee, but after the war was over, the work of promoting the University was resumed under Bishop Quintard. The war had swept away the endowment fund; the soldiers of Rosecrans' army had demolished the corner-stone and carried away chunks of it for souvenirs. But the land was still there, and in 1866 work was resumed on the building of the University of the South, now better known by the name of the mountain on which it stands.

As Bragg's army withdrew in full retreat to Chattanooga, to Forrest's division was assigned the duty of securing and holding the gap through the Cumberland Mountains near Cowan. Dr. Wyeth tells of an amusing incident as Forrest's men sought to check the pursuit:

After the infantry had passed through Cowan and up the mountain, the Federal cavalry, hovering in their rear, came in contact with the rear guard under Forrest in person. Firing and falling back rapidly, the Confederate troopers went through the village and towards the gap. As the general, among the last in retreat, was passing a house, he noticed a woman who was berating his soldiers for not turning on the Yankees and "whipping them back." Shaking her fist at Forrest, the stars on whose collar she was too angry to observe or too nearsighted to see, she shrieked out: "You great big cowardly rascal; why don't you turn and fight like a man, instead of running like a cur? I wish old Forrest was here, he'd make you fight!" The general, unable to control himself, burst into a laugh as he put spurs to his horse and fled the scene. When telling this incident, he said that he would rather have faced a battery than that fiery dame.

With his army now in full retreat, Bragg himself on July 3 proceeded from Cowan to Chattanooga by rail. Jefferson Davis, in his post-war writing about the events of the war, attempted to gloss over Bragg's precipitate retreat in mealy-mouthed words: "In June some movements were made by General Rosecrans which were followed by the withdrawal of our forces from Middle Tennessee and a return to the occupation of Chattanooga."

Bragg himself, however, yielded to no self-delusion. Bishop Quintard writes of encountering Bragg at Cowan on the morning of the 3rd and commenting on his dispirited appearance. When he spoke to the general about it, Bragg replied: "Yes, I am utterly outdone." Then, leaning from his saddle, he whispered sadly to the bishop: "This is a great disaster."

On his way to Chattanooga Bragg stopped at Bridgeport long enough to send a telegram to Richmond advising of his withdrawal. Bragg's message was received in Richmond the next day, July the 4th—a Glorious Fourth indeed for the North, but a sad, bleak day for the Confederacy. On that same day in the East, General Lee was preparing to fall back from Gettysburg. In the West, Pemberton was surrendering Vicksburg to Grant, and with it the control of the Mississippi River. Bragg was giving up Tennessee without a battle.

Gloom rested over the Executive Mansion and the War Department office in Richmond that day. The wave of the Confederate cause had reached and passed its crest. From then on, it was all ebb tide.

Appendix To

CHAPTER IX

During the first half-year of 1863, while the armies of Bragg and Rosecrans were chained into inaction by their own self-imposed strategic and tactical limitations, there were an unusual number of interesting and exciting episodes which shed a revealing light on the conditions surrounding such a militarily unusual situation.

In this Appendix are given an account of a few of these dramatic events.

THE TWO SPIES—OR WERE THEY SPIES?

One of the most mysterious, and tragic, of all the strange things that happened in Middle Tennessee during the first half of 1863 was the strange case of Colonel Lawrence Orton Williams and Lieutenant Walter G. Peter, who paid with their lives for a desperately hazardous escapade, the object of which has never been clear to anybody. Colonel Williams was a graduate of West Point and had served in the United States Army until the secession of Virginia, when he resigned and joined the Regular Army of the Confederacy. He was a first cousin of Mrs. Robert E. Lee, and a distant relative of General Lee himself, and had served with the Army of Northern Virginia during the early days of the war.

This strange episode had its beginning on June 8th, on which date Colonel J. P. Baird, commanding the Federal army post at Franklin, just before midnight telegraphed Brigadier General James A. Garfield, Chief of Staff of the Army of the Cumberland at Murfreesboro:

Two men came in camp about dark, dressed in our uniform, with horses and equipment to correspond, saying that they were Colonel Orton, inspector general, and Major Dunlop, assistant, having an order from Adjutant General Townsend and your order to inspect all posts; but their conduct was so singular that we have arrested them, and they insisted that it was important to go to Nashville tonight. The one representing himself as Colonel Orton is probably a regular officer of the army, but Colonel Watkins, commanding cavalry here, in whom I have the utmost confidence, is of opinion that they are spies, who have either forged or captured their orders. They can give no consistent account of their conduct.

General Garfield, replied promptly and peremptorily:

The two men are no doubt spies. Call a drum-head court martial tonight, and if they are found to be spies, hang them before morning, without fail. No such men have been accredited from these headquarters.

This order was apparently relished by Colonel Baird who said, in his acknowledgement of Garfield's communication, "My bile is stirred and some hanging would do me good". Carrying out Garfield's instructions, a "Court of Commission" was called that very night; the suggested "drumhead court martial" was assembled at 3 A. M., and the prisoners were arraigned on the charge of being spies. The official record of that trial states that, "some evidence having been heard in support of the charges and specifications, the prisoners made the following statement":

That they came inside of the lines of the United States Army at Franklin, Tenn., about dark on the 8th day of June, 1863, wearing the uniform they then had on their persons, which was that of Federal officers; that they went to the headquarters of Colonel J. P. Baird, commanding forces at Franklin, and represented to him that they were Colonel Orton, inspector, just sent from Washington City to overlook the inspection of the several departments of the West, and Major Dunlop, his assistant, and exhibited to him an order from Major General Rosecrans, countersigned by Brigadier General Garfield, chief of staff, asking him to inspect the outposts, and a pass through all lines from General Rosecrans; that he told Colonel Baird he had missed the road from Murfreesboro to this point, got too near Eagleville and run into rebel pickets, and had his orderly shot, and lost his coat containing his money; that he wanted some money and a pass to Nashville; that, when arrested by Colonel Watkins, Sixth Kentucky Cavalry, after examination they admitted that they were in the Rebel army, and that his (the colonel's) true name was Lawrence Orton Williams; that he had been in the Second regular cavalry, Army of the United States, once on General Scott's staff in Mexico, and was now a colonel in the Rebel army, and Lieutenant Peter was his adjutant; that he came in our lines knowing his fate, if taken, but asking mercy for his adjutant.

The prisoners were, not surprisingly, found guilty as charged, the finding was approved by General Rosecrans, and before the day was done Captain J. H. Alexander of the Seventh Kentucky regiment, cavalry, provost-marshal of Franklin, officially reported that he had "carried the sentence into execution by hanging said prisoners by the neck until they were dead."

During the course of the trial neither Colonel Williams nor Lieutenant Peter made any statement or gave any intimation as to the purpose of their hazardous venture into the enemy's lines. Several years after the war, there was printed in the *Confederate Veteran* a letter written by Major Joseph Vaulx, who had served as inspector general on the staff of General B. F. Cheatham at the time of the spies' execution, in which he said:

Colonel Williams had not been with the army since I joined it in 1862. The only time I ever saw him was when I was sick at Columbus, Miss., after the battle of Shiloh. He belonged to the "regular army" of the C. S. by virtue of coming from the regular army of the U. S., and how he was employed from that time in 1862 until June 1863, I do not know. He was (so reputed) very full of exaggerated, personal and military conceit, and had been an aide to General Winfield Scott. In his bearing and dress he was at all times ultra-military, spectacular and erratic. No doubt you remember the small offense for which he ran a soldier through with his sword at Columbus, Ky. I have frequently heard repeated the last sentence of the written statement he made with reference to the killing of this soldier for refusing to salute him the second time he passed him in his morning visit to the stable; it will give some idea of the man's mental and moral organization. He concluded his statement of the killing thus: "For his ignorance, I pitied him; for his insolence, I forgave him; for his insubordination, I slew him".

He was away from the Army of Tennessee after that occurrence till in the spring of 1863 he turned up, by reason of some influence at Richmond, with a cavalry colonel's commission, accompanied by Lieutenant Peter (regular C. S. A.) with orders to report to General Bragg for assignment to a command. At that time there were being organized some new cavalry regiments at Columbia by General Van Dorn. These regiments were formed by consolidating the battalions which had previously been independent organizations. General Bragg sent Colonel Williams with his adjutant, Peter, to General Van Dorn with orders to be assigned to one of these regiments. In compliance, General Van Dorn issued the order assigning him to a Tennessee regiment, in which was Major Richard McCann's splendid old battalion.

Colonel Williams went out to the camp to take command, when he was informed that no officer or soldier of the regiment would obey his orders. The officers believed they had a right to have one of their own number appointed to the command, and neither Tennesseans or volunteer officers nor men would serve under the overbearing man who had killed the soldier at Columbus. The regimental and company officers reported this to Van Dorn, who wisely suspended the order and reported the case to General Bragg who also wisely acquisesced in Van Dorn's action, and Colonel Williams and Lieutenant Peter were left in that anomalous position, termed, "unassigned".

Williams was much mortified by this state of affairs, and after staying in and about Columbia for a short time set out on this journey without orders to do so, or without confiding to anyone in Van Dorn's command his intentions, as I and the army generally understood at the time we heard of his capture and execution. If I recollect further rightly, he passed through the Confederate pickets secretly.

The general belief about the man was that he was out of balance, erratic, full of conceit, personal vanity and distorted views of his military importance and dignity. To sum up—he was not entirely sane. In this mood, after being repudiated by soldiers and generals, he set out to do something sensational. Whether some brilliant and daring exploit to return to Van Dorn's camp, or whether he intended to go through the United States on a survey, or whether, as was published in some Northern papers at that time, he desired to pass on through the army, reach his friends at home and get money to go out of the country, possibly to England or Canada. I read that he made such a statement before his execution.

I never heard at any time in our army a single man express the opinion that Williams' actions in this matter was known to any officer in authority over him, nor could anyone imagine any special service he could have been to the Confederate army by visiting either Franklin or Nashville, for he was a stranger to that section of the country and its inhabitants, and we had many capable and proven men well acquainted with both who could have been far more efficient in such a service than Williams. . . .

Williams' character and quality was appreciated by the army at large in the matter of killing the soldier and in the statement by which he attempted to justify himself. Neither the army nor its generals wanted him; his commission and orders were procured by some influences at Richmond; he was chagrined, and reckless—he was not a sound man, and there is no accounting for the freaks such a one will take. I am sure no Confederate authority was responsible for or cognizant of his intentions in that affair. It was his own misfortune, to which was added the greater one involving Lieutenant Peter's death with his own.

A Spy's Thrilling Escape

John W. Headley, a young Kentuckian who served as a Confederate spy and secret service agent, had many thrilling adventures and hair-breadth escapes during his fantastically exciting cloak-and-dagger activities in Tennessee, in New York and in Canada. An example of his daring and resourcefulness is provided by his escape from a Federal prison in Nashville in 1863, an account of which he wrote after the war. Headley, while engaged in an attempt to ascertain the strength of the Federal forces in Nashville, had been surprised and captured in civilian clothing (along with some uniformed Confederate officers) at the home of S. D. Watkins at Louisa Furnace, near Clarksville. He tells about this thriller:

Here (at the Watkins home) I met Will Baxter, a brother of Mrs. Watkins, Robert Mockbee, her nephew, and Captain "Hick" Johnson, on furlough from Lee's army in Virginia. Johnson was the son of Hon. Cave Johnson, who was Postmaster-General in the Cabinet of President James K. Polk, and was a cousin of Baxter and Mrs. Watkins. The home of these young men was in Clarksville, but they had not considered it safe to venture beyond this point.

We did not retire till after ten o'clock, and it was only twelve o'clock when Mockbee shook me and said the yard was full of Yankees. I asked the others what they intended to do. Captain Johnson said there was nothing to do but surrender. I then arranged with them to say they never saw me before and knew nothing about me, and that I came there after supper. They lighted a candle and began to dress. I cut a small slit in the under side of the bedtick and pushed my pass from Bragg inside without attracting the attention of the others. They were about dressed when the Federals came up. I stayed in bed perfectly unconcerned. The officers in charge questioned the others and got a straight story of their character and the reason of their presence.

They were soon ready to go. The officer then asked Johnson, "Who is that other man?" Johnson answered as I had suggested. I then raised a little and said, "Good-evening." He spoke, asked my name, where I lived, and what I was doing there. I told him my name was Williams, that I was from near the cotton mills on Duck River below Waverly; that the conscript officers were scouring the country to take every one to the Southern army; that I hid out for two weeks until it looked as if I could not stay there any longer and I was now on my way to Shawneetown, Illinois, where I expected to do something until the trouble was over in my section. He looked at my clothing and was satisfied, but several others came up and joined the captain's party and one of them recognized me as the prisoner who ran out of ranks on the way to Clarksville, two weeks before. He called Monroe Adams, who was below, and who identified me without hesitation. It was another joke on me, but the captain told me if I tried to escape this time I would be killed, and he gave orders accordingly. . . .

The next day we were taken down to the river and on board a steamer for Nashville. A crowd of citizens gathered on the wharf as we went down, and Lafayette Wilson, a friend from Madisonville, Kentucky, recognized me, and coming to greet me walked down to the boat. He touched me on the hand as we walked along, my guard being on the other side. I looked and he was trying to put a ten-dollar bill, of greenback money, in my hand. I thanked him in a whisper, telling him I did not need it.

It was late in the afternoon when we started from Clarksville and it was sixty miles up the river to Nashville. I had a great many plans to escape from the boat in the night, but none seemed feasible. The best one, I thought, was to take a plank and jump overboard, but I was afraid I would freeze before I could paddle the plank ashore with my hands. When we reached Nashville the next morning we were marched to the State Capitol, where we were registered at headquarters after ten o'clock, and then marched down to the market square and sent up into the third story of the market-house building, which was used as a temporary prison.

This was a three-story brick building. There were two rooms and a wide hall between on each floor. A winding stair ran up in the hall with iron railing and banisters. The two rooms on the third floor were used for the prisoners and about twenty guards were stationed in the hall. Prisoners were brought in every hour, in squads, and both rooms were crowded. Rosecrans' army was here and at Murfreesboro, and of course a few prisoners on both sides were taken every day. I learned from a guard that the prisoners were sent North every morning at eight o'clock.

I noticed a rather crude restaurant on the first floor as we were brought up. I asked the guard about it and he told me any of us could go down there under guard and buy a meal. This was good news, as the sleeping and cooking were going to be horrible in our prison rooms. I suggested to Baxter that we go down and get a hot dinner. We selected the youngest guard in the bunch, a boy about nineteen years old, to go with us. We made the guard eat with us, which he appreciated, and when we spoke of coming down for supper, he asked us to let him come with us and that arrangement was made.

We could see from our windows that citizens and soldiers crowded the pavements and army wagons crowded the streets. It seemed a poor prospect for making our escape even from the prison, and still worse for getting out of Nashville. I told Baxter in the afternoon we would go late to supper, on the idea that we were not hungry yet, and after dark would try to bribe our guard to let us go in the crowd, while he could slip back, and this was agreed to. We put every small article of our baggage in our overcoat pockets and inside of our other clothing.

At dark we went down, and at the bottom of the stairs I turned to Baxter, as if it made no difference to the guard, and told him that the restaurant in the building was a sloppy place to eat and that we would go across the street to a nice restaurant. I had seen the sign from a window. Baxter agreed, but the guard said he was not allowed to take us over there. He stood by it for a long time through fear, only on his own account, for disobeying orders. I pleaded with him that in such a crowd we would not be noticed and they would never know up-stairs, but he could say that he had taken us to the river bank where he had a right to go with us. He finally consented.

We went to a restaurant on Cedar Street about the middle of the block between the market square and the Commercial Hotel. While there was a crowd along the pavement, there were very few in the restaurant. We sat at a table which stood against the wall, making room for three. The guard sat next to the door, Baxter next to his right, and I on the back side facing the guard and the front door. The cashier's desk was across by the opposite wall and ten feet nearer the front door than our table. I took the lead and ordered a nice supper. While we waited for it, Baxter drew out a half pint bottle of whiskey a friend had given him at Clarksville, and we all made a toddy. We had a good time eating our supper and talking about the war.

An idea of escape occurred to me, and I finished my meal first and carelessly got up, saying I would settle with the cashier and we would be ready to go when they were through eating. I walked on without any more ceremony, getting out my money as I went. I stood for my change with my face turned to the back of the restaurant so the guard would not be uneasy. Taking my change I fumbled with it, turning toward our table. The guard was looking at me, so I took a step slowly while putting my money away. At this moment the guard put his fork to his mouth, bowing his head slightly, which took his eyes from me. I turned and walked to the front door so as not to attract the attention of passers-by. I looked back and the guard had grabbed his gun, which stood against the wall, and was rising hurriedly, but I was out and in the crowd the same as any other person.

I knew the guard could not leave Baxter to follow me, and felt safe after going a few steps, as no one noticed me. Several details of soldiers were passing in both directions, but I passed on in the crowd as though I lived in Nashville. I went several squares toward Broad street and observed that I was getting into the residence part of town. I believed any old citizen would be a friend and I wanted to find one without delay. I went into the first substantial home where there was a light. When the servant answered the door-bell I got a glimpse inside and observed a number of Federal officers in the parlor. I asked the servant if Mr. Wilson lived there. She said "no, sir," and told me who did; but I begged pardon, saying I was mistaken in the house, and excused myself.

A little farther on I came to a small family grocery on the corner. I walked in, and buying a cigar sat down with the proprietor to smoke, which he said was agreeable. I soon learned that he was an old resident and a strong Southern sympathizer. He did not care who knew it. I assured myself fully and then told him the story of my escape. He told me of the large encampments all around the city on both sides of the river. I felt that it was much better for me to go out between picket posts and risk their shots in the dark if I could find any woods. He directed me how to go, to the left of Charlotte pike, where I would probably have the best chance to evade the pickets. I followed his directions for fully a mile and the woodland he had described was in my front. As I approached a fence, at the edge of it I discovered tents on the other side among the trees. I stopped, but had been heard by a sentinel not more than forty feet on the inside of the fence. He shouted "Halt!" It was pretty dark, but I could see my way a few yards. I stooped and ran on tip-toe, swerving to the right, so that I would not be in the range if he heard me. However, I presume he concluded he was mistaken as I heard nothing more.

My new friend in the grocery had told me every one caught on the streets after ten o'clock was arrested. I judged it to be half past eight now, and concluded it would be better to abandon the idea of going out that night. The houses were very scattering in the neighborhood and mostly cottages, where I thought best not to apply for accommodations. When I got on Broad Street I found it was after nine o'clock. I met an old darky, from whom I learned the location of the cemetery on the Nolensville pike inside the city. He said houses extended to the grounds. I went out that way briskly without seeing a light in any dwelling on the street, and began to regret that I had not tried to arrange with my grocery friend for lodging. I looked for his place again in my wanderings but failed to find it.

At the entrance to the cemetery I stopped to look in all directions for a light. I was going into the cemetery and sit up all night among the cedars, because I did not believing I would be disturbed in there; but I saw a light and went to it. I entered the yard gate and saw a two-story dwelling with a hall and room in front. The light was in the front room. When I looked in at the window I saw a lady sitting at the hearth knitting and a man in bed reading by a lamp on a table near by. I sounded the door-bell and the lady came to the door with the lamp in her hand. I bowed, and apologized for being late, but just wanted to speak to her husband a minute. She appeared a little frightened and said he had retired. In a sort of pleading manner I suggested that I would not think of having him get up and would just go in only for a minute. She balked along and showed plainly that she did not want me to come in. I asked her what time it was and tried to relieve her of any apprehension.

We were at the entrance to the door of their bed-room by this time, when her husband spoke up to inquire who was coming in. His wife quickly said she did not know. I laughingly said, "It's a friend; you'll be surprised to see me." His wife stopped in the middle of the room so the light would shine on my face to let her husband see if he could recognize me. I then candidly explained that I had come in for some information only because they had a light burning and I did not think it would be considered an intrusion. I felt that I did not want a gentleman to get up and dress to talk with me a few minutes. I then said frankly that I was a Confederate and told him how I had escaped and the predicament in which I was placed. His wife instantly declared that her husband had taken the oath and could not afford to violate it. I finally got a hearing and told so fair a story that the husband, Mr. Metcalf, said he didn't care if I was a Rebel or a Yankee or neither, if I simply wanted lodging and breakfast and proposed to pay for the accommodation he had a right to entertain me and would do it. After his wife became satisfied she got interested in my story, and when we retired it was midnight.

I was put in their best room up-stairs. Thomas Metcalf was the name of my host. He became thoroughly satisfied that night, and it was agreed that I should be known to the cook, a negro woman, as the cousin of Mrs. Metcalf. The next morning everything was easy. It was agreed that I should stay there until I got tired, unless I had a chance to leave the city. As there were no children in the family I felt perfectly safe.

Mr. Metcalf came home in the afternoon from his business, and had told a friend, who was a grocer, of my case, and after supper we went down town and spent an hour or so in the counting-room of the establishment. I arranged to go the next night to the store of a clothing merchant, who was a friend, where I could fit myself out as a citizen, in the style of a young man. I had been wearing my hair rather long and cropped around the edge. This I now had shingled to change my appearance in every respect as much as possible. I then went about the city freely, having no fears except from Kentucky soldiers from my own locality, who might recognize me on sight. But I carried my discharge from the army for such an emergency.

I soon realized that there was no possible way of escape from Nashville except to get a pass northward. There were over 50,000 soldiers in the army of General Rosecrans, from Nashville to Murfreesboro. The Confederate cavalry under Forrest, Morgan and Wheeler had threatened the east and west picket posts of the city so continually that three different posts were stationed on every road leading to the country, with camp sentinels between the roads. During the next three weeks I visited in the neighborhood with Mr. and Mrs. Metcalf, attending several social parties, and made very pleasant acquaintances.

During the first week, I got an introduction to a Captain Rhodes, of Michigan, who understood from me that I was from Bourbon County, Kentucky, and was visiting relatives in the city and some in the (Federal) Seventeenth Kentucky Cavalry. We did not talk politics, but he was led to infer that I was a Union man. I managed to impress the fact that I would need a pass when I got ready to go home and he very promptly volunteered to say that he would arrange that for me. I now cultivated this gentleman, who was a good man. I was introduced by him to other officers and in a general way, without exciting suspicion, I learned the names of all the brigadiers and major-generals in Rosecrans' army, not only those at Nashville, but at Murfreesboro, Triune, Lavergne, Brentwood, and Franklin. I managed to meet men from nearly all the commands by raking up acquaintance in a casual way and by a little liberality at times with cigars and refreshments. With this information, I knew the number of brigades, and while I did not make any notes there was little else on my mind and I remembered all.

There were funerals every day in the cemetery opposite Metcalf's (my home), and I attended several of these to form casual acquaintances among the soldiers and learn their commands. I frequented all the hotels, where I had generals pointed out to me by soldiers. Here I first saw Governor Andrew Johnson. I was now possessed of information on which a safe estimate could be made, within a few thousand, of the strength and location of the army, and I was ready to go out, but I could not afford to show any special anxiety, though I felt confident now I would have no trouble to use Captain Rhodes.

I was afraid to apply too soon after his offer for fear he might possibly become suspicious. About the third time I met him, after I was ready, the matter came up and I told him when I wanted to start. He cheerfully went with me and introduced me to his personal friend, the provost-marshal, who issued the pass without hesitation. My name was William C. Sims during this sojourn in Nashville.

Before going I bought a gross of good pocket-knives, of small size, that were put up one dozen in a package. These I distributed in my pockets and bootlegs. I managed also to conceal two dozen silk handkerchiefs in my clothes. I passed through two sets of pickets beyond the bridge on my way off on the Louisville Pike. Just beyond Edgefield I turned off to the left on the White's Creek pike. After going about one mile from the pike I met an old gentleman on horseback. His name was Squire White. He lived on White's Creek near by, five miles from Nashville. He eyed me pretty closely and said I looked like a Rebel. I could tell by his look that he hoped I was one. When I concluded it was safe to tell him so, it made me a friend. I went to his home to dinner. He directed me to a man two miles ahead whom I could get to take me to Cumberland River without traveling any public road. I found the place and before sun-down I was on the bank of the Cumberland River, fifteen miles below Nashville. I was soon rowed across in a skiff and spent the night at the home of Mr. Robertson. The next morning he sent me to Charlotte, his son-in-law going with me to bring back the horse I rode. At Charlotte I found a company of about one hundred Confederate cavalry, from Forrest's command at Columbia, on a scout.

I learned afterwards from Mrs. Watkins, at Louisa Furnace, that Baxter went with the guard back to the prison room after failing in an effort to bribe him for liberty. But the next night Johnson, Baxter, and Mockbee succeeded in making their escape.

It was not until nearly forty years later that Headley learned of the fate of his fellow-prisoners, Lieutenant William Baxter, Major J. Hickman Johnson and Captain Robert T. Mockbee. Captain Mockbee, at a reunion of Confederate Veterans in Memphis in 1901, learned Captain Headley's address and wrote to him giving him the particulars of their escape from the Nashville prison after Headley's get-away:

About the third night after you got away, we all three (William Baxter, Major Johnson and myself) went downstairs to the restaurant, accompanied by a poor "green" Yankee boy as our guard, and, after having our supper, in which our guard shared, we went out as if we were going back up-stairs into the prison. When we reached the entrance at the foot of the stairway we halted (as had been prearranged) and Major Johnson said, "Boys, we ought to have a bottle of brandy for to-night," and, turning to the guard, said, "Here, you take this money and go over to the saloon across the square and get us a bottle of brandy and bring it up. We will go on up-stairs. Just put your gun behind the door there until you come back." And the poor simpleton did just as he was told, in the meantime Johnson having given him a five-dollar bill. The guard walked out into the dark, and Baxter and I followed him just as soon as we thought it safe.

Major Johnson stopped to pull off his Confederate overcoat, which he threw behind the door, and took the Yank's gun to guard Baxter and me, after we got outside. In the meantime, Baxter and I had gotten out in the dark and went around the market-house on the side next to the river, and when Johnson came out with his gun he went the other way and so missed us entirely. Putting the gun down, he then hurriedly made his way to the home of his sister, Mrs. Hickman, the mother of John P. Hickman, the present secretary of our Tennessee Confederate Association. She secured a pass from the provost-marshal, took him over the river in a buggy, dressed as a lady, to a sister's, Mrs. Dortch, where he had such a good time he stayed too long, and an old negro servant went in and reported him and the Yankees sent a squad of cavalry out and took him in, putting him in a cell in the penitentiary, until he was sent North.

Baxter and I, after getting safely away, secured us a complete outfit of the latest style citizen's clothes from a friendly Jew, and each of us carried a well-stuffed valise. After going to a barber shop and getting clean shaved and trimmed up we sallied forth and joined a procession of people who had just come on the train from Louisville, and went with the largest crowd to the Sewanee House, then one of the leading hotels of the city. There we registered, Baxter as Charles H. Haynes, and I as John C. Smith, of Louisville, Ky., secured a room and a bottle of brandy, to help keep our nerves quiet, and spent the night. We went down to breakfast the next morning and the room was filled with Yankee officers, at least a hundred at breakfast. Afterwards we went out in the city to try to find some avenue of escape into the country, but failed completely and had to remain two days and until the third night, when we succeeded in getting a skiff and went down the river to Haywood's Landing, where we stopped within ten miles of Mr. Watkins's, where we had been captured. I remained in that section for several weeks getting information, and also some recruits for my regiment in Virginia. I, like you, had orders from the War Department at Richmond, countersigned by General Lee, and slipped them between the feather bed and mattress, and quietly told Mrs. Watkins where to find them. I got back to Richmond just as the battle of Chancellorsville was being fought, and was with my command until Appomattox.

The Adventure of the Hollow-Heeled Boot

Following the battle of Murfreesboro, Rosecrans kept the main body of his army there, but the garrison under General Mitchell was still in Nashville, and the people of the city settled down to the dreary prospect of an existence of indeterminate length under the twin tyrannies of Governor Johnson and the secret police. Now the bloody aspects of the war were forcibly impressed on them as the trainloads of wounded and maimed survivors of the battle of Murfreesboro came pouring into the city during the January days following the battle. Churches, schools and public buildings were taken over for the establishment of 24 Army hospitals, and even private homes were called upon to take care of their share of the wounded, both Federal and Confederate. Convalescent one-armed and one-legged men were a common sight on the streets, and the long low rows of the improvised Federal cemetery in North Nashville filled up with tragic rapidity.

Aside from this constant reminder of the grim side of warfare, conditions in Nashville showed little change during ensuing months. The gestapo-like secret police continued their machinations on an enlarged scale, with scores of spies, many masquerading as escaped Confederate soldiers, ingratiating themselves into the confidence of suspected citizens to spy on them in their homes. The chief of the secret police, William Truesdail, who bore the self-conferred title of Colonel, was a man who seemed to possess an evil genius for this slimy type of work.

Nashville at this time was teeming with spies and counter-spies, both Confederate and Federal. Many of them were known to be in the service of both sides, especially those blockade runners who were buying contraband quinine and other drugs (sometimes from Federal surgeons) and carrying it through the lines to the blockaded Confederacy. The Federals winked at the passage of these smugglers through the lines when arrangements could be made with them to bring back military information from the Confederates—and the Confederates carefully fed these two faced operators with morsels of false or not-very-important information which would encourage the Yankees to permit a continuation of their passage to and fro.

John Fitch, provost judge of the Army of the Cumberland, who had his office in General Zollicoffer's former home on North High Street, published a book in 1864 in which he gloatingly told of the many instances in which guileless and trusting Confederates had been trapped into betraying themselves into the web of his agents. A typical example was that of the Confederate smuggler-spy, Ogilvie Byron Young, the undoing of whom is related in Mr. Fitch's rather turgid style:

In the earlier days of the rebellion there lived in Southeastern Missouri one Ogilvie Byron Young. He was a wild, graceless scamp, rich in the blood of his ancestors, but poor in purse. To the pride of Lucifer he added the courage of Falstaff and the honor of Iago. A scion of Virginia's aristocracy, he deemed himself a statesman from birth and an orator by nature. Showy in manner and superficial in attainments, he could act the accomplished gentleman or the bullying braggart as best suited the occasion. Vain, reckless, and boastful, he was scorned as a visionary enthusiast by some, feared as a bold, bad man by others, but admired as a genuine Southern cavalier of the old school by those who knew him least.

Wildly imaginative, but immensely unpractical, he plunged madly into the first waves of rebellion, and, while Sterling Price was yet a Union general and Claiborne F. Jackson a loyal Governor of Missouri, dared to avow and advocate opinions of the most ultra-Southern character. Fine-drawn theoretical arguments on the right and duty of secession were spread before the people of the state, in column after column of letters published in newspapers and to which was attached the full signature, "Ogilvie Byron Young." The rough backwoodsmen of his county were momentarily swayed by his presumptuous clamor, and he was sent to the first Missouri State Convention. Here he was the only member that took strong ground in favor of secession *per se*, gaining thereby not a little notoriety. The state did not secede; but Ogilvie Byron Young did, and for some months he was not so much as heard from.

In the fall of 1861 he was arrested at the Spencer House, Cincinnati, as a spy. In due time an indictment and trial followed; but, though there was abundant evidence of guilt, he escaped conviction by means of some technical informality in the proceedings. He was ordered to leave the city, however, and did so. In the following spring he was found in Covington, Kentucky, under an assumed name, aiding and abetting the rebels by furnishing information, and was again arrested. He had been cautioned by some one, it would seem; for there was found nothing upon him in the way of papers or letters to warrant his detention, and he was again released, to again disappear from sight for some months.

In November, 1862, he is again met with, in Nashville, where he had been for some weeks as a paroled prisoner, but acting all the while in his old capacity of smuggler and spy. In this business he seems to have had remarkable success, until his career was fortunately arrested by a combination of circumstances and the watchful shrewdness of the army police. About the last of that month Young was introduced to a gentleman who represented himself as a hostage for the return of certain loyal Mississippians captured at Iuka and treated by [General Sterling] Price as traitors, contrary to the terms of the cartel between the Federal and Confederate Governments. At first Young was shy and suspicious, but was finally convinced that his new acquaintance was really what he purported to be, and heartily entered into all his plans for the advancement of the Confederate cause. As his confidence grew stronger, he remarked that he had been of more benefit to the South, as a spy, than any brigade of rebel soldiers. He had encouraged desertions in the Federal camps, and made out paroles in the names of Morgan and Kirby Smith. The business was getting a little dangerous now, however, and he should get beyond the lines as soon as possible. He would have gone long ago, only that he had expected to be saved the trouble and expense of the trip by the fall of Nashville.

Our "Iuka hostage" then informed him that Mrs. Major Ranney—wife of Major Ranney of the 6th Texas Regiment—was in the city, under his charge, and just returned from Europe, whither she had been on diplomatic business for the Confederate

Government. She had in her possession very important despatches, and was anxious to get safely through the lines with them. Young said, in reply, that he would bring his influence to bear upon the army officials in her favor, but in case she should be searched it would be well to provide for such a contingency. There was, he said, in the city a man by the name of Thompson, ostensibly a citizen, but really a rebel lieutenant in Bragg's army, and now acting as a spy. He had made the trip through the lines ten or twelve times, and could do it again. He was now engaged in drawing a map of the fortifications around Nashville and procuring information as to the numbers of the troops, &c., which should be forthcoming in due season. These secret despatches of Mrs. Ranney's, together with this map and other papers, could be hidden in the heel of a boot, which would be made for them by a bootmaker of the city in the employ of the Confederate Government. His name was C. J. Zeutzschell, and his shop was on Union Street.

This plan was agreed to, and Young was to assist in the execution of it; in return for which, he was to be placed in a high position at Richmond. Young's reputation, however, was not of the best, and the bootmaker would do nothing for him when called upon, without first making inquiries among his friends and consulting with our "hostage", for whom the boots were wanted.

Accordingly, Zeutzschell came to his room one evening and said that Young had been to his house and wished him to make a pair of boots and to secrete important documents in them so as to defy detection. He had no confidence in Young's honor, and did not wish to do it for him. He knew him as identified with the Confederates, indeed, but he was a bad man, low in his habits and associates, never had any money, &c. He (Zeutzschell) had been inquiring of the friends of the South—undoubted secessionists—concerning him (our Iuka hostage), and was convinced that he was a gentleman and a true Southerner. He would do any thing to promote the cause,— money was no object,—he would lay down his life for it. If Young could be thrown off the track, he would make the boots and secrete in them a map of the fortifications about Nashville. His brother-in-law, Harris, would go out and see if any new ones had been erected. If not, he had a perfect plan of them in his head, to prove which he immediately sat down and drafted one. He remarked that he had recently sent several to General Morgan. He had made the boots for all the spies in the same way, and not one had ever been detected. He had sent valuable information in a common pipe.

"Can you get a pass for your man?" asked our hostage. "Certainly," was the reply; "as many as you like. There is a German at head-quarters who steals blank passes for me, and I fill them up myself. I give him whiskey for them."

He would like to go South, too, he said, in conclusion. He could describe the fortifications so much better than in a map.

Both parties being satisfied, an agreement for the boots was made. Zeutzschell was to get the exact distances of the defences, the number and disposition of the troops, &c., and secrete them, together with Mrs. Ranney's despatches, in the heel of one of the boots. This he did, according to promise: the boots were made and delivered on the evening appointed. Instead of reaching Generals Bragg and Morgan, as intended, however, the maps, papers, boots, owner, maker, and spy, suddenly found themselves in the hands of the army police, much to the astonishment and chagrin of all parties concerned. Zeutzschell and Young were sent to the military prison at Alton, Illinois.

THE ANDREW JOHNSON KIDNAPPING (?) MYSTERY

With two large hostile armies encamped for so long a time in such close proximity as they were in Middle Tennessee in the summer of 1863, especially with both of the same nationality and speaking the same language, it was inevitable that there should be a constant inter-play of spies and counter-spies and even counter-counter-spies between the two forces. One of the most mysterious and potentially sensational of the plots brewed at this time was one involving the attempt (or, at least, the alleged attempt) to kidnap Andrew Johnson, then in Nashville serving as Military Governor of Tennessee. By his sternly repressive measures he was making himself thoroughly odious to all the citizens loyal to the Confederacy, and it would not have been entirely surprising if one of these oppressed citizens should have hatched some plot against him. The kidnapping plot (or the supposed kidnapping plot), however, did not originate with some revenge-seeking rebel, but was the proposal of one of Johnson's own personal body-guard. A contemporaneous account tells the details of the weird story:

A state of war gives occasion to many strange inconsistencies of conduct on the part of a class of individuals who exhibit the faculty of serving, in turn, both parties to the contest, and that was great zeal; but the strangest instance of this kind, and the hardest to explain, was the case of Dirks, the Captain of Andrew Johnson's Body Guard, at the time he was Military Governor of Tennessee. Those who were concerned most intimately with him in his attempted exploit have never been able to satisfy themselves of his real motives in the part he played. We will give the circumstances, and allow each reader to judge for himself and reach his own conclusion.

Captain Dirks was a trusted officer of Governor Johnson, and the instrument of his will in dealing with the Rebel element at Nashville. He made arrests of citizens almost daily, at the command of his chief, and conducted them to the State Penitentiary for safe keeping. Among these, on one occasion, was Mr. Mat Stratton, a respected citizen, whose active sympathies were with the people of his State, but who, at that time, was living quietly at his home, in the vicinity of Nashville. His arrest, instigated by a native loyalist for what was deemed disloyal utterances, was made by Dirks. On the way to prison, Dirks grew very confidential, though he knew nothing whatever of his prisoner until then, and proposed, with seeming earnestness, to desert to the Confederate army, then stationed at Tullahoma, if he could procure his assistance in getting through the lines. Mr. Stratton, fearing that it was a trap laid for his destruction, refused to seriously entertain the proposition at first; but Dirks insisted with such earnestness that he at length determined to run the risk of probably bad faith, and agreed to see him safely into the Confederate lines, which he could promise confidently to do, on account of his knowledge of the country and extensive acquaintance with the inhabitants on the route.

The arrangement was accordingly made, and in due time the plan was carried out, the party arriving safely at General Van Dorn's headquarters at Columbia, Tenn. They then proceeded without difficulty to General Bragg's headquarters, at Tullahoma, Dirks all the while retaining on the Federal uniform. On the way, or perhaps before starting, the traitor disclosed his design of kidnapping Governor Johnson, of the success of which he had no doubt, as he was familiar with his habits and knew exactly where to find him on certain nights of the week. His plan was to take a small party of horsemen, work his way to the vicinity of Nashville, procure a carriage and drive to the house where his victim would be lodging, and forcibly carry him off through the lines at rapid speed before the alarm could be given.

He disclosed his plan to Captain C. W. Peden, the Confederate Provost Marshal, and pressed him to further his scheme with his influence and provide the means of its execution. This Captain Peden refused to do, saying that he had no authority and would not do so, unless directed by General Bragg. Dirks then besought an interview with the General, which was granted; but the latter—either from scruples of the propriety of the step, or doubts as to the deserter's sincerity—also refused to have any hand in the project, and directed the Provost Marshal to keep strict surveillance over him.

Dirks had some liberties allowed him, however, and was the subject of much speculation when his exploit became known. He soon became aware that he was not trusted, although he had deserted a man and a cause at that time extremely odious to the army; yet he talked very unreservedly of his desertion, saying that he had come to cast his fortunes with the Confederacy and fight his former friends. His air and manner were those of a man who expected that he would be received joyfully and treated with great consideration by the Confederates for what he had done; in other words, to be made a hero of, and to afford the subject of a great sensation.

However, he told off on his late friends so freely and unsparingly that an officer of Bragg's Staff, learning of his kidnapping project, became thoroughly impressed with his sincerity, and besought the General to furnish Dirks with the authority and means to carry out his design. The General again refused, but finally told the officer he had no objection, provided he undertook the matter upon his own responsibility. This the latter agreed to do, and repaired with Dirks to General Van Dorn's headquarters for the purpose of putting the project into execution. A small squad of cavalrymen, under a lieutenant, was permitted to volunteer as an escort, but enjoined to be on guard against treachery. When the expedition reached the vicinity of Nashville, the officer in command became so much dissatisfied with Dirk's claim to the sole management and direction of the affair that a hot altercation ensued between them; whereupon the lieutenant arrested Dirks and, securing his feet with a rope beneath his horse, carried him a prisoner back to Columbia.

Dirks was very indignant at the imputation and harsh treatment put upon him, when he was about to perform an important service for the Confederacy, as he claimed; but his protest was received with general distrust, and he was carried, with his feet still pinioned, back to Tullahoma. On meeting Captain Peden, he exclaimed, "Here's my friend; he will release me," and began to declaim violently against the authors of his bad treatment; but Captain Peden told him that he had no authority in the matter, and that he must go to General Bragg. The General, becoming thoroughly disgusted by this time with the traitor, ordered him to be confined in the guardhouse for safe keeping until further instructions. Dirks resented his confinement by such abuse of everyone whom he failed to impress with the idea of his injured innocence, and annoyed the authorities so much with his importunities for release, that he was at length sent to Atlanta, Ga., and ordered to be kept closely confined. Here he remained for more than a year, still pleading for release, until he finally effected his escape, by burrowing under the wall of his prison.

But the strangest part of this story remains to be told. After his escape from prison, Dirks turned up at Washington City, where he received a colonel's commission and a large amount of back pay. Whether he imposed upon the authorities there with a tale of adventure and cruel treatment in a Rebel prison, or whether they were privy to some plot that Dirks was to execute in the first instance, but not able to effect, is a secret that has never transpired to the general public.

In sifting the facts as they appear for a solution of the mystery, we are of the opinion that Dirks, animated by a morbid fancy for the sensational, did give way to a passing weakness and desert his country's service. This view is supported by the fact of his sudden resolution to desert, and making it known to a prisoner with whom he was unacquainted. Possibly he was animated by an impulse of repugnance for the task assigned him, which required a large share of sternness, and gave way to a feeling of sympathy for his prisoner. At any rate, under the view that he was a deserter, he seemed to think that the very fact that he held an important and responsible office under a Military Governor at that time particularly offensive to the people of the South, would give him *eclat* with these people and create a sensation, making him a hero in his estimation of the qualities and attributes that belong to that character.

Poor fool! If this was the spring and motive of his conduct, he bitterly atoned for it in the treatment he received at the hands of those who, he fondly thought, would receive him with open arms and bursts of applause. Yet he received a balm for his physical suffering in the promotion and emoluments awarded him by the Government he had deserted, and this may have satisfied him in the end. As said before, the strangest part of this story is that he should have been rewarded for his self-imposed sufferings, when the fact of his desertion was made known at Nashville in a short time, by the publicity given to it by the Southern papers. To say the least of it, this story of Captain Dirks is a curious combination of the fickleness and favor of Fortune.

CHAPTER **10**

☆ *Chickamauga*

GEOGRAPHICALLY and physically, the situation of Bragg and the opposing Federal army in July 1863 was about the same as it had been a year previously, just before the Confederate advance into Kentucky. But there was an important difference. In 1862 the initiative had been with Bragg; the Federals under Buell were strictly on the defensive. Now, in 1863, the relationship was reversed. The initiative was with Rosecrans. Bragg in Chattanooga was on the defensive, his movements governed by what his adversary might decide to do.

As a matter of fact, Rosecrans himself appeared to be none too certain just what he wanted to do, and showed no inclination to follow Bragg in hot pursuit. As might have been expected, General Halleck in Washington immediately began a telegraphic bombardment of Rosecrans, urging him to go after Bragg and attack him. But Rosecrans had problems. Van Horne, in his *History of the Army of the Cumberland* tells of the perplexities now confronting the Federal commander:

There were difficulties in the way of an early movement which General Rosecrans deemed insurmountable. In his judgment, three conditions were essential to the successful advance of his army. These were: the repair of the railroad to the Tennessee river, ripe corn in the fields, and support to his flanks. For the actuality of the first, he was himself responsible; the second depended upon time and the weather; and the third rested with the military authorities at Washington, and the commanders of the armies east and west of him, on the line of the Tennessee river. July 13th, the railroad bridge over Elk river was ready for trains, and on the 25th they were running to Bridgeport, Alabama. But corn does not ripen in Tennessee and Georgia in July, and the movement of General Burnside into East Tennessee was long deferred, and no promises had been given that the right flank of the Army of the Cumberland should have protection while advancing against Chattanooga. On the 5th of August, in disregard of General Rosecrans' assigned reasons for not moving his army, General Halleck gave peremptory orders for its advance. The former, however, deferred movement until the middle of the month. By this time his preparations were complete, and the fields promised the forage for which he had been waiting; but no further assurance had been given that he should have supporting forces on right or left. . . .

In view of the strength of Chattanooga against direct attack, General Rosecrans resorted again to maneuver to dislodge his antagonist. As the route to Bragg's right flank penetrated a mountain region almost destitute of forage and water, and involved a wider separation from his communications, he selected his lines of advance over the river and mountains west and south of his objective. He, however, so directed his first movements as to mislead the enemy with regard to his ultimate design, which was to threaten his communications and force him to abandon his position or give battle on equal terms.

Bragg, encamped with his army in Chattanooga, was also enmeshed in indecision. Rosecrans was still on the western side of the Cumberland Mountain range. Bragg, with no inkling of his adversary's intentions and feeling that his own movements must be largely dependent on what Rosecrans might do, was in a haze. Bragg, however, was not bereft of ideas. Soon after his arrival in Chattanooga he wrote to Johnston in Mississippi, suggesting the possibility of taking his army west to join Johnston for a quick blow at Grant. But Johnston did not react favorably. He dismissed the idea with the terse comment: "It is too late", and Bragg did not push the proposal.

Bragg in his perplexity got no help from Richmond. President Davis and the War Department had been so engrossed with the Vicksburg situation and Lee's invasion of Pennsylvania that they seemed to have forgot about the Army of Tennessee. Bragg, in a letter to Beauregard on July 21, deploring his own inaction, said that he had asked for orders three times since July 1 and got no response from Richmond. But, with Vicksburg lost and Lee pushed back south of the Potomac, suddenly Richmond again remembered the Army of Tennessee. General Samuel Cooper, the Confederate Adjutant General in Richmond, coming to life, wrote to Bragg on August 1: "If we can spare most of Johnston's army temporarily and reinforce you, can you attack the enemy?" Bragg, pointing out the geographical difficulty in reaching the enemy's position, told Cooper he felt "it would be unsafe to seek the enemy", even if he were reinforced. And in a letter to Johnston he wrote: "The defensive seems to be our only alternative, and that is a sad one."

Cooper, now showing unwonted combativeness, suggested to Davis that Bragg should be peremptorily ordered to advance and fight Rosecrans. Davis, the old professional soldier, retorted that a commanding general should not be given an order, but only a suggestion, to fight a battle.

So, as the summer drifted by, the Army of Tennessee lay idly at Chattanooga waiting for something to turn up. The men were in fairly good health and spirits; but, as was not unusual under Bragg's command, provisions were scanty and they grumbled much about that. The dearth of provisions in the army and the frugal fare even of the officers is illustrated by an anecdote told by the irrepressible Private Sam Watkins of the First Tennessee Infantry:

About this time my father paid me a visit. Rations were mighty scarce. I was mighty glad to see him, but ashamed to let him know how poorly off for something to eat we were. We were living on parched corn. I thought of a happy plan to get him a good dinner, so I asked him to let us go up to the Colonel's tent. Says I, "Colonel Field, I desire to introduce you to my father, and as rations are a little short in my mess, I thought you might have a little better, and could give him a good dinner." "Yes," says Colonel Field, "I am glad to make the acquaintance of your father, and will be glad to divide my rations with him. Also, I would like you to stay and take dinner with me," which I gladly accepted. About this time a young

African, Whit, came in with a frying-pan of parched corn and dumped it on an old oil cloth, and said to the Colonel, "Master, dinner is ready." That was all he had. He was living like ourselves—on parched corn.

We continued to fortify and build breastworks at Chattanooga. It was the same drudge, drudge day by day. Occasionally a Sunday would come; but when it did come, there came inspection of arms, knapsacks and cartridge-boxes. Every soldier had to have his gun rubbed up as bright as a new silver dollar. . . . The private soldier had to have on clean clothes, and if he had lost any cartridges he was charged twenty-five cents each, and had to stand extra duty for every cartridge lost. We always dreaded Sunday; the roll was called more frequently on this than any other day, and sometimes we would have preaching.

While the army waited there, grumbling at their inactivity, there were some important changes made in organization and in the scope of Bragg's authority, changes that were to make a decided difference in their subsequent campaigning. Hardee had been transferred to Mississippi, to strengthen Johnston there, and to fill Hardee's place was a gravely serious matter. Instead of selecting a replacement from among some of the competent major generals in the Army of Tennessee, President Davis for some unknown reason promoted General D. H. Hill to the rank of lieutenant general, and sent him to Chattanooga to take over Hardee's corps.

Hill, a graduate of West Point and a veteran of the Mexican War, had been serving with the army in Virginia, where he was recognized as a competent division commander and a tenacious fighter. But he was also a sort of stormy petrel—always in a dispute with somebody about something. He was a complete stranger to the troops he was now to command, but he had served in Mexico as a lieutenant in Bragg's battery of artillery, and he looked forward to serving again under his former captain. But when he rejoined his old comrade at Chattanooga, he found him nervous and distraught. "He was," Hill wrote later, "silent and reserved, and seemed gloomy and despondent." And that first chill presaged an unfortunate rift between the old friends which was soon to widen into a chasm of hostility and recrimination.

Aside from this change in personnel, Johnston had been finally relieved of responsibility for Bragg's department (which must have been a relief to both) and the scope of Bragg's own authority was enlarged to include jurisdiction over the Department of East Tennessee. General Buckner, at Knoxville, had been in charge of this department since May. He, however, had no particular craving for authority and had, in fact, suggested the creation of the new "Department of Tennessee" which on July 25th was set up and placed under Bragg's command. However, General Cooper, who sometimes seemed to have a special genius for confusion, in announcing the change said: "General Buckner will continue to correspond directly with this office." Then on August 6th, when Bragg officially took charge of the new Department, he proclaimed that the troops in East Tennessee would now constitute the Third Corps of the Army of Tennessee and be officially known as "Buckner's Corps", and he specified that the administration of the Department of East Tennessee was to remain a part of Buckner's duties. Buckner, faced with this anomalous and well-nigh impossible state of affairs, protested to Cooper that if he was not to have the status of a department commander he did not wish to be saddled with the duties and responsibilities of one; he would rather give his whole time to his troops. Cooper, however, took no notice of the protest, and before this technical matter of jurisdiction could be settled, Buckner was confronted with a pressing military emergency.

Grant's victory at Vicksburg had released the corps of General Burnside that had been sent there to reinforce him, and late in August, after insistent urging from Washington, Burnside with about 20,000 men was brought back to Kentucky to launch a threatening movement out of Lexington toward East Tennessee. Burnside by-passed the Confederate position at Cumberland Gap (held by General Frazier with 2000 men) and went across the mountains through Big Stone Gap. As he neared Knoxville, Buckner (who had only 6,000 men) called on Bragg for help. But Bragg could not send help to anybody at this juncture. He needed help himself, and he ordered Buckner to abandon Knoxville and join him.

Colonel Gilbert C. Kniffen, commanding a regiment in Burnside's corps, tells how the Federal movement into East Tennessee, starting on August 20, was carried out:

General Hascall's division moved from Crab Orchard, crossing the Cumberland at Smith's Ford; General White's division crossed at Jamestown; the cavalry and mounted infantry, Generals Carter and Shackelford and Colonels Foster and Woolford, moving in advance of each column. The two columns were ordered to concentrate after crossing the Cumberland Mountains near Huntsville, and move upon Montgomery in East Tennessee.

From there the movements, as Burnside telegraphed Halleck, would be "according to circumstances, but probably upon Kingston and Loudon, as these seem to be the places to which General Rosecrans desires us to go in order to cooperate fully with him. At all events, our final destination will be Knoxville. We have had very serious difficulty to contend with in bad roads and short forage; in fact the country is about destitute. We shall have still greater difficulties in that way to overcome, but if Rosecrans occupies the enemy fully and no troops are allowed to come down the road from Richmond, from the Eastern army, I think we will be successful."

The army arrived at Montgomery on the first of September, having encountered no opposition. There was nothing there to oppose it. General Carter's cavalry division moved thence in three columns, one under General Shackelford on Loudon Bridge, one under Colonel Byrd on Kingston, and one under Colonel Foster on Knoxville.

Major-General Simon Bolivar Buckner, in command of the Department of East Tennessee, had, in obedience to orders from the Confederate War Department, gathered up all his available force, with the exception of 2000 men under command of Brigadier-General John B. Frazer, who was left in defence of Cumberland Gap, and a few isolated detachments at Knoxville and other places under command of Brigadier-General Jackson, and formed a junction with Bragg's army at Chattanooga.

Previous to leaving Knoxville, General Buckner wrote Major-General Samuel Jones, in command of the Department of Western Virginia, requesting him to look after his department during his absence. Jones' headquarters were at Dublin, Virginia. He had his hands full taking care of Generals Averill and Scammon, who had on several occasions pushed their commands across the mountains from the north and Kanawha Valley, and he was unable with troops at his command to do much besides look after his own department. In compliance with Buckner's request, however, he came down the road as far as Abingdon, whence on the 6th of September he wrote General Frazer, directing him to hold Cumberland Gap as long as possible, as reenforcements were then on the way from the East. . . . General Jones' messenger reached General Frazer too late to prevent his surrender, and 2000 men were thus subtracted from the little force left to oppose the occupation of East Tennessee by the troops under General Burnside.

The cavalry expeditions from Montgomery were all successful. Kingston and

Knoxville were taken without opposition, but at Loudon Bridge Buckner's rear guard was strongly posted. After a brisk skirmish they were driven back by Shackelford's command. The railroad bridge over the Holston, a fine structure, had been saturated with turpentine, and the guard no sooner retreated across it than it was committed to the flames. Colonel Byrd captured at Kingston a steamboat in process of construction, and communicated with Colonel Minty's pickets, who formed the extreme left of General Rosecrans' army.

Leaving Byrd's brigade, 3000 strong, at Loudon and Athens, General Burnside pushed the remainder of the Twenty-third Corps on to Knoxville. Buckner had left Knoxville the day before Colonel Foster's arrival, leaving behind him a small force to guard a considerable quantity of quartermaster's stores, the government workshops, and a large quantity of salt, which fell into Foster's hands. General Burnside reached the city on the 3d.

The East Tennessee troops, separated for many months from their families, were greeted with expressions of the tenderest affection by the people all along the line of march. National flags were brought out from their hiding places and flung to the breeze from nearly every house. There was little use for army rations; a feast awaited the troops at every village. Women stood by the roadside with buckets of water, fruit, and cakes, which they gave freely, refusing all offers of pay. As they drew near Knoxville the city was radiant with flags. Sixty young ladies took their places by the roadside, waving flags and shouting "Hurrah for the Union!" Ladies came out of their houses to greet Generals Burnside and Carter. Seizing their hands, they wept for joy, crying "Welcome to East Tennessee!" Hundreds of people of both sexes and all ages collected in a few minutes, and both General Burnside and General Carter addressed them, promising that they should not again be deserted to their enemies. The demonstrations were not boisterous, but the intense joy imparted by these tidings were exhibited in quiet rejoicing. Men who for months had been hidden in caves in the hills and in mountain fastnesses came in and were overjoyed at their deliverance.

Meanwhile, about the middle of August, Rosecrans had perfected his lines of communication, insuring his source of supplies, and was ready to move against Bragg. Such a move was no easy task. He was separated from Bragg's army by several towering mountain ranges as well as by a deep, wide river. The mountains were rugged and precipitous, passable only by rough and winding roads at widely separated gaps. The river presented a formidable barrier, especially because the retreating Confederates had burned the only bridge at Bridgeport. The country separating the two armies was so exceptionally rugged that Bragg seems to have minimized the probability of a direct approach from that direction. But Rosecrans was not lacking in audacity, and he boldly decided to do what his enemy would least expect him to do. Accordingly he planned to strike directly across the formidable natural barriers toward Dalton, Georgia, in Bragg's rear, cutting his communications to the southward—a bold and hazardous project. In the presence of an alert and enterprising antagonist with skilfully employed cavalry he would have been exposing himself to very grave danger. But Bragg was guilty of inexcusable sloth, and permitted Rosecrans to proceed with his plans practically without molestation.

The actual movement of the Federal army across the Tennessee river began on August 29th, and the last units were over by September 4th. Preliminary of the crossing, Hazen's brigade of Crittenden's corps, about 7000 men, had been detached to make a demonstration opposite to and above Chattanooga for the purpose of leading Bragg to believe that the crossing would be made there. As a part of this demonstration, an Indiana battery unlimbered on the north side of the river and threw shells into the town. This happened to be a day set apart by President Davis for fasting and prayer in the Confederacy, and religious services were in progress when the shelling began. General Hill dryly remarks that there was "a perceptible diminution" of the congregations when the bombardment started.

Despite his vaunted piety, General Rosecrans did not appear to have any compunctions about subjecting the un-warned inhabitants of Chattanooga to bombardment, probably agreeing with his biographer VanCleve that "the vigorous shelling of the city by Wilder's artillery . . . constituted a brilliant feint." But, like the unfortunate frogs in Aesop's fable who admonished the cruel boys: "Consider that though this may be sport to you, it is death to us", the terrified people in Chattanooga found it difficult to identify the shelling of the city as an admirable example of brilliant military tactics. Mrs. S. E. D. Smith, a Confederate hospital matron (better known to her patients as "Grandma Smith"), was just setting up an additional hospital in Chattanooga that memorable day that President Davis had set aside as a day of fasting and prayer.

As the hospital was too far from the city for the inmates to attend divine service, she writes, a goodly number had met in one of the unfinished wards for the purpose of holding a prayer meeting, and I was one of them. . . . A chapter had been read from the Divine Word by one of the company, a hymn sung, and all were in the humble attitude of prayer . . . (when) the whole earth seemed shaken by the thundering roar of one of those mighty death-dealing siege guns of the enemy. . . . In less time than I have been penning this, on came another, and another, until the whole crowd was excited. Still our service continued so long as prudence dictated, when we were dismissed in good order. On leaving the house, the spectacle that attracted my attention, language fails me to describe. Every inmate who had not joined in the service was in the greatest state of excitement and confusion imaginable.

Mrs. Smith did everything possible to calm and reassure the sick and wounded soldiers in her care; then "orders came from headquarters to get ready to leave at a moment's warning". While engaged in these preparations to leave, they were astonished and dismayed to witness the arrival of a number of wagons from one of the other hospitals in town, loaded with disabled soldiers, bringing them to what was considered a place of greater safety although "the shells were whizzing over and around them".

It was painful, she continues, to see the poor, sick, wounded and emaciated soldiers dragged out in the beaming hot sun and laid upon the ground to suffer until beds could be prepared for them. . . . I never shall forget the seeming fear manifested by those helpless sufferers. They had the most perfect horror of falling into the hands of the Federals. I endeavored in every possible way to quiet their fears, telling them that General Bragg's boys would protect them. . . . They, like myself, soon became accustomed to the boom of the cannon, which kept up a brisk fire until late in the day. During the excitement our hearts were made sad by the death of one of our patients. We closed his eyes and dropped a tear of real sympathy for distant friends, who perhaps would never know the fate of their loved one. . . . Is it any wonder that, for the time, there should be a feeling of bitter hatred between the invaded and the invaders? In this instance, if I mistake not, the rules of civilized warfare were entirely disregarded. Without a moment's warning, the city was shelled, thereby not only destroying all private property in their reach, but disregarding the lives of women and children and all other noncombatants.

With the Federal army across the river into northern Georgia, to the south of Chattanooga, Bragg woke up to the fact that he was in an awkward strategic position. If he permitted Rosecrans to move across north Georgia onto his line of communications with his base in Atlanta, he faced being hemmed up in Chattanooga and starved into submission. Tactically it was now not feasible for him to move on Rosecrans' rear. The only course open to him was to throw his army before the mountain gorges and meet the Federal columns as they emerged. That, of course, involved the evacuation of Chattanooga—a move which was sentimentally undesirable but tactically sound. From the standpoint of correct military science, Bragg's plan of seeking out Rosecrans' army and attacking it seems beyond reproach. But, as was all too often true of Bragg's operations, the execution was not so good as the conception.

Rosecrans, in moving across the mountains through the available gaps, wound up with his three corps—under McCook, Thomas and Crittenden—widely separated and wide open to the threat of being assaulted and crushed in detail before they could get in supporting contact with each other. Bragg, however, was not able to take advantage of the opportunity. Thanks to a series of blunders and misunderstandings and displays of glaring ineptitude on the part of the Confederates, Rosecrans was at length able to get his scattered detachments together into a compact body of nearly 50,000 men without any seriously effective opposition from Bragg.

General Hill offers an explanation of Bragg's ineffectiveness in this crisis:

> The trouble with him was: first lack of knowledge of the situation; second, lack of personal supervision of the execution of his orders. No general ever won a permanent fame who was wanting in these grand elements of success: knowledge of his own and his enemy's condition, and personal superintendence of operations on the field. . . . The truth is, General Bragg was bewildered. . . . The wide dispersion of the Federal forces and their confrontal of him at so many points perplexed him instead of being a source of congratulation that such grand opportunities were offered for crushing them one by one. He seems to have had no well-organized system of independent scouts such as Lee had. . . . So General Bragg only learned that he was encircled by foes, without knowing who they were, what was their strength and what were their plans.
>
> The nightmare upon Bragg for the next three days was due, doubtless, to his uncertainty about the movements of his enemy and to the certainty that there was not that mutual confidence between him and some of his subordinates that there ought to be between a chief and his officers to insure victory. Bragg's want of definite and precise information had led him more than once to issue "impossible" orders, and therefore those entrusted with their execution got in the way of disregarding them. Another more serious trouble with him was the disposition to find a scapegoat for every failure and disaster. This made his officers cautious about striking a blow when an opportunity presented itself, unless they were protected by a positive order.

This is a severe indictment of a commanding general, but Hill seems to have put his finger on the weak spot. By now Bragg's officers were convinced that often he did not know what he was doing, and that it was an even chance whether or not the enemy was where Bragg thought he was; consequently they were reluctant to carry out his commands unless their own information justified the action. To this, and to another great fault of his—the loose ambiguity of his orders—may be ascribed his bungling of his first great chance to smash Rosecrans.

Eventually, however, late in September the two armies were maneuvered into position confronting each other in north Georgia a few miles south of Chattanooga in the rolling country between Chickamauga Creek on the east and the foothills of Missionary Ridge to the west, and there the battle of Chickamauga was fought.

While all this preliminary maneuvering was going on, Secretary Stanton in Washington had been growing increasingly fretful because, in his opinion Rosecrans was not showing sufficient enterprise in pushing Bragg more aggressively. So, on August 30th, he started Assistant Secretary Charles A. Dana on a visit to Rosecrans to try to step-up the tempo of Rosecrans' movements, arming him with a letter of introduction stating that his assistant "visits your command for the purpose of conferring with you upon any subject which you may desire to have brought to the notice of the department." Dana had an impressive title, but he was actually a sort of glorified snooper and trouble-shooter for Stanton, and greatly enjoyed this type of work. He tells of how he proceeded to carry out his orders:

As soon as my papers arrived I left for my post. I was much delayed on railroads and steamboats, and when I reached Cincinnati found it was impossible to join Burnside by his line of march to Knoxville and from him go to Rosecrans, as I had intended. Accordingly I went on to Louisville, where I arrived on September 5th. I found there that Burnside had just occupied Knoxville; that the Ninth Corps, which two months before I had left near Vicksburg, was now about to go to him from near Louisville; and that Rosecrans had queerly enough telegraphed to the clergy all over the country that he expected a great battle that day and desired their prayers.

I went directly from Louisville to Nashville, where I found General Gordon Granger in command. As he and Governor Johnson were going to the front in a day or two, I waited to go with them. . . . On the 10th of September we started for the front, going by rail to Bridgeport on the Tennessee River. This town at that date was the terminus of the Nashville and Chattanooga Railroad. The bridge across the river and part of the railroad beyond had been destroyed by Bragg when he retreated in the preceding summer from Tullahoma. It was by way of Bridgeport that troops were joining Rosecrans at the far front, and all supplies went to him that way. On reaching the town, we heard that Chattanooga had been occupied by Crittenden's corps of Rosecrans's army the day before, September 9th; so the next day, September 11th, I pushed on there by horseback past Shellmound and Wauhatchie. The country through which I passed is a magnificent region of rocks and valleys, and I don't believe there is anywhere a finer view than that I had from Lookout Mountain as I approached Chattanooga.

When I reached Chattanooga I went at once to General Rosecrans's headquarters and presented my letter. He read it, and then burst out in angry abuse of the Government at Washington. He had not been sustained, he said. His requests had been ignored, his plans thwarted. Both Stanton and Halleck had done all they could, he declared, to prevent his success.

"General Rosecrans," I said, "I have no authority to listen to complaints against the Government. I was sent here for the purpose of finding out what the Government could do to aid you, and have no right to confer with you on other matters."

He quieted down at once and explained his situation to me.

At Chickamauga the Army of Tennessee, after three days of nose-to-nose, slugging fighting, won the greatest victory of its career—and one of the most complete and impressive victories won by any Confederate army. The climax came on the third day of the fighting, September 20, when a division of Longstreet's corps commanded by General John B. Hood, crashed through a fortuitous opening in the Federal line and sent the whole right wing of Rosecrans' army, routed and reeling, in disorderly retreat into Chattanooga. The Federal left wing, under General George H. Thomas, reinforced by General Granger, clung tenaciously to its position until late in the afternoon, when it was driven from the field under the combined attacks of the Confederates under Longstreet and Polk.

Thomas's stubborn stand won for him the well-earned nickname of "The Rock of Chickamauga", his tenacity standing out in particular contrast to the personal panic of Rosecrans who joined his shattered right wing in their flight from the field. Some of the extravagant claims made by Thomas's too ardent admirers, however, don't stand up under careful scrutiny. That eminent historian John Fiske, for instance, wrote: "Night found Thomas still master of the Rossville road and the Union army saved from destruction." Other writers have repeated the claim that Thomas held his position "until nightfall", and left the field only because of darkness.

As a matter of fact, Thomas was not master of the Rossville road at the close of the day's fighting, and he retreated to Chattanooga not by the Rossville road but through McFarland's Gap. Nor did he hold his ground until nightfall, as has been so widely claimed, and then retire at his leisure. Valiant as his defense had been, he was forced from his position by the combined assaults of Longstreet and Polk. By his own report, his "withdrawal" began by 5:30 PM—which was a long time before night. Actually, the retrograde movement began at some time between four and four-thirty. The whole left wing was off the field by five-thirty; and Thomas himself left his headquarters behind the ridge about four-thirty and in an hour was several miles back arranging for the withdrawal.

Mr. Dana had accompanied General Rosecrans as he effected the concentration of his scattered forces, and on September 19th he sent no less than eleven telegrams to Secretary Stanton, telling of the progress of the fighting. He was with Rosecrans on the morning of the 20th, but relates that

> I had not slept much for two nights, and, as it was warm, I dismounted about noon and, giving my horse to my orderly, lay down on the grass and went to sleep. I was awakened by the most infernal noise I ever heard. Never in any battle I had witnessed was there such a discharge of cannon and musketry. I sat up in the grass, and the first thing I saw was General Rosecrans crossing himself—he was a very devout Catholic. "Hello", I said to myself, "if the general is crossing himself, we are in a desperate situation."
>
> I was on my horse in a moment. I had no sooner collected my thoughts and looked around toward the front, where all this din came from, than I saw our lines break and melt away like leaves before the wind. Then the headquarters around me disappeared. The gray-backs came through with a rush, and soon the musket balls and the cannon shot began to reach the place where we stood. The whole right of the army had apparently been routed. My orderly stuck to me like a veteran, and we drew back for greater safety into the woods a little way. There I came upon General Porter—Captain Porter he was then—and Captain Drouillard, an aide-de-camp infantry officer attached to General Rosecrans' staff, halting fugitives. They would halt a few, get them into some sort of a line, and make a beginning of order among them, and then there would come a few rounds of cannon shot through the treetops over their heads and the men would break and run. . . . I attempted to make my way from this point in the woods to Sheridan's division, but when I reached the place where I knew it had been a little time before, I found it had been swept from the field. . . . I turned my horse and, making my way over Missionary Ridge, struck the Chattanooga Valley and rode to Chattanooga, twelve or fifteen miles away. The whole road was filled with flying soldiers; here and there were pieces of artillery, caissons and baggage wagons. Everything was in the greatest disorder. When I reached Chattanooga, a little before four o'clock, I found Rosecrans there. In the helter-skelter to the rear

he had escaped by the Rossville road. He was expecting every moment that the enemy would arrive before the town, and was doing all he could to prepare to resist his entrance.

The first thing I did on reaching town was to telegraph Mr. Stanton. . . . Having been swept bodily off the battlefield, and having made my way to Chattanooga through a panic-stricken rabble, the first telegram which I sent to Mr. Stanton was naturally colored by what I had seen and experienced. I remember that I began the dispatch by saying: "My report today is of deplorable importance. Chickamauga is as fatal a name in our history as Bull Run."

Chickamauga was, indeed, a crushing Federal defeat, an imposing Confederate victory. When the day was done the Army of Tennessee held the ground over which they had fought for three days. Their enemy had fled in confusion and disorder, narrowly escaping destruction, leaving their dead and wounded behind. But then—as was not unusual when Bragg was concerned—the palsying touch of incompetent and timorous leadership again fell upon them.

Longstreet, writing about it after the war, said: "It did not occur to me on the night of the 20th to send Bragg word of our complete success . . . Everyone in the army was supposed to know on the night of the battle that we had won a complete victory. . . . I know that I had been laying a plan by which we might overhaul the enemy at Chattanooga or between that point and Nashville." But he goes on to say that Bragg had not realized that a victory had been won.

Polk, after his corps' complete success in the later afternoon, established his headquarters on the Chattanooga road within the former Federal works and sent out scouts to locate the enemy. The scouts reported the enemy gone. Polk sent a staff officer to notify Bragg that the Federals were in full retreat, and Bragg then called him to his headquarters for consultation. Polk's aide, Colonel Gale, who accompanied him, tells of the victorious wing commander's call on his confused superior:

General Bragg had gone to bed, but got up to listen to Polk's report of the days' work of his forces. General Polk urged upon him the fact that the enemy was routed and flying precipitately from the field, and that then was the time to finish the work by the capture or destruction of the army by prompt pursuit, before he had time to reorganize and throw up defenses at Chattanooga. General Bragg could not be induced to look at it in that light, and refused to believe that we had won a victory.

Bragg in his preliminary report of the battle on the 24th stated that "a vigorous pursuit" followed the Federal rear-guard into Chattanooga "where we found him strongly intrenched." This was not an exactly accurate statement of fact.

The truth is that the only thing resembling a "vigorous pursuit" was provided by the ever-enterprising Forrest who, with 400 of his troopers, did pursue the retreating enemy and came upon a rear-guard of Federal cavalry at Rossville, charged them and drove them into Chattanooga. Dr. Wyeth, quoting General Armstrong, who was a member of the party tells a dramatic story of this episode:

When nearing Rossville they came upon a rear-guard of Federal cavalry, seeing which Forrest remarked: "Armstrong, let's give them a dare." He immediately ordered a charge, and the two generals, at the head of some four hundred Confederate cavalry, at full speed rode down upon the Federal troopers, who fired a volley and fled in the direction of Chattanooga. Forrest's horse was fatally wounded by this volley, a Minie ball passing through his neck and severing one of the large arteries. The blood spurted from the divided vessel, seeing which Forrest leaned forward from the saddle, inserted the index finger of his hand into the wound and thus, staunching the hemorrhage, the animal was still able to carry his rider onward with the troops pursuing the Federals. As soon as the field was cleared, Forrest, removing his finger from the wound, dismounted, when his noble charger sank to the earth and was soon lifeless.

Forrest's keen intuition had accurately appraised the signs he saw of panic, and the Federals' apparent expectation to withdraw from Chattanooga if pressed. Rosecrans was undeniably in a blue funk. On the evening of the 20th he wired Halleck: "We have met with a serious disaster; extent not yet determined. . . . The enemy overwhelmed us." The next morning he sent a telegram to Lincoln, officially breaking the news and saying sadly that "after two days of the severest fighting I ever witnessed, our right and center were beaten. The left held its position until sunset. . . . Our loss is heavy and our troops worn down. . . . We have no certainty of holding our position here."

Lincoln was greatly alarmed by this shocking news and the same day impressed on Halleck the importance of holding Chattanooga. He did not consider an advance from there necessary, he said, believing that the Federals in a defensive position would so embarrass the Confederates that "the rebellion can only eke out a short and feeble existence, as an animal sometimes may with a thorn in his vitals." Lincoln was assuming that Rosecrans could hold even a defensive position at Chattanooga, which was by no means certain. Two days later he telegraphed Rosecrans for more information, pleading: "Please relieve my anxiety as to the position and condition of your army up to the latest moment", to which Rosecrans replied, none too reassuringly; "We are about 30,000 brave and determined men; but our fate is in the hands of God, in whom I hope."

The panic in the Federal headquarters at Chattanooga and in Halleck's office in Washington subsided when it became apparent that the Confederates had no plans for an immediate follow-up of their victory. Indeed, Halleck a few weeks later, with amazing audacity and mendacity, was officially proclaiming an account of the battle in which he unblushingly stated: "At nightfall the enemy fell back beyond the range of our artillery, leaving Thomas victorious on his hard-fought field." This may have fooled some of the more gullible of the Northern populace; but Grant, the stern realist, says frankly: "Rosecrans was badly defeated."

In connection with a big and bloody battle like Chickamauga there are, of course, countless sad examples of the crushing bereavements and personal family tragedies caused by the war. A particularly touching episode of this kind, involving the family of Tennessee's most distinguished citizen, is related by Mrs. Irby Morgan, refugee from Nashville who was staying in a hotel at Marietta, Georgia, after her flight from Nashville in 1862.

After the battle of Murfreesboro, a train-load of wounded Confederates had passed through Marietta on the way to the hospitals in Atlanta. While the train was making a short stop at Marietta, some of the Tennesseans among the wounded, hearing that there was some "Nashville ladies" staying at the hotel, slipped off the train and made their way to the hotel, hoping to find sympathetic attention—which they did. Among these wounded soldiers was Captain Samuel Jackson, one of the two sons of Andrew Jackson, Jr., the adopted son of President Andrew Jackson.

"The wounded men," Mrs. Morgan relates, "were all dirty, hungry and bloody"; but she tells how, under the ministrations of herself and her willing helpers, their wounds were dressed, and they were bathed and fed and supplied with clean clothing. "Captain Jackson's wound," she says, "proved more serious than we thought it would at first. . . . Erysipelas set in, and he had raging fevers and was delirious." But eventually Captain Jackson recovered and returned to duty with the Army of Tennessee, just before the battle of Chickamauga.

A sense of the painful suspense and shock suffered in such circumstances by those "who only stand and wait" is shown by Mrs. Morgan's recountal of her sensations as it had become apparent that the maneuvering of the two armies was bringing them inevitably to a climactic battle:

I knew most of the cavalry would be there. Gen. John T. Morgan's command and Wheeler's Division had already gone up. My husband was with the cavalry in his brother's command, and I felt miserable. The battle was fought, and such slaughter and carnage was fearful to relate. Both sides suffered terribly. I scarcely ate or slept, and the suspense was maddening. The intelligence came that Captain Jackson was killed. We felt this loss deeply, for we were greatly attached to him. He had won our hearts by his gentlemanly bearing, and he was so handsome and brave. His brother, Colonel [Andrew] Jackson, was at Marietta on parole, having been captured at Vicksburg when that place surrendered. He and many others were waiting to be exchanged, and were in camp near Marietta. Col. Atkinson and himself went up to get the captain's remains to bury in Marietta. After hunting over the field, they found the poor fellow lying on a blanket with straw under his head; badly wounded, but still alive. They took him to Ringgold; but he was exhausted from loss of blood, and they had not time to attend to his wounds. He never rallied, but died in a few hours after getting him there. They brought his body to Marietta and buried him. Since the close of the war his remains have been removed to Nashville, and now rest at the "Hermitage," near Gen. Andrew Jackson's tomb.

The touching aftermath of this young soldier's death is told by Mrs. Morgan:

We were standing one day on the portico watching for the cars to come in, and as the train stopped I saw an aged couple alight, and come feebly up the steps. I heard some one say: "Is this Mrs. Morgan?" I said: "Yes." She threw her arms around my neck and wept as though her heart would break, and said, "I am Captain Jackson's mother, and this is his father," pointing to a venerable-looking old gentleman. I took them to my room and, after she composed herself, she told me in a trembling voice that Captain Jackson had written to them of his being wounded and the kind friends he had met. They had tried and tried to get a pass to come out to see him, and at last succeeded.

They started from the "Hermitage" in a buggy, had their trunk stolen, and after many difficulties got to Cartersville, and there learned that their son had been killed and buried at Marietta. They felt that they must come on and hear all they could about their darling boy. I told them all about his sojourn with us, and sent word to Col. and Mrs. Atkinson that they had arrived; and in a little while the colonel's carriage was at the door, and they were soon conveyed to Mrs. Atkinson's residence.

I can never forget Mr. and Mrs. Jackson. She had a sweet, resigned face, and, for an old lady, was beautiful. And he was a dignified, venerable-looking man. They are indelibly impressed on my mind.

She told me she was born in the North, but was devoted to the South, and the dearest treasure of her heart had died battling for its rights. After spending several days in Marietta, and learning all they could of the death of their boy, they came to bid us good-bye. Ah! how my heart went out in sympathy to those weary old pilgrims whom we would never see again until we meet around our Father's throne. We can teach our children to venerate this noble pair, and to love and admire their brave son, who died defending his country.

CHAPTER **11**

☆ *Interlude After Chickamauga*

ROSECRANS, relieved by the realization that he was not to be pursued, was well content to dig in at Chattanooga and assume the defensive. The redoubts which Bragg had left unfinished when he evacuated the city were hastily occupied and connected by rifle pits. Within two days the Federal forces were protected by what the *Official Records* describe as "formidable earthworks", their demoralization succeeded by a determination to hold the city strongly.

Bragg, realizing now that Chattanooga could not be occupied without a contest, could think of nothing more enterprising than to establish his army in a position of quasi-siege, spread out in a semi-circle six miles long. His left reached to the foot of Lookout Mountain, where the railroad from Chattanooga to Bridgeport squeezed through between the mountain and the river, and cut Rosecrans off from rail connection with his base at Nashville. The Confederate line extended westward across Chattanooga Creek to Missionary Ridge and along the north face of the ridge to Chickamauga Creek about two miles from its confluence with the Tennessee above the city.

Bragg, it soon developed, had no idea of attempting any forward movement. The heart of his strategy was to starve the Federal force into submission—and this aim was by no means impracticable. With the Confederates controlling the rail and wagon roads on the south bank of the river, Rosecrans was forced to haul his supplies from Bridgeport by wagon trains over the roads on the north side. The shortest way to Chattanooga was by the road skirting the north bank, but Longstreet established a long line of artillery and sharpshooters along Raccoon Mountain that soon made this route untenable. The Federal supplies then had to be hauled up through Jasper across the Sequatchie Valley and Walden's Ridge, a roundabout way of sixty miles. This route became increasingly difficult as the fall rains set in and mud grew deep. Food began to get scarce in Chattanooga, and the plight of the beleagured Federals grew steadily more serious from day to day.

Bragg recognized the fact that this supply line was a sort of Achilles heel for

Rosecrans, and his one display of anything resembling energy and enterprise, a raid on this supply line, came within a few days after he moved into position besieging Chattanooga. To command this raid on the Federal line of supply, Bragg selected General Joe Wheeler, and to build up the strongest possible striking force, he sent an unexplained order to Forrest on September 28th ordering him to turn over all his troops to Wheeler. Although infuriated by this order, Forrest dutifully complied, and Wheeler was able to muster a force of some 4,000 men for the projected raid.

Wheeler on October 1st forded the river below Chattanooga, and swept up the Sequatchie Valley where he ambushed and captured a long train of 800 wagons and 4000 mules. He burned the wagons and killed the mules, then pushed on to McMinnville, captured that town and burned its stores. He then fought a running, day-by-day battle with various bodies of Federal cavalry on a wide swooping raid that carried him on to Murfreesboro and nearly to Nashville, then down through Middle Tennessee to Pulaski and finally, on January 8th, across the Tennessee River near Decatur.

By this spectacular raid Wheeler had unquestionably done serious damage to the enemy, but by the time he got to Decatur his own force was so disorganized and exhausted by its hard riding and fighting that it was a long time before he could get it back into fighting trim again.

The relative inactivity of the quasi-siege gave General Bragg time to pursue what seemed to be one of his favorite pastimes—quarreling with his subordinate officers. Although he seemed to be plagued with a constitutional lack of pertinacity when it came to the pursuit of a defeated enemy, he never displayed any lack of zeal in relentlessly pressing any censure he might feel inclined to level at his own colleagues. It was not surprising, therefore, to find his getting promptly into action along these lines within a few days after the battle of Chickamauga.

General Polk (whom Bragg inwardly had never forgiven for his alleged dereliction at Perryville) was the special target for fault-finding in the post-Chickamauga inquest. Polk, so Bragg charged, had not launched the attack by his corps as promptly as ordered on the morning of September 20th. He demanded an explanation of the delay, and then haughtily pronounced the explanation "unsatisfactory", following which he relieved Polk of his command and ordered him to Atlanta. Polk indignantly appealed to President Davis, who unsuccessfully tried to pour oil on the troubled waters. Bragg preferred charges against Polk, which charges were dismissed by the War Department. Polk requested a court of inquiry, which Davis denied as unnecessary, and ordered Polk restored to his command. Polk, however, refused to serve any longer under Bragg, so he was transferred to Mississippi to replace Hardee, who took command of Polk's corps under Bragg.

Bragg's post-battle wrath extended also to Generals Hindman and Hill. Hindman (for reasons he considered sufficient) had not attacked the Federals in McLemore's Cove as Rosecrans was concentrating his scattered commands; and so Hindman was sacked and sent along to Atlanta with Polk. Later Bragg relented and restored him to his command, but Hindman never forgave or forgot. Hill's suspension was asked by Bragg on account of his former messmate's "critical, captious and dictatorial manner" and his "general deportment" by which, Bragg said, he had "greatly demoralized the troops he commanded, and sacrificed thousands at Chickamauga." Hill was suspended, as requested by Bragg, and Breckinridge was placed in temporary charge of his corps. It was understood, however, that Gen.

John B. Hood would command this corps when he had recovered from the serious wound he suffered at Chickamauga, resulting in the amputation of his right leg.

Bragg, in requesting Hill's dismissal, officially placed his request on the grounds of Hill's inefficiency. In writing to Davis on the subject several months later, however, he revealed that personal pique may also have been a factor:

> Having taken active steps to procure my removal in a manner both unmilitary and un-officerlike, in which he failed after a full personal investigation by yourself, he was, at my request, transferred from the army as a necessary consequence of the line of conduct he had pursued.

Bragg here was referring to a strange episode in the history of the Army of Tennessee in which both Hill and Polk had figured. Feeling intense alarm at Bragg's sluggishness after the Chickamauga victory, they had met with Longstreet on September 26th to discuss their commander's "palpable weakness and mismanagement manifested in the conduct of the military operations of this army". Feeling that the matter should be brought to the attention of the Richmond authorities, Longstreet wrote to the Secretary of War and Polk wrote to President Davis, both frankly expressing distrust of Bragg's ability. Following their conference there was a similar indignation meeting on October 4th which was attended by practically all the superior officers of the army, and this session drafted and dispatched to President Davis a remarkable "round robin" petition which rehearsed the woes of the army in restrained but convincing terms:

> Two weeks ago this army, elated by a great victory which promised to prove the most fruitful of the war, was in readiness to pursue its defeated enemy. That enemy, driven in confusion from the field, was fleeing in disorder and panic-stricken across the Tennessee River. To-day, after having been twelve days in line of battle in that enemy's front, within cannon range of his position, the Army of Tennessee has seen a new Sebastopol rise steadily before its view. . . . Whatever may have been accomplished heretofore, it is certain that the fruits of the victory of Chickamauga have now escaped our grasp. . . . The Army of Tennessee, stricken with a complete paralysis, will in a few days' time be thrown strictly on the defensive, and may deem itself fortunate if it escapes from its present position without disaster.

To prevent such a disaster, here predicted with such tragic foresight, the signing officers urged the removal of Bragg, considerately basing their suggestion on the statement that "the condition of his health unfits him for the command of an army in the field."

This round robin, reaching Richmond on the heels of the letters from Polk and Longstreet, could not be disregarded. Davis determined to go and make a personal effort to bring about a peaceful settlement of the difficulty. He reached Bragg's headquarters on October 9th; and, in an amazing display of bad taste, and lack of tact, summoned Longstreet, Hill, Buckner and Cheatham (temporarily in command of Polk's corps) to meet him in Bragg's headquarters. There, in Bragg's presence, the President surprisingly required them to give their personal views of Bragg's fitness to command.

Longstreet, who was astonished at this procedure (as well he might have been), gives an interesting account of this strange conference:

> The President came to us on the 9th of October and called the commanders of the army to meet him at General Bragg's office. After some talk, in the presence of General Bragg, he made known the object of the call, and asked the generals, in turn, their opinion of their commanding officer, beginning with myself. It seemed

rather a stretch of authority, even with a President, and I gave an evasive answer and made an effort to turn the channel of thought, but he would not be satisfied, and got back to his question. The condition of the army was briefly referred to, and the failure to make an effort to get the fruits of our success. The opinion was given, in substance, that our commander could be of greater service elsewhere than at the head of the Army of Tennessee. Major-General Buckner was called, and gave opinion somewhat similar. So did Major-General Cheatham, who was then commanding the corps recently commanded by Lieutenant-General Polk; and General D. H. Hill, who was called last, agreed with emphasis to the views expressed by others.

Longstreet goes on to relate that:

The next morning the President called me to private conference, and we had an all-day talk. He thought to assign me to command, but the time had passed for handling that army as an independent force . . . In my judgment our last opportunity was lost when we failed to follow the success at Chickamauga and capture or disperse the Union army, and it could not be just to the service or myself to call me to a position of such responsibility. The army was part of General Joseph E. Johnston's department, and could only be used in strong organization by him in combining its operations with his other forces in Alabama and Mississippi. I said that under him (Johnston) I could cheerfully work in any position. The suggestion of that name only served to increase his displeasure and severe rebuke.

The net result of all this discussion was that Davis went back to Richmond, leaving Bragg and his generals in an even more intensified state of mutual hostility than when the President came down to wave the olive branch. There had been some desultory talk about a change of base and possibly a movement against Rosecrans at some point, but nothing came of that, and the Army of Tennessee settled down to the investment of Chattanooga with all ranks distressed and perturbed.

The visit of President Davis not only failed to quiet the clamorous discontent of Bragg's subordinates, but before he departed it broke out in a new place—an open breach between Forrest and Bragg over what Forrest considered Bragg's personal prejudice and persecution. Forrest's smoldering resentment had been fanned into flame when he received the order to turn over his troops to General Joe Wheeler, and the more he thought about it the more his anger rose.

Dr. Wyeth, quoting Forrest's aide, Major Anderson, tells how Forrest, when he received this unwelcome order, dictated a letter to Anderson "resenting the manner in which he had been treated, and charging the commander of the army in plain, straight language with duplicity and lying, and informing him that he would call at his headquarters in a few days to say to him in person just what he had written. He concluded by saying he desired to shirk no responsibility incurred by the contents of his letter. When Forrest read the letter over and signed it, it was sealed and handed to the courier and, as he rode away, the general remarked to me, 'Bragg never got such a letter as that before from a brigadier.' "

True to his promise, Forrest did go to Bragg's headquarters on Missionary Ridge, accompanied by Dr. J. B. Cowan, his chief surgeon, and Dr. Cowan has provided a first-hand account of that extraordinary confrontation of these two clashing personalities:

I observed as we rode along that the general was silent, which was unusual with him when we were alone. Knowing him so well, I was convinced that something that displeased him greatly had transpired. He wore an expression that I had seen before on some occasions when a storm was brewing. I had known nothing of the letter he had written General Bragg, and was in utter ignorance not only of what was passing in Forrest's mind at this time, but of the object of the visit to the general-in-chief. As we passed the guard in front of Forrest's tent, I observed that General Forrest did not acknowledge the salute of the sentry, which was so contrary to his custom that I could but notice it. When we entered the tent where General Bragg was alone, this officer rose from his seat, spoke to Forrest and, advancing, offered him his hand. Refusing to take the proffered hand, and standing stiff and erect before Bragg, Forrest said:

"I am not here to pass civilities or compliments with you, but on other business. You commenced your cowardly and contemptible persecution of me soon after the battle of Shiloh, and you have kept it up ever since. You did it because I reported to Richmond facts, while you reported damned lies. You robbed me of my command in Kentucky, and gave it to one of your favorites—men that I armed and equipped from the enemies of our country. In a spirit of revenge and spite, because I would not fawn upon you as others did, you drove me into West Tennessee in the winter of 1862 with a second brigade I had organized, with improper arms and without sufficient ammunition, although I had made repeated applications for the same. You did it to ruin me and my career. When in spite of all this I returned with my command, well equipped by captures, you began again your work of spite and persecution, and have kept it up; and now this second brigade, organized and equipped without thanks to you or the government, a brigade which has won a reputation for successful fighting second to none in the army, taking advantage of your position as the commanding general in order to further humiliate me, you have taken these brave men from me. I have stood your meanness as long as I intend to. You have played the part of a damned scoundrel, and are a coward, and if you were any part of a man I would slap your jaws and force you to resent it. You may as well not issue any more orders to me, for I will not obey them, and I will hold you personally responsible for any further indignities you endeavor to inflict upon me. You have threatened to arrest me for not obeying your orders promptly. I dare you to do it, and I say to you that if you ever again try to interfere with me or cross my path it will be at the peril of your life."

Bragg did not utter a word or move a muscle of his face during this shower of invective from his brigadier. The scene did not last longer than a few minutes, and when Forrest had finished he turned his back sharply upon Bragg and stalked out of the tent toward the horses.

As they rode away, Dr. Cowan remarked, "Well you are in for it now!" Forrest replied instantly, "He'll never say a word about it; he'll be the last man to mention it; and, mark my word, he'll take no action in the matter. I will ask to be relieved and transferred to a different field, and he will not oppose it."

Forrest, having denounced Bragg in characteristic strong terms, went straight to Davis and told him all about it, requesting a transfer. Davis by this time had come to appreciate Forrest's rugged genius, and though probably deploring his insubordination, sought to placate him with praise and soft words. But Forrest was inflexible in his determination to serve no longer under Bragg, so Davis took steps to assign him to an independent cavalry command in West Tennessee "to raise and organize as many troops for the Confederate service as he finds practicable."

Before Davis could get away from Bragg's headquarters he was confronted with another crisis—the breaking out of a bitter controversy between Bragg and Buckner, whose relations had been strained for some time. The new outbreak resulted from the impossible conflict of authority created when Buckner's army was put under Bragg's control but Buckner still left to administer affairs in his old Department of East Tennessee.

Both Bragg and Buckner showed a good deal of petulance in their voluminous correspondence, between themselves and with President Davis, and the harsh things they said about each other gave evidence of their hopeless incompatability. Davis seemed unwilling to take any positive steps in resolving the difficulty, and the wrangle dragged on for months, until the problem eventually solved itself through the developing fortunes of war.

General Bragg, however, was not the only army commander in that area whose subordinates lacked confidence in his ability. A similar backwash of sentiment against General Rosecrans was developing among his generals. Rosecrans, immediately after the battle of Chickamauga, had preferred charges against Crittenden, McCook and Negley, but they were all cleared by a court of inquiry. Chas. A. Dana in his post-war book of recollections, tells of the ferment that reigned "throughout the whole army" growing out of events connected with the battle:

There was at once a manifest disposition to hold McCook and Crittenden, the commanders of the two corps, responsible, because they had left the field of battle amid the rout of the right wing and made their way to Chattanooga. It was not generally understood or appreciated at that time that, because of Thomas's repeated calls for aid and Rosecrans's consequent alarm for his left, Crittenden had been stripped of all his troops and had no infantry whatever left to command, and that McCook's lines also had been reduced to a fragment by similar orders from Rosecrans and by fighting. A strong opposition to both sprang up. . . . The generals of division and brigade felt the situation deeply, and said that they could no longer serve under such superiors, and that, if this was required of them, they must resign. This feeling was universal among them, including men like Major Generals Palmer and Sheridan and Brigadier Generals Wood, Johnson and Hazen. . . .

No formal representation of this unwillingness was made to Rosecrans, but he was made aware of the state of things by private conversations with several of the parties. The defects of his character complicated the difficulty. He abounded in friendliness and approbativeness, and was greatly lacking in firmness and steadiness of will, In short, he was a temporizing man; he dreaded so heavy an alternative as was now presented, and hated to break with McCook and Crittenden.

Besides, there was a more serious obstacle to Rosecrans's acting decisively in the fact that if Crittenden and McCook had gone to Chattanooga, with the sound of artillery in their ears, from that glorious field where Thomas and Granger were saving their army and their country's honor, he had gone to Chattanooga also. It might be said in his excuse that, under the circumstances of the sudden rout, it was perfectly proper for the commanding general to go to the rear to prepare the next line of defense. Still Rosecrans felt that that excuse could not entirely clear him either in his own eyes or in those of the army. In fact, it was perfectly plain that the subordinate commanders' respect for Rosecrans as a general had received an irreparable blow.

The dissatisfaction with Rosecrans seemed to me to put the army in a very dangerous condition, and in writing to Mr. Stanton on September 27th I said that if it was decided to change the chief commander I would suggest that some Western commander of high rank and great prestige, like Grant, would be preferable as Rosecrans's successor to one who had hitherto commanded in the East alone.

The army, however, had its own candidate for Rosecrans's post. General Thomas had risen to the highest point in their esteem, as he had in that of every one who had witnessed his conduct on that unfortunate and glorious day, and I saw that, should there be a change in the chief command, there was no other man whose appointment would be so welcome. I earnestly recommended to Mr. Stanton that, in event of a change in the chief command, Thomas's merits be considered. He was certainly an officer of the very highest qualities, soldierly and personally. He was a man of the greatest dignity of character. He had more the character of George Washington than any other man I ever knew. At the same time he was a delightful man to be with; there was no artificial dignity about Thomas. He was a West Point graduate, and very well educated. He was very set in his opinions, yet he was not impatient with anybody —a noble character.

During all this time the two opposing armies at Chattanooga were in fairly close proximity and, as was not unusual in such circumstances, there was more or less fraternizing between the individual Federal and Confederate soldiers. A private in one of the Kansas regiments tells of one of these informal truces in which he played a part:

Our camp was near North Chickamauga Creek, and when not scouting we picketed the river above Chattanooga. We had a chain of pickets at the river, with supports further back, and the Rebels seemed to watch us from the opposite side on about the same plan.

In daytime we could see each other, and when not exchanging shots—usually a harmless exercise on both sides—we would be talking across the river. If one side wanted to go in bathing, permission was asked from the other; or, by agreement, both parties would go in at the same time, each keeping to its own side. One day a Rebel opened negotiations for the exchange of reading matter. Myself and another man agreed to meet a like number from their side at a sandbar midway of the river. I put a copy of *Harper's Weekly* in my hat (I didn't take any pockets with me), and we swam out to the sandbar. We had a pleasant chat, during which one of the Rebels asked us to mail a letter from him to his mother, who lived in Memphis, inside our lines. He said he had had no chance to get word to or from his family for a year. We stipulated that the letter be delivered next day, unsealed, and promised, if it contained nothing improper in a military sense, to send it on to his mother. We took the letter to the adjutant's office, and it went as mine. Thus at least one Rebel had the benefit of the franking privilege which our Government extended to its soldiers.

That all of this fraternizing was not as innocent and harmless as it appeared on the surface is suggested by Sam Watkins:

The Yankee outpost was on one side of the Tennessee river, and ours on the other. One Sunday I was on the detail commanded by Sergeant John T. Tucker. When we were approaching, going on duty, we heard the old guard and the Yankee picket talking back and forth across the river. We, the new guard, immediately resumed the conversation. We had to halloo at the top of our voices, the river being about three hundred yards wide at this point. But there was a little island about the middle of the river. A Yankee hallooed out, "O, Johnny, meet me half-way in the river, on the island." "All right," said Sergeant Tucker, who immediately undressed all but his hat, in which he carried the Chattanooga *Rebel* and some other Southern newspapers, and swam across to the island. When he got there the Yankee was there, but the Yankee had waded. I do not know what he and John talked about, but they got very friendly, and John invited him to come clear across to our side, which invitation he accepted. I noticed at the time that while John swam, the Yankee waded, remarking that he couldn't swim. The river was but little over waist deep. Well, they came across and we swapped a few lies, canteens and tobacco, and then the Yankee went back, wading all the way across the stream. We found out later that that man was General Wilder, commanding the Federal cavalry, and at the battle of Missionary Ridge he threw his whole division of cavalry across the Tennessee river at that point, thus flanking Bragg's army, and opening the battle. When he waded across he was examining the ford, and the swapping business was but a mere by-play. He played it sharp.

But, although there were such friendly relationships established between the pickets on the front lines, the higher-ups on both sides fully realized the gravity of the military situation at Chattanooga. General Grant, several years after the war, wrote a detailed discussion of the developments at this time, in which he played a leading role:

Soon it was discovered in Washington that Rosecrans was in trouble and needed assistance. The emergency was now too immediate to allow us to give this assistance by making an attack in the rear of Bragg upon Mobile. It was, therefore, necessary to reinforce directly, and troops were sent from every available point. . . . Halleck telegraphed me to send all available forces to Memphis, and thence east along the Memphis and Charleston railroad to cooperate with Rosecrans . . . As fast as transports could be provided, all the troops except a portion of the Seventeenth Corps were forwarded under Sherman, whose services up to this time demonstrated his superior fitness for a separate command.

On the 29th of September Halleck telegraphed me . . . and directed all the forces that could be spared from my department be sent to Rosecrans, suggesting that a good commander like Sherman or McPherson should go with the troops; also that I should go in person to Nashville to superintendend the movement. Long before this dispatch was received, Sherman was already on his way, and McPherson also was moving east with most of the garrison of Vicksburg.

General "Fighting Joe" Hooker was also detached from the Federal forces in Virginia and hurried by rail to Rosecrans' assistance.

Grant goes on to tell how he was ordered, a few day later, to go to Louisville, to receive further instructions from the War Department, how he was met by Secretary Stanton in person, and then:

The secretary handed me two orders, saying that I might take my choice of them. The two were identical in all but one particular. Both created the Military Division of the Mississippi, giving me the command, composed of the Departments of the Ohio, the Cumberland and the Tennessee, and all the territory from the Alleghanies to the Mississippi River north of Banks's command in the southwest. One order left the department commanders as they were, while the other relieved Rosecrans and assigned Thomas to his place. I accepted the latter.

The next night, Grant relates, Stanton received a frantic dispatch from C. A. Dana in Chattanooga, informing him that "unless prevented Rosecrans would retreat, and advising peremptory orders against his doing so." Such a retreat, Grant says, "would have been a terrible disaster. It would not only have been the loss of a most important strategic position to us, but it would have been attended with the loss of all the artillery still left with the Army of the Cumberland, and the annihilation of that army itself, either by capture or demoralization." He then goes on with his narration:

On the receipt of Mr. Dana's dispatch Mr. Stanton sent for me. . . . I hastened to the room of the secretary and found him pacing the floor rapidly in a dressing-gown. Saying that the retreat must be prevented, he showed me the dispatch. I immediately wrote an order assuming command of the Military Division of the Mississippi, and telegraphed it to General Rosecrans. I then telegraphed to him the order from Washington assigning Thomas to the command of the Army of the Cumberland; and to

Thomas that he must hold Chattanooga at all hazards, informing him at the same time that I would be at the front as soon as possible. A prompt reply was received from Thomas, saying "We will hold the town till we starve."

Grant then tells of how he proceeded the next day to Nashville, where he spent the night as "at that time it was not prudent to travel beyond that point by night", and the next morning (after pausing in Nashville long enough to meet Military Governor Andrew Johnson) proceeded by rail to Bridgeport, Alabama, and thence on horseback to Chattanooga, where he arrived on the 23rd and established his headquarters. He telegraphed to Washington that night, notifying Halleck of his arrival, and asking to have Sherman assigned to the command of the Army of the Tennessee, which was done. The next day, he relates, he issued orders for opening the route to Bridgeport, so that food could be brought from the railhead to the troops in Chattanooga who had been on short rations owing to the transportation difficulties. Concerning this, Grant writes:

On the way to Chattanooga I had telegraphed back to Nashville for a good supply of vegetables and small rations, which the troops had been so long deprived of. Hooker had brought with him from the east a full supply of land transporation. His animals had not been subjected to hard work on bad roads without forage, but were in good condition. In five days from my arrival in Chattanooga the way was open to Bridgeport and, with the aid of steamers and Hooker's teams, in a week the troops were receiving full rations. . . . The men were soon re-clothed and well fed; an abundance of ammunition was brought up, and a cheerfulness prevailed not before enjoyed in many weeks.

The casual reader might gather from this that the restoration of the supply line, relieving the scarcity of food and other supplies, was a direct and immediate result of Grant's arriving there and getting the job done before the Federal army was starved out. Lieut.-Colonel H. V. Boynton of the 35th Ohio Volunteers gives an account of this development that takes some of the lustre off Grant's inferential praise of himself and Hooker for this accomplishment:

It is another of the myths of history, which are as thick about these operations as the fogs over Lookout in falling weather, that the coming of Grant had something to do with this opening of the river. True he approved plans which he found perfected down to the smallest details. But these would have been executed exactly in their final form and time if Grant had not been ordered to Chattanooga.

The general plan of opening the Tennessee to the vicinity of Williams' Island was Rosecrans'. The details were committed to that able officer and noted engineer, General W. F. Smith. He fixed on Brown's Ferry as the place for throwing the bridges, and General Rosecrans was engaged with him in general reconnoitering of the river below Lookout the day that the order for his relief from the command arrived. That very day he had ordered Hooker to be ready to move up from Bridgeport along the south bank of the river, and that night, was to direct Hooker to be ready to execute General Rosecrans' last order. Grant came and approved the plans already fully perfected, and gave orders for their execution, nothing more. They were executed, and the line of abundant supplies was open.

It is now possible to fix the responsibility for this lack of supplies at Chattanooga where it properly belongs. When that wonderful transfer of the Eleventh and Twelfth Corps from the Potomac to the Tennessee was ordered, General Rosecrans had a right to suppose that upon General Hooker's arrival at Bridgeport he would be able to cooperate at once for the relief of Chattanooga. Hooker reached that point October

1, and the same day was ordered by Rosecrans to put down his bridges and make immediate preparations for crossing the river to move toward Chattanooga. Then it was found that he had no wagon trains, and so he could not obey.

The finely equipped and throughly efficient trains of those two Eastern corps had been turned in at Alexandria and orders issued that new trains should be furnished at Nashville. But the Nashville depot had been thoroughly depleted, and had only exhausted animals and crippled wagons, a fact that surely should have been known at Washington. When at length apologies for trains had been fitted up at Nashville, the extra Eastern railroad rolling-stock had been sent back to Washington and so the wagon-trains were obliged to march two hundred miles, much of the way over rough and mountain roads, between Nashville and Bridgeport. As a result, Hooker was held immovable at that point from October 1 to 24—in other words, throughout the entire time of short supplies at Chattanooga. Had his trains been shipped from the East so as to follow his troops, he could have occupied the Wauhatchie Valley during the first week in October; or, in other words, before the pinch over short supplies at Chattanooga began.

On October 12 General Rosecrans repeated his order to Hooker to move up from Bridgeport to Wauhatchie to open the river, but Hooker's trains were still behind. On the 19th the order to be ready to move was again given by Rosecrans, and repeated the same night by Thomas. Finally, on the 24th and 26th, Hooker's trains arrived. At daylight of the 27th he crossed the river at Bridgeport, the rear of the column passing the bridge at 9:30 A. M. At three o'clock in the afternoon he was at Wauhatchie in Lookout Valley, and at five o'clock at Brown's Ferry, and the line of supplies was open. It is easily seen that the failure to send Hooker's splendidly equipped trains from the East, upon the erroneous belief that this essential need could be supplied at Nashville, is the historical fact which so nearly caused starvation at Chattanooga.

The hungry Federal soldiers cooped up in Chattanooga were naturally elated at the opening of the so-called "cracker line", and they were not particularly interested in the identity of the individual who broke the blockade and started the food and other supplies flowing into their camps again. Grant himself would probably have got a chuckle if he had overheard the irreverent comment of one of his men, as reported by a Kansas trooper:

General Hooker's forces arrived in the valley and camped between us and Lookout Mountain and a steamboat passed up on the way to Chattanooga loaded with hard bread, bacon and coffee. When the troops near the river saw the steamboat and realized the fact that "the cracker line" flowed unvexed to Chattanooga, they broke forth in wild and vociferous cheers, which started some of us to inquiring the cause. One soldier rushed to the river and inquired of another: "Has Grant come?" "Grant be damned!" said the other; "a boat-load of rations has come."

The authorities in Washington had demonstrated their recognition of the fact that for the Federals to deliver a knock-out blow against Bragg it was necessary for the army at Chattanooga to be materially strengthened. Grant in his new command, therefore, had the satisfaction of knowing that, with the addition of Sherman's and Hooker's troops to those already in Chattanooga, he would have a force of more than twice as many men as Rosecrans had brought there from Chickamauga.

Bragg was kept informed of the heavy forces moving to Grant's assistance by his efficient organization of scouts, but he seemed unable (or unwilling) to recognize the fact that all this force was being built up for no other purpose than to attack him.

One of the scouts operating in lower Middle Tennessee, watching and reporting on the progress of the troops moving from Mississippi, was a young man named Samuel Davis. This young man's willingness to die on the gallows rather than betray a confidence has made his name synonymous with cold-blooded personal heroism and devotion to duty, and his home is preserved by the state of Tennessee as one of its most honored shrines. Sam Davis made but a brief appearance in the spotlight of history, but the dramatic background of his capture and his execution have provided the basis for a wealth of poetry and fiction and more or less historically accurate accounts of his self-sacrifice. What he did, however, does not need the embellishments of poetry or fiction; the plain facts as available in the contemporaneous official records tell a story that needs no embellishment.

DEATH BEFORE DISHONOR

Davis, an 18-year old Rutherford County youth, enlisted in the Confederate army in April 1861, in a company which later became a part of Col. George Maney's 1st Tennessee Infantry. This regiment served under Robert E. Lee in the ill-fated campaign in western Virginia, and later with Stonewall Jackson in the bleak midwinter march to Romney. Early in 1862 the 1st Tennessee was called back to service on its native soil, and Sam Davis served with his regiment at Shiloh and in other engagements.

Some time in 1863 Davis became a member of a group of picked men serving General Bragg as scouts. This group was commanded by Captain H. B. Shaw, but Shaw threw dust in the enemy's eyes by assuming the name of "Captain E. Coleman" for official purposes, calling his outfit "Coleman's Scouts". He was a commissioned officer in the Confederate army and his scouts were all regularly enlisted Confederate soldiers, wearing the Confederate uniform. They were so successful in gaining accurate information, that orders were issued that they must be wiped out and their leader captured.

As the 16th Army Corps of the Federal army, under General G. M. Dodge, was moving from Corinth, Miss., to reinforce Grant at Chattanooga, they were camped briefly at Pulaski, Tenn., and here General Dodge ordered his chief of scouts to be on the lookout for Coleman's men, and to capture them if possible.

Dodge's scouts were commanded by a civilian named L. H. Naron, a Mississippi Unionist who had volunteered to serve the Federal army as a scout, and who was nicknamed "Chickasaw" and sometimes referred as "Captain Chickasaw." He and his men, posing as Confederate conscript officers, frequently wore Confederate uniforms while carrying on their scouting expeditions, and while thus clothed they captured Sam Davis near Pulaski. Davis was carrying, among other things, a letter written by "Captain Coleman" giving Bragg some information about the size and disposition of Dodge's force that was so accurate as to indicate that it must have come from some Federal officer close to Dodge.

Davis at the time of his arrest was wearing his Confederate uniform, together with a once-blue overcoat his mother had bought from a Federal deserter and dyed a dingy brown-black color with walnut hulls. He was, nevertheless, charged with being a spy, was tried as such and condemned to be hanged.

General Dodge, in writing of this tragic event in later years said:

He was a fine soldierly-looking young man, dressed in a faded Federal overcoat, an army soft hat and top boots. He had a fresh, open face, which was inclined to brightness; in all things he showed himself a true soldier. . . .

His captors knew that he was a member of Coleman's scouts, and I knew what was found upon him and desired to locate Coleman and ascertain, if possible, who was furnishing information so accurate to General Bragg. Davis met me modestly. I tried to impress on him the danger he was in; and, as only a messenger, I held out to him the hope of lenient treatment if he would answer truthfully my questions. I informed him that he would be tried as a spy and the evidence would surely convict him, and I made a direct appeal to him to give me the information I knew he had. He very quietly but firmly refused to do it. I pleaded with him with all the power I possessed to give me some chance to save his life. I discovered that he was a most admirable young fellow, with highest character and strictest integrity. He replied, "I know, General, I will have to die; but I will not tell where I got the information, and there is no power on earth that can make me tell. You are doing your duty as a soldier, and if I have to die, I shall be doing my duty to God and my country."

The Military Commission appointed by Gen. Dodge to try Davis was convened at Pulaski on November 24, 1863. The commission was composed of Colonel Madison Miller of the 18th Missouri, Lieutenant Colonel Thomas W. Gaines of the 56th Missouri, Major Lathrop of the 39th Ohio and Captain George N. Elliott of the 39th Iowa, with the latter serving as Judge Advocate. Quoting from the record:

The Commission then proceeded to the trial of Samuel Davis, a person in the service of the Confederate States, who was called before the Commission and having heard the order convening the Commission read, was asked if he had any objection to any member named in the order, to which he replied in the negative. . . . The prisoner was arraigned on the following charges and specifications:

Charge 1st—Being a Spy. Specification: In this that he, Samuel Davis, of Coleman's Scouts in the service of the so-called Confederate States, did come within the lines of the United States forces in Middle Tennessee for the purpose of secretly gaining information concerning their forces and conveying the same to the enemy, and was arrested within the said lines on or about Nov. 20th, 1863. This in Giles Co. Tenn.

Charge 2nd—Being a carrier of mails, communications and information from within the lines of the U. S. Army to persons in arms against the Government. Specification: In this that he, Samuel Davis, on or about Nov. 20th, 1863, was arrested in Giles County, Tenn. engaged in carrying mails and information from within the lines of the United States forces to persons in arms against the United States Government.

To the First Charge and Specifications Davis pleaded Not Guilty; to the Second Charge and Specifications he pleaded Guilty.

L. H. Naron ("Captain Chickasaw") was the first witness sworn. He stated that the prisoner was taken by two of his scouts and brought before him a prisoner on the 19th or 20th, at night, in Giles County. Naron went on:

I had a conversation with him. I asked him how he become arrested. He said the boys played sharps on him. I asked him what he was going to do with them dispatches, papers. He said he was going to carry them through or to Genl. Bragg. . . . I asked him where he got them. He gave me no satisfactory answer. I then took him, papers and all, to Genl. Dodge and delivered the papers to him.

Naron then identified the papers in question, including a yellow envelope directed to General Bragg on the back of which were written the words "Go fast", a dozen or more newspapers and a package of ten or twelve letters. Naron's testimony continued:

He said that he was a soldier in the Confederate army. I told him that he was

in a very tight place. He said that he knew it, and that he never expected to live
through the war; that he didn't care to live through it. And then he said afterwards
life was sweet and he would like to live to see the end of it. . . . He said that he was
bearing a dispatch, and if I was a true Southern man I ought to recognize his pass
and let him go on. He stated that he was right from Bragg's Army. He left there on the
10th of the month and was then on his return.

Joseph E. Farrar, one of the Federal scouts who made the arrest, was the
next witness, and he testified to making the arrest and taking the papers from
the prisoner. Asked how the prisoner was dressed when taken, he said: "He
seemed to have been dressed in his own uniform, except one of our overcoats
dyed black." He also testified that the prisoner was mounted when captured, that
he said he belonged to the 1st Tennessee regiment.

R. S. King, another of the scouts making the capture, said he was not
acquainted with the prisoner; then:

I first saw him last Friday morning 15 miles from here. I met him in the road
and conscripted him. Why I done it, I met him and supposed he was a soldier. I took
his arms away from him, (a Navy pistol I believe it was). I pretended to conscript him
by authority of Col. Cooper for the Confederate service. I asked him his name. He
told me it was Davis, and I asked him if was any kin to Jeff Davis. He said, a distant
relation. He didn't say anything to me about the command to which he belonged or
about his business.

Asked as to how the prisoner was dressed, King testified: "He had on something like a gray suit—dressed in Southern clothes". The Judge Advocate asked:
"Did he wear the uniform of the Confederate army?", to which the witness answered: "Yes, sir, he did."

No further witnesses were called by the prosecution.

The record then continues:

The prisoner, having no testimony to offer, made the following statement: "I
met Coleman on Thursday morning 19th Nov. 1863, in the road. He asked me where
I was going. I told him that I was trying to get to Dixie, and he asked me how I was
going. I told him that I did not know—anyway to get out. He asked me if I could not
cross below Decatur. I told him I did not think so. He told me it would be the best
way to go, and he wanted me to carry something for him. I told him I would if it was
not too heavy. He told me it was not heavy, and no trouble. I told him I would carry
it. I told him I would take it but it must take me some time to get there, that my
horse was tired. He said he had a good horse and I told him that I would swap with
him and give him one hundred dollars to boot. He said he would trade. I left him. He
went west and I went South. I was captured the next morning by two Federal soldiers."

The prisoner desired to make a further statement, which being granted he proceeded as follows: "At the retreat from Shelbyville I was sick, too sick to walk. I rode
in a wagon from Shelbyville to near Columbia and there I left it and stayed near
Columbia until the Federals came there. I then went farther South, bought me a horse
and started to Williamsport, and met this man Coleman. He told me he would like for
me to go with him. I told him that I had no pass and was afraid to travel about. He
told me he would give me a pass. I asked him by what authority he could give me a
pass. He said by Genl. Bragg's. I told him I would like to have one if he could give me
one that would be of any service to me. He gave me a pass and said I could go anywhere I wanted to. Then I went back with him eight or ten miles in the direction
of Mt. Pleasant. I stayed one night with him and left him next morning and never
saw him any more till last Thursday morning. The reason I went to Chattanooga was
for the purpose of carrying clothes to my brother."

The prisoner having nothing further to offer and not desiring to make any address to the Commission, the case was closed on both sides.

The commission met again the next morning, "and having maturely considered the evidence adduced" found the prisoner, Samuel Davis, guilty of both the First and the Second Charges and Specifications, and sentenced him "to be hung by the neck until he is dead, at such time and place as the Commanding General shall direct, two-thirds of the Commission concurring in the sentence." The Commanding General duly approved the sentence and ordered the execution for Friday morning. November 27.

The letter that Davis was carrying, written by Captain Coleman to Bragg's Provost Marshal General at Chattanooga, giving the information which indicated some close contact with Federal official sources, is preserved in the records of the trial:

> Giles Co. Tennessee,
> Thursday morning Nov. 19th, 1863

Col. A. McKinstry
Pro Mar Gen A. Tenn Chattanooga
Dear Sir: I send you seven Nashville, three Louisville and one Cincinnati papers, with dates of the 17th—in all eleven.

I also send for Genl Bragg three wash-balls of soap, 3 more tooth brushes & two blank-books. I could not get a large size diary for him. I will send a pr. shoes & slippers, some more soap, gloves and socks soon.

The Yankees are still camped on the line of the T & A R R. Genl Dodge's hdqrs are at Pulaski. His main force is camped from that place to Lynnville, some at Elk River and 2 Regts at Athens. Dodge has issued an order to the people in those counties on the road to report all the stock, grain & forage to him & says he will pay or give vouchers for it. Any refusal to report he will take it without pay. They are now taking all they can find. Dodge says he knows the people are all Southern & does not ask them to swear to a lie.

All the spare forces around Nashville and vicinity are being sent to McMinnville. Six batteries & 12 Parrot guns were sent forward on the 14th 15th & 16th. It is understood there is hot work in front somewhere.

Telegrams suppressed

Davis has returned—Gray is gone below

Everything is beginning to work better

I sent Roberts with things for you & Genl B with dispatches

I do not think the Feds mean to stay here. They are not now repairing the main points on the road. I understand part of Sherman's force has reached Shelbyville. I think a part of some other than Dodge's div. came to Lynnville from the direction of Fayetteville. I hope to be able to post you soon.

I sent Billy Moore over in that country & am sorry to say he was captured. One of my men has just returned from there. The general impression with the citizens is they will move forward soon some way. Their wagon train has returned from N.

Davis tells me the line is in order to Somerville. I send this by one of my men to that place. The dispatches sent you on the 9th with papers of the 7th reached Decatur on the 10th at 9 PM. Citizens were reading the papers next morning after breakfast. I do not think the Major will do to forward them, from reports.

> I am with high regard
> Capt. E. Coleman

During the last year of the war Mr. Naron ("Chickasaw") wrote his reminiscences, in the course of which he told the details of how his men captured Sam Davis:

(In November 1863) I sent out two of my scouts, dressed in Confederate uniform. While on their return to camp they met a young man dressed in rebel uniform, who they conscripted for the rebel army. The young man was very indignant at first, and told them they were doing wrong, that he was on special business from General Bragg, all of which was of no avail, my scouts persisted in taking him before their Captain, who could act at his pleasure. They then demanded his arms which he hesitated some time before delivering up, and said he did not believe they were Confederate soldiers, he would never give them up, that the whole Federal army could not take them from him alive. They had now approached to within about two miles of our camp, when this young man discovered that he was a prisoner in the hand of Federal scouts. He attempted to escape by putting spurs to his horse, but the scouts were on the watch, and the moment he made the effort one of the men caught his horse by the bridle rein.

He was taken to headquarters, and upon examining his person was found a water-proof haversack filled with letters and papers for General Bragg. Among them was a despatch from General Bragg's chief of scouts in Middle Tennessee, giving the exact number of men in General Dodge's command, together with all his late orders and a late paper from Nashville. Other papers were found proving this young man to be a spy.

The General then turned him over to me, with orders to deliver him to the Provost Marshal and to have him put into a cell, also to tell him that he had only a few days to live; except on one condition would his life be spared, that was to tell who the person was that furnished him with those papers. He replied that he would not confess anything, that when he entered the army he did not expect to live through the war, and if Tennessee could not be restored to the Southrn Confederacy he would rather die than live. I could not but admire his brave manly spirit. At no time, while in my presence, did he seem to be depressed. The next day a commission was called to give him a trial. The prisoner was called out, who confessed to the charge preferred against him. He was sentenced to be hung on the following Friday.

When he was taken to the scaffold I was permitted to talk to him. I addressed him thus: "Davis, you are not the man that should be hung, and if you would yet tell me who General Bragg's chief of scouts was, so I might capture him, your life would yet be spared." He looked me steadily in the eye and said: "Do you suppose, were I your friend, that I would betray you?" I told him I did not know, but life was sweet to all men. His reply to this was: "Sir, if you think I am that kind of a man you have missed your mark. You may hang me a thousand times and I would not betray my friends."

I then left him only to witness in less than two minutes afterwards his fall from the scaffold, a dead man. Thus ended the life of Samuel Davis, one of General Bragg's scouts, a noble, brave young man, who possessed principle. I have often regretted the fate of this young man, who could brave such a death when his life rested in his own hands.

Singularly enough, while Grant was so energetically and successfully building up the strength of his army, Bragg was incredibly doing the opposite—dividing his strength by sending Longstreet on a wild-goose chase after Burnside, who was hovering between Chattanooga and Knoxville. This foolhardy project seems to have been conceived by President Davis at the time he was visiting Bragg soon after the Chickamauga battle. "You might advantageously assign General Longstreet with his two divisions to the task of expelling Burnside," Davis wrote to Bragg during a stop-over in Atlanta on his way back to Richmond. Grant, in later commenting on this move, said that "Mr. Davis had an exalted opinion of his own military genius. . . . On several occasions during the war he came to the relief of the Union army by means of his *superior military genius.*" Grant did admit that Davis might have taken this step as a means of separating two incompatible commanders; and that this idea might not have been without foundation is suggested by Bragg's letter to Davis on October 31: "The Virginia troops will move in the direction indicated as soon as possible. This will be a great relief to me." And as he might have surmised, it was a great relief to Grant also.

Colonel G. Moxley Sorrell, one of Longstreet's staff officers, has left us a succinct account of this ill-advised movement and its outcome:

The troops of the expedition were to be the two divisions (nine brigades of infantry) brought from Virginia and Alexander's fine battalion of artillery, six batteries; also Leyden's artillery, and Wheeler's powerful body of cavalry (four brigades) and horse artillery. We were also to take up all the loose bodies of troops to be found in the wide district to be covered. A force of about 3,000 men was promised from southwest Virginia.

The cavalry was an ill-disciplined body, not well organized, but accomplished wonders under Wheeler as a screen to the army, and an unceasing menace to the enemy's communications. . . . When Wheeler let us with instructions for a movement calling for some night work his cheerful words to his fellows were: "Come, boys, mount. The War Child rides to-night" that being, it seems, one of his pet names among the men. But Major-General Wheeler was not long with us, Bragg, to whom his services were invaluable, having sent for him. . . .

Burnside's force south of Knoxville was computed at about 15,000 and if we could get all the troops Bragg held out to our commander, there would be enough of us to crush Burnside. But the Federal general had within reach some 5000 more men than General Bragg estimated.

The expedition, glad to be on the move, set out smartly for Tyner's Station, where it was to be entrained for Sweetwater, but things went decidedly wrong. We had brought no transportation from Virginia. General Bragg's officers supplied us with wagons and teams, but they held themselves under Bragg's order—a most inconvenient disposition, then and until we parted company with that commander for good.

With these and other difficulties it was November 12th before the last of our brigades came to Sweetwater. Here there were more disappointments as to rations, supplies and transportation. We were dependent on Bragg's provisions, which cruelly failed us. Not to dwell too long on these mishaps, I need only add that they beset the entire campaign.

The cars and railway by which we helped the transportation were almost comical in their inefficiency. The railroad was of heavy grades and the engines light-powered. When a hill was reached the long train would be instantly emptied—platforms, roofs, doors, and windows—of our fellows, like ants out of a hill, who would ease things by trudging up the dirt road and catching on again at the top; and so it went on as far as the railroad would serve us.

A bridge train had been prepared by the engineers, and it had been our intention to use it across the Little Tennessee, or Holston, above its confluence and through Maryville. But here again was disappointment; there were pontoons but no wagon train for hauling.

We were thus forced to throw our bridge across at Loudon, where fortunately, the boats could be floated direct from cars without need of wagons, and there that curious bridge was laid by our worthy engineers. It was a sight to remember. The current was strong, the anchorage insufficient, the boats and indeed entire outfit quite primitive, and when lashed finally to both banks it might be imagined a bridge; but it was with its graceful reverse curves, a huge letter "S" in effect. But no man should abuse the bridge by which he safely crosses, and this one took us over, using care and caution. I shall always love the looks of that queer bridge. . . .

A fine opportunity of crushing Burnside was lost at Campbell's Station. Burnside's retreat was in time to cover the roads leading into it, and there he had to make a stand. We would have beaten him badly, but he escaped and was soon safe in Knoxville. The roads were deep in mud and caused us hard travel and labor—but they were no better for the Union force.

Campbell's Station cannot be termed a serious battle. It was principally an artillery fight, in which the gallant Alexander was tormented by defective ammunition. It should have been a strong and decisive battle, but things went wrong with the infantry divisions and an effective cooperation was not secured. Ah! would that we could have had Hood again at the head of his division!

As it was, the five brigades of this fine command were practically paralyzed by the differences between the senior brigadier in command, Jenkins, and his competitor, General E. M. Law. It was a most unhappy condition of things, but by no fault of Longstreet. When Mr. Davis visited us at Chickamauga, Longstreet laid the situation before him and urged the promotion and appointment of Jenkins, to which Mr. Davis would not listen. He was asked then to appoint Law, but his also met the Executive's "No", that officer being junior. Then Longstreet begged the assignment of any good major-general to be found elsewhere. But none came. . . .

Thus it came about that the enemy eluded us at Campbell's Station, and the next day was behind his works at Knoxville, except his cavalry, which lingered to retard our march. Our army followed closely, at once put the enemy's works under fire, and so began what is called the "Siege of Knoxville."

By many it is thought to have been a serious error on the part of the Confederate commander, the resorting to so slow a process. "He should have attacked immediately" it was said; and I am disposed to consider intelligent statements of Union officers and citizens of Knoxville, long after, as indicating that an energetic movement then, without the slightest delay, would have carried us into the town and brought Burnside to terms. . . .

Burnside's strongest defense was Fort Loudon, later called Fort Sanders, for the gallant officer of that name who fell in its defense. It was a strong earthwork, closely under [Gen. Lafayette] McLaws' eye, who was expected to capture it. Of course he had done much work toward it—ditches, parallels, and many devices for success. A night attack was proposed and at one time favored.

On the 22d General McLaws thought the time had come and he was ordered to prepare his assaulting column, supported by the division. Longstreet also ordered up other troops for support and following up a success. Later on McLaws reported that his officers preferred daylight for the work before them and the movement was for the time being deferred. . . .

On the 25th, Bragg's chief engineer, General Leadbetter, brought orders from the former to attack immediately. Longstreet was reluctant. Troops from Virginia were on the march, due with us in eight or ten days, and with them the investment could be made complete. . . . But Leadbetter felt that Bragg's orders were imperative and the assault must be attempted. Minute orders were then sent to McLaws for the effort. . . . It was intended for the 28th, but because of bad weather put off until the 29th.

At the appointed time the vigorous assault was made in fine form by the brigades of Wofford, Humphreys, and Bryan in the early gray of the morning. At first we seemed to be going right ahead, shoving everything aside, but some stops were made and the wounded men began coming back. General Longstreet says that when Major Goggin, an old Army man on McLaws' staff, reported to him that it would be useless to persevere, that the fort was so surrounded with net-works of wire that no progress could be made without axes and not an axe was to be found—"Without a second thought, I ordered the recall." He says later that the accounts of General Poe, the Federal engineer in charge of the works, convinced him that the few wires met with were far from being the serious obstacle reported and that we could have gone in without axes. It also seemed sure that the fort was nearly ours by the retirement of part of its garrison, only some two hundred men being kept with the guns.

General Longstreet takes upon himself the failure of the assault. It seems conclusive to him that it was due to the order for recall. He had long known Goggin. Some of our men pushed into the fort. One gallant young officer, Adjutant Cumming, from Augusta, Georgia leaped through an embrasure and instantly demanded the surrender of fort and garrison. The Union troops cheered the feat while making him a prisoner of war.

Almost immediately after the repulse General Longstreet received a telegram from the President to the effect that "Bragg had been forced back by numbers" and that we were to co-operate with his army. This was a euphemism on the part of the President—Bragg had suffered a severe defeat and was in full retreat. He made for Dalton, which put out of the question any co-operation by us. Our own safety was to be considered and how it could be accomplished.

General Sorrell's explanation of the failure of the assault on Fort Sanders is not entirely convincing. Brigadier General Orlando M. Poe, who took part in the defense of Fort Sanders, has this to say pridefully about the reason why Longstreet's attack was not successful:

Many reasons have been assigned for the failure of this assault, and there is some difference of opinion in regard to the matter. Some of those opposed to us, of unquestioned ability and fairness, have attributed it to the warning given us by taking our picket line the night before, the insufficient use of their artillery, and the improper direction taken by two of the columns, resulting in their intermingling and consequent confusion. The opinion has been confidently expressed that a subsequent assault would have been successful.

All this assumes, first, that we were not already vigilant and waiting for the attack; second, that a heavy and continued artillery fire would have greatly damaged and demoralized us; third, that the confusion arising from the convergence of the advancing columns would not have occurred again; fourth, that the works were "very faulty in plan and very easy to take by a properly managed assault"; and last, but not least, that the troops of the enemy were better than ours. The first of these assumptions is erroneous; the second greatly exaggerated; the third might have been verified, but again might not; the fourth is correct only within the limits and to the extent already explained; and the last has no evidence to sustain it.

The conduct of the men who stood in the trenches at Knoxville cannot be overpraised. Half-starved, with clothing tattered and torn, they endured without a murmur every form of hardship and exposure that falls to the lot of the soldier. The question with them was not whether they could withstand the assaults of the enemy, but simply whether sufficient food could be obtained to enable them to keep their places in the line. That they were not reduced to the last extremity in this regard is due to the supplies sent in by the loyalists of the French Broad settlements, who took advantage of Longstreet's inability to invest the place completely, and under cover of the night-fog floated down to us such food and forage as they could collect.

What General Poe says about the "half-starved" Federal troops defending Knoxville is particularly interesting in view of General Sherman's caustic comments on the same subject when, after forced marches, he reached Knoxville a few days later with his troops, ordered there to reinforce Burnside. Sherman, whose sour words might seem to suggest that he was disappointed to find that Burnside's men were not starving, says in his memoirs:

With the head of my infantry column I reached Maryville, about fifteen miles short of Knoxville, on the 5th of December, when I received official notice from Burnside that Longstreet had raised the siege, and had started in retreat up the valley toward Virginia. Halting all the army, except Granger's two divisions, on the morning of the 6th, with General Granger and some of my staff I rode into Knoxville. Approaching from the south and west, we crossed the Holston on a pontoon bridge, and in a large pen on the Knoxville side I saw a fine lot of cattle—which did not look much like starvation. I found General Burnside and staff domiciled in a large, fine mansion, looking very comfortable, and in a few words he described to me the leading events of the previous few days, and said he had already given orders looking to the pursuit of Longstreet. I offered to join in the pursuit, though in fact my men were worn out, and suffering in that cold season and climate. Indeed, on our way up I personally was almost frozen, and had to beg leave to sleep in the house of a family at Athens.

To accentuate Sherman's disgust with what he found there, some of the Unionist citizens of Knoxville gave a sumptuous ceremonial dinner to Sherman and Burnside. The blunt Sherman, instead of accepting this courtesy in the spirit in which it was proffered, did not hesitate to express his surprise at finding the citizens able to produce such a lavish display of supposedly scarce food. The citizens had their feelings hurt, Burnside was embarrassed, and Sherman did not tarry in Knoxville any longer than was necessary before returning to Chattanooga.

CHAPTER 12

☆ *Missionary Ridge*

B UT ALL THIS by-play at Knoxville was really just a side-show to what was meanwhile happening at Chattanooga. On November 14th, the day after Longstreet left Loudon in his advance to Knoxville, Sherman had reached Bridgeport in person and the next day proceeded to Chattanooga to report to Grant. Reinforced by the troops under Hooker and Sherman, Grant now had a great numerical superiority over Bragg, and he lost no time in preparing to assume the active offensive in an attack on the Confederate position. As to his plans, Grant says:

My orders for the battle were all prepared in advance of Sherman's arrival, except the dates, which could not be fixed while troops to be engaged were so far away. The possession of Lookout Mountain was of no special advantage to us now. Hooker was instructed to send Howard's corps to the north side of the Tennessee, thence up behind the hills on the north side, and to go into camp opposite Chattanooga; with the remainder of the command Hooker was, at a time to be afterward appointed, to ascend the western slope between the upper and lower palisades of Lookout Mountain and so get into Chattanooga Valley.

The plan of battle was for Sherman to attack the enemy's right flank, form a line across it, extend our left over South Chickamauga River, so as to threaten or hold the railroad in Bragg's rear, and thus force him either to weaken his lines elsewhere or lose his connection with his base at Chickamauga Station. Hooker was to perform like service on our right. His problem was to get from Lookout Valley to Chattanooga Valley in the most expeditious way possible; cross the latter valley rapidly to Rossville, south of Bragg's line on Missionary Ridge, form line there across the ridge, facing north, with his right flank extended to Chickamauga Valley east of the ridge, thus threatening the enemy's rear on that flank and compelling him to reinforce this also. Thomas, with the Army of the Cumberland, occupied the center, and was to assault while the enemy was engaged with most of his forces on his two flanks.

There were some modifications of these orders, and some delays due to high water and other causes, but it was essentially the plan of operation expected to be followed when the Federal attack was eventually launched on the 24th. Like many well-laid plans, however, this scheme did not work out according to expectations.

While Grant was making these elaborate arrangements looking to a massive assault on Bragg's line of defense, Bragg seemed strangely oblivious to what was going on. Although his efficient staff of scouts kept him fully informed of the heavy forces coming to Grant's assistance, he seemed blissfully blind to the fact that all this concentration of striking power meant anything dangerous to him and that the enemy might be about to attack. On the contrary, instead of trying to strengthen his defenses, he went on unaccountably dissipating his already slim force. Not only was Longstreet gone, but on November 22, the very day that Grant's arrangements for attack were completed, Bragg sent Buckner to reinforce Longstreet. Not satisfied with that, on the 23rd, when the first movements of the Federal advance were actually launched, Cleburne's division was also ordered to entrain at nearby Chickamauga Station to join Longstreet. Fortunately for Bragg he was able to recall Cleburne just in time for part of his division to return with him and take its position on the right flank, where it was to add to its already great fame for dogged courage by effectively repulsing Sherman's attack.

Stripped of the forces of Longstreet and Buckner, Bragg's army was now reduced to two corps—one commanded by Hardee, the other temporarily by Breckinridge. The main part of the army was arrayed on the crest of Missionary Ridge, with a thin skirmish line down the slope in its front. Hardee was on the right and Breckinridge on the left, with Bragg's headquarters about in the center. The line extended across Chattanooga Creek on the left to Lookout Mountain, the troops on this extreme left being under the immediate command of General C. L. Stevenson. The position on the slope of Lookout Mountain, now recognized by both side as of relatively minor importance, was lightly held by the three brigades of Walthall, Moore and Jackson, with a token force on the summit together with some artillery and sharpshooters.

Lookout Mountain is actually more of a stupendous long ridge than an isolated mountain as the word is generally understood. At its northern tip it abuts on the Tennessee River in a declivity so abrupt that rights of way for the railroad and the highway had to be blasted out of its face. Here the promontory rises almost vertically from the river, but about midway between the water level and the mountain-top the steep slope is interrupted by a gently sloping bench, a rugged sort of tilted plateau, upon which in wartime days were a farm and farmhouse occupied by the Cravens family. It was across this bench that the ensuing action took place, with another vertical cliff rising from the slope to the famous peak where countless tourists have stood and gazed at the imposing panorama below them.

When Hooker, on the morning of the 24th crossed Lookout Creek and moved against the Confederates on the slope near the Cravens house, the brigades of Walthall and Moore were not able to put up much opposition, and carried out their instructions, if attacked, to "fall back fighting over the rocks." The engagement took place in a dense fog rising from the Tennessee River, giving it the doubly misleading label of "The Battle Above the Clouds". The correspondent of the New York *Tribune* accurately expressed it when he said: "There were no clouds to fight above—only a heavy mist." Asked about it in later years, General Grant frankly said: "The battle of Lookout Mountain is one of the romances of the war. There was no such battle, and no action even worthy to be called a battle on Lookout Mountain. It is all poetry." So it would seem that there was neither battle nor cloud in the famous "Battle Above the Clouds."

But for the men engaged it was a serious affair. Hooker's army and Walthall's outnumbered brigade fought desperately over the rugged mountain bench throughout the morning. Both were hampered by the thickness of the fog, but the Confederates were gradually forced back. When they reached the Cravens House and Moore's brigade came to Walthall's support they tried to establish a line and make a stand there, but they soon had to fall back to another line behind the house, and this position they held until nightfall stopped the fighting. At midnight General Stevenson ordered the battered survivors to withdraw and join Breckinridge's force on Missionary Ridge, where it was now evident the main Federal attack was to be centered.

Hooker woke up in the morning to find that he was in complete possession of the mountain, and he celebrated by sending an unopposed detachment to plant the Stars and Stripes on the mountain peak, while the army cheered. From then on he did not do so well. The Confederates having destroyed the bridge over Chattanooga Creek, he experienced difficulty and delay in carrying out his instructions to cross and operate on the Confederate left and rear, and did not arrive on the battlefield until late in the afternoon when the fighting was just about over.

Grant in his official account of the battle glosses over Hooker's misadventure, which was overshadowed by his supportable claim that he captured Lookout Mountain—although possession of the mountain did not seem to be of any special value to either army.

Grant is similarly disingenuous in seeking to give the impression that Sherman's carrying out of his orders was an unqualified success. In the first place, Grant tells with some pride of the elaborate arrangements and precautions taken to bring Sherman's forces into position when they arrived on the scene, although Colonel H. V. Boynton suggests that all such precautions were entirely unnecessary:

As this movement of Sherman's on Bragg's right flank was designated by General Grant as the central feature of the battle, its execution merits close attention, says Colonel Boynton.

General Thomas had favored bringing Serman's troops directly into the city, together with the cooperating forces from Hooker's columns, and marching them by night along the south bank of the river to the north end of Missionary Ridge. But General Grant, after finding that this portion of the ridge was unoccupied, thought its possession could be more certainly effected by a night crossing of the river near the ridge, and an advance upon it at daylight.

So General Thomas sent from his army, by Grant's direction, a division of infantry, a brigade of cavalry, and two batteries, (the latter contributing toward making up forty guns) to form a covering party for Sherman's crossing. A pontoon train was brought up from Bridgeport and Stevenson and sent floundering up the North Chickamauga; and 116 boats, mostly built in Chattanooga, requiring 750 oarsmen, were carried up and secretly floated in that stream. General Thomas furnished half of the latter force. To reward these tremendous efforts the crossing was completely successful under the direction of those eminent engineers, General W. F. ("Baldy") Smith and General James H. Wilson.

That no such exhaustive work was necessary is shown by the fact that General Howard, who had ridden up from Chattanooga unmolested, accompanied only by his escort and three regiments of infantry, appeared on the south bank to welcome General Sherman as he came first over the bridge. As if to emphasize the meaning of this, he left his troops with Sherman, and rode back to the city with his escort alone. If there could be anything comical in war, this meeting would deserve the attention of the wits. Think of the tremendous effort to prepare at such a season and in such a country for this crossing of over 20,000 men, and of the comment on its needless character furnished by Howard's unmolested ride from Chattanooga.

To make this situation more remarkable, at daylight (when General Sherman had two divisions of 8000 men in line facing Missionary Ridge) there was no enemy in force, either on the ridge or along its base within two miles and a half of General Sherman's position. Further than this, there were no Confederate forces nearer than a mile and a quarter from the hill over the tunnel, which was his objective, until after two o'clock of the day he crossed the river, nor were any ordered towards it till that hour. If he had marched at daylight for Tunnel Hill, as was contemplated by the order of battle, he could have occupied the entire north end of Missionary Ridge not only to the tunnel but for some distance south of it without encountering a Confederate in arms.

Sherman moved to attack the ridge at one o'clock in the afternoon, having five divisions in his columns, and it was not until two o'clock that Cleburne, then a mile and a quarter south of Tunnel Hill, was instructed to move to that point to resist Sherman's advance. Cleburne did not occupy the position until 2:30 P.M. It was not entrenched when he reached it, and throughout the afternoon he had only three brigades (and one battery with each), with which to hold it against Sherman's five divisions.

But the astonishing error, an error which caused utter failure to the whole movement against Bragg's right, and which ever since has been covered thick in official reports and misleading histories, was Sherman's first day's occupation of a range of detached hills north of Missionary Ridge, and completely separated from it. Since the plan of battle turned on occupying the north end of the ridge, it was certainly one of the most remarkable oversights of the war that this position was not thoroughly identified.

So, at daylight of the 25th Sherman found himself on a crest one thousand yards distant from Cleburne's works on the real north point of Missionary Ridge, with a deep gorge between the lines; and in order to assault Cleburne's position he was obliged to move down an open slope under the direct fire of the Confederate guns and rifles, and then up the steep ascent to Cleburne's fortified lines.

Captain Irving A. Buck, who served as A.A.G. of Cleburne's Division, soon after the war wrote for the *Southern Historical Society Papers* an account of the activities of that division in the battle on November 25th. Cleburne had been held in reserve when Hardee moved his corps into position on the ridge on the 24th, but in the afternoon of that day he was ordered to proceed to the right and take possession of the rising ground near the mouth of Chickamauga River. "The troops moved at double quick and arrived none too soon," Buck says. "Sherman's advance was endeavoring to occupy the ground, and Cleburne had to fight for position—the men firing by file as they formed into line." Buck goes on:

Cleburne's line, with his left resting near the right of the tunnel, extended over a circular wooded hill occupied by Smith's (Texas), Liddell's (Arkansas), and Polk's (Tennessee) brigades. The right flank was protected by Lowry's (Mississippi and Alabama) brigade, thrown some half a mile distant and somewhat in advance of the remainder of the division. Immediately over the tunnel, and connecting with Cleburne's left, was a strong battery of Napoleon guns commanding the open ground in front. By direction of General Hardee the railroad bridge over the Chickamauga was burned.

Cleburne's artillery had been halted by him on the opposite side of Chickamauga river, and was not now brought up because of his impression (based upon the reduction of General Bragg's force by the detachments referred to, the increase of General Grant's by the arrival of Sherman, and the loss of Lookout Mountain) that General Bragg would not attempt longer to hold the extended line of Missionary Ridge.

About 9 o'clock P. M., Cleburne, unable to restrain his anxiety, turned to me and said: "Go at once to General Hardee's quarters, ask what has been determined upon, and say that if it is decided to fight it is necessary that I should get my artillery into position." Upon reaching corps headquarters I ascertained that General Hardee had been called to a council of war at General Bragg's quarters, some miles further up the ridge, to the left. I proceeded to and reached army headquarters some half an hour before the council adjourned. The remark of General Breckinridge, who commanded the left corps, as he came out, that "I never felt more like fighting than when I saw those people shelling my troops off Lookout to-day," indicated the result of the conference even before General Hardee's response to Cleburne's message. I gathered that General Breckinridge and urged in favor of a stand, that it was now too late to withdraw his troops before daylight would discover the movement. General Hardee said: "Tell Cleburne we are to fight, that his division will undoubtedly be heavily attacked, and that he must do his very best." I replied that the division had never yet failed to clear its front, and would do so again—no vain boast, as the morrow proved. As the party rode down the crest of the ridge in the stillness of the night the sparse camp fires burning low along the rifle-pits at its western base showed how thin the line was—less than shoulder to shoulder, in single rank. This was remarked upon, and it was suggested that an energetic dash by the enemy upon the centre held by such a line might prove a serious matter. I remember General Hardee observed that the natural strength of the position would probably deter such an attempt; and that the enemy had been massing on the flanks, where the heaviest work was to be expected.

Cleburne ordered up his artillery, and made such other preparations for the approaching conflict as practicable in the night; now rendered abnormally dark and sombre by an eclipse of the moon. General Hardee, who, from its liability to be turned, felt most solicitude about Cleburne's position, arrived at this part of the line between 2 and 3 o'clock in the morning, and afterwards, in company with Cleburne, made a personal and careful inspection of it.

A heavy mist had prevailed throughout the day on the 24th, but the morning of the 25th of November broke bright and clear. Before the sun was fairly up the troops were called to arms by picket firing, followed soon after by the line and artillery, and the conflict soon rose to the dignity of a general engagement. Repeated attempts were made to carry Cleburne's position, and the assaulting columns were repulsed and hurled bleeding down the slope, only to reform and charge again in gallant but vain effort. Cleburne's veterans found foeman worthy of their steel in the army commanded by Sherman and led by such Lieutenants as Corse, Ewing, Leightburn, and Loomis. Almost the entire day was thus consumed. The enemy, met at every advance by a plunging and destructive artillery fire, followed, when in range, by a withering fire of infantry, were repulsed at all points, and slowly and stubbornly fell back. In some instances squads of them finding shelter behind the obstructions afforded by the rugged sides of the hill, kept up a damaging sharp shooting until dislodged by stones hurled down upon them by the Texans.

Meanwhile the enemy had shown in force and made demonstrations at points further to the left. Early in the forenoon they had occupied a farm-house and outbuildings near and to the left front of the tunnel, whence their sharp-shooters were beginning to do effective work. From this position they were driven by a charge, directed by General Hardee and handsomely executed by the Twentieth Alabama regiment, and the buildings were destroyed. About the middle of the afternoon a strong Federal brigade approached Cleburne's left through an open field, and under heavy artillery and infantry fire. The Napoleon guns posted over the tunnel, which had been rapidly and continuously served, were turned upon this advancing brigade with deadly precision. Every discharge plowed huge gaps through the lines, which were promptly closed up, as the troops moved forward with a steadiness and order that drew exclamations of admiration from all who witnessed it. The brigade advanced to an old fence row, where planting their colors and lying down they opened and kept up a damaging fire, and held their position with a tenacity which seemed proof against all efforts to dislodge them.

About this time Cleburne dispatched a staff officer to ascertain the condition of affairs in Lowry's front. Finding all well there, the officer returned by a detour, made necessary by the conformation of the ground, which brought him in view of the flanks of the contending forces. Arrested by the sound of heavy firing and the sight of opposing lines in closer proximity than the relative positions justified, he moved towards the scene of action and discovered a considerable body of Federal soldiers coming through the woods. Supposing the right flank had been turned and was about to be attacked in rear, he galloped up to Cleburne and made his report. He was met with the reply that the soldiers he had seen were prisoners of war being sent to the rear. Such, indeed, was the fact. Seeing a column of assault advancing up the hill, Cleburne had placed himself at the head of the Texas brigade, and jumping the works met and repulsed the charge, and returned with a number of prisoners and several stands of colors.

Simultaneously with the last assault on Cleburne's left, General Hardee, from his post of observation near the tunnel, had opportunely directed an effective charge of a brigade, conducted by Brigadier-General Cummings, against the attacking force.

No further attempts were made on Cleburne's front, and the sun was getting low. General Hardee, secure of the right, now proceeded up the ridge to his left as the ringing cheers raised by the whole of Cleburne's division over their victory extended and were taken up and reechoed by the entire line.

Flushed with justifiable pride in the accomplishment of Cleburne's men in driving off Sherman's attack, Hardee was shocked to discover when he reached the left end of his line that the left-center of the Confederate position had been carried by assault, and the elated Federals were streaming over the crest of the ridge where they had breached the supposedly invulnerable Confederate position. Walthall's brigade of Cheatham's division had hastily changed front under fire and formed a weak, short line at right angles with the crest of the ridge. This line, strengthened and prolonged by reinforcements drawn from the right, was able to hold its position until nightfall put an end to the fighting and, in the darkness, the Confederate forces abandoned their position and began their retreat into Georgia which did not stop until they had passed through Ringgold Gap.

What had happened constituted one of the most astounding happenings in the course of the whole war, as the "impregnable" Confederate center unaccountably melted away under the assault of Thomas' veteran infantrymen. General Joseph S. Fullerton of the Fourth Army Corps was with Grant and Thomas on Orchard Knob when the attack was ordered, and he tells how this successful attack started late in the afternoon after the other Federal efforts had failed:

Early in the morning of the 25th General Grant and General Thomas established their headquarters on Orchard Knob, a point from which the best view of the movements of the whole army could be had. At sunrise General Sherman commenced his attack, but after repeated assaults and severe fighting, it appearing to be impossible for General Sherman to take the enemy's works, operations ceased early in the afternoon.

Meanwhile Hooker was detained three hours at Chattanooga Creek, while a bridge that the retreating enemy had burned was being rebuilt . . . It was by this time nearly sundown. Hooker reached the south end of the ridge too late in the day to relieve the pressure on Sherman, who was at the north end six miles off. Bragg's right had not been turned. Success had not followed Sherman's movement. The battle as planned had not been won. . . .

On Orchard Knob and opposite the center of Missionary Ridge were four divisions of the Army of the Cumberland. . . . all under the personal command of Thomas. It was past 3 o'clock. General Sherman had ceased operations. General Hooker's advance had not yet been felt. The day was dying and Bragg still held the ridge. If any movement to dislodge him was to be made that day it must be made at once. At half-past three o'clock an attack was ordered by General Grant.

Montgomery C. Meigs, Quartermaster General of the Army, was an eyewitness of the charge of Thomas' men that broke the Confederate line, and after the battle he dutifully sent to Secretary Stanton at Washington a graphic report of the great Federal victory. Of the climax of the battle, the surge of Thomas' force up the face of Missionary Ridge, Meigs says:

A strong line of skirmishers, followed by a deployed line of battle some two miles in length, moved rapidly and orderly forward. The Rebel pickets discharged their muskets and ran into their rifle pits. Our skirmishers followed on their heels. The line of battle was not far behind, and we saw the grey rebels swarm out of their long line of rifle pits in numbers which surprised us, and over the hill.

A few turned and fired their pieces, but the greater number collected into the many roads which cross obliquely up its steep face and went on to the top. Some regiments pressed and swarmed up the steep sides of the ridge. Here and there a color was advanced beyond the lines. The attempt appeared most dangerous, but the advance was supported and the whole line ordered to storm the heights, upon which not less than forty pieces of artillery and no one knows how many muskets stood ready to slaughter the assailants. With cheers answering to cheers, the men swarmed upwards. They gathered to the position least difficult of ascent, and the line was broken.

Color after color was planted on the summit, while musket and cannon vomited their thunder upon them. A well directed shot from Orchard Knob exploded a rebel caisson on the summit, and the gun was seen galloping to the right, its driver lashing his horses. A party of our soldiers intercepted them and the gun was captured with cheers. A fierce musketry fight broke out to the left, where between Thomas and Sherman a mile or two of the ridge was still occupied by the Rebels. Bragg left the house in which he had held his headquarters, and rode to the rear as our troops crowned the hill on either side of him.

Ralph J. Neal, a private in the Twentieth Tennessee Infantry, was one of those in the Confederate line receiving the brunt of Thomas' attack, and his account of the action there helps give a clearer idea of just what happened and how it happened. He mentions the total eclipse of the moon the night before, and says this had a depressing influence on the men, giving them a sense of "impending disaster". Such depression, he admits, was unreasonable on their part, asking the rhetorical questions: "Why should it presage defeat to us? Why not to the Yankees?" (And he might well have asked: "Why not to Cleburne's men?") Anyhow, he says, the "gloom of the preceding night still hung over us" the next morning as they moved into position.

We moved along the ridge about a mile north of Bragg's headquarters and took our place on the line of battle. Our brigade (Tyler's) formed the right of Bate's Division. The 4th Georgia Battalion to the right, the 20th Tennessee next and so on. The enemy had formed outside his works and was moving across the valley towards us, we being on the crest of the ridge. It was indeed a grand spectacle for our little band to see—perhaps in modern times an entire army had not witnessed such a scene. The valley between the ridge and Chattanooga had been occupied by both armies for near two months, and was now almost destitute of timber; and across this denuded valley Grant's army of from 80,000 to 100,000 were marching in plain view of every Confederate soldier. We could plainly see every movement. When about half-way across the valley our artillery opened up on them and they could not well reply. How we did enjoy that cannonading—no shells were disturbing us. But on they came, and when they reached the foot of the ridge our guns could not be depressed sufficiently to play on them any longer, and now our small arms were brought to bear on them as they climbed up the ridge.

In order to cover a long front, we were formed in one rank. At the right of our regiment our line turned from north to the northeast, conforming to the crest of the ridge. In about a hundred yards it turned north again. This hundred yards was occupied by the 4th Georgia Battalion. As the enemy came up, everything in our front was driven back, so also in the front of the Georgia Battalion, and to the north of this, as they came steadily on, never halting.

Our regiment could only look on; we could not fire to the right oblique, for that would endanger our Georgia Battalion—and from the lay of the land they could not see the enemy. With bated breath we waited to see the result, there being no enemy in our own front. Steadily Deas' men, with their weak line, fired into that brave as well as overwhelming host of the enemy. They staggered up to the half-finished rifle pits, then three stands of Federal colors in a bunch mounted the works. Deas' line was broken—not to their discredit, however; they were too heavily outnumbered.

The Yankees first turned right and left, flanking our men out of the ditches. They next went for one of our batteries in position between Deas' and Tyler's brigades. Our men wheeled two guns and fired, at not more than a hundred feet distance, at the Yankees; but many of them were now over the works, and they rushed at the battery with fixed bayonets. The cannoneers fought them with their swab sticks, but they were soon overpowered and killed or captured with their guns . . . The enemy now turned the guns down our trenches, but fortunately it was infantry and they could not sight a cannon with any degree of accuracy, and the charges of cannister for the most part went wild . . . Colonel Shy commanded us to move out by the left flank . . . As we were moving back we noticed that our entire line south towards Bragg's headquarters was broken and our men in full retreat. As we moved back our brigade continued to fire at the pursuing enemy, until we got them checked in a measure, and other brigades now began to reform, and order was partially restored. Colonel Shy discovered our field band in the rear, and ordered them to play "Dixie". This seemed to do more toward rallying the men than all else.

We came to a field, and just across the field was General Bragg, sitting on his horse with a large flag, appealing to the men to stand. Finley's brigade now reformed, and our brigade was placed with the field in our front, Finley to our left. Before we finished our formation the enemy advanced on us. Night was fast approaching and they made no determined charge, but kept up a pretty heavy firing until darkness had gathered around us, so we were firing only at the flashes of each other's guns. It was thus that the enemy was checked, giving the left wing of our army a chance to cross the Chickamauga River.

Bragg, schocked by the debacle, determined to retreat to Dalton on the Western & Atlantic railroad; or, as his report expressed it in the circumlocution generally used, "It was decided to put the army in motion for a point further removed from a powerful and victorious army, that we might have some little time to replenish and recuperate for another struggle." As Cleburne had given such signal evidence of steadfastness and fighting quality, to his division was assigned the honor of holding off any possible pursuit until the rest of the army could be concentrated somewhere in the rear, and Cleburne again gave proof of his mettle for resistance in an emergency.

The Federal pursuit was launched the next day by Hooker's force of 16,000 men; but Cleburne had skillfully located his men and his artillery in control of Ringgold Gap, through which the road to Dalton passed, and after some fierce fighting there, Hooker turned back to Chattanooga and Cleburne's battered division went on the next day in the wake of the retreating army.

On November 30th General Bragg made a brief report of the Missionary Ridge debacle, in the conclusion of which he said:

No satisfactory excuse can possibly be given for the shameful conduct of our troops on the left in allowing their line to be penetrated. The position was one that ought to have been held by a line of skirmishers against any assaulting column, and wherever resistance was made the enemy fled in disorder after suffering heavy loss. Those of the enemy who reached the ridge did so in a condition of exhaustion from the great physical exertion in climbing which rendered them powerless, and the slightest effort would have destroyed them. Having secured much of our artillery, they soon availed themselves of our panic, and turning our guns upon us enfiladed the lines, both right and left, rendering them entirely untenable. Had all parts of the line been maintained with equal gallantry and persistence, no enemy could ever have dislodged us, and but one possible reason presents itself to my mind in explanation of this bad conduct in veteran troops who never before failed in any duty assigned them, however difficult and hazardous: They had for two days confronted the enemy, marshaling his immense forces in plain view, and exhibiting to their sight such a superiority in numbers as may have intimidated weak-minded and untried soldiers. But our veterans had so often encountered similar hosts when the strength of position was against us, and with perfect success, that not a doubt crossed my mind.

In writing to his friend, Jefferson Davis, on December 1, however, Bragg spoke much more frankly and with great bitterness:

I send by Lieutenant-Colonel Urquhart a plain, unvarnished report of the operations at Chattanooga, resulting in my shameful discomfiture. The disaster admits of no palliation, and is justly disparaging to me as a commander. I trust, however, you may find upon full investigation that the fault is not entirely mine . . . I fear we both erred in the conclusion for me to retain command here after the clamor raised against me. The warfare against me has been carried on successfully, and the fruits are bitter. You must make other changes here, or our success is hopeless. Breckinridge was totally unfit for any duty from the 23rd to the 27th—during all our trials—from drunkenness. The same cause prevented our complete triumph at Murfreesborough. I can bear to be sacrificed myself, but not to see my country and my friends ruined by the vices of a few profligate men who happened to have an undue popularity. General Hardee will assure you that Cheatham is equally dangerous.

CHAPTER **13**

☆ *After Missionary Ridge - 1864*

B RAGG, in his telegram to General Samuel Cooper on the night of November 28th, had closed his report with the terse sentence: "I deem it due to the cause and to myself to ask relief from command." He followed this up with another letter to President Davis on December 2nd, in which he reverted to the defeat of his army at Missionary Ridge "by sheer force of numbers", and went on:

No one estimates the disaster more seriously than I do, and the whole responsibility rests on my humble head. But we can redeem the past. Let us concentrate all our available men, unite them with this gallant little army, still full of zeal and burning to redeem its lost character and prestige, and with our greatest and best leader at its head, yourself if practicable, hurl the whole upon the enemy and crush him in his power and glory. I believe it practicable, and trust that I may be allowed to participate in the struggle which may restore to us the character, the prestige and the country we have just lost.

Whether Bragg was sincere in suggesting that Davis himself fill the requirements of "our greatest and best leader" or was merely indulging in a little flattery of his official commander in chief, Davis ignored this part of Bragg's letter—and also disregarded the offer to stay and "participate". Nobody in Richmond, however, disputed Bragg's suggestion that the time had arrived for him to relinquish command of the Army of Tennessee. Cooper on November 30 notified Bragg he had acceded to his request, and ordered him to transfer the command of the Army to the official next in rank, General Hardee, which was done.

This, of course, created two new problems: whom to put in Bragg's place, and what future assignment to give to an officer of the high rank of Bragg, a full general.

After many suggestions and much discussion, it was decided to place General Joseph E. Johnston at the head of the Army of Tennessee. Then, to the surprise of practically everybody and to the satisfaction of practically nobody, Davis solved the problem of Bragg's future by kicking him upstairs to the post of military adviser to the President, where he acted as a sort of chief of staff or ex officio commander in chief. The official description of his new duties specified that "under the direction of the President" he was "charged with the conduct of military operations in the armies of the Confederacy."

E. A. Pollard, the sharp-tongued editor of the Richmond *Examiner* wrote a vitriolic editorial about the appointment, with the bitterly sarcastic comment that "This happy announcement should enliven the confidence and enthusiasm reviving among the people like a bucket of water on a newly kindled grate." But, for better or worse, the change had been made, and the Army of Tennessee settled down into its winter quarters at Dalton under a new commander they soon learned to love and respect—"Old Joe" Johnston.

While all this was going on, General Longstreet, hovering on the outskirts of Knoxville was spending some uneasy moments wondering just what to do. He had first been ordered to re-unite his force with Bragg. Before he could move in that direction, however, he was informed that a Federal force under Sherman was on its way to Knoxville to succor Burnside, so a southward movement by Longstreet was impossible. General E. P. Alexander, Longstreet's artillery chief, tells of their eventual movement northward in East Tennessee, seeking a suitable location for winter quarters:

We remained before Knoxville until the night of December 4th. About noon the next day we encamped at Blain's Cross-roads, having made eighteen miles. That was, I think, about the very worst night march I ever went through. The roads were in fearful condition, and in the inky darkness and pouring rain neither men nor animals could see. Frequently guns or wagons would be mired so that the column behind would be blocked in the mud until extra teams and men at the wheels could set the column going for a few minutes. Strict orders had been given that the men should not use fence rails for fuel, but that night the orders were ignored, and miles of fence were fired merely to light up the road.

I recall some incidents illustrating how poorly our army was provided with even prime necessaries, although we were in our own country. We were so badly off for horse-shoes that on the advance to Knoxville we had stripped the shoes from all the dead horses, and we killed for the purpose all the wounded and broken-down animals, both our own and those left behind by the enemy. During the siege the river brought down to us a number of dead horses and mules, thrown in within the town. We watched for them, took them out, and got the shoes and nails from their feet. Our men were nearly as badly off as the animals—perhaps worse, as they did not have hoofs. I have myself seen bloody stains on frozen ground, left by the bare-footed where our infantry had passed. We of the artillery took the shoes off the drivers and gave them to the cannoneers who had to march.

Early in the advance Longstreet gave permission to the men to "swap" shoes with the prisoners whenever any were taken, but each man was strictly required to have something to "swap", and not leave the prisoner barefoot. It was quite an amusing sight (to us) to see a ragged rebel with his feet tied up in a sort of raw beef-hide moccasin, which the men learned to make, come up to a squad of prisoners, inspect their feet, and select the one he would "swap" with. Generally, however, the prisoners took it all very good-humoredly, guyed one another, and swapped jokes also with the swappers. It looked a little rough, but, as one of the victims said, "When a man is captured, his shoes are captured too."

Late in December Longstreet ordered his army to cross to the east side of Holston River, and he tells with obvious satisfaction of the ensuing improvement in the condition of his destitute and suffering men:

Before Christmas we were in our camps along the railroad, near Morristown. Blankets and clothes were very scarce, shoes more so, but all knew how to enjoy the beautiful country in which we found ourselves. . . . The country contains as fine farming lands and has as delightful a climate as can be found. Stock and grain were on all farms. Wheat and oats had been hidden away by our Union friends, but the fields were full of maize still standing. The country about the French Broad had hardly been touched by the hand of the foragers. Our wagons immediately on entering the fields were loaded to overflowing. Pumpkins were on the ground in places like apples under a tree. Cattle, sheep and swine, poultry, vegetables maple-sugar, honey, were all abundant for immediate needs of the troops. . . .

With all the plentitude of provisions and many things which seemed at the time luxuries, we were not quite happy. Tattered blankets, garments, and shoes (the latter going—many gone) opened ways, on all sides, for piercing winter blasts. There were some hand-looms in the country from which we occasionally picked up a piece of cloth, and here and there we picked up other comforts—some kind and some from unwilling hands, which nevertheless could spare them. For shoes we were obliged to resort to the raw hides of beef cattle as temporary protection from the frozen ground. Then we began to find soldiers who could tan the hides of our beeves, some who could make shoes, some who could make shoe-pegs, some who could make shoe-lasts, so that it came about that the hides passed rapidly from the beeves to the feet of the soldiers in the form of comfortable shoes. Then came the opening of the railroad, and lo and behold! a shipment of three thousand shoes from General Lawton, quartermaster general! Thus the most urgent needs were supplied, and the soldier's life seemed passably pleasant—that is, in the infantry and artillery. Our cavalry were looking at the enemy all of this while, and the enemy was looking at them, both frequently burning powder between their lines.

The presence of Longstreet's corps in East Tennessee was a constant source of worry to Halleck and Grant, and they continued to impress on General Foster (who had succeeded Burnside at Knoxville) that Longstreet must be driven out of the state. Grant went personally to Knoxville about the first of the year and spent a week there, the result of which was an order to Foster to drive Longstreet "at least beyond Bull's Gap". Preparatory to this effort there was a concentration at Dandridge of Federal cavalry, and in connection with these developments the First [Federal] Regiment of Tennessee Volunteer Cavalry, made up largely of Knoxville recruits, had an opportunity to visit their home-town as they passed through there on their way to the front. W. R. Carter, a private in that regiment, tells of their movement and of the enthusiastic reception they received in Knoxville:

While we were lying in camp at Sparta, an order was received from General Thomas directing General Elliott, chief of cavalry, to march at once with all of the First Division and report to General Burnside at Knoxville. Early on the morning of December 7, camp was broken and soon the long, dark lines of McCook's division could be seen slowly winding along the crooks and turns of the old state road toward Kingston. . . .

On the morning of the 15th we entered Knoxville by the Middlebrook and Clinton roads, and on the range of hills just west of town we passed through Longstreet's main line of works. . . . We proudly entered our native town about 3 P. M., and marched down Gay Street in platoons, with colors flying and bands playing, and were warmly greeted by the loyal people of Knoxville who lined the streets to witness the parade of McCook's veterans. Where Reservoir street crossed Gay, we passed through Burnside's main line of works, the yellow clay towering high above our heads. . . . Turning west on Cumberland street, we passed the home of Rev. W. G. Brownlow, whose son

Jim was colonel of our regiment. The parson—as he was familiarly called—and his family came out and witnessed with a great deal of interest the regiment as it marched by, under the command of its youthful colonel. We gave the parson and his interesting family three rousing cheers as we marched by . . .

But they were soon to find out that this was no picnic outing. On the day of their arrival at Knoxville, they were ordered to cross Holston River and attack the Confederate cavalry under General Martin at or near Morristown. This, writes Mr. Carter, was the beginning of "the ever-memorable East Tennessee campaign." On Christmas Eve Campbell's Brigade (of which the First Tennessee Cavalry was a part) encountered the Confederates at Dandridge and, after a brief but brisk skirmish, the Federals fell back to New Market. On Christmas Day McCook advanced his division along the Mossy Creek road. He tells of how, upon reaching Mossy Creek, the next two or three days were spent in picketing, scouting and skirmishing "in the midst of bitter cold weather, with bad roads, scanty rations and a hostile foe near by." Then he goes on:

On the morning of the 29th General Sturgis, who was in command of all the cavalry then operating in East Tennessee, learned that a brigade of the enemy's cavalry had moved to Dandridge, and decided to surprise and destroy it. He sent the most of the cavalry off on this "Tom Fool" trip, leaving only Campbell's brigade to hold Mossy Creek. . . . The First Tennessee and the Second Michigan were formed in line of battle across the valley early in the morning. The Ninth Pennsylvania and the three remaining guns of Lilly's battery were placed in position a short distance east of Mossy Creek.

As soon as the troops had reached their respective positions, Campbell moved up the valley with the First Tennessee and Second Michigan. About a mile beyond our camp Campbell halted his brigade and threw out a line of skirmishers. He remained in this position until about 10 A. M., when word was sent in by his pickets on the Morristown road that the enemy was advancing in force, with eight or ten pieces of artillery. The enemy continued to advance, and after driving in the pickets encountered the skirmishers, which were some distance out.

There was a sharp rattling fire along the skirmish line, after which they fell back, closely followed by the enemy in line of battle, with flags waving and arms flashing in the sunlight. It was an exciting moment, and we began to think it was another Dandridge scrape. But Campbell was equal to the occasion. Seeing that his little brigade was greatly out-numbered, he gave orders to fall back. The enemy pressed forward, showing several lines of battle, and with superior numbers attempted to out-flank him, at the same time using the artillery at close range.

We fell back to the residence of Stokely Williams, a large two-story brick house and during the engagement it was struck several times by flying shells. Here Campbell was compelled to halt this brigade and fight. The enemy was close upon us and at the same time opened a severe fire from a battery at close range, and soon the air about us was filled with missiles of all sizes, shapes and kinds, whirling and whizzing, producing a most unearthly sound that would chill the blood of the bravest veteran. Some of our boys at the pack-train went so far as to investigate these strange-sounding missiles when they had stopped, and reported that Longstreet was shooting railroad iron at us.

Colonel Campbell ordered the First Tennessee to charge the enemy on the right of the brick house, which it did with a yell, driving back their center and halting their whole line. At the same time the Second Michigan, which was fighting dismounted, opened a destructive fire with their Colt's rifles at close range, which completely staggered their line. During this temporary check, Campbell ordered his brigade to fall back and take up a new position near where Lilly's battery and the Ninth Pennsylvania were stationed, hotly contesting every inch of ground as he fell back. . . .

Our lines were hardly formed when the enemy opened on us with ten guns, and it began to look like the regiment and battery would be swept from the field. It was the most terrific artillery fire the regiment had ever been under, but we lay there and took it all, not firing a shot. It was exceedingly monotonous lying there taking all their old scrap-iron, giving nothing in return. Men and horses were going down at almost every discharge. . . .

Once more the order came to fall back, and as we moved to the left, the solid shot and exploding shells went crashing through the trees, doing no harm except cutting off limbs and tearing up trees. We moved only a short distance to the left, where a new line of battle was formed, with the First Tennessee in the center. Our lines were hardly formed when the enemy came charging upon us in such overwhelming numbers that we were driven back and the day seemed lost.

The day was fast wearing away and the sun was almost lost behind the western hills. The fighting was severe all along the line, and we were again compelled to give ground, falling back a short distance to the edge of the woods. The enemy, seeing us falling back, now rushed on after us with their well-known "rebel yell".

Colonel Brownlow, seeing the boldness and courage that the enemy were displaying in still advancing upon him under so hot a fire, suggested to Campbell the propriety of making a spirited saber charge. . . . The order was given to draw sabers, and with a yell the First Tennessee, with its well-known gallantry, rushed upon the enemy in one of the most daring charges of the war. The spirit, courage, boldness and audacity with which the charge was made has scarcely ever been equalled in the war, and the important effect that it produced was a matter of astonishment to those who witnessed it. We drove the enemy back into the woods, retaking a part of the lost ground, but were forced back with some loss. . . . At this critical moment a portion of Mott's brigade, Second Division, came upon the field. Cavalry, infantry and dismounted men now charged upon the enemy, who began to show signs of wavering, driving them through the woods in great confusion The Second Brigade, which had been recalled, now reached the field and entered heartily into the case, which was continued for some distance, halting only when it became too dark to distinguish friend from foe.

The intensely cold weather and the condition of the roads made campaigning difficult for both armies, but Grant was insistent in his repeated demands that Longstreet be "routed and pursued beyond the limits of the state of Tennessee." General Sorrell, Longstreet's aide, tells how the East Tennessee campaign gradually fizzled out:

On February 9th General Schofield took command at Knoxville of the Union army in East Tennessee. The pressure on him continued from Halleck, whose uneasiness at one time became almost uncontrollable. Grant at first made strong effort to carry out these wishes, but we were not moved. Later on he found the field too far from his other operations and likely to interrupt plans for the summer. He preferred resting on the apparent apathy at the South and using his East Tennessee strength in Virginia and Georgia where he should have full need for it. This view was to leave us in inactivity in East Tennessee, and no further serious effort was made. Longstreet had to move east when he was refused more troops for extended aggressive operations and received orders for return of Martin's cavalry to Georgia. Our march was begun about February 20, 1864, and was not disturbed. A fair position was found at Bull's Gap, and then we distributed our commands in good camps from the Holston to the Nolachucky.

General Longstreet writes with pride of the strong position he was able to take for his winter quarters at Bull's Gap:

It would be difficult to find a country more inviting in agriculture and horticulture than East Tennessee, and its mineral resources are as interesting; but for those whose mission was strategic, its geographical and topographical features were more striking. Our position at Bull's gap was covered by a spur of the mountains which shoots out from the south side of the Holston River towards the north bend of the Nolachucky, opening gaps that could be improved by the pick and shovel until the line became unassailable. In a few days our line was strong enough, and we looked for the enemy to come and try our metal, until we learned that he was as badly crippled of the cavalry arm as we.

Secure in this stronghold, and relieved from the threat of immediate attack by the Federal forces in East Tennessee, Longstreet devoted his leisure time to dreaming up various plans for movements of the combined Confederate armies into Kentucky or Tennessee. These suggestions were not considered practical by the Richmond authorities, although Longstreet went to Richmond in person to press them. At length, on April 7th, he was ordered to move back with his army to Virginia, to rejoin General Lee on the Rapidan, where Lee was preparing to resist the advance by Grant's army expected to come as soon as the weather permitted.

The Confederate Congress adopted a resolution of thanks to "Lieutenant General James Longstreet and the officers and men of his command for their patriotic services and brilliant achievements", with praise for Longstreet's "great ability, skill and prudence in command"; but, despite these flowery words, it was generally recognized that Longstreet's East Tennessee campaign had been considerably less than brilliant or successful.

There was little or no military activity in East Tennessee during the summer of 1864, but before the year ended there was a flare-up of combat in that area, resulting in the tragic ending of the meteoric career of General John Hunt Morgan, whose spectacular exploits during the early days of the war had thrilled the whole South. Morgan and several of his officers had been captured at the unsuccessful conclusion of their Indiana-Ohio raid in the summer of 1863, and since then had been imprisoned in the Ohio state penitentiary at Columbus. On the cold, drizzly night of November 28th, 1863, Morgan and his six fellow-officers made their escape from the prison by tunneling under its walls. By a circuitous route through the South, Morgan made his way to Richmond, Virginia, where he arrived on January 7th and was given a tumultuous welcome.

Morgan was expecting to have his old command restored to him, and was ready to resume active service at once; but, to his surprise, discovered that General Bragg was using his influence to prevent this. At length, however, he was given official authority to reorganize his command, and he issued a proclamation for his scattered men to get together with him at a rallying point. Eventually, in the face of great and unexpected difficulties, and after an expedition into Kentucky, which was the source of much subsequent controversy, he was stationed in southwestern Virginia with what was left of his force—less than two thousand men, some of whom had no horses and some without arms. Aside from the duty of protecting the valuable salt works at Saltville, Virginia, Morgan seemed to have no definite objective in this area.

In September he and his force were ordered to move southward out of Abingdon, to meet a Federal column reported advancing in that direction from Knoxville. On the afternoon of September 3rd, at the head of 1600 men, he rode into Greeneville, where he planned to spend the night and advance the next morning. Basil Duke writes movingly of the tragic events of the next few hours:

Reaching Greeneville about 4 P. M., on the 3rd of September, he determined to encamp there for the night and move on Bull's Gap the next day. The troops were stationed on all sides of the place, and he made his headquarters in town at the house of Mrs. [Catherine D.] Williams. The younger Mrs. [Lucy] Williams left Greeneville, riding in the direction of Bull Gap at the first rumors of the approach of our forces, to give, we have always believed, the alarm to the enemy.

The Tennesseans of Vaughan's brigade (under Colonel Bradford) were encamped on the Bull's Gap road, and were instructed to picket that road and the roads to the left . . . The town, if all instructions had been obeyed and the pickets correctly posted, would have been perfectly protected. The enemy gained admittance unchallenged, through an unaccountable error in the picketing of the roads on the left. . . . About daylight a body of perhaps one hundred cavalry dashed into Greeneville and were followed in a short time by General Gillem's whole force.

It was the party that came first which killed General Morgan. His fate, however, is still involved in mystery. Major Gassett, of his staff, stated that they left the house together and sought to escape, but found every street guarded. They took refuge once in the open cellar of a house, expecting that some change in the disposition of the Federal forces would leave an avenue for escape, or that they would be rescued by a charge from some of the troops at the camps. They were discovered and pointed out by a Union woman. Gassett succeeded in effecting his escape. General Morgan made his way back to the garden of Mrs. Williams' house. Lieutenant X. Hawkins, a fearless young officer, charged into town with fifteen men and strove to reach the point where he supposed the general to be, but he was forced back. General Morgan was killed in the garden—shot through the heart. It is not known whether he surrendered or was offering resistance.

His friends have always believed that he was murdered after his surrender. Certain representations by the parties who killed him, their ruffianly character and the brutality with which they treated his body, induced the belief; and it was notorious that his death, if again captured, had been sworn. His slayers broke down the paling around the garden, dragged him through and, while he was tossing his arms in his dying agonies, threw him across a mule and paraded his body about the town, shouting and screaming in savage exaltation. No effort was made by any one except Lieutenant Hawkins to accomplish his rescue.

Thus, on the 4th of September, 1864, in a little village of East Tennessee, fell this almost unequalled partisan leader. But not only was the light of genius extinguished then and a heroic spirit lost to earth—as kindly and as noble a heart as was ever warmed by the constant presence of generous emotions was stilled by a ruffian's bullet. When he died the glory and chivalry seemed gone from the struggle and it became a tedious routine, enjoined and sustained only by pride and duty. . . .

His body was taken from the hands which defiled it by General Gillem, as soon as that officer arrived at Greeneville, and sent to our lines under flag of truce.

That General Duke may have been in error in his suspicion that General Morgan was betrayed by the younger Mrs. Williams is indicated by an account written in the *Confederate Veteran* in later years by the Hon. A. B. Wilson, of Greeneville:

In relation to the defeat and death of General Morgan many sensational and improbable stories have been published. The principal of these may be given under the following heads:

First. That he was betrayed by Mrs. Lucy Williams, a daughter-in-law of Mrs. Catherine D. Williams, who left the house after the arrival of General Morgan and, proceeding to the Federal camp, informed General Gillem as to the position of General Morgan and the disposition of his forces.

Second. That General Morgan was murdered, having been shot wilfully after he had surrendered.

Third. That after being killed and, as some writers have stated, before he was in fact dead, the body of General Morgan was placed on a horse before a Federal soldier and was paraded up and down the streets of the town. As to all these matters the true facts as evidenced by eye-witnesses will be given.

Mrs. Catherine D. Williams of Greenville was an aged lady, the widow of Dr. Alexander Williams who was a brother of Senator John Williams and Chancellor Thomas L. Williams, men of prominence in the early history of the state. Mrs. Williams was herself the only daughter of William Dickson, one of the earlier settlers of Greenville who in the mercantile business amassed a handsome fortune, all of which was given to Mrs. Williams, his child. The family of Mrs. Williams consisted originally of (a daughter) Mrs. Sneed, and three sons, William D. Williams, Thomas L. Williams and Joseph A. Williams. Thomas L. Williams was a captain in the Confederate army. William D. Williams was a volunteer member of General Morgan's command and came with him and his command to Greenville. Mrs. Joseph A. Williams was living with Mrs. Catherine D. Williams, her husband's mother. She was previous to her marriage a Rumbough of a prominent Virginia family and she had one brother, a captain in the Confederate army and another, probably a major in the quartermaster's service of the Confederacy. It was generally understood that she strongly sympathized with the Confederate cause in which her brothers were serving. At that time the Williams family at home consisted of the old lady, her daughter-in-law (Lucy Williams) and a sister of the latter—a Miss Rumbough, who was a visitor.

Mrs. Williams was the owner of a very large farm situated about three or four miles south of Greenville, containing more than 1,000 acres. From this farm Mrs. Williams drew her supplies, it being occupied by renters. . . . The road leading to this farm did not lead in the direction of Bull's Gap but led off at right angles to the Bull's Gap road.

On the afternoon of the day when General Morgan and staff arrived at the Williams mansion Mrs. Lucy Williams left the house, not on horseback as has been often stated, but in a buggy and with a small boy. From this fact and perhaps from other circumstances it was assumed that young Mrs. Williams proceeded all the way to Bull's Gap and as a traitor informed General Gillem as to Morgan's position and surroundings. Instead of doing so, she went to the farm . . . where she procured a lot of watermelons and placed them in the buggy with the evident intention of returning that evening and furnishing the melons as a treat for their distinguished guests. There had been that afternoon a very hard rain, and on account of the rain she could not return but spent the night at the farm house occupied by the renters, returned to the town the next morning and was conducted in by the Federal pickets—which added to the suspicion that she was the traitor. It is undoubtedly true that she encouraged this belief and in her conduct sought to ingratiate herself with the Federal officers to a degree that subjected her to serious censure. But the facts here stated have been substantiated by the witnesses who saw her, and as to these facts there can be no question. . . .

The person who actually did give the information as to the position of General Morgan's forces and where he was quartered, was a boy named James Leady whose father resided in Greenville. The following account is given as to his adventures and escape, but they are not vouched for as being absolutely authentic: He started down the road on an old gray horse after General Morgan's arrival and, being halted by the pickets and asked where he was going, said he was going to mill. It appears that he had a sack under him on the horse. There was a mill on the road, as was known to the pickets, and he was permitted to pass but was watched until he was seen to go beyond the mill. He was followed and asked further about where he was going and said that he had to go to the house of his uncle near Blue Spring more than half-way to Bull's Gap. He was near that point and was informed that he must be placed under arrest, but begged that at least he be permitted to go to his uncle's house. The guards agreed to go with him and await his coming out of the house, keeping charge of his horse. It was then growing dark and he hastily went into the house of his uncle, but passed immediately through the house into a corn field in which he made his escape and went on foot from there to Bull's Gap. From what he told, and explained by Colonel Edwin B. Miller, General Gillem and his officers, several of whom were perfectly well acquainted with Greenville and its surroundings, a good idea was easily formed as to the position of General Morgan and his forces. . . . As a reward for his services, the boy Leady was afterwards sent to school as the protege of General Gillem.

It was well in the night when General Gillem broke camp and started on his daring expedition. Those who were along say that the night was extremely dark and that it rained all the way with much thunder and lightning and but for the constant flashes of lightning they could scarcely have found their way. From Greenville to Bull's Gap the direction is nearly due west and consequently they were marching nearly due east.

It is stated that during the night Lieutenant Wilbur Carter reported to General A. A. Withen at headquarters that the Federals were advancing on the Warrensburg road. This appeared so improbable that it was not believed. It was remarked by one of the officers that no force would advance on such a night as this was; that General Morgan was tired and needed rest and there was no use in disturbing him with such an improbable tale. In the morning when the firing commenced on the streets it was believed by some of General Morgan's staff that it was only the soldiers firing off their guns on account of the rain the previous day, for the purposes of reloading that they might be sure that their charges were all right.

It seems that it was Miss Rumbough who first informed General Morgan that the Federals were in town and all around the square. He immediately got up and hastily putting on his pants, socks and his pistol belt with his pistols, but without his other clothing, he went out of the door leading into the garden. He went in the direction of Main street hoping to escape that way, but about this time the Federals appeared on Main street and he turned back. . . . in the direction of the vineyard, apparently with the idea that after the passage of the forces along that street he could cross the street and secure his horse, then in the Williams stable, and escape. He was in the vineyard about fifty yards from Depot street when another squad came along and, seeing him, the firing commenced, he also shooting with his pistols. He was shot and instantly killed by one James Campbell, a member of the Thirteenth Tennessee cavalry, a soldier of fortune who had deserted from the Confederate army and who, it appears, knew General Morgan personally. At the time he was killed General Morgan had two pistols on his person and, of one, four chambers were empty. He evidently fired these from the place where he was killed and those in the party with Campbell saw him shooting at them. . . .

Campbell after killing General Morgan threw his body on a horse in front of him and carried it back with him to the main force, where it was thrown or laid off on the ground. This was certainly an unjustified and unwarranted indignity, but he did not parade the body up and down the street on his horse as stated by some writers, and in fact had no time to do so, for they were close to the main force of the Confederates and it was necessary for them to retreat as soon as possible. It seems that the object of Campbell was to let it be known certainly that he was the man that killed General Morgan in the hope of a reward by promotion. He was given a lieutenancy in the Federal army.

When the body of General Morgan was identified after delivery at the main force of the Federals it was ordered to be placed in an ambulance and returned to Greeneville where, by order of General Gillem, it was washed and dressed and a burial case was ordered to be made for it, which was done by J. J. Mitchell, after which it was turned over, under a flag of truce, to his friends.

Following Morgan's death, the remnants of his force were placed under the command of Basil Duke, who was promoted to the rank of brigadier-general, under General John C. Vaughn. This organization made one more abortive effort to advance in East Tennessee, but it was beaten back. This was about the last activity in Tennessee of Morgan's renowned cavalry, that dynamic outfit the very name of which was during its heyday a source of pride to all those who rode with Morgan and a source of uneasy apprehension to its enemies as long as it existed.

Following the battle of Missionary Ridge and the failure of Longstreet's attack at Knoxville, General Grant on the 20th of December moved his headquarters to Nashville.

Nashville, says Grant, was the most central point from which to communicate with my entire military division, and also with the authorities at Washington. . . . Nothing occurred at Nashville worthy of mention during the winter, so I set myself to the task of having troops in position from which they could move to advantage, and in collecting all necessary supplies so as to be ready to claim a due share of the enemy's attention upon the appearance of the first good weather in the spring. I expected to retain the command I then had, and prepared myself for the campaign against Atlanta.

The Army of the Ohio had been getting supplies over Cumberland Gap until their animals had nearly all starved. I now determined to go myself to see if there was any possible chance of using that route in the spring, and if not to abandon it. Accordingly I left Nashville in the latter part of December by rail for Chattanooga. From Chattanooga I took one of the little steamers that had been built there, and, putting my horses aboard, went up to the junction of the Clinch with the Tennessee. From that point the railroad had been repaired up to Knoxville and out east to Strawberry Plains. I went by rail therefore to Knoxville where I remained for several days. General John G. Foster was then commanding the Department of the Ohio. It was an intensely cold winter, the thermometer being down as low as zero every morning for more than a week while I was at Knoxville and on my way from there on horseback to Lexington, Kentucky, the first point where I could reach rail to carry me back to my headquarters at Nashville.

The road over Cumberland Gap, and back of it, was strewn with debris of broken wagons and dead animals, much as I had found it on my first trip to Chattanooga over Waldron's Ridge. The road had been cut up to as great a depth as clay could be by mules and wagons, and in that condition frozen; so that the ride of six days from Strawberry Plains to Lexington over these holes and knobs in the road was a very cheerless one, and very disagreeable.

I found a great many people at home along that route, both in Tennessee and Kentucky, and, almost universally, intensely loyal. They would collect in little places where we would stop of evenings, to see me, generally hearing of my approach before we arrived. The people naturally expected to see the commanding general the oldest person in the party. I was then forty-one years of age, while my medical director was gray-haired and probably twelve or more years my senior. The crowds would generally swarm around him, and thus give me an opportunity of quietly dismounting and getting into the house. It also gave me an opportunity of hearing passing remarks from one spectator to another about their general. Those remarks were apt to be more complimentary to the cause than to the appearance of the supposed general, owing to his being muffled up, and also to the travel-worn condition we were all in after a hard day's ride. I was back in Nashville by the 13th of January, 1864.

Grant's plans to lead a spring campaign against Atlanta were upset by his unexpected advancement to the command of all the Federal armies, with the newly revived rank of lieutenant-general. This milestone in his career is simply recorded by Grant in his Memoirs:

The bill restoring the grade of lieutenant-general of the army had passed through Congress and became a law on the 26th of February. My nomination had been sent to the Senate on the 1st of March and confirmed the next day (the 2d). I was ordered to Washington on the 3d to receive my commission, and started the day following that. The Commission was handed to me on the 9th. It was delivered to me at the Executive Mansion by President Lincoln in the presence of his Cabinet, my eldest son, those of my staff who were with me and a few other visitors.

Grant's promotion also meant advancement for Sherman. Sherman, who was now making his headquarters in Memphis, tells of how he got the news of his promotion, and of the subsequent ceremonies at Nashville honoring Grant:

On the 14th of March I received from General Grant a dispatch to hurry to Nashville in person by the 17th, if possible. Disposing of all matters then pending, I took a steamboat to Cairo, the cars thence to Louisville and Nashville, reaching that place on the 17th of March.

I found General Grant there. He had been to Washington and back, and was ordered to return East to command all the armies of the United States, and personally the Army of the Potomac. I was to succeed him in command of the Military Division of the Mississippi, embracing the Departments of the Ohio, Cumberland, Tennessee, and Arkansas. General Grant was of course very busy in winding up all matters of business, in transferring his command to me, and in preparing for what it was manifest would be the great and closing campaign of our civil war. Mrs. Grant and some of their children were with him, and occupied a large house in Nashville [the residence of Major Cunningham] which was used as an office, dwelling, and everything combined.

On the 18th of March I had issued orders assuming command of the Military Division of the Mississippi, and was seated in the office, when the general came in and said they were about to present him a sword, inviting me to come and see the ceremony. I went back into what was the dining-room of the house; on the table lay a rosewood box, containing a sword, sash, spurs, etc., and round about the table were grouped Mrs. Grant, Nelly, and one or two of the boys. I was introduced to a large, corpulent gentleman, as the mayor, and another citizen, who had come down from Galena to make this presentation of a sword to their fellow-townsman. I think that Rawlins, Bowers, Badeau, and one or more of General Grant's personal staff, were present.

The mayor rose and in the most dignified way read a finished speech to General Grant, who stood, as usual, very awkwardly; and the mayor closed his speech by handing him the resolutions of the City Council engrossed on parchment, with a broad ribbon and large seal attached. After the mayor had fulfilled his office so well, General Grant said: "Mr. Mayor, as I knew that this ceremony was to occur, and as I am not used to speaking, I have written something in reply." He then began to fumble in his pockets, first his breast coat pocket, then his pants, vest, etc., and after considerable delay he pulled out a crumpled piece of common yellow cartridge-paper, which he handed to the mayor. His whole manner was awkward in the extreme, yet perfectly characteristic, and in strong contrast with the elegant parchment and speech of the mayor. When read, however, the substance of his answer was most excellent, short, concise, and, if it had been delivered by word of mouth, would have been all that the occasion required.

I could not help laughing at a scene so characteristic of the man who then stood prominent before the country, and to whom all had turned as the only one qualified to guide the nation in a war that had become painfully critical.

CHAPTER 14

☆ *"That Devil Forrest"*

D URING 1864 the principal military activity in the state of Tennessee was
that of General Nathan Bedford Forrest, who was constantly in motion
from the first till the last day of the year. Grant and Sherman, preparing
for an advance against Joe Johnston in the spring, were fearful that the Confederates would assign Forrest to the duty of crippling the railroad supply line
between Nashville and Chattanooga. So, their strategy was to keep Forrest so
busy in northern Mississippi, where he was then operating, that he would not be
able to move into Tennessee.

As a first step in this strategy, in February a formidable force was sent
out against him from Memphis under General Wm. Sooy Smith, but Forrest
crushingly defeated this task force, and sent Smith scurrying back to Memphis.

In March Forrest's strength was increased by the addition of 700 Kentucky
troopers, who joined him at his headquarters at Columbus, Mississippi. With this
addition to his command, he felt strong enough to move again into West Tennessee, marching through Corinth (to be used as a base) and Bolivar. On March
23rd a part of the command was detached under Colonel Duckworth to move
against Union City. The next day, as a result of Duckworth's success in giving
the Federals an exaggerated impression of his strength, the Federal garrison of
475 men, with their arms, equipage and horses were surrendered.

Forrest himself, with Buford's division, had moved against Paducah, Kentucky.
He was able to occupy the city for the greater part of March 25th, during which
time his men replenished their supply of stores, clothing and horses. Forrest quickly
realized, however, that the Federal troops in the fortification, supported by two
gunboats in the river, were too strong to be taken by storm, so he withdrew
and went into camp four miles south of the town, with 50 prisoners, about 400
horses and mules, and a much-needed addition to his supply of clothing and
military material.

Forrest, with the force under his immediate command, then moved back into
West Tennessee, establishing his headquarters at Jackson. Buford retired to

[256]

Dresden; and Chalmers, who had been left in Mississippi was ordered to join Forrest.

Forrest's next aggressive move, his attack on Fort Pillow on the Mississippi, was one which precipitated a long-lasting controversy, involving sensational charges of Forrest's "massacre" of the defending garrison. An account of the events leading up to the movement against Fort Pillow is given by Colonel Jordan:

Ever since his advent into West Tennessee Forrest had been distressed by well-authenticated instances, repeatedly brought to his notice, of rapine and atrocious outrage upon non-combatants of the country by the garrison at Fort Pillow. (Fort Pillow, abandoned by the Confederates in 1862, had only recently been re-activated and garrisoned by the Federals) And a delegation of the people of the town of Jackson and surrounding region now waited upon and earnestly besought him to leave a brigade for their protection against this nest of outlaws. According to the information received, the garrison in question consisted of a battalion of whites, commanded by Major W. F. Bradford (a Tennessean), and a negro battalion under Major L. F. Booth, who likewise commanded the post.

Many of Bradford's men were known to be deserters from the Confederate army, and the rest were men of the country who entertained a malignant hatred toward Confederate soldiers, their families and friends. Under the pretense of scouring the country for arms and "rebel soldiers", Bradford and his subalterns had traversed the surrounding country with detachments, robbing the people of their horses, mules, beef cattle, beds, plate, wearing apparel, money and every possible movable article of value, besides venting upon the wives and daughters of Southern soldiers the most opprobrious and obscene epithets, with more than one extreme outrage upon the persons of these victims of their hate and lust.

The families of many of Forrest's men had been thus grievously wronged, despoiled and insulted, and in one or two cases fearfully outraged, and many of his officers, uniting with the citizens of the country in the petition, begged to be permitted to remain to shield their families from further molestation. Of course this was impossible; but Forrest determined to employ his present resources for the summary repression of the evil and grievances complained of, by the surprise, if possible, and capture, at all hazards, of Fort Pillow; and the orders necessary to that end were issued on the 10th of April; Bell's and McCulloch's Brigades, with Walton's Battery—four mountain howitzers—being selected for the operation. . . .

Leaving Jackson on the morning of April 11th, Forrest overtook General Chalmers at Brownsville at 2 P. M., and to add another to the chances of success, ordered that officer to push ahead with the troops by a forced march, so that they might be in close proximity to Fort Pillow by daylight the next morning. The distance was 38 miles; it was raining, and so dense the darkness after midnight that it was difficult to distinguish the road or to see a file-leader. . . . Just before dawn the advance guard surprised the Federal pickets and captured all except one or two who, escaping to the fort just at sunrise, gave the first warning of the danger impending.

Just exactly what happened at Fort Pillow has long been a matter of controversy. The account of the affair in *Battles and Leaders of the Civil War* (one of the most restrained of all the Northern comments) gives some quotations from Forrest's official report, after making these introductory remarks:

Major Lionel F. Booth, 6th United States Heavy Artillery, who commanded Fort Pillow April 12th, 1864, was killed in the battle of that date, of which there is no circumstantial official Union report. From the data attainable it appears that the garrison consisted of 557 soldiers (about half of them colored troops), and that the killed, wounded and captured numbered about 400. According to the Confederate reports the prisoners, including wounded, numbered 237. The percentage of killed was extraordinarily large. The news of this fight created much excitement in the North and led to an investigation by the (Congressional) Committee on the Conduct of the War. This Committee reported that the Confederates entered the works shouting "No quarter"; and there then began "an indiscriminate slaughter, sparing neither age nor sex, white or black, soldier or civilian", and that this slaughter was not due to the excitement of the combat but was the result of "a policy deliberately decided upon".

This report of the Congressional Committee was printed by the Government and so widely circulated as a Republican campaign document in the 1864 elections that it was accepted as gospel truth by the Northern public, forming the foundation for the distorted view of Forrest and his character that was then and is still widely held in the North.

On the other hand, the people in the South denounced the Committee report as mendacious propaganda based on the testimony of survivors of the fort's garrison who were either deliberate perjurers or ignorant and tractable individuals who were led into giving the desired testimony concerning things of which they could not have had any actual knowledge. The report did develop the fact that there was never any actual, formal surrender of the fort, and that armed resistance continued even after Forrest's men had overpowered the defenders, the refusal to surrender accounting for most of the loss of life.

R. R. Hancock of the 2nd Tennessee Calvary unit in Forrest's command, who was a participant, gives his first-hand account of what happened at the storming of the fort, as he saw it:

Fort Pillow, first established in 1861 by the State of Tennessee, and still better fortified by the Confederate States Engineers, under the orders of General Beauregard, in March and April, 1862, is on the east bank of the Mississippi River, in Lauderdale County, some three and a half miles above Fulton, and just below the mouth of Coal Creek. The lines of works erected by the Confederates were upon a very extended scale—far too large to be of the least use or value to a garrison so small as that which the Federals habitually kept there, therefore they had freshly thrown up breastworks upon the highest part—perhaps fifty feet above the water level—of a bank or bluff which extended for several hundred yards nearly parallel with the river, leaving a space, comparatively level, between its base and the river bank proper, perhaps thirty to fifty yards wide. The fort was near the southern extremity of this bluff, it being the highest, and about seventy-five yards from the river. About one acre of land was inclosed by earth-works thrown up on three sides—north, south, and east. The wall was about eight feet high, exterior to which there was a ditch six feet deep and twelve feet broad. . . .

Upon the capture of the pickets, McCulloch's Brigade was pressed rapidly on with instructions to take up a position southward of the fort, and as near as possible to the river bank and work; therefore, McCulloch soon seized a position with his left flank on the river bank, about half a mile southward of the fort, the remainder of his line disposed in the ravines extending around and toward the north-east, in close proximity to a high ridge upon which were the old Confederate works, the most elevated point of which was occupied at the time by a Federal detachment. He then and there came to a halt to wait for Bell's Brigade (which was about two miles from the fort when the Federal guns first opened, a little after sunrise) to come up and take position.

As soon as up, Wilson's Regiment of Bell's Brigade was deployed directly in front to occupy the close attention of the garrison by an immediate, virgorous skirmish, while Colonel Barteau led the Second Tennessee rightward, winding his way as best he could through the woods to Coal Creek bottom, and there dismounting threw his men forward to a good position a few hundred yards north of the fort along the north-east face of a hill. From this position skirmishers were thrown forward to brush the small force of Federal sharp-shooters back from their advanced positions; this drew the Federal guns from both fort and gunboat upon our position. Meanwhile Colonel Russell threw his regiment forward to a position between Barteau and Wilson.

The investment was now complete, though it was at long range; and about this time, too (nine A. M.), General Forrest came upon the field, and about the same hour Major Booth, the Federal commander, and his adjutant by his side, were killed. Coming immediately to our position, thence along the top of the bluff upon which the fort stood, General Forrest made as close an inspection of the fort and its surroundings as he possibly could, thus ascertaining that the conformation of the ground around the Federal works was such as to afford protection to his troops, while two ridges, from four to five hundred yards distant, eastward and north-eastward from the enemy's position, gave the Confederate sharpshooters excellent cover, from which they completely commanded the interior of the Federal works, and might effectually silence their fire. He therefore decided at once to make a close investment, returned to our position and ordered Colonel Barteau to "move up".

Accordingly the Second Tennessee "moved up" to the top of the bluff and opened fire upon the Federal garrison. By dropping over a little to the right and moving along the side of the bluff facing the river, it gave us some protection from the garrison, while at the same time this move placed us in easy range and plain view of the gunboat, which moved up as we moved down, and when about opposite to us she turned broadside as though she was going to give us "Hail Columbia;" however, after maneuvering around for a while, as though she was trying to scare us off of that bluff without firing a gun, she finally came to a halt several hundred yards above the fort, and (to our great relief) remained a "silent spectator" during the rest of the engagement. (I do not know why Captain Marshall, the commander of the gunboat, ceased firing when he could have used his guns with such telling effect upon our regiment, unless it was because he was scarce of ammunition or afraid to open his port-holes, fearing we would kill his gunners.) Moving along this bluff to within about one hundred yards of the north side of the fort—perhaps some were nearer— Colonel Barteau halted and waited for the rest of the command to close up.

After advancing a short distance with our regiment, Forrest turned and went round leftward to move up the rest of Bell's Brigade as well as McCulloch's. Accordingly Russell's and Wilson's Regiments were thrown forward, to the left of Barteau's, to a position in which their men were well sheltered by the conformation of the ground. McCulloch, advancing about the same time, soon brushed the Federals back from the old Confederate intrenchments on the highest part of the ridge immediately in front of the south-eastern face of the work. The Federals fell back without further stand to their main work and the rifle-pit in its front, closely pressed by McCulloch, who seized and occupied the cluster of cabins on the southern face of the work, which were only about sixty yards from it, foiling an attempt on the part of the enemy to burn the buildings. He also carried and occupied the rifle-pit rightward, thus completing the investment at short range, extending from the river bank north of the fort to the river bank south.

These positions thus secured were fatal to the defense, for the Confederates were now so placed that artillery could not be brought to bear upon them with much effect, except at a mortal exposure of the gunners, while rearward of the advance line were numerous sharp-shooters, favorably posted on several commanding ridges, ready to pick off any of the garrison showing their heads above, or indeed, any men moving about within the circuit of, the parapets.

Fully satisfied of his ability to carry the position without difficulty or delay, but desiring to avoid the loss of life that must occur in storming the works, Forrest determined to demand the surrender of the place. Accordingly, causing the signal for a cessation of hostilities to be given, he deputed Captain W. A. Goodman, Adjutant-General on the staff of General Chalmers, to bear a flag of truce with a formal demand in writing, addressed to "Major L. F. Booth, commanding United States forces," as he was thought to be still in command. However, as we have seen, he had been dead for several hours, and the command had fallen into the feeble hands of W. F. Bradford, the commander of the odious Thirteenth Tennessee Battalion of Cavalry. Nevertheless, the answer received, after some delay, bore the name of Major L. F. Booth, and required an hour for consultation with his officers and those of the gunboat in regard to the demand for the surrender of his post and the vessel. On receiving this communication Forrest immediately replied, in writing, that he had not asked for, and did not expect, the surrender of the gunboat, but that of the fort and garrison, and that he would give twenty minutes for a decision. Moreover, so great was the animosity existing between the Tennesseans of the two commands, he added, that he could not be responsible for the consequences if obliged to storm the place.

During the period of the truce the smoke of several steamers were discovered ascending the river; and speedily one (the *Olive Branch*), crowded with troops and her lower guards filled with artillery, was distinctly seen approaching near at hand, and manifestly bearing directly for the beleaguered fortress. Apprehensive that an attempt would be made to land reinforcements from these steamers, Forrest promptly dispatched his aide-de-camp, Captain Anderson, with a squadron of McCulloch's Brigade, down to the river bank under the bluff and just below the southern face of the invested work. The *Olive Branch*, in her course, soon came so near that by opening with a volley on the mass of men with whom she was laden a heavy loss of life must have been inflicted; but Captain Anderson, limiting himself strictly to preventing the landing of any reinforcements during the truce, caused two or three admonitory shots to be fired at the pilot-house, with the immediate effect of making her sheer off to the opposite shore, and pass on up the river.

Some minutes later the answer to the second demand was brought out of the fort and handed to Forrest by Captain Goodman. It ran as follows: "Your demand does not produce the desired effect." The Confederate General exclaimed: "This will not do; send it back, and say to Major Booth"—whose name was attached—"that I must have an answer in plain English—yes or no!" Captain Goodman returned not long after with the Federal answer, a brief but positive refusal to surrender the post.

As soon as he had read this communication, turning to his staff and some officers around him, Forrest ordered that his whole force should be put in readiness for an immediate and simultaneous assault. After stimulating his troops with a few energetic words he, with a single bugler, rode to a commanding eminence, some four or five hundred yards east of the fort, from which he had a complete view of the field of operations, and scanning the field, and observing that all was ready, caused the signal to be given for the resumption of hostilities.

At the first blare of the bugle the Confederate sharp-shooters, at all points, opened a galling fire upon the hostile parapet, to which the garrison replied for a few moments with great spirit. But so deadly was the aim of the Confederates from their enfilading positions that their enemies could not rise high enough from their scanty cover to fire over at their foes, nor use their artillery on the southern face without being shot down. Consequently there was practically little resistance, when, a few moments later, the bugle still sounding the charge, the main Confederate force, surging onward as with a single impulse, leaped headlong into the ditch, and helping each other, they clambered nimbly, swiftly and simultaneously over the breastworks beyond, opening from its crest a fearful, converging fire, from all its forces, upon its garrison within.

In anticipation of this contingency Major Bradford, it appears, had arranged with the captain of the gunboat that, if beaten at the breastworks, the garrison would drop down under the bank and the gunboat would come to their succor and shelter them with its canister. The prearranged signal was now given, and the whole garrison, white and black, for the most part with arms in their hands, broke for the place of refuge and naval aid there expected, leaving the Federal flag still aloft on its staff. The gunboat, however, was recreant at this critical moment, and failed to give the least assistance; and no timely shower of canister came from its ports to drive back the Confederates, who swiftly and hotly followed after the escaping negroes and Tennesseans. As soon as we entered the fort two of the captured guns were turned upon the gunboat, which caused her to move further up the river in place of coming to the relief of the garrison, as the commander had distinctly agreed to do.

The left of the Second Tennessee entered the fort at the north-west corner, while the right extended westward down the bluff toward the river; and while they were pouring a volley into the right flank of the retreating Federals, the troops that had been stationed below the fort to watch the steamers, did likewise for the enemy's left flank. Thus being exposed to a fire from both flanks, as well as rear, their ranks were fearfully thinned as they fled down that bluff toward the river.

Finding that the succor which they had been promised from the gunboat was not rendered, nor at hand, they were greatly bewildered. Many threw themselves into the river and were drowned in their mad attempt to swim away from the direful danger which they apprehended; while others sought to escape along the river bank southward, as well as northward, and, still persisting in their efforts to get away, were shot or driven back. In the meantime, or as soon as he could reach the scene, Forrest, as well as Chalmers and other officers, interfered so energetically to stop the firing that it ceased speedily—ceased, in fact, within fifteen minutes from the time the bugle first sounded the charge.

The garrison, as a whole, be it remembered, did not surrender at all. When we poured over, on all sides, into the work they did not lay down their arms nor draw down their flag, but fled (some returning the fire of their pursuers) toward another position in which they were promised relief. Such was the animosity between the Tennesseans of the two commands, and as such is frequently the case in places taken by storm, some, no doubt, were shot after they had thrown down their arms and besought quarter; no such cases, however, happened to come under my immediate observation.

The first order now issued by Forrest was to collect and secure the prisoners from possible injury, while details were made from them for the burial of the Federal dead. Among the prisoners taken unhurt was Major Bradford, the commanding officer of the post since nine in the morning, and at his special request Forrest ordered the Federal dead to be buried in the trenches of the work, the officers to be interred separately from their men. Bradford was then temporarily paroled to supervise the burial of his brother, Captain Bradford, after which, under a pledge not to attempt to escape, he was placed for the night in the custody of Colonel McCulloch, who gave him a bed in his own quarters, and shared with him his supper. This pledge Major Bradford violated; taking advantage of the darkness and his knowledge of the locality, when his host was asleep, he effected his escape through the careless line of sentinels, and, in disguise, sought to reach Memphis.

Colonel Jordan tells of the ultimate fate of Major Bradford:

Major Bradford . . . was, several days afterward, recaptured in disguise. At first he affected to be a conscript, but being recognized was remanded to custody as a prisoner of war. He was then sent in charge of a party—a subaltern and some five or six men—to Brownsville. On the way he again attempted to escape, soon after which one of the men shot him. It was an act in which no officer was concerned, mainly due, we are satisfied, after the most rigid inquiry, to private vengeance for well authenticated outrages committed by Bradford and his band upon the defenseless families of the men of Forrest's Cavalry.

C. R. Barteau, colonel of the Second Tennessee Cavalry, and at one time during the battle in temporary command of Bell's Brigade, offers a plausible explanation of the large proportion of the defenders who were killed or wounded:

The troops in the fort had evidently been made drunk, for those we took were more or less intoxicated, and we found barrels of whisky and ale and bottles of brandy open, and tin cups in the barrels out of which they had been drinking. We also found water-buckets sitting around in the fort with whisky and dippers in them, which showed very clearly that the whisky had been thus passed around to the Federal troops. . . .

They made a wild, crazy, scattering fight. They acted like a crowd of drunken men. They would at one moment yield and throw down their guns and then would rush again to arms, seize their guns and renew the fire. If one squad was left as prisoners, it was soon discovered that they could not be trusted as having surrendered, for taking the first opportunity they would break loose again and engage in the contest. Some of our men were killed by negroes who had once surrendered.

As the summer of 1864 wore on and General Joe Johnston slowly fell back southward in Georgia before the steady and overwhelming pressure of Sherman's forces, Sherman spent much of his time looking back nervously over his shoulder, worrying about his attenuated supply line, growing longer every day. To his trained military mind it seemed inevitable that the enemy would recognize this as his Achilles heel and take action against it. He was particularly concerned about the activities of "that devil, Forrest" (as Sherman called him), and he grew increasingly insistent that sufficient Federal offensive activity should be maintained in Mississippi to keep Forrest occupied there and keep him off Sherman's back.

Sherman's fears were well founded. Early in May the Confederate authorities in Richmond, acting under Johnston's prodding, authorized a "prompt and vigorous" movement by Forrest into Middle Tennessee. Before this movement could get under way, however, General Stephen D. Lee (who had been placed in charge of operations in Mississippi and was now Forrest's superior officer) received word that Sherman in Georgia had telegraphed orders for "a threatening movement from Memphis to Columbus, Miss.", to prevent Forrest's moving on his communications. The Middle Tennessee invasion, therefore, was temporarily postponed in favor of an immediate defense against this raid.

The threatened raid from Memphis not materializing as promptly as had been expected, Forrest was again authorized to move into Tennessee, and was preparing to do so on June 1st; but on that very day the expedition ordered by Sherman moved out of Memphis with the boldly announced plan to "smash things" in Mississippi. The Federal force seemed amply capable of doing a smashing job, consisting of some 8,000 men—cavalry, infantry, artillery, wagon trains, etc.—under the command of General Samuel D. Sturgis. Forrest was hastily called back from the beginning of his movement to Tennessee, and on the 10th of June, with less than half as many men as Sturgis, he met the advancing Federal force at Brice's Cross Roads, near Guntown, Mississippi, and audaciously attacked them. The result was a surprisingly complete victory for Forrest, and Sturgis fled in disorder to Memphis, where he arrived to report the loss of 2,240 of his men, all his artillery and most of his wagons.

Sherman was enraged at the failure of Sturgis's effort against Forrest—even though it had at least temporarily effected his chief aim, to keep Forrest occupied elsewhere than on his supply line. And when Sherman was enraged he made himself heard. "I can not understand how he could defeat Sturgis with 8000 men," he complained in a letter to Secretary Stanton. He wasted no time in regrets, however, but at once started making plans for another similar (but larger) movement against Forrest. "I have two officers in Memphis that will fight all the time, A. J. Smith and Mower," he wrote Stanton. "I will order them to make up a force and go out and follow Forrest to the death if it costs 10,000 lives and breaks the Treasury. There will never be peace in Tennessee until Forrest is dead."

Accordingly, elaborate preparations were made in Memphis for another anti-Forrest expedition, to be headed by Major General Andrew J. Smith and Brigadier General Joseph R. Mower. General Cadwallader C. Washburne, in command at Memphis, was ordered by Sherman to give these two competent commanders a sufficient force of infantry, cavalry and artillery "to deal with Forrest handsomely". Mower was personally promised by Sherman that he would be promoted to the rank of major general if he could, as ordered, "pursue and kill Forrest".

On June 26th the Federal force moved out of Memphis. It consisted of 14,000 men, fully equipped, an army described by General Washburne as "ample to whip anything this side of Georgia". Forrest, now operating under the immediate command of General S. D. Lee, who was personally present, kept his scouts' eyes on Smith as he moved through New Albany and Pontotoc, proceeding cautiously and slowly. As was his custom, Forrest had no idea of fighting Smith until he could do so on his own terms. On July 14th, however, Lee decided to dispute the further advance of the Federal force at Harrisburg (on the outskirts of Tupelo), although the total Confederate force was about 9,000, opposed to Smith's 14,000.

The Confederates launched their attack early in the morning, but there was a lack of coordination in their efforts, and the assault was repulsed with considerable loss of life. Then and later there was controversy as to where the fault lay; but, regardless of the reason, it was indisputably a Confederate defeat. Surprisingly, however, the victorious General Smith started a retreat to Memphis the next morning, closely pursued by Forrest, who had been restored to command of the troops by General Lee. But Forrest was wounded in the foot during the fighting, and command devolved on General Chalmers, who hung on Smith's flanks until he was back at his starting point.

Smith lamely explained his retreat by stating that his supply of bread was running low, and Washburne accepted this explanation—but it was unsatisfactory to Sherman. "Order Smith to pursue and keep after Forrest all the time", Sherman telegraphed Washburne, and he notified Halleck that he had ordered Smith to advance again and "hang on to Forrest to prevent his coming to Tennessee." Spurred by Washburne and Sherman, Smith lost no time in making preparations for another go at Forrest and by the first of August had assembled a force of 18,000 men and was getting his movement under way. Forrest was still crippled by his wound, and active command of the Confederate force was in the hands of Chalmers—but, Forrest, riding in a buggy, was on hand and kept up with what was going on. General Lee was no longer on the scene, having been called to Georgia to take command of Hood's corps in the Army of Tennessee, after Hood had replaced Johnston as commander of that army. Lee was succeeded as department commander by General Dabney H. Maury, who made his headquarters at Mobile; and Maury promptly notified Forrest: "I intrust to you the operations against the enemy threatening an invasion of North Mississippi."

Forrest, in replying to Maury, pointed out that he had lost a large proportion of his officers and men in his recent engagements, but he concluded: "Nevertheless, all that can be done shall be done. I have not the force to risk a general engagement, and will restort to other means."

As Smith moved cautiously into Mississippi, proceeding to Holly Springs by rail, and then marching southward from the Tallahatchie, Forrest had his greatly inferior force divided into separate bodies designed to watch every possible route of advance and harass Smith as much as he could. Smith, waiting for delayed supplies, was progressing at a snail's pace, almost at a standstill, but about August 20th he moved on in the direction of Oxford, where Forrest (now back in the saddle) had stationed himself with about 4000 men.

Obviously with this meagre force he could not expect to make an effective fight against Smith's 18,000; the time had come to resort to those "other means" referred to in his letter to General Maury. On the evening of August 18th Forrest made known what he planned to do, and even his own men were amazed at the audacity of his plan. Leaving Chalmers in command of half of the force, Forrest with 2,000 picked men started out on a forced march around Smith's flank in a surprise raid on Memphis, far in Smith's rear. Chalmers was ordered to keep up a vigorous demonstration against the Federals for at least two days, to prevent Smith's discovery of Forrest's absence.

Memphis had been held by the Federal forces since its occupation in June, 1862, and had been so long removed from any suggestion of attack that the possibility of it was literally unthinkable. On the evening of Saturday, August 20th, the soldiers and civilians in the city retired to their night's rest with every reason to consider their security complete—but they had a surprise awakening ahead of them. As they slept, Forrest and his hardy riders were splashing through the mud and fog, approaching the city's outskirts, preparing to launch the thunderbolt of a dawn attack.

The Second Tennessee Cavalry was one of the units in this daring expedition, and R. R. Hancock of that outfit, wrote in his *Diary* an account of it replete with colorful details:

In spite of the mud, fog, darkness, and the great fatigue of our horses, General Forrest drew rein about three o'clock this morning at Cane Creek, only four miles from Memphis. By this time he was well informed in regard to the numbers and positions of the Federal troops, and the location of their prominent officers, as well as the exact position of the pickets on that particular road. There were fully five thousand troops, of all arms, in and around the city, for the most part negroes and one hundred days' men.

Directing his force to be closed up, and summoning the commanders of his brigades and detachments to the front, Forrest gave to each definite and comprehensive instructions as to the part assigned their respective commands in the approaching drama, and at the same time the necessary guides were distributed.

To a company commanded by Captain William H. Forrest was given the advance, with the duty of surprising, if possible, the pickets; after which, without being diverted by any other purpose, it was to dash forward into the city, by the most direct route, to the Gayoso House to capture Major-General Hurlbut and some staff officers who were known to be quartered at that hotel. Lieutenant-Colonel Logwood was to press rapidly after Captain Forrest to the Gayoso House, with the Twelfth (Green's) and Fifteenth (Stewart's) Tennessee Regiments, placing, however, detachments to hold the junction respectively of Main and Beale and Shelby and Beale streets, and to establish another detachment at the steamboat landing at the foot of Union street. Lieutenant-Colonel Jesse A. Forrest (with Wilson's Regiment from Bell's Brigade) was ordered to move rapidly down DeSoto Street to Union, and thence leftward, along that street, to the headquarters of General Washburne the Federal commander, whose capture it was his special duty to make. Colonel Neely was directed to attack, by an impetuous charge, the encampment of the one hundred days' men, across the road in the outskirts of Memphis, with a command composed of his own regiment (Fourteenth Tennessee), the Second Missouri, and the Eighteenth Mississippi. Colonel Bell, being held in reserve, with Newsom's, Russell's, and Barteau's Regiments—the latter under Captain DeBow—with Sale's section of artillery, was to cover the movement. And upon all commands the most rigid silence was enjoined, until the heart of the city was reached, and the surprise had been secured. These dispositions and orders having been made, the several detachment commanders rejoined their troops, formed them immediately into column of fours, and, at about a quarter past three A. M., the whole command was again put in motion at a slow walk.

Captain Forrest preceded the rest of his company some sixty paces with ten picked men. When within two miles of Court Square, the sharp challenge of the picket, "Who comes there?" was suddenly heard to break the stillness of the morning hour, also the Confederate Captain's cool and prompt reply: "A detachment of the Twelfth Missouri Cavalry with rebel prisoners." The customary rejoinder quickly followed, "Advance one." Captain Forrest rode forward in person, having previously, in a low tone, directed his men to move slowly but closely behind him.

As soon as he was in reach of the unsuspecting picket, mounted, in the middle of the highway, the Confederate officer felled his adversary to the ground by one blow with his heavy revolver, while, at the same instant, his men sprang forward and captured the picket-post of some ten or twelve men—dismounted at the moment—a few paces rearward, to the left of the highway, without any noise or tumult, except the discharge of a single gun, which, with no little anxiety, was heard by General Forrest, who was moving with the head of the main column only about one hundred yards rearward. Sending the prisoners immediately to the rear Captain Forrest pressed on for a quarter of a mile, when he encountered another outpost, which greeted him with a volley. The daring Confederates dashed forward, however, and scattered the enemy in every direction. But, unhappily, forgetting the strict orders to be as silent as swift in their operations, Captain Forrest's men shouted lustily, and the contagion spreading, the cheer was taken up and resounded rearward through the whole column, now roused to a state of irrepressible eagerness for the fray.

By this time the head of the column was in a few paces of the Federal camp, on the outskirts of the city; day was breaking, and a long line of tents was visible, stretching across the country to the eastward and westward of the highway nearly a mile. The alarm having been given, and the orders prescribing silence generally forgotten by his men, General Forrest directed his bugler (Gaus) to sound the charge, and all the bugles of several regiments took up and repeated the inspiring notes. Another cheer burst forth spontaneously from the whole line, and all broke ardently forward in a swift, impetuous charge.

Captain Forrest, dashing rapidly by the infantry encampment with his little band (some forty strong) encountered an artillery encampment (six guns) eight or nine hundred yards beyond. Sweeping down with a shout and a volley from their pistols, the Confederates drove the Federals from their guns, after killing or wounding some twenty of the gunners. This effected, they pressed forward into the city, and did not halt until they drew rein before the Gayoso Hotel, into the office of which Captain

Forrest and several of his companions entered without dismounting. In a moment his men, spreading through the corridors of that spacious establishment, were busily searching for General Hurlbut and other Federal officers, to the great consternation of the startled guests of the house. Some of the Federal officers, roused by the tumult, rushing forth from their rooms, misapprehending the gravity of the occasion, offered resistance, and one of their number was killed and some others captured, but General Hurlbut was not to be found. Happily for that officer, his social habits having led him out of his quarters the evening before, they had also held him in thrall and absent from his lodging throughout the night.

Unfortunately, Logwood was moving in rear of Neely, and, in attempting to pass, his men became so intermingled with Neely's that he was unable to push on and enter the city as soon as had been expected. The time thus lost proved to be precious moments, for the Federals, having been aroused by Captain Forrest, were flying to arms and into line and the artillery was being remanded. Order to push on into the heart of the city without halting to give battle on the wayside, Logwood, placing himself at the head of his men, pressed onward for some distance, running a gauntlet of small-arm volleys from the right, until a turn of the road brought him in the presence of a line of infantry directly across the way and sweeping it with their fire. Unswerved, on rushed the Confederates with their well-known yell, and burst through the opposing ranks.

Hastening onward, a battery was seen to the leftward, but commanding a straight reach of the road ahead, the gunners of which were busily charging the pieces. In view of the danger his command incurred from this battery, Logwood was obliged to charge and disperse those who manned it; and, giving the command to charge, his men swooped down upon their luckless enemy, a number of whom were knocked down at the pieces, while the rest were driven off before they were able to fire a gun. Resuming his charge toward the city, Logwood in a few minutes entered and galloped down Herando street to the market-house and up Beale, across Main to the Gayoso House, and his men were soon busily engaged in completing the search of that hotel for Federal officers.

The women and children and some men were screaming or crying with affright, or shouting and clapping their hands and waving their handkerchiefs with joy as they recognized the mud-bespattered, gray uniforms of the Confederate soldiery in their streets once more. Soon, indeed, the scene was one of memorable excitement. Memphis was the home of many of those gray-coated young riders who thus suddenly burst into the heart of their city that August morning, and the women, young and old, forgetting the costume of the hour, throwing open their window-blinds and doors, welcomed their dear countrymen by voice and smiles and every possible manifestation of the delight inspired by such an advent.

During the same time, Lieutenant-Colonel Forrest, speeding with his regiment toward the headquarters of Major-General Washburne, on Union Street, reached that point without serious resistance to find, however, the Federal commander had already flown, but several of his staff were captured before they could dress and follow their fleet-footed leader.

Colonel Neely dashed into the Federal encampment on the right of the road, while Captain DeBow threw the Second Tennessee into position (mounted) on the left, in support of Lieutenant Sale's section of artillery, which was thrown into position and opened upon the enemy about daybreak.

Meanwhile Neely had met serious resistance in the execution of his orders. The infantry—at least a thousand strong—which it was his part to attack, had been formed in line in time to receive his force with a warm fire of small arms. Seeing this check, General Forrest, who had remained with the reserves under Colonel Bell, led them rapidly by the right flank to reinforce Neely, but on the way developed a cavalry encampment just eastward of the infantry, from which the Confederates received a heavy fire. Being in advance, Forrest charged promptly with his escort (mounted) over intervening fences and through some gardens, dispersing the dismounted occupants of the encampment, and capturing nearly all their horses, with a number of prisoners.

Neely, at the same time making a vigorous onset upon the infantry, succeeded in driving them, with some loss, from their position; whereupon they and the dispersed dismounted cavalry took refuge in the extensive brick buildings of the "State Female College," several hundred yards distant, a strong defensive position. Followed by the Confederates, the enemy poured a noisy and annoying fire from behind the cover afforded by the college.

At this Forrest ordered up Captain DeBow with the Second Tennessee (dismounted), and also Lieutenant Sale with the artillery, and dismounting some other troops, made an effort to dislodge the Federals, and an animated skirmish ensued. A number of shells were thrown and exploded in the main building, but it soon became apparent the position was only to be gained at a loss far greater than was required for the success of the expedition, therefore the troops were withdrawn; not, however, until after we had suffered some loss, for the Federals had decidedly the advantage—they behind brick walls, while we had no protection. The Second Tennessee, being directly in front of the college, suffered more, perhaps, than any other portion of the command.

Finding that the enemy were rapidly rallying and assembling, Forrest had previously ordered the troops to evacuate the city and concentrate at the Federal infantry camp, which I have mentioned. This order found the Confederates greatly dispersed and widely spread over the city, many with the hope and object of meeting and greeting friends and kindred, but for the most part intent upon the discovery and appropriation of horses. Few, indeed, retained their regimental or, in fact, company organizations. As soon, however, as they could be collected, and Lieutenant-Colonels Logwood and Forrest then hastened to rejoin their commander, as directed; and as all the Confederates were now withdrawn from the city except some stragglers and those who had been captured or killed, General Forrest gave orders (about nine A. M.) for the whole force to withdraw. The object of the expedition having been in the main attained by the confusion and consternation into which the garrison had been thrown by his operations of that morning, it only remained, to secure the entire success of Forrest's plans, that General Smith should receive as early intelligence of the occurrence as possible, and therefore he retired to give General Washburne leisure and opportunity to telegraph the menacing situation at Memphis and ask for succor, which it was felt assured he would do.

Meanwhile, some of the Confederates who had lingered in the city, or had lost their way in the general dispersion which occurred, were chased out by a body of several hundred Federal cavalry, a strong detachment of which made a dash at some of Forrest's men still in the infantry camp, and just in the act of mounting. Seeing their jeopardy, Forrest sprang forward with a small detachment of the ever-reliable Second Missouri, that happened to be most convenient, and a close, sanguinary collision took place. Among the slain on this occasion was a Federal field officer (Colonel Starr), who, while urging his men forward, was mortally wounded by the hand of General Forrest. With this affair the contest terminated, and the Confederates moved back southward on the Hernando road for about a mile, when they were halted and directed to exchange their jaded horses for those captured in the city, some four hundred in number.

Company C, Second Tennessee, under the gallant A. B. McKnight, stood on guard in the rear while the command was halted here. It was now found that some six hundred prisoners had been brought away, including some citizens, and many convalescent soldiers, who, when the alarm was given, having fled from their hospitals into the streets, had been captured. Nearly all were bare-headed, and numbers were without shoes or clothing, except that in which they slept. After some delay at this point the march was resumed about noon, but on reaching Cane Creek it was apparent that few of the prisoners were able to walk in their shoeless condition, while the convalescents were utterly unable to make such a march as was impending. General Forrest therefore dispatched a flag of truce by Captain Anderson, accompanied by a captured staff officer, to propose, as an act of humanity, that the prisoners in his possession be exchanged for those of his own command taken that morning, and that the rest would be turned loose on parole, provided General Washburne would accept the arrangement as binding; but in the event that this proposition was rejected, he would wait at Nonconnah Creek for the necessary clothing to be sent out. A little after two P. M. Captain Anderson returned with General Washburne's reply, to the effect that, having no authority to recognize the proposed parole of the prisoners, he could not do so, but thanking Forrest for the proffered privilege of supplying them with clothing, that should be done as speedily as possible. After some delay, Colonel W. P. Hepburne and Captain H. S. Lee, two officers of the Federal army, appeared with a flag of truce and clothing for both officers and men, which was promptly and properly distributed.

This done, the prisoners were drawn up, and after examination by surgeons, the able-bodied men were selected, some four hundred in number, and mounted upon the led horses to accompany the command. The others—that is, the sick or disabled and all citizens—were then marched back across the Nonconnah and turned adrift to return to Memphis, but with the promise exacted not to bear arms, or otherwise injure the Confederate cause, until they should be regularly exchanged.

General Forrest took advantage of this opportunity to return to General Washburne his handsome blue uniform which one of the raiding troopers had picked up as a trophy when Washburne's bedroom was invaded. Not to be outdone in the amenities of warfare Washburne shortly afterwards sent through the lines to Forrest under a flag of truce a full suit of Confederate gray he had had made by Forrest's own Memphis tailor.

Private Hancock goes on with his story:

Another difficulty now presented itself in connection with the remaining prisoners. Exposed since leaving Oxford to the continuous heavy rains, and in the swimming of streams, the rations of the command, it was found, had been almost all destroyed, and there were consequently none for issue to the prisoners. In this dilemma, with that readiness which ever served him, General Forrest, before leaving Nonconnah, wrote to General Washburne, and setting forth in emphatic terms this inability to feed his prisoners, suggested, as Washburne would not receive them on parole, that he should at least send something that night for them to eat on the road to Hernando, where he would be found. This communication having been dispatched, Forrest resumed his movement toward Hernando, at which place—seventeen miles distant—he arrived in four hours, and then halted for the night.

Monday, 22d.—About daylight, Colonel Hepburne, Captain Lee, and several Federal officers, overtook the Confederate command with two wagon-loads of supplies, of the contents of which, after issuing two days' rations to the prisoners, enough was left for the whole command for a day.

Remaining at Hernando, as if intending to retire no further, Forrest gave his men rest until the Federal officers with the subsistence wagons had left to return to Memphis, when, about eight A. M., he rapidly resumed his march to Panola, which place he reached by ten o'clock that night.

Forrest's sensational raid into Memphis immediately had the hoped-for effect —General Smith's invasion of Mississippi was brought to a sudden stop and he and his forces ordered back to the defense of the city. Forrest established his temporary headquarters at Grenada, Mississippi, where his force was reorganized and given a short rest. Soon, however, they were in the saddle again. This time they were actually started on what had been so long planned—a raid into Middle Tennessee to disrupt Sherman's supply line and disrupt his communications.

Forrest moved swiftly through north Alabama, capturing (by strategem) the strong Federal blockhouse and its garrison at Athens, and destroying other blockhouses, railroad bridges and trestles as they pressed on into Tennessee. As they approached Pulaski, the Federal pickets were encountered and pushed back; but before they could proceed further they encountered stronger opposition:

A heavy Federal force was developed in line of battle, stretched across the turnpike and railroad—here about 400 yards apart—and on a range of hills affording an excellent position. It was a mixed force of cavalry, artillery and infantry, apparently not less than 6,000 strong; while the Confederates present did not number over 3300 men and four guns. Nevertheless their leader resolved on the offensive, dismounting them, deployed Buford's and Johnson's small divisions across the roads as Kelley, still mounted was launched to make a detour to the eastward and gain the Federal rear. . . . A running skirmish was kept up for five or six miles, in the course of which, the enemy halting frequently, turned and made battle at every favorable position, until Forrest, concentrating his forces, deployed and threw his men forward with his wonted aggressive tactics. Then, in each instance, they withdrew till finally, about three P. M., they filed into position behind their works in Pulaski. These consisted of a chain of detached redoubts of commanding positions, interlinked by rifle-pits, the whole furnished with artillery and bristling with abatis.

Manifestly nothing was to be achieved by the sword-in-hand process here, and it had been folly to have attempted the offensive, even had not the force in occupancy been greatly superior to that under Forrest. However, he made a menace of an attack upon the southern and eastern faces; pushing forward a strong skirmish line, he pressed it slowly but steadily up to within 400 yards of the Federal intrenchments by nightfall. After dark a broad long belt of campfires, by his orders, blazed on a ridge about a mile and a half from the threatened part of the Federal works. Maintaining his pickets close up to the enemy, and renewing the campfires about nine o'clock, the Confederates were quietly formed and at ten o'clock drew off by the road to the eastward, in the direction of Fayetteville, with the purpose of striking the Nashville and Chattanooga Railroad at and in the vicinity of Tullahoma. That railroad was the main channel of supply and recruitment for Sherman's army, then at Atlanta, Georgia, and Forrest's object was to destroy as much of the track and as many of the bridges upon it as possible. The rain, however, began to pour down, and the night became soon so dark that the ordnance train could not be forced along over the miry, rugged roads of the country, and the command was halted for the night after a short march of six or seven miles.

But at daybreak on the 28th [of September] the movement was resumed, and though the route was by narrow cross-ways, through a broken, extremely rough country, made boggy by recent hard rains, nevertheless the command, much of the time at a sharp trot, marched forty miles and bivouacked at dark five miles beyond and northward of Fayetteville. Still pressing on the next day toward Tullahoma, till within fifteen miles of that place, Forrest there was met by scouts with the tidings that a heavy column of Federal infantry was advancing from Chattanooga to meet him, and that the forces which he had left in the lurch, intrenched at Pulaski, were now on the way by rail through Nashville to confront him at Tullahoma. Thus anticipated, the Confederate commander found it expedient to make a radical change in his plan of operations.

Captain John W. Morton with his artillery was taking an active part in this expedition, and he tells an amusing story of an episode on the march where General Forrest was tricked by one of his own men into showing some of that discretion which is reputed to be the better part of valor:

The roads were ordinary country roads, very muddy after the recent rains and much cut up by the passage of the artillery. Captain Andrew McGregor was struggling with a captured caisson which had stuck in the mud and refused to budge, when General Forrest road up. General Forrest, thinking the men were not expending sufficient energy in the effort, began to upbraid them.

"Who has charge here, anyhow?" he thundered.

"I have, General," replied Captain McGregor.

"Then why in hell don't you do something?" shouted General Forrest, proceeding to utter other emphatic utterances.

Captain McGregor sprang up. "I'll not be cursed out by anybody, even a superior officer," he roared and, seizing a torch, he rammed it violently into the caisson. General Forrest seemed stupefied for a moment by the insanity of thrusting a lighted torch into a caisson full of powder, then clapped spurs to his horse and rode away as fast as he could, shouting a warning to the others. Reaching his staff, he asked: "What infernal lunatic is that just out of the asylum down there? He came near blowing himself and me up with a whole caisson full of powder."

The members of the staff knew the caisson was empty, and everybody laughed heartily, General Forrest readily joining in as he saw the point. It was noticed, however, that he never used profanity to Captain McGregor after that.

Realizing the futility of continuing his efforts to break the Nashville and Chattanooga Railroad, in the face of so much opposition being brought to bear on him, Forrest quickly decided to exert his efforts in another direction. "The situation", Colonel Jordan says advisedly, "was extremely precarious, and one indeed that required a large measure of coolness and judgment for extrication." Fortunately for Forrest, however, coolness and judgment were two qualities with which he was generously endowed, and he promptly began to exercise them. As Jordan tells it:

Forrest, therefore, resolved to sub-divide his command. One detachment, of 1500 men and the artillery and wagon train, he placed under General Buford, with orders to move swiftly upon Huntsville, seize that place if practicable, and afterward, destroying as much of the railroad thence to Decatur as he could, throw his command south of the Tennessee at that point, if the means were found there. Putting himself at the head of the other detachment, likewise about 1500 strong, he proposed to move rapidly across the country to Spring Hill, strike the railroad there and break it up between that point and Columbia, and at the same time drawing after him hostile forces that otherwise would be sure to follow Buford and prevent, most probably, the escape of the Confederate wagon-train and artillery across the Tennessee river. He had also received information, through citizens, that a vast amount of army stores had been collected at Johnsonville, on the Tennessee River, the terminus of the Nashville and Northwestern Railroad, destined and essential for the Federal forces at Chattanooga and Atlanta. This depot, and the bridges on the railroad leading to it, it was likewise his purpose to destroy, if the condition of his horses on reaching Spring Hill would warrant him in undertaking it.

Detachments of Federal troops were converging on Forrest from all directions in an effort to cut him off before he could across the Tennessee River on his withdrawal from Middle Tennessee, and there were confident predictions that he would be hemmed in and destroyed. The resourceful Forrest, however, was able by the exercise of characteristic energy and ingenuity to get his men and equipment safely across the river, and on October 6th he was back again at Cherokee, Alabama, where he had started out on September 21st. In his official report he summarized the effects of his foray:

During the expedition I captured 86 commissioned officers, 1274 non-commissioned officers and privates, 67 government employees, 933 negroes, besides killing and wounding in the various engagements about 1000 more, making an aggregate of 3360, being an average of one to each man I had in the engagements. In addition to these I captured about 800 horses, seven pieces of artillery, 2000 stands of small arms, several hundred saddles, fifty wagons and ambulances, with a large amount of medical, commissary and quartermaster's stores, all of which have been distributed to the different companies. The greater damage done to the enemy was in the complete destruction of the railroad from Decatur to Spring Hill, with the exception of the Duck River bridge. It will require months to repair the injury done to the road.

Forrest's own casualties in the expedition were 47 killed and 293 wounded, a total of 340.

Among the Federal forces put into motion to intercept Forrest and prevent his crossing the Tennessee was a detachment of infantry from Johnsonville, under Colonel George S. Hoge, supported by a flotilla of gunboats. Their objective was Eastport, where they were supposed to land and fan out and break the Memphis and Charleston railroad at and near Iuka. Forrest had arrived safely at Cherokee before he heard of this expedition, but he promptly sent Colonel D. C. Kelley with 500 men and a section of artillery to take position at Eastport to prevent the Federals' landing there. Kelley arrived at his destination in time to conceal his men and his guns on the river bank, before the Federal expeditionary force (two gunboats and three transports loaded with three regiments of infantry and a battery of artillery) got there. Colonel Hoge in his official report tells of his hot reception:

On nearing Eastport the gunboat *Key West* went above the landing, and seemed to be satisfied that there was no enemy near, and I immediately landed the troops. Lieutenants Lytle and Boals, as soon as they could land their horses, started out to reconnoitre, and about 500 yards off the landing came upon the pickets of the enemy. A masked battery (I think it was a battery of at least six rifled guns), and shortly after a battery of at least three rifled guns at Chickasaw, opened on us. I immediately went on shore and had a line of battle formed. The enemy had got a perfect range of the transports, every shot doing more or less execution. One of the gunboats (*Undine*) had become disabled and was dropping down the river, and the *Key West* followed her. I ordered the troops to be placed on board. I then went on board the transport *City of Pekin*, when a shell from the enemy struck a caisson of the battery on board the *Kenton*, exploding it and setting fire to the boat. Immediately after this a caisson exploded on the *Aurora*, setting fire to her, and also bursting her steampipe. A scene of confusion then began. The boats, in spite of all I could do, backed out, parting their lines, leaving about two-thirds of the command on the shore. The troops that were left on the bank were commanded to keep in good order and proceed down under the river-bluff and they would all be taken on board. A number were thus rescued. I am sorry to have to report the loss of the four guns of the battery.

Keeping supplied with food and clothing was a never-ceasing problem to the armies on both sides. It was an equally serious and painful problem to the civilian population on the "home front", becoming increasingly severe as the war-

time years rolled by. Since the Federal occupation of Memphis in 1862 the surrounding area of Tennessee and northern Mississippi had been thoroughly drained
of foodstuffs, livestock, and other supplies. The women, children and old men
living in this devastated area, to a great extent, had no other source of food
than Memphis, and from that source only with the greatest difficulty. Permits to
purchase food must be obtained and then arrangements must be made for hauling
it. The experience of a woman living in Holly Springs at this time was typical.
She was fortunate enough to be able to get a pass to go through the lines to
Memphis, carrying her young baby in her arms, as there was no one at home with
whom to leave it; also she was able to arrange for transportation in a wagon
driven by a neighbor friend who was doing some more or less surreptitious trading
with the enemy. She has left an enlightening account of her trip to Memphis and
back in October of 1864:

Starting very early in the morning, we arrived in Memphis before the close of
the day. At this time the purchase of goods was hedged about with many difficulties.
You had to beg them before you could buy them.

The General in command of the post had refused to grant any permits, but he
being temporarily absent, his substitute granted a number to his friends, of whom my
brother happened to be one. After a permit was obtained it was subjected to a board
of supervisors, who hacked it to their heart's content, and it frequently came back
to its owner so much mutilated as to be hardly worth having. These permits were
limited to a very few days, and if by any accident the owner was detained in the city
beyond the limit they were forfeited. . . .

My neighbor's wagon and mules were on his plantation, fifteen miles below Memphis, and Nonconnah Creek having been rendered unfordable by a recent freshet, I
waited, in the greatest anxiety, day after day for their arrival. Finally the last day of
grace arrived, and I found myself obliged to have my effects hauled on drays outside
the picket lines, there to await the coming of the wagon. The picket lines were three
miles from the city, and if I could have gone so far on my way home it would have
been convenient enough; but, while my road lay directly east, the wagon was coming
from the south, and I had to go in that direction to meet it.

On every road leading out of the city there were stations where traveller's effects
were overhauled, and every package compared with the permit. In addition to this, we
were subjected to a most disagreeable personal examination. Fortunately the woman
who performed this most disgraceful duty was out of the way, and a young officer had
undertaken to perform the task of personal inspection. I could not resist the temptation
to tease the young fellow a little, and insisted on his undressing the baby, who I
assured him from his weight might have any amount of gold and silver hidden about
him. He positively declined to touch the baby, and thoroughly ashamed of his un-
dignified position and occupation, passed us by with a very cursory examination.

On arriving at the farm-house where we were to pass the night, we were delighted to find that the wagon had already arrived, and we soon had it filled with
meal, flour, bacon, dry goods, children's toys, etc., ready for a very early start in the
morning. Next morning, just at daybreak, I took my seat on a hard box, hemmed in
on all sides by packages and barrels, with my baby in my lap, and no companion but
the driver, an old family servant. These were the circumstances under which I set
out on my long, weary, perilous journey homeward.

We were obliged to make a wide circuit in order to keep outside the picket lines,
for if we had once gotten inside of them we would not have been allowed to come
out again. There was no road, so we had to find our way through woods and hollows,
often retracing our steps. Whenever we came in sight of a picket station we were
halted, catechised and overhauled. I underwent six of these detentions during the day.

Once when a number of negro soldiers had been nursing and romping with my baby, I found that his shoe was gone, and from that time his chief occupation was in kicking off his stocking.

After many worries and detentions we at last emerged from the woods into our homeward road, but the last beams of the setting sun as they shot down the long, dusty track, reminded me that the day was done, and we were just six miles from Memphis. We pushed on for six miles more, but our team was jaded, we had eaten nothing all day, and the air growing chill we determined to seek a shelter for the night. But where should we stop? I knew that the country was infested by robbers and desperate characters of every kind, and I remembered with horror an encounter we had had with a drunkard on our way to Memphis.

I would say to myself, "I will certainly stop at the next place," but as I approached it my courage would fail, and I would decide to drive on a little further. At last the old man grew so tired and sleepy that he began to remonstrate, and seeing a light about a quarter of a mile away in the woods I ordered him to make for it. In response to our application we were told that we could not be accommodated, so we had to find the main road and take up our weary journey again.

After going what seemed to us for hours, we drew up in front of a little white house, and in response to our "hallo," a woman's voice said, "Who's there?" I shall never hear a sweeter voice than that woman's! All my fears were gone in a moment, and I walked into the house perfectly confident that I should receive care and protection, and I certainly did need it. I had sat all day long in one position, on a hard box, with a heavy baby in my arms, who, at every jolt of the wagon, pounded me as though I had been in a mortar. I could not sit up for a moment longer, but went supperless to bed, while two sweet girls (shall I every forget them?) took charge of the child.

After various disturbing and dangerous vicissitudes the next day and evening, she finally reached Holly Springs late at night, and it is easy to appreciate the sincerity of her words as she writes: "As I laid my tired head upon my pillow that night (or rather morning), I prayed that the Lord would "shorten those days" and send us peace.

Forrest had hoped that when he got back to Cherokee from his Middle Tennessee raid he might be able to take a short leave of absence for rest and some badly needed relaxation from the pressure under which he had been operating so long. But there was no rest for the weary. On the contrary, he had hardly arrived at Cherokee before he received orders from Lieutenant General Richard Taylor, now in command of the department, "to start at the earliest practicable moment into West Tennessee, in order to interrupt the navigation of the Tennessee River and to destroy at Johnsonville the immense stores which the Federal government were gathering at that important center of distribution".

General Taylor gave no indication as to why this movement against Johnsonville was considered so imperative, but subsequent developments showed that it was of particular importance and significance in the over-all Confederate strategy at this time. Sherman in Georgia had stretched his lifeline almost to the breaking point, and it was thought that a successful blow at Johnsonville could be effective in stopping the steady stream of supplies flowing his way from this important rail-head.

Forrest was fully aware of the fact that the assignment given him was one of those things that is easier said than done, but he sensed the great importance of it, and on October 12th he dutifully replied to General Taylor:

I will move into West Tennessee in a few days, and you may rely on my doing all I can towards accomplishing your desires and in facilitating your suggestions. . . . It is my present design to take possession of Fort Heiman, on the Tennessee River below Johnsonville, and thus prevent all communication with Johnsonville by transports. It is highly important that this line be interrupted, if not entirely destroyed, as I learned during my recent operations in Middle Tennessee that it was by this route that the enemy received most of his supplies at Atlanta. . . . The great, predominating, absorbing desire is to cut Sherman's line of communication.

By the 29th of October Forrest had his depleted force (now down to about 3,000 men) pretty well deployed at strategic points along the west bank of the Tennessee. Buford, with Chalmers in cooperation, had his men and his artillery judiciously placed at Fort Heiman, and a few miles up the river Bell's brigade, with part of Morton's battery was in position near Paris Landing, with his guns commanding a mile-long straight stretch of the river. All this had been accomplished without the Federals having any idea that this formidable ambush had been prepared for them—but who would ever have suspected that a cavalry force would have the impudence to think of attacking enemy naval vessels?

Forrest in his official report gives a modestly condensed account of how quickly and thoroughly his ambush scheme was crowned with success:

On the morning of the 29th, the steamer *Mazeppa*, with two barges in tow, made her appearance. As she passed the battery at Fort Heiman supported by Brigadier-General Lyon, she was fired upon by one section of Morton's battery and two 20-pounder Parrott guns. Every shot must have taken effect, as she made for shore after the third fire and reached the opposite bank in a disabled condition, when she was abandoned by the crew and passengers, who fled to the woods. A hawser was erected on this side of the river and she was towed over, and on being boarded she was found to be heavily loaded with blankets, shoes, clothing, hard bread, &c. While her cargo was being removed to the shore, three gun-boats made their appearance and commenced shelling the men who were engaged in unloading the *Mazeppa*. They were forced to retire and, fearing the boat might be captured, Brigadier-General Buford ordered her to be burned.

On the 30th the steamer *Anna* came down the river and succeeded in passing both the upper and lower batteries, but was so disabled that she sunk before she reached Paducah. The *Anna* was followed by two transports (the *J. W. Cheeseman* and the *Venus*) and two barges under convoy of the gun-boat *Undine*. In attempting to pass my batteries all the boats were disabled. They landed on the opposite side of the river and were abandoned by the crews, who left their dead and wounded. Lieutenant-Colonel Kelley, with two companies of his regiment, was thrown across the river and soon returned to Paris Landing with the boats. The steamer *J. W. Cheeseman* was so disabled that she was ordered, with the two barges, to be burned; the gun-boat was also burned while moving up the river to Johnsonville. The *Venus* was recaptured by the enemy on November 2, but was destroyed November 4 at Johnsonville by my batteries.

Fortunately, Dr. Wyeth in his account of the affair, gives considerably more of the colorful details of this unusual and sometimes amusing day's activities. In telling of what happened when the *Mazeppa* was riddled by the Confederate artillery and driven aground on the far side of the river, where she was abandoned by all on board except the captain, he says:

As the Confederates did not have even a canoe or skiff, volunteers were called for to swim the river and take possession of the boat. Private W. C. (Claib) West of

Company G, Barteau's Second Tennessee regiment, bravely offered his services. Stripping himself, although the water at this season of the year was cold, and strapping his six-shooter around his neck and shoulders in order to keep it dry, the plucky soldier, seated astride a piece of driftwood, with a fragment of plank as a paddle, encouraged by the cheers and jocular remarks of his comrades, who lined the bank to witness this daring feat, made his way safely across. The captain of the steamer, who had refused to desert his boat, promptly surrendered to the intrepid Confederate and, in courteous recognition of his daring, reached down over the gunwale of the boat and assisted the volunteer from his frail raft on to the steamer's deck. Private West and the captain now launched the boat's yawl and rowed to the opposite shore and returned with a detail of troopers who proceeded to make a hawser fast to the steamer and, carrying the other end across, soon warped the prize to the western shore. Forrest's men now found themselves bountifully supplied with blankets, shoes, clothing and all the necessaries and not a few of the luxuries of life. It was the richest capture in many a day.

Captain Morton tells that General Buford accompanied the boarding party that returned to the *Mazeppa* in the yawl, and of what he found there:

Among the luxuries on board a jug of French brandy came to light, and as the boat was being pulled across General Buford, who was on the hurricane deck, raised the jug to his lips. The men on the bank chaffingly called to him not to take it all, and the General replied: "Plenty of meat, boys; plenty of hard-tack, shoes and clothes for all the boys; but just whisky enough for the General."

R. R. Hancock supplies a footnote to this by-play, telling how the redoubtable Private Claib West, who had effected the capture of the *Mazeppa*, managed to obtain possession of the demijohn and fled with it, hotly pursued by Buford. West was able to evade the general long enough to fill his own canteen, whereupon he dutifully returned the demijohn to his thirsty superior officer.

Dr. Wyeth goes on with his story, telling how

Forrest now conceived the novel idea of manning the captured boats and using them in cooperation with his land force in the proposed attack on Johnsonville and the Federal flotilla there. Colonel W. A. Dawson was ordered to take charge of the fleet, and with a volunteer crew of "horse marines" raised the spurred commodore's flag on the *Undine*. The two twenty-pounder Parrotts were placed upon the *Venus*, and Captain Gracey was placed in command. . . .

"Commodore" Dawson was directed to proceed up the river towards Johnsonville, but not to venture beyond the support of the batteries, which with the troops would march along the road parallel with the bank of the river. As Dawson went on board his vessel he said to Forrest: "General, I will go with these boats wherever you order, but I tell you candidly I know very little about managing gunboats. You must promise me that if I lose the fleet you won't give me a cursing when I wade ashore and come back on foot." Forrest said: "No, Colonel, you will do the best you can; that is all I want. I promise not to haul you over the coals if you come home wet; but I want you and Gracey, if you see that you are going to be caught, to run your boats into the bank, let your men save themselves as best they can, and then set the steamers on fire." A trial-trip was now made with the fleet, and although the boats behaved awkwardly enough to frighten a river-man, since these land-lubbers were able to maintain steam enough to overcome the force of the current and to keep the boats from running into the woods it was deemed a sufficient experience to justify an engagement with the enemy.

On November 1st the "horse marines" steamed slowly and cautiously up the river, keeping in close touch with the troops and artillery that were plodding along the bank in the direction of Johnsonville. Forrest's sailors were, for the present at least, enjoying their novel situation and, as occasion would offer, spoke words of affected sympathy to their unfortunate comrades who had to ride horses and drive artillery. Their sarcasm even went so far as to offer to carry their guns and forage-sacks if the cavalry-men would only wade out in the stream and hand them on board. The men on shore, however, were equal to the emergency and, while appreciating the kindness of their "web-footed" comrades, declined assistance on the ground that the sailors would soon be drowned by the Yankee gunboats, and their guns and forage sacks were too valuable to be risked in such hands.

These words, spoken in jest, proved next day to be painfully close to the truth. The two boats, forgetting Forrest's cautionary words, ran ahead of the artillery and were attacked by two Federal gunboats. The *Venus* was quickly dis-abled, so that Colonel Dawson ran her into the bank and escaped with all his men, although he neglected to burn the vessel as instructed. The next day the *Undine* was also attacked and forced ashore, but Captain Gracey was able to set her on fire before escaping to the canebrakes on the bank.

All this horse-play with the gunboats was a side-show to the main purpose of Forrest's expedition: the destruction of Johnsonville and its immense stock of stores intended for the use of Sherman's army. During the night of the 3rd and early morning of the 4th, Forrest (without being observed by the Federals) got all his artillery into position on the west bank of the river, concealed by the lay of the land and the undergrowth there.

Johnsonville, on the eastern bank of the river, was the terminus of the railroad line from Nashville, and was the transfer point for stores brought by river boats to this rail-head. The Federal government had built warehouses at this location, and on the hills immediately back of the town there were gun emplacements for a strong defensive artillery force.

Captain Morton, who was to open the attack by the firing of his guns, (writing in the third person) tells of looking across the river that morning and sizing up the situation of the enemy, who were evidently unaware of any impend-ing attack:

Two gunboats with steam up were moored at the landing. . . . A number of barges clustered around, negroes were loading them, officers and men were coming and going, and passengers could be seen strolling down to the wharf. The river banks for some distance back were lined with quantities of stores, and two freight trains were being made up. It was an animated scene, and one which wore an air of complete security. . . . Above the whole frowned the guns and the fort. . . .

Then the opening shot was fired by Captain Morton's two guns opposite Johnson-ville, and immediately the remaining nine guns followed with a deafening roar. The scene changed, as if a magician's wand had been suddenly waved over it. Spurts of steam and smoke broke from the boats, showing that the range had been gauged with pretty fair accuracy; the crews dropped their washing, hauling, and packing, and jumped into the water like rats deserting a sinking ship; the passengers who had been sauntering around in the neighborhood of the wharf rushed wildly up the hillside, and everybody made for shelter.

The gunboats and the fort returned the fire with spirit and some damage, but, owing to the advantageous position selected for the Morton Battery, it could not be reached, and continued to ply the enemy with unabated energy. The sharpshooters joining in, the opposite bank was soon enveloped in a steady rain of fire. At the third discharge of the Confederate battery the boiler of one of the gunboats was perforated, and the agonized screams of the wounded and scalded could be plainly heard across the river. For forty minutes the cannonade continued with one unceasing roar. Flames spread from boat to boat, and spread rapidly to the warehouses and piles of hay, corn, and other stores along the bank. Soon the whole bank was a solid sheet of flame, soaring splendidly into the air.

As Captain Morton passed from battery to battery, directing the firing, he encountered General Forrest at one of the guns. The General was accompanied by Generals Bell and Buford and Major Allison. Forrest was himself acting as gunner, Major Allison, from his post of observation behind a tree near the bank, acquainting him with the effect of his shots. When a shot fell short, General Forrest would exclaim: "A rickety-shay! A rickety-shay! I'll hit her next time!" In ordering the range changed, he called: "Elevate the breech of that gun lower!" With ready good humor he joined in the laugh that greeted these amateur orders and continued to bombard the enemy steadily. After the recoil occasioned by the shots, General Bell and General Buford would push the gun back up the bank.

The fumes of roasting meats and coffee, burning sugar and liquor, and other tantalizing odors floated across the river, causing the always hungry Confederates to caper in an ecstasy of appetite, but there was no way of crossing the river. Also there was no way of saving the stores, as was evidently the opinion of the Federals, for they made but few efforts to check the flames, as their appearance was greeted with such an effective shower of shot that, according to the official reports, the soldiers could not be forced to expose themselves. The buildings and stored supplies that had covered acres of ground were soon reduced to mere heaps of ashes and crumbling piles of blackened refuse.

General Forrest, mud-stained and smoke-begrimed, rode from point to point, encouraging the men and keeping a close watch on the movements of the enemy. When it became apparent that the Federals had given up all hope of saving the situation, he ordered the firing to cease.

Forrest, in making his report, said:

Having completed the work designed for the expedition, I moved my command six miles during the night by the light of the enemy's burning property. The roads were almost impassable, and the march to Corinth was slow and toilsome, but we reached there on November 10th, after an absence of over two weeks, during which time I captured and destroyed four gunboats, fourteen transports, twenty barges, twenty-six pieces of artillery, and $6,700,000 worth of property, and captured one hundred and fifty prisoners. General Buford, after supplying his own command, turned over to my chief quartermaster about nine thousand pairs of shoes and one thousand blankets. My loss during the entire trip was two killed and nine wounded.

Captain Henry Howland, assistant quartermaster at Johnsonville, in his report to Brigadier General J. L. Donaldson, Chief Quartermaster of the Department of the Cumberland, at Nashville, tried to minimize the loss and damage as much as possible, but it was impossible to conceal the fact that the affair was of disaster proportions from the Federal standpoint:

At about 2 p.m. the enemy were discovered planting batteries directly opposite, also above and below, our warehouses and levee. The gun-boats opened fire upon them, as did also our batteries upon the hill. After some twenty minutes' firing a reply was received from all the rebel batteries, and for nearly thirty minutes the cannonading was the most terrific I have ever witnessed. The gun-boats fought magnificently, and continued firing for more than twenty minutes after they were all disabled, when Lieutenant Commanding King was compelled to order them abandoned and burned.

Our position was now most critical, our whole front, with the large warehouse and transfer building, stores, and transports, uncovered and almost unprotected. A large rebel force (as it has since been ascertained by trustworthy and reliable men who were captured from the transports below) of 13,000 men under Generals Forrest, Chalmers, Buford, Bell, and Lyon, with thirty-six pieces of artillery, twenty of them 20-pounder Parrotts, was on the opposite bank of the river, the small force of volunteer employes under Colonel Peterson, being the only force we could rely upon to face the enemy and defend our position. It was at the juncture—it having become evident the rebels would endeavor to cross sufficient force under the cover of their guns to obtain possession of our transports, they already having in their possession the cutter and gig of the *Undine*—that Colonel Thompson, upon the recommendation of Lieutenant Commanding King and other officers, directed me to destroy by fire all the transports, which direction was immediately complied with (the water being of insufficient depth to submerge them below the main deck by scuttling, which would therefore only temporarily disable them).

Soon as the transports were fired the enemy directed their fire upon the warehouses and the large pile of stores on the levee. The bursting of a shell soon fired the stores on the levee; also, the intense heat of the burning boats, which had been driven against the wharf by the strong wind, fired the stores in another place. The flames spread rapidly, and soon communicated to the small transfer building, which, with its contents, was speedily consumed. Soon as I learned that the stores on the levee had caught fire, I directed Captain Montandon with a large force of employes to extinguish the flames, if possible, but owing to the great heat and the constant fire of the sharpshooters, together with the batteries, they were able to accomplish but little; an occasional shell was thrown into town at intervals during almost the entire night.

At about 7 o'clock on the morning of the 5th the rebels again opened their batteries upon the town and shelled it right vigorously for about one hour as a farewell salute, when, all hope of crossing the river in any large force having been destroyed by the destruction of the transports, they moved away, thus terminating the attack upon Johnsonville. I cannot at this time state with accuracy the whole amount of loss, yet from our most careful estimates (including the transports and barges) I am confident the loss will but little, if any, exceed $1,000,000.

That Captain Howland's report was not entirely convincing or satisfactory is indicated by the fact that Colonel James A. Hardie, Inspector General of the U. S. Army at Washington, promptly sent his assistant, Lieutenant Colonel William Sinclair, to Johnsonville to conduct an investigation into "the circumstances attending the destruction of a large amount of property on the Tennessee River between October 28th and November 5th". After giving a detailed description of the military activity involved, Colonel Sinclair's report concluded with these damning words:

It is claimed by Colonel Thompson and others that there was danger of the steamboats falling into the hands of the rebels, as they had the two small boats of the *Undine* in their possession with which to cross the river and seize them. The armed force at Johnsonville was sufficient to have prevented any of the rebel force from crossing the river in two small boats at or near Johnsonville. The firing of the boats was premature. They could have been temporarily disabled by scuttling and removing parts of their engines. The boats were fired at 3 p.m. at the time the wind was blowing on the levee, whereas if they had waited until the wind changed, the stores on the levee and in the warehouse, where the loss was the greatest, would have been saved. The property on the steam-boats and barges should have been landed between October 30 and November 4.

After the fire a general system of theft was inaugurated, stealing clothing, hospital stores, and anything they could lay their hands upon. I was informed that some of the officers of the gun-boats helped themselves to clothing, and directed their men to take what they wanted. The soldiers and quartermaster's employes came in for their share of the plunder.

On the evening of the fire the railroad agent at Johnsonville, C. H. Nabb, ran off with a train of cars loaded with clothing and some 400 men from gun-boats. On arriving at Waverly, twelve miles from Johnsonville, he detached the engine and tender and went to Nashville, leaving the train at Waverly. The boxes on this train were broken open and a considerable amount of clothing stolen. This man, Nabb, was still in the employ of the Government when I was at Johnsonville.

The total money value of the property destroyed and captured during the operation of the rebels on the Tennessee River, including steam-boats and barges, is about $2,200,000.

Colonel Thompson estimated the rebel force operating on the left bank of the Tennessee at 13,000 men. . . . I think this estimate of the rebel force is too large.

Colonel Thompson and Captain Howland are responsible for the destruction of the boats and other property at Johnsonville.

Before leaving Johnsonville Forrest had received a message from General Beauregard instructing him, as soon as he had accomplished his purpose at Johnsonville, to move to Middle Tennessee and cooperate with General Hood in his advance on Nashville. On the night of the 6th of November Forrest camped at Perryville, where he had planned to cross the river with his complete command and move to join Hood. No boats could be found there, and he undertook to build rafts; but the rising river was so full of driftwood that it was found unsafe to use the rafts for the transfer of men or horses. After working at it all day of the 7th, some 400 of Rucker's men had been transferred to the other side of the Tennessee, but it was seen that it would be impossible to cross the whole command here. Accordingly, Rucker was ordered to proceed with his men to Mt. Pleasant, there to await Forrest and the rest of the command, who would march in the direction of Corinth, and there to Florence. One of those on this march tells that the roads were in such wretched condition that as many as sixteen horses were used to haul a single cannon, and the ox-teams of farmers were impressed to help move the guns through the mud. Eventually, however, the command reached Cherokee, where they were transferred by railroad to Florence, where they reported to General Hood on November 18th.

CHAPTER **15**

☆ *Hood's Invasion of Tennessee*

THE Army of Tennessee had been having a rough time of it in Georgia during the long, hot summer of 1864. Under General Joseph E. Johnston it had been falling back slowly but steadily ever since Sherman had moved out of Chattanooga early in May and attacked Johnston's army in its position around Dalton. There had been almost constant, daily skirmishing, and two or three full-scale battles such as New Hope Church and Kennesaw Mountain; but Johnston's tactics were entirely defensive—and such tactics maddened President Jefferson Davis in Richmond.

When Johnston had at length retreated south of the Chattahoochee River, followed by Sherman, getting closer and closer to Atlanta, it was more than Davis could stand. On July 17th he curtly telegraphed Johnston that he was relieved from command of the Army and Department of Tennessee, which he should immediately turn over to General John B. Hood, who had been advanced to the temporary rank of General for this purpose.

Hood was a native of Kentucky, where he was born June 1, 1831. He graduated from the Military Academy at West Point in 1853, and in 1861 was serving in Texas as a first lieutenant in the Second Cavalry regiment of the United States Army commanded by Colonel Albert Sidney Johnston, with Robert E. Lee as lieutenant colonel. When Texas seceded Hood resigned his commission and offered his services to the Confederacy. Serving with the Army of Northern Virginia he distinguished himself for headlong gallantry and leadership, commanding successively a regiment, a brigade and a division. He was wounded at Gettysburg, losing the use of his left arm; at Chickamauga (serving under Longstreet) he was severely wounded in his right leg, which was amputated. When he returned to active duty in February 1864 he was promoted to the rank of lieutenant general to command a corps in Johnston's Army of Tennessee, and he was serving in this capacity when he superseded Johnston.

Hood, recognizing that he was expected to abandon the defensive and assume the offensive, fought Sherman in a series of engagements around Atlanta which resulted in the Confederates' defeat and loss of possession of the city. Following this disaster, President Davis left Richmond for a visit to Hood and his army at Palmetto, Georgia. The only change resulting from this visit was that General Beauregard was called to a meeting with Davis at Augusta, where he was placed at the head of a new "Military Division of the West", embracing the departments of both Hood and General Richard Taylor.

In the ensuing discussion between Davis and his generals, it was agreed that the most effective immediate strategy would be for Hood to move his army back north of the Chattahoochee and strike the railroad in Sherman's rear. This movement, put into effect about the first of October, had the desired effect, causing Sherman to strike out with some 65,000 of his men in pursuit of Hood, leaving only one corps of his army to hold the depopulated city of Atlanta.

Maneuvering and skirmishing northward along the line of the Western & Atlantic Railroad, within two weeks both armies were in North Georgia just about where they had started in May. After resting a day or two at Dalton, Hood surprised Sherman by marching his army across to Gadsden in northeastern Alabama, whereupon Sherman moved his force to Gaylesville, about 25 miles northeast of Gadsden, where he encamped for a week of inactivity while waiting for Hood to make the next move. In leaving Atlanta he had belligerently declared that he would follow Hood "wherever he goes"; but when Hood stopped, Sherman stopped—at a safe distance—and showed no aggressive tendencies.

Beauregard joined Hood at Gadsden for a discussion of strategy, and here it was that Hood proposed the daring idea of a bold movement into Tennessee aimed at the destruction of the Nashville and Chattanooga Railroad (Sherman's lifeline) and the possible capture of Nashville. After talking the matter over for two days, poring over their maps, Beauregard authorized what Hood proposed. The only condition he imposed was that Wheeler and his cavalry must be left south of the Tennessee; but, to take Wheeler's place, he promised that Forrest would be ordered to join Hood after he had crossed the river.

So, on October 22 Hood started with his army for Guntersville, where he intended to cross the Tennessee and make a direct strike against the railroad at Stevenson and Bridgeport. But the ambitious Tennessee campaign had not been under way twenty-four hours before it struck a snag. Hood relates that the first night out from Gadsden he got word that Forrest was then in West Tennessee, and could not immediately join him. He could hardly be expected to operate north of the river without cavalry, so he changed his line of march to a route westward to cross at Decatur. Decatur, however, was found to be too strongly held to be taken by storm.

Beauregard, who had joined the march before the army reached Decatur, was upset by these delays; but there was nothing for him to do with make the best of it. Now that they had deviated so far to the westward from their original target, Beauregard thought they might as well abandon the idea of doubling back to attack Stevenson and Bridgeport but should instead go straight on into Middle Tennessee and try to capture Nashville with its garrison and great store of supplies, while the cavalry operated to destroy the railroad between Nashville and Chattanooga. Hood agreed to this, so they marched on to Tuscumbia, where the river could be crossed more easily and where Hood hoped to be able to find shoes and other supplies for his men.

Sherman, dozing at Gaylesville, did not learn of Hood's march from Gadsden until October 26th, and by then Hood was at Decatur. This decided Sherman's own plans. He made up his mind to leave Hood to General Thomas, who had been sent back to Nashville, with such force as could be concentrated there, while he took the principal part of his army and marched off southward through Georgia to the seacoast. Sherman returned from Gaylesville directly to Atlanta and, after burning the city, set forth on the morning of November 16th on his famous March to the Sea. Thus was created a situation unique in military history: two opposing armies, theoretically campaigning to destroy each other, deliberately marching in opposite directions.

When Hood had arrived at Tuscumbia, Sherman thus summarizes the Federal defensive force opposed to him:

General Thomas was at Nashville, with Wilson's dismounted cavalry and a mass of new troops and quartermaster's employes amply sufficient to defend the place. The Fourth and Twenty-third Corps, under Generals Stanley and Schofield, were posted at Pulaski, Tennessee, and the cavalry of Hatch, Croxton and Capron were about Florence watching Hood. Smith's (A. J.) two divisions of the Sixteenth Corps were still in Missouri, but were reported as ready to embark at Lexington for the Cumberland River and Nashville. Of course General Thomas saw that on him would likely fall the real blow, and was naturally anxious. He still kept Granger's division at Decatur, Rousseau's at Murfreesboro, and Steedman's at Chattanooga, with strong railroad guards at all the essential points intermediate, confident that by means of this very railroad he could make his concentration sooner than Hood could possibly march up from Florence.

Sherman in his *Memoirs* says of the status of things before he cut loose from Thomas and started on his march to the sea:

On November 11th General Thomas and I exchanged full despatches. He had heard of the arrival of General A. J. Smith's two divisions at Paducah, which would surely reach Nashville much sooner than General Hood could possibly do from Florence, so that he was perfectly satisfied with his share of the army.

If Sherman actually thought that Thomas was satisfied with the force allotted him, he was very much mistaken. Thomas's biographer Van Horne, reflecting the general's real sentiments, says:

General Thomas did not state that he had heard of the arrival of A. J. Smith's two divisions at Paducah, but said that he had "heard nothing from him since last report." He did not assure Sherman that he was all ready; he did not urge him to go ahead, nor did he promise unconditionally that he would ruin Hood if he advanced from Florence. . . . Thomas was conscious on the 12th of November that he was not then prepared to engage the enemy.

But if Thomas was unhappy, so was Hood. The success of Hood's plan of campaign depended on celerity of movement, but the delays he encountered at Tuscumbia were many and maddening. In spite of his request weeks before that the railroad from Corinth be repaired, nothing had been done when he got there, and a gap of ten miles existed between Tuscumbia and Cherokee, near Corinth. This thwarted his expectation of picking up supplies and getting promptly across the river. Plagued by one harassing difficulty after another, he spent three valuable and fateful weeks chafing at the delay but unable to do anything about it. The fall rains had set in, and the work of repairing the railroad slowed almost to a standstill. A pontoon bridge had been thrown across the river, but the continuous rainfall brought a sharp rise in the waters of the Tennessee, and after part of Lee's corps had got across and gone into camp at Florence the bridge was partly submerged, the approach roads were impassable, and the crossing had to be suspended. Word came from Forrest on November 4th that he was still west of the river across from Johnsonville, following his destruction of that railhead and its supplies, transports and gunboats. Hood, of course, was glad to learn of the damage done the enemy, but he was growing impatient for Forrest to join up.

While Forrest was still floundering in the seemingly bottomless mud of the West Tennessee roads, Hood telegraphed President Davis on November 6th that he hoped to march for Middle Tennessee by the eighth or ninth of the month, and that "General Beauregard agrees with me as to my plan of operation." Davis in reply advocated that Hood should endeavor to beat Sherman in detail "and subsequently, without serious obstruction or danger in your rear, advance to the Ohio River." Hood responded that he had been delayed by the rains, lack of supplies and Forrest's delay in joining him, but he said: "You may rely upon my striking the enemy whenever a suitable opportunity presents itself, and that I will spare no effort to make that opportunity."

Hood was not able to launch his march on the eighth or ninth, as he had promised Davis, for unavoidable delays continued to multiply. On the 13th he crossed over the river himself and established his headquarters at Florence, a few days later the remainder of Lee's corps was able to get across, then Forrest and his men arrived; but renewed rains held up the crossing of Stewart and Cheatham a few more days, and it was not until the morning of November 21st that Hood and his army were able to move forward.

The three corps, aggregating about 30,000 men, marched along separate roads, all in a generally northward direction, the immediate goal being Columbia to the northeast, forty-four miles south of Nashville on Duck River. "I hoped," Hood says, "by a rapid march to get in rear of Schofield's forces, then at Pulaski, before they were able to reach Duck River." Leaving Florence, Cheatham's corps was on the left (west) marching on the road to Waynesboro; Stewart on the right on the Lawrenceburg road; with Stephen D. Lee's corps on the country roads between the two main highways. Forrest's cavalry to the number of about 8,000, operated in front of the infantry, having left Florence two days ahead, and Hood relates that Forrest had no trouble in driving the enemy cavalry, under Hatch and Croxton, "from one position to another."

Hood's hope for a "quick march" soon faded as his columns set out in the midst of a prematurely early blast of sleet and snow and rain, accompanied by freezing temperatures, with the roads soon churned up into quagmires which alternately froze into hard ruts and thawed into tenacious mudholes.

W. J. Worsham of the Nineteenth Tennessee Infantry, in Strahl's Brigade, writes feelingly of a private soldier's impression of that opening march:

We started out from Florence early in the morning of November 21st, one of the coldest days of the winter, in rain, sleet and snow. The wind blew almost a hurricane in our faces and, with the snow, was almost blinding. All day long we plodded through this storm, so slow we could hardly keep warm. Late in the evening we halted for the night, passing it without rest or comfort to our weary and and cold bodies. We had gone only about twelve miles, and a hard day's travel. The next morning the storm had not abated, but had grown in intensity; yet on we went, combatting wind, sleet and snow. The second night we went into camp about eighteen miles from our camp the night before, filed into the woods after dark. The snow and ice covered everything, and we had a jolly time in starting our fires. The trees, being frozen, fell quickly and with a crash and a rattle, falling among the men, which kept them on the lookout all the time from being caught beneath them. It is needless to say, we began our third day's march under difficulties and hardships, and we camped that night in four miles of Waynesboro.

General Schofield, in command of the Federal advanced forces at Pulaski, was a young man of almost exactly the same age as General Hood, and they had been classmates at West Point. Schofield, in writing of his West Point days, describes Hood as "a jolly good fellow, a little discouraged at first by unexpected hard work; but he fought his way manfully to the end. He was not quite so talented as some of his great associates in the Confederate army, but he was a tremendous fighter when occasion offered." Schofield goes on to say of his old school-mate:

Hood was not well up in mathematics. The first part of the course he found very hard—so much so that he became discouraged and seemed much depressed. He asked me which I would prefer to be, "an officer of the army or a farmer in Kentucky?" I replied in a way which aroused his ambition to accomplish what he had set out to do in coming to West Point, without regard to preference between farming and soldiering. He went to work in good earnest, and passed the January examination, though by a very narrow margin. From that time on he did not seem to have so much difficulty. When we were fighting each other so desperately, fifteen years later, I wondered whether Hood remembered the encouragement I had given him to become a soldier, and came very near thinking once or twice that perhaps I had made a mistake. But I do not believe that public enmity ever diminished my personal regard for my old friend and classmate.

Schofield also explains the details of how he happened to be in Pulaski, charged with the duty of checking Hood's advance into Tennessee. This resulted, he points out, from the change made by Sherman in his proposed plan of operations after he learned of Hood's movement towards Tennessee:

General George H. Thomas, commanding the Department of the Cumberland, whose headquarters were at Nashville, was already at that place, and was directed by General Sherman to assume command of all the troops in the three departments under Sherman's command, except those with the latter in Georgia, and to direct the operations against Hood.

Thomas had in his department at that time only the garrisons and railroad guards which had been deemed essential during the preceding operations in Georgia; and many of those were soon to be discharged by expiration of their terms of enlistment, their places to be supplied by new regiments coming from the rear. General A. J. Smith's corps, then in Missouri, about ten thousand strong, was ordered to Tennessee, and Sherman also ordered Stanley, with the Fourth Corps, about twelve thousand men, to return from Georgia to Tennessee and report to Thomas. Stanley had started by rail to Tullahoma, and was to march, as he did, from the latter point to Pulaski, Tennessee, which had been selected as the point of concentration for Thomas's forces. This was the situation when I returned to the army and reported to General Sherman.

Schofield, who had been absent from the front after the fall of Atlanta, attending to the business of his own department, goes on to tell how, upon his return to the army, he heard for the first time of Sherman's proposed "march to the sea" and of the troops he had provided for Thomas. He says that he told Sherman that the force at Thomas's command was much too small to stop Hood if he advanced into Tennessee, and requested Sherman to send him back with his Twenty-Third Corps to join Thomas. Accordingly, on October 30, Sherman ordered Schofield to march with his corps to the nearest point on the railroad and report by telegraph to General Thomas for orders. Telling about it, Schofield says:

At first General Thomas ordered me to move by rail to Tullahoma, and then march across to Pulaski, as Stanley was doing. But just then Forrest with his cavalry appeared at Johnsonville, on the Tennessee River west of Nashville, and destroyed a great quantity of property, General Thomas not having sufficient force available to oppose him; hence on November 3 Thomas ordered me to come at once by rail to Nashville with my corps, where I reported to him with the advance of my troops on November 5. He then ordered me to go at once with some of my troops to Johnsonville and dispose of the Confederate cavalry there, and then to return to Nashville and proceed to Pulaski, to take command of all the troops in the field, which would then include the Fourth Corps, my own Twenty-third, except the detachment left at Johnsonville, and the cavalry watching Hood toward Florence. My duty at Johnsonville, where I left two brigades, was soon disposed of; and I then returned to Nashville and went at once by rail to Pulaski, arriving at that place in the evening of November 13. . . . On the 19th General Thomas repeated to me the same orders he had sent to General Stanley, in these words: "If the enemy advances in force, as General Hatch believes, have everything in readiness either to fight him at Pulaski if he advances on that place, or cover the railroad and concentrate at Columbia should he attempt to turn your right flank."

Commenting on the fact that "the season of Hood's invasion of Tennessee was extremely unfavorable for aggressive operations, and hence correspondingly favorable for the defense", Schofield says candidly that "we had ample time in which to make the necessary dispositions to oppose him".

Our cavalry, writes Schofield, gave us accurate information that the enemy was advancing on the 21st, when Cox with Wagner in support, was ordered to interpose between the enemy's cavalry and Columbia; while Stanley, with two divisions of the Fourth Corps, marched from Pulaski to that place, and our cavalry moved on the enemy's right to cover the turnpike and railroad. The whole army was in position at Columbia November 24, and began to intrench. Hood's infantry did not appear in sight until the 26th. . . . We held our intrenched position in front of Columbia until the evening of November 27, inviting an attack, and hoping that Thomas would arrive with, or send, reinforcements in time to assume the offensive from Columbia; but reinforcements did not come, and the enemy did not attack. It became evident that Hood's intention was not to attack that position, but to turn it by crossing Duck River above; hence the army was moved to the north bank of the river in the night of the 27th.

It is interesting now to read Hood's account of his own thoughts and plans and activities at this juncture, after he arrived at Columbia and found Schofield there ahead of him:

The enemy having formed line of battle around Columbia, Lee's Corps filed into position with its right upon the Mount Pleasant pike; Stewart's formed on Lee's right, his own right flank extending to the Pulaski pike; and Cheatham established his left on the latter pike, with his right resting on Duck river. Army headquarters were established at the residence of Mrs. Warfield, about three miles south of Columbia.

The two armies lay opposite each other during the 27th. The Federals being entrenched, I determined not to attack them in their breastworks, if I could possibly avoid it, but to permit them to cross undisturbed to the north bank of Duck river that night, as I supposed they would do; to hasten preparations, and endeavor to place the main body of the Confederate Army at Spring Hill, twelve miles directly in the enemy's rear, and about mid-way upon the only pike leading to Franklin; to attack as the Federals retreated, and put to rout and capture, if possible, their army which was the sole obstacle between our forces and Nashville—in truth, the only barrier to the success of the campaign.

I was confident that after Schofield had crossed the river and placed that obstruction between our respective armies, he would feel in security, and would remain in his position at least a sufficient length of time to allow me to throw pontoons across the river about three miles above his left flank, and, by a bold and rapid march together with heavy demonstrations in his front, gain his rear before he was fully apprised of my object.

The situation presented an occasion for one of those interesting and beautiful moves upon the chess-board of war, to perform which I had often desired an opportunity. As stated in a letter to General Longstreet, I had urgently appealed for authority to turn the Federal left at Round Top Mountain. I had beheld with admiration on the noble deeds and grand results achieved by the immortal Jackson in similar maneuvers; I had seen his Corps made equal to ten times its number by a sudden attack on the enemy's rear, and I hoped in this instance to be able to profit by the teaching of my illustrious countryman.

As I apprehended unnecessary and fatal delay might be occasioned by the appearance of the enemy on the line of march to the rear, I decided to bridge the river that night, and move at dawn the next morning with Cheatham's Corps—whose right was then resting near the point selected for a crossing—together with Stewart's Corps and Johnson's Division, of Lee's Corps, and to leave Lieutenant General Lee with Stevenson's and Clayton's Divisions and the bulk of the artillery, to demonstrate heavily against Schofield, and follow him if he retired.

Since I had attempted this same movement on the 22d of July (at Atlanta), and had been unable to secure its success, I resolved to go in person at the head of the advance brigade, and lead the army to Spring Hill.

Colonel Prestman and his assistants laid the pontoons during the night of the 28th, about three miles above Columbia; orders to move at dawn the following day having been issued to the two corps and the division above mentioned, I rode with my staff to Cheatham's right, passed over the bridge soon after daybreak, and moved forward at the head of Granberry's Texas brigade, of Cleburne's Division, with instructions that the remaining corps and divisions follow, and at the same time keep well closed up during the march.

General Forrest had crossed the evening previous and moved to the front and right. I threw forward a few skirmishers who advanced at as rapid a pace as I supposed the troops could possibly proceed.

Forrest's cavalrymen, having crossed the Duck ahead of the infantry, had competently set about their appointed task of keeping the enemy cavalry out of the way. The Federal cavalry was now under the command of General James Harrison Wilson, a young West Pointer, 27 years old, who had shown so much ability while commanding a division under Sheridan in Virginia that he was sent to Sherman when that general asked Washington for a competent man to command all his cavalry. Wilson tells of the launching of his activities in his new sphere of duty:

Toward the close of October I reported to Sherman at Gaylesville, Alabama . . ., and after a full and interesting conference I was announced on October 24th as chief-of-cavalry, and placed in absolute command of all the mounted forces of the three armies. . . . I arrived at Nashville on the 6th of November, and by the aid of a large staff, mostly from the regular army, pressed forward the preparations of the corps for the campaign which it was now evident the resolute Hood was about to begin for the capture of Nashville and the possession of Middle Tennessee. . . . On the 19th of

November the enemy was reported by the cavalry pickets as marching north in force on the west side of Shoal Creek, and this was confirmed without delay by a cavalry reconnaissance. . . . Constant marching, accompanied by heavy fighting and many skirmishes followed. The Federal cavalry, under the immediate direction of Hatch, who showed great coolness and steadiness, fell back through Lexington, Lawrenceburg, Pulaski and Lynnville to Columbia, where all its detachments then in that theatre of operations were for the first time collected under my command. Having as far as possible completed my arrangements at Nashville, I had taken the field in person a few days before.

Wilson was an able, energetic and well-trained young man, and he soon developed into a cavalry commander of exceptional ability, as was later demonstrated by his handling of his force in the battle of Nashville. When his initial assignment in his new command was to stop Forrest, however, he was out of his depth. Forrest, operating with his customary vigor and effectiveness, soon forced Wilson so far off to the northeast as to remove him temporarily from the field of action. Then, leaving one of his brigades to keep Wilson occupied, Forrest with the bulk of his command rode across country to Spring Hill.

Up to this point, there is general agreement among both Federal and Confederate participants and observers as to just what was done. As regards subsequent developments, however, there is such confusion and disparity between the accounts of those involved as to make it difficult to give an absolutely final and convincing answer to the question that is so frequently asked, even today, when Hood's Tennessee campaign is discussed: What happened at Spring Hill?

Bearing in mind that the reports and recollections of practically all army commanders are to a certain extent colored by self-interest, let us read what General Schofield and General Hood had to say when they wrote about it in later years. Hear General Schofield:

In the afternoon of November 28 I received information that the enemy's cavalry had forced the crossing of Duck River above Columbia and driven our cavalry back; and, about two o'clock that night, the prisoners reported the enemy laying pontoon bridges, and that Hood's infantry would begin to cross that morning. The army was ready to march at a moment's notice. It could have retired to Spring Hill or to Franklin without molestation or delay, but that would have given the enemy the crossing of Duck River at Columbia and the turnpike road for his advance with his artillery and trains. . . . One thing was clear, and that was that I must hold Hood back, if possible, until informed that Thomas had concentrated his troops. . . . After considering the matter some time in the night, I decided to hold on at least until morning. Early in the morning a brigade of infantry was sent up the river to reconnoiter and watch the enemy's movements; at the same time Stanley was ordered, with two divisions of his corps, back to Spring Hill to occupy and intrench a position there covering the roads and trains, which were ordered to be parked at that place, and General Thomas H. Ruger was ordered to join him.

About 8 A. M. on the 29th came a despatch from Thomas, dated 8 P. M. of the day before, conveying the information that Smith had not arrived, expressing the wish that the Duck River position be held until Smith arrived; and another despatch designating Franklin behind the Harpeth River as the place to which I would have to retire if it became necessary to fall back from Duck River. I then decided to hold on to the crossing of Duck River until the night of the 29th, thus gaining twenty-four hours more for Thomas to concentrate his troops. I did not apprehend any serious danger at Spring Hill, for Hood's infantry could not reach that place over a wretched country road much before night, and Stanley with one division and our cavalry could easily beat off Forrest. Hence I retained Ruger's division and one of Stanley's, and disposed all the troops to resist any attempt Hood might make by marching directly from his bridges upon my position on the north bank of Duck River to dislodge me from that position. . . .

Specifically, about 10 A. M. Schofield had his force in position as follows: Stanley, with one of his divisions (Wagner's) of the Fourth Army Corps was nearing Spring Hill. Stanley's other two divisions, (Kimball's and Wood's) were in position on the Franklin Pike between Duck River and Rutherford's creek; and Ruger's division of the Twenty-third Corps was on the pike, north of that creek, about half-way to Spring Hill. Schofield himself left Duck River about 3 P. M. and, picking up Ruger's division on the way, arrived at Spring Hill about dusk. He had left instructions that "at nightfall" Cox's division, who had been left at Duck River, should march to Spring Hill, and that Wood's and Kimball's brigades should fall in and follow Cox after he had passed them on the pike.

As Schofield accurately says in his account of the troop movements, "Stanley arrived at Spring Hill in time to beat off Forrest and protect our trains. Then he intrenched a good position in which to meet Hood's column when it should arrive, which it did late in the afternoon." But this greatly over-simplifies what happened.

The primary purpose in sending Wagner's division to Spring Hill was to guard the wagon trains and reserve artillery, which had been sent there. Wagner's men, double-quicking through the village, got there barely in time to forestall Forrest, who was arriving from the east by the Mount Carmel road. Wagner's men (about 5,500) were stretched out in an intrenched line roughly encircling the village. Opdyke's brigade was on the north, extending eastward from the railroad station, about a mile northwest of the village, across the Franklin pike north of town. Lane's brigade was in a line east of Spring Hill, across the Mt. Carmel pike. Bradley's brigade, of four regiments, which constituted the right of the Federal line, was placed in an advanced, detached position on a wooded ridge to the southwest, covering approach by the Rally Hill (or Kedron) road. The reserve artillery, or a substantial part of it, was placed in position in the defensive line close to the pike, facing to the south and southeast.

As Wagner's column was approaching Spring Hill, just before noon, the 26th Ohio regiment with a section of artillery was detached to guard a country road entering the pike a mile southwest of the town. Also, as some of Forrest's reconnoitering troops were seen in the fields to the east of the pike, the 64th Ohio infantry regiment, which was bringing up the rear of the Federal column, was dropped off to drive them away. Captain Shellenberger, commanding Company B in this latter regiment, tells of the incidents of this initial clash:

With the right wing deployed as skirmishers and the left wing in reserve, the regiment advanced steadily, driving before it the cavalry, without replying to the harmless long-range fire they kept up with their carbines, but always galloping away before we could get within effective range.

About a mile east of the pike we crossed the Rally Hill road. This was the road by which Hood's infantry column approached. There it runs north, nearly parallel with the pike, to a point five hundred yards east of Spring Hill where it turns west to enter the village. Leaving one of the reserve companies to watch the road, the rest of the regiment kept on in pursuit of the cavalry until our skirmishers were abreast of the Caldwell house, about eight hundred yards east of the road, where a halt was called. A few minutes later, at two-thirty o'clock, the left of our skirmish line, north of the

Caldwell house, was attacked by a line of battle in front while the cavalry worked around our left flank.

At the time we believed the battle line to be a part of Hood's infantry; and, in a letter from General Bradley, he states that it caused great consternation at headquarters in Spring Hill when Major Coulter of the 64th came galloping back with the information that the regiment was fighting infantry. But investigation has disclosed that the battle line was composed of mounted infantry belonging to Forrest's command. They were armed with Enfield rifles and always fought on foot like ordinary infantry, using their horses for traveling rapidly from place to place.

The four reserve companies were thrown in on a run at the point of contact, but our line was soon forced to fall back by the cavalry turning our left flank. . . . Eventually the 64th was driven back across the Rally Hill road, where a last stand was made in a large woods covering a broad ridge abutting on the road three-fourths of a mile southeast of Spring Hill. . . . Some of the enemy had secured a position on our right flank, where they opened an enfilading fire. To get out of that fire the regiment fell back towards the interior of the woods, where it was so close to our main line [Bradley's line, that is] that it was called in.

Captain James Dinkins of General Chalmers's escort company, who was active in the skirmishing with Wilson all the morning and took part in Forrest's attack on Spring Hill, gives a colorful account of it from his point of view:

At Spring Hill we found a cavalry force in line of battle, which Colonel Rucker easily dispersed, but they retired behind a long line of breastworks, which were filled with a corps of infantry. Rucker withdrew and reported the fact to General Chalmers, when they both rode forward to investigate further, and found as Colonel Rucker had stated. . . .

This was the situation when General Forrest rode up, but in the meantime about two hundred of the enemy's cavalry had returned to the position from which General Rucker had driven them, and General Forrest, observing them, said to General Chalmers: "Why don't you drive those fellows off?" General Chalmers answered: "Why there are three divisions of infantry in breastworks behind the cavalry; and, further, my men are out of ammunition and broken down." Said General Forrest: "I think you are mistaken; that is only a small cavalry force . . . General Chalmers felt that he could not argue the matter further, so said: "All right; I will try it."

Soon the line was formed, with the general and his staff and escort on the right. He gave the command, "Forward, gallop", and immediately Carson (the bugler) sounded the charge. . . . We charged through a beautiful grove, the men urging their horses. General Chalmers was leading and they were determined to be with him. General Forrest watched the charge, which also put the men on their mettle, and there was not a laggard in the line. We had almost reached the edge of the woods when the shock came. Twenty pieces of artillery opened upon us, followed by the fire of a long line of infantry. Horses tumbled over each other and fell, men were shot, and horses galloped away riderless, and limbs and bark covered the ground. It was a dreadful few minutes, and it all happened very quickly. There was no command given to fall back, but when the smoke rose above there were only four men in their places: General Chalmers, Lieutenant Elbert Oliver, Frank M. Norfleet and Carson, the bugler. They were together, but the next moment Oliver and Carson were shot down. Then Norfleet said: "General, everybody but you and me have been killed or wounded; let us get away", and they rode to the rear.

When Chalmers got back to where Forrest had been watching the charge, according to the account given by one who was there, Forrest said: "They was in there sure enough, wasn't they, Chalmers?" To which Chalmers replied dryly: "Yes, that is the second time I found them there."

Forrest's men, during the Spring Hill action, were to a great extent immobilized by lack of ammunition. Captain Dinkins indicates this in telling of Forrest's efforts to lend his support when Cleburne came up and prepared to go into action. "It was well understood," says Dinkins, "that our command had no ammunition, and the only thing we could do was to yell".

Colonel Jordan gives us a detailed account of what Forrest did after he arrived at Spring Hill and had his first brush with the enemy there:

Every disposition was now made to attack and check the infantry in movement, and some sharp skirmishing had taken place when General Forrest received a dispatch from General Hood, directing him to attempt to hold the enemy in check at that point until Cheatham's and Stewart's corps, then en route, should come up. The skirmishing therefore was continued, and with such effect that the enemy withdrew all their pickets and outposts behind their fortifications, and about four o'clock Forrest, dismounting his whole force, disposed it as if in menace of a general attack.

Jordan then tells of the coming of Cleburne's infantry, and its advance, driving back the enemy infantry, going on to say:

It was now dark; Forrest's men, engaged in action since sunrise, had exhausted their ammunition and were worn down from hard work—without intermission for the past week; therefore they were withdrawn to feed their horses and bivouac out of immediate contact with the enemy's pickets, the infantry being left to hold the ground acquired.

About nine that night General Stewart's Corps came up to the immediate vicinity of General Forrest's headquarters, and these two officers meeting, after a short conversation, found that their orders appeared to conflict. Accordingly they rode together to General Hood's headquarters, a mile distant . . . On the way thither . . . a dispatch overtook him from Jackson, who had been thrown round with his division across the turnpike northward of Spring Hill, reporting that, being over-matched and pressed back from the road, he stood in need of immediate aid. Buford and Chalmers, having already expended sixty rounds of ammunition during the day, were without a cartridge. Forrest, therefore, hurried on to report the situation to the General-in-chief.

Hood, according to Jordan, was surprised to learn that Cheatham was not in possession of the turnpike, and asked Stewart if he could not establish his corps in that position, but it developed that Stewart could not do so. Then, says Jordan:

Hood now asked Forrest if he could not throw his cavalry upon the turnpike in time to check the Federal retreat. The Cavalry general replied: "That, as Chalmers and Buford were without ammunition, their commands would be inefficient, leaving him only Jackson's division for the service. Jackson, luckily, had captured enough ammunition in his operations of the day for present purposes. But he would do the best he could in the emergency." General Hood then remarked that he would order his corps commanders to furnish the requisite ammunition . . . but neither Cheatham nor Stewart could supply it. . . . Returning to his own headquarters, Forrest found General Jackson awaiting him. Explaining the situation of affairs, as well as General Hood's expectation, Jackson, engaging to establish his division upon the road at Thompson's Station, and endeavor to hold the enemy in check at that point, left at once with that object.

Having thus done all in his power to interpose a barrier between the divided portions of the Federal army, Forrest reported, through a staff officer, to his superior his inability to obtain ammunition, and what he had done in the exigency. By midnight, Jackson's guns began to be heard in an animated engagement in the north, and a continuous uproar of musketry resounded from that direction throughout the night; and never did so small a force fight more tenaciously or stoutly than Jackson's little division on this occasion. The force encountered a heavy column of infantry pressing on toward Franklin, was too powerful, however, for Jackson's slender force. He was unable to do more than harass the masses that forced their way by him during the night, and to oblige them to abandon a number of wagons, which he burned, while a considerable number of the enemy were killed and captured; and one of his brigades (Ross's) came upon and destroyed a train of cars near Thompson's Station.

After having given an outline of just what he planned to do at Spring Hill, Hood, in his post-war book *Advance and Retreat,* published in 1880, gives his account of what happened there:

Thus I led the main body of the army to within about two miles and in full view of the pike from Columbia to Spring Hill and Franklin. I here halted about 3 p.m., and requested General Cheatham, commanding the leading corps, and Major General Cleburne to advance to the spot where, sitting upon my horse, I had in sight the enemy's wagons and men passing at double-quick along the Franklin pike. As these officers approached, I spoke to Cheatham in the following words which I quote almost verbatim, as they have remained indelibly engraved upon my memory ever since that fatal day: "General, do you see the enemy there, retreating rapidly to escape us?" He answered in the affirmative. "Go," I continued, "with your Corps, take possession of and hold that pike at or near Spring Hill. Accept whatever comes, and turn all those wagons over to our side of the house." Then addressing Cleburne, I said, "General, you have heard the orders just given. You have one of my best divisions. Go with General Cheatham, assist him in every way you can, and do as he directs." Again, as a parting injunction to them, I added, "Go and do this at once. Stewart is near at hand, and I will have him double-quick his men to the front."

They immediately sent staff officers to hurry the men forward, and moved off with their troops at a quick pace in the direction of the enemy. I dispatched several of my staff to the rear, with orders to Stewart and Johnson to make all possible haste. Meantime I rode to one side, and looked on at Cleburne's Division, followed by the remainder of Cheatham's Corps, as it marched by seemingly ready for battle.

Within about one-half hour from the time Cheatham left me, skirmishing began with the enemy, when I rode forward to a point nearer the pike, and again sent a staff officer to Stewart and Johnson to push forward. At the same time, I dispatched a messenger to General Cheatham to lose no time in gaining possession of the pike at Spring Hill. It was reported back that he was about to do so.

Listening attentively to the fire of the skirmishers in that direction, I discovered there was no continued roar of musketry, and being aware of the quick approach of darkness, after four o'clock at that season of the year, I became somewhat uneasy, and again ordered an officer to go to General Cheatham, inform him that his supports were very near at hand, that he must attack at once, if he had not already so done, and take and hold possession of the pike. Shortly afterwards, I entrusted another officer with the same message, and, if my memory is not treacherous, finally requested the Governor of Tennessee, Isham G. Harris, to hasten forward and impress upon Cheatham the importance of action without delay.

Then, showing how seriously ignorant he was of the actual state of affairs, he continues:

I knew no large force of the enemy could be at Spring Hill, as couriers reported Schofield's main body still in front of Lee, at Columbia, up to a late hour in the day. I thought it probable that Cheatham had taken possession of Spring Hill without encountering material opposition, or had formed line across the pike, north of the town, and entrenched without coming in serious contact with the enemy, which would account for the little musketry heard in his direction. However, to ascertain the truth, I sent an officer to ask Cheatham if he held the pike, and to inform him of the arrival of Stewart, whose Corps I intended to throw on his left, in order to assail the Federals in flank that evening or the next morning, as they approached and formed to attack Cheatham. At this juncture, the last messenger returned with the report that the road had not been taken possession of. General Stewart was then ordered to proceed to the right of Cheatham and place his Corps across the pike, north of Spring Hill.

By this hour, however, twilight was upon us, when General Cheatham rode up in person. I at once directed Stewart to halt, and, turning to Cheatham, I exclaimed with deep emotion, as I felt the golden opportunity fast slipping from me, "General, why in the name of God have you not attacked the enemy, and taken possession of that pike?" He replied that the line looked a little too long for him, and that Stewart should first form on his right. I could hardly believe it possible that this brave old soldier, who had given proof of such courage and ability upon so many hard-fought fields, would ever make such a report. After leading him within full view of the enemy, and pointing out to him the Federals, retreating in great haste and confusion, along the pike, and then giving explicit orders to attack, I would as soon have expected mid-day to turn into darkness as for him to have disobeyed my orders. I then asked General Cheatham whether or not Stewart's Corps, if formed on the right, would extend across the pike. Darkness, however, which was increased by large shade trees in that vicinity, soon closed upon us, and Stewart's Corps, after much annoyance, went into bivouac for the night, near but not across the pike, at about eleven or twelve o'clock.

It was reported to me after this hour that the enemy was marching along the road, almost under the light of the camp-fires of the main body of the army. I sent anew to General Cheatham to know if at least a line of skirmishers could not be advanced, in order to throw the Federals in confusion, to delay their march, and allow us a chance to attack in the morning. Nothing was done. The Federals, with immense wagon trains, were permitted to march by us the remainder of the night, within gunshot of our lines. I could not succeed in arousing the troops to action, when one good division would have sufficed to do the work. One good division, I re-assert, could have routed that portion of the enemy which was at Spring Hill; have taken possession of and formed line across the road; and thus have made it an easy matter for Stewart's Corps, Johnson's Division, and Lee's two Divisions from Columbia, to have enveloped, routed, and captured Schofield's Army that afternoon and the ensuing day. General Forrest gallantly opposed the enemy further down to our right to the full extent of his power; beyond this effort, nothing whatever was done, although never was a grander opportunity offered to utterly rout and destroy the Federal Army.

General Cheatham, when he read these statements in General Hood's book, was overcome with indignation, and he made a spirited denial of the accuracy of Hood's statements in an article in the *Southern Historical Society Papers.*

Concerning Hood's account of his conversation with Cheatham and Cleburne "about 3 P. M." on the afternoon of November 29th, Cheatham says:

There is not a bit of truth in this entire paragraph. At the hour named, 3 PM, there was no movement of "wagons and men" in the vicinity of Spring Hill. Moreover, from the crossing at Duck River to the point referred to by General Hood the turnpike was never in view, nor could it be seen until I had moved up to within three-quarters of a mile of Spring Hill. Only a mirage would have made possible the vision which this remarkable statement professes to record.

Contradicting other statements made by Hood, General Cheatham caustically remarks that "General Hood conveniently forgot the facts". Rebutting Hood's recountal of his alleged conversation with Cheatham "at twilight", when "with deep emotion" he childed Cheatham, Cheatham simply says:

Here again General Hood's memory proved treacherous. . . . The dramatic scene with which he embellishes his narrative of the day's operations only occurred in the imagination of General Hood.

Having blasted his former commander with these blistering allegations of mendacity, General Cheatham proceeds with his account of just what was done by him and his three divisions (Cleburne's, Bate's and Brown's) that fateful November 29th afternoon:

About 3 o'clock P. M. I arrived at Rutherford's creek, two and one-half miles from Spring Hill. At this point General Hood gave me verbal orders, as follows: That I should get Cleburne across the creek, and send him toward Spring Hill, with instructions to communicate with General Forrest, who was near the village, ascertain from him the position of the enemy, and attack immediately; that I should remain at the creek, assist General Bate in crossing his division, and then go forward and put Bate's command in to support Cleburne; and that he would push Brown forward to join me.

As soon as the division of General Bate had crossed the creek, I rode forward and, at a point on the road about one and a half miles from Spring Hill, I saw the left of Cleburne's command just disappearing over a hill to the left of the road. Halting here, I waited a few minutes for the arrival of Bate, and formed his command with his right upon the position of Cleburne's left, and ordered him forward to the support of Cleburne. Shortly after Bate's division had disappeared over the same range of hills, I heard firing toward Cleburne's right, and just then General Brown's division had come up. I thereupon ordered Brown to proceed to the right, turn the range of hills over which Cleburne and Bate had crossed, and to form line of battle and attack to the right of Cleburne. The division of General Brown was in motion to execute this order, when I received a message from Cleburne that his right brigade had been struck in flank by the enemy and had suffered severely, and that he had been compelled to fall back and reform his division with a change of front.

It so happened that the direction of Cleburne's advance was such as had exposed his right flank to the enemy's line. When his command was formed on the road by which he had marched from Rutherford's creek, neither the village of Spring Hill nor the turnpike could be seen. Instead of advancing directly upon Spring Hill, his forward movement was a little south of west and almost parallel with the turnpike, instead of northwest upon the enemy's line south and east of the village. General Cleburne was killed in the assault upon Franklin the next day, and I had no opportunity to learn from him how it was that the error of direction occurred.

Meanwhile General Bate, whom I had placed in position on the left of Cleburne's line of march, continued to move forward in the same direction until he had reached the farm of N. F. Cheairs one and a half miles south of Spring Hill.

After Brown had reached the position indicated to him and had formed a line of battle, he sent to inform me that it would be certain disaster for him to attack, as the enemy's line extended beyond his right several hundred yards. I sent word to him to throw back his right brigade and make the attack. I had already sent couriers after General Bate to bring him back and direct him to join Cleburne's left.

In sending this order to Bate, Cheatham (unwittingly, of course) seems to have made the greatest contribution to the failure of Hood's hope to intercept Schofield's marching men on the pike.

General Bate, in his official report, tells of his movements after he had crossed Rutherford's creek and had led his division along the Rally Hill road to the point where he was ordered to march his men westward across the fields to form and move on Cleburne's left:

Not seeing General Cheatham at the moment of forming my line of battle, General Hood, who was personally present, directed me to move to the turnpike and sweep toward Columbia. General Cleburne, being in advance, formed and moved forward

Before it was possible for me to do so, and "changed front" without stopping and without my knowing the fact, owing to intervening hills obstructing the view. As soon as ascertained, I conformed to the movement as well as I could, and pushed forward in the direction of the enemy, who held the turnpike. It was now getting dark and I had moved more than a mile in line of battle. Cleburne had been engaged, with what success I did not know.

At this juncture, it seems clear, Bate and Cleburne (supposed to be acting in concert) were so far apart as to be entirely out of sight of and out of touch with each other. Indeed, each was now aiming at a different target—Bate at the turnpike and whatever troops might be on it, and Cleburne at the Federal force already in position at Spring Hill, with which he had been in combat. Bate continues with his account of how, in the gathering darkness, he pressed on:

Procuring a guide, learning the exact location of the enemy and the general direction of the turnpike, I "changed direction to the right" again, and was moving so as to strike the turnpike to the right of Major Nat Cheairs's residence, which I believed would bring me near to Cleburne's left. Caswell's battalion of sharpshooters, deployed as skirmishers, was within a hundred yards of and commanded the turnpike, checking the enemy's movement along it in my front, and my lines were being adjusted for a further forward movement, when I received an order, through Lieutenant Schell, from General Cheatham to halt and join my right to General Cleburne's left. My main line was in two hundred yards of the turnpike, when Major Caswell's battalion fired into the enemy on the pike. He (the enemy) veered to his left, as I subsequently ascertained, and took a road leaving the pike near Dr. McKissick's.

I obeyed the order of General Cheatham, and with delay and difficulty (it being in the night and near the enemy) I ascertained the left of Cleburne's line, which had retired some distance to the rear of my right. . . . I made known to General Cheatham the fact of the enemy threatening my left, and called for force to protect it. My left brigade was retired to confront any movement from that direction, and during the night, perhaps 10 o'clock, General Johnson's division of Lee's corps moved to my left. I bivouacked between 9 and 10 o'clock for the night.

Cheatham, continuing with his account of his maneuvering of his divisions, gives the impression that at this critical time he had a strikingly foggy idea of the position of the Confederate troops as well as of those of the enemy. He says:

Going to the right of my line, I found Generals Brown and Cleburne, and the latter reported that he had re-formed his division. I then gave orders to Brown and Cleburne that, as soon as they could connect their lines, they should attack the enemy, who were then in sight; informing them at the same time that General Hood had just told me that Stewart's column was close at hand, and that General Stewart had been ordered to go to my right and place his command across the pike. I furthermore said to them that I would go myself and see that General Bate was placed in position to connect with them, and immediately rode to the left of my line for that purpose.

During all this time I had met and talked with General Hood repeatedly, our field headquarters being not over one hundred yards apart. . . . I had been along my line and had seen that Brown's right was outflanked several hundred yards. I had urged General Hood to hurry up Stewart and place him on my right, and had received from him the assurance that this would be done, and this assurance I had communicated to Generals Cleburne and Brown.

When I returned from my left, where I had been to get Bate in position, and was on the way to the right of my line, it was dark; but I intended to move forward with Cleburne and Brown and make the attack, knowing that Bate would be in position to support them. Stewart's column had already passed by on the way toward the turn-pike, and I presumed he would be in position on my right.

On reaching the road where General Hood's field headquarters had been established, I found a courier with a message from General Hood, requesting me to come to him at Captain Thompson's house, about one and a fourth miles back on the road to Rutherford's creek. I found General Stewart with General Hood. The commanding General [Hood] there informed me that he had concluded to wait till morning, and directed me to hold my command in readiness to attack at daylight. . . .

What reason General Stewart gave for not reaching the turnpike I do not know. General Hood said to me repeatedly, when I met him between 4 and 6 o'clock in the afternoon, "Stewart will be here in a few minutes." Stewart's column did not come up until about dark.

In a letter written to General Cheatham after the war, General Bate tells how, after placing his men in biovouac, he went to General Hood's headquarters (between 10 and 12 o'clock at night) to acquaint Hood with the situation on his front.

On my arrival at his quarters, Bate says, I found General Hood in conference with General Forrest, consequently I waited some time for an interview. I informed the General of having about dark come near to and in line of battle, and commanded with my skirmish line, the turnpike south of Spring Hill, and caused a cessation in the move-ments of wagons, horsemen, etc., which were passing; but I did not "pass onto the turnpike and sweep toward Columbia" as you (General Hood) had directed me to do, because just at that time I received an order from my corps commander, General Cheatham, to halt and align the right of my division with the left of Cleburne's, which I declined to do until I received a second order to the same effect, and then I did so. General Hood replied in substance: "It makes no difference now" or "It is all right anyhow, for General Forrest, as you see, has just left and informed me that he holds the turnpike with a portion of his forces north of Spring Hill, and will stop the enemy if he tries to pass toward Franklin, so in the morning we will have a surrender without a fight." He further said, in a congratulatory manner: "We can sleep quiet tonight."

The net result of all the shifting of Cheatham's divisions and brigades was that, when activities ended for the night, Cleburne and Brown (on Cleburne's right) were in a line facing northward towards Spring Hill; Bate was on Cleburne's left, with his left brigade refused so as to face westward, parallel to the pike; and, later, Johnson's division was placed on Bate's left. It was presumably Ruger's division (led by Schofield) that had been fired upon by Bate's sharpshooters; and it was in front of Bate and Johnson that the troops of Cox, Wood and Kim-ball marched quietly by later in the evening.

General Stewart, in a letter written after the war, sheds some light on the question as to why he was held so long in battle array south of Rutherford's creek, and why it was more than "a few minutes" before he was ordered to move to the support of Cheatham:

I was not allowed to cross Rutherford's creek until dark. When I reached the creek, riding in advance of my troops, Cheatham's corps was crossing. A staff officer of his informed me that an attack was to be made. I expected to be hurried forward to support the attack. Instead, I was ordered to form in line of battle *before crossing* the creek, and about at right angles to it. This, in my poor judgment, was the fatal error. . . . When, about dusk, I received orders to move on across the creek, and rode forward to find the Commanding General [Hood], he complained bitterly that his orders to attack had not been obeyed. But *he was there himself*. I asked him why he had halted me at Rutherford's creek. He replied that he confidently expected Cheatham would attack and rout the enemy; that there was a road leading to Murfreesboro on the other side of the creek. He wished me there to prevent the escape of the routed foe in that direction. Here, I think was the error. Johnson's division of Lee's corps was with me. That division, reinforced if necessary by one of mine, would have been sufficient to guard that road. The rest of my command should have been pressed forward to reinforce Cheatham and Forrest. I have a note from General Hood, written after we moved round into North Carolina, fully exonerating me from all censure on that occasion.

Evidently, Hood had a fatally confused impression of the local geography and of the position of the Federal troops at that time. If Cheatham's attack on the troops in his front (the units of Wagner's division occupying Spring Hill) had been successfully executed, causing the rout of the enemy, it would have resulted in driving the routed Federals further to the north rather than back southward where they might have sought to escape by any cross-road held by Stewart's deployed troops. And, anyhow, the road from Spring Hill to Murfreesboro was the Mt. Carmel road, then held by Forrest.

Stewart's account of just exactly what he did after he had at last advanced with his men across Rutherford's creek is given in a subsequent letter written by him to General Samuel Cooper in Richmond:

Riding in advance of the column, about dusk, I found General Hood some half mile from the creek and about as far west of the (Rally Hill) road on which we were marching and which led to Spring Hill. The Commanding General gave me a young man of the neighborhood as a guide and told me to move on and place my right across the [Franklin] pike beyond Spring Hill, "your left," he added, "extending down this way." This would have placed my line in rear of Cheatham's, except that my right would have extended beyond his. The guide informed me that at a certain point the road made a sudden turn to the left, going into Spring Hill; that from this bend there used to be a road leading across the pike meeting it at the toll-gate some mile and a half beyond Spring Hill, toward Franklin. I told him if he could find it, that was the right road.

Arriving at the bend of the road we passed through a large gateway, taking what appeared in the darkness to be an indistinct path. Within a short distance I found General Forrest's headquarters and stopped to ascertain the position of his pickets covering Cheatham's right and of the enemy. He informed me that his scouts reported the enemy leaving the direct pike—leading from Spring Hill to Franklin and Nashville —and taking the one down Carter's creek.

While in conversation with him I was informed that a staff officer from General Hood had come up and halted my column. It turned out to be a staff (engineer) officer of General Cheatham's, who informed me that General Hood had sent him to place me in position. It striking me as strange that the commanding general should send an officer not of his own staff on this errand (or indeed any one, as he had given directions to me in person), I inquired of the officer if he had seen General Hood since I had. He replied that he had just come from General Hood and that the reason why he was sent was that I was to go in position on General Brown's right (the right of Cheatham's corps) and he and General Brown had been over the ground by daylight.

Thinking it possible the commanding general had changed his mind as to what he wished me to do, I concluded it was proper to be governed by the directions of this staff officer, and therefore returned to the road and moved on toward Spring Hill. Arriving near the line of Brown's division, General Brown explained his position, which was oblique to the pike, his right being farther from it than his left. It was evident that if my command were marched up and formed on his right, it being now a late hour, it would require all night to accomplish it, and the line, instead of extending across the pike, would bear away from it. Feeling satisfied there was a mistake, I directed the troops to be bivouacked, while I rode back to find the commanding general to explain my situation, and get further instructions.

On arriving at his quarters I inquired of him if he had sent this officer of General Cheatham's staff to place me in position. He replied that he had. I next inquired if he had changed his mind as to what he wished me to do. He replied that he had, "But," said he, "the fact is, General Cheatham has been here and represented that there ought to be somebody on Brown's right." I explained to him (Hood) that in the uncertainty I was in, I had directed the troops (who had been marching rapidly since daylight, and it was now 11 p. m.), to be placed in bivouac, and had come to report. He remarked, in substance, that it was not material; to let the men rest; and directed me to move before daylight in the morning, taking the advance toward Franklin. Subsequently General Hood made to me the statement: "I wish you and your people to understand that I attach no blame to you for the failure at Spring Hill; on the contrary I know if I had had you there the attack would have been made."

The record shows that soon after Hood crossed Rutherford's creek in the early afternoon he met Forrest, who reported his action against the enemy during the preceding three hours. In spite of this clear evidence that there was a substantial part of Schofield's force already entrenched there, Hood seemed unable to disabuse his mind of the delusion that Lee's demonstration at Columbia was holding all, or most of, the Federal force there. This is clearly evidenced by the fact, as stated in his own words, that when he was giving his final orders to Cleburne (in Cheatham's presence) he was not directing an assault on the enemy troops already entrenched around Spring Hill but rather had in mind assailing whatever force might be advancing on the pike. He did not say to Cleburne: "Go, and attack those troops that General Forrest has been fighting at Spring Hill"; but, according to his own account, he said: "Go, take possession of and hold that pike at or near Spring Hill". And that the pike was his objective for Bate's division is shown further by his instructions to Bate to "move to the turnpike and sweep toward Columbia."

Cleburne seems to have had no idea of the close proximity of enemy troops (Bradley's) as he moved westward across the fields from the Rally Hill pike—which was the direction in which he had to move if his objective was the Franklin pike. That his clash with Bradley's brigade was entirely accidental is shown by the account of it told by Captain Shellenberger of the 64th Ohio of that brigade, who was there and saw it all and took part in the fighting:

Shortly before four o'clock, having completed his formation, Cleburne started to march across to the pike. . . . He had three brigades in line—Lowrey's on his right, then Govan's, then Granbury's . . . First crossing a field in his front, Lowrey entered the extension of the woods, and on emerging on the other side his right came in view within easy range of the 42nd Illinois, on Bradley's flank, and that regiment opened an enfilading fire, Lowrey's line being then almost perpendicular to the line of the 42nd. It was this accident of Lowrey's right passing within range of the 42nd that led to the failure of Hood's plan which, up to that minute, had been a great success. When the 42nd opened fire the two guns at the pike also opened, their fire crossing that of the 42nd, and the 64th, running forward, poured in their fire.

When our fire had thus developed our position, out in those wide fields, they could see just what we had. They pulled down the rims of their old hats over their eyes, bent their heads to the storm of missiles pouring upon them, changed direction to their right on double-quick in a manner that excited our admiration, and a little later a long line came sweeping through the wide gap between the right of the 42nd and the pike, and swinging in towards our rear. Our line stood firm, holding back the enemy in front until the flank movement had progressed so far as to make it a question of legs to escape capture, when the regimental commanders gave the reluctant order to fall back. The contact was then so close that as the men on our right were running past the line closing in on them, they were called on with loud oaths, charging them with a Yankee canine descent, to halt and surrender; and, not heeding the call, some of them were shot down with the muzzles of the muskets almost touching their bodies.

By the recession of the two regiments on the flank [the 42nd Illinois and the 64th Ohio] the rear of the four regiments in the woods became exposed. They were attacked at the same time by Forrest in front and by Cleburne on their right and rear and were speedily dislodged. The attack was pressed with so much vigor that, in a few minutes after the 42nd had opened fire, Bradley's entire brigade was in rapid retreat towards Spring Hill, with Cleburne in close pursuit and pouring in a hot fire. In falling back we had to cross the valley of a small stream. . . . As we descended into the valley, we uncovered our pursuers to the fire of the battery at the village, which opened with shrapnel shells firing over our heads. General Stanley, who was in the battery, reported that not less than eight guns opened fire. As soon as Cleburne encountered that fire, he hastily drew back over the ridge out of sight. . . .

When Cleburne changed direction . . . Lowrey and Govan made the change in line of battle, while Granbury faced to the right and followed their movement in column of fours. Afterwards, Granbury about-faced and, moving back some distance in column, then fronted into line and advanced to a farm fence paralleling the pike at a distance variously stated at from 80 to 100 yards. His line there halted and laid down behind the fence. Cleburne and Granbury were both killed next day, and it is not known why Granbury did not go on and take possession of the pike.

The brigades of Lowrey and Govan had become so badly mixed up in the pursuit of Bradley and in the recoil from the fire of the battery that their line had to be reformed. When this was accomplished, the intrepid Cleburne was about to resume his attack towards Spring Hill, when he was stopped by an order from Cheatham, who had brought up Brown's division on Cleburne's right, and had also sent a staff officer to recall Bate with an order for him to close up and connect with Cleburne's left.

This proves that developments, probably the fire of so many guns opening on Cleburne, had convinced Cheatham that the force holding Spring Hill was strong enough to demand the attention of his entire corps. His intention was for Brown to lead in an attack, Cleburne to follow Brown, and Bate, when he got up, to follow Cleburne. But on getting into position Brown reported to Cheatham that he was outflanked several hundred yards on his right, and that it would lead to inevitable disaster for him to attack. . . . Cheatham then concluded that the force holding Spring Hill was too strong for his corps alone to attack, for he reported to Hood that the line in his front was too long for him, and that Stewart's corps must first come up and form on his right. But before Stewart could get up, night and come.

Schofield in his *Memoirs,* published after the war, volunteers his comments as to why Hood's plans miscarried:

Much bitter controversy arose between Hood and some of his subordinates because of their failure to dislodge Stanley's division and get possession of the turnpike at Spring Hill. While I have no wish to take any part in that discussion, I must say that I think the mistake was Hood's. I think he attempted a little longer march, over a very bad road, than could be made in so short a time. The 29th of November is a very short day, and the march of troops across pontoon bridges and through deep mud is very slow. If Hood had turned down the north bank of Duck River, across the fields, which were no worse than his road, he could have got into a fight about noon; but he thought, according to his own account in "Advance and Retreat," that he was deceiving me by his thundering demonstrations at Columbia, and that I did not know he was marching to Spring Hill. He thought he was going to "catch me napping," after the tactics of Stonewall Jackson, while in fact I was watching him all day. Besides, Hood went to bed that night, while I was in the saddle all night, directing in person all the important movements of my troops. Perhaps that is enough to account for the difference between success and failure, without censuring subordinate commanders. Mine did all I could have asked anybody to do that night.

Schofield, after indulging in this self-satisfied philosophising, continues with his story of what happened that afternoon and night:

As soon as I was satisfied that Hood was gone to Spring Hill and would not attack me on the bank of Duck River, I took the head of my troops—Ruger's division—and marched rapidly to Spring Hill, leaving staff officers to give orders to the other division commanders (Kimball and Wood and Cox) to follow immediately in proper order as then formed in line. These orders were somehow misunderstood. The order of march was reversed, and the troops, except Ruger's, and Whitaker's brigade of Kimball's division, did not move at once. But the delay did no harm, and I did not know of the mistake until several days afterward. If Hood had only known of that mistake, he might have troubled me no little, perhaps, by pushing a column across from his camp, south of Whitaker's right flank at Spring Hill, until it reached the Columbia turnpike. But I had prepared even for that, as well as I could, by sending a company of infantry to occupy the only crossroad I could see near Spring Hill as we approached that place. . . .

On arriving at Spring Hill, Whitaker's brigade was put in line on the right of the troops then in position, so as to cover the turnpike on which we were marching. This was about dark. In a few minutes the Confederate camp-fires were lighted a few hundred yards in front of that brigade. It was a very interesting sight, but I don't think any of Whitaker's men cared to give the Confederates a similar view of them.

After stopping to see Stanley a few minutes, and learning that some of Forrest's troopers had been seen at Thompson's Station, three miles farther north, about dusk, I went with Ruger's division to drive them off and clear the way to Franklin. To my great surprise, I found only smoldering fires—no cavalry. This was where our men passed so close to the "bivouac" that they "lighted their pipes by the enemy's camp-fires"; and that is the way romance is woven into history! . . .

When Schofield's army began its retreat from Duck River the morning of November 29th, Colonel Issac R. Sherwood and his regiment (111th Ohio infantry. Moore's Brigade) were detailed to occupy the line on the north bank of the Duck until midnight, and then fall back and rejoin his brigade in the rear. Just about nightfall Sherwood heard the roar of artillery and the rattle of musketry in his rear at Spring Hill. Although ordered to hold his position until midnight, he realized that the military situation had changed since he received those orders, and that he must act quickly to save his regiment from capture. He goes on to tell how his regiment, the rearmost unit of Schofield's retreating army, made its way out of an uncomfortable position:

I decided to fall back and take all desperate chances, as a new emergency had happened. I moved my regiment to the left until I reached the Franklin and Columbia pike, near the blockhouse protecting the railroad bridge. Here I found a captain of the 24th Missouri regiment with his company guarding the bridge. He had no orders to fall back, but he joined his fate with mine and ordered his company to fall in behind my regiment. He said: "I approve your action and will share your peril."

Together we started our march to the north, with no guide but the North Star. Just about midnight, as we were approaching Spring Hill, we saw the glimmer of bivouac fires, but didn't know whether this army was friend or foe. I halted my small command, ordered silence in the ranks, and rode forward to make observations. It was a star-lit night with occasional clouds, but no moon.

When I arrived near enough to make observations I saw stacks of guns revealed by the light of the bivouac fires and I saw human figures moving about, indicating the presence of a large army. I saw a man approaching on horseback, but it was too dark to distinguish his uniform and I couldn't tell whether he was friend or foe. As he drew nearer I called out: "Whose division is that on the left?" He replied: "General Cleburne's." I answered: "All right," and turned and rode back at a gallop to tell my boys that we were in the immediate presence of the whole Confederate army. The officer I met was evidently putting out his outposts in the rear of the army. I have always been grateful to an over-ruling Providence, who guided our destiny that night.

Sherwood, realizing what a precarious position he was in, decided to make a flank movement of his own:

I felt our only safety from capture was a silent march to the left to avoid the enemy pickets and cavalry outposts. I felt sure the enemy cavalry was on the right flank. I made a detour to the left across fields and fences and plantations for at least three miles, when I turned to the right. At four o'clock on the morning of November 30 we reached the Franklin pike, where we met the last section of our wagon trains with the muleteers hurrying north, whipping and cursing the animals. Just at dawn, when my tired and sleepy veterans were marching alongside the wagon train, a battalion of enemy cavalry that had formed over a hill at our right swooped down on us with drawn sabres and that defiant rebel yell that we heard so often in the Atlanta campaign. I gave the command: "By the right flank halt! Commence firing!" Ad Fulton strung out our regimental colors, and the Missouri captain lined up on our right. We fired a volley at the bold raiders, who thought to capture our last wagon train. Then I gave the order to fix bayonets. The bold captain of the raiders pulled up his charging steed, his followers soon followed, and the cavalry cavalcade scattered in swift retreat. . . .

Schofield (in writing about it in later years) expresses the greatest possible confidence in the successful outcome of his movements that day and night, and gives himself a few pats on the back for the skill and sagacity he displayed:

There was no anxiety in my mind about what might happen at Spring Hill after dark. The danger which actually developed there between dark and midnight— of which I knew nothing until several days afterward—resulted entirely from faulty execution of my orders.

I arrived at Spring Hill at dusk with the head of the main column, having ordered all the troops to follow in close order, and (except Ruger's troops, which I took to Thompson's) to form line on the right of Stanley's division at Spring Hill, covering the pike back toward Columbia. Cox's division, being the last, was to form our extreme right. In that contemplated position, if Hood had attacked at any time in the night we would have had decidedly the advantage of him. I had no anxiety on that point. When informed, about midnight, that Cox had arrived, I understood that my orders had been exactly executed, and then ordered Cox to take the lead and the other divisions to follow, from the right by the rear, in the march to Franklin.

But it happened that only Whitaker's brigade of Kimball's division, to which I gave the orders in person, followed Ruger's. Hence that one brigade was the only force we had in line between Hood's bivouac and the turnpike that night. If that fact had been known to the enemy, the result would have been embarrassing, but not very serious. If the enemy had got possession of a point on the pike, the column from Duck River would have taken the country road a short distance to the west of Spring

Hill and Thompson's Station, and marched on to Franklin. The situation at Spring Hill in the night was not by any means a desperate one. Veteran troops are not so easily cut off in an open country.

It is interesting to consider what would probably have been the march of events if we had retreated from Duck River in the night of November 28, upon first learning that Hood had forced the crossing of that river. We would have reached Franklin early on the 29th, could have rebuilt the bridge and crossed the Harpeth that day and night, and Hood could not have got up in time to make any serious attack that day. So far as our little army was concerned, for the moment all would have been well. But Hood would have been in front of Franklin, with his whole army, artillery, and ammunition-trains, by dawn of day on the 30th; he could have forced the crossing of the Harpeth above Franklin early that day, compelled us to retire to Nashville, and interposed his cavalry between Nashville and Murfreesboro that night or early on December 1. Thus Thomas's remaining reinforcements from the south and east would have been cut off, and he might have been attacked in Nashville, not later than December 2, with several thousand fewer men than he finally had there, a large part of his army— A. J. Smith's three divisions—not fully ready for battle, and with fewer effective cavalry; while Hood would have had his whole army, fresh and spirited, without the losses and depression caused by its defeat at Franklin, ready to attack an inferior force at Nashville or to cross the Cumberland and invade Kentucky. In short, the day gained at Duck River and Spring Hill was indispensable to Thomas's success.

However, Captain Shellenberger, who was very definitely a non-admirer of General Schofield, in a talk he made to the Missouri Commandery of the Loyal Legion in 1907, challenged not only the military competence of Schofield but also the accuracy of his statements about the Spring Hill affair. Captain Shellenberger says:

After the campaign Schofield claimed that its success was due to the intimate knowledge of Hood's character, gained when they were classmates at West Point, which enabled him to foresee what Hood would do under any given conditions, and then make the best dispositions for defeating him . . . But there can be no question that Schofield's dispositions were made under the conviction that Hood would march down the river after crossing, to clear the way for Lee to cross. And so deeply infatuated was he with this self-imposed delusion that, disregarding the order of Thomas and the advice of Wilson, he cherished it for about five hours after Post had reported that Hood was marching towards Spring Hill.

"There was no anxiety in my mind," Schofield wrote later, but Shellenberger quotes General Stanley in support of the assertion that when Schofield arrived at Spring Hill about dark he was in a state of uncertainty and anxiety as to whether it would be possible to get to Franklin. Says Shellenberger:

It was then Schofield's belief that Hood had possession of the Franklin pike; that the army was caught in a trap; that the only way out was the desperate expedient of forcing a passage by a night attack and, failing in that, he must fight a battle next day under so many disadvantages that ruinous defeat, with the probable loss of the army, was staring him in the face. . . .

The prime purpose of Schofield's campaign was to delay Hood. How well he succeeded in that purpose can be significantly stated in a single sentence: the evening of November 29th he was at Duck River and the morning of December first he was at Nashville, more than forty miles away. . . . If Schofield's orders at Duck River had been to make no effort to delay Hood but to get inside the fortifications of Nashville with the least possible delay, he would not have covered the distance in so short a time without the spur of Hood's flank movement. The celerity with which he ran out of the country was due to the scare he got at Spring Hill.

Hood, in what he says about the Spring Hill affair in his *Advance and Retreat,* not only attempts to unload on others the blame for his failure there, but also indulges in some unbecoming and undeserved censure of the fighting qualities of the Army of Tennessee which aroused the deep resentment of the officers and men of that army when they read what their former commander said:

The best move in my career as a soldier, I was thus destined to behold come to naught. The discovery that the Army, after a forward march of one hundred and eighty miles, was still, seemingly, unwilling to accept battle unless under the protection of breastworks, caused me to experience grave concern. In my inmost heart I questioned whether or not I would ever succeed in eradicating this evil. It seemed to me I had exhausted every means in the power of one man to remove this stumbling block to the Army of Tennessee. And I will here inquire, in vindication of its fair name, if any intelligent man of that army supposes one moment that these same troops, one year previous, would, even without orders to attack, have allowed the enemy to pass them at Rocky-faced Ridge, as he did at Spring Hill.

Lieutenant General Lee performed his duty, at Columbia, with great skill and fidelity which were crowned with entire success: he attained the object of the demonstration, which was to keep the Federals in ignorance of our movements till sufficient time had been allowed the Army to reach the desired point. Colonel Beckham, chief of artillery in Lee's Corps, and one of the most promising officers of his rank, was unfortunately killed on the 29th, during the heavy cannonade in front of that town. On the morning of the 30th of November, Lee was on the march up the Franklin pike, when the main body of the Army, at Spring Hill, awoke to find the Federals had disappeared.

I hereupon decided, before the enemy would be able to reach his stronghold at Nashville, to make that same afternoon another and final effort to overtake and rout him, and drive him in the Big Harpeth river at Franklin, since I could no longer hope to get between him and Nashville, by reason of the short distance from Franklin to that city, and the advantage which the Federals enjoyed in the possession of the direct road.

General Cheatham, in concluding his article in the *Southern Historical Society Papers* in rebuttal of General Hood's account of the Spring Hill affair, delivers this withering blast at Hood's unmanly and undeserved reflection on the personal bravery of the men composing the Army of Tennessee:

During my service as a soldier under the flag of my country in Mexico, and as an officer of the Confederate armies, I cannot recall an instance where I failed to obey an order literally, promptly and faithfully. Military operations, however well conceived, are not always successful; and I have had my share of failures and disappointments, but I have never found it necessary to seek for a scape-goat to bear my transgressions, nor to maintain my own reputation by aspersion of my subordinates. No chieftan since the world began has ever commanded an army of men more confident in themselves, more ready to endure and to dare whatever might be required of them, or more capable of exalted heroism than that which obeyed the will of their General from Peach Tree Creek to Nashville. The Army of Tennessee needs no defense against the querulous calumnies which disfigure General Hood's attempt at history.

An interesting (and significant) sidelight on the Spring Hill mystery is provided by a letter written in 1877 to Governor James D. Porter of Tennessee by Isham

G. Harris, wartime governor of the state and a volunteer aide, on General Hood's staff. This letter as published in Drake's magazine *Annals of The Army of Tennessee* for May 1877, reads as follows:

In answer to yours of the 12th instant, I have to say that on the night the Army of Tennessee, under command of General J. B. Hood, halted at Spring Hill on its march from Columbia to Nashville, General Hood, his adjutant-general Major Mason, and myself occupied the same room at the residence of Captain [Absalom] Thompson, near the village. Late at night we were aroused by a private soldier, who reported to General Hood that on reaching the camp near Spring Hill, he found himself within Federal lines; that the troops were in great confusion, a part of them were marching in the direction of Franklin, others had turned toward Columbia, and that the road was blocked with baggage-wagons and gun carriages, rendering it impossible to move in order in either direction. Upon the receipt of this report, General Hood directed Major Mason too order General Cheatham to move down the road immediately and attack the enemy. General Hood and myself remained in bed. I went to sleep, and I suppose that General Hood did the same. At daylight on the following morning we learned that the Federal Army had left Spring Hill and was being concentrated at Franklin.

On the march to Franklin, General Hood spoke to me, in the presence of Major Mason, of the failure of General Cheatham to make the night attack at Spring Hill, and censured him in severe terms for the disobedience of orders. Soon after this, being alone with Major Mason, the latter remarked that "General Cheatham was not to blame about the matter last night. I did not send him the order." I asked if he had communicated the fact to General Hood. He answered that he had not. I replied that it is due to General Cheatham that this explanation should be made. Thereupon Major Mason joined General Hood and gave him the information. Afterwards General Hood said to me that he had done injustice to General Cheatham, and requested me to inform him that he held him blameless for the failure at Spring Hill. And, on the day following the battle of Franklin, I was informed by General Hood that he had addressed a note to General Cheatham, assuring him that he did not censure or charge him with the failure to make the attack.

CHAPTER 16

☆ *Battle of Franklin*

WHEN Hood on the morning of November 30th woke up in his bed at the home of Captain Absalom Thompson, where he had established his headquarters and spent the night, he discovered that Schofield had eluded him while he slept. When he realized what had happened he was, as General John C. Brown later said, "wrathy as a rattlesnake". Hood and several of his generals ate breakfast that morning at the nearby home of Major Nat Cheairs, and there are legends of a violent quarrel at that breakfast table. Whether there were actually any such angry accusations and recriminations can not now be established. It is safe to say, however, that there was a distinct feeling of frustration and disappointment at the events of the preceding twenty-four hours. Hood was undeniably bitter. As he wrote later: "The best move in my career as a soldier, I was thus destined to behold come to naught." It was indeed a brilliant conception of strategy, frustrated by amazingly poor tactical work. But whose fault was it? After all, Hood was in command. Whatever was done or was left undone was his responsibility.

Schofield was ungenerous and boastful when he later wrote: "Hood went to bed that night, while I was in the saddle all night, directing in person all the important movements of my troops. Perhaps that is enough to account for the difference between success and failure." Immodest as this may sound, there is an element of truth in it. Hood, during the fateful hours of that night, was certainly out of touch with what was actually going on. In his defense, it should be remembered that he was painfully crippled, suffering with his withered left arm and the stump of his amputated right leg. In this condition, in the pain that he must have suffered, he simply was not equal to the sustained physical and mental activity demanded by such an emergency. The spirit was willing, but the flesh was weak—but sympathy for a crippled man can not be extended to condone his efforts to blame the failure on a scapegoat, instead of manfully saying, as did Robert E. Lee in similar circumstances, "It was all my fault."

But, regardless of how he felt and who was to blame, on the morning of

November 30 Hood had a new and pressing problem—how to retrieve his lost advantage over his adversary. In his frame of mind that morning, angry at his subordinates (and probably angry at himself), he evidently could think of nothing better to do than to try to overtake the flying Schofield, fight him and punish him. In his own words, he arrived at the desperate resolve "to make that same afternoon another and final effort to overtake and rout him, and drive him in the Big Harpeth River at Franklin."

So, the men of the Army of Tennessee were roused and pressed forward from Spring Hill "at early dawn", their van not far behind Schofield's rear guard which, according to one of the Federal chroniclers, did not leave the village "till it was fairly daylight." Stewart's corps marched first, followed by Cheatham's. Lee, who had followed the last of Schofield's men as they fell back from Duck River, reached Spring Hill about nine o'clock on the morning of the 30th, with Clayton's and Stevenson's divisions of his corps, and they fell in behind Cheatham. Then came the wagons and the artillery.

Probably no army ever marched to battle in such a temper as pervaded the Army of Tennessee that morning, plodding along the dusty road from Spring Hill to Franklin, fifteen miles away. The army's commander was disappointed and angry; his subordinates were in equally bad humor; and the feeling of frustration had permeated the ranks and engendered in the men as well as the officers a resolution to overtake and whip the enemy who had slipped through their fingers the preceding night. Before the day was done Hood was to learn that the Army of Tennessee need not be behind breastworks to fight, was not afraid to charge an enemy in his entrenchments.

The Federal withdrawal from Spring Hill that night was not accomplished without a full measure of anxiety on the part of all concerned. Schofield, in pushing on ahead with Ruger's division, left Stanley with the responsibility of saving the artillery and the wagon trains, which was no small task. Wagner's division, which had been the first to arrive at Spring Hill, was the last to leave. Captain Shellenberger, who was among those called under arms about midnight to take part in the withdrawal, makes no secret of their nervous apprehension as they waited for the other units of Schofield's army to move down the pike.

While standing in column we could hear to our left the rumble of wheels where the artillery and the wagons were pulling out, and much of the time could be heard the dull tread of many feet and the clicking of accoutrements that told of the march of a column of troops along the pike; but there was no other sound—nor even the shout of a teamster to his mules or the crack of a whip. All the surroundings were so impressive as to subdue the most boisterously profane man. In expressing their dissatisfaction with the situation, they were always careful to mutter their curses in a tone so low as to be inaudible a short distance away, for, looking to our right, we could see the glow on the sky made by the bivouac fires of the enemy, and in some places could see the fires with a few men about them cooking something to eat, or otherwise engaged, while most of their men were lying on the ground asleep.

Every minute of those anxious hours we were looking for them to awake to the opportunity that was slipping through their fingers and grab hold of it by advancing and opening fire on the congested mass of troops and trains that choked the pike. Occasionally our column would move a short distance. Any orders that may have been given were spoken in a low tone at the head of the column. You would be apprised that the column was moving by the silent disappearance in the darkness of your file leader. You would hurry after him and taking, perhaps, not more than a dozen steps, would be brought to a sudden halt by running against him, immediately followed by the man in your rear bumping up against yourself. Then would follow an indefinite wait until the column would again move on a short distance.

The wearing suspense of the long waiting, while standing on our feet, the exasperating halts following those false starts, when everybody was almost frantic with impatience to go on, the excessive physical fatigue, combined with the intense mental strain when already haggard from much loss of sleep during the three days and night preceding, make that night memorable as by far the most trying in nearly four years of soldiering. It afforded unspeakable relief when, just as daylight was beginning to dawn, our column finally got away in rapid motion for Franklin, the enemy dogging our heels with their close pursuit.

Captain Levi T. Scofield, engineer officer of Schofield's 23rd Army Corps, tells how the general and his staff, galloping ahead of the column, arrived at Franklin about 3 o'clock in the morning. Here they established their headquarters at the home of Fountain B. Carter and his family, "the last house in the suburbs of the town, on the Columbia pike." To Captain Scofield was assigned the duty of placing the Federal troops in a defensive position when they arrived, and he sat down in front of the house and waited for their coming.

Presently, he relates, the tramp of horses in the distance and the rattle of tin cups against bayonet clasps foretold the coming of the troops. First the brigade officers, mounted, appeared, and they were led off to the right of the road, where a hasty inspection of the ground was made in the darkness; then the weary men came marching by the left flank. The night tramp had been wearing to those on foot, for they had been pressed to unusual speed, and their anxiety about the train, that was strung along by their side, kept them peering out into the dim distance, lest Forrest's cavalry might strike them at any point, although every regiment had a company deployed in the fields to our right.

The Third Division (Cox's) of the Twenty-third Corps was led into position on the east side of the pike . . . all facing to the south. General Cox was placed in command of the two divisions, his own (on the east of the road) and Ruger's, (on the west), and was instructed—as soon as the troops could get a short breathing spell, a few winks of sleep and their morning coffee—to strongly intrench themselves.

It was deemed expedient by General Schofield to make our stand on the south side of the town and river, so that the trains could mass in the streets and open spaces in the village, while a wagon-road bridge was being built and planks laid on the sleepers of the railroad bridge for their transfer across. . . . There was nothing to do but construct the bridges with the meager facilities at hand; so, with his Engineer Battalion and details of troops, the work was performed, requiring the General's constant personal attention. He remained in this position up to the time of the engagement, so as to better superintend the crossing, and at the same time be near the railroad and telegraph station; while from Fort Granger, on the bluff east of the railroad and near the river, he had perfect command during the battle of the entire field, and to direct the fire of the artillery stationed there with him.

These necessary activities requiring all his personal attention, General Schofield temporarily assigned command of the Twenty-third Corps to General Cox, emphatically impressing on him that he must "hold Hood back at all hazards, till we can get our trains over and fight with the river in front of us." As General Stanley was slightly wounded at the very beginning of the ensuing battle and had to retire from the field, it came about that Cox was virtually in charge of the entire Federal force during the battle of Franklin.

Continuing his account of the placing of the troops in position, Captain Scofield says:

During the forenoon the troops, in close order, kept pouring in, the infantry on the right side of the road and wagon trains and artillery to their left. The march was not so rapid as during the night, for they were continually harassed by Forrest's cavalry attacking in weak points on the road. Wood's Division of the Fourth Corps passed through the town and formed in position on the north side of the Harpeth; Kimball's Division of the same corps was ordered to report to General Cox, and was placed by him on the right of the Twenty-third Corps, with its right flank resting on the Harpeth River. Lane's and Conrad's brigades of Wagner's division were counter-marched and placed something over 100 rods in our front, across the Columbia pike, to watch the approach of the enemy, and to their right and front on a little knoll, a section of Marshall's Battery, supported by an infantry regiment. Opdyke's Brigade, of the same division, which had been acting as rear-guard from Spring Hill, passed through our line and was ordered to take up a position in reserve behind Carter's Hill. The two regiments of Reilly's Brigade that were left back in the skirmish line at Duck River arrived, and formed the second line behind the main works.

Franklin is on the south side of the Harpeth River, on elevated ground enclosed within a bend of that stream. From the south the town is approached by three turnpikes and by the Nashville & Decatur (now the Louisville & Nashville) Railroad. The most important of the three turnpikes is the road from Columbia, there running about due north and south, with the railroad almost parallel a half mile to the east. Further east, running about parallel with the river, is the Lewisburg pike; and from the southwest the town is approached by the Carter's Creek pike. Leaving the town on the north the Nashville highway and the railroad cross the river on bridges not far apart, but at the time of the battle the bridge had been destroyed.

The crossing of the Harpeth was commanded by a strong fortification called Fort Granger, bristling with artillery, and by other batteries along the banks of the river on the north side. The line of works occupied by Schofield's army made a wide crescent, stretching from a stout position on the extreme left, where the railroad passed through a deep cut near the river, westward across the Columbia pike, where the works were strongest. There was a gap left in the breastworks where the turnpike passed through, and back of this gap was a retrenchment extending across the road just south of the Carter house on the west side of the road, and extending for a short distance westward, on a line with the Carter smoke-house, providing a double line of breastworks in this sector for about a hundred yards. On the east side of the road the entrenchments passed, at a sharp angle, just in front of the Carter cotton gin. Just outside the front line on the west side of the pike was a grove of locust trees, and on the east side an osage orange hedge, both of which had been felled to form a rude abatis at each of those points.

The position occupied by Wagner's two brigades in their exposed position in front of the main line turned out to play an important part in the action to take place in the next few hours. In the Federal retirement from Spring Hill, Wagner's division was kept in position there until the trains and all the other troops were moving in the direction of Franklin; and Opdyke's brigade of this division, which was the rear guard of the whole movement, did not get under way until six o'clock in the morning of the 30th.

When Wagner and his three brigades came up after the other Federal troops had been placed in position in the main defense works, he was ordered to form a line across the road about a half-mile in front of the breastworks, to act as a sort of buffer skirmish line. Colonel Bradley had been wounded at Spring Hill and his brigade was now commanded by Colonel Joseph Conrad. Conrad's and Lane's brigades were placed in position without protest; but, Captain Shellenberger relates,

When Opdyke's brigade came up to the position occupied by Conrad and Lane, Wagner rode forward and ordered Opdyke into line with them. Colonel Opdyke strenuously objected to this order. He declared that troops out in front of the breastworks were in a good position to aid the enemy and nobody else. He also pleaded that his brigade was worn out, having been marching for several hours during the morning, while covering the rear of our retreating column, in line of battle in sight of the enemy, climbing over fences and passing through woods, thickets and muddy corn-field, and was entitled to a relief. While they were discussing the matter they rode along the pike together, the brigade marching in column behind them, until they entered the gap in the breastworks left for the pike, and finding the ground in that vicinity fully occupied by other troops, they kept along until they came to the first clear space, which was 200 yards inside the breastworks. There Wagner turned away with the final remark: "Well, Opdyke, fight when and where you damn please; we all know you'll fight." Colonel Opdyke then had his brigade stack arms on the clear space; and his persistence in thus marching his brigade inside the breastworks proved, about two hours later, to be the salvation of our army.

In subsequent accounts of the battle it was stated by Wagner's superior officers that he had been given "instructions not to be caught fighting out there, but to fall back immediately behind the breastworks if Hood made a forward movement in force." Captain Marshall P. Thatcher says that "a staff officer was sent a second time to see if Wagner understood the order, but the poorest charity we can extend him (Wagner) is that he must have been drunk," and he quotes Colonel Edward H. Wolfe, commander of one of Wagner's regiments, as saying he was. Thatcher also quotes General Stanley as saying that "Wagner was full of whisky, if not drunk. He told Conrad's aide to tell Conrad to 'fight the rebs till hell freezes over' which was directly contrary to my instructions."

Captain Shellenberger, who was directly involved, has this to say about it:

When Conrad's brigade took up its advanced position we all supposed it would be only temporary, but soon an orderly came along the line with instructions for the company commanders, and he told me that the orders were to hold the position to the last man, and to have my sergeants fix bayonets and to instruct my company that any man, not wounded, who should attempt to leave the line without orders would be shot or bayonetted by the sergeants.

The men in the two brigades immediately began to fortify . . . but, in spite of our utmost exertions, when the attack came we had only succeeded in throwing up a slight embankment which was high enough to give good protection against musket balls to the men squatting down in the ditch from which the earth had been thrown, but on the outside, where there was no ditch, it was so low that a battle-line could march over it without halting. We were out in a large old cotton-field, not under cultivation that year. The ground ascended with an easy grade from our position back to Cox's line, and all the intervening space, as well as a wide expanse to our left, was as bare as a floor of any obstruction. . . .

It took two hours, from two till four o'clock, for the corps of Cheatham and Stewart to come up and get into position, and then they advanced to the assault in heavy lines of battle. . . . We kept our entrenching spades flying until they had approached within range of our skirmish line, which fired a few shots and then began to retreat rapidly. Then the spades were dropped and the men, taking their muskets, squatted down below the low streak of earth they had thrown out, to receive the coming onset. . . .

It was a pleasant, hazy Indian summer day, and so warm that I was carrying my overcoat on my arm. When the line squatted down I folded the coat into a compact bundle and, placing it on the edge of the bank in rear of my company and sitting on it, with my feet in the shallow ditch, by craning my neck could look over our low parapet. . . . Our line opened fire on the approaching rebel line, and our fire checked them in front, for they halted and began to return it, but for a minute only, for, urged on by their officers, they again came forward.

Their advance was so rapid that my company had fired only five or six rounds to the man when the break came. The salient of our line was near the pike, and there the opposing lines met in a hand-to-hand encounter in which clubbed muskets were used, but our line quickly gave way. I had been glancing uneasily along our line, watching for a break as a pretext for getting out of there, and was looking towards the pike when the break first started. It ran along the line so rapidly that it reminded me of a train of powder burning. I instantly sprang to my feet and looked to the front. They were coming on the run, emitting the shrill rebel charging yell, and so close that my first impulse was to throw myself flat on the ground and let them charge over us. But the rear was open, and a sense of duty, as well as a thought of the horrors I had heard of rebel prisons, constrained me to take what I believed to be the very dangerous risk of trying to escape. I shouted to my company, "Fall back!" and gave an example of how to do it by turning and running for our breastworks. . . . I had forgotten my overcoat, but had run only a rod or two when I thought of it and stopped and looked back with the intention of returning to get it, but the rebels then appeared to be as close to the coat as I was and very reluctantly, for it was a new one, I let them have it. After running a few rods farther I again looked back. They were then standing on the low embankment we had left, loading and firing at will; but just as I looked some of their officers waved their swords and sprang forward. The fire then slackened, as they started in hot pursuit to get to the breastworks with us.

General Hood, in writing his book several years later, gives a colorful account of the action at Franklin which is interesting as coming from the Confederate commanding officer, but which is somewhat misleading and not entirely accurate in some of its statements and implications:

Within about three miles of Franklin, the enemy was discovered on the ridge over which passes the turnpike. As soon as the Confederate troops began to deploy, and skirmishers were thrown forward, the Federals withdrew slowly to the environs of the town.

It was about 3 p. m. when Lieutenant General Stewart moved to the right of the pike and began to establish his position in front of the enemy. Major General Cheatham's Corps, as it arrived in turn, filed off to the left of the road, and was also disposed in line of battle. The artillery was instructed to take no part in the engagement, on account of the danger to which women and children in the village would be exposed. General Forrest was ordered to post cavalry on both flanks, and, if the assault proved successful, to complete the ruin of the enemy by capturing those who attempted to escape in the direction of Nashville. Lee's Corps, as it arrived, was held in reserve, owing to the lateness of the hour and my inability, consequently, to post it on the extreme left. Schofield's position was rendered favorable for defence by open ground in front, and temporary entrenchments which the Federals had had time to throw up, notwithstanding the Confederate forces had marched in pursuit with all possible speed. At one or two points, along a short space, a slight abatis had been hastily constructed, by felling some small locust saplings in the vicinity.

Soon after Cheatham's Corps was massed on the left, Major General Cleburne came to me where I was seated on my horse in rear of the line, and asked permission to form his Division in two, or, if I remember correctly, three lines for the assault. I at once granted his request, stating that I desired the Federals to be driven into the river in their immediate rear and directing him to advise me as soon as he had completed the new disposition of his troops. Shortly afterward, Cheatham and Stewart reported all in readiness for action, and received orders to drive the enemy from his position into the river *at all hazards.* About that time Cleburne returned, and, expressing himself with an enthusiasm which he had never before betrayed in our intercourse, said, "General, I am ready, and have more hope in the final success of our cause than I have had at any time since the first gun was fired." I replied "God grant it!" He turned and moved at once toward the head of his Division; a few moments thereafter he was lost to my sight in the tumult of battle. These last words, spoken to me by this brave and distinguished soldier, I have often recalled; they can never leave my memory, as within forty minutes after he had uttered them, he lay lifeless upon or near the breastworks of the foe.

The two corps advanced in battle array at about 4 p. m., and soon swept away the first line of the Federals, who were driven back upon the main line. At this moment, resounded a concentrated roar of musketry, which recalled to me some of the deadliest struggles in Virginia, and which now proclaimed that the possession of Nashville was once more dependent upon the fortunes of war. The conflict continued to rage with intense fury; our troops succeeded in breaking the main line at one or more points, capturing and turning some of the guns on their opponents.

Just at this critical moment of the battle, a brigade of the enemy, reported to have been Stanley's [it was Opdyke's] gallantly charged, and restored the Federal line, capturing at the same time about one thousand of our troops within the entrenchments. Still the ground was obstinately contested, and, at several points upon the immediate sides of the breastworks, the combatants endeavored to use the musket upon one another, by inverting and raising it perpendicularly, in order to fire; neither antagonist, at this juncture, was able to retreat without almost a certainty of death. It was reported that soldiers were even dragged from one side of the breastworks to the other by men reaching over hurriedly and seizing their enemy by the hair or the collar.

Just before dark Johnson's Division, of Lee's Corps, moved gallantly to the support of Cheatham; although it made a desperate charge and succeeded in capturing three stands of colors, it did not effect a permanent breach in the line of the enemy. The two remaining divisions could not unfortunately become engaged owing to the obscurity of night. The struggle continued with more or less violence until 9 p. m., when followed skirmishing and much desultory firing until about 3 a. m. the ensuing morning. The enemy then withdrew, leaving his dead and wounded upon the field. Thus terminated one of the fiercest conflicts of the war.

Nightfall which closed in upon us so soon after the inauguration of the battle prevented the formation and participation of Lee's entire Corps on the extreme left. This, it may safely be asserted, saved Schofield's Army from destruction. I might, with equal assurance, assert that had Lieutenant General Lee been in advance at Spring Hill the previous afternoon, Schofield's Army never would have passed that point.

When General Hood stood under a linn tree on the side of Winstead Hill and examined the terrain through his field glasses, he must have been impressed by Schofield's well-manned and well-constructed works, but his battle ardor was not cooled by what he saw. "We will make the fight!" he announced crisply, as he snapped shut the case of his glasses and turned to his subordinates at his side. Cheatham, the oldest of Hood's corps commanders, did not "like the looks of the fight", and was bold enough to say so, but Hood held to his determination. Forrest also advised against a direct frontal attack on Schofield's strong position. He thought they should try to flank Schofield by crossing the Harpeth to the right, and he offered to attempt this himself if given a brigade of infantry to support his cavalry. Hood, however, says in his report that "the nature of the position was such as to render it inexpedient to attempt any further flanking movement". It was essential, he reported, to attack Schofield "before he could make himself strong"—but Schofield had already made himself strong in his works, with headlogs on top of the earthworks to protect the double and triple lines of riflemen ensconced there.

Having made his rash decision to attack the Federal works in his front, Hood seemed consumed with a burning impetuosity and could not wait even long enough to make proper preparations—could not wait for Lee to come up with his divisions; could not wait for the artillery to arrive. It was getting late, and if he was going to fight he must get into action without delay. Stewart and Cheatham were up; he would attack with them immediately, as quickly as they could get into line.

Stewart's corps was deployed to move up on the right along the Lewisburg pike and the Nashville & Decatur Railroad. They were aligned in the grove behind the John M. McGavock house, with Loring's division on the right, Walthall in the center and French on the left. Cheatham moved directly forward along the Columbia pike, with Cleburne on the right (east) side of the road and Brown on the left. Bate's division was marched by the left flank around behind Merrill's hill, toward the Carter's Creek pike, to come in on Brown's left as they neared the works. Johnson's division of Lee's corps, which had moved from Spring Hill with Cheatham, was held in reserve. Forrest was ordered to divide his cavalry between the two flanks.

As soon as Stewart and Cheatham announced that their lines had been formed and adjusted to each other, Hood ordered the assault. At four o'clock they went forward under the declining autumn sun, their bayonets flashing, their tattered battle-flags flying in the November breeze; eighteen brigades of infantry marching in a straight line across an open field.

Captain Scofield was standing on the Federal parapet as the attacking Confederate forces swept over the fields of the Carter farm in what he described as "a solid human wave". He gives a vivid picture of the sight he saw there:

> The firing had slackened and the smoke cleared, so that we could plainly see the splendid advance. It was a grand sight! Such as would make a lifelong impression on the mind of any man who could see such a resistless, well-conducted charge. For the moment we were spellbound with admiration, although they were our hated foes and we knew that in a few brief moments, as soon as they reached firing distance, all of that orderly grandeur would be changed to bloody, writhing confusion and that thousands of those valorous men of the South, with their chivalric officers, would pour out their life's blood on the fair fields in front of us.
>
> As fore-runners well in advance could be seen a line of wild rabbits, bounding along for a few steps, and then they would stop and look back and listen, but scamper off again, as though convinced that this was the most impenetrable line of beaters—in that had ever given them chase; and quails by the thousands in covies here and there would rise and settle, and rise again to the warm sunlight that called them back;

but no, they were frightened by the unusual turmoil and back they came, and this repeated until finally they rose high in the air and whirred off to the gray skylight of the north.

The day had been bright and warm, reminding us of the Northern Indian Summer; the afternoon sun, like a ball of fire, was settling in all its Southern splendor in a molten sea of bronze, over the distant hills; and in the hazy, golden light, and with their yellowish-brown uniforms, those in the front ranks seemed to be magnified in size; one could almost imagine them to be phantoms sweeping along in the air.

On they came, and in the center their lines seemed to be many deep and unbroken, their red-and-white tattered flags, with the emblem of St. Andrew's cross, as numerous as though every company bore them, flaring brilliantly in the sun's rays, with conspicuous mounted groups of general and staff officers in their midst, and a battery or two in single line charging along between the divisions.

James Barr, of Company E, Sixty-Fifth Illinois Volunteers, in Cox's division, writing after the war, gives another account of the Confederate attack from the viewpoint of one of those in the Federal line anxiously waiting for the moment of contact with the attackers:

I was a re-enlisted veteran, and went through twenty-seven general engagements, but I am sure that Franklin was the hardest fought field that I ever stood upon.

Gen. J. D. Cox (in his "Franklin and Nashville") censures Gen. Wagner for holding to his advanced position too long, calls his action a gross blunder, etc.; but, as one of Cox's men, I looked upon the matter in a different light. I think, if Cleburne had not struck Wagner's two brigades as he did, that his brave lads would have broken our line successfully; but, as it was, his men were badly winded with his work with Wagner, which gave Opdyke's and White's men a better chance to check him at the cotton gin.

The way I saw it was this: I was acting as orderly and standing a few paces east of the cotton gin. The first Confederate troops that came in view were Stewart's Corps on our left with Cheatham's Corps to the left of Stewart. The Confederate line moved easily and steadily on, until Cleburne was checked for the time by Wagner. The short time lost by Cleburne threw Stewart's line too far in advance. Stewart was first to receive the fire from our main line, and was unable to carry our works, his men who were not killed or wounded being compelled to retire. Now Cleburne, who had been delayed by Wagner, came up just in time to receive a heavy right oblique fire from the men who had repulsed Stewart's Corps. I never saw men in such a terrible position as Cleburne's Division was in for a few minutes. The wonder is that any of them escaped death or capture.

General John C. Brown, in a report to General Cheatham of the operations of his division during the ensuing action, in which Brown was seriously wounded, says:

Cleburne and myself were directed (by General Hood) to form in conjunction, Cleburne on the right and I on the left of the turnpike, and threaten and (if not routed before we reached the works) attack the enemy's center; but were instructed not to move until further orders from him, as he desired Bate and Stewart, having a longer distance to march, to move in advance of us.

After the expiration of half an hour or more, Cleburne and myself were directed to commence our movement. We advanced our line, attacking simultaneously the enemy's front line of works (being a lunette some 400 or 500 yards in advance of the main works). We routed and drove that line back upon the enemy's main line with but slight loss to ourselves and without impeding the advance of our line. General Cleburne and myself met several times upon the turnpike road and conferred and acted in harmony in the movement.

When we assaulted the main line, we carried the works in many places. General [George W.] Gordon, commanding the right brigade of my front line, stormed and carried the enemy's works at the turnpike road and advanced a considerable distance within the works, when he and a part of his command were captured. The enemy rapidly reinforced his center from his flanks, and the slaughter in our ranks was frightful, considering the very short time in which we were engaged. The loss was so heavy to my front line that I immediately brought forward the supporting brigades (Strahl's and Carter's), and we held the works in a hand-to-hand fight, with varying fortune, until night closed upon the bloody conflict.

The engagement lasted but little more than one hour, during which time the fire of the enemy's infantry was terrific. Generals Gist and Strahl were killed on the field, with nearly all of their staff officers. General Carter received a mortal wound from which he died in a few hours. When I was shot from my horse near nightfall, I had only one staff officer and two couriers on duty.

I regret very much that the loss of my papers will not allow me to give you in detail the list of casualties and to mention the conduct of very many officers and men conspicuous for their gallantry during the engagement. It is just to say, however, that the entire command did its full duty. The enemy were intrenched in strong works protected in front by an abatis of black locust, which was almost impassable, and our advancing lines were met by successive volleys of musketry that would have repulsed any but well-tried and dauntless veterans.

The "reinforcements" mentioned by General Brown were the men of Colonel Opdyke's brigade, who were standing in reserve when the battle started. But for the fortuitous presence of Opdyke's men in the right place at the right time and their prompt action in counter-charging into the melee where the Confederates' initial charge had punched through the Federal line, the outcome of the battle of Franklin might well have been different. It is interesting to read Opdyke's own account of how his brigade turned the tide of battle at the critical moment:

At about 4 PM General Cox sent me orders to have my brigade ready. . . . The fighting was now heavy, and I commenced moving the command to the left of the pike for greater security to the men and for easier maneuvering in case of need. While thus moving, a most horrible stampede of our front troops came surging and rushing back past Carter's house, extending to the right and left of the pike. I at first thought them the Second and Third Brigades of our [Wagner's] division, that were left nearly a quarter of a mile to the front, with orders to fall back; but I soon saw that the troops at the main works had left them. When I gave the order "First Brigade, forward to the works", bayonets came down to a charge, the yell was raised, and the regiments rushed most grandly forward, carrying many stragglers back with them. We deployed as we charged, which took us up in echelon forward on the center.

The enemy were following our troops with great celerity and force. He was met this side of Carter's house by our charge, and at once put to rout, with a loss of 394 prisoners. . . . A battery and a section of another near Carter's house were abandoned to the enemy in the stampede, and were retaken by this charge and worked by the officers and men of this command. Our lines were now restored, and the battle raged with indescribable fury. The enemy hurled his masses against us with seeming desperation. Officers devoted their mightiest energies to bringing up the stragglers to the breast-works, and we soon had the position impregnable. These desperate assaults continued till after dark, when the enemy ceased all heavy efforts against our position. I twice stepped to the front of the works on the Columbia pike to see the effect of such fighting. I never saw the dead lay near so thick. I saw them upon each other, dead and ghastly in the powder-dimmed starlight. My withdrawal was under General Cox's instructions, and was accomplished at midnight.

Ellison Capers (after the war an Episcopal minister who became Bishop of South Carolina) was colonel of the 24th South Carolina Infantry in Gist's brigade of Brown's division, and he led his regiment in that historic and bloody charge against the Federal breastworks at Franklin, moving into action to the left (west) of the Columbia pike. General Gist was killed in this action and the adjutant general of the brigade was wounded, so Capers wrote a report of the brigade's action for the record. He tells how

Just before the charge was ordered the brigade passed over an elevation, from which we beheld the magnificent spectacle the battle-field presented—bands were playing, general and staff officers and gallant couriers were riding in front of and between the battle lines, 100 battle-flags were waving in the smoke of battle, and bursting shells were wreathing the air with great circles of smoke, while 20,000 brave men were marching in perfect order against the foe. . . .

General Gist ordered the charge in concert with General Gordon. In passing from the left to the right of the regiment the general waved his hat to us, expressed his pride and confidence in the Twenty-fourth, and rode away in the smoke of the battle, never more to be seen by the men he had commanded on so many fields. His horse was shot and, dismounting, he was leading the right of the brigade when he fell, pierced through the heart.

On pressed the charging lines of the brigade, driving the advance force of the enemy pell-mell into a locust abatis, where many were captured and sent to the rear; others were wounded by the fire of their own men. This abatis was a formidable and fearful obstruction. The entire brigade was arrested by it. Fortunately for us, the fire of the enemy slackened to let their advance troops come in, and we took advantage of it to work our way through. Gist's and Gordon's brigades charged on and reached the ditch of the work, mounted the work, and met the enemy in close combat. The colors of the Twenty-fourth were planted and defended on the parapet, and the enemy retired in our front some distance, but soon rallied and came back, in turn, to charge us. He never succeeded in retaking the line we held. About dusk there was a lull in the firing west of the pike. Brown's division had established itself in the ditch of the work and so far as Gist's brigade front, on the crest. Torn and exhausted, deprived of every general officer and nearly every field officer, the division had only strength enough left to hold its position.

Strahl's and Carter's brigades came gallantly to the assistance of Gist's and Gordon's, but the enemy's fire from the houses in rear of the line and from his reserves, thrown rapidly forward, and from guns posted on the far side of the river so as to enfilade the field, tore their line to pieces before it reached the locust abatis. Strahl and his entire staff were killed . . . and Carter was mortally wounded. But there was no backward movement of this line. Its momentum, though slackened by its terrible losses, carried it on to the ditch.

S. A. Cunningham, a sergeant-major in Strahl's brigade, was one of those who took part in that hand-to-hand fighting over the breastworks and he wrote a graphic account of it in the *Confederate Veteran,* of which he was editor and publisher after the war:

I was near General Strahl, who stood in the ditch and handed up guns to those posted to fire them. I had passed to him my short Enfield (noted in the regiment) about the sixth time. The man who had been firing, cocked it and was taking deliberate aim, when he was shot and tumbled down dead into the ditch upon those killed before him. When the men so exposed were shot down, their places were supplied by volunteers until these were exhausted, and it was necessary for General Strahl to call for others. He turned to me, and though I was several feet back from the ditch, I rose up immediately, and walking over the wounded and dead, took position with one foot upon the pile of bodies of my dead fellows, and the other upon the embankment, and fired guns which the General himself handed up to me until he, too, was shot down. One other man had position on my right, and assisted in the firing.

The battle lasted until not an efficient man was left between us and the Columbia Pike, some fifty yards to our right, and hardly any behind us to hand up guns. Indeed but few of us were then left alive. It seemed as if we had no choice but to surrender or try to get away. When I asked General Strahl for counsel, he simply answered, "Keep firing." But just as the man to my right was shot, and fell against me with terrible groans, the General too was shot. He threw up his hands, falling on his face, and I thought him dead, but in asking the dying man, who still lay against my shoulders as he sank forever, how he was wounded, the General, who had not been killed, thinking my question was to him, raised up saying that he was shot in the neck, and called for Colonel Stafford to turn over his command. He crawled over the dead, the ditch being three deep, about twenty feet to where Colonel Stafford was. Staff officers and others started to carry him to the rear, but he received another shot, and directly the third, which killed him instantly. Colonel Stafford was dead in the pile, as the morning light disclosed, with his feet wedged in at the bottom, other dead across and under him after he fell; leaving his body half standing as if ready to give command to the dead!

By that time but a handful of us were left on that part of the line, and as I was sure that our condition was not known, I ran to the rear to report to General John C. Brown, commanding the division. I met Major Hampton of his staff, who told me that General Brown was wounded, and that General Strahl was in command. This assured me that those in command did not know the real situation, so I went on the hunt for General Cheatham.

Captain Irving A. Buck, adjutant general of Cleburne's division, has written an impressive account of the action east of the pike as Cleburne's division encountered Wagner's advanced line and then pressed on:

Wagner's men broke in confusion and fled to the protection of their main line of works. For a long time there had existed a rivalry between Cheatham's (now Brown's) division and that of Cleburne, and as the line rushed forward, the former troops shouted to the latter, as the Federals scattered, "We will go into the works with them," and the two divisions were pushed so rapidly that on the right of the Franklin-Columbia pike Cleburne's reached the entrenchments almost as soon as did Wagner's demoralized men.

To describe truly that which followed is beyond the power of tongue or pen. In the reckless disregard of life, and in the tenacity of purpose displayed, the attack has rarely been equalled, never excelled. The men fought like demons. Often the combatants were near enough to use clubbed muskets and the bayonet. The first desperate charge by Cheathan was repeated again and again, while Stewart on his right threw his force upon the Federals in their entrenchments and fought with the same daring and determination that Cheatham's men had shown. Inside the Federal works a new raw regiment broke and ran to the rear, and into the gap thus created Brown's and Cleburne's men rushed, but from losses they were too weak to hold the ground against the reinforcements of the seasoned and well-disciplined brigade of General Emerson Opdyke. Besides, of their leaders the inspiring voice of Cleburne was already hushed in death, and Brown lay wounded on the field. The division were driven only to the ditch outside, into which they dropped fighting, as they thus lay, as opportunity offered to fire at any exposure by the troops defending the works; these in turn discharging their guns by inverting and holding them perpendicularly over the fortifications. Neither antagonist at the time was able to retreat without risk of certain death. Lieutenant Mangum, Cleburne's aide, in delivering an order, finding himself between the embrasures of two Federal batteries, found it safer to remain where he was, with only the ditch separating him from the enemy, than to attempt to return, until the simultaneous discharge of the guns to his right and left enabled him to ride back in safety.

While the infantry fight was in progress Forrest ordered Chalmers to the left, where his cavalry charged and dislodged the enemy from every position. Forrest also directed General Jackson's cavalry division to cross Harpeth river and drive the enemy from a hill from where he was firing upon the Confederate troops on the Lewisburg pike. General Buford's cavalry was dismounted and took position in line of battle to the right of Stewart's corps, covering the ground from the Lewisburg pike to Harpeth River. Skirmishing began at once, and Buford rapidly advanced, driving the enemy's infantry across the river, where it joined General Wilson's cavalry. Jackson engaged this united force of infantry and cavalry and held them in check until night, when he threw forward his pickets and drew back across the river to replenish his exhausted ammunition. . . .

Darkness came, but the struggle continued. Flashes of the guns upon one side would furnish light by which a volley would be directed by the other. The opposing lines at points were within easy reach of each other, and kept up the fusilade until between 9 and 10 o'clock, when it abated, simply because both sides were actually worn out physically and human endurance would bear no greater strain. Between 11 o'clock and midnight the Federals took advantage of the cessation to slip quietly in retreat towards Nashville.

Strangely enough, nobody seems to have seen Cleburne when he received his fatal wound. General Govan tells of his last contact with his division commander:

General Cleburne had two horses killed under him in the attack on Franklin. I was very near him when his first horse was killed. The impetus at which he was moving carried the horses forward after his death wound, and he fell almost in the ditch on the outside of the entrenchments. One of the couriers dismounted and gave Cleburne his horse; and, while in the act of mounting, this second horse was killed by a cannon-ball fired, as well as I remember, from the gin house. General Cleburne then moved forward on foot, waving his cap, and I lost sight of him in the smoke and din of battle, and he must have met his death a few seconds afterwards. All of this occurred near the intersection of the pike, and his body was found within twenty yards of where I last saw him waving his cap and urging his command forward.

John McQuaide, a Mississippi private in Cleburne's command, tells of the finding of the body of his commander "at early dawn the next morning":

He was about 40 or 50 yards from the works. He lay flat upon his back as if asleep, his military cap partly over his eyes. He had on a new gray uniform. The coat was unbuttoned and open; the lower part of his vest was unbuttoned and opened. He wore a white linen shirt, which was stained with blood on the front part of the left side. This was the only sign of a wound I saw on him, and I believe it is the only one he had received. I have always been inclined to think that, feeling his end was near, he had thus lain himself down to die, or that his body had been carried there during the night. He was in his sock feet, his boots having been stolen. His watch, sword belt and other valuables were all gone, his body having been robbed during the night.

Rev. Thomas R. Markham, a Presbyterian minister of New Orleans, was the chaplain of Featherston's brigade of Loring's division, and in charge of the brigade ambulance. McQuaide, seeing him nearby, removing the body of General Adams, called on him for help. Mr. Markham, in a post-war letter to McQuaide, takes it from there:

The men were in the act of lifting General Adams's body into the ambulance, when you rode up and reported that General Cleburne's body lay on the field. The ambulance was at once driven to the spot indicated by you. His body was placed beside that of General Adams and both taken to Colonel McGavock's residence. The two were placed together on the lower gallery, perfectly protected and cared for until their friends removed them.

On the Confederate right, the units on the right of Stewart's corps, almost as soon as the forward movement started, struck an unexpected obstacle in the railroad cut that anchored the left end of the Federal works. Forced to change front and move by the left flank, they were subjected to a massed artillery fire from across the river. Those who were able to make their way through the osage orange abatis struck the line where it was defended by Casement's brigade armed with the new repeating rifles. It has been said that never before in the history of warfare had a command the size of Casement's killed and wounded so many in so short a time. The quick-firing repeaters seemed to blaze out a continuous sheet of destruction. This, coupled with the enfilading fire of the artillery across the river, was more than Stewart's men could stand, and they fell back. The savagery of the fighting and the frightful loss of life among the officers in this charge are indicated by Walthall's report that in Quarles's brigade the highest ranking officer left was a captain.

Just one repulse was not enough to check the Army of Tennessee. Cheatham's and Stewart's men re-formed for another assault, with the attack concentrating along the line before the cotton gin. Again they were thrown back, again they re-formed and once more they charged. Repeatedly, in the teeth of the blinding storm of musketry and the devastating volleys of the guns, they forced their way up to those bloody breastworks and hung on in a hand-to-hand struggle with the defenders, battling man to man across the parapet.

Colonel Henry Stone, one of Thomas's staff officers, pays an admiring tribute to the bravery and tenacity of the attacking forces:

Time after time they came up to the very works. More than one color-bearer was shot down on the parapet. It is impossible to exaggerate the fierce energy with which the Confederate soldiers, that short November afternoon, threw themselves against the works, fighting with what seemed the very madness of despair. There was not a breath of wind, and the dense smoke settled down upon the field, so that after the first assault it was impossible to see at any distance. Through this blinding medium, assault after assault was made, several of the Union officers declaring in their reports that their lines received as many as thirteen distinct attacks.

On the left, Bate had further to move than Hood had estimated, and did not get up in time to take part in the grand charge. When he did reach the front, it was to discover that the Federal line angled away to the north, and when H. R. Jackson's brigade on his right was in contact with the enemy's works, the brigades on his left were still far away from it. Consequently Bate never got into effective cooperation with the other Confederate forces, although Jackson maintained his position at the works. Telling about it in his report, Bate says:

I moved forward through the open plain in good order. My skirmish line drove back that of the enemy. . . . The line moved steadily on, not waiting for the cavalry, driving the enemy from his outer works, which covered the right but not the left of my line. The cavalry (dismounted) not touching my left, nor being on a line with it, exposed that flank to a furious fire. . . . My line, now a single one, without support, charged the works of the enemy. My right got to the works (the second line) and remained there until morning; the left was driven back. The enemy's works were strong and defiant, constructed on a slight elevation, with few obstructions in front for several hundred yards. . . . The left of my line was reformed . . . but not in sufficient numbers to justify another effort to carry the works. . . . My loss in this engagement was 47 killed, 253 wounded and 19 missing. . . . Captain Carter, on staff duty with Tyler's brigade, fell mortally wounded near the works of the enemy and almost at the door of his father's house. His gallantry I witnessed with much pride, as I had done on other fields, and here take pleasure in mentioning it especially.

The death of Captain Theodoric (Tod) Carter, was one of those truth-is-stranger-than-fiction incidents, in which this war abounded. His father, Fountain B. Carter, tells us in simple words of the tragic home-coming of his son:

A Confederate soldier brought the sad tidings that Captain Theodoric Carter, a son and brother, lay wounded on the field. An elder brother (Colonel Moscow B. Carter) went immediately in search, but by misdirection went to another part of the field. In the meantime, General Thomas B. Smith, of whose staff young Carter was a member, reported the casualty and led the way, followed by the father, three sisters and sister-in-law, to where the young officer lay, mortally wounded. They lifted him gently and bore him back to die in the home he had not seen for two years and more. He had fallen when his heart's wish was almost attained, only a few rods distant from the home of a lifetime.

The harrowing experience of the Carter family, with a big-scale battle raging in their very door-yard, was one never to be forgotten. Fountain B. Carter, the elderly master of the household, early in the day had asked General Cox what he ought to do. Cox had advised him not to leave the house, "unless it should become certain that a battle was imminent"; but Cox had gone on to say that if there should be a battle "it would be no place for women and children". Col. Moscow B. Carter, the elder son, was a paroled prisoner of war who happened to be at home at the time. He took charge in the emergency, and tells how the family sweated it out:

While the preparations for the impending battle were going on, the Carter family were not inattentive observers, They had witnessed on other occasions sharp skirmishes between Rebel cavalry raiders and the Federal pickets stationed about the premises, in which men were killed and wounded, some in the yard, and even in the house itself. They felt somewhat inured to the casualties of war; but the great number of men now so hurriedly and so intently engaged in demolishing houses and constructing works of defence, looked to them painfully ominous. The scene presented was on a bigger scale than anything they had ever seen before. It created a feeling of profound anxiety. Whether to abandon home and the little that was left to them after three years and more of devastation, and to seek personal safety by flight, was the all-absorbing thought. In either aspect the prospect was discouraging. To leave home, pillage was almost certain, and blackened ruins might be all that would be left to greet their return. With one accord it was determined to remain: perhaps their presence would be respected and the house spared. They would trust to God to shield themselves from harm. . . .

Although Hood was said to be a rash fighter, it was hardly thought he would be reckless enough to make a determined assault on the formidable works in front of him; but to be prepared for any emergency, it was directed that a bundle of clothing proportioned to the strength of each one be prepared, for the twofold purpose of having that much saved in case all else were lost, and for partial protection should they be forced to leave the house. If the latter became necessary, all were instructed to throw their respective bundles over their backs, and follow the leader withersoever he led.

In a little while all doubts were solved as to Hood's intentions. His solid lines, to the right, to the left, and in front, advancing at a rapid pace, showed plainly enough that the crash was at hand. Although the house had withstood the shock of former conflicts, they seemed as child's play to the approaching storm. The cellar afforded the securest retreat, and hardly was it reached before the din of battle grew appalling. In the gloom of the cellar the children cowered at the feet of their parents, and while the bullets rained against the house, and a cannon ball went crashing through, all seemed in a state of acute expectancy, but gave no audible sound of fear.

The first onset having passed and no one harmed, reassurance returned, and hope revived with some: with others the comparative lull increased the tension and awakened fears of unknown dangers yet to come. In this state of alternating hope and fear, they dragged through the weary hours until the last shot was fired and deliverance assured.

Considering the short length of time, this was one of the bloodiest battles of the whole war. Schofield's casualties were given as 2,326, of which total about 1,000 were prisoners. But Hood's loss was a staggering 6,202. A crippling feature of Hood's casualties was the loss in general officers. In no other battle did any army have so many generals killed and wounded. In the short action that afternoon Generals P. R. Cleburne, S. R. Gist, H. B. Granbury, John Adams and O. F. Strahl were killed outright, and General John C. Carter was mortally wounded. General George W. Gordon was captured; and Generals John C. Brown, A. M. Manigault, William A. Quarles, F. M. Cockrell and T. M. Scott were wounded. That morning five of these generals had sat down to breakfast at the hospitable table of Major Nat Cheairs at Spring Hill. The next day the dead bodies of all five of them lay on the long back gallery of the McGavock house near Franklin.

The fury of the fighting was such that it did not end with the coming of darkness, but went on fitfully as late as 9 P.M. The still indomitable Hood, when his artillery came up late in the evening, ordered that the guns should fire a hundred rounds each into the Federal works at daybreak the next morning, after which the troops would charge again. The guns did fire a few volleys, but there was no reply. Investigation revealed that the works were deserted. Schofield had given the order to retire at 11 P.M., and as soon as the men could be moved out of the breastworks they had so valorously defended, they filed over the Harpeth and along the highway to Nashville.

Schofield, in his dispatches and in his report, refers to the battle as a victory —this in spite of the fact that just as soon as he possibly could he retreated with all haste, leaving the field and his dead and wounded in the possession of the enemy. True, that enemy had failed in his effort to storm the works; but Thomas had wanted Schofield to hold Hood at Franklin for three days—and Schofield held him scarcely three hours. Hood, of course, could scarcely claim a victory, in view of his repulse and his crippling casualties. Accurately it should be classified as a drawn battle, a heartbreaking, murderous unnecessary battle that settled nothing—unless it settled in Hood's mind the question whether the Army of Tennessee would charge breastworks.

CHAPTER 17

☆ *Battle of Nashville*

O N the morning of December 1st the Confederates found themselves in possession of the Franklin battlefield, with their preceding day's opponents in
precipitate flight. Hood, if he was willing to delude himself, might claim a
technical victory, but he knew very well as he looked at the six thousand Confederate dead and wounded on the field that he could not stand any more "victories" of that kind. His immediate problem was to bury the dead of both armies,
where they fell, and give such medical attention as was possible to the wounded.
Having done that, he must answer for himself the vital and vexing question, What
to do next?

Subsequently, second-guessing writers and arm-chair military experts seem to
agree that what Hood did in his dilemma was fatal. Even after the passage of
a century, however, there is still no agreement among his critics as to just what
he should have done. What he did finally decide to do, and why, he explains in
the book he wrote after the war. His explanation is none too convincing, but
here is what he says:

After the failure of my cherished plan to crush Schofield's army before it reached
its strongly fortified position around Nashville, I remained with an effective force of
only twenty-three thousand and fifty-three (23,053). I was therefore well aware of our
inability to attack the Federals in their new stronghold with any hope of success, although Schofield's troops had abandoned the field at Franklin, leaving their dead and
wounded in our possession, and had hastened with considerable alarm into their
fortifications—which later information, in regard to their condition after the battle, I
obtained through spies. I knew equally well that in the absence of the prestige of
complete victory I could not venture with my small force to cross the Cumberland
River into Kentucky without first receiving reinforcements from the Trans-Mississippi
Department. I felt convinced that the Tennesseans and Kentuckians would not join
our forces, since we had failed in the first instance to defeat the Federal army and
capture Nashville. The President was still urgent in his instructions relative to the
transference of troops to the Army of Tennessee from Texas, and I daily hoped to
receive the glad tidings of their safe passage across the Mississippi River.

Thus, unless strengthened by these long looked for reinforcements, the only remaining chance of success in the campaign at this juncture was to take position, entrench around Nashville and await Thomas's attack which, if handsomely repulsed, might afford us an opportunity to follow up our advantage on the spot and enter the city on the heels of the enemy.

I could not afford to turn southward, unless for the special purpose of forming a junction with the expected reinforcements from Texas, and with the avowed intention to march back again upon Nashville. In truth, our army was then in that condition which rendered it more judicious the men should face a decisive issue rather than retreat—in other words, rather than renounce the honor of their cause, without having made a last and manful effort to lift up the sinking fortunes of the Confederacy.

I therefore determined to move upon Nashville, to entrench, to accept the chances of reinforcements from Texas, and even at the risk of an attack in the meantime by overwhelming numbers, to adopt the only feasible means of defeating the enemy with my reduced numbers, viz., to await his attack and, if favored by success, to follow him into his works. I was apprised of each accession to Thomas's army, but was still unwilling to abandon the ground as long as I saw a shadow of probability of assistance from the Trans-Mississippi Department or of victory in battle; and, as I have just remarked, the troops would, I believed, return better satisfied even after defeat if, in grasping at the last straw, they felt that a brave and vigorous effort had been made to save the country from disaster. Such at the time was my opinion, which I have since had no reason to alter.

So, leaving a sufficient force at Franklin to bury the dead and care for the wounded, Hood started in pursuit of Schofield the morning of December 1, but even Forrest's cavalrymen were unable to overtake the fast-flying Federals, who were safe within the Nashville fortifications that afternoon.

In spite of his strong fortifications, however, General Thomas did not feel secure. Colonel James F. Rusling, chief of staff of Quartermaster General Donaldson at Nashville, tells us of the justifiable apprehension suffered by Thomas during the tension-packed days in late November as Hood's army approached nearer and nearer, and there was so much unexpected delay in the arrival of the Sixteenth Army Corps commanded by General Andrew J. Smith. Then he tells of the relief experienced by Thomas as the belated Smith arrived the night of November 30:

I happened in his quarters the night General A. J. Smith arrived at Nashville, by way of the Cumberland, from St. Louis, with thirteen transports and eight armored gunboats swarming with veteran soldiers, and I shall never forget the scene. It was the night of the battle of Franklin (November 30) and our news of matters there was as yet uncertain. Judge Campbell, of the United States Supreme Court, then residing at Nashville, gave a reception that night, and on my way to it I dropped into General Thomas's headquarters (about nine o'clock) to inquire more about Franklin. Thomas, his face all aglow, handed me a telegram from Schofield, announcing that he had defeated Hood; putting thirteen of his general officers alone and over six thousand of his men *hors de combat*—a terrific blow to the Confederates—but was now falling back on Nashville in pursuance of his orders. Thomas eagerly inquired if I had any news from A. J. Smith. I answered, no; that I had sent a swift steamer down the Cumberland early in the afternoon to hurry him forward, but it was not yet time for his arrival.

"Well", he said, "if Smith does not get here tonight, he will not get here at all; for tomorrow Hood will strike the Cumberland and close it against all transports."

I replied he need not fear, for Smith would certainly "arrive soon"; and went on to Judge Campbell's.

About midnight I left Judge Campbell's, and on my way back dropped in at Thomas's headquarters again, and there I found Schofield and T. J. Wood just arrived from Franklin, and all three in conference over what was to be done next day. Wood was still on crutches, from a wound received in the Atlanta campaign; but in command of his corps, and handling it ably and gallantly. Thomas introduced me to the other two, and again eagerly inquired about A. J. Smith.

"O", I replied, "he is all right. Just as I came in I heard his steamers tooting along the levee!"

And, even as I spoke, the door opened and in strode General A. J. Smith, a grizzled old veteran but a soldier all through. They all four greeted each other eagerly; but Thomas (undemonstrative as he was) literally took Smith in his arms and hugged him; for he now felt absolutely sure of coping with Hood, and defeating him duly. They first discussed Franklin and rejoiced over it, and then Thomas spread his maps on the floor and pointed out his Nashville lines, explaining their bearings and significance. I left them at 1 AM, all four down on their knees and examining attentively the positions to be assumed next morning, as Schofield's and Wood's men fell back on Nashville and Smith marched out from the Cumberland.

As the Confederates reached the outskirts of Nashville on their advance from Franklin, General Hood established his headquarters at Travelers' Rest, the home of John Overton on the Franklin pike six miles south of Nashville. Here he immediately issued to his three corps commanders an order covering the establishment of the Confederate line, specifying the positions they were to take as they arrived:

General Lee will form his corps with his center upon the Franklin Pike; General Stewart will form on General Lee's left; and General Cheathan on General Lee's right.

The entire line of the army will curve forward from General Lee's center so that General Cheatham's right may come as near the Cumberland as possible above Nashville, and General Stewart's left as near the Cumberland as possible below Nashville. Each position will be strengthened as soon as taken, and extended as fast as strengthened. Artillery will be placed in all favorable positions. All engineer officers will be constantly engaged in examining the position of the enemy and looking to all his weak points. Corps commanders will give all necessary assistance. Not a cartridge of any kind will be burned until further orders, unless the enemy should advance on us.

So on December 2nd, Hood deployed on the hills south of Nashville what was left of the badly battered Army of Tennessee. As the corps commanders moved to take their assigned positions, it immediately became apparent that there were not nearly enough troops to form a line which would come close to reaching the Cumberland river on either the right or the left. Cheatham's corps could reach no further to the right than just across the Nolensville pike, a mile away from the Cumberland; Stewart, on the left, barely reached the Hillsboro pike, leaving an interval of four miles to the river.

As Hood undoubtedly knew, for his spies sifted freely into and out of the city, Nashville was at this time a strongly defended place—probably the most thoroughly and skilfully fortified city on the North American continent. Soon after the Federal occupation of the city in 1862, Captain James St. Clair Morton of the Corps of Engineers of the United States Army, had been ordered by General Don Carlos Buell to go to Nashville and select sites for redoubts to protect the city. After surveying the situation, Morton devised a defensive system based on three large forts: Negley, Morton (named for himself), and Houston, with a blockhouse on Casino Hill, west of Fort Negley. In deference to Governor Andrew Johnson's forcibly expressed fears of raiding rebels, Morton also built some earth parapets and cedar log stockades around the State Capitol. These were supplemented by breastworks made of cotton bales, manned with a regiment of infantry and mounting fifteen guns, and the Military Governor felt a little more secure. Interspersed with redoubts on strategic hilltops, the Federal defense lines stretched entirely around Nashville, from the river above the city to the river below.

Colonel James F. Rusling, in a letter written December 11 to friends at home, boasts of the strength of the Federal defenses—and, incidentally, reveals the reason for the scarcity of large trees in the immediate environs of Nashville today:

Our line of defense is a semi-circle, drawn around the city, from the Cumberland around to the Cumberland again, with the enemy's line one-half or three-quarters of a mile distant.

Our line is immensely strong, crowned with forts and bristling with cannon; and both ends of it covered by gunboats. The Rebs might as well butt their brains against the Rocky Mountains as attempt to take it. Besides, our force is quite as numerous as theirs, if not more so; and if they don't "skedaddle" soon, we shall have one of the biggest fights you ever did see.

Just now, both armies are doing their best to keep warm. For three days we have had bitterly cold, winter weather; diversified with rain, hail, sleet and snow. The troops on both sides must have suffered terribly. As a consequence, the beautiful woods and groves that surrounded Nashville on all sides, and made it one of the most lovely towns I ever saw, are all going remorselessly down before the axes of the soldiers. We are getting in wood by rail and river for the hospitals here; but the army beyond has to take care of itself. . . .

Of course the Rebs must have wood too; and away it goes by the thousands of cord daily. If the Rebs coop us up here another fortnight, there won't be a tree left within five miles of Nashville.

To cover the excessive intervals between the ends of his infantry line and the Cumberland on both wings, Hood planned to use his cavalry. But the cavalry force also was inadequate to the assigned task—especially as Hood immediately dispersed Forrest's forces in a masterpiece of suicidal military ineptitude.

When the foot soldiers were leaving Franklin on the morning of December 2, Hood sent Bate's infantry division of Cheatham's corps to Murfreesboro, about twenty-eight miles eastward, with orders "to destroy the railroad from Murfreesborough to Nashville, burning all the bridges, and taking the blockhouses and burning them." Bate, with his 1600 men, when he approached Murfreesboro discovered that it was more strongly held than had been thought, and he appealed for help.

Forrest's force, upon arrival in front of Nashville, had been divided by Hood. The division of General Chalmers was assigned to duty on the left of the Confederate line, between Stewart's left and the river. The other two divisions (Buford's and Jackson's) were placed on the Confederate right, under the immediate command of Forrest, instructed to destroy the Nashville-Murfreesboro railroad. When Bate called for help, Forrest was ordered to join forces with Bate, together with two small infantry brigades sent from the Confederate main line, and operate against Murfreesboro and its garrison. Eventually Buford's division was sent back to the neighborhood of the Hermitage, east of Nashville, to watch the Cumberland river and protect that flank. Forrest, with Jackson's division, continued his assignment aimed at the destruction of the railroad.

As a result of these moves, Hood fought the battle of Nashville with only a single under-manned cavalry division on each wing, and with Forrest, the most able and successful cavalry commander on either side, thirty miles away from the scene of battle, engaged in superintending the job of damaging the railroad track. On December 10, Chalmers was ordered to send Biffle's brigade of his division to the right of the line to strengthen Buford, leaving Rucker's brigade the only cavalry force on the Confederate left. To strengthen Rucker, Hood sent what was left of Ector's infantry brigade, (about 700 men), and they took a precarious position near the Harding pike, between Rucker's cavalry and Stewart's infantry.

The day after the battle of Franklin, Thomas had reported to General Halleck that he intended to remain on the defensive in the Nashville fortifications until General Wilson could get his cavalry recruited and equipped. This was duly reported to President Lincoln, and on December 2 Stanton telegraphed Grant:

> The President feels solicitous about the disposition of General Thomas to lay in fortifications for an indefinite period "until Wilson gets equipments". This looks like the McClellan and Rosecrans strategy of do nothing and let the rebels raid the country. The President wishes you to consider the matter.

Thus nudged by the armchair strategists in Washington, Grant (although entirely ignorant of conditions at Nashville) started a barrage of telegrams to Thomas urging him to move out at once in an attack on Hood, ready or not ready. Thomas explained the impossibility of operating without the cavalry, but Grant and Stanton continued to nag him, and Thomas made arrangements to move against Hood on December 10. But on December 10 there came a sudden turn in the weather. There was a swift drop to freezing temperatures, with snow, sleet and freezing rain that covered the country around Nashville with a solid sheet of ice. Thomas advised Halleck of this, but the nagging telegrams continued; and on December 13, General John A. Logan was ordered to proceed from Washington to Nashville and take over the command from Thomas. Then, on the next day, feeling that the matter required his personal attention, Grant started for Nashville himself.

But on the morning of December 14 there was a quick rise in the temperature, and under a warm sun the ice and frozen ground began to melt rapidly. Several days before, Thomas had explained to his corps and division commanders the details of the attack he planned to launch against Hood as soon as the weather permitted; and on the 14th he called another council of war, at which it was explained that the attack as planned would be made the following morning. Detailed, written orders were given each of the corps commanders, and through them to the commanders of divisions, explaining just exactly what each was expected to do in the forward movement to begin at 4 A.M. the morning of the 15th.

Thomas's plan of battle consisted of an opening diversionary attack by Steedman's corps on his left against Cheatham's corps on the Confederate right. The principal attack in strength was to consist of a great turning movement by Smith's corps on the Federal right, supported by Wilson's cavalry, against Stewart's corps on the Confederate left along the Hillsboro pike. His general idea was that he could mass a sufficiently superior force against the Confederate left to crush it, and that Steedman's attack on Cheatham would serve to prevent Hood's drawing any reinforcements from that wing. It was a tactically sound plan, backed up by ample man-power and armament, and Thomas faced the coming battle with calm confidence in its successful outcome.

Captain Marshall P. Thatcher, an officer in the Federal army who happened to see Thomas as he was leaving his quarters at the St. Cloud Hotel the next morning, tells of the lasting impression made on him by the glimpse he had of the Federal commander at this critical moment of his life:

The nearly twenty years that have intervened since that memorable morning have not in the least dimmed the picture of human grandeur that riveted my attention as, when passing the St. Cloud Hotel at 8 o'clock A. M., December 15, 1864, I saw the familiar form of General Thomas standing at the hotel desk, paying his bill as any ordinary traveler. His horse was at the door and a colored servant was bearing to the headquarters ambulance a small valise. A part of his staff stood to horse, awaiting the General's pleasure, and as without a word he marched out, it seemed to me at that moment the most perfect soldier in his bearing that I have ever set admiring eyes upon. There was no haughtiness nor ostentatious parade, but a quiet dignity that well became his handsome face—with its short, smooth-cut, red and gray beard, that finished off his well rounded figure. And as he walked out grandly, modestly, and vaulted into his saddle, there was an unmistakable air of "business" about him which boded no good for Mr. Hood. He seemed to say, "Well, boys, we will go out and settle this little business now—it's about the right time to stop fooling."

I could plainly read in his face, "We are going to stay. We will not be back to-night, landlord." I turned to my comrades and remarked, "You will hear music to-day."

Steedman's attack on the Confederate right wing was launched promptly, but was not made with sufficient vigor and determination to accomplish the desired result. Lieutenant-Colonel Charles H. Grosvenor of the 18th Ohio Infantry was commanding the Third Brigade of the Provisional Division in Steedman's corps, and in his official report he tells how "at daylight" he moved his brigade into action, supporting the movement of Colonel Thomas J. Morgan's First Colored Brigade, "near Rains's House", driving back the Confederate skirmishers. Then, he goes on to say:

I led the Second Battalion in person to the assault of the right and southern angle of the enemy's work. In this I was ably assisted by Captains Henderson, Brown and other officers of the battalion, and all that could be was done to bring the line to an assault of the work. But the troops were mostly new conscripts, convalescents and bounty jumpers, and on this occasion, with but few honorable exceptions, behaved in the most cowardly and disgraceful manner. The enemy, seeing the men hesitating and wavering, fired a heavy volley and stampeded the whole line. In vain the officers tried to rally the men; in vain the old soldiers rushed forward themselves. The line broke, and nearly all the men fled from the field.

Colonel Morgan in his official report, telling of this action on the morning of the 15th, when his attacking brigade was thrown back, says:

About the time of the repulse of Colonel Grosvenor, Colonel Shafter was compelled to withdraw his line from the range of the artillery. The entire command was then withdrawn, by order of General Steedman, and moved to the north of Rains's house. . . . Sharpshooters loop-holed a dwelling house and outbuildings, and silenced the enemy. Thus the day wore away. The general's purpose had been accomplished; the enemy had been deceived and, in expectation of a real advance upon his right, had detained his troops there while his left was being disastrously driven back.

Morgan, however, is trying to gloss over his own failure. As a matter of fact, Hood was not at all deceived by the attack on his right, and as the heavy assault later developed on his left he, during the afternoon, withdrew all of Cheatham's divisions from their position facing Steedman and moved them to the support of Stewart. That this withdrawal of Cheatham's force was not detected by the Federals is evidenced by the statement of Col. Charles R. Thompson, commanding the Second Colored Brigade, in his report of the defensive steps taken by his command the night of the 15th against the enemy who wasn't there.

> During the night we strengthened our rifle-pits and threw up an earthwork for the protection of the artillery, which had been much exposed during the day to the fire of the enemy's sharpshooters.

Smith's infantry and Wilson's cavalry (some of them unmounted) on the Federal right were delayed by the early morning fog and by some mix-up in marching orders, but they soon got their turning movement under way, swinging in a wide sweep directed at Stewart's left wing position. Stewart's infantry were mostly strung out behind the stone wall on the east side of the Hillsboro pike; but he also had on his flank five hastily thrown up slight fortifications, called redoubts, each containing some artillery. Redoubts No. 1 (which was the main salient) and No. 2 were embodied in the line east of the Hillsboro pike, but Redoubts 3, 4 and 5 were in separated positions on the western side of the road, the latter two located several hundred yards in advance of the main line.

Captain James Dinkins was in command of the escort company of General Chalmers, whose cavalry near the Charlotte pike, beyond Richland creek caught the first impact of the Federal advance in that sector as Johnson's brigade of Wilson's cavalry on the morning of the 15th swept out the Charlotte pike until they came under the fire of Chalmers' guns on the high ground beyond Richland Creek.

Dinkins tells how, at about 2 A.M. that morning, Chalmers at his headquarters in the Belle Meade mansion on the Harding pike was aroused by a courier with a note from General Hood telling Chalmers that his position would be attacked that morning. So, Dinkins later wrote:

> We hurried over to Davidson's Landing, on the Charlotte pike, and found Rucker in a desperate fight with a greatly superior force. It was about the break of day, and the enemy was forming a column of cavalry to charge down the pike, this force in addition to the troops fighting Rucker.
>
> General Chalmers quickly got a battery of smooth-bore guns in position, and, when the column of cavalry crossed the branch [Richland Creek] and started up the hill, grape shot were used with fearful effect. It was a terrible scene. Men and horses were killed, and others stumbled and fell over them. Our guns continued to fire, and the enemy on the right, shocked by the result, began to retreat. Rucker saw the opportunity, and, grasping a flag, raised it above his head and ordered a charge. He dashed along in front of his line, urging his men to push on. At the same time, General Chalmers with his escort charged them on the left, and within three minutes the enemy was on the run. We followed about a mile, until they reached their breast-works.
>
> As we drove them back, we were joined by Colonel Mark Cockrill, [a local civilian] mounted on a good horse. He rode in front, and called to our men to come on. The field belonged to Colonel Cockrill, who was not less that seventy-five years of age, and had little, if any, use of his right arm. He held the reins in his mouth and his hat in his right hand. He was a picture, and his presence and bravery inspired our men to superhuman efforts. . . . During that charge we lost many good men. All of

the officers of the escort were severely wounded, and two were left in the enemy's lines and died in prison.

In the meantime, General Hood's line had been driven back, and we found ourselves some three miles in advance of any other troops. We fell back to Davidson's Landing, and the gunboats on the river began to throw their big shells over us. They, however, did little damage. We could hear firing far to our rear, and the indications seemed that we were cut off. About 4 P. M., General Chalmers decided to fall back and, if possible, join the main body of our army.

He ordered me ahead with the escort company, as advance guard, with instructions to cross Walnut Ridge, and find the wagons which had been left on General Harding's race track. General Chalmers followed with Kelley's regiment, and Colonel Rucker with his brigade. With the escort, we reached a point oposite "Belle Meade" and, though the ridge was very steep, succeeded in crossing, the men dismounting and leading their horses. General Chalmers, with Kelley's regiment, passed about a mile beyond and crossed. The weather was intensely cold, and snow and ice covered the ground.

When I reached the race track (where Chalmers' wagon train had been parked) I found the wagons had been burned. I rode down near the pike, and saw Federal soldiers moving about in the yard of Belle Meade. Several of them had no guns; some were on foot, others were mounted. I concluded it was a good opportunity, and moved the escort company around and behind the barn, where they formed for a charge.

The boys went yelling and firing as they passed through the yard. The enemy, some two hundred in number, were surprised and ran. They had no idea there was a Confederate soldier in the neighborhood. We pushed through the park but, when near the creek, found a line of infantry behind a rock fence and fell back. The enemy opened a hot fire and, as the boys returned through the yard, the bullets were clipping the shrubbery, and striking the house. Nine of the enemy were killed or wounded, and some fifteen captured.

As we rode back, I saw Miss Selene Harding standing on the stone arm of the front steps waving her handkerchief. The bullets were falling thick and fast about her, but she had no fear in her heart. She looked like a goddess. She was the gamest little human being in all the crowd. As I rode past I caught the handkerchief and urged her to go into the house, but she would not, until the boys had disappeared behind the barn. They fell back across the pike, and awaited the coming of General Chalmers, who soon arrived.

While Johnson's brigade of Wilson's cavalry was engaged with Chalmers, the rest of Wilson's force, along with all of Smith's infantry, were swinging steadily around like a turning wheel until they were approaching Stewart's position. The force now rolling against the Confederate left consisted of about 20,000 men— Smith's corps of close to 12,000 and some two-thirds of Wilson's cavalry. About three-fourths of Wilson's men were mounted, the rest on foot; all of them were armed with the deadly seven-shot Spencer repeating rifle, which gave them tremendous fire-power in addition to their mobility.

The only Confederate infantry confronting this powerful force when it first started its advance was Ector's little brigade, on the ridge north of the Harding pike and west of the present White Bridge Road. General Ector having lost a leg at Atlanta, the brigade was now commanded by Colonel David Coleman of the 39th North Carolina. Lieutenant J. J. Tunnell of the 14th Texas infantry was one of the officers in Ector's picket line that morning, and he tells of their brief clash with the Yankee juggernaut before they were brushed aside:

On the morning of December 15th the brigade was camped on Harding Pike, with a picket line in front, extending across the pike at the mouth of a lane, in charge of Captain House of the Tenth on the right and the writer on the left. We soon discovered a vast body of cavalry maneuvering on our left front, and a little later we saw a large brigade of infantry advancing upon our left front in line of battle, followed by a battery of artillery. We reported to Colonel Coleman, who came to our line and examined the situation. He instructed us to hold the line until forced to retire, then to fall back over the ridge in order, and make a run of about two miles to the Hillsboro Pike, where we could find him with the brigade. The enemy threw forward a skirmish line and moved slowly but steadily forward. Our thin line in rifle pits gave them a warm reception. When they got uncomfortably near, we hastily fell back, but in order, over the ridge. We then made a run for the brigade, fearful of being cut off by cavalry.

The first collision of the enveloping Federals and the Confederate forces defending the left wing came late in the forenoon, when Colonel Datus E. Coon, with his brigade of Hatch's cavalry, found himself on the exposed flank of Redoubt No. 5, the detached and unsupported outermost outpost of Stewart's line. Coon's men quickly dismounted and, with their Spencer repeaters, moved to the attack, supported by the first brigade of McArthur's infantry division and a battery of artillery. After an artillery duel of an hour or more, the charge of the combined Federal infantry and dismounted cavalry swept over the defenders like an engulfing wave, and Redoubt No. 5 with its four guns and its 150 men were captured.

The captured guns were then turned on Redoubt No. 4, which was already under fire from Smith's massed artillery, 24 guns, on the opposite ridge. Redoubt No. 4, however, proved to be not such an easy nut to crack. It was defended by a battery of four smooth-bore Napoleon guns, manned by forty-eight artillerymen under the command of Captain Charles L. Lumsden, a graduate of Virginia Military Institute who had been commandant of cadets at the University of Alabama when the war started. The battery was supported by one hundred infantry under Captain Foster of the Twenty-ninth Alabama, these men being in shallow breastworks stretching for a short distance on each side of the redoubt.

Lumsden had been ordered to hold this position "at all hazards", and by some miracle of stubborn courage he and his men did cling to their beleagured position for more than three hours, banging away with their smooth-bores as fast as they could be served. Sergeant James R. Maxwell, in command of the left section of the battery, has left a graphic account of the battery's brave defense of the position and the final scene, as the defenders of the little hill were overwhelmed by the tidal wave of bluecoats:

Major Foster of the Engineers, with a detail of 100 men, had started the redoubt shortly after the remnant of Hood's army had aligned itself before Nashville. Hood's orders were that it should be a regular fort enclosing the top of the hill; but as yet it was simply a redoubt, facing a ridge some 800 yards away that ran nearly perpendicularly to the general direction of the army's line of battle at the extreme left end of the army. Between the ridge and the location of the redoubt were cultivated fields, and had been some woods, through which a branch of Richland Creek meandered towards the northwest. The woods our engineers had cut down, so as to give an uninterrupted view of the lands in our front, and give a cover for skirmishers who might be driven back towards the redoubts—and also give cover for an enemy line of skirmishers to approach to within 100 yards of the redoubt under cover, when they had driven back the defending skirmishers.

From the date of our arrival at the fort location we had rain, snow and sleet, and the ground frozen hard, so that it was impossible to make any rapid progress on the redoubt laid off for four embrasures for our four Napoleon guns. Stretched blankets and the tarpaulins for our guns and ammunition were the only cover for officers or men. I well remember that, the day before the battle of the 15th, my servant Jim Bobbett brought me a change of clean underclothing, for which I had to scrape off the snow on a log at Richmond Creek, strip and bathe in its icy waters to make a change.

By the 15th (the day of the battle) we had managed to get our redoubt front with four embrasures in fairly good condition to face direct fire from the front, but with no side protection at all. For perhaps 100 feet at each end, a trench about three feet deep had been dug for the supporting infantry. The inside wall of the redoubt was about eight feet high between the four embrasures, so that men working the guns were well protected except from fragments of shell that might explode just before passing above the embankment, which did not often happen when enemy was using percussion shell. We had done well to get so good protection in the 10 days we had been at work.

On the morning of 15th December the Federal General A. J. Smith's Corps, just arrived at Nashville from Missouri, moved out from Nashville, forcing back, with little trouble, the Confederate cavalry and its skeleton infantry brigade. There was a dense fog early in the morning, but by 11:00 A. M. four six-gun batteries had aligned themselves along that ridge in our front covering a length of about one-half mile.

Lieut. John Caldwell, with the horses and drivers, had been sent to the rear to the Cook Camp, and only the cannoneers under Captain Lumsden and Lieutenant A. C. Hargrove remained at the guns. Captain Lumsden had charge of the right section of two guns and Hargrove had guns No. 3 and 4 or the left section. Besides a sergeant, it takes a corporal acting as gunner, and seven men to handle a gun properly. (We had 10 men to each gun at the battery, three extras to take place when casualties occur, who take the best protection possible till needed) . . . .

From 11:00 A. M. when the 24 guns opened on our four, to 2:00 P. M., or three full hours, we kept our four guns replying. Above our heads was a network of shrieking shells. At one time a Federal battery opened on us from a position on our left, near some haystacks, that directly enfiladed our four guns in rear of our redoubt. Captain Lumsden ran his two guns at right of battery back out of their embrasures on top of the hill far enough to fire to the left behind our left section. Ed. King, my gunner, had been knocked out by a fragment. I, having been gunner a long time, had to take his place. I too turned my gun on the enfilading battery, which soon got away from that position and troubled us no more. Then our four guns had to use cannister against A. J. Smith's infantry and dismounted cavalry, the 11th Missouri, which swarmed over and past our guns at both ends and through the embrasures. . . .

When the charging Federals passed my gun, on left of redoubt, Lieutenant Hargrove ordered us to leave it. I ran towards Captain Lumsden's section (guns 1 and 2) where Sergeant Jim Jones had turned No. 2 to fire cannister at Federals near gun No. 4. He called to me "Look out, Jim", and I dropped on hands and knees whilst he fired that cannister right over my head. I took my place between his gun and the embrasure, helping handle the gun and he gave them the double cannister again. Captain Lumsden was standing with another charge of cannister in his hands. The command had been given "fire", but the man with the friction primers had run. I called out "Captain, he's gone with the friction primers". Says Captain Lumsden: "Take care of yourselves, boys".

As he said that, down by my side, between gun and embrasure, dropped a Federal soldier with his rifle. I left him right there and lit out down the hill. As I got about half way to the creek at bottom of hill, I ran over an infantry-man's Enfield rifle. Noticing it cocked with cap shining on its nipple, I grabbed it up and fired at a Federal soldier waving his hat at the guns I had just left. I did not stop to see if I hit him, but ran for the creek—and I don't think I put but one foot in the creek. Several Federals on horses had got between me and the Hillsboro pike where a Confederate line of infantry was forming. There was a high stone wall that ran off from the pike, so I made for that stone wall and got it between me and those horsemen, then took it more leisurely to our new line. Resting a little while, I went down past Mr. Castleman's house, in front of which Captain Lumsden was reporting to General Stewart, who was congratulating Captain Lumsden for detaining the advance of the Federals so long.

During this reduction of Redoubts 4 and 5, the main body of Smith's infantry force was marching across the fields between the Harding and Hillsboro turnpikes, swinging into position to storm Stewart's main line. The Seventh Minnesota Volunteers was one of the infantry regiments in Smith's command, and Captain Theodore G. Carter, commanding Company K of that regiment, was right in the midst of the action when the clash occurred. Here's what he says about it:

Previous to the battle our regiment (7th Minnesota, in the Third Brigade, First Division, Sixteenth Army Corps) lay along the outer line of works in front of Nashville, our right resting on the railroad running to Johnsonville. On the morning of December 15 we marched out through the fog and formed in column of brigades on the left of the Harding Pike, and about a mile and one half in front of our works. Here we deployed into line, and I think our regiment was the extreme left of our corps. We then marched in line of battle for some distance, when it was discovered that there was a long interval to our left which was unoccupied. We lay here until some time in the afternoon, out of range of small arms, but subject to the fire of a battery on a high point just to the left of the Hillsboro Pike [Redoubt No. 2], which was annoying, the guns being well served by experienced gunners. Late in the afternoon we were ordered to storm the works in our front, being stone walls (on both sides of the Pike) with a redoubt [No. 3] on the right of the Hillsboro Pike, just opposite the battery mentioned above.

We advanced on the run down a gentle slope and through open woods until out of breath, when we lay down for a few minutes; then we ran down across a little brook and lay down under cover of the slope ascending the redoubt. We went into the redoubt, or such portion of our regiment as fronted on it did, which included my company. Of course all this was not done without opposition on the part of the Confederates. We suffered from the direct fire from the works assaulted, and also from a crossfire, enfilading our line part of the time, from the fort on the hill across the pike.

We had scarcely gained possession of the works when the fort across the way opened upon us, not regarding the fact that there were about as many Confederates with us inside the redoubt as there were of our own men.

It is almost a miracle that anyone was left alive in that redoubt, for the gunners cut their fuses so that every shell burst inside of it, and there did not seem to be ten seconds' interval between the discharges. Colonel S. G. Hill, our brigade commander, gave the order to charge the fort on the hill [No. 2], and was shot through the head the next moment. Our major heard the order and repeated it; we jumped down from the wall and, led by Colonel (W. R.) Marshall, crossed the pike and climbed the hill, the Confederates leaving the fort as we got to it. We followed on through the woods until dusk, when we bivouacked for the night. As we followed the Confederates who evacuated the fort on the hill, we did not leave any one to take possession of the guns, and I saw a line of our troops advancing toward it from the front, but several hundred yards distant. They bravely marched up to it and carried the works (then unoccupied) and received the credit which their commander claimed in his report and which, so far as I know, was never disputed, as the reports were never seen until published by the government.

As the full power of the Federal assault developed, Hood realized that his left wing was in extreme peril. Too late, he started to reinforcing it from his relatively inactive center. First Manigault's brigade from Edward Johnson's division was double-quicked to the scene of the impending disaster. Here they were placed in support of Walthall's line behind the stone wall, across the pike from Redoubt No. 4 before it fell. Then Deas's brigade from the same division came up and filled in the gap between Manigault's right and Walthall's left. But by then the redoubts were lost. The irresistible blue flood swept on to the pike, and the two reinforcing brigades broke from their cover and fled.

With nothing to impede their progress, Smith's men crossed the pike and pushed on to the east a full half-mile, turning the flank and gaining the rear of both Walthall and Loring, in the salient, who had doggedly withstood all frontal attacks. Walthall, to save his men from capture, was now forced into precipitate retreat, and the flanking Federals swept northward east of the pike. Stewart, recognizing that his men were being overpowered, gave orders to both Walthall and Loring to withdraw to escape capture, and Loring promptly did so, but by this time Walthall's brigades were already in retreat.

General Thomas J. Wood, who commanded the Federal center at Nashville, had the largest corps in Thomas's army—an aggregate effective force of 16,645, with 13,526 "present for duty equipped". He was an old Regular Army officer, having graduated from West Point in 1845, and had served in the Mexican War and in the Indian fighting on the Western frontier. When General Stanley was wounded at Franklin, he succeeded to the command of the Fourth Corps.

In the Federal advance on the morning of the 15th, his corps was closest to the hub of the turning wheel, and had the shortest distance to go to come in contact with the enemy. The swinging advance of the troops threw Wood's third division in front of Montgomery Hill, the salient of the advanced skirmish line in front of the left of the Confederate solid line. Wood's men carried the thinly defended Montgomery Hill without very much trouble; but, having done so, he recognized that the true key to the Confederate position in his front was the main salient (Redoubt No. 1) on the high hill at the angle in the Confederate line. He also recognized that it would be a difficult position to carry by direct frontal attack. In fact, he spent almost the entire afternoon in artillery bombardment of the salient, with some intermittent, ineffective infantry sallies. Finally, at 4:30 P.M., Wood ordered Kimball's division to attack the salient, and in his report he says:

> With the most exalted enthusiasm and with loud cheers, it rushed forward up the steep ascent and over the intrenchments . . . capturing several pieces of artillery and stands of colors, many stand of small arms and numerous prisoners.

What Wood neglects to say in his report is that Kimball's men entered the fortification along with those of the flanking third brigade of McArthur's division, who had just stormed Redoubts 3 and 2; and that when they got there Loring's defending force was already in retreat, having been ordered by Stewart to withdraw and form along the Granny White pike, to the rear.

W. D. Gale, who served as Assistant Adjutant General of Stewart's Corps, following the battle wrote a detailed account of Hood's Tennessee campaign in a letter to his wife, who was the daughter of Bishop-General Leonidas Polk. After telling of how the army had moved up to Nashville after the battle of Franklin, establishing Stewart's headquarters at the home of John Johns on the Granny White pike, he gives his wife a brief but impressive account of the first day's battle. Of its disastrous climax he says:

I remained in my office until the Yankees advanced to within three hundred yards. I then mounted and made my escape through the back yard, with my clerks, and joined General Stewart in front of Mr. Plater's, where General Sears lost his life very near me. . . . As our men fell back before the advancing Yankees, Mary Bradford ran out under heavy fire and did all she could to induce the men to stop and fight, appealing to them and begging them, but in vain—Deas's brigade was here. General Hood told me yesterday that he intended to mention her courageous conduct in his report, which will immortalize her. The men seemed utterly lethargic and without interest in the battle. I never witnessed such lack of enthusiasm, and began to fear for tomorrow, hoping that General Hood would retreat during the night, cross Duck River, and then stop and fight; but he would not give it up. However, he sent all his wagons to Franklin, which prepared his men still more for the stampede of the next day.

Colonel Coleman and his battered brigade (Ector's) had a rough time of it that first day of the battle. After receiving the first shock of the over-powering advance of the Federal right that morning, they fell back (as ordered) to the main Confederate line along the east side of the Hillsboro pike. Here Walthall put them in position as an extension of the left of his line, trying to stretch it as far as possible to the south. When the flanking Federal force began to seep across the Hillsboro pike, Walthall moved the brigade still further south, "down near [Felix] Compton's house" to hold the pike for the protection of the left wing. After the redoubts fell and the victorious Federals came streaming across the road, Coleman was forced back to the eastward, and a spearhead of advancing Federals drove in between him and Walthall's left, effectually isolating Ector from Walthall's ensuing action.

General Hood, to get closer to the scene of the action, had left his head-quarters at Lealand early that morning and had taken up a post of observation on top of a high hill southeast of Felix Compton's house—the hill now known as Shy's Hill, in honor of Colonel William M. Shy who was killed there the next day. Lieutenant Tunnel tells of the brigade's encountering Hood at this point, as they fell back:

We could see the Confederate line moving to the rear and to our right, but fighting desperately as they retreated. They and the Federals that were pressing them passed our position and left us in the rear. A prompt retreat was ordered, and we moved at a double-quick on a line parallel with the movement of the troops in the battle. When we got to the Brentwood range of hills, General Hood and his staff were on the hill. General Hood rode down the line, saying to all the soldiers as he passed, "Texans, I want you to hold this hill regardless of what transpires around you," and the spontaneous answer was: "We will do it, General." Our line was formed on the brow of the hill fronting west.

In the meantime the battle had ceased and General Bate was reforming his lines to our right and in plain view of our line. Soon they attacked him again, and for a time we stood watching a terrific battle. A battery of artillery close in the rear of Bate's infantry on a little eminence did splendid work. The line of infantry wavered back and forth as long as we saw the fight. Before very long, however, a strong force of infantry attacked our line and made a desperate but unsuccessful effort to drive us from the hill. Night closed the conflict with our line unmoved. Our losses were pretty heavy.

General Bate and his division, after skirmishing ineffectively with Forrest against Murfreesboro for several days, had been recalled to their position in Cheatham's right wing of Hood's main line facing Nashville, near the Nolensville pike. He says:

Nearly one fourth of the men were still barefooted, Bate says in his official report, many with bleeding feet. I remained in the intrenched line, with the men uncomfortable from the extreme cold and the scarcity of wood, until the evening of the 15th, when I was ordered by General Cheatham to move to the left, where the fighting was going on, and should he not be there to report to General Hood. When I passed the Franklin turnpike streams of a stragglers and artillerists and horses without guns or caissons, the sure indicia of defeat, came hurriedly from the left. I formed my division for battle at once, its right resting near the turnpike, and communicated the situation to General Cheatham, who meanwhile had come up. It was nearly dark. I received an order from General Hood to move straight forward and take a skirt of woods beyond the field, in the rear of which I had formed my line, and near which the firing was going on. I did so, and made known that fact to my corps commander and awaited orders. The firing had now slackened.

About 8 o'clock Major General Cheatham came to me and took me with him to find the line I was to occupy. He informed me that he was directed by the general commanding to extend a line of battle from the apex of the hill occupied by Ector's brigade in direction of Mrs. Bradford's house, on the Granny White turnpike, so that a prolongation of the same would strike the line then occupied by General Stewart. We went together and found General Sharp's brigade on left of that corps, in the rear of Mrs. Bradford's house, somewhat parallel to the turnpike, its right resting near the woods in which we were informed the balance of that corps was. A fire was kindled, by General Cheatham's order, to indicate the direction of my line from the given point on the left. I moved my command in the position indicated, but with much difficulty, attributable to the darkness of the night and the marshy fields through which I had to pass. The artillery was unable to get up. . . .

Having a personal interview with Colonel Coleman, commanding Ector's brigade, and agreeing upon the point where the right of his line rested, I adjusted mine, as ordered, between that and the point designated on General Sharp's line, taking such advantage of the ground in its exact locality as I could the night. My left then rested near the crown on that slope of the hill, facing the turnpike, and my right in the corn-field, advanced toward Nashville, hence not quite at right angles with the turnpike.

Seeing that my line at its junction with Coleman's made a right angle, and the enemy already immediately under the brow of the hill annoying me with sharpshooters, within 100 yards, and my right unconnected with anyone, I went in person to my corps commander and remonstrated as to the position of my line. He informed me that he was not authorized to change it, and that General Stewart was to connect with my right. I at once put the men to making defenses with such tools as I had. They worked with alacrity the balance of the night, and constructed works along my entire front impervious to ordinary shots.

A vivid contemporaneous account of how the first day's battle looked to a young man engaged in it is given in a letter written to his father by a member of Major Trueheart's artillery battalion, from their camp in the rear of the battle-line on December 16th:

> Camp Wagon-Train, Trueheart's Battery,
> Near Franklin, Tennessee,
> December 16, 1864

My Dear Father—Before this reaches you, the news of our defeat yesterday will have been received. As you will be anxious, let me say, in the first place, that I came through without a scratch.

Yesterday morning early the enemy began sharp-shooting in our front; that is, the front of Stewart's Corps, which was the extreme left of Hood's line. We soon received orders—that is, our ordnance train and forage wagons, which are under command of the battalion quartermaster, Captain Spindle, with whom I am detailed as clerk—to be ready to move at any moment. This must have been about 2 o'clock, and was the first notice we received that there was any danger. No one had any idea that the enemy were then massing on our left. The firing soon became heavy, and. . . . Major Trueheart being in the line, Captain Spindle dispatched a courier to him, to know whether he would move his train out or not, as the enemy's shells began to fall pretty thick. Before the courier returned, Captain Spindle decided to move all his train, except the ordnance, further to the rear, and ordered me to go with him.

I started, and got upon a high hill, where I could see the Yankees moving on our left, and preparing to charge Lumsden's battery.

And here, in order that you may understand the whole affair better, I will give you a description of our position, as far as I saw it, from the left toward the right.

It was in the form of a half circle, the center about a mile and a half from the Yankee line around Nashville. Cheatham was on the right, Lee in the center, and Stewart on the left. Walthal's division of Stewart's corps was on the extreme left of our corps. Our battalion was with Walthal's division, Lumsden's battery being on the left; one section of Tarrant's battery came next; one of our (Seldon's battery) about a half mile further to the right; the other section of Tarrant's battery came next, and the remaining two guns of our battery on the extreme right of Walthal's division.

The enemy first flanked and took Lumsden's battery, the captain and most of his men making their escape. They immediately turned our guns on us, and took Tarrant's two guns. About this time I succeeded in getting to the section of our battery to which my gun belongs. I saw the enemy advance and take Lumsden's battery. On getting to my piece, I took a blow, and then went to work. I found Major Storrs in charge of the section.

The enemy soon began to appear in two lines of battle on our immediate front, and we poured shell and solid shot on them very heavily, causing them to halt. Our ammunition getting scarce, the major ordered us to reserve our fire. Our infantry support, consisting of about one hundred men of Sayre's [Sears'] brigade (the general himself in our works), continued to fire a few rounds now and then. The Yankees about this time commenced a furious cannonading, and we had to remain idle behind our works.

We received orders about this time to hitch up and save our guns, as the enemy was now seen coming up the pike, in our rear, and at the same time charging in two or three lines of battle on our front and right flank.

We got our two pieces about four hundred yards from our works, in a muddy field, where we had to abandon one of them; two of the horses being shot, leaving only four, and they were not able to pull it. Our other gun and our ammunition wagon we brought off. Just as we arrived in this field, the last brigade, either Shelly's (Canty's old brigade) or Reynolds', being flanked, and the Yankees two hundred yards, in two lines of battle, on their left and rear, broke, General Walthall himself giving the order. From this time it was one perfect stampede for a mile. As I came out, I saw a pony rearing and pitching, and being nearly worn out, went back and got him. But after doing this I got so far behind, and the shells and minies came so thick and fast, I could not mount the pony until I reached a skirt of wood. As soon as I got on him I felt so relieved that I did not care much what came, I was so nearly worn out, that had I not got the horse I do not know what I should have done.

After falling back nearly a mile (I may not be correct in the distance, as the fatigue made it seem much longer than it really was, I suppose) we formed a second line of battle, and there I left the front, as my piece had gone on, and we had no ammunition with which to fire any longer. As I had nothing to eat, and no blanket, I started to find our wagons, which I did after walking three or four miles, en route for this place. Being tired out, I got in a wagon and remained in it till we reached our present camp, which is a mile and half south of Franklin. We reached here about 1 or 2 o'clock in the morning; I am not certain whether this is the 15th, 16th or 17th; I think it is Friday, the 16th.

I am so tired and sleepy that I can scarcely write, and only do so because an opportunity of sending a letter to-morrow offers, and I know you will want to hear from me. I fear many of our infantry were captured. All of Trueheart's battalion of artillery was taken except Sergeant Riddle's piece (eleven out of twelve), to which I belong. I gave up hope once or twice, and felt sure that by this morning I would be on my way to some Yankee prison; but, God be thanked, I am safe and sound.

When I left the front, about 8 P. M., no one knew whether we were going to stand and form a new line, or fall back to this point. I never had such a fine view of the enemy approaching before. If we had only had some works; but even without these, had we only been reinforced, we might have done better, for it was very evident to every one that the Yankees had massed on the extreme left.

Give my sincere love to mother, sisters, and all the family, and many kisses to the little ones. God grant that we may yet be victorious, and that peace may soon spread her balmy wings over this troubled land.

I do not know how General Hood intended to protect his flank; I do not see how he could have expected to do so, but I am no general. If he does not take some stronger position than he has at present, I fear the enemy will do him more damage yet, by taking possession of the pike, and cutting him off entirely.

If anything happens, I will add before closing. With much love, etc., H.

P. S.—Two of our men have just come in from the front; they report the Yankees advancing down a pike which intersects the Nashville and Franklin pike, between our position and Franklin. I hope this is not so.

THE SECOND DAY

The end of the fighting, as night closed down on the battlefield the evening of the 15th, found the units of both armies badly scattered as they bivouacked where nightfall found them. Both Thomas and Hood, as they sought to extemporize new positions during the night and early morning of the next day, found themselves greatly hampered by the unavoidable confusion and the traditional "fog of battle".

Hood found it particularly hard to re-form his scattered units and establish some sort of effective defensive formation for the survivors of the day's crushing defeat. Locating a new right wing was not so difficult: Lee's corps in the center, which (with the exception of Johnson's division) had been relatively inactive during the day and had also escaped the slaughter at Franklin, two weeks before, simply fell back to the high ground about two miles southward along the Franklin turnpike. Here, some four miles north of Brentwood, they formed a line with Stevenson's division in the center and Edward Johnson's division (which had rejoined the corps after its ineffective effort to help Stewart) on the left, both these divisions being to the west of the road. Clayton's division, forming Lee's right—and the right of the whole line—was strongly posted on a hill just east of the pike and south of the present Elysian Fields Road. This hill is referred to in the battle reports as Overton's Hill, presumably because it was located on the Overton property, but it was known locally and by the family as Peach Orchard Hill. Holtzclaw's brigade, on the left of Clayton's division, was astride the pike. Gibson's and Stovall brigades were to Holtzclaw's right, with their lines refused southward along the eastern face of the hill for several hundred yards.

For the second day's action Cheatham's corps was transferred to the left wing

of the army—most of his men being already in that area or on the way there at
the end of the first day. Stewart's corps, which had absorbed the principal Federal attack that day, was to constitute the center of Hood's new line, connecting
on his right with Lee and on his left with Cheatham.

There was some confusion on the morning of the 16th when Bate (on
Cheatham's right) discovered that during the night Stewart's corps had been
moved back, south of the present Battery Lane, with his left division (Walthall's)
west of the Granny White Pike, in echelon to the rear of Bate's right. Stewart
had established his men in a strong position, entrenched behind a stone wall that
ran along the southern boundary of the Lea property, which they were able to
defend against all frontal attacks all day. Bate, however, was discomfited to find
that the breastworks on top of Shy's Hill, which Ector's brigade had started and
his men had completed during the night, were so far back from the crest of the
hill as to make it practically impossible to see an approaching attack. But it was
too late to do anything about it that morning.

Thomas, so Schofield says, thought it likely that Hood would retreat during
the night and that the next day's action would be a pursuit rather than a combat.
As Schofield tells it:

> After darkness had ended the first day's battle, I received an order in writing from
> General Thomas [not in the *Official Records*], which was in substance to pursue the
> retreating enemy early the next morning, my corps to take the advance on the Granny
> White pike, and was informed that the cavalry had been or would be ordered to
> start at the same time by a road to the right and cross the Harpeth below Franklin.
> These orders seemed to be so utterly inapplicable to the actual situation that I rode
> to the rear to where General Thomas's headquarters were supposed to be, and there
> found that he had gone back to his house in Nashville, to which place I followed him.
> He appeared surprised at my suggestion that we would find Hood in line of battle ready
> to receive us in the morning, or even ready to strike our exposed right flank before we
> could renew the attack, instead of in full retreat as he had assumed. I told him I knew
> Hood much better than he did, and I was sure he would not retreat. Finally, after
> considerable discussion, I obtained a modification of the order so far as to direct the
> cavalry to remain where it was until Hood's action should be known, and an order
> for some of A. J. Smith's troops to support the right if necessary. But no orders
> whatever were given, to my knowledge, looking to a battle the next day—at least none
> for my troops or the cavalry.

Thomas makes no mention of any such discussion as Schofield reports, and
some of Thomas's biographers have expressed doubts as to whether it actually
occurred. General Cox (commanding a division under Schofield) says in his
report that Thomas "held a conference with his corps commanders in the evening." General Wood reports that after placing his corps in bivouac for the night
he sought out Thomas to receive orders for the next day's operations, and that
these orders were "to advance at daylight the next morning, the 16th, and if the
enemy was still in front to attack him; but if he had retreated to pass to the
eastward of the Franklin pike, to face southward and pursue him till found."

Schofield, now on Thomas's right, did not have to make much adjustment
of his troops' position in preparation for the second day. Late in the afternoon
of the first day, his force had come up on the right of Smith's corps, and just
before dark had crossed the Hillsboro pike. Cox on his right had attacked Ector's
brigade on Shy's Hill, but was repulsed. Couch's division, on Schofield's left, had
attacked and occupied the hill opposite Shy's Hill, where Bate's division had

stopped when it first came up. "After dark," says Schofield in his report, "the troops intrenched their position and bivouacked for the night." His line was in an awkward position, with Cox's division roughly parallel with the Hillsboro pike, running north and south, and Couch almost at right angles with Cox, with his left turned back northward.

General Smith, in his report of the first day of the battle, says nothing about whether he received any orders for the ensuing day, but merely: "Night coming on, the troops bivouacked in line of battle. During the night, a request coming from General Schofield for reinforcements, I sent him the Third Division just before daylight." Smith goes on to say:

> On the morning of the 16th, advancing my lines in the same order as the preceding day, it was discovered that the enemy had taken position at the base of a chain of hills called the Brentwood Hills, and had strongly intrenched themselves. . . . Changing my front by a half wheel by brigades, the command moved slowly in echelon from the right, so as not to break connection with the Fourth Corps [Wood's], and took a position directly in front of the enemy at a distance of about 600 yards, my right resting at the base of a hill on the top of which was the enemy's left [Shy's Hill], and my line, being the whole front of the two divisions, extending about one mile. . . . The Twenty-third Corps [Schofield's] was on my right in the intrenchments thrown up by them the night before, and nearly at right angles with my present line. Expecting that corps to take the initiative, as they were on the flank of the enemy, I held the command in its position, keeping up a slow artillery fire at their lines without eliciting any reply.

General Wilson, the Federal cavalry leader, always energetic and enterprising, had bivouacked where night overtook him along the Hillsboro pike. He got into action early on the morning of the 16th, and by 9:30 had Hatch's division moving to take position on the right of Schofield's right, with orders to connect with Hammond's cavalry brigade and "drive the enemy from the hills and push them as vigorously as possible in flank and rear".

The Confederate left, with Shy's Hill as a main salient, had a main line that was curved back in the shape of a fish-hook, and it was against the southward face of this backward curve that Wilson's planned attack was to be aimed.

At daylight the next morning, in pursuance of Thomas's orders, Wood started to move toward the Franklin pike. He soon encountered Lee's skirmishers, who fell back southward with Wood following—Elliott's division deployed across the pike, facing southward, Beatty's division on the left of Elliott, and Kimball's massed near the pike in rear of Elliott. After advancing about a mile they encountered Lee's skirmish line about a half mile in front of his intrenched main line at Peach Orchard Hill. Wood tells how he formed his men into a battle line:

> The troops moved handsomely into position under a sharp fire of musketry and artillery. Thus formed, the entire corps advanced in magnificent array, under a galling fire of small-arms and artillery, and drove the enemy's skirmishers into his main line. Further advance was impossible without making a direct assault on the enemy's intrenched lines, and the happy moment for the grand effort had not yet arrived. I hence ordered the division commanders to press their skirmishers as near to the enemy's intrenchments as possible, and to harass him with a constant fire.

General Steedman, on Thomas's left, in his report tells how he woke up on the morning of the 16th and found that Cheatham's corps had slipped away from his front during the preceding evening:

December 16th, at 6 AM, in obedience to the orders of Major General Thomas, my command moved on the enemy's works, and found that he had evacuated the right of his line in my front during the night. Rushing out my troops on the Nolensville pike, rapidly driving his cavalry, I took up a position between the Nolensville pike and the left of the Fourth Corps [Wood's], my right resting on the railroad, my left refused near the Nolensville pike, and covering the entire left of our line, engaging and putting to flight a portion of the enemy's cavalry.

Early in the forenoon of the 16th Thomas had his lines deployed in accordance with his ideas, but except for intermittent skirmishing and a few scattered attacks which were easily repulsed, there was no general activity of the ground forces until several hours later. Throughout the morning, however, the whole Confederate line was subjected to an exceptionally heavy and continuous bombardment by the superior Federal artillery. This was particularly severe on the Confederate right and left salients at Peach Orchard Mill and Shy's Hill.

Commenting on the bombardment of Lee's position on Peach Orchard Hill, General Wood (whose guns were contributing the major share of the shelling) said in his report:

In a conflict of this nature I knew that we would have greatly the advantage of the enemy, as our supply of ammunition was inexhaustible and his limited. All the batteries of the corps on the field were brought to the front, placed in eligible position in short range of the enemy's works, and ordered to keep up a measured but steady fire on his artillery. The practice of the batteries was uncommonly fine. The ranges were accurately obtained, the elevations correctly given; and, the ammunition being unusually good, the firing was consequently most effective. It was really entertaining to witness it. The enemy replied spiritedly with musketry and artillery, and his practice with both was good. In the progress of the duel he disabled two guns in Ziegler's battery.

General Carter L. Stevenson, commanding a division in Lee's corps, on the receiving end of this bombardment, has these words of praise for the attackers:

Their success the previous day had emboldened them, and they rushed forward with great spirit, only to be driven back with dreadful slaughter. Finding at last that they could make no impression on our lines, they relinquished their attempt and contented themselves with keeping up an incessant fire of small arms at long-range and an artillery fire which I have never seen surpassed for heaviness, continuance and accuracy. This state of things continued until evening, doing, however, but little damage, my men keeping closely in the trenches and perfectly cool and confident.

General Holtzclaw of Clayton's division, in his report also emphasized the severity of the artillery fire on this front:

At 10 o'clock the enemy made a desperate charge, but was driven back with loss. He then commenced a most furious shelling from three six-gun batteries, concentrating his fire mainly upon my right. One battery of unusually heavy guns was brought down the pike to within 600 yards of my line. The conformation of the ground prevented me sharpshooting it sufficiently to drive it away. . . . The shelling of the enemy's batteries between 12 and 3 PM was the most furious I ever witnessed, while the range was so precise that scarce a shell failed to explode in the line. The enemy now seemed to be satisfied that he could not carry my position, and contented himself by shelling and sharpshooting everything in sight.

General Wood was well aware of the importance and strength of the position of the Confederate right wing in his front, with "a strongly intrenched line running around the northern slope of Overton Hill [Peach Orchard Hill], about midway between its summit and base, with a retired flank, running nearly southward, prolonged along its eastern slope." As he recognized, this position commanded the Franklin pike; and, as he says in his report, "A close examination of the position satisfied me that if the Overton Hill could be carried the enemy's right would be turned, his line from the Franklin pike westward would be taken in reverse and . . . the capture of half of the rebel army would almost certainly have been the guerdon of success." Despite the repulse of his first attack in the morning, he laid careful plans for another concerted attempt in the afternoon, spearheaded by Post's brigade.

His artillery and that of Steedman on his left intensified a continuous fire on the Confederate position. Steedman agreed to move his infantry forward with Wood's assaulting column to support its left. "Everything being prepared for the attack, near 3 P. M." Wood says, "I gave the order for the assaulting brigade to advance.

The troops were full of enthusiasm, and the splendid array in which the advance was made gave hopeful promise of success. Near the foot of the ascent the assaulting force dashed forward for the last great effort. It was welcomed with a most terrific fire of grape and canister and musketry; but its course was onward. When near, however, the enemy's works (a few of our men, stouter of limb and steadier of movement, had already entered his line) his reserves on the slope of the hill rose and poured in a fire before which no troops could live.

Unfortunately, the casualties had been particularly heavy among the officers, and more unfortunate still, when he had arrived almost at the abatis, while gallantly leading his brigade, the chivalric Post was struck down by a grape-shot and his horse killed under him. The brigade, its battalions bleeding, torn and broken, first halted and then began to retire: but there was little disorder and nothing of panic. . . .

After the repulse, our soldiers, white and colored, lay indiscriminately near the enemy's works at the outer edge of the abatis. But while the assault was not immediately successful, it paved the way for the grand and final success of the day. The reinforcements for the Overton Hill, which the enemy had drawn from his left and left center, had so much weakened that part of his line as to assure the success of General (A. J.) Smith's attack.

General Clayton, whose division bore the brunt of this afternoon attack by Wood's brigades, has this to say about it:

In these assaults the enemy suffered great slaughter, their loss being estimated at 1,500 or 2,000 killed and wounded. It was with difficulty that the enthusiasm of our troops could be repressed so as to keep them from going over the works in pursuit of the enemy. Five color-bearers with their colors were shot down in a few steps of the works, one of which having inscribed on its folds "Eighteenth Regiment U. S. Colored Infantry; Presented by the Colored Ladies of Murfreesborough."

General Holtzclaw, whose brigade was stationed squarely across the pike, tells how

The enemy made a most determined charge on my right. Placing a negro brigade in front, they gallantly dashed up to the abatis, forty feet in front, and were killed by hundreds. Pressed on by their white brethren in the rear, they continued to come up in masses to the abatis, but they came only to die. I have seen most of the battlefields of the West, but never saw dead men thicker than in front of my two right regiments; the great masses and disorder of the enemy enabling the left to rake them in flank while the right, with a coolness unexampled, scarcely threw away a shot at their front. The enemy at last broke and fled in wild disorder. With great difficulty I prevented my line from pursuing.

As Thomas's plan of battle contemplated a high-pressure effort at turning Hood's left flank, there was an especially heavy concentration of artillery fire from three Federal positions against Bate's line on Shy's Hill. Says Bate:

The enemy opened a most terrific fire of artillery, and kept it up during the day. In the afternoon he planted a battery in the woods in the rear of Mrs. Bradford's house and fired directly across both lines composing the angle; threw shells directly in the back of my left brigade; also placed a battery on a hill diagonally to my left, which took my first brigade in reverse. The battery on the hill in its front, not more than 300 yards distant, that had borne the concentrated fire of my Whitworth rifles all day, must have suffered heavily, but were not silenced. These rifled guns of the enemy being so close razeed the works on the left of the angle for fifty or sixty yards.

While Cheatham's men on Hood's left were absorbing the storm of artillery fire that poured into their position all day, anxiously watching the enemy lines in their front, they were unaware of a climaxing attack that was about to burst on them from the rear. During the late evening and night of the 15th Wilson's cavalry divisions commanded by Hammond, Hatch and Croxton had swept entirely around their own right wing and had established a line across the hills in the rear of Cheatham's left, stretching from Schofield's right through the tangled underbrush of the Brentwood hills across the Granny White pike, facing to the north.

In an account written some twenty years after the war, Wilson gives a colorful account of the proceedings at this juncture.

The dismounted men, urged on by their gallant officers, continued their pressure and by noon had driven the skirmishers close in upon Hood's main line, and had formed a continuous line from the right of Schofield's corps to and beyond the Granny White turnpike, which passed north and south through Hood's left center. Thus it will be seen that Hood's entire left wing was enveloped front and rear, and would be obliged to give way whenever it was vigorously and simultaneously assailed from opposite sides. Riding close up to the front, and perceiving the advantageous position which my men had gained, I sent my staff-officers, one after another, to Generals Schofield and Thomas with information of the success, accompanied by suggestions that the infantry should attack with vigor.

It was during this stage of the battle that a dispatch from Hood to Chalmers (Forrest was still absent) was captured and brought to me, and forwarded by me at once to General Thomas. The dispatch seems to have been lost after the battle; at all events it has disappeared, but its character impressed it upon the memory of all who saw it. It ran, in substance, as follows: "For God's sake drive the Yankee cavalry from our left, and rear, or all is lost."

I found Thomas with Schofield in rear of the right of the line, and explained to them the situation, which was fortunately made entirely clear to them by the sight of the dismounted cavalrymen in full view, skirmishing heavily with the Confederate left, and also by the fire of a section of horse artillery which had been dragged up the steep hillsides to a commanding position in rear of the Confederate works, and was pouring a heavy fire into them. Occasionally a shot would pass over the heads of the enemy and fall into our own lines. Seeing all this, Thomas turned to Schofield and indicated that the time had come for the infantry to advance.

This was between half-past three and four o'clock. Schofield ordered his men forward at once, and as they charged the Confederate lines in front Hatch's dismounted cavalrymen entered them from the rear. Pressed on all sides, and perceiving that further resistance was futile if not impossible, the Confederates broke and fled in confusion from the field,

In a book he wrote in 1912, Wilson writes of the climax with even more color:

... Thomas turned to Schofield and as calmly as if on parade directed him to move to the attack with his entire corps. Fully realizing that the crisis was now on, I galloped as rapidly as my good gray, Sheridan, could carry me back to my own command, but when I reached its front the enemy had already broken and was in full but disorderly retreat. ... This was shortly after 4 P. M.

It is interesting to read General Schofield's post-war account of the climactic action on the afternoon of December 16th. He makes no mention of Wilson's reporting to him and Thomas, dismisses the action of Wilson's cavalry in a few words, and gives credit to McArthur's infantry division, not mentioned by Wilson:

The whole forenoon was passed by me in impatient anxiety and fruitless efforts to get from General Thomas some orders or authority that would enable us all to act together—that is, the cavalry and the two infantry corps on the right. At length the cavalry, without orders from General Thomas, had worked well round on the enemy's left so as to threaten his rear; I had ordered Cox, commanding my right division, to advance his right in conjunction with the movement of the cavalry, and at the proper time to attack the left of the enemy's intrenchments covering the Granny White pike, and that movement had commenced; while, having been informed by General Darius N. Couch, commanding my left division, that one of Smith's divisions was about to assault, I had ordered Couch to support that division, which movement had also commenced. Then General Thomas arrived near our right, where I stood watching these movements. This, about four o'clock PM, was the first time I had seen or heard from General Thomas during that day. He gave no order, nor was there time to give any. The troops were already in motion, and we had hardly exchanged the usual salutations when shouts to our left announced that McArthur's division of Smith's corps had already carried the enemy's work in its front, and our whole line advanced and swept all before it.

Thomas's biographer, Van Horne, in his account, of the preliminary activities on the 16th, presumably supplied by Thomas himself, does not present Schofield in as favorable light as does Schofield's own story. He tells of Thomas's meeting Wilson on the Hillsboro pike about 9 or 10 o'clock in the morning, at which time Thomas emphasized the importance of Wilson's getting in the rear of Hood's left flank. "The attainment of this position," Van Horne says, "was to be the signal for a general attack from right to left, Wilson and Schofield to take the initiative in conjunction." He goes on to say that Wilson had attained the desired position about noon, and so notified Thomas and Schofield that he was ready to move against the enemy, but Schofield demurred, saying that he needed reinforcements. Wilson, says, "impatient at the delay of Schofield . . . finally rode around the left of Hood's line to learn the cause of the failure of the infantry to attack." Thomas meanwhile had gone to his left to consult with General Wood, just before his unsuccessful attack on Hood's right wing.

Continuing, Van Horne says:

After this action on his left, General Thomas rode towards his right flank to hasten if possible the cooperative attack by Schofield and Wilson. As he reached the position of the Sixteenth Corps, Smith referred to him a request from General [John] McArthur for permission to assault the salient in Hood's line directly in front of Couch's division of the Twenty-third Corps. Thomas said: "No; the prescribed order of attack gives the initiative to General Schofield in conjunction with the cavalry, and I desire the maintenance of this order; I will ride to General Schofield's position and hasten his attack." When he met Schofield he directed him to advance against the fortified position in his front. Schofield was reluctant to move from fear of the loss such an assault would produce, and Thomas said: "The battle must be fought, if men are killed."

While the matter was under discussion, Thomas looked to the left, and, observing that McArthur was moving upon the angle in the enemy's line, said to General Schofield: "General Smith is attacking without waiting for you; please advance your entire line." At this moment General Wilson called the attention of the commanding general to the movement of the cavalry upon the fortified hill on the extreme flank of Hood's line. Both assaults were successful, and almost at the same instant McArthur's division, moving southward, carried the angle of Hood's line and Wilson's troops, moving in the opposite direction and striking the enemy in reverse gained the other important position.

General A. J. Smith, in his report of the battle, tells about the more or less spontaneous attack on Shy's Hill by McArthur's division, which seems to have triggered the action which precipitated the collapse of the Confederate left:

About 3 P.M. General McArthur sent word that he could carry the hill on his right by assault. Major-General Thomas being present, the matter was referred to him, and I was requested to delay the movement until he could hear from General Schofield, to whom he had sent. General McArthur, not receiving any reply, and fearing that if the attack should be longer delayed the enemy would use the night to strengthen his works, directed the First Brigade, Colonel W. L. McMillen commanding, to storm the hill, on which was the left on the enemy's line. . . . Throwing out a strong party of skirmishers, under a rapid fire from them and his artillery, he commenced the ascent. He had no sooner fully commenced his movement than the Second Brigade, also took up the attack, followed by the Third Brigade, and lastly the Second Division. The enemy opened with a fierce storm of shell, canister and musketry, sadly decimating the ranks of many regiments, but nothing save annihilation could stop the onward progress of that line. Sweeping forward, the right of the line up the hill and the left through mud and over walls, they gained the enemy's works, calling forth the remark from one of their general officers that "powder and lead were inadequate to resist such a charge." The enemy were whipped, broken and demoralized.

Colonel Henry Stone, one of General Thomas's staff officers, who was not always a stickler for accuracy but who had a gift for the purple prose favored by so many of the contemporaneous Civil War writers, witnessed the charge of McMillen's division and the collapse of the Shy's Hill defense, and he describes it in eagle-screaming eloquence:

The bravest on-lookers held their breath as these gallant men steadily and silently approached the summit amid the crash of musketry and the boom of artillery. In almost the time it has taken to tell the story they gained the works, their flags were wildly waving from the parapet, and the unmistakable cheer, "the voice of the American people", as General Thomas called it, rent the air. It was an exultant moment; but this was only a part of the heroic work of that afternoon.

While McMillen's brigade was preparing for this wonderful charge, Hatch's division of cavalry, dismounted, had also pushed its way through the woods and had gained the tops of two hills that commanded the rear of the enemy's works. Here, with incredible labor, they had dragged, by hand, two pieces of artillery, and just as McMillen began his charge, these opened on the hill where Bate was, up the opposite slope of which the infantry were scrambling. At the same time Coon's brigade of Hatch's division with resounding cheers charged upon the enemy and poured such volleys of musketry from their repeating-rifles as I have never heard equaled.

Thus beset on both sides, Bate's people broke out of the works and ran down the hill toward their right and rear as fast as their legs could carry them. It was more like a scene in a spectacular drama than a real incident in war. The hillside in front, still green, dotted with the boys in blue swarming up the slope; the dark background of high hills beyond; the lowering clouds; the waving flags; the smoke slowly rising through the leafless tree-tops and drifting across the valleys; the wonderful outburst of musketry; the ecstatic cheers; the multitude racing for life down into the valley below—so exciting was it all that the on-lookers instinctively clapped their hands, as at a brilliant and successful transformation scene, as indeed it was.

Lieutenant James Litton Cooper was a staff officer serving General Thomas Benton Smith, who was now commanding Tyler's brigade of Bate's division. Several years after the war in a newspaper article, he wrote of his experience in the battle:

This brigade did no fighting on the 15th. Late in the afternoon Bate's division was ordered from the right, near the Nolensville Pike, to our left, which had been sorely pressed during the day. . . .

After dark we crossed the Granny White Pike and, with our line extended from a little beyond the summit of a very steep hill, probably half a mile beyond the pike, well down upon the south side, were told to set every man at work fortifying.

General Bate, as usual, was with the head of the column, and I well remember his impressive words to me that night: "Tell General Smith to get every pick and shovel he can find, and don't let a man stop until they are well sheltered. We will fight here and the result of the battle may depend upon this brigade."

We did the best we could, but tools were very scarce, about one to every ten men, and some points were so rocky that it was almost impossible to make an impression.

When morning came we had very poor works—at some places only old logs and rocks piled together and a few shovels of dirt thrown on them. Worst of all, we found that the line had been located by the command who occupied the position before us so far back from the crest of the hill that at several points a six-foot man could not be seen twenty yards in front, thus rendering it possible to mass an attacking party within a few yards of the position and be perfectly sheltered from our fire. This was actually done before the final charge. This, of course, was not discovered till after daylight and the enemy gave us no chance to remedy it then. . . .

Between Smith's brigade and Cheatham's (Lowrey's) division, occupying the position to the left, my recollection is that there was a considerable gap not occupied, through which a road ran.

At daylight we had a fair line of battle, but during the day it was stretched and prolonged till it was less than one-man thickness. There was a brigade in rear of the hill, as reserve, part of the forenoon, but as the enemy kept driving back our men on the hills to our left and rear, they were moved off to the left.

From 10 o'clock the hill was exposed to a cross-fire from sharpshooters and artillery that made a staff officer's life a burden. After 2 o'clock it was swept by the most searching fire of shell it had ever been our fortune to experience. Three or four batteries at short range were playing upon the few acres about the top of the hill, and if a man raised his head over the slight works he was very apt to lose it.

About 4 o'clock, as things seemed approaching a crisis, I was ordered by General Smith to go to the left of the brigade. His adjutant, Captain Jones, was sent to the right, while he remained in the center, where we were to make report if necessary. . . .

In a few minutes what had been feared all day occurred. A large force of the enemy massed under the crest of the hill, and, by a gallant charge, dashed over the flimsy works before some of the men had time to fire a single shot. More than half the brigade were killed, wounded or captured in a hand-to-hand struggle, prominent among the killed being Colonel Shy. General Smith, after surrendering, was struck across the head with a sword and received wounds from which he has never recovered.

General Bate, in the official report he wrote after the army reached Tupelo on its retreat from Nashville, gives this account of the events leading up to the collapse of his line:

The line established by Ector's brigade had been located in the darkness of the night and was, unfortunately, placed back from the brow of the hill, not giving a view and range on the front of more than from five to twenty yards, and the curvature of the hill, as well as the gradual recession of the lines from the angle, forbade any flank fire giving protection to the front of the angle. The works were flimsy, only intended to protect against small arms, and had no abatis or other obstruction to impede the movements of an assaulting party. From the hour this became a part of my line it was impossible to remedy it. The constant fire of sharpshooters from the neighboring hills made it fatal to attempt a work in front. . . .

Ector's brigade was withdrawn from its supporting position in rear of the angle, and left me without any support whatever, at which transfer I remonstrated. The enemy was in two lines in my front, and in the afternoon moved by his right flank from direction of the Granny White turnpike, and massed by advancing a skirmish line under the brow of the hill near the angle. I made this known to General Cheatham by a staff officer (Lieutenant Rogan), and asked for re-inforcements. The general informed me that he had nothing that could possibly be spared, and desired me to extend still farther to the left, as he had to withdraw strength from his front to protect his left, which had been turned. About this time, the brigade on the extreme left of our infantry line of battle was driven back, down the hill into the field in my rear, and the balls of the enemy were fired into the backs of (killing and wounding) my men.

The lines on the left (as you go into Nashville) of the Granny White pike at this juncture were the three sides of a square, the enemy shooting across the two parallel lines. My men were falling past. I saw and fully appreciated the emergency, and passed in person along the trenches in the angle built by Ector's brigade, where I had placed troops who I knew to be unsurpassed for gallantry and endurance, and encouraged them to maintain their places. The men saw the brigade on the left of our line of battle give way and the enemy take its place on the hills in my rear, yet they stood firm and received the fire from three directions with coolness and courage. Anticipating a disaster, I ordered Captain Beauregard, who commanded my artillery, to move his battalion back to the Franklin turnpike, as the enemy already had the Granny White pike in our rear, which was my channel of escape as per order in the forenoon.

About 4 PM the enemy with heavy force assaulted the line near the angle and carried it at that point where Ector's brigade had built the light works, which were back from the brow of the hill and without obstructions; not, however, until the gallant and obstinate Colonel Shy and nearly half of his brave men had fallen, together with the largest part of the three right companies of the Thirty-seventh Georgia, which regiment constituted my extreme left. When the breech was made, this command still contested the ground, under Major Lucas, and finally when overwhelming numbers pressed them back, only sixty-five of the command escaped, and they not as a command but individuals. The command was neary annihilated, as the official reports of casualties show. Whether the yielding of gallant and well-tried troops to such pressure is reprehensible or not, is for a brave and generous country to decide.

The breach once made, the lines lifted from either side as far as I could see almost instantly and fled in confusion.

Colonel Isaac R. Sherwood, commanding an Illinois infantry regiment in Couch's division of Schofield's corps, tells of how, on the first day of the battle, "Citizens of Nashville, nearly all of whom were in sympathy with the Confederacy, came out of the city in droves. All the hills in our rear were black with human beings watching the battle, but silent. No army on the continent ever played on any field to so large and so sullen an audience." Then, concerning the second day's action, Colonel Sherwood gives some interesting details:

The next day opened bright and clear, but there was still a mantle of snow over the fields and especially in the woods. The audience from Nashville was not so large . . .

An hour before sunset our commanding general, George H. Thomas, appeared along our line of battle. He was an idol of the boys in blue and was loudly cheered. Sixty-five pieces of artillery had been thundering on our line more than two hours. Just before sunset, with long lines of infantry in line, the grand charge was ordered. When the brigade bugles sounded the advance I looked back to the rear in range of the enemy cannon on the heroic figure of General Thomas sitting calmly on his tired horse. There was still a mantle of snow on the field, flecked here and there with the red life blood of some hero.

This charge ended the battle with the defeat and practical destruction of the last Confederate army of the West.

Just before culmination of this victorious charge I saw a sight never witnessed before on any battlefield. I saw a group of the Sisters of Charity on our line of battle, each with a decanter of wine, going from wounded comrade to wounded comrade, lifting their heads from the snow and giving wine with words of comfort and cheer. I never shall forget the spectacle.

Following the collapse of the Confederate left the victorious Federals swept down on the exposed left flank of the line occupied by Stewart's corps. Captain Theodore G. Carter, whose company was on the extreme left of McArthur's division, facing Stewart, tells of how his company played its part in this flanking operation, routing Stewart's men:

We were in line at right angles to the Granny White Pike, our left slightly in advance of the [Bradford] house but a little to the right of it, the Twelfth Iowa being between us and the pike. Here we lay in the rain skirmishing until about 3 P. M., when we saw one of our regiments on the extreme right of our line begin a charge on the Confederate works [on Shy's Hill]. As we saw them go over the works and heard the cheering, we realized that the business was "catching", and that in a few minutes we would have to do the same thing.

About the time the first regiment had reached the Confederate works the next one to it started, and in that order they kept on until but a short distance away from us, when our colonel, who was commanding the brigade that day, rode from our right and rear and ordered us to charge.

We rose and, throwing down the fence, advanced on the run until we reached the Confederate rifle pits, made of rails, where we halted for breath. The field was a hard one to travel over, the mud being ankle deep. Directly we advanced, the regiment obliqued to the right to get through the only gap in the wall; in fact the only one for a long distance either way. My company was directly in front of the Point Coupee Battery, which had poured grape, cannister and shrapnel into us from the moment we started, and the supporting line had also done their share with their rifles.

The works, a stone wall built up very high with rails laid a part of the way from the top and sloping to the ground toward us, had no opening in our front except a slight notch at the top, just to the left of the battery. The greater part of my company had, as was right, "touched elbows" to the right, while ten or twelve had touched to the left; and, as I was looking to the front, calculating how we could get over the wall, I had not noticed the oblique movement. As soon as I saw it, there being a wide gap in my company, I told the boys that we would go right ahead. We reached the wall just as the "break" came, and the notch in the wall was so high, and I was so badly used up with a stitch in the side, that the boys had to boost me up to the notch, through which I climbed and dropped to the ground, just as my colonel came along inside the line on the gallop, calling out: "Lay down your arms and surrender." There were but four or five men in the battery, one the commander, Captain Alcide Bouanchaud, and they had ceased resisting. I told the men who were with me to follow me, and went to the support of my colonel, who was entirely alone and surrounded by, apparently, thousands of the Confederates.

In the morning, before we advanced, I had told my second Lieutenant, James B. Burrittin, that in the event of our capturing any cannon that day, to take a guard and stay with them. This he did, as our company, after getting inside of the works, advancing by the left flank, were the first to reach the battery. And now I learn from "history", if the reports of officers are history, that the brigade directly on our right captured the battery; and, in fact, the brigade commander with his staff rode down and ordered my lieutenant to take his men and rejoin his regiment. But the lieutenant told him flatly that he would only be relieved by his own officers . . . The two brigade commanders got together—I think they were politicians—and agreed to divide the guns, each taking two.

Just before the break came, General Stewart was absent from the position of his corps, having been called by General Hood to consult with him at his headquarters near the Lea home. His official report, therefore, has meagre details of the attack on his line. He says:

About 2 or 3 o'clock in the afternoon the commanding general sent for me, and while in conversation with him an officer of his staff announced that the line had given way. Not being present at the moment this took place, at least where I could witness it, and not yet being in possession of the official reports of subordinate commanders, I do not deem it proper to attempt to decide where the line first yielded. It would seem, however, that when once broken it very soon gave way everywhere and the whole army made for the Franklin pike.

Colonel W. D. Gale of Stewart's staff, who was there, tells vividly of those action-packed last few minutes in that sector of the battle:

As soon as I found all was lost, and the enemy closing in around us, I sent a courier to General Stewart, who had gone to General Hood's headquarters in the rear of Lea's house, to inform him of the fact, that he might save himself. . . . Finding the enemy closing in around us, and all indeed gone, I ordered the couriers and clerks who were there to follow me, and we rode as we could to where I thought General Stewart and General Hood were. They were gone and in their places were the Yankees.

I turned my horse's head toward the steep knobs and spurred away. It was the only chance of escape left. This first place I struck, the hill was too steep for my horse to climb, and I skirted along the hills hoping to find some place easier to ascent, but none seemed to exist. Finally I reached a place not too steep, and in the midst of a thousand retreating soldiers I turned my horse's head for the ascent, resolved to try it. The bullets began to come thick and fast. Now I found my saddle nearly off, and was forced to get down, but on I went on foot. The poor frightened fellows were crying out to me, "Let me hold on to your stirrup, for God's sake." "Give me your hand, and help me, please." Some were wounded and many exhausted from anxiety and over-exertion.

On I struggled until I, too, became exhausted and unable to move. By this time the enemy had gotten to the foot of the hill and were firing at us freely. What was I to do? I twisted my hands into my horse's mane and was borne to the top of the hill by the noble animal, more dead than alive. I was safe, though, and so were my men.

We descended the southern slope and entered the deep valley, whose shades were darkened by approaching night. The woods were filled with our retreating men. I joined the crowd and finally made my way to the Franklin Pike, where I found General Stewart, who was much relieved, for I had been reported as certainly killed or captured.

All night long we fled. . . . On we marched through ice and rain and snow, sleeping on the wet ground at night. Many thousands were barefooted, actually leaving the prints of blood upon the ground as the enemy pressed us in the rear.

The men in Lee's corps, on the Confederate right, were taken completely by surprise by the rout of their left and center. They had just successfully repulsed the vigorous assault on their position by Wood and Steedman, and, says Lee in his report, "were in fine spirits and confident of success."

But suddenly (Lee continues) all eyes were turned to the center of our line of battle near the Granny White pike, where it was evident the enemy had made an entrance, although but little firing had been heard in that direction. Our men were flying to the rear in the wildest confusion, and the enemy following with enthusiastic cheers. The enemy at once closed toward the gap in our line and commenced charging on the left division (Johnson's) of my corps, but were handsomely driven back. The enemy soon gained our rear, and was moving on my left flank, when my line gradually gave way. My troops left their line in some disorder, but were soon rallied and presented a good front to the enemy.

Lee's official report modestly omits any reference to his own zeal and gallantry manifested in attempting to turn the tide, but one of his men gives a stirring picture of the heroic young commander in this fateful crisis:

At the time of the break (on the left) General Stephen D. Lee was sitting, mounted in the rear of Clayton's Division. Over on the left he could see the confusion, and a Federal line advancing from the rear and attacking the left wing of Lee's corps. Everything else had apparently been swept before it. Clayton's Division was divided by the Franklin pike. General Lee rode across the pike, taking both stone fences, followed by one of his staff and two of his escourt. He rode until he reached the rear of Stevenson's Division of his corps, rode right into the midst of fugitives and in the face of the enemy who by this time had reached the rear of Pettus's brigade.

General Lee seized a stand of colors from a color bearer and carried it on horseback, appealing to the men to rally. "Rally, men, rally; for God's sake, rally! This is the place for brave men to die." The effect was electrical. Men gathered in little knots of four or five, and he soon had around him three or four other stands of colors. The Federals, meeting this resistance, hesitated and halted. (It was late in the evening and misty). The rally enabled Clayton's Division to form a nucleus and establish a line of battle. General Lee came back from his advanced position to this line, which was formed on one of the Overton hills, and crossing the Franklin pike. Here he was joined by a few pieces of artillery and a little drummer boy who beat the long roll in perfect time, as Gibson's brigade came up and formed a rear guard. This line, formed across the pike, was in a woods near Col. Overton's house. . . . It was Lee's prompt action in rushing to the rear of Stevenson's Division and rallying the men that created the idea of organized resistance and caused the Federals to halt, thus giving Clayton's Division (and some of Stevenson's) time to fall to the rear in good order and form a new line. The Federals were advancing on the rear and would have cut Clayton off.

Evidence of the somewhat haphazard, though highly effective nature of the Federal action on December 16 is supplied by the fact that the culminating assault on Shy's Hill by McMillen's brigade seems to have come as a complete surprise to the rest of the Federal forces, even to those comprising the left of Smith's own corps. Captain Carter, in that part of McArthur's brigade on the east side of the Granny White pike, tells about it:

There was no intention of charging the Confederates on the 16th, as we had received orders to intrench, and our details sent for intrenching tools had nearly reached our lines when the charge took place. Besides, Col. Marshall told me a few days after, that he went to General Smith's headquarters and urged the general to make a charge, and that the General said: "No, there will be no charge. We are going to intrench." While talking he heard the noise of the charge, the increased fire, and the cheering, and he said to the General: "They are charging now," to which the General replied: "No, I don't understand that there is to be a charge." But the Colonel did not wait for any more words—he put spurs to his horse and dashed up, as I have described, and ordered the charge.

As a matter of fact, the collapse of the defenders of Shy's Hill surprised even Bate's brigades on his own right. Charles B. Martin, a member of the First Georgia Volunteers of General H. R. Jackson's brigade, was having a pleasantly easy time of it when the blow fell. The ground in front of Jackson's brigade, he relates, was so rough that no assault was made on them, "although our pickets had a lively time with the enemy." Jackson's men were watching with keen interest the destructive effect of the Federal bombardment on Stewart's stone wall across the road, and Martin was seated on the edge of the ditch in the rear of his brigade's works, watching the show, when "a loud hurrah was heard in our rear," and the bluecoats were seen pouring in on them from their left flank. At Jackson's command, Martin hurried to the left of the brigade with orders to move out by the right flank, and then hurried back to where he had left the general.

Assisted by Lieutenant Colonel Gordon of my regiment, (Martin continued) the general was walking to where his horse had been sent; but the ground was thawing and the walking was slow and tedious. At every step our feet became encumbered with two or three pounds of stiff mud. The enemy were trying to cut us off and, though at some distance, were firing at us and calling out: "Surrender!" The general was becoming exhausted and requested the colonel and myself to leave him. Being near the pike, Colonel Gordon told him that he thought we might get away. The general's horse was in the edge of the woods just beyond, and we felt we could reach the animal. I remained with the general, however.

After crossing the pike and while getting over the stone fence, It rolled from under him and threw him into the ditch beyond. I assisted him out and persuaded him to pull his heavy boots off, as they were so loaded with mud that he could scarcely walk. He had got one off and was trying to remove the other when we heard the cry: "Surrender, damn you!" Looking up, we saw the muzzles of four guns aimed at us across the fence, not more than seventy or eighty yards distant. "They have got us, general," I said, and called out: "We surrender."

The general commenced to pull on his boot, and I turned his coat collar down to prevent our captors from discovering his rank, as I hoped we might be recaptured. The men—one corporal and three privates—sprang over the fence and came up to where we stood just as General Jackson succeeded in getting his boot on, and in pulling at it his collar assumed its natural position. The corporal walked around the general once or twice, then standing in front of him said: "You are a general". "That is my rank," was the reply. The corporal, taking off his hat, waved it around his head and cried out: "Captured a general, by God! I will carry you to Nashville myself."

At a command in German from the corporal, two men took charge of the general and with the corporal crossed the fence to the pike and started with him toward the city, leaving me in charge of the other men, who in very strong language informed me that if I tried to run he would shoot my head off. I told him not to worry; I had run as far as I could. Then he started with me to Nashville.

Prominent among those surprised by the sudden turn in the battle at the close of the day was General Wood on the Federal right. After withdrawing and re-posting the troops engaged in the unsuccessful assault on Peach Orchard Hill, Wood rode to his right to look to the condition of Garrad's and Kimball's divisions. Shortly after reaching his right, he says in his report,

An electric shout, which announced that a grand advance was being made by our right and right center, was borne from the right toward the left. I at once ordered the whole corps to advance and assault the enemy's works, but the order was scarcely necessary. All had caught the inspiration, and officers of all grades and the men, each and every one, seemed to vie with each other in a generous rivalry and in the dash with which they assaulted the enemy's works. So general and so combined an attack on all parts of the enemy's line was resistless. It rushed forward like a mighty wave, driving everything before it. The sharp fire of musketry and artillery did not cause an instant's pause. I advanced with the First Division and witnessed with the highest satisfaction the gallant style in which it assaulted and carried the enemy's works.

Wood's florid rhetoric, and the reports of his division commanders gave the distinct impression that they carried the Confederate position on Peach Orchard Hill by another brave charge in the face of great resistance, and there are some highly colored—and highly imaginative—prints showing such action taking place. "The Third Division re-assaulted the Overton Hill, carrying it," Wood says in his official report, and Beatty (the commander of the Third Division) uses similar terms. In truth, however Clayton had evacuated his works on the hill before Beatty's men got there, and the only men captured were the unresisting ones who stayed in the line, too tired or too discouraged to run. This fact is shown by the words used in the reports of Beatty's regimental commanders: "We advanced in pursuit of the enemy, who had been flanked from their works"; ". . . the enemy, having been routed on our right, fell back rapidly from their works in our front, and we advanced, pursuing them"; "We saw the enemy leaving their works on the hill. The First Brigade was ordered forward, and our brigade followed them"; "The rebel works in our front were occupied with little or no resistance," etc.

Lee's corps, in the event of disaster, had been entrusted with the responsibility of holding the Franklin pike until the retiring Confederates could use it as an avenue of escape, and they performed this function in an eminently capable manner. As soon as it became obvious that the day was lost and that the only hope was to save what they could out of the wreckage of defeat, Lee moved to his appointed task with alacrity and efficiency.

Informed by Hood that the Federals were already near Brentwood, Lee quickly abandoned the line he had formed across the pike near the Overton house and hastened everything to the rear. A new rear-guard line was established at Hollow Tree Gap, beyond Brentwood and seven miles north of Franklin, at about 10 P.M. Wood's pursuit was not particularly energetic, and he bivouacked several miles short of Hollow Tree Gap when night fell.

Chalmers' cavalry had been relatively inactive during the second day of the battle, but they had the distinction of offering the last organized opposition to the Federal pursuit after Hood's infantry had been routed. Morning had found Chalmers with Rucker's brigade where he had bivouacked on the Hillsboro pike at its intersection by the road to Brentwood. He held this position until late in the afternoon when he was ordered to move across to Granny White pike and hold that road until Cheatham's ambulance train had withdrawn in the direction of Franklin.

In the unusual tactical situation then existing, Chalmers was now in the rear of Wilson, who was in the rear of Cheatham; but Chalmers lacked sufficient force to make his position effective.

About 4:30 P.M. Chalmers received Hood's frantic appeal to "hold the Granny White Pike at all hazards". The brigade was accordingly moved onto that pike, and took a position just north of the cross-road to Brentwood, constructing a stout barricade of logs, fence rails and brush. Here they waited for the onslaught of the enemy cavalry, and it was not long coming. Soon the victorious and elated troopers of Hatch, Hammond and Croxton, now back in the saddle, came plunging out the pike, through the gathering darkness and the downpour of rain, that was freezing as it fell. Wilson tells of the contact:

It had become so dark before they were well under way in pursuit that the men could scarcely see their horses' ears. It was a rainy and disagreeable night . . . Hatch's column had not gone more than two miles when its advance under Colonel Spalding encountered Chalmers' cavalry strongly posted across the road behind a fence-rail barricade. They charged it at once, and a spirited hand-to-hand melee ensued, in which many men were killed and wounded on each side. Colonel Spalding had the honor of capturing Brigadier-General Rucker in a personal encounter, in which each had seized and wrested the other's saber from him and used it against its owner.

It was a scene of pandemonium, in which every challenge was answered by a saber stroke or pistol shot, and the flash of the carbine was the only light by which the combatants could recognize each other's position. The gallant Confederates were driven in turn from every fresh position taken up by them, and the running fight was kept up until nearly midnight. Chalmers, however, had done the work cut out for him, gallantly and well. He was over-borne and driven back, it is true, but the delay which he forced upon the Federal cavalry by the stand he had made was sufficient to enable the fleeing Confederate infantry to sweep by the danger-point that night, to improvise a rear-guard, and to make good their retreat the next day.

Sam Watkins, the chronicler of the activities of Company H of the Maury Grays, had been wounded twice during the day, but was still with his company when it was caught up in the rout. He says:

Such a scene I never saw. . . . Hood's whole army was routed and in full retreat. . . . Wagon trains, cannon, artillery, cavalry, and infantry were all blended in inextricable confusion. Broken down and jaded horses and mules refused to pull, and the badly-scared drivers looked like their eyes would pop out of their heads from fright. Wagon wheels, interlocking each other, soon clogged the road, and wagons, horses, and provisions were left indiscriminately. . . . General Frank Cheatham and General Loring tried to form a line at Brentwood, but the line they formed was like trying to stop the current of Duck river with a fish net. . . .

I saw a wagon and team abandoned, and I unhitched one of the horses and rode on horse-back to Franklin, where a surgeon tied up my broken finger, and bandaged up my bleeding thigh. My boot was full of blood, and my clothing saturated with it. I was at General Hood's headquarters. He was much agitated and affected, pulling his hair with his one hand (he had but one), and crying like his heart would break. I pitied him, poor fellow. I asked him for a wounded furlough, and he gave it to me. I never saw him afterward. I always loved and honored him, and will ever revere and cherish his memory. . . . Hood was a good man, a kind man, a philanthropic man. . . . As a soldier, he was brave, good, noble, and gallant, and fought with the ferociousness of the wounded tiger, and with the everlasting grit of the bull-dog; but as a General he was a failure in every particular.

Of the part played by General Forrest in protecting the retreat of Hood's retreating survivors of the battle of Nashville, Dr. Wyeth has written:

In the desperate straits in which he found himself towards the close of that disastrous day of December, 1864, General Hood turned to his famous lieutenant for help, and Forrest never showed himself a greater soldier or a more successful fighter than in this trying emergency. When on the afternoon of the 15th of December, he had received by courier a message stating that the battle in front of Nashville had been begun, his sound military judgment told him that the contest between the greatly superior army of Thomas and the troops under General Hood would end in the overthrow of the latter. . . .

With this in mind, as soon as he heard that the battle was in progress, although the Confederates were still holding their position, Forrest hastened Buford's division in the direction of Nashville and Franklin, where it would be ready to unite with Chalmers and offer what resistance it could in the protection of the army when it should retreat. It will be seen that this division arrived just in the nick of time to unite with Chalmers at Franklin on the early morning of the 17th of December.

He (Forrest) had already started southward in the direction of the Tennessee River, his prisoners (some 400 in number), the wagon-trains, the sick and wounded, and several hundred infantry who were unfit for active duty by reason of being barefooted, and with these a considerable drove of beef cattle and hogs which had been gathered up for the use of the army. Thus encumbered, his march along the almost impassable road was unavoidably slow, and had he not started in advance he would not have been able in safety to reach Duck River and unite with General Hood there as he did on the 18th of December.

When the courier arrived with the information that Hood's lines were broken, from Triune Forrest hastened Armstrong's brigade westward in the direction of Spring Hill, and threw the remainder of Jackson's division on that route to unite with the rear-guard, then under Chalmers and Lee, struggling against the onslaughts of Wilson's corps. The single brigade of Ross accompanied his train across Duck River near Columbia on the 18th, and early on this morning Forrest, in person, reported to General Hood and was immediately assigned to the command of the rear-guard of the Army of Tennessee.

Hood had originally intended to make a stand when he got across Duck River, but when he saw the shattered condition of his army he quickly realized the futility of that. Accordingly he moved on from Columbia with the main body of his troops on the morning of December 20th, determined to get them south of the Tennessee River before stopping. Before leaving Columbia, however, Hood formally assigned the command of the rear guard to Forrest, with instructions to hold the town as long as possible and then follow Hood through Pulaski in the direction of Florence, Alabama. Forrest pointed out that his cavalrymen could not alone handle this difficult assignment, so Hood ordered General Walthall and an infantry force of about 2,000 men to serve under Forrest in holding off the Federal pursuers.

Forrest was given a little breathing spell in which to organize his makeshift command into workable condition. The heavy rains had resulted in a freshet in Duck River which made it unfordable; so, as Forrest had destroyed all the bridges, it was not until December 22nd that the Federals were able to get across and take up the pursuit. They soon encountered the rearmost pickets of Forrest's force, and there was a more or less continuous running fight for the next four or five days.

The service rendered by this rear-guard force, and the difficulties they encountered in their day-to-day combat with the pursuing Federals, are impressively related by Dr. Wyeth:

Of the infantry which volunteered its services to cover the Confederate retreat, fully 300 were without shoes, and their feet were so badly cut by the ice and the rough marching that they could scarcely hobble along on foot. The brave fellows, however, had not lost heart, and were ready to fight to the death if needed. They wrapped pieces of blankets around their raw and swollen feet, tied them on with thongs, and still trudged on, staining the snow and slush as they went, until Forrest ordered some of the wagons to be emptied of their contents in order to give transportation to these unconquerable men. When it became necessary to fight off the Union advance-guard they left the wagons, took their place in line, and did effective service.

On a cold Christmas morning the advanced ranks of Hood's infantry reached the Tennessee River at Bainbridge, a few miles above Florence, where they crossed the river on a pontoon bridge and began the long march to Tupelo, Mississippi, their designated destination. On that same Christmas day Forrest and the rear guard made a stand near Pulaski, checking their pursuers; and on the 26th maneuvered the Federals into a sort of ambush which, Forrest reported, resulted in their "complete rout" and the capture of one piece of artillery. His report continues: "The enemy was pursued for two miles, but showing no disposition to give battle my troops were ordered back."

That was about the last flicker of an effort by the Federals to impede the Confederate retreat. Forrest and the last of the rear-guard crossed the Tennessee River on December 27th, and on the 29th General Thomas issued General Orders declaring the pursuit at an end.

The war dragged on for a few more months until Lee in Virginia and Joe Johnston in North Carolina had surrendered; but when Wilson's tired troopers turned back from their pursuit of the retreating Army of Tennessee, it marked the end of the war in Tennessee, insofar as were involved the organized forces of the Union and Confederate armies.

CHAPTER **18**

☆ *The Long Way Home*

BROMFIELD L. Ridley, a young man from Rutherford County, was a lieutenant on the staff of General A. P. Stewart. He was with Stewart until the last dark day in April, 1865, when General Joseph E. Johnston surrendered in North Carolina to General William T. Sherman. Lieutenant Ridley was an observant and sensitive young man, fully aware of the historical significance of the events in which he was taking part, and fortunately for posterity, he kept a journal in which he set down a day-by-day account of his experiences in making his way home, more than a thousand miles, through a war-torn country, after the surrender:

April 27th: To-day we received the order to surrender, and now we are prisoners of war. We will start for our homes in a day or two, just as soon as our paroles can be made out. The war is over. In the terms we pledge ourselves to make no more war and remain quietly at home until released. For preservation and the eye of my old age, I transcribe in my journal the famous General Order No. 18, which is the last I am to receive from General Joseph E. Johnston, and the last of the organized army of the Confederacy:

"Headquarters, Army of Tennessee, near Greensboro, N. C., April 27, 1865. General Order No. 18.

"By the terms of a military convention made on the 26th inst. by Major-General W. T. Sherman, U. S. A., and General J. E. Johnston, C. S. A., the officers of the army are to bind themselves not to take up arms against the United States until properly relieved from the obligation, and shall receive guarantees from the U. S. officers against molestation by the United States authorities so long as they observe that obligation and the laws in force where they reside. For these objects, duplicate muster rolls will be made immediately, and after the distribution of the necessary papers, the troops will march under their officers to their respective States, to be there disbanded, all retaining their personal property. The object of this convention is pacification to the extent of the authority of the commanders who made it. Events in Virginia, which broke every hope of success by war, imposed on its general the duty of sparing the blood of this gallant army and saving our country from further devastation and our people from ruin.

[353]

"(Signed) J. E. Johnston, General; Archer Anderson, Lieutenant-Colonel and Assistant Adjutant-General; W. D. Gale, Assistant Adjutant-General; Lieutenant Bromfield Ridley, Aide de Camp to Lieutenant-General A. P. Stewart, Army of Tennessee."

And now around the camp fires to-night we are discussing the surrender. All is confusion and unrest, and the stern realization that we are subdued, and ruined, is upon us. The proud-spirited Southern people, all in a state of the veriest, the most sublimated sorrow. Oh! how is it in the Yankee camp to-night? Rejoicing, triumphing and revelling in the idea of glory. Think of it, the big dog has simply got the little dog down. Two million seven hundred thousand have gotten the upper hand of six hundred thousand, who have worn themselves weary after losing half—the giant has put his foot on the Lilliputian and calls it glory! Bosh! Confucius says "Our greatest glory is not in the never falling, but in rising every time we fall." And so let's philosophize, "What can't be cured, must be endured." "Let's laugh and not sigh; A silver lining by and by." Our courage will command respect, and our devotion will enlist admiration.

But the question is how to get home. Colonel Gale goes by Asheville for his wife; Terry Cahill by Wilmington; the rest of us will divide up the transportation, load with commissaries, to exchange for forage on our long journey. We have fears that there is no organization and that the soldiers will take our teams. Major Wilbur F. Foster, corps engineer, and his attaches will take one route; Dr. Darby, medical director from South Carolina, won't have far to go; Major Murphy of Memphis, and attaches, another road. But as Major Lauderdale, our acting Quartermaster, knows where the stores are, we will take his wagon and also Colonel Sevier's in our party, and "go as you please" so as to get out of the line of the army. Assistant Adjutant Inspector General Minnick Williams is to strike out with a separate party. 'Tis now eleven o'clock p. m. Our plan is settled upon. Lieutenant Stewart [General Stewart's son] and I are off to ride all night, leaving our general and Lauderdale to care for the troops and provide for their exit.

Major Smith, our acting ordnance officer, will take charge of the guns after stacked, and deliver them to Uncle Sam. I will keep this journal up until I get home and show it to my children, if I ever have any, in the "sweet by and by."

April 28th, 1865: After the famous battle order No. 18, Lieutenant R. C. Stewart and I concluded to get ahead of the disbanded army on the way home, so we could find forage for man and beast. We left town last night with three headquarters' wagons (Stewart's, Lauderdale's and Sevier's) and one ambulance. Rode all night and and now in camp, seven miles from Lexington, on the Danville road.

April 29th: Remained here to-day. A great many people visited us to exchange forage for spun thread; that is our currency, now. Sent messenger to General Stewart, who waited to see men paroled, to bring our paroles.

April 30th: Made a Sabbath day's journey across the Yadkin, finding forage scarce. Left a letter for General Stewart and drove ten miles further before learning that the ferryboat at Brown's Ferry had been removed. Went into camp about five miles from river and sent out Captain Hughes and two others to examine and report a safe place for crossing; also sent courier back to General Stewart. When we cross the Yadkin will await orders for fear of falling in with the "Philistines," who might give us trouble, without our proper papers. Omitted to mention that my father (Chancellor Bromfield Ridley, of Tennessee) joined our company yesterday at Lexington, and will be of our party to Georgia and Tennessee. Camp to-night in Davidson county.

May 1st: This beautiful day augurs pleasant weather for our long journey homeward. The fact of our surrender will occupy a noticeable place in history, that the "Military Convention," as it is called in General Johnston's order, took place near Greensboro, N. C., in the county of Guilford, within five miles of the battlefield of

Guilford, celebrated in the history of the Revolution as one of the bloodiest of that war. It was fought by General Greene and Cornwallis, with success to the American arms. Aiken, our courier, just returned 5 p. m., reports that the army is being paroled rapidly, but friends will not overtake us before tomorrow or next day.

May 2nd: Forage scarce; strike tents; cross the Yadkin at Haiston's Ferry and wait for our friends; in the meantime have the mules shod and mend the ambulance. Are now on the Knoxville road, near Peter Haiston's elegant residence, and, upon invitation, partake of the hospitality of his home. The lady of the house was Miss Fannie Caldwell, daughter of Judge Caldwell of Salisbury, and a grand-daughter of the celebrated Bailey Henderson, of North Carolina. Her husband is a man of wealth and lives in magnificent style. It is a home for Southern soldiers. This Mr. Haiston is the wealthiest man in North Carolina. He was the owner of seven hundred and fifty negroes, and twenty-five thousand acres of land in North Carolina and Virginia. Stragglers made an effort to get our mules last night, but failed, after a few shots from our Irish guards who are sleeping on this campaign with one eye open.

May 3rd: Major Lauderdale has arrived with tidings from our General, and our paroles. The troops of different states are to be placed under a general of their States, and transportation so divided that soldiers can get home. Enough arms were given to guard duty while en route. General J. B. Palmer takes charge of Tennesseans, and General Stewart hopes to overtake us, whenever everything touching his corps is completed.

May 4th: On our journey of over twelve hundred miles, to-day we traveled over fourteen miles, crossing the south fork of the beautiful Yadkin. Camp on another plantation of Peter W. Haiston's, twelve miles northwest of Salisbury. Have fared well; struck forage, eggs, coffee, onions and fish; found a little oasis in the arid desert. While our hearts are heavy over the recent surrender, we are glad that we are going home.

Oh, that word Peace! Peace is the sweetest word I ever heard, except that other word Home! "Sweet, sweet home." Our march hence is through to Lincolnton, forty-five miles. Start to travel now at the rate of twenty-five miles a day. Captain John Oliver, who dammed Mill Creek under General Stewart's supervision, near Rocky Face Ridge, in January, 1864, and changed Sherman's course, came up with me yesterday, and gave me an elegant Colt's pistol.

May 5th: Stoneman in his last raid through this part of North Carolina burnt the bridges, so while striving to go the nearest way to Lincolnton, we changed our route three or four miles. Have traveled twenty-six or seven miles to-day, and pitched tents twelve miles from Beattie's Ford, on the Catawba river. At this ford live the families of the late Judge Burton and Alfred Burton, first cousins of my paternal grandfather.

May 6th: Crossed the beautiful Catawba at Beattie's Ford, one-fourth mile wide. It is full of historic interest connected with Revolutionary times. Our party called to see, and was warmly received by Robert A. Burton and a number of ladies. Overtook our wagons seven miles from Lincolnton in camp, having traveled twenty-two miles.

May 7th: Started at seven; came to Lincolnton; called to see Mrs. Fannie Hoke, daughter of Judge Robert Burton and the mother of Major-General Hoke, the hero of the battle of Plymouth. She treated us royally; remembered to have met my father when he was only fifteen. Having lost our coffee pot in camp, she generously provided another. Overtook our wagons at Mr. McGill's, eighteen miles from Lincolnton. Our cook, Jim, made us an excellent pot of coffee in our "Hoke coffee pot." Near camp we found Colonel James E. Bailey, of Clarksville, Tennessee, Hardee's command, who was likewise en route to Tennessee.

May 8th: Left our camp this morning at seven and in a few hours were in the state of South Carolina, Spartanburg district. We passed in view of King's Mountain, N. C., near to which the celebrated battle was fought Oct. 7th, 1790, by General

Campbell on the American side, and General Ferguson commanding the British forces. My recollection is that the Americans had a force of 1,500, and the British 800 men only, but they were stationed on the cone shaped mountain almost impregnable; yet, after a hard fought battle, victory perched on the American arms. Colonel T. F. Sevier, our Inspector-General, is of the same ancestral line as our first governor of Tennessee, Colonel John Sevier, who attained great prominence in that battle. (In the Tennessee Historical Society there is a gold mounted sword given to Colonel John Sevier for his achievements at King's Mountain.)

We have crossed Broad river at Cherokee iron works, owned partly by Colonel Campbell, of Chester, S. C. Have gone into camp, having traveled twenty-two miles on the roughest road yet encountered. Near King's Mountain, I saw a woman who was my ideal of a veritable mountain maid. She emerged from a little cabin after a bucket of water, bare-footed, bare headed, and evidently with but a single garment on. She had the pearliest teeth, "eyes like twin forget-me-nots beneath the moonbeam's glint," lips like the cherry, hair as glistening as black polished ebony, a nose as beautifully carved as that of any fabled nymph. Gosh! she was a beauty. I approached, and with her lily-white hand she dipped the bucket in the spring, and gave me a drink. Zounds! she was the top blossom of the mountain, and prettier than any flower in the valley. "And the dimple in her chin was like the flower the bee sits in."

We are getting restless about our stock—no organization—straggling soldiers threaten to take them. They swarm everywhere; some travel fifty miles a day, going to see father and mother, and wife and children and loved ones—and oh, the young bloods going to see "The Girl I Left Behind me." That old song comes impressively before me now. We have sung "Just Before the Battle, Mother," "Tramp, Tramp, Tramp, the Boys are Marching," "Joe Bowers," "Lorena," "Maryland," "Dixie," and "When This Cruel War is Over." But light up the camp fire, boys; tune up the fiddle and the bow; bring in the old tambourine; and listen, oh listen! to the tune of "The Girl I Left Behind Me." As the spirit-stirring strains fall on old Jim's (our cook) ears, he begins to pat, and the soul-inspiring sound attracts servant Hannibal who begins to dance, and the welkin fairly rings when we come to that verse:

> "If I ever get through this war,
> And Lincoln's chains don't bind me,
> I'll make my way to Tennessee—
> To the girl I left behind me."

Tuesday, May 9th, 1865: Have halted here at Cherokee iron works, in Spartanburg district, South Carolina, to have mules shod and clothes washed. Works extensive on Broad river, which, after receiving the Pacolette a few miles below, is navigable for flat-boats to Columbia, 110 miles distant. We are fishing and bathing and will our journey pursue to-morrow.

Had the war lasted a few weeks longer, the staff, by special act of Confederate Congress, would have been promoted—Lieutenant, Colonel and Major. Well, Caruthers, Stewart and I have lost the glory. The staff was not in line of promotion, hence Congress, on account of the efficiency of this arm of the service, was endeavoring to recognize it.

I often reflect how I got picked up on this staff duty. As a private in Company F, Ward's regiment, Morgan's cavalry, I caught the enemy's fire at and over my line; but horrors! instead of being far enough in the rear to escape minies, I have found that the staff had to go where the fighting was, in a battle and out, and take the fire, cross-fire and enfilades at the whole corps, and was always a target for batteries and sharpshooters. But, with the military courtesy of being called a grade higher than our real rank, the staff (whose loss quadrupled any other branch) had to content itself.

May 10: Left camp this morning at seven, and have traveled twenty miles, having crossed Thickelty creek and Pacolette river. We have passed within a few miles of

Cowpens, a notable place in the history of the Revolution as the locality of a bloody battle between General Morgan and Colonel Tarleton; also passed the scene of another battlefield on Pacolette river—believe it was Eutaw Springs, but may be mistaken. We passed through Spartanburg and are now in Union District, ten miles west of Unionville. The road is full of returning soldiers. Feed is scarce, but the people are very kind to us. A Mr. Jones invited Major Lauderdale and my father to breakfast with him a half mile off. Some one tried to steal a mule last night, but we were on the alert. A fellow came to our camp and by false pretenses got a spool of spun thread from us, promising to bring corn, but he decamped and we never heard of him again. Our circulating medium, cotton yarns, tobacco, and hams, is about to give out. But as Jacob Faithful in one of Marryatt's novels used to say:

> "Life's a river, and a man is a boat
> That over its surface is destined to float;
> But Joy is a cargo so easily stored,
> That he is a fool who takes sorrow on board."

May 11th: Have traveled twenty-five miles to-day: camped on the east bank of Tiger river. The country is sterile, and the contrast with Tennessee lands is striking. Road jammed with soldiers. Expecting to meet General Stewart at Cross Anchor, but found he had passed on with his corps, though our informant said he had disbanded them.

May 12th: Are now in camp at Laurens Court House, South Carolina. Stop at two o'clock to have broken wheel repaired.

May 13th: Have traveled rapidly to-day over a smooth road, and are now seventeen miles from Laurens Court House at half past one. Write this hasty memorandum on the south bank of the Saluda river, Puckett's Ferry. Whilst we are crossing it, it was rumored at Lawrenceville, and. the report is rife all along the way, that Bob Lincoln had killed Andrew Johnson at Washington. A man said he had seen a gentleman who had informed him that it was reported in the Knoxville *Whig* and the Augusta *Chronicle*. Don't believe it, yet am "prepared now to believe anything." Have also heard another rumor that a French fleet is in sight of Wilmington. Don't I wish that President Davis could get on it!

Mr. Puckett's ferryman says that President Davis, with his Cabinet, crossed the river here on Monday, May 1st, also his escort, Dibrell's division together with Vaughan's brigade from East Tennessee. President is in good health. Escort was disbanded at Washington, Ga. The last Cabinet meeting was held there in a bank building.

Have found a returning soldier of Vaughan's brigade who says there are forty or fifty Yankees at Abbeville Court House, a few miles ahead of us. If so, we will probably fall in with them to-morrow. Have not seen one since the surrender. We are twenty-two miles from Abbeville. Passed to-day Ninety-Six, a place which has become historical from the fact that it was the station during the Revolution for the British—the surrounding country of Laurens and Abbeville being distinguished for Tories. The British General Cruger commanded it when Greene attempted once unsuccessfully to take it. It was at this place that the brave Kosciusko, who afterward became Dictator of Poland and filled so large a place in European history, directed the siege for General Greene. In camp now after traveling twenty-five miles.

May 14th: Passed through Cokesbury twelve miles from Abbeville, a village distinguished for its excellent schools. Passed Abbeville at half past twelve; the town full of soldiers. Saw my friend, John Young of McMinnville, who came near being hanged by Andrew Johnson in Nashville, charged with being a spy. General Loring's wagon train had stopped one mile south of the town for the purpose of avoiding the crowd en route to Washington, Ga. We have taken a road leading across Savannah river at Barksdale's Ferry. Yankees occupy Washington, hence to avoid them we will go directly after crossing river at Warrenton, to Sparta. General Stewart sent forward a courier to say that he was in the rear, and to wait for him. Courier missed us and went to Washington, we suppose. Have pitched tents four miles south of Abbeville.

May 15th: Have decided to wait; and sent General Stewart's son back to meet him. An accident occurred in camp last night. Mr. Hill, of Tennessee, who is one of our company, lost his mule. Lieutenant Stewart and his brother Alphonso have returned and bring no tidings of the General. We are in trouble, not knowing what to do, but will go on in the morning. I went back to Abbeville last night, and got a supply of commissary stores—bacon, hams, flour, salt, sugar, etc. Camped near Mr. Tolmand's.

May 16th: Returned from the village last night where I saw twelve Yankees who looked scared. Their mission, I hear, is to take charge of the commissary stores there; also heard that the Yankees had captured President Davis on his Mississippi tour. The rumor is pretty well authenticated, therefore I mention it. Our faithful man Jim gave us a poor breakfast this morning. The coffee and biscuit were both badly prepared; but he said he was all the time "thinking of his wife and how she would receive him." He promised next time to put more beans and less water in the coffee pot.

May 17th, 1865: As I write this memorandum for the eye of my old age and to recur to when I strike some old soldier who is on this tramp with us, I will take a bird's-eye view and make short pencilings of our party:

Major Lauderdale of Kentucky is our chief of staff on this campaign, a lawyer by profession, a five-year practitioner at Hickman, Kentucky, and a partner of our Captain Roulack. He was at the time of surrender Acting Corps Quartermaster—quits the army with high character.

Robert Caruthers Stewart is another of our party, a young man nineteen years old, and my associate as aide-de-camp to his distinguished father (Lieutenant-General A. P. Stewart). We have been together in all the battles of the Army of Tennessee, beginning with McLemore's Cove, Chickamauga, Lookout Mountain, and Missionary Ridge. Then we were in the 100 days' fight from Dalton to Atlanta, the battles around Atlanta, Franklin, and Nashville. Alphonso, another son of the General, is with us—a sprightly lad and very agreeable, but too young to have been a soldier.

Captain Hughes of Memphis, Tennessee, is the Major-Domo of our party and very popular. He is on his way to meet a lady friend at Memphis, and we expect that he'll lead her soon to the "hymeneal halter."

Captain Jim Rawlings is the Chevalier Bayard. He wears the heaviest mustache, the longest beard, and rides the best saddle-horse in the company. He hails from Chattanooga, Tennessee, was clerk in Lauderdale's department for several years, and one of the best book-keepers in America. It is doubtful whether the Captain is more careful of himself or of his horse. Jeff. This protracted war has postponed the nuptials with his lady love, but when he gets home there will be heard the voice "of joy and gladness."

We have five Irish teamsters along with us, all useful well-behaved fellows: John Daily, Aiken, "Tennessee," O'Neil and McLaughlin. They mess to themselves—the last named is cook. They can smell pine-top whiskey further, and get more onions and eschallots than anybody. O'Neil has a cart and a mule of his own—is greatly attached to this mule, "Jerry." Says he is twenty years old, and has stolen much corn and fodder for him. He wanted to get a furlough for Jerry, and had it in his mind to ask the "Gineral," but feared if he did, he and Jerry would both be sent to the "Divil". These Irishmen came from Memphis, Tennessee, with General Polk, and are now returning thither. They speak with great veneration and affection of General Polk.

Mr. McKee of Columbus, Ga., is traveling with us. He is a private of some artillery company, and has been a pleasant member of our party. Messrs. Hill and Jones, of Tennessee, and a Mr. Ledford of Texas, are also in our company.

This finishes the group, except my father who seemed as cheerful as any soldier, even if he has been a wanderer from the family altar for years; my servant, Hannibal;

General Stewart's cook, Jim, and his historic rooster, "Old Dick." This chicken has accompanied the army through Tennessee, Alabama, Mississippi, Georgia, South and North Carolina. After winning fifty pitched battles, old Jim regards him as the champion cock of Stewart's corps.

We have traveled twenty miles to-day. Crossed the Savannah river, and pitched tents one mile from Barksdale Ferry, six miles from Lincolnton. We are "on the heels" of General Stewart. Heard at the crossing that he passed there to-day at ten o'clock with his escort company, Captain Greenleaf's Light Horse from New Orleans, and Colonel Sevier of his staff. Will overtake him to-morrow.

And now we are in the State of Georgia, County of Lincoln, Passed Lincolnton, a poor village—never could have been a Rome or an Athens in its palmiest days. Have passed from Lincoln into Wilkes county, but avoided Washington, the county seat, the home of Bob Toombs, having heard that Yanks occupied it—don't care to see them. Called at a house to get a drink of water and found a note from General Stewart, saying he would go on ten miles farther, crossing Little river, and wait for us. We have now overtaken the General. He traveled a road parallel to ours.

Have this moment heard that President Davis is certainly captured.

May 18th: We are striking for the residence of Colonel John Bonner, who lives in Hancock County. Have flanked Crawfordsville, leaving it to the left, hearing that the Federals are there. Crawfordsville is a small town, the home of Vice-President Stevens [Stephens] of the Confederacy. Camped at White Plains—hear that Stevens, Governor Jos. E. Brown and President Davis and family have been arrested, also Bob Toombs and General Cobb.

May 19th: Nothing to-day—have traveled sixteen miles. Will go from here via Sparta and Milledgeville, to Dr. C. L. Ridley's on the Ocmulgee.

May 21st: Arrived at John Bonner's. He is a man of wealth, finely educated, but peculiar. At the breaking out of the war he filled his store room with coffee and sugar, and has had an abundance all through the war. He is not a drinking man, but is possessed of this eccentricity: When he married he put up a cask of wine, and when his son was born, forty years ago, he put up a barrel of peach brandy. As this son (being the only child) had children, he commemorated the birth of each one with putting up wines, and also certain notable events, until he had a storeroom full of fine liquors. A sip from that forty year old barrel was sweeter to me than the fruits of the Hesperides, the honey of Hymettus, or the nectar of the gods. This old gentleman had his coffin made out of the lumber of a tree, under whose shade some incident took place, forming an episode in his history. In that beautiful coffin was a jug to be filled with that forty-year old brandy, to be drunk up after his death by his pall-bearers. He was a Southern nabob—at one time he defied a regiment. Glittering wealth seemed to be around him—a magnificent plantation, once stocked with Devon cattle, Berkshire hogs, Cockrill sheep and blooded horses.

The next morning he called up one of his little grand-daughters, whose heart, he said, was on her right side. We placed our hand over the little girl's heart, on the right side, and it thumped away as naturally as if there were no freak of nature. (By the way I have never heard of but one freak of nature, in the last thirty years, that excelled this: There is said to be a young man, near Sabinal, Texas, who has no ears, nor the sign of ears, and yet he talks to you like other people, and hears like others—sound is imparted through the mouth).

From near Colonel Bonner's, Colonel Sevier and our escort company, Captain Greenleaf's Light Horse, go via Macon to Columbus. They expect to dispose of the wagon and team assigned them for funds to pay the transportation of the company to their homes in New Orleans, by steamboat down the Chattahoochee to Apalachicola, Fla., and thence by schooner.

The echo of the surrender is still preying upon me, and when I think of the future of the Southland, I am filled with dark forebodings. Had we succeeded, we had been patriots; as we did not, we are called rebels. No monument of marble, nor brass, now to commemorate the sacred principles for which we fought, no shaft to be erected by a nation in our honor, but in our hearts will live the memories and convictions that only force has smothered. The monument to the Southern cause can only be, as we said of Audubon, the naturalist, who died and has no tombstone to mark his grave: "The little wren will only whisper our names and memory about our Southern homes, the robin and the red-bird will pipe our principles from the meadows, the ring-dove will coo it from the dewy depths of our Dixie woods, and our mountain eagles scream it to the stars."

May 21st, 1865: We start from John Bonner's for Eatonton, Putnam County, Ga., crossing the Oconee at Lawrence Ferry; camp to-night at Spivey's during a heavy rain storm; my father and General S. shelter at Spivey's house, the rest of us drenched.

May 22nd: Murder creek full; ran into ambulance and wagon camp six miles from Hillsboro. It has been intimated that a part of our company who left this morning in a *sub silentio* way, went to the house of a Mr. Turner, editor of a newspaper called "The Countryman," who has a large distillery and a manufactory of hats, and supplied themselves with a canteen of the creature comfort. All have returned, and Captain Roulack says in a thick-lipped, "how come you so" way, that, "he is the most elegant man in Georgia; that his liquor beats pine-top, pop-skull, or Jeff Davis busthead."

Whilst this party are exuberant over their kind treatment, I must not forget the square meal that Jim Rawlings and I struck in their absence. The kind-hearted old man said at the table, "Now, men, turn over and take out, and you'ns just help yourselves." The old woman asked us if we would have sweet potato coffee. Rye, okra seed, parched wheat and meal coffees are our national substitutes for the pure bean, and our sugar is "long sweetening."

May 23rd: Arrived at Cornucopia to-day, near the residence of Dr. Chas. L. Ridley, on the Ocmulgee. The postoffice was formerly called by the uncanny name of Grab-all. That recalls to me some of the names I have met with in my peregrinations and perambulations as a soldier boy: Hard-up, Lick Skillet, On Top, Snatch, Stop and Swap, Buzzard Roost, Low Down, Tooth Pick, Frog Level, Possum Trot—names not euphonious, nor aristocratic, but often significant. Names of people have also attracted me, such as Goosefoot, Shinbone, Swingletree, Goodenough, Hog, Gander, Dossen-berry, and Blowhard.

We are "Tenting to-night on the Old Camp Ground" at County Line Meeting House—same occupied by me last summer with General Stewart's stock and wagons during his absence at Savannah, whilst disabled from a wound in the forehead received 28th of July, near Atlanta. Whilst my brigade will dwindle now, I'll gather a few recruits for Tennessee; Dr. James A. Ridley, of the late Colonel Keeble's Twenty-Third Tennessee, and son Granville, of the Fourth Tennessee cavalry. He came out with Hood, and only in time to receive his baptism of fire.

May 24th: Captain Lee S. Stewart arrives from Macon and reports that Mrs. Stewart and little son, who have been refugeeing there, will be at Forsythe to-morrow. She will be escorted here, where she will recruit for ten days, preparatory for Tennessee trip.

May 25th: There is a general separation to-day. Lauderdale exchanges for a buggy and goes to Marianna, Fla., for his wife, thence to his home in Kentucky; Mr. McKee goes with him; Captains Hughes and Roulack go to Memphis; Jerry Jones and John Hill to Nashville, Tennessee; O'Neil with his cart and mule, strikes out for Macon, also McLaughlin, leaving in camp with us, Tennessee and Daily and servants Hannibal and Jim.

From May 25th to June 5th: And now we are in the red clay hills of Jones county, Ga., twenty miles from Macon, fifteen from Forsythe, in the land of the goober, the "watermillyun," the kershaw, the muscadine and the scuppernong. We have met North Carolina belles, South Carolina beauties; but, hear me! the Georgia girl takes the cake!

June 5th, 1865: And now after a delightful stay of ten days at Cornucopia, we start for Tennessee. Have taken this circuitous route to avoid the bushwhackers of the mountains. We have the pleasure of Mrs. Stewart's company, her little son Alex., Dr. Jas. A. Ridley and son Granville—one Judge, one General, one Surgeon, one lady and little boy, and four attaches, besides our two Irish teamsters and two servants. Camped to-night five miles east of Jackson. Lieutenant Stewart and I went by Forsythe for news. I pointed out to him, in that hospitable town, the old church where in 1864 Colonel Cunningham and Lieutenant Smith, of General Hood's staff, Lieutenant Hawkins, of Major-General Smith's staff, and I attended a swell wedding—the occasion being the marriage of Lieutenant Eth B. Wade, one of General Hood's Aides, to Miss Dora Cochran, when in our $1,500 uniforms of Crenshaw gray, we moved down the aisle to the tune of Mendelssohn's march, each swinging one of Forsythe's inimitable beauties. As Scott said of Rebbeca and Rowena in *Ivanhoe,* they were "roses of loveliness, gems of wealth, bundles of frankincense and clusters of camphire."

June 6th: Camped to-night one and a half miles north of McDonough, a journey of twenty-five miles. Saw Andrew Johnson's proclamation and find little encouragement in it.

Understanding from citizens that anyone who wears rebel uniform through Atlanta is liable to have his buttons, bars, stars and lace cut off, we have changed our coats.

Camp to-night near Griffin. It was in Griffin that General John C. Brown, last year, married Miss Bettie Childress, a niece of Mrs. James K. Polk, she being a refugee there from Murfreesboro, Tenn. Immediately after the ceremony was over, a telegram announced the advance of the enemy, and called the General from his bonnie bride to return at once to the front.

June 7th: And now, our Irish teamsters are alarmed about their mules. The two that General Stewart intended for them are branded U. S. It is amusing to see them stop occasionally and put mud on their brands to hide them from the Yanks. They also let a piece of sack hang over their shoulders. We pass Lovejoy, the point from which General Hood had his controversy with Sherman about driving the women and children out of Atlanta—also the point to which Jefferson Davis came and reviewed the Army of Tennessee before making the campaign to Nashville.

We conclude to shun Atlanta with the wagons and strike for Howell's Ferry on the Chattahoochee; General Stewart and party to go direct; my father to make a detour; Granville Ridley and I go into the city and report news, but all to meet at Howell's Ferry.

It turned out that there were three Howell's Ferries on the Chattahoochee, all wide apart. Each party went to a different one, and we never met again until we got to Tennessee. The country was such a barren waste that we could not follow in Sherman's and Johnston's trail from Atlanta to Dalton, because of nothing for man or beast. All animated nature was so nearly starved that, in crossing the trail, a hungry horse-fly popped me on the lip, producing such torturing pain that for a day I thought myself poisoned.

(In the city, the lone chimneys show that arson had held sway, but the old shelter during the storming of Atlanta, remained. We passed our headquarters during the siege, and went by our old quarters near Peachtree creek, where General Hood took breakfast with us the morning he took command of the army. Oh! how we were shocked when we heard of that change! Ah! the gloom with which the army was filled! It looked for the time as if the soldiers, who idolized Joe Johnston, would throw down their muskets and quit.)

Granville Ridley and I journeyed along somehow until we struck the railroad at Cartersville; sold our two horses for $15. We got free transportation, and, on arriving at Chattanooga, went to a hotel room and remained until the train of boxcars was ready to take us home. From our windows we could see those who wore the blue promenading the streets with the composure of victors. I thought of the Turkish executioner with his scimitar, of the old Indian chief with his scalps dangling by his side. It did not take us long, though, to size them up as quartermasters, commissaries, and hangers-on to an army far enough in the rear to hear no bullets whiz, but to blow and put on airs as if they were the United States Government.

My old father wandered through North Georgia over the Cumberland Mountains on a little mule; General Stewart and party likewise, aided by his maps, crossed over via Short Mountain. Here my journal ends.

AT HOME

We beat the party home by at least three weeks. (*June 12.*) My dear old mother threw her arms around me and wept. Old "black mammy," Eliza, and other darkies who remained at home, rushed up and hugged me; and Old Henry, the faithful servant who had taken care of my mother through the war, with its maelstrom-like swirl of fire and persecution, got a bottle of whiskey and was soon "gloriously" drunk. My faithful dog Carlo, that gave the alarm that kept my mother and sister from burning up, seemed as if he realized the situation and would go crazy with delight. For a moment I forgot the gloom of surrender.

I had reached home in time to join with mother in meeting her absent ones. One by one my brothers came in—Major J. S. Ridley, of Stevenson's division; Captain George C., and Lieutenant Charles L. Ridley, of General Ben Hill's staff, and Dr. J. L. Ridley, Surgeon in Dibrell's cavalry, and then our little sister, a refugee at Lagrange, Ga., returned, and next came my venerable father from across the mountains on his little mule. Last of all, my servant Hannibal, to whom I am indebted for bringing home the diary from which this journal was written. Old "black mammy's" joy upon Hannibal's return may be imagined.

General Stewart and family were back home at Lebanon, and we at home at Old Jefferson, Tennessee, within a few miles of the battlefield of Murfreesboro. Two dwellings had been laid in ashes by Federals, and my oldest sister had died from fright created by these fires.

"The old home" was not what it used to be, "yet there was no place like the old place." In pondering over these sorrows, I took fresh courage in the sentiment:

"Behold, we live through all things:
Famine, thirst, bereavement, pain,
All grief and misery, all woe and sorrow.
Life inflicts its worst on soul and body,
But we cannot die, though we
Be sick, and tired and faint and worn—
Lo! all things can be borne."

In a short time everybody went to work to drive "the wolf from the door"; all was gone but the wallet and staff. I went off to school to supplement my broken education, interrupted by the war.

BIBLIOGRAPHY

Alexander, E. P.: *Military Memoirs of a Confederate,* Scribner's, New York, 1907.

Annals of the Army of Tennessee, The, Vol. 1 (All published). Nashville, 1878.

(Bickham, William D.): *Rosecrans' Campaign With the Fourteenth Army Corps,* by W. D. B. Cincinnati, 1863.

Bierce, Ambrose: *The Collected Works Of.* Neale, New York, 1909.

Blackburn, J. K. P.: *Reminiscences of the Terry Rangers.* The Southwestern Historical Quarterly, Vol. XXII.

Boynton, H. V.: *Sherman's Historical Raid,* Cincinnati, 1875.

Buck, Irving A.: *Cleburne and His Command,* Neale, New York, 1908.

Carter, W. R.: *History of the First Regiment of Tennessee Volunteer Cavalry.* Knoxville, Tenn., 1902.

Confederate Veteran, The, 40 volumes, Nashville, 1893-1932.

Cox, Jacob D.: *The Battle of Franklin, Tennessee, November 30, 1864.* Scribner's, New York, 1897.

—*The March to the Sea—Franklin and Nashville,* Scribner's, New York, 1906.

Cumming, Kate: *Journal of Hospital Life.* Louisville, 1866.

Davis, Jefferson: *The Rise and Fall of the Confederate Government,* 2 volumes. Appleton, New York, 1881.

Dinkins, James: *1861 to 1865—by an Old Johnnie.* Cincinnati, 1897.

Duke, Basil W.: *Morgan's Cavalry.* Neale, New York, 1906.

Dyer, John Will: *Reminiscences, or Four Years in the Confederate Army.* Evansville, Indiana, 1898.

(Fitch, John): *Annals of the Army of the Cumberland,* by An Officer. Lippincott, Philadelphia, 1864.

Fremantle, Lieut. Col. Arthur Lyon: *Three Months in the Southern States.* New York, 1864.

French, Gen. S. G.: *Two Wars—an Autobiography.* Nashville, 1901.

Grant, Ulysses S.: *Personal Memoirs,* 2 volumes in 1. Webster, New York, 1894.

Hancock, R. R.: *Hancock's Diary.* Nashville, 1887.

Head, Thomas A.: *Campaigns and Battles of the Sixteenth Regiment, Tennessee Volunteers,* Nashville, 1885.

Headley, John W.: *Confederate Operations in Canada and New York.* Neale, New York, 1906.

Hesseltine, William B. (Edited by): *Dr. J. G. M. Ramsey, Autobiography and Letters.* Nashville, 1954.

Hood, J. B.: *Advance and Retreat.* New Orleans, 1880.

Johnson, Robert Underwood, and Buel, Clarence Clough (Editors): *Battles and Leaders of the Civil War,* 4 volumes. Century, New York, 1887.

Johnston, Joseph E.: *Narrative of Military Operations.* Appleton, New York, 1874.

Johnston, William Preston: *Life of General Albert Sidney Johnston.* Appleton, New York, 1878.

Jordan, Gen. Thomas, and Pryor, J. P.: *The Campaigns of Lieut. Gen. N. B. Forrest.* Blelock, New Orleans, 1868.

Land We Love, The, 6 volumes. Louisville, 1866-1869.

Livermore, Thomas L.: *Numbers and Losses in the Civil War.* Houghton Mifflin, Boston, 1900.

Longstreet, James: *From Manassas to Appomattox.* Lippincott, Philadelphia, 1896.

Morgan, Mrs. Irby: *How It Was—Four Years Among the Rebels.* Nashville, 1892.

McMurray, W. J.: *History of the Twentieth Tennessee Regiment.* Nashville, 1904.

Morton, John Watson: *The Artillery of Nathan Bedford Forrest's Cavalry.* Nashville, 1909.

Nash, Chas. E.: *Biographical Sketches of Gen. Pat Cleburne and Gen. T. C. Hindman.* Little Rock, 1898.

Noll, Arthur Howard (Editor): *Bishop Quintard's Memoirs of the War.* Sewanee, 1905.

Oates, William C.: *The War Between the States.* Neale, New York, 1905.

Otis, Ephraim A.: *The Nashville Campaign.* Chicago, 1899.

Papers of the Military Historical Society of Massachusetts. Vol. XII: Campaigns in Kentucky and Tennessee. Boston, 1908.

Polk, Wm. M.: *Leonidas Polk, Bishop and General,* 2 volumes. Longmans, New York, 1893.

Powers, Elvira J.: *Hospital Pencilings.* Boston, 1866.

Reed, Major David W.: *Campaigns and Battles of the Twelfth Regiment Iowa Veteran Volunteer Infantry.* n.p.; n.d.

Ridley, Bromfield L.: *Battles and Sketches of the Army of Tennessee.* Mexico, Missouri, 1906.

Roman, Alfred: *The Military Operations of General Beauregard,* 2 volumes. Harper, New York, 1884.

Rusling, James F.: *Men and Things I Saw in Civil War Days.* New York, 1899.

Sarmiento, F. L.: *Life of Pauline Cushman, the Celebrated Union Spy and Scout.* New York, n.d.

Schofield, Lieut. Gen. John M.: *Forty-Six Years in the Army.* Century, New York, 1897.

Shellenberger, Captain John K.: *The Battle of Franklin, Tennessee, November 30, 1864.* Cleveland, 1916.

—*The Battle of Spring Hill, Tennessee, November 29, 1864.* Cleveland, 1913.

Scofield, Levi T.: *The Retreat From Pulaski to Nashville.* Cleveland, 1909.

Sherman, W. T.: *Personal Memoirs,* 2 volumes. Webster, New York, 1892.

Sherwood, Gen. Isaac R.: *Memories of the War.* H. J. Chittenden Co., Toledo, Ohio, 1923.

Smith, Mrs. S. E. D.: *The Soldier's Friend.* Memphis, 1867.

Sorrell, Gen. G. Moxley: *Recollections of a Confederate Staff Officer.* Neale, New York, 1905.

Southern Bivouac, The, 6 volumes. Louisville, 1886-1887.

Southern Historical Society Papers, 49 volumes. Richmond, 1876-.

Stanley, Henry M.: *Autobiography of Henry M. Stanley.* Houghton Mifflin, Boston, 1906.

Stevenson, A. F.: *The Battle of Stone's River.* Osgood, Boston, 1884.

Stevenson, William G.: *Thirteen Months in the Rebel Army.* New York, 1862.

Surby, R. W.: *Grierson Raids . . . The Life and Adventures of Chickasaw, the Scout.* Chicago, 1865.

Taylor, Richard.: *Destruction and Reconstruction.* Appleton, New York, 1879.

Thatcher, Captain Marshall P.: *A Hundred Battles in the West.* Detroit, 1884.

Van Horne, Thomas B.: *History of the Army of the Cumberland.* (2 volumes and atlas). Clarke, Cincinnati, 1875.

—*The Life of Major-General George H. Thomas.* Scribner's, New York, 1882.

War of the Rebellion, Official Records of the Union and Confederate Armies, 128 volumes. Washington, 1881-1900.

Watkins, Samuel R.: *Co. "Aytch"—First Tennessee Regiment.* Nashville, 1882.

Watson, William: *Life in the Confederate Army.* New York, 1888.

Worsham, Dr. W. J.: *The Old Nineteenth Tennessee.* Knoxville, 1902.

Worthington, T.: *Shiloh: The Only Correct Military History of U. S. Grant.* Washington, 1872.

Wyeth, John Allan: *Life of Gen. Nathan Bedford Forrest.* Harper, New York, 1899.

Young, John R.: *Around the World With General Grant.* New York, 1879.